RRAC

ENCYCLOPEDIA OF THE JAZZ AGE

Volume One

ENCYCLOPEDIA OF THE JAZZ AGE

From the End of World War I to the Great Crash

Volume One

Edited by **James Ciment**

SHARPE REFERENCE

an imprint of M.E. Sharpe, Inc.

SHARPE REFERENCE

Sharpe Reference is an imprint of M.E. Sharpe, Inc.

M.E. Sharpe, Inc.
80 Business Park Drive
Armonk, NY 10504

Library of Congress Cataloging-in-Publication Data

Encyclopedia of the Jazz Age: from the end of World War I to the great crash / James Ciment, editor.
   p. cm.
Includes bibliographical references and index.
ISBN 978-0-7656-8078-5 (hardcover: alk. paper)

1. United States—History—1919–1933—Encyclopedias. 2. Nineteen twenties—Encyclopedias.
I. Ciment, James.

E784.E53 2007
973.91'503—dc22   2007023928

Cover Images provided by Getty Images and the following: (top row, left to right) Time & Life Pictures; Hulton Archive/Stringer; Hulton Archive; Stringer/Hulton Archive; (middle row) American Stock/Hulton Archive; Transcendental Graphics; Edward Gooch/Stringer/Hulton Archive; Kirby/Stringer/Hulton Archive; (bottom row) Harold Lloyd Trust/Hulton Archive; Getty UK/Hulton Archive; Frank Driggs Collection/Hulton Archive; Stringer/Hulton Archive.

Printed and bound in the United States of America

The paper used in this publication meets the minimum requirements of
American National Standard for Information Sciences
Permanence of Paper for Printed Library Materials,
ANSI Z 39.48.1984.

MV (c) 10 9 8 7 6 5 4 3 2 1

Contents

Sidebars

Topic Finder

Art, Literature, and Music

Algonquin Round Table
American Mercury
Anderson, Sherwood
Armstrong, Louis
Art, Fine
Baker, Josephine
Beiderbecke, Bix
Berlin, Irving
Blues
Bohemianism
Burroughs, Edgar Rice
Country Music
Cummings, E.E.
Dance, Performance
Design, Industrial
Dos Passos, John
Dreiser, Theodore
Eliot, T.S.
Fiction
Gershwin, George
Harlem Renaissance
Hemingway, Ernest
Hood, Raymond
Hughes, Langston
Jazz
Lewis, Sinclair
Locke, Alain
Lost Generation
McKay, Claude
Mead, Margaret
Mencken, H.L.
Music, Classical
New Yorker, The
O'Keeffe, Georgia
Oliver, Joe "King"
O'Neill, Eugene
Parker, Dorothy
Poetry
Radio
Ross, Harold
Smith, Bessie

Stein, Gertrude
Theater

Biographies

Anderson, Sherwood
Armstrong, Louis
Atlas, Charles
Baker, Josephine
Baldwin, Roger
Beiderbecke, Bix
Berger, Victor
Berlin, Irving
Bernays, Edward L.
Borah, William
Bow, Clara
Brandeis, Louis
Burroughs, Edgar Rice
Byrd, Richard E.
Capone, Al
Chaplin, Charlie
Coolidge, Calvin
Cummings, E.E.
Darrow, Clarence
Daugherty, Harry M.
Davis, John W.
Dawes, Charles
DeMille, Cecil B.
Dempsey, Jack
DePriest, Oscar
Dewey, John
Dos Passos, John
Dreiser, Theodore
Du Bois, W.E.B.
Ederle, Gertrude
Eliot, T.S.
Fairbanks, Douglas
Fisher, Carl
Fitzgerald, F. Scott, and Zelda Fitzgerald
Flynn, Elizabeth Gurley
Ford, Henry
Fosdick, Harry Emerson
Garvey, Marcus

Business, Economics, and Labor

Consumer and Popular Culture

Religion

Science and Technology

Women's Issues

General Editor
James Ciment

Contributors

John Barnhill
Independent Scholar

Christopher Bates
University of California, Los Angeles

Sarah Boslaugh
Washington University, St. Louis

Dino E. Buenviaje
University of California, Riverside

Michael H. Burchett
Limestone College

Tom Cerasulo
Elms College

April Smith Coffey
University of Alabama

Guy Patrick Cunningham
Independent Scholar

Charles E. Delgadillo
University of California, Santa Barbara

Kerry Dexter
Independent Scholar

Charles M. Dobbs
Iowa State University

Catherine W. Dolinski
Independent Scholar

Kathleen Drowne
University of Missouri, Rolla

Matthew Drumheller
McMurry University

Jon M. Eckert
Vanderbilt University

Erik P. Ellefsen
Boston University

Michael Faubion
University of Texas, Pan American

Abigail B. Feely
American River College

Richard M. Filipink, Jr.
Western Illinois University

John Fiorini
College of William and Mary

Russell Fowler
University of Tennessee, Chattanooga

Margaret L. Freeman
College of William and Mary

Gene C. Gerard
Independent Scholar

Rachel Gillett
Northeastern University

Kevin Grace
University of Cincinnati

Rob Hardin
University of Tennessee

John Paul Hill
University of Georgia

Matthew Hiner
Lakeland Community College

Sam Hitchmough
*Canterbury Christ Church University,
    United Kingdom*

Patrick Huber
University of Missouri, Rolla

William Hughes
Independent Scholar

Justin F. Jackson
University of Massachusetts

Michael Jacobs
University of Wisconsin, Baraboo

Steven B. Jacobson
University of Hawaii

Thomas F. Jorsch
Ferris State University

Beth Kattelman
Ohio State University

Kevin Kern
University of Akron

Leigh Kimmel
Independent Scholar

James E. Klein
Georgia State University

Steven Koczak
New York State Senate Research Service

Jodi Lacy
Adler Planetarium and Astronomy Museum

Tim Lacy
Loyola University, Chicago

Darin D. Lenz
Northwest University

Steven R. Loomis
Wheaton College, Illinois

Patrick Mallory
Loyola University, Chicago

David Malone
Wheaton College, Illinois

Robert F. Martin
University of Northern Iowa

Michael McGregor
Independent Scholar

Matthew K. McKean
Queen's University, Canada

Scott Merriman
University of Kentucky

Eric Paras
Independent Scholar

Jenifer Paras
Independent Scholar

Alison M. Perry
University of Texas

Justin H. Pettegrew
Independent Scholar

Kimberly K. Porter
University of North Dakota

Leslie Rabkin
Independent Scholar

Michael A. Rembis
University of Arizona

Maria Reynolds
Loyola University, Chicago

Marty Roth
University of Minnesota

Kathleen Ruppert
Independent Scholar

Erica J. Ryan
Brown University

Kelly Boyer Sagert
Independent Scholar

Margaret Sankey
Minnesota State University, Moorhead

Cord Scott
Loyola University, Chicago

David A. Serafini
Western Kentucky University

Charles J. Shindo
Louisiana State University

Adam Shprintzen
Loyola University, Chicago

Jason Stacy
Southern Illinois University, Edwardsville

Bruce E. Stewart
University of Georgia

David Stiles
University of Toronto, Canada

Gregory D. Sumner
University of Detroit Mercy

Jennifer Aerts Terry
American River College

Rebecca Tolley-Stokes
East Tennessee State University

William Toth
Mercy College

David Treviño
Donna Klein Jewish Academy

Marcella Bush Treviño
Barry University

Thomas Adams Upchurch
East Georgia College

Jennifer Jensen Wallach
Georgia College and State University

Andrew J. Waskey
Dalton State College

Tim J. Watts
Kansas State University

Simon Wendt
Free University of Berlin, Germany

Elizabeth Penn Whittenburg
Independent Scholar

Kevin Wozniak
Independent Scholar

Ben Wynne
Gainesville State College

Introduction

The Jazz Age was a decade of contrasts. While the popular image of the Roaring Twenties—one of a booming economy and carefree cultural excess—captures the general spirit of the times, the reality was far more nuanced and diverse.

Rarely had American big business done better than in the 1920s, with productivity and profits, not to mention stock prices, rising to unprecedented levels. The decade also saw stagnating wages, a labor movement in retreat, and persistent hard times on America's farms. The early part of the decade was marked by one of the most corruption-ridden administrations in U.S. history—that of Warren G. Harding—while its middle years saw the White House occupied by one of the most restrained and sober presidents of modern times—Calvin Coolidge.

New technology, most notably the automobile and the radio, united city and country as never before, forging a truly national popular culture. Yet the 1920s also witnessed a new divisiveness. Native-born Americans erected barriers against new immigrants, race relations deteriorated into rioting, and a mass exodus of blacks from the segregated and oppressive South swelled the urban centers of the Northeast, Midwest, and West.

Women gained the right to vote, but the impact on electoral politics and government policy promised by many who had fought for the Nineteenth Amendment went largely unrealized. An urban culture that celebrated, or at least tolerated, the lawlessness surrounding Prohibition and a new openness toward sexuality helped spark a reaction in rural and small-town America. And while writers and critics such as Sinclair Lewis and H.L. Mencken lambasted the cultural pretensions of a middle-class "booboisie," the 1920s were also a time of great artistic and literary expression—be it the writings of the Lost Generation or the efflorescence of African American culture in the Harlem Renaissance.

Few decades in American history are as clearly defined chronologically as the Jazz Age, which began on November 11, 1918, with the armistice that ended World War I, and concluded on October 24, 1929, the first day of the great stock market crash on Wall Street. In a sense, then, the 1920s are defined by what came before and after.

The period's probusiness conservatism and foreign-policy isolationism represented a reaction to the crusading spirit of the Progressive Era that had prevailed in the previous two decades and the Wilsonian idealism that had helped draw America into World War I. By contrast, the Jazz Age's flamboyant embrace of materialism is highlighted by the dark years of the Great Depression that followed. Indeed, the myth of Jazz Age abundance was largely a creation of those bleak economic times, when Americans looked back fondly—and a bit unrealistically—on a decade when their country seemed much more confident and hopeful.

If the Jazz Age represented a lighthearted hiatus between two more serious periods, the period also marked a national beginning of sorts. Social and intellectual historians frequently cite the 1920s as the birth of the modern era in America, emphasizing the growth of mass culture, public spectacle, and popular fads, as well as the more lasting contributions of artists and literary figures who broke from traditional influences—both home-bred and European—and forged a uniquely modern and American mode of expression. Indeed, the 1920s witnessed the full flowering of the modernist movement in the arts and letters. Writers, musicians, and visual artists experimented with new forms and content, attempting to capture the spirit of an age defined by the machine, the metropolis, and the dislocations of modern society.

None of this was entirely new, of course. Big business had begun to dominate the American economy at least a half century earlier, in the decades following the Civil War. American politicians' deference to the masters of finance and industry was hardly unique to the Jazz Age. Nor was the search for a uniquely American cultural expressiveness invented by writers such as F. Scott Fitzgerald, Gertrude Stein, and Ernest Hemingway or modernist painters such as Joseph Stella and Georgia O'Keeffe. Nineteenth-century poets and novelists, including Mark Twain,

Walt Whitman, and Herman Melville, already had created masterpieces in that quest, as had the visual artists of the nineteenth-century Hudson River and early twentieth-century Ashcan schools.

The great cultural divides of American life were nothing new either. No serious student of the country's history would date the origins of America's ambivalence about immigration, race, or the role of women in society to the decade that followed World War I. Indeed, the 1920s are remembered not so much as the beginning of the modern age but as the decade that embraced and glorified the modern. Something about the Jazz Age makes it seem more familiar to Americans of the early twenty-first century than any previous era in the nation's history.

For all the new technology, new media, modernist art, and power of big business, what makes the Jazz Age seem so modern is the contrast that defined it—the tension between centralization and democratization. Never before had so few dominated the lives of so many, whether it was the board members of major corporations determining the economic fate of millions of workers and investors, the advertisers of Madison Avenue dictating the tastes of consumers, or the producers of Hollywood movies and network radio programs purveying cultural offerings for countless moviegoers and radio listeners.

Yet the centers of American power and influence did not wield control in the service of some totalitarian order, as in the new Soviet Union or, during the following decade, in Nazi Germany. Far from it. In Jazz Age America, power and influence were exercised in the name of a new kind of democracy—not of politics, but of the pocketbook. Every successful entrepreneur, advertising executive, and purveyor of mass culture in the 1920s understood—as their counterparts do today—that all the power and wealth they enjoyed rested with the individual decisions of millions of consumers. Never before had so many had so many choices.

How to Use this Encyclopedia

The *Encyclopedia of the Jazz Age* is divided into three main sections. The first is a series of thematic essays on politics, business, society and culture, and foreign affairs. This section is followed by the major body of the work, a collection of more than 300 entries, organized alphabetically. These entries cover the important ideas, events, trends, institutions, and people of the period. Several dozen of these articles are accompanied by a sidebar feature that further explores a related theme or subject of interest.

The main A–Z section is followed by special material collected under the title "Cultural Landmarks" and divided into the categories of art and architecture; fiction, nonfiction, and poetry; and film, theater, and music. "Cultural Landmarks" provides descriptions of more than 100 of the most influential cultural offerings of the Jazz Age, including brief commentary on their historical and cultural significance.

The primary means of finding a subject of interest appears at the front of each volume: the Table of Contents, which is organized alphabetically, and the Topic Finder, which is organized by subject category. To help you locate special features within the entries, a list of sidebars also is provided. All articles feature bibliographies, and those in the A–Z section are cross-referenced to related entries. Also included in this work is a general bibliography, listing more than 500 of the most important titles on the Jazz Age, as well as a general index.

James Ciment

Essays

Politics

The Jazz Age, or 1920s—here defined as the period between the end of World War I, in November 1918, and the Wall Street crash of October 1929—was a period of both continuity and flux. Socially and economically, the nation experienced sweeping change. The U.S. Census of 1920 revealed that, for the first time in the nation's history, more Americans lived in towns and cities than in rural areas. The new urbanism was reflected in risqué fashions and carefree lifestyles. Meanwhile, according to historians, the economy also became increasingly modern, with a mass market for consumer products—most notably the automobile—and a growing reliance on credit buying. Yet in one critical arena—national politics—the Jazz Age was a throwback to earlier times.

While the Progressive Era, from the 1890s to World War I, had seen a host of reforms and an expansion of federal involvement in the daily lives of Americans, the 1920s were marked by a more laissez-faire approach to governance. Politicians in Washington turned away from the Progressive Era crusades that sought to rein in big business and to provide more services to ordinary Americans.

Between 1918 and 1929, the country was led by four presidents: Woodrow Wilson, Warren G. Harding, Calvin Coolidge, and Herbert Hoover. Wilson and Hoover, however, presided only at the very beginning and very end of the period. For the majority of the decade, the White House was occupied by Harding (1921–1923) and Coolidge (1923–1929). Both were conservative, probusiness Republicans who believed in limited government, and both practiced an executive style that delegated the day-to-day running of the government to others. Moreover, Republicans controlled the legislative branch, and the Supreme Court was presided over by conservative Chief Justice William Howard Taft, the former Republican president.

Wilson and the End of Progressivism

Historical eras do not always fall into neat categories. During the first several years of the Jazz Age, the country was led by the progressive Wilson, a Democrat. In 1917, the former Princeton University president and New Jersey governor had brought the country into World War I, calling it a crusade to make "the world safe for democracy." He had grand hopes for the postwar era, projecting the United States as a great power at the head of a League of Nations that would make war obsolete and lead to the spread of democracy worldwide. Seeking the support of Congress, Wilson campaigned vigorously in 1918 to retain Democratic control of Capitol Hill, hinting that Republicans were not fully supportive of the war effort and hence were disloyal. But the mood of the country was changing. The Republicans, campaigning in favor of laissez-faire government and an isolationist foreign policy, took control of both houses of Congress for the first time since 1911.

The supremely self-confident and somewhat self-righteous Wilson was undeterred. When the war was over, rather than send a representative to the Paris Peace Conference, Wilson headed a handpicked delegation that included but one Republican—and he was a foreign service officer, not a prominent politician. The president intended to speak for the United States himself. In Paris, Wilson was greeted as a hero by the French people for having aided them in their hour of need, but he was stonewalled by Allied leaders. His ambitious plans for peace—including self-determination for the colonized peoples of the world and a more forgiving attitude toward defeated Germany—were largely ignored in the Treaty of Versailles, signed in June 1919. The only major idea Wilson was able to sell to his European counterparts was the League of Nations.

Wilson came home to a hostile Senate, the branch of Congress charged by the Constitution with approving treaties negotiated by the president. He virtually ordered Congress to ratify the treaty. Still angry over the 1918 campaign and stung by Wilson's decision to close them out of the Paris talks, Republicans in the Senate were not ready to concede total

The inauguration of President Warren G. Harding (hatless, at center) on March 4, 1921, marked the beginning of a decade of Republican ascendancy in Washington, D.C. *(General Photographic Agency/Stringer/Hulton Archive/Getty Images)*

control of the peace process. There were also ideological differences between the president and the Republicans. Wilson was an internationalist, believing that the United States had a vital role to play in world affairs. Many Republicans were isolationists, believing that the United States, protected as it was by vast oceans, was best served by remaining aloof from foreign involvement outside the Western Hemisphere.

The Senate majority leader, Henry Cabot Lodge (R-MA), stood somewhere in the middle. As head of the Foreign Relations Committee, he sought a middle ground, favoring the League of Nations but wanting to ensure that U.S. membership would not subject the country's foreign policy to the dictates of international bureaucrats. President Wilson, however, convinced of the rightness of his plan, refused to compromise and embarked on a strenuous national speaking tour in the summer of 1919 to win public support for the peace treaty and U.S. membership in the League. Exhausted by his efforts, he suffered a serious stroke in early October and was left largely incapacitated for the rest of his term in office; day-to-day management of the administration was turned

over to his wife, Edith. In November, the Senate voted to reject the peace treaty.

Twelve months later, in November 1920, the nation faced its first general election since the end of the war. Wilson, still ailing, wanted the election to be a referendum on the treaty. Indeed it was, though not in the way the president hoped. Republicans dramatically increased their majorities in the House and Senate and took control of the presidency after eight years of Democratic leadership. Indeed, the losing Democratic candidate for president, Ohio Governor James Cox, while supporting the League, distanced himself from Wilson during the campaign. Sweeping to victory (in the first national elections in which women could vote) was another Ohioan, Republican Senator Warren G. Harding, who campaigned on the platform of "normalcy," a term he had coined but never fully defined. Most voters, it seems, took it to mean a shift away from government crusades at home and abroad, an end to U.S. involvement in European affairs, and a dramatic scaling back of federal involvement in the economy.

Wilson had utterly misjudged the mood of a newly conservative American people, who were distrustful of foreigners—both cynical European leaders and the alien immigrants flooding American cities—and fearful of radicalism. In 1919–1920, the country was gripped by a "Red Scare," partly in reaction to the Communist revolution in Russia. Thousands of radicals were arrested in nationwide raids, and hundreds of aliens were deported from the United States.

Overall, most Americans were interested in pursuing private interests rather than public crusades. As the 1920s began, they wanted an end to government involvement in economic affairs and a retreat from U.S. involvement in world affairs. In a word, they wanted "normalcy."

Harding and Coolidge: Republican Ascendancy

Critics said Harding was underqualified for the job of president, considering him "a good second rater," and by Harding's own account, he was no crusading chief executive. Indeed, he admitted publicly that he did not "seem to grasp" that he was president of the United States. Still, the new president did make some ripples upon taking office. He pardoned a number of war critics the Wilson administration had jailed under harsh wartime antisubversion legislation. Among those pardoned was the Socialist Party presidential candidate and labor leader Eugene V. Debs. Conservatives, including the American Legion, denounced the president for his decision. Nor was Harding's term in office devoid of reform. In 1921, he signed the Sheppard-Towner Act, which authorized federal funds for health care for pregnant women and young children. The program was controversial, as it marked the first time that Washington stepped into the medical marketplace in a significant way.

The president did appoint several esteemed figures to his cabinet, including former presidential candidate Charles Evans Hughes as secretary of state and future president Herbert Hoover as secretary of commerce. More controversial was the appointment of former banking magnate Andrew Mellon as secretary of the treasury. Extremely conservative, Mellon helped pushed through a major tax cut as part of his overall economic philosophy of limiting government involvement in economic affairs.

The Harding administration, however, is probably best remembered for its scandals. Whatever one thought of his politics, Mellon was at least an honest public servant. That could not be said of several other Harding appointees. Secretary of the Interior Albert Fall, a former Republican senator from New Mexico, was convicted in 1924 of receiving bribes in exchange for leases on government oil reserves at Teapot Dome, Wyoming. Fall would be fined $100,000 and spend a year in jail for his crimes. The head of the Veterans Bureau, Charles Forbes, went to prison for accepting bribes and committing fraud. And closest to the president among those accused of wrongdoing was Attorney General Harry Daugherty, a member of Harding's campaign staff who escaped prosecution—also on bribery and fraud charges—only by refusing to testify against himself.

Harding's problem, his father once noted, was that he trusted others too much. "I have no trouble with my enemies," Harding told a journalist in the midst of the scandals, "but my friends . . . they're the ones that keep me walking the floor nights." To borrow a phrase from the late twentieth century, Harding was no "hands-on" manager. Indeed, he seemed more at home at the poker table than behind his desk in the Oval Office. In the spirit of the Roaring Twenties, he enjoyed his parties, his mistresses, and his hidden cache of liquor (the manufacture and sale of alcohol were illegal during the Prohibition years, 1920 to 1933). Perhaps it was for this reason that Harding remained popular in spite of the scandals—that and the

A series of scandals involving government oil reserves in Wyoming—collectively known as Teapot Dome—brought down a number of major figures in the Warren Harding administration. President Harding died in August 1923, before the scandal became a major public embarrassment. (*MPI/Stringer/Hulton Archive/Getty Images*)

prosperity the country was enjoying after a short but sharp postwar recession. In either case, Harding's premature death in August 1923, while he was on a tour of the Western states, was much mourned.

It would be hard to imagine a more striking contrast to Harding than his vice president and successor, Calvin Coolidge, at least as far as their private lives were concerned. A native of Vermont, Coolidge had earned his stripes as the Massachusetts governor who took a hard line against striking Boston police in 1919 (he fired the lot and brought in the National Guard to restore order). Where Harding was something of a playboy, Coolidge was a dour family man.

Ideologically, however, the two were of a piece. Like his predecessor, "Silent Cal" was a probusiness Republican who believed in limited government and a reserved executive. His nickname came from his proclivity to say little in public, and he was famous for his afternoon naps. Whether because of his laissez-faire policies—he kept Mellon on as treasury secretary—or despite them, Coolidge's America enjoyed unprecedented prosperity. Moreover, the new president also was sympathetic to the nativist mood of the country, signing into law the Immigration Act of 1924, establishing national quotas that were especially harsh on immigrants from Southern and Eastern Europe.

By the time of the 1924 election, the Republicans were in no mood for change; they nominated Coolidge as their presidential candidate. The Democrats, meanwhile, were in a state of almost total disarray. Divided on economic, immigration, and race issues—failing to condemn the resurgent Ku Klux Klan, whose virulent antiblack, anti-immigrant message attracted some 5 million members by the mid-1920s—the party took 103 convention ballots to nominate dark horse candidate John W. Davis, a former one-term congressman from West Virginia. The Democrats had come a long way from the progressive Wilson of the 1910s. Davis was a corporate lawyer whose probusiness proclivities differed little from those of Coolidge, who aptly characterized the dominant political spirit of the 1920s when he stated, "the chief business of the American people is business." Coolidge won in a landslide, with 54 percent of the vote to Davis's 29 percent. Still, the crusading spirit of the prewar era was not entirely dead, as Progressive Party candidate Robert M. La Follette of Wisconsin won 17 percent of the vote. Much of La Follette's support came from those parts of America not sharing in the general prosperity—the depressed agricultural sector and immigrant poor of the nation's largest cities.

As the renowned journalist Walter Lippmann once remarked, "grim, determined, alert inactivity . . . keeps Mr. Coolidge occupied constantly." Indeed, Coolidge considered it a badge of honor that he did little to govern, believing that the nation could take care of itself. He resisted introducing major domestic legislation and left foreign policy largely in the hands of his secretaries of state, Hughes and Frank Kellogg. His administration, however, was not without legislative and regulatory highlights. Coolidge signed the McNary-Haugen bills of 1927 and 1928, which established government price supports for staple crops and represented the first major federal intervention in the agricultural marketplace. And Hoover, an activist commerce secretary, established regulations for the burgeoning aviation and radio industries.

Coolidge also departed somewhat from the isolationism of the Harding administration, particularly late in his term. Secretary of State Frank Kellogg helped negotiate the ambitious 1928 Kellogg-Briand Pact with French Foreign Minister Aristide Briand, renouncing war "as an instrument of national policy." Coolidge also sent a high-level delegation to the 1928 Havana Conference of the Pan American Union (now the Organization of American States), which attempted to present a less interventionist foreign policy toward the United States' hemispheric neighbors.

The nation continued to prosper—at least most of it. By 1928, the national economy seemed to be in permanent growth mode, with the stock market reaching new highs by the month. Had he asked for it, Coolidge surely would have been renominated by his party and most likely re-elected by the American people. But "Silent Cal" declined a second term, saying only "I do not choose to run for president in 1928." Leading the pack for the Republican nomination was Hoover, who, despite his role in some of the most conservative Republican administrations of the twentieth century, was somewhat of a progressive.

Hoover and the Decline of Republican Hegemony

A native Iowan, Herbert Hoover had made a fortune in international mining ventures before leading U.S. relief efforts to aid refugees in the aftermath of World War I. Unlike Harding and Coolidge, Hoover did not believe in laissez-faire government, nor did he subscribe to the view that the capitalist system was most efficient when left to its own devices. Yet neither did he share Wilson's or Theodore Roosevelt's penchant for government regulation or trustbusting. Instead, as commerce secretary, Hoover had tried to establish cooperative relations between business and government, whereby the latter would establish rules for fair competition and plans for economic efficiency. Compliance would always be voluntary, however, as businesses could never be forced or coerced by government dictate. Hoover hoped that business leaders could be persuaded, by idea and example, that following the government's lead would result in greater profits and growth. "Associationalism" was the underlying principle of Hoover's thinking; businesses should create associations, which in turn would create stable yet competitive sectors of industry and efficient systems of manufacturing.

Even more than the reserved Coolidge and the controversial Mellon, Hoover was widely credited with the prosperity of the late 1920s. His reputation was such that he faced virtually no competition at the 1928 Republican convention, winning the nomination on the first ballot.

The Democrats offered a very different choice, nominating New York Governor Al Smith as their candidate. A product of the rough-and-tumble school of New York City politics, Smith had risen through the ranks of the Tammany Hall political machine. A descendant of Irish immigrants, Smith was also something no other major party candidate had ever been—a Roman Catholic. As reflected by the rise of the Ku Klux Klan and the Immigration Act of 1924, there was a strong anti-immigrant strain in America in the 1920s; much of that sentiment was premised on the idea that foreigners were members of a church regarded as alien to the democratic spirit of the country. Many Americans felt that a Roman Catholic owed first allegiance to the pope and was therefore implicitly disloyal and un-American. There was also a great urban-rural divide to the country in the 1920s, with many residents of small-town America believing that cities were the source of crime, sin, and radical politics. Given these handicaps and the continued prosperity of the country under Republican leadership, it was not surprising that Smith lost in a landslide, winning almost all of his eighty-seven electoral votes in the solidly Democratic South, still so hostile to the party of Abraham Lincoln that they would choose a Catholic New Yorker over a Republican.

Unlike his two Republican predecessors, Hoover was determined to be an activist president. His appointments—including a number of businessmen in high-level cabinet posts and young professionals in lower-level positions—reflected his own background of business and philanthropy infused with technocratic expertise. While there were warning signs of potential economic troubles—manufacturing indices were down slightly from the previous year—Hoover took office at a time of great optimism, and the stock market surged to new heights during the first eight months of his administration.

Then came the crash. On a series of trading days in late October 1929, stock prices plummeted, wiping out vast paper fortunes. Efforts by banks and wealthy investors failed to rally the market. Within months, the general economy was slipping into depression, as business profits disappeared and unemployment and bankruptcies soared. Hoover tried some limited government measures to revive the economy, including the creation of the Reconstruction Finance Corporation, which provided federal loans to struggling financial institutions, large corporations, and eventually local and state governments, in the hope that rescuing these institutions would lead to jobs and income for those lower on the economic ladder. But the president, committed to the ideology of nineteenth-century individualism, refused to provide large-scale government job programs or relief for the expanding population of impoverished Americans. That reluctance, along with his inability to convey a sense of hope and the public's perception that his administration did not seem to have an appropriate level of concern for the state of the nation's poor, doomed him and the Republican Party at the polls.

In the 1930 congressional elections, the first of the Great Depression, the Democrats erased their deficits on Capitol Hill, taking control of the House and coming within one seat of the Republicans in the Senate. But it was in the election of 1932 that the Republicans fully paid the price for presiding over the worst economic collapse in the nation's history. Not only did the Democratic candidate for president, New York Governor Franklin D. Roosevelt, trounce Hoover in a landslide, but Democrats won huge majorities in both houses of Congress. Just as the Republicans had reaped the political benefits of 1920s prosperity over which they presided, so they paid the price for the economic collapse of the early 1930s.

With their victory in 1932 and subsequent Depression-era elections, Roosevelt and the Democrats had put together a coalition of Southern party stalwarts and Northern workers that would dominate the country's politics almost continuously through the 1970s.

Scott Merriman and James Ciment

Further Reading

Allen, Frederick Lewis. *Only Yesterday: An Informal History of the 1920s.* New York: Perennial Classics, 2000.

Bernstein, Irving. *The Lean Years: A History of the American Worker, 1920–1933.* Boston: Houghton Mifflin, 1960.

Braeman, John, Robert H. Bremner, and David Brody, eds. *Change and Continuity in Twentieth-Century America: The 1920s.* Columbus: Ohio State University Press, 1968.

Carter, Paul A. *The Twenties in America.* 2nd ed. Arlington Heights, IL: Harlan Davidson, 1987.

Goldberg, Ronald Allen. *America in the Twenties.* Syracuse, NY: Syracuse University Press, 2003.

Hicks, John Donald. *Republican Ascendancy, 1921–1933.* New York: Harper, 1960.

Miller, Nathan. *New World Coming: The 1920s and the Making of Modern America.* New York: Scribner's, 2003.

Perrett, Geoffrey. *America in the Twenties: A History.* New York: Simon and Schuster, 1982.

Schlesinger, Arthur, Jr. *The Crisis of the Old Order, 1919–1933.* Boston: Houghton Mifflin, 2003.

Business, Economics, and Labor

It is perhaps the most frequently quoted comment on the relationship between American economics and politics. Notably, it was uttered by one of the most taciturn presidents in the country's history. "The chief business of the American people," said Calvin Coolidge in a 1925 speech, "is business." Silent Cal may have said little, but in this case he spoke volumes.

Business—more specifically, big business—dominated virtually every aspect of life in the United States during the Jazz Age. Captains of industry such as Henry Ford and General Electric's Gerard Swope were lauded as national heroes; Ford's name was even bandied about as a possible presidential candidate. Advertising executive Bruce Barton wrote *The Man Nobody Knows,* a 1924 best seller depicting Jesus as the founder of modern business, having "picked up twelve men [the apostles] from the bottom ranks of business and forged them into an organization [the Christian church] that conquered the world."

Probusiness Republicans occupied the presidency from 1921 through 1932, and the party controlled both houses of Congress—at times with overwhelming majorities—from 1919 through 1931. The GOP used that power to promote a probusiness governing agenda, significantly lowering taxes on business and the wealthy and halting antitrust action initiated during the earlier Progressive Era. Probusiness justices on the U.S. Supreme Court issued rulings that consistently favored business interests, ruling child labor and minimum wage laws unconstitutional.

Manufacturers offered all kinds of new consumer durables—most notably the automobile, but also household appliances such as the radio and the refrigerator—that profoundly changed the way Americans lived, traveled, and entertained themselves. Advertising was transformed from the purely informational to the seductive, altering how people viewed themselves and their lives. New credit schemes were introduced, giving consumers the ability to purchase goods beyond their immediate means and, in the process, overturning centuries-old admonitions about the dangers and immorality of debt. Business came to dominate the world of entertainment through the media of radio and motion pictures and the promotion of mass spectator sports like baseball.

Indeed, not since the Gilded Age of the late nineteenth century or until the administration of Ronald Reagan in the 1980s would big business play such a central role in American society. And, as in those other eras, what business offered was not economic equality or justice but material abundance. Thus, while the 1920s represent one of the great economic booms in U.S. history, the era also saw millions of Americans unable to reap the benefits of the good times. Of course those times came to an abrupt end in the Wall Street crash of 1929, triggering the Great Depression, the worst economic calamity in the history of the republic.

Like so much else about the Jazz Age, the economy of the 1920s was riddled with contradictions. The popular image is one of unbridled prosperity, though this view first emerged in the depths of the Great Depression. By contrast to those hard times, the economy of the 1920s—for all its flaws—seemed positively buoyant. Still, there is some truth to the image. Business, particularly big business, rarely had it so good. With a supportive federal government behind them, the nation's corporations chalked up huge profits and productivity gains, all reflected in share prices that, with a few bumps along the way, rose steadily throughout the decade, soaring to positively giddy heights by 1929. This economic exuberance leant the Jazz Age its other nickname—the Roaring Twenties.

Millionaires and corporations were not the only ones to share in the good times. Millions of Americans, particularly skilled workers and the educated white-collar middle class, saw their wages and salaries increase, even as prices held steady, allowing them to purchase an enticing array of new products. Moreover, after the dislocations of World War I demobilization and a sharp but brief recession early in the decade, unemployment remained consistently

9

American manufacturing in general and the automobile industry in particular boomed during the 1920s. Here, workers at the Ford Motor Company's massive Dearborn, Michigan, plant assemble one of the millions of Model Ts that put Americans behind the wheel. *(Hulton Collection/ Hulton Archive/Getty Images)*

low, offering unskilled and semiskilled workers a steady paycheck.

The drawback was that these paychecks did not go up. Compared to the wage gains of the skilled and educated, not to mention the huge profits enjoyed by corporations, workers at the bottom slid further behind. Although a number of factors were behind the unequal distribution of the nation's growing bounty, surely one of the most important was the weakness of organized labor. After an unprecedented wave of strikes in the first years following the armistice of 1918, most of the labor activity in subsequent years was defeated by the combined forces of government and management, and unions saw their membership decline significantly over the course of the decade. Unable to bargain collectively, workers were hard put to insist on their fair share of the gains enjoyed by Jazz Age businesses. For those who made their living off the land, the decade was especially trying, with crop prices depressed and farm debt at record heights.

Early Troubles

America's economy was far from roaring in the first years of the Jazz Age, as the transition from a wartime to a peacetime economy was anything but smooth. During World War I, the federal government expanded its spending manyfold, from several hundred million dollars annually at the outset to nearly $2

billion a month for the duration of the conflict. The money kept factories humming with defense production while unemployment virtually disappeared, the latter due to the fact that nearly 4 million Americans were in uniform. When the war ended, pent-up demand for consumer products sent prices soaring; inflation ran at over 30 percent in 1919. Fearing that inflation would eat into their savings, Americans spent their money even faster, creating new demand and further fueling inflation. With wages failing to keep up with demand, a wave of strikes spread across the country in 1919 and early 1920. Roughly 4 million workers—about 20 percent of the nation's industrial workforce—walked off their jobs in more than 3,000 strikes during 1919 alone. While most of the strikes went against the workers, the disruptions caused by labor agitation further crippled productivity and contributed to rising prices.

To curb the inflationary spiral, the administration of Woodrow Wilson and the newly formed, semi-independent Federal Reserve Board instituted measures that helped plunge the economy into recession. Believing that government debt soaked up financial resources needed by business to expand production and thereby bring down inflation, the White House dramatically cut back federal spending. Meanwhile, the Federal Reserve, convinced that its expansive, low-interest monetary policies during the war had encouraged excessive consumer spending and debt, tightened credit drastically. Further compounding the problem was a steep decline in exports—down from $13.5 billion in 1920 to less than $7 billion in 1921—due to the drop in demand for American products from European nations recovering from the war. The resulting recession from late 1920 to early 1922 was one of the sharpest, but briefest, in American history. Unemployment soared from roughly 3 percent to more than 10 percent at the depths of the downturn in late 1921. In the end, the budget and monetary policies, however disruptive in the short term, had their intended effect, at least as far as inflation was concerned. During the recession, prices fell by almost 20 percent, wiping out most of the gains of the early postwar period.

Economic Takeoff

By early 1922, the economy was in full recovery mode. With a few mild downturns along the way, it remained healthy throughout the decade; unemployment never rose above 4 percent, and inflation was almost nonexistent. Between 1922 and 1929, the gross national product rose from $74.1 billion to $103.1 billion, an expansion of roughly 40 percent. Meanwhile, per capita income rose from about $640 in 1921 to nearly $850 in 1929, a nearly one-third increase.

Several factors contributed to the solid economic performance. First and foremost were technology-driven productivity gains. The expansion of the electricity grid allowed businesses to replace steam engines with smaller, cleaner, more efficient electric motors. While home usage accounted for some of the gains, much of America's dramatically increased electricity output—from nearly 39 million kilowatt hours in 1919 to more than 97 million in 1929, a nearly 150 percent increase—was consumed by business and industry. Communications also improved in the 1920s; the number of telephone lines in the country grew from fewer than 30 million in 1920 to about 70 million by 1930, an increase of about 133 percent.

Head offices could now communicate more effectively with branches, factories, and customers. If the telephone facilitated better business communication, so the internal combustion engine made it easier to move goods and people. And just as electricity allowed businesses to decentralize operations—replacing one big steam engine with several small electrical motors—so the motor truck, powered by an internal combustion engine, freed businesses from established rail lines. It also made delivering goods to customers far more efficient, as the truck could move faster and carry more than the horse-drawn vehicles they replaced for short-haul loads.

But technology was only one factor behind the growing productivity of business and industry. The 1920s also saw the widespread implementation of new management techniques. Known as "scientific management" or Taylorism—after Frederick Taylor, the management theorist who first developed the idea—the new techniques included tight managerial control over workers, extensive on-the-job training,

After expanding rapidly to meet the needs of World War I, America's agricultural sector languished in recession throughout the 1920s. African American sharecroppers, such as these farmers bringing their cotton to a gin in Alabama, were particularly hard hit. *(MPI/Hulton Archive/Getty Images)*

and rigid time limits and rules for how long a worker should take and what methods should be used to complete a task. If this kind of rigid control seems counterproductive by modern standards, it worked wonders in both the assembly-line factories and bureaucratic, precomputer offices of the day.

Meanwhile, forward-looking executives like Alfred Sloan, Jr., at General Motors (GM) were reconfiguring the way management itself operated. Sloan relieved GM's top managers from overseeing day-to-day production, allowing them to concentrate on overall strategy and long-term planning. The GM model soon became the norm for big business. To find the right people, executives came to rely increasingly on graduates of leading business and engineering schools. Indeed, during much of the decade, top companies like Singer, DuPont, and Goodyear were headed by engineering graduates of the Massachusetts Institute of Technology. Recognizing the importance of new technology, these engineering and management experts expanded their companies' research and development divisions. By 1927, more than 1,000 major American corporations had set up research programs, the most famous being the Bell Labs division of American Telephone and Telegraph, incorporated as a separate company in 1925.

The buoyant 1920s economy was not solely attributable to changes at the supply end. Increased demand, particularly for consumer durables, contributed as well. While neither the automobile nor the many popular household appliances of the era were invented in the 1920s, demand for them increased dramatically between 1919 and 1929. In 1920, U.S. manufacturers produced roughly 2.2 million automobiles; by 1929, that figure had climbed to 5.3 million, a 140 percent increase. Similar gains were being recorded for other consumer durables. In 1914, American manufacturers produced less than $7 million worth of washing machines; by 1927, the figure was close to $75 million. Before World War I, the number of home refrigerators in America could be counted in the hundreds; by 1927, U.S. manufacturers were producing nearly $100 million worth.

Nor was the demand confined to consumer durables. With banks beginning to offer more affordable mortgages, millions of Americans were buying their own homes for the first time. Expanding businesses were building new office headquarters and new factories. Together, these forces created a boom in both real estate and the construction industry. Be-

tween 1921 and 1927, the value of new construction doubled from $6 to $12 billion annually.

The 1920s were not only a time of high productivity and demand but also one of the great eras of consolidation in American business history. More corporate mergers took place in the six years from 1924 through 1929 than in any equivalent period in U.S. history to that time. In 1929 alone, there were nearly 1,250. The wave of consolidation, much of it financed by New York banks, firmly established Wall Street as the center of American finance, with just 1 percent of banking firms controlling almost 50 percent of the nation's banking assets. Nevertheless, banking across the country boomed, with assets rising from $48 billion in 1919 to $72 billion in 1929. The United States became the world's financial leader, emerging from World War I as the largest creditor nation. Nearly twelve years after the war, America's allies still owed the United States some $4.3 billion. U.S. businesses were also active overseas. By 1929, American corporations had made direct overseas investments of more than $15 billion. The investments were a mixed lot, in everything from automobile manufacturing plants in Great Britain and Germany to cattle farms in Argentina, banana plantations in Central America, and oil wells and refineries in Mexico and Venezuela.

Probusiness Government

Big business had an active and sympathetic partner in the federal government of the 1920s. Banker and industrialist Andrew Mellon served as secretary of the treasury through three presidential administrations, beginning his term in 1921 with a massive tax cut—largely for wealthy Americans and corporations—designed to spur private investment. An old-school conservative, Mellon believed that government should intervene as little as possible in the economy by keeping taxes and regulations to a minimum. This was a dramatic change from the reformist Progressive Era that witnessed the creation of new regulatory agencies like the Food and Drug Administration as well as ratification of the Sixteenth Amendment to the U.S. Constitution, establishing the graduated income tax. Meanwhile, the Justice Department dropped its long-running antitrust case against U.S. Steel, signaling a retreat from the trust-busting advocated by presidents going back to Theodore Roosevelt.

While the efforts of Mellon and the Justice Department enjoyed a certain conservative ideological consistency—less government interference allowed the markets to function more efficiently—Congress's decision to pass one of the toughest tariff laws in U.S. history, the Fordney-McCumber Tariff of 1922, was a sop to manufacturing interests. Republicans had long supported high tariffs to protect infant industries against stiff foreign competition, and by the 1920s, America's manufacturers were among the wealthiest, most powerful, and most efficient in the world, needing little in the way of protection. In fact, the growing number of big American businesses with foreign operations, including General Motors and Standard Oil of New Jersey, opposed the tariff. Moreover, the tariff had a negative effect on international finances, making it difficult for countries in debt to the United States to sell their products in America, thereby making it even harder for them to pay off their debts.

Perhaps the most interesting ideas about how government could aid business in the 1920s came from the mind of Herbert Hoover. Now most remembered for his unpopular economic policies in the early years of the Great Depression, Hoover was something of a business hero during much of the 1920s. As head of the Commerce Department under presidents Harding and Coolidge, Hoover pioneered a program for cooperation between government and business that he labeled "associationalism." Under this program, the federal government would assist industries in setting up voluntary trade organizations, or associations, that would gather useful market information and promote the industries to the public, both American and foreign. The associations would encourage businesses to pool their resources for research and development purposes. Most significantly, in the interests of promoting efficiency and avoiding the destructive competition of pure laissez-faire capitalism, the associations would foster cooperation among businesses with respect to price and wage stability. Normally, such associations would be viewed as illegal restraints on trade, but in the probusiness climate of the era, the Federal Trade Commission decided not to enforce applicable antitrust laws and allowed the agreements that set up these associations to stand.

Labor's Hard Times

Government in the 1920s was far less supportive of the interests of labor. During the great wave of strikes in 1919 and 1920, local and state governments followed the traditional practice of using police and National Guard troops to help protect strikebreakers and business property, with the usual effect of forcing striking workers to return to their jobs. Even after the labor militancy had come to an end, however, American workers and their unions faced a sustained assault from government, and particularly the courts. In 1922 and 1923, the U.S. Supreme Court issued a string of rulings that rendered Progressive Era laws designed to protect workers unconstitutional. In *Bailey v. Drexel Furniture Company* (1922), the Court held that a special tax on child labor represented an unconstitutional penalty against businesses, and in *Adkins v. Children's Hospital* (1923), the Court declared minimum wage laws an unconstitutional infringement on an individual's right to make a contract of his or her own choosing. Perhaps the most devastating for organized labor was *Colorado Coal Company v. United Mine Workers* (1923), in which the Court declared that a union and its officials could be prosecuted under the nation's antitrust laws because calling for workers to go on strike represented an illegal restraint of trade.

Labor faced more than a hostile legal climate in the 1920s. Management was particularly active in its efforts to break the power of unions. By instituting scientific management principles, companies took away the power of shop foremen to set the work pace. Many corporations set up "company unions," worker organizations under company control, as a way to prevent workers from joining independent trade unions. Still others tried to negate unions altogether by offering workers some of the benefits that traditionally only organized labor could obtain for them—such as sick leave, health plans, vacation time, and shorter work hours. By the end of the 1920s, the five or five-and-a-half day workweek had replaced the traditional six-day week in many industries. Moreover, the general prosperity of the times and the steadily rising wages of skilled workers—the backbone of the labor movement until the 1930s—encouraged many to leave unions and others never to join. The impact of these various factors on the ranks of organized labor was nothing short of devastating. Between 1917 and 1920, union membership had climbed by some 70 percent, from just under 3 million to roughly 5 million, but by 1930, it had fallen back to 3.4 million, or just 11.6 percent of the labor force—the lowest figure in twentieth-century labor history.

Structural Weaknesses and the Great Crash

While wages for skilled workers rose slowly but steadily during the decade, for the masses of unskilled laborers they were virtually stagnant. Given the impressive productivity gains of the 1920s—and the drastically lower taxes on the wealthy put into place by Mellon—this meant that most of the vast new wealth generated by corporate America was accruing to fewer and fewer people. In fact, the 1920s saw the gap in income and wealth between America's wealthiest and poorest citizens grow dramatically. While per capita disposable income rose 9 percent from 1921 to 1929, that of the top 1 percent of the population rose 75 percent, accounting for most of the overall increase.

Some of that wealth was eaten up by conspicuous consumption, but much of it went into speculation. Early in the decade, real estate was the most popular investment. By the late 1920s, however, virtually everyone with disposable wealth and income was investing in the stock market. In the two years leading up to the great crash of October 1929, the average price of stocks rose nearly 50 percent. Soon the middle class was joining in; by 1929, some 10 percent of American households owned stock, many having purchased it on margin (buying a percentage of the stock with one's own capital and borrowing the rest from banks and brokerage houses). All of the speculation and margin buying represented a financial house of cards; when stock prices began to decline in the fall of 1929, there was little to stop them from collapse. Overleveraged investors were forced to sell their stock for whatever they could get in order to meet their margins, which they often failed to do, bringing down banks and brokerage firms with them.

Still, most economic historians agree that the crash of 1929 might have been confined to Wall Street and stock speculators but for other underlying weaknesses in the national economy. One of these was the widening gap between rich and poor. With the wages of the working class essentially stagnant, millions of Americans went into debt to buy the shiny new goods presented to them by the increasingly sophisticated advertisers of the 1920s. While the demand for new housing and automobiles peaked in 1928, the level of debt generated by this degree of consumption could not be sustained forever and inevitably led to a lowering of demand. This had an inevitable ripple effect, as merchandisers began to

The Hollywood trade paper *Variety* responds to the stock market crash of October 29, 1929, with a tongue-in-cheek headline. Black Tuesday, as it came to be called, marked the unofficial end of the Jazz Age. *(Library of Congress, LC-USZ62–70085)*

accumulate larger inventories, which forced them to cut back on their orders to manufacturers.

Meanwhile, a host of weakened industries—from coal (facing growing competition from oil) to textiles (too much capacity) to railroads (under assault from trucks and buses)—continued to drag on the economy. No sector of the 1920s economy was weaker than agriculture. Indeed, some economic historians speak of a continuous agricultural depression that ran from the end of World War I through the beginning of World War II. The problem for American agriculture dated to World War I, when growers expanded their output to meet demand from Europe. At that time, American farmers had borrowed heavily to buy new land and equipment to meet wartime demand. But when the European agricultural sector revived after the war, American farmers found themselves saddled with debt—and an excess of capacity. The result was depressed crop prices and farm incomes. While nonfarm incomes averaged roughly $750 during the decade, farm incomes averaged just over $250. Given that farmers represented roughly one-fourth of the U.S. workforce in 1920 and one-fifth in 1930, a depressed agricultural sector represented a major weakness in the national economy.

Nor was business as healthy as it appeared. Not only did it face declining demand by the late 1920s, but many corporations found themselves deeply in debt. While consumers had gone into the red to buy new products and farmers had never emerged from the debt they accumulated in World

War I, businesses borrowed heavily during the frenzy of corporate consolidation in the second half of the decade.

Given all of these structural weaknesses, it is not surprising that the 1929 stock market crash pre-cipitated an even greater depression throughout the American economy. As America had become the global financial leader by the end of World War I, much of the rest of the world was also plunged into economic hard times.

In the United States, the economic excesses of the 1920s led to a dramatically altered political cli-mate. Government no longer deferred to big busi-ness; instead, under Franklin D. Roosevelt's New Deal, it sought to regulate and control the private sector through agencies such as the National Recov-ery Administration and the Securities and Exchange Commission. Organized labor was given a new lease on life with the National Labor Relations Act (1935), which offered the protection of the federal govern-ment to workers trying to set up or join unions. And the public seemed much less enamored with big business and wealthy executives. Having credited the titans of industry with the boom times of the Jazz Age, it was only natural that those same business leaders would receive the blame when the economy of the Roaring Twenties ground to a halt.

James Ciment

Further Reading

Allan, Frederick Lewis. *Only Yesterday: An Informal History of the 1920s.* New York: John Wiley and Sons, 1997.

Arnesen, Eric. *Black Protest and the Great Migration: A Brief History with Documents.* Boston: Bedford/St. Martin's, 2003.

Atack, Jeremy, and Peter Passell. *A New Economic View of American History.* 2nd ed. New York: W.W. Norton, 1994.

Best, Gary Dean. *The Dollar Decade: Mammon and the Machine in 1920s America.* Westport, CT: Praeger, 2003.

Carter, Susan B., Scott Sigmund Gartner, Michael R. Haines, Alan L. Olmstead, Richard Sutch, and Gavin Wright, eds. *Historical Statistics of the United States, Millennial Edition.* New York: Cambridge University Press, 2006.

Earle, Jonathan. *The Routledge Atlas of African American History.* New York: Routledge, 2000.

Heilbroner, Robert. *Teachings from the Worldly Philosophy.* New York: W.W. Norton, 1996.

———. *The Worldly Philosophers: The Lives, Times, and Ideas of the Great Economic Thinkers.* 7th ed. New York: Touch-stone/Simon & Schuster, 1999.

Heilbroner, Robert, and Aaron Singer. *The Economic Transfor-mation of America: 1600 to the Present.* 4th ed. Fort Worth, TX: Harcourt Bruce College, 1999.

Hing, Bill Ong. *Making and Remaking Asian America Through Immigration Policy, 1850–1990.* Stanford, CA: Stanford University Press, 1993.

Hoffert, Sylvia D. *A History of Gender in America: Essays, Doc-uments, and Articles.* Upper Saddle River, NJ: Prentice Hall, 2003.

MacMillan, Margaret. *Paris 1919: Six Months That Changed the World.* New York: Random House, 2003.

Temin, Peter. *Lessons from the Great Depression.* Cambridge: Massachusetts Institute of Technology Press, 1989.

Family, Community, and Society

Historians are wont to say that significant social changes occurred in whatever period they happen to be discussing. That claim may be truer for some periods than for others. One of those periods is the Jazz Age. No decade in twentieth-century American history, other than perhaps the 1960s, saw greater change in virtually every aspect of family, community, and society—from where people lived and how they earned their livelihoods to courting and dating habits, marriage and child rearing, and leisure time activities. These changes were demographically broad based, affecting every major cohort of the population: whites and blacks, immigrants and the native born, young and old, men and women.

Population Shifts

The U.S. censuses of 1920 and 1930 confirmed that Americans were becoming increasingly concentrated in cities, living in conditions very different from those in agricultural-based rural areas. In 1920, for the first time in the nation's history, more than half the total population—54 million of 106.5 million, or 50.7 percent—lived in settings described as urban. By the end of the 1920s, that figure had risen to 69.2 million of 123.2 million, or 56.2 percent. The urban setting was defined as an incorporated community of 2,500 or more residents—hardly a metropolis—but the proportion of Americans living in geographically compact communities was increasing. Meanwhile, movement to truly large cities was also under way. By 1920, a dozen U.S. cities had passed the half-million population mark, with New York, Chicago, and Philadelphia each exceeding 1 million. By 1930, several more cities had joined the ranks of those larger than 500,000, while Detroit and Los Angeles were now included in the list of metropolises with populations over 1 million.

A variety of factors were behind the shift to urban living. Rural, agricultural America had experienced great prosperity during the first two decades of the twentieth century, providing farm products to meet the demands of urban populations, the needs of

the military during World War I, and the food shortages in wartime European nations. However, farmers had borrowed large amounts of money to put more land into cultivation and to buy machinery. With the end of the war, the market for crops and livestock shrank and land values declined. Farmers were left with heavy debt. The last year of agricultural prosperity was 1920, after which American farm income and land values sank into what would be a twenty-year depression. Even in that relatively good year, more than half a million of the nation's 6.5 million farms were sold. As the nation drifted into recession, Midwestern farm bankruptcies quadrupled in 1922 and doubled again in 1923. These distressing conditions prompted an exodus to towns and cities in search of employment.

During the war, half a million African Americans had moved from the rural South to cities in both the South and the North in search of jobs. When the fighting was over and the ranks of the U.S. military shrank from 4 million in late 1918 to roughly 130,000 by the end of 1920, many of the demobilized soldiers settled in urban areas, where the jobs were. New immigrants from Southern and Eastern Europe represented yet another group that made their homes in American cities. These groups typically did not travel beyond their city of debarkation, making the ports of Boston, Philadelphia, and above all New York home to vast numbers of newcomers. Those seeking family members and ethnic enclaves established by earlier waves of immigrants found their way to such cities as Pittsburgh, Cleveland, Detroit, and Chicago, the latter having a foreign-born population of nearly 750,000. All told, nearly 27 million immigrants arrived on U.S. shores—most of them settling in cities—between 1880 and the middle of the 1920s, when anti-immigration legislation—including national quotas—went into effect.

Daily life in America's growing cities was quite different from that in rural areas and small towns. The city conferred anonymity on its residents. In a modern metropolis, where there were fewer family members or community authorities, such as clergy, to regulate people's behavior, individuals were free to decide with whom to associate and how to act. City dwellers could choose for themselves whether to embrace new ways of living, from fashions to sexual practices. But liberation came with new anxieties. The pressures of a rigid and narrowly traditional community might be absent, but so were the reassurances of family and community in times of distress. The city also represented those elements that rural America most feared: Europe and its immigrants, Wall Street money and power, competing religions or religious skepticism, political radicalism, cultural relativism, intellectual arrogance, and contempt for small-town values.

Mass Production and Mass Consumption

By the end of World War I, the United States had achieved the highest standard of living any people had ever known, and workers were paid the highest wages in the nation's history. The decade's prosperity was largely due to the stunning increase in production efficiency, a result of Frederick W. Taylor's theory of "scientific management" and the development of technological innovations, such as Henry Ford's moving assembly line, which in 1925 rolled out a complete new automobile every ten seconds. With more efficient management, greater mechanization, intensive corporate research and development, and

As evidenced by the bustle on New York City's Fifth Avenue, the decade of the 1920s brought the great urbanization of America. Indeed, the 1920 U.S. Census marked the first time more Americans lived in urban areas than in rural areas. *(General Photographic Agency/Hulton Archive/Getty Images)*

innovative advertising and sales methods, U.S. industrial production almost doubled from 1921 to 1929. And the increase in productivity was achieved without a major expansion in the labor force: manufacturing employed the same number of workers in 1929 as it had in 1919. Overall, from 1919 to 1929, the nation's gross national product rose 39 percent, manufacturing output and corporate profits nearly doubled, and wages for skilled workers increased 25 percent (those for unskilled and semiskilled laborers remained flat).

The flip side of mass production was mass consumption. American consumers were enjoying greater purchasing power and experiencing new forms of consumer debt. Discretionary spending increased from 20 percent to almost 35 percent in the first three decades of the century. Prosperity allowed many middle-class and skilled workers to purchase automobiles, washing machines, refrigerators, electric irons, gas stoves, telephones, and ready-to-wear fashions. And people had more time to enjoy these goods: the average workweek had decreased by about 10 hours between 1900 and 1926, to 50.6 hours.

The product with the most dramatic impact on family, community, and society was the automobile. With its popular Model T, introduced in 1908, the Ford Motor Company extended ownership to a widening market by reducing the price to a mere $290 in 1925 and offering improved design and engineering. Henry Ford had promised to "build a motor car for the great multitude," and he did: 15.5 million Model Ts were sold during its nineteen years of production (1908–1927). All in all, the total number of cars manufactured in the United States rose from 180,000 in 1910 to 4 million by 1925; by 1929, there was one car for every five Americans. The automobile, along with the mobility it offered, became the symbol of American life.

Mass consumption also changed life in the home. Among the cornucopia of household appliances that appeared in the 1920s, the radio provided the most personal experience of mass culture. In the privacy of their homes, people listened to voices and music that were simultaneously shared by millions nationwide. From a few scattered stations in 1920, the number of radio broadcasters climbed to 600 by 1929. Radio sets began to appear widely in stores in 1922; within a decade, 55 percent of American homes had a radio. The radio proved to be a great leveler, introducing isolated farmers and immigrant factory workers alike to a broader American culture.

Of central importance in accelerating the pace of consumerism was the newly minted installment plan. Purchases of cars, pianos, and other big-ticket items nearly doubled, reaching 7.6 percent of household income between the turn of the century and the beginning of World War I. By 1924, almost three-quarters of new cars in America were bought on time. By 1925, 70 percent of furniture, 75 percent of radios, 80 percent of appliances, and 90 percent of pianos were also purchased on the installment plan. Buying on time reduced the gap between the purchasing power of the rich and the middle class. It also encouraged the notion that nothing was beyond the reach of the family with a steady paycheck. Those promoting the new consumer debt culture—advertisers and merchandisers most of all—argued that it taught positive economic lessons by encouraging Americans to budget their money each month in order to make their payments. Many social commentators, however, worried that installment buying and the new consumer culture of the 1920s were undermining traditional American values of thrift, hard work, and saving.

Manners, Mores, and Morals

The post–World War I change in American values was reflected in an unprecedented revolution in the manners and morals of society's younger generation. One reason for this was the growing secularization of the country, particularly in urban areas, which greatly weakened religious sanctions and the authority of those who had set American moral standards—the professional classes, especially ministers, lawyers, and teachers. Even more important, the authority of the family had been sharply eroded as millions of young people moved to cities.

The war itself had a great impact on the manners and morals of young Americans. More than 70 percent of the men in the U.S. Army were drafted under the Selective Service Act of May 1917. Some 4 million soldiers were mobilized, of which 2 million were sent to Europe to fight, and two-thirds of these saw action; more than 120,000 were killed and almost 200,000 wounded. Soldiers were far away from America's moral code and its defenders, and they had an ample number of prostitutes at their disposal. Meanwhile, the more than 30,000 young women who served in the U.S. Army, Navy Nurse Corps, Marines, and Coast Guard also experienced more relaxed European manners and standards about sex. For many of these young men and

women, the result was a breakdown of traditional restraints and taboos concerning sexuality. It was nearly impossible for this generation of Americans to return home from the war unchanged and willing to accept without question the morality of their elders.

The revolution of mores was accelerated by the growing independence of American women. During World War I, roughly 1 million women on the home front joined the workforce for the first time, while many of the 8 million already employed moved from low-paying positions such as domestic service to higher-paying manufacturing and service positions outside the home. Americans became used to women working in defense plants and other traditional bastions of male employment, although most people expected that women would return to the home once men returned from the front and reassumed their former positions as breadwinners.

Still, the number of employed women rose steadily after the war, climbing some 25 percent between 1920 and 1930, and the number of married women workers reached 29 percent. Most of the work was still in traditionally female occupations. As late as 1930, one-third of American working women were employed in domestic service—one-half among African American and foreign-born white women. For those who did retain positions outside domestic service, most worked in the lowest-paying jobs, notably retail trade and secretarial positions. Even female professionals made little progress, consistently receiving less pay than their male counterparts and concentrated in traditionally female occupations such as teaching. As for high-paying manufacturing jobs, the American Federation of Labor, the nation's largest trade union federation, remained openly hostile to women members because it did not want them competing for men's jobs.

For young women, the availability of jobs often varied according to race and ethnicity. European immigrant daughters often left school at age sixteen to contribute to family income and remained in the labor force until marriage. Clerical work was the second-largest field for female workers; by the end of the decade, 19 percent of working women over sixteen, the vast majority single, held these jobs. Saleswomen and store clerks represented about 6 percent of the female labor force. These positions widened the job opportunities for immigrant daughters while bringing in middle-class workers as well.

While middle-class young women in white-collar work contributed to the image of the new working woman portrayed in fiction, advertising, and the movies, in 1920, only about 9 percent of working women in America were professionals; by 1929, the figure had increased to 14 percent. This group represented the "New Woman," who was most likely to achieve autonomy and personal satisfaction in her work. These new women were generally clustered in teaching, nursing, and social work, all feminized fields of endeavor. In the 1920s, only 3 percent of lawyers and 5 percent of physicians in America were women. By 1930, however, with medical schools employing admissions quotas and many hospitals refusing to accept woman doctors as interns, the latter number declined to 4.4 percent. In the 1920s, eight out of ten teachers in America were women, but only one in sixty-three were school superintendents.

African American women were mostly concentrated in domestic service, laundry work, and agricultural labor. Well-educated African American women had some professional opportunities—especially in social work, with YWCAs and the Urban League hiring—and teaching was a viable option, but it was hard to find such jobs in the urban North. In 1920, Chicago employed only 138 black female teachers. Nurses faced discrimination; public health jobs, even if they could be found, paid significantly less to black women than to their white counterparts, and white women were often unwilling to work with them.

Yet the increased number of women working, even if the positions were low paying, had a significant effect on American society. Many single working women put off marriage and enjoyed an autonomy they never had before, avoiding the traditional route from their parents' household directly into that of their husband. Combined with their new voting rights, won in 1920, young women were becoming more independent and more self-assured, as reflected in risqué fashions and lifestyle habits, including dating and (illegal) drinking, that would have shocked their mothers.

Courting and Dating

American family life was also undergoing fundamental change in the 1920s. The shifts that occurred came at a faster pace in urban areas, but they gradually spread throughout the nation. Courtship, the process of identifying and engaging a life partner, changed most radically, as "dating" began to replace "calling."

Up to the first decade of the twentieth century, most courtship took place in the home according to well-defined customs. In this social ritual—originating with the upper classes, common in the middle classes, and copied as far as possible by families of more modest means—a young man called on a young woman in her home, met her parents, talked to her in the family parlor, was offered a refreshment, was entertained by her piano playing, and ultimately received encouragement or discouragement about calling again. This routine gave eligible women and watchful parents basic control over the courtship process.

Dating in the modern sense became common among the youth of the 1920s, not only in the cities, where the practice started, but in suburbs and smaller communities as well. Young urban men and women who had not married found that they could meet each other at dance halls, speakeasies and bars, coffee shops, movie theaters, restaurants, skating rinks, and other public places in which they experienced no supervision and greater privacy than in the parlor. Only in rural areas and especially the South,

Newly available technologies such as the automobile and the telephone gave young people new freedom and new ways to meet each other, undermining the traditional authority of parents. *(H. Armstrong Roberts/Stringer/Retrofile/ Getty Images)*

where there was little surplus income, access to automobiles, or commercial entertainment, did older patterns persist.

Dating soon became a primary means of casual social entertainment among adolescents and young people, and frequent use of the family automobile for dating became a source of tension between teens and their parents. In high schools and colleges, dating became a measure of one's popularity. For many young people, dating served as a form of social affirmation, not necessarily the courtship of a potential life companion.

Dating often involved an outlay of cash and, as males were far more likely to have money for such purposes, men now had greater control over courtship. It was considered improper for a woman to propose a date, though she might hint that she would welcome a man's invitation. And, as costs of dating increased, so did the female sense of obligation and male expectation of more than verbal expressions of appreciation.

Engaged couples had long enjoyed what was coming to be called "heavy petting," and enough couples engaged in premarital intercourse that in the late nineteenth century nearly one in ten American brides were pregnant on their wedding day. Dating, without the commitment of marriage, also encouraged greater intimacy and sexual exploration. In fact, one of the most common date destinations, the movies, with its passionate love scenes, provided a kind of "how-to" guide for the inexperienced. Consequently, more young people were comfortable with sexual experimentation. Kissing and embraces were accepted aspects of romantic relationships. Necking and petting (the distinction depending on whether the contact was above or below the shoulders) were customary if not universal practices.

Not surprisingly, there was a notable rise in premarital sexual intercourse after World War I, with more than four-fifths of males and nearly half of females acknowledging participation. The gender difference reflected the persistence of a double standard, the widespread attitude that sexually active males were just "sowing wild oats" and could not be expected to be faithful to a single mate, while women who behaved in the same fashion were considered to have abandoned their virtue. Although sexual attitudes were beginning to change, most of the sexual activity that did take place was only with a single partner whom an individual expected to marry.

Marriage and Family

As courtship practices evolved and dating provided young people with a greater variety of potential partners, the decision to marry was cast in a new light. Fewer people now participated in family economies such as farming, and more people were involved in work that provided cash wages, allowing individuals to purchase daily necessities. Moreover, other institutions were taking more control of educational and welfare responsibilities. The mutual dependency that had held couples together began to diminish. In divorce petitions in the 1920s, a mate's lack of attention, consideration, or romantic appeal came to be mentioned far more as a reason for marital dissatisfaction.

A new notion had emerged, popularized by psychologists, social workers, and educators, that a successful marriage was based on affection and companionship. The new spousal relationship, dubbed the "companionate marriage," was built on mutual devotion, sexual attraction, and respect for equality. Pressure from society, church, or state to stay together could not produce a happy marriage, and the absence of emotional fulfillment was likely to prove harmful to a couple and any children they might have. Marriage could not be expected to be free of tension or conflict, but husbands and wives who were loving companions could communicate and resolve difficulties. Couples unable or unwilling to do so were better off separating.

In the 1920s, U.S. marriage rates remained fairly stable, but childbearing continued its long-term decline. Slightly more than 60 percent of Americans over the age of fifteen lived as married couples, while 36.9 percent of males and 29.4 percent of females remained unmarried. Six percent of men and 14.6 percent of women were widowed. In the nineteenth century, the average number of children born to American white women fell from 7 to 3.5; between 1900 and 1929, the birthrate dropped by another third. The latter decline was greater among middle-class than working-class families, among white families than nonwhite families, and among native-born than immigrant women. In fact, the rate of childbearing among immigrant women was nearly twice that of native-born women, while the educated classes were choosing not to reproduce.

The drop in birthrate reflected decisions to limit family size, and practice birth control to do so. During the 1920s, birth control became increasingly more available, largely due to the work of family planning pioneers like Margaret Sanger. Many upper-class American couples used some means of contraception—male condoms primarily, but increasingly female diaphragms. One significant result of these deliberate actions was that growing numbers of women completed their child rearing by their early thirties and spent more of their life in other occupational pursuits. Among working-class couples, however, few understood or practiced birth control.

Some policy makers became concerned about the decline in births among the native born and the educated, seeing a trend in which the poor, uneducated, and foreign born and their descendants would overwhelm the middle and upper classes. To encourage population growth among the latter, nativists (those who opposed unlimited immigration) persuaded Congress in the 1920s to adopt legislation that prohibited the sale of contraceptives, the publication of abortion-related advertising, the distribution of abortion-inducing drugs, and the dissemination of birth control information.

The ongoing revolution in manners and morals was accompanied by a revolution in female sexual conduct. Women who came to maturity after the turn of the century were much more likely than their forebears to have sex both before marriage and outside it. One study found that of fifty women born before 1890, seventeen had engaged in intercourse outside of marriage; of fifty women born after 1890, however, thirty had. Psychologist Lewis M. Terman noted that nearly 90 percent of the women surveyed who were born before 1890 were virgins at marriage, compared to 74 percent of those born between 1890 and 1899, 51 percent born between 1900 and 1909, and just 32 percent born after 1910.

The sexual researcher Alfred Kinsey, in his studies conducted in the 1940s, also described a dramatic shift in sexual behavior among women born around 1900 who came to sexual maturity around 1916. These women were two to three times as likely to have premarital intercourse than women born before 1900 and were also more likely to experience orgasm. Premarital sexual experience among men did not increase, but it occurred less often with prostitutes and more frequently with women they knew. Women, it appeared, were beginning to regard sex as a normal part of life. To help the process along, a number of textbooks and pamphlets about reproduction were being published, and the first marriage-counseling center appeared in the mid-1920s.

Child Rearing

The relationship between American parents and their children was undergoing change in the 1920s, most notably in middle-class families. The shift stemmed from what many social commentators of the day described as a decline in parental authority. In general, strict discipline and harsh punishment became less evident in many homes, while parent–child communication was emphasized by the newly popular science of psychology. Young children came to be treated with more open affection, while adolescents were given far greater freedom than in earlier decades. Young people in immigrant families, who found it easier than their parents to deal with the new circumstances of an alien land, gained greater influence within the family.

In all social classes, both urban and otherwise, fewer adolescents were spending much time at home. In their famous 1929 study, *Middletown: A Study in Modern American Culture,* sociologists Robert and Helen Lynd focused on the behaviors of what they considered the typical middle American community of Muncie, Indiana. They found that 55 percent of high school boys and 44 percent of high school girls were at home three evenings per week or less; nearly 20 percent of the high school boys did not spend any evenings at home. Fathers and mothers typically resented this mass exodus of their children: high school boys and girls cited disputes about how often they went out on school nights as the leading cause of friction between themselves and their parents. But adolescents were not likely to give up their time away from home. Asked to recall their most enjoyable occasion during the previous year, only 5 percent of high school boys and 17 percent of high school girls cited an incident or experience that took place in the family home. Moreover, what they enjoyed—sports, outdoor activities, parties, dancing—was experienced in the company of other young people, not parents.

Marital and Family Relations

Researchers like the Lynds were struck by the psychological gulf separating husbands and wives. The husbands' main preoccupations were earning a living and taking care of such practical matters as car repairs, and they felt little involvement in their families' day-to-day concerns. Wives, in contrast, were responsible for organizing household affairs, caring for and disciplining children, and arranging the family's social life. Few fathers maintained the old role of domestic patriarch responsible for shaping the moral character of their children; fathers who came of age at the turn of the century tended to associate fatherhood with being a reliable provider and breadwinner. Primary responsibility for the guidance and discipline of children had clearly shifted to the mother.

The narrowing definition of fatherhood developed as more and more middle-class men were employed some distance from their residence. The time spent at work and in commuting to and from their jobs greatly reduced the amount of time fathers spent in the presence of their families. Aside from a lingering male resistance to traditional domestic responsibilities, the rising business culture preached that the highest levels of personal accomplishment could only be achieved outside the home, in the world of business.

The shift away from the patriarchal father was apparent in immigrant families as well. Among Irish, Italian, and Jewish families, for example, the second generation often viewed as irrelevant the mores and character traits of their fathers in a dramatically changed social environment. In America, the father's traditional sources of authority were weakened, and the mother became the most important figure in helping the children adjust to new conditions, providing them with parental approval and emotional support. Financially, by the 1920s, fewer working-class families expected their working children to hand over their entire paycheck to their parents; instead, children might retain some of their earnings to spend as they pleased.

Despite the varied and dramatic changes in America during the 1920s, there was not a complete break with the past. In most respects, the new decade witnessed the continuation of well-established patterns and long-term developments. Changes in everyday life took place bit by bit, often in ways that did not immediately attract much attention. Furthermore, changes in the character of daily life would occur at different rates for Americans in various locations and situations. Many would adopt new ideas, practices, technologies, and fashions reluctantly and selectively, if at all. Yet awareness that shifts were taking place in the circumstances of everyday life would permeate American society, influencing the outlook and behavior of those who resisted change as well as those ready to embrace it.

Leslie Rabkin

Further Reading

Allen, Frederick L. *Only Yesterday: An Informal History of the 1920s.* New York: Harper, 2000.

Dumenil, Lynn. *The Modern Temper: American Culture and Society in the 1920s.* New York: Hill and Wang, 1995.

Fass, Paula S. *The Damned and the Beautiful: American Youth in the 1920s.* New York: Oxford University Press, 1979.

Gidlow, Liette. *The Big Vote: Consumer Culture and the Politics of Exclusion, 1890–1920s.* Baltimore: Johns Hopkins University Press, 2004.

Goldberg, David J. *Discontented America: The United States in the 1920s.* Baltimore: Johns Hopkins University Press, 1999.

Lynd, Robert, and Helen Lynd. *Middletown: A Study in Modern American Culture.* New York: Harcourt, Brace, 1929.

Miller, Nathan. *New World Coming: The 1920s and the Making of Modern America.* New York: Scribner's, 2003.

Parrish, Michael E. *Anxious Decades: America in Prosperity and Depression, 1920–1941.* New York: W.W. Norton, 1992.

Perret, Geoffrey. *America in the Twenties: A History.* New York: Simon & Schuster, 1982.

Consumer and Popular Culture

The decade of the 1920s has gone down in history as a time of frivolity and excess, as Americans enjoyed a rise in productivity and prosperity after World War I. Mass-production techniques, such as those used in the automobile industry, enabled Americans to buy more goods and enjoy more leisure time than ever before. Consumerism became the driving force of the nation's economy, with manufactured goods, advertising, and popular culture all benefiting from the good times.

The changes in the economy were reflected in changes in the values and morals of Americans as well, with a pronounced shift from subdued Victorian mores to a looser, more fun-loving, sometimes even hedonistic sensibility. The new values did not go unchallenged, however, as various social movements sought to limit the influences of modernity.

Production and Consumption

In the 1920s, American business reigned supreme. U.S. industry could boast the most efficient and productive workforce in the world, utilizing the most technologically advanced production equipment and techniques, operating under trained management professionals, and creating the most advanced products in the world. Led by the automobile industry, the nation's manufacturing sector produced more than enough goods for American consumers.

The economic boom of the 1920s, epitomized by Henry Ford's dominance of the automobile industry through the use of assembly-line production, led to a high standard of living for many Americans as wages increased, working hours decreased, and mass production lowered the cost of consumer products. Ford's River Rouge plant, outside Detroit, in which raw materials were processed, parts fabricated, and products assembled under one roof, exemplified the transformation. The company was able to produce a high-demand product, the Model T car, that required little highly paid skilled labor and could be sold at a relatively cheap price.

The automobile industry, in turn, fueled growth in related industries such as construction, glass, rubber, oil, and tourism. New industries developed to create even more products, such as cigarettes, cosmetics, telephones, electric refrigerators, and radios. As businesses grew, so did the paychecks and benefits of many workers. In 1923, U.S. Steel was able to reduce the working hours of its employees from twelve to eight hours a day, employ 17,000 additional laborers, increase wages, and increase profits—all as a result of the company's increasingly efficient productivity. With more money with which to buy goods and services, and more of these to choose from, consumers found it increasingly easy to acquire what they needed and wanted.

Part of that ease had to do with the development of chain stores, which implemented the same principles of efficiency and economy of scale used by manufacturers. From gasoline stations such as Standard Oil of New Jersey (which grew from 12 stations in 1920 to 1,000 stations in 1929) and auto parts stores such as Western Auto Supply (3 stores in 1920; 54 stores in 1929) to specialty outlets such as United Cigar Stores (2,000 stores in 1920; 3,500 stores in 1929) and clothing stores such as Lerner Shops (6 stores in 1920; 133 stores in 1929), chain retailers bought goods in volume and were able to sell them at a lower price than smaller competitors. Most effective were grocery chains such as Safeway Stores (766 stores in 1920; 2,660 stores in 1929) and the Great Atlantic and Pacific Tea Company, better known as A&P (4,621 stores in 1920; 15,418 stores in 1929).

Piggly Wiggly grocery stores (515 stores in 1920; 2,500 stores in 1929) introduced the idea of self-service in food retail. Previously, customers asked a clerk behind a counter to collect items for them; under the new system, shoppers walked around the store selecting items off the shelves for themselves. Following the new concept of "scientific merchandising," Piggly Wiggly was able to reduce the number of employees needed to work the stores and further increase profits and lower prices. Such self-service stores were popularly known as "grocerterias" until the term "supermarket" was coined.

23

With an expanding middle class and new forms of consumer credit, Americans during the Jazz Age went on a mass shopping spree, bringing huge profits to department stores such as New York City's Gimbel Brothers, pictured here in 1920. *(Edwin Levick/Stringer/Hulton Archive/Getty Images)*

In addition to chain stores, the consumer spending spree was also fueled by the use of credit. Installment purchases increased fourfold during the 1920s, reaching $6 billion a year. At the peak, 90 percent of all pianos, sewing machines, and washing machines; 80 percent of all vacuum cleaners, radios, and refrigerators; 70 percent of all furniture; and 60 percent of all automobiles were purchased on credit. While some economists pointed out the dangers of overextending personal credit, most Americans enjoyed the new opportunities to "have today what you can afford tomorrow." And there were products galore from which to choose.

Indeed, American industry was producing more than was needed. Before the 1920s, manufacturers generally could be guaranteed a market for their goods, and growth in the economy was driven by how much industry could make. During the 1920s, production began outpacing demand. Rather than cut back on manufacturing, businesses sought to increase consumer demand.

Advertising

Products, as well as credit opportunities, were marketed to consumers through the growing business of advertising. No less than 60 percent of all newspaper column inches and 80 percent of all mail were devoted to advertisements, while the new medium of radio depended on selling airtime to pay for programming. Advertising became a necessary means for producers to increase demand for their products, which were being produced at an ever-growing rate.

While many companies hired celebrities to endorse their products or relied on the testimony of experts to validate their claims of product effectiveness, the most significant advance in advertising came with the introduction of psychology into marketing. Although it was nearly twenty years old, Walter Dill Scott's book *The Psychology of Advertising* (1903) led the way, with popularized versions of Sigmund Freud's ideas about dreams, repression, and sexuality.

Advertisements in the nineteenth century had emphasized information over image, since most producers were marketing not directly to consumers but to retailers. In the 1920s, however, ads began emphasizing the particular appeal or cachet of products, as well as what they could do for the consumer. Advertising also played on people's fears about what they looked like, the clothes they wore, and even how they smelled. Bad breath could lead to a love lost; body odor could mean the loss of a promotion. Some ads equated ownership of a product with desirable attributes, such as the envy of friends and family. One ad for the American Radiator Company claimed that its radiators were so "clean and handsome," owners could use their cellars as entertainment space, since they would not be embarrassed for guests to see them. And, given the changing morals of the day, advertisements indulged in sexual innuendo, such as the ad in which a woman seated next to a man who is smoking a Chesterfield cigarette says, "Blow some my way" (also suggesting the liberation of women who want to smoke).

Advertising enabled American companies to continue to produce goods at levels that outpaced need by creating new demand for their products. But advertising was seen as more than just a way to sell products in the 1920s. Ad executive Bruce Barton (of the highly successful Batten, Barton, Durstine & Osborn advertising agency) held that modern sales principles provided a model by which to live. In his best-selling books *The Man Nobody Knows* (1925), *The Book Nobody Knows* (1926), and *What Can a Man Believe?* (1927), Barton argued that effective advertising is based on the same principles as the teachings of Jesus Christ. "He would be a national advertiser today, I am sure," Barton wrote of Jesus, "as he was the great advertiser of his own day." Barton himself was an exemplary marketer, having coined the slogan for the Salvation Army, "A man may be down, but he is never out," and creating the quintessential American homemaker, Betty Crocker.

The emphasis on image, gratification, and self-expression went beyond the realm of advertising and was evident in the popular culture of the era as well. From novels such as F. Scott Fitzgerald's *The Great Gatsby* (1925) and Sinclair Lewis's *Babbitt* (1922) to the increasingly frenetic sound of jazz and new dances such as the Lindy Hop (named after famous aviator Charles Lindbergh), American popular culture reflected the modern emphasis on personal pleasure and self-expression.

Even clean-cut, all-American celebrities such as the Hollywood stars Douglas Fairbanks and Mary Pickford now were challenged by more sexually expressive personalities, such as Rudolph Valentino and Greta Garbo. Modern media, such as the radio, phonograph, and talking pictures, reinforced the new ethics and values. Both the form and content of 1920s popular culture reflected a sense of modernity.

Literature

Gertrude Stein called them the Lost Generation, writers of the 1920s—such as Fitzgerald, Lewis, Ernest Hemingway, John Dos Passos, T.S. Eliot, Ezra Pound, E.E. Cummings, and Sherwood Anderson—who lived in Europe and produced works of literature that critiqued American society, especially the traditions and values of rural life or, in their words, "the village." Disillusioned by their involvement in World War I, these writers reflected that mentality in their characterization of the period. Theirs was a lost generation, according to Malcolm Cowley in *Exile's Return: A Literary Odyssey of the 1920s* (1934), "because it was uprooted, schooled away and almost wrenched away from its attachment to any region or tradition."

Although the Lost Generation authors are most often associated with the 1920s, they were not that decade's best-selling authors. Instead, the most popular were children's and romance writer Gene Stratton Porter and novelist Harold Bell Wright. Both of these writers appealed to traditional American values of optimism, love of nature, and triumph over adversity, as well as clean living and the ultimate victory of good over evil. Also popular were western writer Zane Grey and adventure writer Edgar Rice Burroughs, whose Tarzan of the Apes series consistently topped the best-seller lists. Women writers attempted to capitalize on the less repressive atmosphere of the 1920s. The poet

Edna St. Vincent Millay, for example, flaunted sexual expression in her verse and her life. African American writers such as the poets Langston Hughes and Countee Cullen and the novelists Claude McKay, Jean Toomer, Jessie Faust, and Zora Neale Hurston joined artists such as Aaron Douglas and Augusta Savage in leading the Harlem Renaissance.

Yet the reading habits of most Americans were geared primarily to newspapers and magazines. Newspapers in the 1920s came increasingly under the control of powerful publishing tycoons such as William Randolph Hearst and Joseph Pulitzer, while tabloids satisfied an audience hungry for sensationalized news of crime, passion, and entertainment. Tabloids, or magazine-type newspapers with large sports sections, comic strips, and puzzles, soon boasted circulations that exceeded those of traditional newspapers.

Magazines likewise illustrated the preference for entertainment over serious news, with popular publications such as *The Saturday Evening Post* and *Ladies' Home Journal*. The newly introduced, easy-reading newsmagazine *Time* outsold serious journals such as *Atlantic* and *Harper's*. Magazines featuring genre fiction sold well, as western, gangster, mystery, and sports stories kept readers entranced. Most popular of all were "true confession" magazines, which featured supposedly real-life stories of life, love, crime, and the quest for fame and fortune.

Movies

In the 1920s, motion pictures emerged as a popular form of mass entertainment. More than 8,000 movie theaters were built during the course of the decade, many of them palatial. The Roxy in New York City, for example, seated 6,200 patrons served by 125 ushers and entertained by a 110-piece orchestra. Much in the way vaudeville shows had featured several forms of entertainment, most movie programs included a newsreel, a comedy short, previews, an episode of a serial drama, and a feature film. The major studios produced so many films that theaters could change their entire program every week or so.

Americans flocked to movies that featured adventure, romance, mystery, and glamour. Wholesome stories featuring "America's Sweetheart" Mary Pickford and swashbuckling adventures starring her husband, Douglas Fairbanks, not only increased attendance but also created a whole industry designed to promote celebrity. Magazines and newsreels were filled with stories and gossip about movie stars, while episodes in celebrities' lives became public events—such as the 1921 sex and manslaughter scandal involving film comedian Fatty Arbuckle, and the premature death of the great romantic hero Rudolph Valentino in 1926. One of the most popular stars of the decade was Clara Bow, the "It Girl," who embodied the "new woman" of the 1920s. Her characters were independent, carefree women who went after what they wanted, though what they usually wanted in the end was a husband.

But the genre most suited to silent film—which prevailed until the introduction of the sound motion picture, or "talkie," in the late 1920s—was comedy. Charlie Chaplin, Harold Lloyd, Buster Keaton, and Stan Laurel and Oliver Hardy all made films that were easily understood because the humor was primarily visual. Immigrants who spoke no English especially liked Charlie Chaplin's Little Tramp character, since they could relate to his perpetual outsider status, wit, and charm. For many immigrants, movies became a way to understand American culture, while for other Americans, divided by religion, race, class, or region, movies became a shared language, a part of a national culture.

The most important film of the decade was *The Jazz Singer* (1927), which transformed the industry virtually overnight. Using a combination of silent film and synchronized sound sequences, the film was an immediate hit. Once the success of this film became apparent, audiences expected sound with all their films.

Few stars of the silent films made a successful transition to sound. Some, like Chaplin, refused to give a voice to their characters. Chaplin felt that his Little Tramp should not have a specific identity, nationality, or ethnicity.

While Chaplin continued to make silent films through the 1930s, the rest of Hollywood converted to sound films and created whole new genres to take advantage of the new technology, such as the movie musical. One of the lasting legacies to come out of the transition to sound film was Mickey Mouse, introduced in Walt Disney's 1928 cartoon *Steamboat Willie*.

Jazz

The introduction of music in film provided jazz musicians with another outlet for their creativity beyond live performance, radio, and recordings. This new venue enabled them to reach a wider audience. Although the jazz heard in *The Jazz Singer* bore little resemblance to the music being produced by the leading jazz artists of the day, its use did imply a broader acceptance of that form than ever before.

Earlier, World War I had helped in the spread of jazz music. The military's closure of Storyville, the New Orleans red-light district, forced many jazz musicians who had been employed there to travel north in search of other opportunities, and war mobilization forced greater contact between the races at military installations and wartime manufacturing plants. These two factors led black musicians to adapt black blues and jazz to the expectations of a white audience.

Jazz spread first among younger audiences, mainly because of its spontaneous nature and association with chaotic dancing. While critics denounced it as unmusical, intoxicating, and immoral, jazz became the most popular form of music during the 1920s, dominating the radio airwaves and record sales, and even influencing movies.

As jazz music became more popular, however, it also became more standardized, organized, and arranged. What had once been music that emphasized improvisation throughout a piece became a highly structured genre in which improvisation was limited to specific breaks in the arrangement of jazz "riffs."

What had been "hot" jazz by musicians such as Louis Armstrong and his Hot Five became "sweet" jazz in the hands of band leaders such as Guy Lombardo and his Royal Canadians, or "symphonic" jazz in the work of Paul Whiteman. In 1924, Whiteman's orchestra debuted George Gershwin's *Rhapsody in Blue*, subtitled "for jazz band and piano," a primarily symphonic work with jazz motifs. Orchestras and large bands developed what would become Big Band swing music in the 1930s and 1940s.

Radio

Jazz spread primarily through radio. From amateurs broadcasting in basements and garages to fully formed and regulated networks that resulted from the Radio Act of 1927, the radio industry developed into Americans' most used and trusted source of news, information, and entertainment.

The 1920s were a period of growth for the radio industry, not only in its technical aspects, but also in regard to programming. Stations learned what worked well on radio and what did not. For listeners, the most attractive aspect of the medium was its immediacy. Broadcasts of boxing matches and baseball games, political conventions and election returns,

No invention had a greater impact on popular culture in the 1920s than the radio, which broadcast news, live music, and sports to the homes of millions of Americans—rural and urban alike—for the first time. *(Stringer/Time & Life Pictures/Getty Images)*

live remote broadcasts from big-city ballrooms, and news reporting all became mainstays of the industry.

Variety entertainment, homeless after the decline of vaudeville, found a new home on radio. The most popular radio comedy, *Amos 'n' Andy,* featured white vaudevillians Freeman Gosden and Charles Correll portraying two black Southerners whose simple ways and common misunderstandings provided the humor for the show. The pervasive nature of radio reinforced, to a national audience, many regionally held stereotypes, especially of minorities.

Many people believed what they heard on the radio, not only because the medium was capable of presenting news as it occurred, but also because the radio produced a special form of intimacy. The presence of the radio set in one's home, and the need for listeners to create mental images from the sounds presented, led audiences to create a personal version of the program, unique to each individual. The transformation in communications and entertainment, with their immediacy and national appeal, reinforced the feeling that the 1920s were the start of the "modern" era.

Sports

Mass spectator sports also came into their own during the Jazz Age. Never before were major sports so widely followed, as tens of thousands attended athletic competitions in person or listened to games over the new medium of radio, often to follow the larger-than-life heroes who seemed to dominate several sports.

No spectator sport was more widely followed in the 1920s than professional baseball. The sport quickly recovered from the 1919 "Black Sox" scandal, in which players with the Chicago White Sox were paid by gamblers and organized crime figures to throw the World Series to the Cincinnati Reds. To clean up the sport's image, major league baseball owners hired a tough federal judge named Kenesaw Mountain Landis as baseball's first commissioner. They also changed the rules of the game and the baseballs themselves to produce more fan-pleasing home runs. The results quickly became evident, as a record 300,000 spectators came to see the six games of the 1921 World Series between the New York Giants and New

York Yankees. Nobody did more to revive the game than the Yankee slugger George Herman "Babe" Ruth. Also known as "the Bambino" and "the Sultan of Swat," Ruth led the Yankees to six World Series appearances and three championships during the 1920s, hitting a record 60 home runs in 1927.

College football also became a nationally followed sport in the 1920s. Prior to World War I, the better teams were confined to the Northeast and football rivalries were largely local affairs, attended primarily by students and alumni. Spearheaded by Notre Dame's head coach Knute Rockne, national rivalries developed, and a whole new style of playing, featuring the dramatic forward pass, drew millions of new fans to modern stadiums across the country.

Nor were team sports the only ones to gain a new mass following during the 1920s. By winning no fewer than thirteen major championships from 1923 through 1930, Bobby Jones helped popularize golf as a spectator sport, even as the construction of hundreds of new courses drew tens of thousands of middle-class duffers to the game. The flamboyant Bill Tilden did much the same for tennis. Still, both tennis and golf were largely confined to middle- and upper-class participants and spectators during the Jazz Age.

A sport particularly popular among immigrants and the working class was boxing. Unabashedly professional—as opposed to the largely amateur sports of tennis, golf, and college football—boxing had a great champion, too, who drew unparalleled crowds to his performances. No less than 80,000 fight fans were on hand to see the immigrant Irish heavyweight Jack Dempsey knock out French fighter Georges Carpentier in 1921 in what sportswriters dubbed the "fight of the century." In September 1926, Dempsey lost his title to U.S. Marine Gene Tunney with more than 120,000 spectators on hand.

Resistance to Change

Several social movements of the era can be understood as revolts against the changes taking place in American society. Nativism, Prohibition, and opposition to the teaching of evolution represented efforts to defend traditional values in the face of change.

Nativist sentiment reflected anxiety over the changes in American society resulting from immigration. The antiradicalism of the Red Scare was a form of nativism in which people who disagreed with the government were seen as undesirable, disloyal, and alien. The Palmer Raids of 1919–1920 were a campaign initiated by U.S. Attorney General A. Mitchell Palmer against purported leftist subversives, and the controversial 1921 murder trial of immigrant anarchists Nicola Sacco and Bartolomeo Vanzetti in Massachusetts was also part of the fear of political radicals that followed the 1917 Russian Revolution. The fear of radicals spilled over into fear of non-Protestants, including Catholics and Jews. Michigan and Nebraska both passed laws prohibiting parochial schools, and critics of President Woodrow Wilson called him "the puppet of the pope."

The fear of others often translated into fierce support of white Anglo-Saxon Protestants. Sociologist Madison Grant, in the book *The Passing of the Great Race* (1916), describes a hierarchy of races, with whites being at the top, and further dividing white Europeans into three main groups—Mediterraneans, Alpines, and Nordics—with Nordics being the superior group. A widespread belief in the inferiority of Asians, Africans, and Southern and Eastern Europeans led to passage of the Immigration Act of 1924, also known as the National Origins Act, in which immigration quotas were designed to increase the number of Nordic immigrants, while decreasing all others. It resulted in the virtual exclusion of Asian immigrants and small quotas for Southern and Eastern Europeans.

The most dramatic example of nativism during the 1920s was the revival of the Ku Klux Klan (KKK). Unlike the period after the Civil War, when the purpose of the Klan was to intimidate African Americans, the 1920s Klan advocated white supremacy over not only blacks, but Jews, Catholics, and any immigrants who were not white Anglo-Saxon Protestants. The Klan modernized by using expert advertisers to promote the organization and recruit new members. By 1923, more than 3 million Americans were members of the Klan. The strongest organizations were in America's Midwest and Far West rather than the South, which experienced relatively little immigration during this period.

The KKK also advocated the prohibition on alcohol, as its consumption was seen as yet another way that immigrants were destroying American society. The proliferation of saloons in the late nineteenth and early twentieth centuries had been seen by many Americans as an expression of encroaching foreign influence, and halting this change was considered reinforcing traditional values. The movement for prohibition started in the nineteenth century, but only when it gained the support of nativists was the campaign able to pass the high hurdles needed for the prohibition of alcohol to become part of the U.S. Constitution. January 1919 brought ratification of the Eighteenth Amendment, which prohibited the manufacture, sale, or transport of intoxicating beverages in the United States. The Volstead Act, intended to enforce the amendment and passed over President Woodrow Wilson's veto, defined intoxicating beverages as any that contain more than 0.5 percent alcohol.

In the attack on things foreign and new, science was also a target, especially in areas where scientific theory and practice conflicted with deeply held religious beliefs—as in the conflict between the theory of evolution and belief in the biblical story of creation. In 1925, the state of Tennessee passed a law prohibiting the teaching of evolution in public schools and colleges. In a test case in July 1925, John T. Scopes, a high school teacher in Dayton, Tennessee, was indicted and tried under the law.

The Scopes case became a national sensation, with two of America's most prominent attorneys representing the opposing sides. The American Civil Liberties Union hired the famous trial lawyer Clarence Darrow to argue on Scopes's behalf, and the former presidential candidate and statesman William Jennings Bryan argued the other side. Although the "Monkey" trial highlighted the issue of evolution versus creationism, the judge ruled simply that Scopes had, in fact, taught evolution and therefore was guilty under the law. Scopes was fined $100, but that penalty was ultimately suspended by the state supreme court. It was a Pyrrhic victory for the creationists.

Each of these social movements—nativism, Prohibition, and opposition to the theory of evolution—seen in conjunction with the rise of economic prosperity, the automobile and other consumer goods, advertising, and the radio and film industries, underscores the conflicted state of American culture during the 1920s. While many Americans reveled in the modern, celebrating the Jazz Age with exuberance and optimism, others sought to hold the modern at bay, trying to retain or regain traditional values in the face of cultural change.

Charles J. Shindo

Further Reading

Cowley, Malcolm. *Exile's Return: A Literary Odyssey of the 1920s.* New York: Penguin, 1976.

Dumenil, Lynn. *The Modern Temper: American Culture and Society in the 1920s.* New York: Hill and Wang, 1995.

Hentoff, Nat, and Albert J. McCarthy, eds. *Jazz: New Perspectives on the History of Jazz.* New York: Da Capo, 1959.

Marchand, Roland. *Advertising and the American Dream: Making Way for Modernity, 1920–1940.* Berkeley: University of California Press, 1985.

May, Lary. *Screening Out the Past: The Birth of Mass Culture and the Motion Picture Industry.* Chicago: University of Chicago Press, 1980.

Nash, Roderick. *The Nervous Generation: American Thought, 1917–1930.* New York: Ivan R. Dee, 1990.

Riess, Steven A. *City Games: The Evolution of American Urban Society and the Rise of Sports.* Urbana: University of Illinois Press, 1989.

Sklar, Robert. *Movie-Made America: A Cultural History of American Movies.* New York: Vintage Books, 1975.

Smith, Terry. *Making the Modern: Industry, Art, and Design in America.* Chicago: University of Chicago Press, 1993.

Susman, Warren I. *Culture as History: The Transformation of American Society in the Twentieth Century.* New York: Pantheon, 1973.

Townsend, Peter. *Jazz in American Culture.* Jackson: University Press of Mississippi, 2000.

Foreign Affairs

World War I, or more precisely, the war's immediate aftermath, proved a disappointment to many of the American people and their elected representatives in Washington. President Woodrow Wilson had led the country into war with grand promises about a better world to come—a world of democracy, national self-determination, and international law. It did not turn out that way. At the Paris Peace Conference in 1919, Great Britain and France insisted on maintaining their empires and harshly punishing Germany. Disillusioned, the American people turned inward. The Senate rejected Wilson's efforts to bring the United States into the League of Nations, an international conflict-resolution organization, and Warren G. Harding won the 1920 election in part by pledging that the United States would stay out of world affairs.

The latter proposition proved easier said than done. The United States emerged from World War I as the world's largest creditor nation. Even before it entered the war—in April 1917, nearly three years into the fighting—the United States had been lending vast sums of money to the British, French, and other Allies. To enable them to repay this debt, as well as to punish Germany and facilitate the rebuilding of their own countries, these powers imposed harsh reparations on Germany and devised a precarious financial scheme: Germany would pay France and Britain, who would then pay back the United States. By the mid-1920s, the process had collapsed, forcing the United States to take the lead in setting up a more workable global financial system.

Although the Republican administrations that governed the country during the 1920s had won office pledging to keep America out of world affairs, the commitment was not ironclad. The United States participated in various League of Nations undertakings, such as maritime treaties, on an ad hoc basis. Washington also helped negotiate treaties limiting navies and, most significantly, the Kellogg-Briand Pact of 1928, which called on all nations to renounce "war as an instrument of national policy." And in the Western Hemisphere, its traditional sphere of influ-

ence, the United States continued, for a time at least, to occupy several politically troubled nations in the Caribbean and Central America.

Prewar Background

For much of its history through the beginning of World War I, the United States remained largely aloof from, or indifferent to, world affairs. There were good reasons for this. Geographically, America was protected from the conflicts and political intrigues of Europe and Asia by vast oceans. For more than a century following independence in 1776, the United States had extensive territories to settle; its formidable energies were focused on westward expansion, obviating any need for overseas colonies.

The troubling experiences of the French Revolution and the Napoleonic wars of the late eighteenth and early nineteenth centuries also contributed to this resolve. Despite George Washington's famous warning to stay out of European affairs—uttered in his farewell address of 1796—the new nation had been drawn into these European convulsions. The result was bitter political fighting, with supporters of France arrayed against supporters of Britain. There was also an undeclared naval war with France and a disastrous war with Britain from 1812 to 1815. For nearly seventy-five years thereafter, America's relationship with the world beyond its surrounding oceans was largely confined to trade and, compared to the size of its economy, rather limited trade at that.

The great exception to American avoidance of foreign entanglements was the Western Hemisphere. In 1823, President James Monroe articulated his famous eponymous doctrine, declaring that the United States would resist any European effort to seize new colonies or territories in the hemisphere. The Monroe Doctrine, however, did not apply to the United States. In the 1840s, it fought a war with Mexico in which it seized the northern half of that country; it also signed a treaty with Great Britain that divided the Oregon Territory between them.

America's noninvolvement in world affairs began to change in the last decade of the nineteenth century, when a number of policy makers began to grow concerned that, with the closing of the continental frontier, America would soon lack for natural resources, as well as an outlet for its prodigious economic output. Some of the more philosophical among the new American imperialists also expressed concern that a great nation of enterprising and energetic people would stagnate unless it had room to grow. With the continent settled, the only place to expand was overseas. Once a relative miser when it came to spending on the military, in the 1890s the United States began to build a great navy to project its power around the world. A new era in American foreign affairs began in 1898, when the nation went to war with Spain and seized most of that nation's colonial possessions in the Caribbean and Pacific.

Wilsonianism

Another factor played into the new expansiveness of American foreign policy at the turn of the twentieth century: progressivism. In the decades following the Civil War, the U.S. economy had grown enormously; by 1900, it was the largest in the world. But headlong business expansion had come at a price: political corruption, a damaged environment, impaired consumer safety, and growing inequalities in income and wealth. By the late 1890s, a new political movement—transcending regions and party lines—swept the nation, a movement that embraced the idea that government could play a role in improving people's lives and regulating the economy.

President Wilson was a proponent of progressivism, and his administration saw a number of significant economic and social reforms, from the progressive income tax to the prohibition of alcohol.

U.S. President Woodrow Wilson (center) is flanked by French Prime Minister Georges Clemenceau (left) and British Prime Minister David Lloyd George at the Paris Peace Conference following World War I. Wilson's hopes that the United States would become more engaged in world affairs were dashed by isolationist sentiment at home. *(Stringer/Hulton Archive/Getty Images)*

Wilson also believed that what had worked for America could work for the world. If new government institutions could help alleviate social problems at home, then a global governing body could overcome international problems, most notably war. Thus, while America was drawn into World War I for strategic and economic reasons—German submarine warfare was wreaking havoc on U.S. shipping, costing the lives of American seamen and threatening the principle of freedom of the seas—Wilson "sold" the war at home as a means to end war forever and to spread American-style democracy and progressivism around the world.

Even before the war ended, Wilson had worked out his vision for the postwar world—his famed Fourteen Points. These included a host of progressive ideas, among them free trade, arms reduction, national self-determination, and an end to the kind of secret treaty-making that had led Europe into war in the first place. But it was the last of the Fourteen Points that was the most revolutionary and, in the United States at least, the most controversial. The League of Nations, "a general association of nations," would help make the other elements of the Fourteen Points possible and would serve as a forum for resolving international disputes before they led to war.

It was a grand vision, and a doomed one. At least two major obstacles stood in the way of this new and democratic world order. The first was the combined efforts of Great Britain and France. Neither wanted to give up its empire or the economic barriers it had erected to protect the home nation. And neither was in a particularly forgiving mood toward its former enemies. France, in particular, had good reason for exacting economic vengeance. Much of the fighting on the war's western front had taken place on French soil, leaving some of the most productive agricultural and industrial regions of the country in ruins. France wanted Germany to pay, and at the Paris Peace Conference, it got its way. While Wilson had insisted in the first of his points that there would be no room for secret diplomacy in his new world order, he and the leaders of Britain, France, and Italy—heads of the "big four" nations at the conference—met behind closed doors and came up with a final sum for Germany to pay as reparations: $33 billion. It was a staggering sum for its day, and one that proved crippling for the German economy. Wilson protested, but he could do little except watch as his Fourteen Points were discarded or watered down. Rather than discussing an end to

their own empires, Britain and France, as well as Japan, divided up Germany's overseas possessions among themselves.

Still, the progressive president hoped that the League of Nations he envisioned might ameliorate the worst aspects of the Treaty of Versailles. The keystone of the League of Nations charter he had worked on so diligently in France was Article X, which committed member states to respect and preserve the independence of all other members and to renounce all armed aggression. If armed aggression did occur, the League would be committed to halting it. To Wilson, this collective security clause was critical to an effective League. He refused to talk of compromise, and Article X was approved in the League charter.

The second obstacle to Wilson's vision came from Washington. A new isolationist spirit was gripping both the capital and the nation at large, fueled by disenchantment with the Machiavellian politics at Versailles, a fear of foreign-inspired subversion after the 1917 Russian Revolution, and a revived nativism that would lead to tight legal restrictions on immigration in 1921 and 1924. Thus, even while the president was still negotiating at Versailles, the political battle lines over American participation in the League were forming back home. In March 1919, thirty-nine senators—enough to deny treaty passage—signed a petition complaining that League membership compromised American sovereignty by committing it to the principle of collective security. The United States had avoided entangling alliances since the end of the American Revolution, the petition-signing senators contended, and it should continue to avoid them now.

Wilson argued that membership in the League of Nations would serve American interests, since the United States, as the world's greatest economic power, would be able to impose its will on the body. That idea proved tough to sell. Traditional American isolationism, rising nativist sentiment, and weariness with progressivism ultimately sank Wilson's efforts. Despite working himself into a stroke campaigning for passage across the country, Wilson was unable to win Senate approval, and America never joined the League. Without the most powerful economic nation on board, the League proved ineffective in halting the aggressive actions of Germany, Italy, and Japan that plunged the nations of the world into an even more devastating global conflict in the 1930s and 1940s.

Normalcy in Foreign Affairs

Like any presidential and congressional contest, the 1920 election was about many small issues: agricultural aid, antitrust action, and the continuing U.S. military occupation of Nicaragua, the Dominican Republic, and Haiti. The 1920 contest, however, was like other critical elections in the nation's history in that it was also about one big issue: the progressive agenda. Did Americans want a continuation of the crusading reform spirit—both at home and abroad—of the last quarter-century, or did they want a return to what Republican presidential candidate Harding called "normalcy"? What exactly he meant by that newly coined term was never made clear to the electorate, but as far as foreign affairs were concerned, it implied a return to the traditional American isolationism of the nineteenth century and a turning away from any world leadership position. Normalcy won the day decisively. Harding held more than 60 percent of the popular vote in the greatest landslide to that date in modern American history. On his coattails, the Republicans won sixty House and ten Senate seats, giving them an overwhelming majority in both houses of Congress.

Domestically, the administrations of Harding and his successor, Calvin Coolidge, fulfilled the promise—and the perils—of normalcy. Federal efforts at social legislation and economic regulation withered. Big business flourished, and Americans focused on private concerns—buying a car and a radio, attending the movies and sports events—rather than public crusades. At the same time, the corruption of the late nineteenth century returned, with a number of Harding administration officials forced from office for their too-cozy deals with business interests.

The Jazz Age Republican administrations of Harding, Coolidge, and Herbert Hoover did their best to return America to a more isolationist foreign policy, but with mixed results. One impediment was the sheer dynamism of the American economy. The nation's huge growth in productivity and corporate wealth during the 1920s needed overseas outlets more than ever. Whether it was Standard Oil of New Jersey (now ExxonMobil) drilling for petroleum in Mexico and Venezuela, or General Motors building cars in Britain and Germany, American corporations were investing, acquiring, manufacturing, hiring, and selling overseas to an unprecedented extent. By the end of the 1920s, U.S. corporations had invested

more than $15 billion in foreign countries. In short, the American people may have wanted to retreat from the world stage, but their business leaders had no intention of doing so.

The United States found itself tied into the world economy—and an increasingly troubled economy at that—in other ways as well. There was the huge war debt—still exceeding $4.3 billion in 1930—which a combination of U.S. policies made only more burdensome to the country's World War I allies. The era's conservative economic values dictated that borrowers were responsible for their obligations. When asked about his administration's position on debt relief for the British and French, Coolidge famously remarked, "They hired the money, didn't they?" At the same time, however, traditional Republican protectionism led to high tariffs on imported manufactured goods. This had once made sense, when American industry was in its infancy and needed protection from more competitive English manufacturing. But now American industry was a behemoth, and the world was in debt to America. Unable to sell to the United States, the indebted nations could not raise the funds they needed to pay

When Germany proved unable to pay war reparations to the victorious Allies in the mid-1920s, American envoy Charles Dawes (seated, in dark suit) attempted to negotiate a more workable plan. (*Library of Congress, LC-USZ62–36724*)

back their foreign creditors, nor could Germany raise the funds to pay its reparations.

In the early 1920s, the weakest player in this precarious game of financial musical chairs—Germany—collapsed into economic depression and hyperinflation. At that point, America could no longer act as simply a huge loan-collection agency; it would have to take the lead in restructuring global finances. Under the leadership of Chicago banker Charles G. Dawes, a plan was devised whereby the United States would make new loans, this time to Germany, which that country would then use to pay its reparations to France and England; they, in turn, would use the funds to pay back their debts to the United States. The Dawes Plan offered no permanent fix to the world's balance of payments problem. It would work only so long as capital, in the form of loans and direct investment, continued to flow out of America, a fact that helps to explain why the Wall Street crash of October 1929 plunged not just America but the whole world into severe economic depression.

Beyond Europe

Financial interests also played a role in America's relations with Latin America. Between 1914 and 1929, direct American investment in that region grew from $1.26 billion to $3.52 billion, representing nearly a quarter of all overseas investment. However, many of the nations in the region were politically unstable and unable to pay their foreign debts, making them vulnerable to interference by the creditor nations in Europe. As part of the Monroe Doctrine, at least as interpreted by such turn-of-the-century American expansionists as President Theodore Roosevelt, the United States was committed to ensuring political stability and fiscal responsibility in Latin America. To those ends, the United States in the 1910s dispatched troops to the Dominican Republic, Haiti, Mexico, and Nicaragua. In all but Mexico, the troops remained in place as the following decade began. During his 1920 campaign, Harding had made U.S. withdrawal from those countries part of his platform of normalcy and a less aggressive foreign policy. While political turbulence prevented Harding from fulfilling that pledge, the Coolidge and Hoover administrations completed the process, paving the way for a new and more cooperative relationship between the United States and its Latin American neighbors under Democratic President Franklin D. Roosevelt.

In Asia, strategic concerns rather than financial ones dictated U.S. foreign policy. While Americans had always been wary of involvement in European affairs, there was a long-standing view that the country's overseas destiny lay across the Pacific in East Asia. China was of particular concern, with many American missionaries traveling there to spread the Christian faith in the nineteenth and early twentieth centuries and American businesses forever eyeing China's huge potential market. But China's lack of a strong central government and an escalating civil war made it virtually impossible for America to establish regular relations in the 1920s.

More significant for U.S.-Asia relations was the rising nation of Japan. Once closed to the outside world, Japan had emerged as a regional power by the early twentieth century. Many U.S. policy makers regarded Japan as a potential economic and strategic competitor in East Asia. It was in part to counter that threat that the Harding administration organized the Washington Naval Arms Conference of 1921. Conferees, including the United States, professed the idealistic goal of limiting the size of national navies and thereby reducing the threat of conflict. But the American agenda also included placing a check on Japanese power, by limiting its navy to 60 percent of the size of America's.

While much of American foreign policy of the 1920s was guided by either isolationism or narrow self-interest, Wilsonian idealism was not entirely dead. In 1927, French foreign minister Aristide Briand approached the United States about a treaty guaranteeing France's security and outlawing war between the two nations. U.S. Secretary of State Frank Kellogg offered a bolder idea—a multilateral treaty that called on signatories to "condemn recourse to war for the solution of international controversies, and renounce it as an instrument of national policy." Praised by U.S. peace groups and eventually signed by more than sixty nations, the Kellogg-Briand Pact was ratified by the U.S. Senate by a vote of 85–1. It passed so easily in the still-isolationist body, however, because the treaty had virtually no teeth, lacking any enforcement machinery. America's legislators, effectively representing the will of the people, were still in no mood for serious foreign entanglements.

In the context of America's world role, the 1920s and early 1930s represented a lull between storms—between the progressive-inspired Wilsonianism of the World War I era and the rising threat of international fascism of the late 1930s and early 1940s. Even as the United States basked in isolationism—protected by two great oceans, buoyed by unprecedented economic growth, and diverted by the pleasures of mass popular culture—forces still largely hidden from the American people were at work, drawing the country into world affairs and preparing it for global leadership later in the century. Among these forces were economic expansion abroad, the decay of the traditional European-controlled imperial order, and the rise of revolutionary and expansionist ideologies on both the Right (fascism, militarism, and Nazism) and the Left (communism in its various guises). But those were still years away from the Jazz Age—the last era in which America could maintain its distance from foreign entanglements.

James Ciment

Further Reading

Buckley, Thomas H. *The United States and the Washington Conference, 1921–1922.* Knoxville: University of Tennessee Press, 1970.

Cohen, Warren I. *Empire Without Tears: American Foreign Relations, 1921–1933.* Philadelphia: Temple University Press, 1987.

Ellis, L. Ethan. *Republican Foreign Policy, 1921–1933.* New Brunswick, NJ: Rutgers University Press, 1968.

Hoff, Joan. *American Business and Foreign Policy, 1920–1933.* Lexington: University Press of Kentucky, 1971.

Kent, Bruce. *The Spoils of War: The Politics, Economics, and Diplomacy of Reparations, 1918–1932.* New York: Oxford University Press, 1989.

Louria, Margot. *Triumph and Downfall: America's Pursuit of Peace and Prosperity, 1921–1933.* Westport, CT: Greenwood, 2001.

A-Z
Entries

Adkins v. Children's Hospital (1923)

In its landmark 1923 decision in *Adkins v. Children's Hospital,* the U.S. Supreme Court ruled 5–3 that Congress could not mandate a national minimum wage. Writing for the majority, Associate Justice George Sutherland held that such laws violate the constitutional guarantee of life, liberty, and property, in that they infringe upon an individual's right to make a contract of his or her choosing. The case has been viewed by historians as part of a conservative, probusiness backlash to the liberalized labor laws of the Progressive Era before World War I.

The struggle over the government's right to establish working conditions was several decades old when the *Adkins* case came before the nation's highest court. In its 1905 decision in *Lochner v. New York,* the Supreme Court had ruled that a state could not set a maximum number of hours that employees—in this case, bakers—could work each week. In 1908, however, the Court reversed itself, at least in part, ruling in *Muller v. Oregon* that states are free to limit the number of working hours for female employees. Writing for the majority in that case, Associate Justice David Josiah Brewer argued that the state has a special interest in protecting the health of women, given their roles as child bearers and mothers. Nine years later, in *Bunting v. Oregon* (1917), the Supreme Court extended the rule on maximum working hours to men; the Oregon statute under litigation was declared constitutional because it regulated hours rather than wages.

In 1918, the U.S. Congress authorized the wartime National War Labor Board (NWLB) to set an appropriate minimum wage for female employees in the District of Columbia, which Congress directly governed at the time. Like the Supreme Court in *Muller,* Congress argued that women constitute a special class and therefore require special protections. In this instance, it was argued, an adequate minimum wage was necessary for the "health and morals of women." That is, a woman worker who was not adequately paid might be led into a life of sin.

The *Adkins* case pitted the Children's Hospital of the District of Columbia against its many female employees under contract; some of these women were being paid less than the minimum established by the NWLB. Hospital officials appealed the board's decision, claiming that it violated their freedom to contract, and the case made its way to the Supreme Court.

In the *Adkins* decision, the Court ruled that Congress could not mandate a minimum wage because to do so was an unconstitutional infringement on the Fifth Amendment. Specifically, the Court held that individuals and commercial firms have the right to contract for whatever pay both parties agree upon. To infringe on that right, the justices held, is to deny individuals a constitutionally guaranteed freedom; as a denial of "life, liberty, or property, without due process of law," it was deemed a violation of the Fifth Amendment. Justice Sutherland also cited the recently ratified Nineteenth Amendment (1920), which granted women the right to vote. With that measure, he argued, women were clearly becoming more equal citizens and therefore no longer needed special protections under the law.

The *Adkins* decision had broad implications for the country as a whole. Since the Fourteenth Amendment applied the due process clause to the individual states, the ruling in *Adkins* extended beyond the District of Columbia and Congress. Implicitly, the Supreme Court denied the right of any state to pass similar minimum wage laws.

The two main dissents in the case came from Chief Justice William Howard Taft and Associate Justice Oliver Wendell Holmes. Taft argued that Congress indeed has the right to regulate wages or other terms of employment when health is at issue, and that the *Bunting* decision had upheld that right. According to Taft, Sutherland's Nineteenth Amendment argument was irrelevant. Holmes argued that the *Lochner* decision, on which Sutherland had based much of his decision, had been superseded by later Court decisions in *Muller* and *Bunting.*

Given the increasingly conservative, probusiness climate of the day, the decision aroused little immediate controversy. Moreover, with the urban economy booming from 1923 to 1929, the issue of wages was largely being settled in workers' favor by low unemployment and market forces.

With the coming of the Great Depression in 1929, however, the political climate began to change. An increasingly restive labor movement, public opinion, and President Franklin D. Roosevelt's landslide reelection in 1936 may have had an impact on the Supreme Court's thinking. In *West Coast Hotel v. Parrish* (1937), the justices reversed their decision in *Adkins,* ruling 5–4 that state minimum wage laws—in this case, for women workers—are indeed constitutional. The Court agreed with the many labor advocates who contended that employees are at a disadvantage in negotiating contracts with employers and not at liberty to set whatever terms they please.

In 1938, Congress passed the Fair Labor Standards Act, setting minimum wages and maximum hours for all workers. The legislation was upheld by the Supreme Court in *U.S. v. Darby Lumber Co.* (1941).

Scott Merriman and James Ciment

See also: *Bailey v. Drexel Furniture Company* (1922); Holmes, Oliver Wendell, Jr.; Labor Movement; Law and the Courts; Taft, William Howard; Women and Gender.

Further Reading

Arkes, Hadley. *The Return of George Sutherland: Restoring a Jurisprudence of Natural Rights.* Princeton, NJ: Princeton University Press, 1994.

Burton, David Henry. *Taft, Holmes, and the 1920s Court: An Appraisal.* Madison, NJ: Fairleigh Dickinson University Press, 1998.

White, G. Edward. *Oliver Wendell Holmes: Sage of the Supreme Court.* New York: Oxford University Press, 2000.

Advertising

The advertising industry came of age during the Jazz Age. Total U.S. advertising expenditures, which were almost $1.5 billion in 1918, increased to $2.82 billion in 1919, nearly $3.1 billion by 1925, and $4 billion by 1929. Gross revenues from advertising in magazines, which stood at $58.5 million in 1918, reached $129.5 million by 1920 and $196.3 million by the end of the decade. *The Saturday Evening Post,* one of the nation's most popular magazines, nearly doubled in size after World War I, to approximately 200 pages, most of which were filled with advertisements. But during the 1920s advertising was more than just big business; it was a glamorous, exciting,

and powerful social force that permanently altered popular consumption in the United States.

Among other things, American advertising during the Jazz Age became bolder, more colorful, and eye-catching, appealing to an American public freed from Victorian modesty and eager to consume. Ad agencies took advantage of new technology that enabled high-speed, four-color printing in magazines. Ad budgets grew, campaigns became more elaborate, and new products were developed and brought to market in a fraction of the time it had taken in the past.

Rise of the Advertising Professional

Advertisers came to be praised as the geniuses of American popular culture. Magazines glorified the qualities of good advertising. Social observers claimed that advertising was the foundation of any good newspaper or magazine, and that much of the serious writing of the decade was being published in advertisements. A best-selling book, *The Man Nobody Knows* (1925), by ad executive Bruce Barton, went so far as to characterize Jesus Christ as a business executive, salesman, and yes, adman.

Advertising methods became increasingly sophisticated. Ad agencies preyed on people's fears, their vanity, and their need to be socially accepted. Ads encouraged consumers to keep up with their neighbors. Women were told they could be as glamorous and beautiful as any Hollywood movie star, and men were told they could be as successful and charismatic as any multimillionaire, if only they used the right products. Advertising copywriters even invented new diseases or afflictions, which people could avoid if they bought the right product. In their quest for increased profits, advertisers changed the thoughts and habits of many Americans.

Many of the products that are ubiquitous to modern consumers were first thrust onto the national market during the 1920s, backed by full-scale advertising. Harvey Firestone embarked on a major campaign to sell pneumatic truck tires after World War I. Robert B. Wheelan became the first entrepreneur to set an exercise routine to music, record it, and market it to a mass audience. His "Daily Dozen" became an immediate success, and doing routine calisthenics became known as doing one's daily dozen. The country's three largest tobacco producers spent billions to recruit new smokers, and Camels, Chesterfields, and Lucky Strikes became American consumers' favorite cigarettes. For the first time, tobacco producers appealed directly to women, marketing cigarettes as an appetite suppressant and something that would help women preserve their newly acquired social freedom. By 1925, American Tobacco was selling 17.4 billion cigarettes each year, 13 billion of them Lucky Strikes; R.J. Reynolds was selling 34 billion Camels, and Liggett & Myers was selling more than 20 billion Chesterfields. The three major tobacco producers controlled over 82 percent of the U.S. cigarette market.

Soap was also successfully marketed during the 1920s. The B.J. Johnson Soap Company assured women that they could "Keep that Schoolgirl Complexion" if they used Palmolive, which by 1927 had become the best-selling soap in the world. Johnson soon expanded its offerings to include shampoo and shaving cream. Lux soap, according to its ads, was used by nine out of ten movie stars to maintain their beautiful skin. Users of Lifebuoy soap, it was said, could avoid a condition so horrifying that one needed to utter only two letters to identify it, "B.O." Women could use Odorono deodorant to avoid offending a prospective marriage partner.

Advertising also helped Jazz Age consumers find relief for aches, pains, and other personal health problems. In 1922, Gerard B. Lambert, a son of the creator of Listerine—a surgical antiseptic used by dentists—found himself $700,000 in debt. He went to his four brothers, all vice presidents at the Lambert pharmaceutical company, and demanded to be put on the payroll. When they made him general manager, one of his first tasks was to boost sales of Listerine, which until 1914 had been sold only by prescription. By 1928, the company was spending $5 million a year on advertising its mouthwash and had the profits to show for it. Similarly, a product created by W.F. Young, Inc., called Absorbine Jr. (originally intended for use on horses) found a vast new consumer market during the 1920s when advertisers discovered that, in addition to treating sore muscles, sunburn, and insect bites, Absorbine Jr. could be used to cure a condition that later became known as "athlete's foot."

Testimonials were the ad of choice during the 1920s. Celebrities hawked everything from soaps, lotions, and hair tonics to storage batteries, cars, motorcycles, and typewriters. Madison Avenue—the New York City street where the leading agencies maintained their offices—had lists of opera stars, society figures, athletes, and movie stars who, for $5,000, would endorse nearly any product. Although the validity of such testimonials was suspect—movie idols who did not smoke, for ex-

ample, might extol the virtues of their favorite brand of cigarettes—few Americans seemed to mind. The Federal Trade Commission and the Better Business Bureau made passing attempts at regulating testimonial advertising, but neither the industry nor the consuming public paid them much heed.

Soaring Consumption

Consumer purchasing soared during the 1920s largely because advertisers, manufacturers, and retailers promoted installment purchases. The earlier reluctance of the American people to accumulate debt disappeared almost completely during the 1910s, when auto manufacturers began selling cars on the installment plan. After World War I, installment selling expanded beyond cars and houses to include every new appliance and electronic gadget coming to market. By 1927, Americans possessed more than $4 billion in unpaid merchandise. Washing machines, electric refrigerators, pianos, sewing machines, and radios were just some of products bought on credit during the 1920s. Increasing debt put a strain on many American households during the Jazz Age. Perhaps more important, it placed increasing pressure on consumers' future earning potential.

In October 1929, consumption came to a grinding halt for the millions of Americans who lost their jobs, farms, homes, or life savings with the collapse of the stock market and the onset of the Great Depression. During the Roaring Twenties, however, advertising had reigned supreme, ushering in the conspicuous consumption of modern American society.

Michael A. Rembis

See also: Beauty Industry and Culture; Bernays, Edward L.; Cigarettes and Tobacco; Credit and Debt, Consumer; Lasker, Albert; Radio; Retail and Chain Stores; Sarnoff, David.

Further Reading

Ewen, Stuart. *Captains of Consciousness: Advertising and the Social Roots of the Consumer Culture.* New York: Basic Books, 2001.
Turner, E.S. *The Shocking History of Advertising!* New York: E.P. Dutton, 1953.
Wood, James P. *The Story of Advertising.* New York: Ronald, 1958.

African Americans

For many African Americans, the 1920s were a time of rising aspirations. The vast migration of black people

African American soldiers hoped that wartime service would win them respect and equality upon returning home from World War I. Instead, they would be met by continued discrimination and even violence. Here, members of the celebrated 369th Colored Infantry, known as the Harlem Hellfighters, arrive in New York City in 1919. *(Paul Thompson/Stringer/Time & Life Pictures/Getty Images)*

out of the rural South and into urban areas, especially in the North, continued a trend which had begun in the early twentieth century, and offered an escape from the worst abuses of segregation and the abject poverty of tenant farming. The new urban setting not only presented economic opportunities in the form of factory work, it also created communities where African American culture could flourish.

The decade brought modest improvements in the lives of rural black Southerners; Jim Crow remained firmly entrenched, but extralegal violence against blacks in the form of lynchings declined. In urban areas, however, the vast influx of blacks resulted in a series of deadly attacks by white mobs. Between 1917 and 1921, major riots occurred in East St. Louis, Chicago, and Tulsa, while lesser outbreaks took place in other locales.

Despite serious challenges, it was clear as early as 1918 that a "New Negro" had emerged in the United States. African Americans of the 1920s were willing to leave the oppressive living conditions of

the rural South and fight to make a better life for themselves and for future generations.

Great Migration

Approximately one-fifth of America's nearly 12 million African Americans, or 2.4 million people, left the rural South between 1910 and the end of the Jazz Age, in what is called the Great Migration. In 1935, the U.S. Census Bureau issued a special report that documented the historic demographic shift in the black population during the preceding two decades. Whereas earlier over 90 percent of African Americans had lived in the rural South, between 1910 and 1920 the figure dropped to 85 percent, and by 1930 it fell to 78.5 percent. While more than three-quarters of African Americans still lived in the rural South in 1930, barely making a living as sharecroppers and tenant farmers, many African Americans were on the move geographically, socially, politically, and economically.

Most blacks left the rural South in search of

better-paying jobs and relief from Jim Crow discrimination. Since the end of Reconstruction in the 1870s, Southern blacks had faced an increasingly oppressive system of institutionalized segregation, discrimination, and disenfranchisement, as well as mounting white hostility and violence. Southern blacks were forced into displays of humiliating deference to whites. This social oppression was made worse by deteriorating economic conditions. The cotton crop, the mainstay of Southern farmers, was destroyed by a boll weevil infestation in 1915, followed by declining cotton prices during the 1920s. These conditions added to African Americans' plight and compelled many of them to abandon the fields for city life. New job opportunities created by a shortage of workers during World War I and a prospering manufacturing sector after the 1921–1922 recession provided African Americans with means to escape the oppressive living conditions in the South.

Most of the migrants settled in the industrial states of the North. Lured by jobs at Henry Ford's River Rouge plant in Detroit, as well as those of other automakers, nearly 170,000 African Americans flocked to Michigan in the 1920s. The African American populations of New York and Wisconsin more than doubled, while Illinois, New Jersey, and Ohio had a combined total of 360,000 black residents by 1930. In absolute numbers, New York showed the largest increase in African American residents, with a gain of nearly 215,000. Pennsylvania, which had a long history of taking in blacks from the South, had more than 430,000 black residents according to the 1930 census, more than any other Northern state.

In 1920, more than 3.5 million African Americans lived in urban areas (defined by the U.S. Census as places with a population of 2,500 persons or more). By 1930, the figure had risen to 5.2 million, or 43.7 percent of the country's black population.

The majority of black urbanites lived in cities with more than 25,000 residents. New York City's black population more than doubled from 1920 (152,467) to 1930 (327,706). In the process, the Harlem section of Manhattan became the center of African American cultural expression and civil rights activity during the 1920s, attracting black migrants from all over the South. Chicago's black population also more than doubled between 1920 and 1930 (to 233,903), making it the second largest black community in the United States.

African Americans also moved to urban centers in the South and West. Houston's black population almost doubled in size during the 1920s, while the Memphis African American community increased to 96,550. Baltimore reached a total of 142,106 black residents by 1930, an increase of 31.2 percent for the decade. Washington, D.C., New Orleans, Birmingham, Memphis, St. Louis, and Atlanta also experienced dramatic rises in their black populations during the course of the decade. Los Angeles's black population more than doubled, to 38,894.

Whether they remained in the South or moved to the West or North, African Americans continued to face hostility, violence, segregation, and discrimination during the 1920s. Job opportunities and living conditions were much better in the West and the North than they were in the South, but even in those areas, African Americans encountered a host of obstacles. Fearing unrest from hostile white workers, or acting on prejudices of their own, factory owners typically put blacks in menial janitorial or maintenance positions, rather than in higher-paying assembly-line jobs. Nor could black workers turn to unions for help, as union membership was only open to skilled craft workers. As a result, black workers faced a kind of double discrimination—because of their skin color and because of their unskilled status.

Like foreign immigrants, African Americans often moved into neighborhoods where they had friends and family and could find goods and services that appealed to their culture. As blacks poured into the cities, they competed for limited housing, or they moved in with family or friends. Landlords took advantage of de facto segregation by charging higher rents to blacks, while often failing to maintain their buildings. White hostility kept many African Americans confined to overcrowded and rundown slums. Often there was no way out. Even those who had the financial resources to leave the ghetto were prevented from doing so by realtors who would not sell to them or by hostile whites who used intimidation, terror, and even violence to prevent black families from relocating to white neighborhoods.

Institutions of Community

Despite the obstacles and limitations, segments of the African American community managed to thrive during the 1920s. The most important institution in the black community had always been the church, and church membership continued to grow during the Jazz Age.

A 1926 census of religious institutions in the United States counted twenty-four different African American denominations. African Americans owned or leased 37,790 church buildings, with a combined membership of more than 5 million. Women outnumbered men in church membership by more than two to one. The various Baptist denominations together accounted for approximately 60 percent of all black church members. Four Methodist denominations accounted for another 30 percent of parishioners in 1926. Although 90 percent of black churches were located in the South during the 1920s, church membership expanded wherever African Americans settled. Cleveland's forty-four black churches grew to over 149 by 1933. One Alabama church moved its entire congregation to Cleveland during the 1920s.

African Americans created business districts that provided goods and services, stabilized black communities, and formed the foundation for an expanding black middle class. They established their own insurance companies, banks, real estate companies, funeral parlors, and other enterprises during the Jazz Age, many of these businesses made possible by the growing urban black communities. Black-owned grocery stores, pharmacies, barbershops, and other services catered to an all-black clientele.

Perhaps the best-known African American entrepreneur was Madame C.J. Walker, who sold beauty products to the black community. Born Sarah Breedlove to Louisiana tenant farmer parents in 1867, Walker got her start as a washerwoman in St. Louis, where she developed a hair treatment involving hot combs and ointments. By 1910, she had established her own company, Madame C.J. Walker Manufacturing Company, in Indianapolis. Throughout the 1920s, her company generated millions in revenues, employing thousands of salespeople, mostly women. Despite such successes, most black businesses remained marginal in the overall American economy, and when the country sank into the Great Depression during the early 1930s, only the strongest ones survived.

Civil Rights

As African Americans built their own institutions and communities during the 1920s, they also continued their struggle for civil rights. Northern black communities established branches of the National Association for the Advancement of Colored People (NAACP), which fought against lynching, disenfranchisement, segregation, racism in the criminal justice system, and economic inequality. By 1920, the NAACP had an all-black national leadership and was the most influential civil rights group in America. The organization's most prominent leader was W.E.B. Du Bois, the founding editor of its monthly magazine, *The Crisis*. During the 1920s, Du Bois became one of the most influential black intellectuals and civil rights leaders in America, and *The Crisis* became a well-respected, widely read outlet for black art and literature and social and political commentary. NAACP leaders James Weldon Johnson and Walter White fought throughout the 1920s to end lynching and to get an anti-lynching bill through Congress. Although Congress never passed federal legislation, the work of the NAACP and other civil rights groups, including the National Association of Colored Women's Clubs, helped raise public awareness and ultimately reduced the number of lynchings in the United States.

To further promote African American civil rights worldwide, Du Bois organized four pan-African conferences. Delegates from around the world met in Paris in 1919; London, Paris, and Brussels in 1921; London and Lisbon in 1923; and New York in 1927. Although there had been earlier meetings (the first in 1905), the conferences of the 1920s were more ambitious in their goals and received better press coverage, especially in the European press. Delegates from Africa, the Caribbean, Europe, and the United States issued a powerful manifesto to the world, demanding an end to colonialism, as well as a declaration against the exploitation of African labor and natural resources.

At home, meanwhile, African Americans won an important political victory in 1928, when Chicago's black community elected Oscar DePriest, a longtime community activist, to the U.S. Congress. For the first time since 1900, an African American sat in the U.S. House of Representatives.

One prominent trend in black activism during the 1920s eschewed electoral politics. Founded by Jamaican-born black nationalist Marcus Garvey, the United Negro Improvement Association (UNIA), based in Harlem, attracted thousands of supporters by calling on black people to reject white society and to build a separate economic and social existence outside of it. Garvey argued that African Americans had to focus on their own institutions rather than worry about their rights as whites defined them. Garvey encouraged black Americans to think of themselves as part of the wider African diaspora and to fight for the liberation of all Africans. Garvey created the Black Star Shipping Line in 1919, in part to provide African Americans with a means of returning to Africa. When it became known that Garvey did not actually own the ships he claimed to, he was convicted of conspiracy to commit mail fraud and spent two years in prison. President Calvin Coolidge commuted his sentence in 1927, but Garvey was deported to Jamaica and his movement went into steep decline.

Other groups, such as the Urban League, helped African Americans make gains in employment by providing social services to as many as 40,000 African Americans annually during the 1920s. Wealthy whites contributed most of the money to the Urban League, which had branches in Northern cities. The organization helped Northern black migrants acquire job skills and find work in an era when there were virtually no laws prohibiting employment discrimination. Urban League volunteers trained migrants for industrial jobs, ran adult education courses for various trades, promoted health education and child welfare, and engaged in social work.

Black women only partially shared in the contemporaneous gains of their gender. While women had technically won the right to vote, African American women were prevented from doing so by antiblack voting laws in the South. Thus, African American women pressed the recently formed National Women's Party to join the fight for African American civil and voting rights. Black women, such as longtime activist Ida B. Wells, and the National Association of Colored Women's Clubs also played a critical role in pressing Congress to pass antilynching legislation. Women organized fund-raising events, contributed money, and distributed literature for the NAACP and other civil rights groups. Throughout the 1920s, black women such as educator Mary McLeod Bethune also fought to promote schooling—at both the secondary and college levels—for young black women.

Culture

In its new urban setting, African American cultural expression blossomed during the 1920s with musicians, artists, and writers finding a growing audience for their work. In New York City, the artistic movement called the Harlem Renaissance found creative writers and artists in all fields sharing the African American historical experience, celebrating the Great Migration, and grappling with the many legacies of slavery.

For the most part, the emergence of a new generation of black artists during the 1920s was a spontaneous organic process, but black civil rights leaders and white benefactors recognized the power of artists to shape public perceptions of African Americans and possibly break down long-standing racial barriers. These groups and individuals quickly became involved in the movement as patrons and by providing places for black artists to exhibit their work. The NAACP provided black writers, poets, and artists with a forum in its journal *The Crisis*. The Urban League provided a similar outlet for artists in its journal *Opportunity*. White benefactors included William E. Harmon, who provided black painters and sculptors an opportunity to present their work and to win acclaim and awards through the William E. Harmon Foundation.

While black writers, painters, sculptors, and actors played a critical role in shaping the culture of the 1920s, it was a black musical form that defined the era. F. Scott Fitzgerald, author of *The Great Gatsby* (1925) and other modern classics, referred to the 1920s as the "Jazz Age." Jazz music, which emerged out of black New Orleans around the turn of the twentieth century, had become an international phenomenon by the 1920s. Black and white audiences and performers flocked to bars, cabarets, juke joints, saloons, and dance halls to hear live jazz performances. The blues, a product of the Mississippi Delta, also became highly popular during the 1920s and influenced the emergence of rock and roll thirty years later.

African American creativity influenced all art forms during the Jazz Age. Black artists painted and sculpted, made movies, transformed the Broadway musical, and created serious dramatic roles on stage and film. They wrote some of the most engaging prose and poetry and composed timeless blues and jazz classics, as well as spirituals and gospel music. As cultural critic Alain Locke and other figures in the black community claimed, a "New Negro" had indeed emerged in Jazz Age America.

Michael A. Rembis

See also: Blues; Chicago Race Riot of 1919; DePriest, Oscar; Du Bois, W.E.B.; Garvey, Marcus; Harlem Renaissance; Jazz; Ku Klux Klan; Locke, Alain; Lynching; Migration,

Great; National Association for the Advancement of Colored People; Rosewood Massacre (1923); Tulsa Race Riots of 1921; Universal Negro Improvement Association.

Further Reading

Arnesen, Eric. *Black Protest and the Great Migration: A Brief History with Documents.* Boston: Bedford/St. Martin's, 2003.

Cronon, E. David. *Black Moses: The Story of Marcus Garvey and the Universal Negro Improvement Association.* 2nd ed. Madison: University of Wisconsin Press, 1981.

Schneider, Mark Robert. *African Americans in the Jazz Age: A Decade of Struggle and Promise.* Lanham, MD: Rowman and Littlefield, 2006.

Trotter, William, Jr., ed. *The Great Migration in Historical Perspective: New Dimensions of Race, Class, and Gender.* Bloomington: Indiana University Press, 1991.

Wintz, Cary D. *Black Culture and the Harlem Renaissance.* Houston, TX: Rice University Press, 1988.

Agricultural Marketing Act of 1929

In the aftermath of World War I, American farmers faced significant difficulties. With the return of peace in Europe, demand fell, and inevitably prices tumbled. As service personnel were demobilized, the armed forces no longer needed as much food, and Americans did not rapidly return to their prewar diets, heavy with meats and breads. In addition, Europe recovered quickly from the war and thus was less reliant on American foodstuffs than had been expected. Indeed, Europeans produced more food for themselves and their livestock in 1919 than they had in 1913 (the last full harvest before the outbreak of war).

Smaller markets were but one factor; production contributed to the chronically low prices as well. Throughout the war years, farmers had plowed up orchards, pastures, and farmyards to produce food and fodder. They also listened to their county agents on methods of improving poultry production and butterfat content, raising meaty swine, and growing better strains of corn and healthier fruit trees, enhancing productivity every step of the way.

A further contribution to agricultural production came in the form of mechanization: the gasoline-powered tractor. Throughout the 1920s, farmers retired an average of about 500,000 horses and mules annually for the noisy demands of a Case, John Deere, Allis-Chalmers, or Farmall tractor. Not only did the tractors enable farmers to tend their fields more rapidly, but gasoline replaced the need for homegrown oats and fodder, making more acreage available for crops. It has been estimated that the retirement of each draft animal opened up an additional five acres.

As farmers struggled to keep up with mortgage payments, foreclosures became commonplace and tenancy increased. The situation was hardly brightened by years of dry weather, particularly in the Midwest and Great Plains. Adding insult to injury, young people abandoned farms to make their living in urban areas. With skills gained in military service, former soldiers left the farm in droves to serve as mechanics, electricians, and factory workers or as entry-level, white-collar workers.

Those who remained on the farm attempted a variety of solutions to their woes. Cooperative buying and selling became popular, as did reducing overhead by keeping strict account of livestock and crop productivity, and using only the best seed and livestock. Spurred by the farm bloc, Congress enacted legislation to prohibit monopoly and restraint of trade in the slaughterhouses, to exempt farmers' cooperatives from antitrust laws, and to provide cheaper credit. Still the farm crisis continued.

Farmers, desperate for relief, sought help through a subsidized export corporation operated by the federal government. Named after its sponsors, Senator Charles McNary (R-OR) and Representative Gilbert Haugen (R-IA), the exceedingly complex proposal—the McNary-Haugen Farm Relief Bill—passed Congress three times (1924, 1926, 1928), only to be vetoed by President Calvin Coolidge. In his veto, Coolidge had the support of Secretary of Commerce Herbert Hoover, who held fast to his belief that farm conditions would improve when farmers operated cooperatively from informed positions.

Conditions did not improve, and by the election of 1928, the "farm problem" seemed to be on everyone's mind. In fact, presidential hopeful Herbert Hoover promised that, if elected, he would call a special session of Congress to tackle the issue. As president, he supported, and Congress passed, the Agricultural Marketing Act of 1929. The measure authorized the federal government to create a revolving fund of $500 million to lend to agricultural cooperatives. Cooperatives could then purchase price-depressing surpluses, keeping them off the market until prices improved. With orderly marketing and an increasing demand, cooperatives could then sell their surplus products, return a profit to the nation's farmers, and commence the organization of orderly marketing associations.

Within the Agricultural Marketing Act, Congress included language to establish the Federal Farm Board, which was to institute a number of agricultural stabilization corporations for grains and cotton. The stabilization corporations also held authorization to purchase excess commodities, withhold them from the marketplace, and release them only with improved prices. Some surpluses found their way to relief lines, distributed as charity.

As the depression, both agricultural and general, worsened, it became clear that a single organization, regardless of its backing, could not return prosperity to the farms of America. By 1932, the Federal Farm Board had not proven itself up to the task and stood some $184 million in debt. Despite the efforts and expenditures, farm conditions had actually worsened during its brief existence.

Regardless of its failure, the Agricultural Marketing Act and the accompanying Federal Farm Board did mark the onset of closer relations between farmers and the government, ultimately setting the stage for the revolutionary agricultural measures of the New Deal.

Kimberly K. Porter

See also: Agriculture; American Farm Bureau Federation.

Further Reading

Benedict, Murray R. *Farm Policies of the United States, 1790–1950: A Study in Their Origins and Development.* New York: Twentieth Century Fund, 1953.

Hurt, R. Douglas. *American Agriculture: A Brief History.* Ames: Iowa State University, 1994.

Shideler, James H. *Farm Crisis, 1919–1923.* Berkeley: University of California Press, 1957.

Agriculture

The 1920s were a difficult period economically for America's farmers. During this time, the prosperity generated during World War I gave way to crop surpluses, falling crop prices, rising farm debt, and widespread poverty in agricultural regions, particularly the South.

Paradoxically, the motion pictures, music, and popular literature of the time extolled the farmer as the backbone of America, offering up idealized images of farm life for the consumption of newly expanding urban audiences. Although farmers were sometimes portrayed as hayseeds, they also were seen as a font of homespun wisdom, unsullied by the worldliness of cosmopolitan cities. Writers and moviemakers depicted the innocent pride and competition of farmers showing off the best of their livestock and crops at state fairs. Magazines, ignoring the labor that farming involved, portrayed the countryside as a clean, unpolluted place and farmers as healthy, apple-cheeked citizens.

Farm Work

Work on America's farms was heavy indeed, for agricultural mechanization was still in the pioneering stages by the 1920s. For most farmers, life followed the ancient biblical injunction about earning one's bread by the sweat of one's brow. In 1919, most tractors were ten-ton behemoths, practical only on the largest spreads. Or they might be shared power sources for a threshing machine that was owned by a number of neighboring farmers and moved from field to field. The few small gasoline tractors that were available often proved inadequately powered, breaking down under the challenges of farm work. In 1917, when Henry Ford, a farmer's son, entered the market with his small but rugged Fordson—the first mass-produced farm tractor—he joked that his only competition was the horse.

Although the Fordson had serious problems, including a dangerous tendency to tip over backward and crush its driver, it was successful enough that other companies had to produce small tractors or get out of the business. International Harvester, the descendant of Cyrus McCormick's reaper company, in 1924 introduced the Farmall, a nimble little red tractor whose very name proclaimed its suitability for a diversity of farm chores. Even so, tractors were still rare on American farms. As late as 1928, there were just 800,000 tractors—versus about 20 million mules and horses—on America's roughly 8 million farms. Many farmers could not afford to switch from four-legged to mechanized power.

During and immediately after World War I, agriculture had enjoyed a brief era of prosperity because of the need for food for soldiers, federal price supports, and the demand from war-torn Europe. After the war, however, prices for grain and other farm products steadily declined, while the prices farmers paid for manufactured goods remained the same or rose.

Between 1918 and the depths of the 1921–1922 recession, wheat prices fell by 40 percent, corn by a third, and hogs by roughly half. Farmers had barely recovered lost ground when the Depression hit in 1930. From 1919 to 1930, farm income fell from 16 percent of the national income to 8.8 percent. The

Boll Weevil

In the early twentieth century, agriculture in the southern United States remained concentrated on a small number of cash crops. Most farms, in fact, focused on a single crop as a source of income: cotton. First cultivated in the British American colonies along the southern coast, cotton spread westward into the Mississippi River valley and beyond during the early nineteenth century. It remained the dominant cash crop in most of the South until 1918, when a number of factors began to force southern agriculture to abandon its traditional one-crop economy and move toward diversification and mechanization. Among these factors was the boll weevil.

Approximately a quarter inch in length, the boll weevil (*Anthonomus grandis*) is a beetlelike insect that damages cotton crops by depositing its eggs in the square, or boll, of the cotton plant—the pod that yields cotton as the plant matures. The weevil hibernates in the ground during the winter, emerging in the spring to lay its eggs in the bolls, causing them to rot before the cotton can mature. Boll weevils also feed on the bolls, resulting in additional injury to the plant.

The boll weevil migrated into the southern United States from Mexico in 1892. By the middle of the first decade of the twentieth century, it had reached the cotton fields of Louisiana and Mississippi; by the early 1920s, it had infested all cotton-producing regions of the South.

Cotton production declined sharply during this period—in some regions by as much as 50 to 75 percent. Production began to recover in the years immediately preceding the Great Depression as farmers modified their planting schedules to allow the cotton to mature early, and the locus of cotton production shifted northward and westward to the drier and more fertile lands of West Texas, Arkansas, and the Mississippi Delta.

The boll weevil created an acute economic crisis for landowners, tenant farmers, and farm laborers in cotton-producing regions. Poor farm laborers, for whom mechanization had already reduced employment opportunities, were particularly hurt by the devastation the insect brought to the cotton crops.

This situation contributed significantly to the mass migrations of African Americans and poor whites to urban areas in the East, Midwest, and West. African Americans who left the South during the Great Migration of the early twentieth century often cited racism, reduced demand for farm labor due to mechanization, and the boll weevil as their reasons for leaving.

Boll weevil infestations also led to agricultural diversification and an increase in the cultivation of foodstuffs such as peanuts and soybeans, forcing cotton-producing regions of the South to end their dependence on a single cash crop. The boll weevil remained a problem for southern cotton farmers for decades, until intensive eradication campaigns in the late twentieth century succeeded in eliminating the pest as an economic threat.

Michael H. Burchett

situation was made even worse by the fact that many farmers had borrowed money to make capital investments during the period of prosperity, believing that the tractor and other mechanical innovations would soon pay for themselves in increased productivity.

With the farm population continuing its steady decline—the 1920 U.S. Census reported a greater urban than rural population for the first time in the nation's history—the agricultural sector lost some of its political clout. An effort to pass a crop price support bill in 1924 was defeated by urban members of Congress, who called it special-interest legislation.

Although American agriculture during the 1920s moved increasingly away from a subsistence to a cash-crop basis, most farmers remained relatively diversified. Even as the tractor began to replace the draft horse as a source of power, relatively few farmers were ready to abandon livestock and concentrate entirely on producing grain for sale. Most farms had a cow or two for milk, a few pigs to turn kitchen waste into edible pork, and a small flock of chickens to lay eggs, which might be consumed by the farm family or sold in town. Tending these animals was often the responsibility of the children; almost as soon as they were able to walk, they would be given such simple tasks as scattering grain for chickens and gathering eggs. As they grew older and stronger, they would graduate to feeding hogs and mucking out stables. Only the oldest boys and girls would shoulder the difficult task of handling full-grown cattle, which could try a grown man's strength.

Because livestock were still an important part of a farm, at least a portion of its acreage had to be devoted to pasture, generally alfalfa or clover, on which cattle might graze. Farmers were also beginning to grow fields of alfalfa or clover to be cut and baled as hay, which could be fed to cattle later in an enclosed yard. Many farmers were encouraged to make the switch because feeding cut hay meant less waste than did open grazing; it also gave them better control over the animals' diets and protected livestock from the hazards of open grazing.

The women of the family were generally responsible for the farmstead, keeping not only the house but also the barn lots and a large garden that produced most of the vegetables the family consumed. Who would consider purchasing factory-canned vegetables when one could can and preserve home-grown produce? The farmwife also was responsible for supervising the children's performance of barnyard chores.

Mechanization, including the introduction of the Ford Motor Company's first tractor—the Fordson—helped American farmers increase their output during the 1920s. Given the large crop surplus and falling prices of the era, this proved to be a mixed blessing for many farm families. *(Hulton Archive/Gerry Images)*

If eggs, milk, or vegetables were to be sold in town, women managed the task as well as the money from the sales, which would go into a fund for household incidentals rather than into the general farm-operating fund. As a result, most farm women enjoyed a small measure of financial independence that was unknown to many urban housewives, who usually were entirely dependent on their husbands for their incomes.

End to Isolation

The 1920s marked the end of the isolation that had been one of the most difficult characteristics of American farm life. Unlike traditional European peasants, who lived in a village and enjoyed the constant company of other peasant families, American farmers tended to live on their own farms. The nearest neighbor might well be a mile or more away. Trips into town were rare affairs, made only when the horses had no other work to do.

Mechanization changed that situation, allowing a farm family to get into their automobile and drive to town with ease. Indeed, farmers bought more automobiles than did any other occupational group in the 1920s; as early as 1921, there were about 3 million cars on American farms, or more than one for every three farms. Farmers too poor to afford an automobile might drive into town on a tractor.

Radio further diminished a farm's isolation.

While electrification had reached relatively few farms in the 1920s, most farmers could afford battery-operated radios, although the batteries were expensive enough that they had to be used carefully. Many times, a family would crowd around the radio, straining to hear the faint sounds generated by a battery's last bits of power. The radio brought not only weather and market reports, of immediate interest to the farmer, but also news, dramas, and music. Young members of a farm family in Idaho or Utah might dance the Charleston to music heard on the radio, just like their urban compatriots in New York or Chicago.

The telephone had an even greater effect on farmers, since it was a two-way medium. Approximately six out of ten telephones were owned by rural households in 1927. The technology was simple enough, so that, instead of waiting for an urban telephone company, a group of farmers could set up their own circuit, with a switchboard in one farmer's house. Tornado and other storm warnings could be passed along the party line, and, once a connection with town was established, help could be called for the sick or injured. The party line also offered an opportunity to visit with neighbors, if only by voice.

Yet these changes were not unmixed blessings. Not only did farmers become more closely tied to the cash economy, making them dependent on the prices they could get for crops such as corn and wheat, but technological progress also led to social changes. Mechanization meant longer workdays, since tractors required no rest breaks and there was no danger of working them to exhaustion. Furthermore, the fast-moving parts of tractors offered far more possibilities for crippling or deadly accidents than did horse-driven implements. The radio that connected the farm family with the national culture helped erode local culture and encourage passive consumption of entertainment. The telephone that passed lifesaving messages also could be an instrument of idle or malicious gossip.

The 1920s was a period of transformation for American farmers and a difficult time for many. While some left the farm for urban jobs, most farmers persevered, adapted to the changes, and moved into the new era of agriculture as a business rather than a folkway.

Leigh Kimmel

See also: Agricultural Marketing Act of 1929; American Farm Bureau Federation; Farmer-Labor Party; Recession of 1921–1922.

Further Reading

Blandford, Percy W. *Old Farm Tools and Machinery: An Illustrated History.* Fort Lauderdale, FL: Gale Research, 1976.

Dregni, Michael, ed. *This Old Farm: A Treasury of Family Farm Memories.* Stillwater, MN: Voyageur, 1999.

———. *This Old Tractor: A Treasury of Vintage Tractors and Family Farm Memories.* Stillwater, MN: Town Square, 1998.

Green, Harvey. *The Uncertainty of Everyday Life: 1915–1945.* New York: HarperCollins, 1992.

Kyvig, David E. *Daily Life in the United States, 1920–1939: Decades of Promise and Pain.* Westport, CT: Greenwood, 2002.

Shearer, Stephen R. *Hoosier Connections: The History of the Indiana Telephone Industry and the Indiana Telephone Association.* Indianapolis: Indiana Telephone Association, 1992.

Air-Conditioning

While air-conditioning was a technology nearly twenty years old when the Jazz Age began, it was still largely confined to industrial settings, providing climate control in factories that required controlled temperatures or humidity (air-conditioning cools by regulating humidity), such as candy factories and textile mills. The 1920s saw air-conditioning expand beyond the factory to public spaces, including stores, theaters, and hotels; home and vehicular units remained rare until after World War II. The spread of air-conditioning altered not only the way Americans lived—contributing to the popularity of moviegoing and department store shopping in summer—but also where they lived. With the advent of air-conditioning, hot and humid environs such as South Florida—once largely a winter haven for wealthy Americans—became increasingly popular places for year-round living.

Mechanical engineer Willis Carrier, who was employed by the Buffalo Forge Company, a heating-system company in Buffalo, New York, designed air-cooling systems as early as 1902. The systems were originally designed for factories that needed to regulate humidity in order to maintain a quality product, such as paper mills. In 1906, Carrier received a patent for his "Apparatus for Treating Air." That same year, the term "air-conditioning" was introduced by a North Carolina engineer named Stuart W. Cramer, who filed his own patent claim using the term.

By 1911, air-conditioning had become a well-established branch of engineering, involving primarily humidity control but also dealing with the control of air temperature, purity, moisture, and ventilation. In 1915, Carrier, along with a group of young engineers, raised the funds to found the Carrier Engineering Corporation, the first independent firm dedicated entirely to air-conditioning development, sales, and service.

The 1920s marked the beginning of the use of more powerful and efficient centrifugal compressors for the refrigerating machines at the heart of the modern air-conditioning system. On March 26, 1923, Carrier Engineering made its first sale of a centrifugal compressor-based system, to a candy manufacturer. Carrier also invented the restriction disc to lubricate the spinning driveshaft without the oil contaminating the refrigerant system, overcoming a frequent complaint about petroleum odors. As the compressors were perfected, replacing toxic substances such as ammonia or methyl chloride with the safer Freon as a refrigerant, they enabled air-conditioning systems to become much smaller and thus opened the way for air-conditioning in nonindustrial venues, such as the chamber of the U.S. House of Representatives, which became air-conditioned in 1928. Senators had to wait another year for summertime relief.

Department stores were early customers. In 1924, the J.L. Hudson store in Detroit was having trouble with its bargain basement overheating from the press of warm bodies radiating heat. Customers were fainting from heat exhaustion. When the store installed three centrifugal air-conditioning machines from Carrier Engineering, shoppers found the newly cool basement area so inviting that sales increased, and the store soon installed air conditioners on other floors as well.

Movie theaters also reaped the benefits of air-conditioning. Previously, movie theaters would close or run at a loss during the hot months, since few moviegoers would tolerate sweltering in a crowded movie theater full of other sweating patrons. In 1925, the Rivoli in New York became the first air-conditioned movie theater, after Carrier personally demonstrated that the system's chemicals were safe. On the first night the Rivoli operated with air-conditioning, California filmmaker Adolph Zukor was in the audience to witness the effect. At first the audience members fanned themselves out of sheer habit, but one by one they put down their fans. Soon people were coming to movie theaters in the summer to enjoy the air-conditioning as much as to watch a motion picture, and movie theaters began to advertise their air-conditioned premises as a selling point. By 1930, Carrier's company had installed air-conditioning in some 300 movie theaters.

Carrier also undertook air-conditioning Madison Square Garden's outdoor ice rink in 1925. On even the hottest of days, the rink owners had the doubly daunting task of maintaining both a frozen rink and a pleasant garden atmosphere. Madison Square Garden was more difficult than previous installations because it was outdoors, which meant that a certain portion of the chilled and dehumidified air would constantly be escaping. As a result, the installation required much larger compressors.

Carrier introduced a gas-powered home air conditioner in 1926. In 1928, he began production of the Weathermaker, a year-round residential air-conditioning system. His company also provided individual offices in a large office building with individually controlled air-conditioning units, while preserving the economies of central refrigeration supply. In 1927, General Electric introduced the first mass-produced air conditioners; previously each unit had been custom built for a particular venue.

Air-conditioning also contributed to real estate booms in regions such as south Florida and Arizona, where tropical or desert climates had made life uncomfortable, particularly in the summer months. Florida saw 300,000 new residents between 1923 and 1925 alone, but a hurricane devastated the Florida real estate market and put an end to the boom there in 1926. Air-conditioning's spread to other areas was set back by the economic downturn of the Great Depression, and many appliance factories were diverted to war production during World War II.

Leigh Kimmel

See also: Appliances, Household; Florida Land Boom; Technology.

Further Reading

Ingels, Margaret. *Willis Haviland Carrier: Father of Air Conditioning.* Garden City, NY: Country Life, 1952.

Kyvig, David E. *Daily Life in the United States, 1920–1939: Decades of Promise and Pain.* Westport, CT: Greenwood, 2002.

Will, Harry M., ed. *The First Century of Air Conditioning.* Atlanta: American Society of Heating, Refrigerating, and Air-Conditioning Engineers, 1999.

Algonquin Round Table

The Algonquin Round Table, also known as the "Vicious Circle," was a group of writers and critics that met almost daily from 1919 to 1929 at the Algonquin Hotel in New York City (59 West Forty-fourth

Street, between Fifth and Sixth avenues). Known for its individual and collective wit, often in the form of acerbic quips and biting criticisms, the group was at the center of literary culture during the 1920s. Although the composition of the Round Table changed over the years, the members' sensibilities and writings epitomized a modernist attitude and style that resonated through the twentieth century.

The original members—writer Dorothy Parker, humorist Robert Benchley, and playwright Robert Sherwood—began meeting regularly for lunch at the Algonquin Hotel because of its proximity to the offices of the magazine *Vanity Fair,* where they worked. The hotel manager and later owner, Frank Case, provided free appetizers for the low-paid writers and reserved their own table and waiter in the Rose Room.

Although there was no formal membership in the Algonquin Round Table, prominent members and frequent attendees included playwrights George and Beatrice Kaufman; columnist Franklin Pierce Adams (pen name F.P.A.); sportswriter Heywood Broun; journalist Ruth Hale; Alexander Woollcott, a *New Yorker* critic who wrote the popular "Shouts and Murmurs" column; journalist and *New Yorker* founder Harold Ross; composer and music critic Deems Taylor; author and screenwriter Donald Ogden Stewart; actress Peggy Wood; lyricist and librettist Howard Dietz; historian Peggy Leech; novelist and playwright Edna Ferber; comedian and musician Harpo Marx; actor Douglas Fairbanks; violinist Jascha Heifetz; and humorist Corey Ford.

Round Table conversation ran from art and literature to popular culture and politics. Although a number of members were sympathetic to the political Left of the 1920s (Parker actively supported the condemned anarchists Sacco and Vanzetti, and Woollcott visited the Soviet Union in the 1930s), as a group, they were not overtly inclined to any particular political direction. (Leech, for example, published a sympathetic biography of the moral crusader Anthony Comstock in 1927.)

The members were eminently quotable. Parker's quip "Brevity is the soul of lingerie," for example, captures the combination of high literary taste and playful revision of traditional Victorian values common at the Round Table. *The New Yorker* magazine, which debuted in February 1925 at the height of the group's popularity, reflected its combination of dry wit, incisive analysis of current events, and high aesthetic sensibility. Harold Ross, the founder and longtime editor of *The New Yorker,* se-

cured funding for the magazine at the Algonquin Hotel in 1924.

Edna Ferber called the core members of the Algonquin Round Table the "Poison Squad" and described them as "merciless" in their criticisms. Franklin Pierce Adams, for example, publicly ridiculed the spelling errors in F. Scott Fitzgerald's novel *This Side of Paradise* (1920). At the same time, the members of the group openly celebrated work they considered up to their standards, and with all the journalists and critics involved, their praise often found its way into print. Members of the Round Table lent assistance to the reputations and publishing fortunes of Fitzgerald, Ernest Hemingway, and other luminaries. Dorothy Parker, for example, edited *The Portable F. Scott Fitzgerald,* an anthology of his work.

By 1925, the Algonquin Round Table had become something of a public spectacle, and tourists often came to the hotel to dine within earshot. Popularity began taking its toll, however. Sherwood and Benchley, who had been living at the Algonquin, moved to quieter locations in the city to concentrate on their writing. In addition, the August 1927 execution of Sacco and Vanzetti, whose case had stimulated debate at the Algonquin Round Table since 1920, permanently divided the group. By 1929, the Vicious Circle had stopped meeting on a regular basis.

Jason Stacy

See also: Fiction; *New Yorker, The*; Parker, Dorothy; Poetry; Ross, Harold.

Further Reading

Drennan, Robert, ed. *The Algonquin Wits.* New York: Replica, 2000.

Gaines, James. *Wit's End: Days and Nights of the Algonquin Round Table.* New York: Harcourt Brace Jovanovich, 1979.

Kaufman, George, with Edna Ferber, et al. *Kaufman and Co.: Broadway Comedies.* New York: Library of America, 2004.

Meredith, Scott. *George S. Kaufman and the Algonquin Round Table.* New York: Allen and Unwin, 1977.

Parker, Dorothy. *The Complete Poetry and Short Stories of Dorothy Parker.* New York: Modern Library, 1994.

Alien Property Custodian Scandal

Among the many scandals associated with the administration of President Warren G. Harding, the one concerning the Alien Property Custodian has received the least attention from historians. Even so, it was one of the most blatant examples of corruption in the U.S.

federal government to that time. Thomas Woodnutt Miller, the custodian for U.S. property seized by the federal government from enemies, enemy aliens, and naturalized U.S. citizens born in enemy countries during World War I, was convicted of fraud in 1927 and sent to prison for his part in the conspiracy.

The office of Alien Property Custodian was created by the Trading with the Enemy Act of 1917. When the United States declared war on Germany, government leaders realized that large amounts of enemy-owned property, both real and intellectual, existed in the United States. The custodian was charged with seizing the property and disposing of it in ways that would benefit the U.S. war effort. As a result, German-owned property worth $556 million was confiscated by the U.S. government over the next eighteen months. Possessions of naturalized citizens also were seized. Confusion and scandal marked the process, since no list of the properties had been prepared. Some property belonging to German firms and enemy aliens was effectively hidden from the U.S. government.

The custodian's office tried to dispose of most of the property before the war ended. A. Mitchell Palmer, later the U.S. attorney general, was the first to hold the position of custodian. He and his successor, Francis P. Garvan, approved the sale of much of the property, including stocks and patents, for prices far below market value.

Thomas W. Miller was appointed Alien Property Custodian early in the administration of President Warren G. Harding, in 1921. Miller came from a prominent political family of Delaware and had been active in forming the American Legion, a patriotic organization. He had supported Major General Leonard Wood for the Republican presidential nomination in 1920 before switching his allegiance to Harding. As custodian, Miller was charged with disposing of all remaining confiscated property and disbursing the funds received from their sale.

The scandal centered on Miller's handling of proceeds from the sale of American Metal Company stock. Forty-nine percent of the firm's stock had been owned by two German concerns, Metallbank and Metallgesellschaft, then seized by Palmer during the war and sold for $7 million. In December 1920, the Société Suisse pour Valeurs de Métaux wrote to the custodian's office, claiming to be the rightful owner of the stock, having acquired it from the two German firms. Richard Merton, president of the Swiss company, traveled to the United States to press his case. Merton was a German national and former

president of the German companies. He contacted Jesse Smith, a personal friend of U.S. Attorney General Harry Daugherty. Smith held no formal office in the government, but he served as a conduit for businesspeople seeking favors from government officials. Smith arranged for Miller to meet with Merton.

When the two met for a private dinner, Miller gave $7 million in checks to Merton. The next morning, Merton gave John T. King, a close associate of Miller, $391,000 in Liberty Bonds. He had already given King $50,000 in cash. Some of the bonds were later deposited in Daugherty's account at his brother's bank. Some went to King, and Miller received a share as well.

Rumors of the scandal surfaced before the death of President Harding on August 2, 1923. An investigation of Attorney General Daugherty in January 1923 failed to turn up anything, but other investigations followed. Although Daugherty apparently destroyed many of the records incriminating him, he and Miller were indicted for their part in the transfer of funds in the American Metal Company case—Miller for taking a $50,000 bribe in connection with the transfer and Daugherty for certifying an illegal transfer. They were placed on trial in New York in September 1926. The case received widespread coverage. Daugherty went through two trials in 1926 and 1927. The first ended in a hung jury and the second in acquittal. Federal prosecutors were unable to prove a case for bribery against Miller, but he was convicted of conspiracy to defraud the government. Miller served eighteen months in jail in 1928 and 1929 and was fined $5,000.

Tim J. Watts

See also: Daugherty, Harry M.; German Americans.

Further Reading

Daugherty, H.M., and Thomas Dixon. *The Inside Story of the Harding Tragedy.* New York: Churchill, 1932.

Kurland, Gerald. *Warren Harding: A President Betrayed by Friends.* Charlotteville, NY: SamHar, 1971.

Mee, Charles L. *The Ohio Gang: The World of Warren G. Harding.* New York: M. Evans, 1981.

Russell, Francis. *The Shadow of Blooming Grove: Warren G. Harding in His Times.* New York: McGraw-Hill, 1968.

American Civil Liberties Union

In 1920, the Boston aristocrat and government adviser Roger Nash Baldwin, along with such other social activists as Jane Addams, Norman Thomas, and Helen Keller, founded the American Civil Liberties Union (ACLU), an organization dedicated to the defense of individual rights and liberties as enumerated in the U.S. Constitution and expressed in national law and custom. The organization traces its origins to the National Civil Liberties Bureau (NCLB), of which many of its founders were members. Established during World War I, the NCLB provided legal assistance to conscientious objectors and individuals charged under new federal and state laws designed to suppress dissent.

From its inception, the ACLU demonstrated a nonpartisan approach to legal advocacy, defending parties on the left and right of the political spectrum. The organization monitored the activities of the resurgent Ku Klux Klan during the 1920s but also represented its members in cases involving First Amendment rights to free speech, expression, and assembly. Its defense of unpopular and controversial organizations, individuals, and viewpoints provoked criticism from a variety of perspectives, particularly those who feared that its actions would precipitate civil disorder or political revolution. Despite its advocacy of the Constitution, and the Bill of Rights in particular, the ACLU was often labeled "un-American."

The ACLU provided legal assistance and other support to defendants in a number of important cases during the 1920s. Among these were the trials of Italian immigrants Nicola Sacco and Bartolomeo Vanzetti, two political dissidents who were executed for murder in 1927, and the case of the "Scottsboro Boys," nine young African American men accused of raping two white women in Alabama in 1931.

Perhaps the most famous case was the 1925 Scopes "Monkey" trial, which constituted the first test of a state law banning the teaching of evolution in public schools. Tennessee science teacher John T. Scopes had volunteered to challenge the measure and lost at trial. When Scopes's conviction was overturned on a technicality, the ACLU lost its chance to challenge the constitutionality of the law through the appeals process. The Scopes case, despite being a defeat in court for the ACLU, helped to propel the organization to national prominence in the mid-1920s.

During the remainder of the twentieth century, the ACLU influenced such landmark legal opinions as the 1954 Supreme Court decision in *Brown v. Board of Education,* which outlawed public school segregation, and the Court's 1966 ruling in *Miranda v. Arizona,* which required police to advise arrested persons of their constitutional rights. The organization continues to participate in controversial cases involving defendants of diverse political persuasions and concerning numerous social and legal issues. In addition to its legal advocacy, it conducts educational programs, public awareness campaigns, and legislative lobbying. The ACLU experienced a resurgence of membership in the early twenty-first century in reaction to civil liberties restrictions following the terrorist attacks of September 11, 2001.

Michael H. Burchett

See also: Baldwin, Roger; Darrow, Clarence; *Gitlow v. New York* (1925); Law and the Courts; Red Scare of 1917–1920; *Schenck v. United States* (1919); Scopes Trial (1925).

Further Reading

Cottrell, Robert C. *Roger Nash Baldwin and the American Civil Liberties Union.* New York: Columbia University Press, 2001.

Walker, Samuel. *In Defense of American Liberties: A History of the ACLU.* Carbondale: Southern Illinois University Press, 1999.

American Farm Bureau Federation

A national self-help, educational, and advocacy organization founded by and for farmers and ranchers, the American Farm Bureau Federation was formed in Chicago in 1919, when twenty-eight state farm bureaus joined together to pool their financial resources and better serve their members.

The roots of the federation lay in the Morrill Act of 1862, which created state land-grant agriculture colleges with the specific mission of developing and teaching improved agriculture techniques. In 1914, the Smith-Lever Agriculture Extension Act created the cooperative extension system. This network of county extension agents, or locally based government agricultural experts, supported by the state land-grant colleges, was designed to provide farmers with information about innovative farming techniques.

The cooperative extension system served as an impetus to form local farm bureaus. The first local organization to call itself a farm bureau was located in Broome County, New York. Often the local farm bureau and cooperative extension office were located in the same building, owned by the former and rented to the latter, with a donation provided by the farm bureau for each year's rent.

The two organizations worked together to develop outreach programs to better the lives of farm families. Farm women benefited from home extension programs, which taught new methods of housework and other aspects of home economics. Youth organizations such as the 4H program were set up to reach farm youth, encouraging them to seek self-improvement and be receptive to new developments in farming and homemaking.

The first state federation of farm bureaus was formed in 1915 in Missouri, and other states soon followed suit. The precise organization of state associations varied, but many adopted systems like the one in Indiana, in which the state organization was not owned by farmers directly, but through farmers' county bureau organizations.

The movement to become a national federation was largely a response to the economic troubles resulting from World War I, which left farmers deep in debt. Many hoped that, by working together, they could develop more leverage in markets that often saw them as rubes ripe for exploitation. However, there was considerable opposition to this movement from railroads, elevator operators, and other businesses that bought crops from or offered services to farmers. These institutions, as well as the politicians who sided with them, frequently accused Farm Bureau representatives of being Socialists or Communists in a time when people were alarmed by the Russian Revolution and the Red Scare. In Indiana, the Ku Klux Klan burned crosses to protest the Wheat Pool, a Farm Bureau cooperative marketing effort, and denounced it as a Jewish conspiracy to fix prices.

In spite of even violent opposition, the federation worked hard to improve farmers' position in the market, both as sellers and as purchasers. One of the most successful programs targeted high prices for binder twine, used in baling hay. During the 1919 harvest season, the federation located the best prices on this vital product and spread the word so that local suppliers had to match the price in order to be competitive. Other attempts to use marketplace pressures to collectively bring down prices for farmers were less successful. This led to the creation of farmers' cooperatives, such as the Farm Service in Illinois, to buy farm supplies in bulk at advantageous prices and resell the supplies to individual farmers.

During the 1920s, the federation also turned its attention to providing farmers with affordable insurance. This resulted in the "country companies," or Farm Bureau Insurance agencies, created in various states, through which county Farm Bureau members were able to purchase various kinds of insurance, including such farm-specific policies as hail insurance.

In 1920, the federation created an office in Washington, D.C., to lobby the government on behalf of farmers, whose interests had often been ignored by politicians. Throughout the decade, the Washington office of the American Farm Bureau Federation was instrumental in pushing for programs such as rural electrification and soil and water conservation. Many of its efforts did not bear fruit until the Great Depression, when President Franklin D. Roosevelt was able to create federal programs as part of his economic recovery package.

Leigh Kimmel

See also: Agricultural Marketing Act of 1929; Agriculture; Farmer-Labor Party.

Further Reading

Berger, Samuel R. *Dollar Harvest: The Story of the Farm Bureau.* Lexington, MA: Heath Lexington, 1971.

Colby, Edna Moore. *Hoosier Farmers in a New Day.* Indianapolis: Indiana Farm Bureau, 1968.

Howard, Robert P. *James R. Howard and the Farm Bureau.* Ames: Iowa State University Press, 1983.

American Federation of Labor

The American Federation of Labor (AFL) was organized in 1886 to bring skilled workers into a system of national craft unions—a sort of union of unions. From the beginning, the AFL was an exclusive organization, with no provision for unskilled workers. Among the early member unions were the United Brotherhood of Carpenters and Joiners and the Brotherhood of Locomotive Engineers.

From its foundation, the AFL was led by Samuel Gompers. Gompers, who had grown up in the Cigarmakers' Union, flirted with socialism in his youth but ultimately turned against it. He rejected both the idealism of groups such as the Knights of Labor, who wanted to abolish wages and replace them with cooperation at all levels, and the extremism of groups such as the Industrial Workers of the World (IWW, or Wobblies), who wanted to bring about a Socialist revolution. Instead, the AFL would approach labor relations pragmatically, accepting the existence of capitalism and seeking to obtain the most for workers through disciplined negotiation.

The AFL's rejection of socialism and revolutionary ideology was critical to the public's perception of it as a stable, respectable labor organization during the Red Scare following the Russian Revolution and World War I. Unlike the Wobblies, the AFL was not targeted in the notorious Palmer Raids of 1919–1920, in which labor agitators and suspected anarchists were rounded up by the thousands.

The AFL claimed more than 4 million members in 1920, but its membership and influence declined during the course of the decade. Its failure in the national steel strike of 1919, brought about largely by its refusal to admit unskilled and nonwhite workers, had been a significant blow to its power and influence. By restricting its membership, the AFL inadvertently created a pool of alienated workers for the steel mill owners to hire as temporary workers, or scabs, to keep the mills running during the strike. It was the government, not any of the unions of the AFL, that pressured the steel industry in the early 1900s to end the twelve-hour day and the seven-day workweek.

Furthermore, social changes throughout the 1920s made union membership less necessary and less desirable to American workers. Big business, not organized labor, was seen as raising the standard of living by producing a flood of new consumer goods at affordable prices. Workers enjoying the prosperity of being able to buy an automobile, a radio, and household appliances for a newly electrified home were not likely to be interested in risking their jobs by agitating for higher wages or shorter hours. Moreover, with the economy booming and well-paying jobs to be had everywhere, it was that much harder to convince workers that "open shops" and "right-to-work" laws were a bad idea.

With Gompers's death in 1925, the AFL fell into an organizational slump that incoming president William Green could not reverse. In that year, the United Mine Workers of America (UMWA), one of the AFL's strongest member unions, began a bitter strike against the anthracite coal mine owners. As the strike dragged on, the UMWA granted thousands of dollars of relief to coal miners and their families to keep them from breaking ranks and returning to work before the contract issues were resolved. The strike lasted for over a year. As a result, the UMWA became less able to pay its dues to the AFL, leading to friction with other unions of skilled workers. Such internal squabbling further weakened the AFL's position and credibility.

In the face of a hostile probusiness government and tough anti-union corporate attitudes and tactics, the AFL saw its membership shrink to 2.9 million in 1929. Still, unlike earlier efforts to create national unions in the late nineteenth century, the AFL survived the onslaught of the anti-union 1920s and the economic collapse of the 1930s.

With a prolabor administration in Washington coming to power in 1933, and a new labor militancy spreading across the country, unionism saw its fortunes rise again by the mid-1930s, though it took some time for the AFL to adjust to the new labor climate. Instead, a new organization, the Congress of Industrial Organizations (CIO)—led by John L. Lewis, who had pulled the United Mine Workers out of the American Federation of Labor in 1935—spearheaded a union revival that would continue through the early post–World War II period.

Leigh Kimmel

See also: *Adkins v. Children's Hospital* (1923); *Bailey v. Drexel Furniture Company* (1922); Coal Strike of 1919; Gastonia Strike of 1929; Industrial Workers of the World; Labor Movement; Lawrence Textile Strike of 1919; Lewis, John L.; Passaic Textile Strike of 1926; Railroad Shopmen's Strike of 1922; Railway Labor Act (1926); Seattle General Strike of 1919; Steel Strike of 1919–1920.

Further Reading

Bernstein, Irving. *The Lean Years: A History of the American Worker, 1920–1922.* Boston: Houghton Mifflin, 1960.

Foner, Philip S. *History of the Labor Movement in the United States.* New York: International Publishers, 1964.

Reed, Louis S. *The Labor Philosophy of Samuel Gompers.* Port Washington, NY: Kennikat, 1930.

American Mercury

In the fall of 1923, writers H.L. Mencken and George Jean Nathan, with publisher Alfred A. Knopf, founded *American Mercury* magazine, a pathbreaking monthly journal of social, political, and cultural commentary. The three men had shared a long, close professional relationship, and Mencken quickly embraced Knopf's idea of a new magazine that would focus on culture, society, and politics. Despite serious reservations concerning the magazine's focus, Nathan, who was more interested in theater and the arts than social commentary, agreed to co-edit the new project with Mencken.

The publishing team began acquiring advertisers and advanced subscriptions for the new magazine in September 1923, and Mencken began soliciting articles from such well-known writers as Upton Sinclair, James Weldon Johnson, and Theodore Dreiser. By mid-November, most of the organizational work for *American Mercury* had been completed, and Knopf placed a print order for 10,000 copies. The first issue, dated January 1924, went on sale on Christmas Day 1923—and quickly sold out.

Knopf ordered a second and then a third printing, ultimately selling more than 22,000 copies. The success of the magazine surprised the three founders, who had assumed a readership composed largely of middle- and upper-class urbanites. Trade publications and the popular press hailed *American Mercury* as one of the most significant literary events of the 1920s.

American Mercury was revolutionary in both form and content. At fifty cents a copy and $5 for a one-year subscription, the new magazine cost more than its competitors. Knopf and Mencken made sure the high cost was reflected in every aspect of the magazine. It had a rich Paris-green cover and was printed on high-quality imported paper. There were no full-page illustrations, but the artwork in the margins was crafted by the finest artists of the day. And readers found thought-provoking articles written by America's best-known writers.

The content of the first issue, which closely resembled Mencken's own interests and concerns, set a pattern for *American Mercury* that would remain consistent for the rest of the 1920s. The magazine included portraits of important social, political, and historical figures that revealed new insights into their lives. It also included a poem by the acclaimed author Theodore Dreiser and three short stories. By far the strongest section of the magazine was arts and sciences, which contained short essays on medicine, architecture, and language and would eventually include articles on eugenics, evolution, law, theology, pedagogy, music, and other topics. Many of the magazine's articles were largely critical of political and military matters. Mencken's influence on *American Mercury* was especially evident in a section called "Americana," in which he ridiculed conservative and racist ideologies and practices, as well as lampooning other popular publications. *American Mercury* was also the first popular monthly to establish a music department, giving Mencken more influence on music criticism that any other editor of his day.

At a time when black writers and black culture were not featured in white publications, *American Mercury* made an effort to dispel racist stereotypes and portray the complexity of African American life.

Mencken published a total of fifty-four articles and fifteen editorials by or about African Americans on a number of subjects, including politics, religion, art, folklore, and music.

The magazine helped spur widespread changes in the magazine industry. Other publishers modernized the appearance of their magazines. Older, established magazines began including articles that they would not have considered publishing before *American Mercury,* and industry leaders such as *The Saturday Evening Post* and *The New Yorker* openly imitated many of the magazine's profiles and sections.

In spring 1924, philosophical disputes between Mencken and Nathan erupted when Nathan insisted on a clearer balance between literature and the social and political commentary in the magazine. Nathan reluctantly submitted his resignation in November 1924, but he continued to contribute articles. He also remained a member of the board of directors and retained financial holdings in the magazine, until Knopf bought him out for $25,000. Nathan's departure from *American Mercury* seemed to have little effect on the magazine's success. By the end of 1925, its circulation had reached 75,000, and its first few issues were collectors' items, selling for $20 each.

Although highly influential during the 1920s, *American Mercury* suffered during the economic downturn following the stock market crash of October 1929. Americans were less willing to pay fifty cents for a magazine during the Great Depression, and advertising revenues dropped to less than half of precrash levels by 1931. Mencken remained the editor of *American Mercury* until 1934. The magazine's editorial slant shifted conspicuously to the right during the 1950s, and it ceased publication in 1980.

Michael A. Rembis

See also: Journalism; Mencken, H.L.

Further Reading

Rodgers, Marion Elizabeth. *Mencken: The American Iconoclast.* New York: Oxford University Press, 2005.

Spivak, Lawrence E., and Charles Angoff, eds. *The American Mercury Reader.* Garden City, NY: Blue Ribbon, 1944.

Americanization

In the wake of World War I, America experienced a massive influx of immigrants from Southern and Eastern Europe and, to a lesser extent, Mexico. At the same time, hundreds of thousands of rural Southern blacks were migrating to the cities. Along with the postwar Red Scare, these conditions prompted some concern about the racial, social, economic, and political organization of American society.

One response was the reemergence of the Ku Klux Klan—now nativist as well as racist. There were also programs to compel newly arrived immigrants and African Americans to adopt mainstream white American values and culture, a process known as Americanization, which gained popularity in nearly every part of the country, in urban areas and small towns alike. At the local, state, and federal levels, white middle-class reformers and politicians advocated the use of education and various social and economic incentives to induce cultural conformity. In fact, the U.S. Bureau of Education held an Americanization Conference in 1919 to address this concern.

Most Americanization efforts were aimed at women and children. Women were targeted based on the general assumption that they were responsible for the transmission of values in the home, and that the woman's role as mother and homemaker was her most highly valued asset, and in some cases her biological destiny. Reformers hoped to bring immigrant and, to a lesser extent, African American mothers into conformity with white middle-class standards of child rearing and homemaking. The intent was to instill "traditional" American culture and values in future generations of citizens. Proponents of Americanization argued that racial and cultural differences could be transcended and that good American citizens could be made through a "proper" education, including instruction in the English language, "proper" meal preparation, homemaking, health, nutrition, and child care.

The federal Bureau of Education and local groups, such as the Los Angeles Commission on Immigration and Housing, used an army of social workers, teachers, nurses, and other white middle-class professionals to implement their numerous programs. Reformers in Los Angeles used the Home Teacher Act, passed by the California legislature in 1915, to enter the homes of Mexican immigrants to instruct mothers and their children about proper school attendance, hygiene, use of the English language, housekeeping, and basic principles of the American system of government and citizenship responsibilities. Although Governor Friend Richardson dismantled the Commission on Immigration and Housing in 1923, its Americanization programs persisted under the state's Department of Education. Similar programs existed in Chicago's immigrant and

African American neighborhoods and New York City's immigrant-populated Lower East Side, as well as other cities, throughout the 1920s.

During the 1920s, a variety of state-sponsored welfare programs, including those that provided income assistance to women with dependent children, were initiated. These programs, known as Mothers' Pensions, were yet another attempt at institutionalized Americanization. Reformers categorized possible welfare recipients as either "deserving" or "undeserving" poor, and they linked the allocation of funds to a woman's perceived competence as a mother and homemaker. In most cases, reformers insisted that even "deserving" mothers required continuing direction and oversight.

Thus, the creation and implementation of welfare programs such as Mothers' Pensions resulted in increased supervision and interference in recipients' home life, creating a link between the provision of income assistance and a perceived right by the larger society to monitor and control the behavior of welfare recipients. Mothers' Pensions programs did not outlive the Jazz Age, but many elements of the programs found their way into the New Deal, as well as other AFDC legislation.

The idea of Americanization persisted well into the twentieth century but was ultimately displaced by an emphasis on multiculturalism following the civil rights movement of the post–World War II era. Still, in the twenty-first century, with concerns about immigration and illegal immigrants rising, various Americanization proposals, such as English-only laws, have resurfaced.

Michael A. Rembis

See also: Anti-Catholicism; Anti-Semitism; Eugenics; Immigration; Immigration Laws of 1921 and 1924; Italian Americans; Jewish Americans; Ku Klux Klan.

Further Reading

Mink, Gwendolyn. *The Wages of Motherhood: Inequality in the Welfare State, 1917–1942.* Ithaca, NY: Cornell University Press, 1995.

Sánchez, George J. *Becoming Mexican American: Ethnicity, Culture, and Identity in Chicano Los Angeles, 1900–1945.* New York: Oxford University Press, 1993.

Anarchism

Anarchism is a political philosophy based on the shared ownership of production, a society bound by voluntary agreements among individuals, and the elimination of organized government. This movement reached its zenith in America in the years immediately preceding the country's entry into World War I, though it never counted more than a few tens of thousands of adherents.

Anarchism experienced a number of blows during and immediately after the war that rendered it largely impotent by the late 1920s. Anarchists were subject to government repression during World War I because of their opposition to the conflict, and many of the movement's leaders were exiled after the war. Moreover, the success of the Russian Revolution in 1917 established communism as a more compelling political alternative for many American radicals.

By the end of the 1920s, there were probably just a few thousand anarchists in the United States (as anarchists eschew formal organizations, hard numbers are difficult to come by). Still, a diminished movement continued to promote anarchist ideals in newspapers, union halls, and educational and cultural institutions as the prosperity of the 1920s gave way to the economic depression of the 1930s.

Repression and Reprisal

Two branches of anarchism coexisted in the United States in the late nineteenth and early twentieth centuries. One consisted of both native-born and immigrant workers in the extractive industries of the West, notably in the Western Federation of Miners. This branch of anarchists expanded and was organized as the Industrial Workers of the World (IWW) in 1905. The other form of anarchism could be found in East Coast and Midwest cities, largely among communities of immigrants from Eastern, Central, and Southern Europe. This branch gained national notoriety after a number of its activists were convicted (and four executed) for throwing a bomb that killed several policemen during a strikers' rally in Haymarket Square, Chicago, in May 1886.

While most anarchists adhered to nonviolent means to overthrow the capitalist system, a few did advocate violence. Both in the United States and internationally, some anarchists advocated the use of selective acts of violence—specifically assassinations of business and political leaders—as a way to spark revolution. In 1892, immigrant anarchist Alexander Berkman attempted to assassinate steel magnate Henry Frick during the bloody Homestead steel strike of 1892. In 1901, a mentally unbalanced immigrant named Leon Czolgosz, who claimed to be an anarchist but had no real connection to the movement, assassinated President William McKinley.

Given this track record of violence and their radical anticapitalist, antigovernment philosophy, anarchists had long been the target of government repression. But it was their vocal and militant opposition to America's entry into World War I that brought the full weight of the federal government down on the anarchist movement. When Berkman and Emma Goldman organized the antidraft No Conscription League and held mass antiwar protests in New York City in 1917, both were arrested under the Espionage Act, a 1917 law that allowed for the arrest of anyone seen to be aiding an enemy of the United States. The two activists were sentenced to two years in federal prison, while postal authorities shut down Goldman's magazine, *Mother Earth,* and Berkman's newspaper, *The Blast.*

In 1918, the federal government supplemented the Espionage Act with additional laws aimed at radicals. The Sedition Act, an amendment to the Espionage Act, made it a crime to use "disloyal, profane, scurrilous, or abusive language" when referring to the U.S. government, flag, or armed forces during wartime. Congress also passed the Alien Act, sometimes referred to as the anti-anarchist act, which allowed for the deportation of any immigrant who had joined an anarchist organization after coming to the United States.

With strikes and social unrest embroiling the country after World War I—and the specter of the Communist revolution in Russia haunting many—Attorney General A. Mitchell Palmer conducted a number of raids on Communist and anarchist organizations, arresting thousands of alleged radicals. In December 1919, Palmer used the Alien Act to deport several hundred radicals and anarchists to the Soviet Union. Among those on board the deportation ship *Buford,* dubbed the "Soviet Ark" by the press, were Berkman and Goldman.

The mass arrests and deportations intimidated most remaining anarchists, leading many to retreat into ethnic organizations that tried to organize workers locally. A zealous group of Italian anarchists, however, responded to the arrests and deportations through violent reprisals.

Luigi Galleani, an Italian anarchist who had emigrated to America in 1901 to avoid persecution in Europe, had developed an ultramilitant following among Italian American anarchists through incendiary oratory and his newspaper, *Cronoca Suvversiva*

Morgan Bank Bombing

On Thursday, September 16, 1920, a man in downtown New York City drove a horse-drawn wagon inconspicuously to the corner of Wall and Broad streets. He parked the wagon across the street from the headquarters of J.P. Morgan and Company, a prominent banking firm and symbol to many of the power of modern capitalism. The man jumped off the wagon and disappeared, unnoticed by the hundreds around him. At exactly 12:01 P.M., a massive explosion rocked the financial district. The wagon had carried a large dynamite bomb packed with cast-iron slugs. The blast caused widespread damage and suffering, killing thirty people outright, severely injuring more than 200 others (three mortally), and causing more than $2 million in property damage to nearby buildings. While Morgan himself was vacationing in England at the time, the bomb killed one of his employees and devastated the bank's offices. Most of the victims were messengers, stenographers, and clerks.

A federal investigation failed to identify the bomber, and no one was ever charged with the crime. However, law enforcement officers did discover leaflets nearby, signed "American Anarchist Fighters," that warned of more attacks unless "political prisoners" were freed. Investigators recognized similarities between these leaflets and ones left at the sites of previous bomb attacks, the suspected trademarks of Italian American anarchists associated with the notorious Luigi Galleani.

In May 1918, the federal government had shut down Galleani's radical newspaper, the *Cronoca Suvversiva* (Subversive Chronicle), under the Sedition Act. Early the next year, immigration authorities arrested him and several of his associates and prepared to deport them. A series of bombing reprisals followed. On April 29, 1919, a bomb intended for Georgia Senator Thomas Hardwick, a cosponsor of a 1918 anti-anarchist immigration law, maimed one of his maids. At a New York City post office, authorities discovered thirty mail bombs set to detonate upon opening on May 1, a traditional day of labor protest. The bombs were addressed to officials and businessmen associated with recent crackdowns on unions and immigrants, including Attorney General A. Mitchell Palmer, Postmaster General Albert S. Burleson, Supreme Court Justice Oliver Wendell Holmes, and financiers John D. Rockefeller and J.P. Morgan.

Then, on the night of June 2, bombs accompanied by pamphlets signed "The Anarchist Fighters" exploded at the residences of political and business leaders in Boston, New York, Philadelphia, Pittsburgh, Cleveland, and Paterson, New Jersey, as well as Washington, D.C. One of the bombers and a night watchman died in the explosions—which in turn led to further repression of the radical movement.

The dragnet that followed the 1919 bombings focused on Italian American anarchists associated with Galleani. In May 1920, Nicola Sacco and Bartolomeo Vanzetti, two Galleanists from the Boston area, were arrested for a robbery and murder not associated with any bombings. Historian Paul Avrich has speculated that an Italian American anarchist close to Sacco and Vanzetti carried out the Wall Street bombing in response to their arrests.

Whether or not this was the case, the 1920 incident reinforced public impressions of anarchists as dangerous foreigners, prejudiced many Americans against Sacco and Vanzetti and other radicals in the 1920s, and provoked calls for further immigration restrictions (adopted in 1924). No major anarchist bombings followed the Morgan Bank incident.

Justin F. Jackson

(Subversive Chronicle). In its pages, he openly advocated the use of revolutionary violence, including bombings and assassinations of government officials, as a means to accelerate the destruction of the political and economic order. In 1919, Galleani's followers launched a national series of bomb attacks against government and business figures, including Standard Oil founder John D. Rockefeller. These bombing attacks culminated in the Wall Street bombing of the Morgan Bank on September 16, 1920.

International Influences

Like Goldman and Berkman, many American anarchists hailed the Russian Revolution as the first truly successful Socialist revolution. They welcomed news of the workers' soviets in Russia, in which workers self-managed factories, as evidence of the coming of an anarchist society without capitalism or the state. Only later would it become evident that Soviet leaders believed in the necessity of a strong state in the early stages of revolution. Indeed, a growing number of American anarchists, forever suspicious of state power in any form, soon received worrisome news from Russia about Bolshevik arrests and imprisonment, as well as executions of anarchists who criticized Soviet policies.

Goldman and Berkman, in particular, became disillusioned after they arrived in Russia in 1921. Berkman criticized Vladimir Lenin as an incipient dictator and denounced Leon Trotsky for his role in crushing the anarchist-influenced rebellion of sailors at the Kronstadt naval base in March 1921. Berkman and Goldman started to warn anarchists in Europe and America about the Bolsheviks through numerous letters, articles, and pamphlets. By the mid-1920s, only a few anarchists continued to support the Soviet government. Despite some misgivings, a number of anarchists supported Trotsky for his critique of the authoritarianism inherent in the increasingly bureaucratic Soviet state.

Russia was not the only international concern of anarchists in this period. Most American anarchists remained active within their own ethnic communities and organized themselves through foreign-language publications. They were keenly interested in news of anarchist and radical activity not only in their European homelands but also in Asia, the Far East, and Latin America.

Jewish anarchists active within two New York–based labor unions, the International Ladies' Garment Workers' Union (ILGWU) and the Amalgamated Clothing Workers of America, rallied around the *Fraye Arbeter Shtime* (Free Voice of Labor), a Yiddish newspaper founded in 1890 and published until the 1970s. Other major ethnic anarchist publications in the 1920s included the Spanish *Cultura Obrera* (Working Culture) of New York City and the Russian *Golos Truzhenika* (Worker's Voice), published in Chicago. But anarchists in this period often complained about a lack of cohesion and communication across ethnic and linguistic boundaries.

Italian American anarchists were especially active in developing an antifascist movement in America to oppose Mussolini's rise to power in Italy. Carlos Tresca, a well-known anarchist and labor and free-speech agitator in New York, edited the influential *Il Martello* (The Hammer), the leading Italian American radical newspaper of the 1920s. In *Il Martello* and numerous speeches, Tresca tirelessly denounced the Italian fascists, organized protests against Mussolini's representatives in New York, and battled the fascist movement within the Italian American community. Followers of Luigi Galleani continued his provocative message in *L'Adunata dei Refrattari,* a newspaper founded in 1922.

When Nicola Sacco and Bartolomeo Vanzetti were convicted of the 1920 murder of a Massachusetts factory paymaster and guard during a robbery aimed at raising money for the anarchist cause, anarchists were joined in their protests by liberals and civil libertarians. Many believed that the government's case was weak and that Sacco and Vanzetti were prosecuted simply because of their immigrant origins and their political philosophy. The Sacco and Vanzetti case became a cause célèbre of the political Left in the United States and around the world.

Throughout the 1920s, anarchist clubs and organizations sponsored lecture series, plays, picnics, and even anarchist schools and summer camps. The most important of these schools was the Stelton Modern School, in Stelton, New Jersey. Based on the principles of Spanish educational reformer Francisco Ferrer, the Modern School encouraged students to develop their own curriculum of self-directed learning and play.

The Stelton "colony" also became a cultural center for anarchists in the New York area. From the colony, in 1924, Czech immigrant anarchist Hippolyte Havel began to publish *Road to Freedom,* the only major English-language anarchist publication of this period. The *Road to Freedom* group involved several anarchists who later became leaders in social movements during the Great Depression, such as Rose Pesotta, a union organizer for the ILGWU and the union's vice president from 1934 to 1944.

Justin F. Jackson

See also: Communist Party; Red Scare of 1917–1920; *Schenck v. United States* (1919); Socialism and the Socialist Party of America.

Further Reading

Avrich, Paul. *Anarchist Voices: An Oral History of Anarchism in America.* Princeton, NJ: Princeton University Press, 1995.

———. *The Modern School Movement: Anarchism and Education in the United States.* Princeton, NJ: Princeton University Press, 1980.

———. *Sacco and Vanzetti: The Anarchist Background.* Princeton, NJ: Princeton University Press, 1991.

Green, James. *Death in the Haymarket: A Story of Chicago, the First Labor Movement, and the Bombing That Divided Gilded Age America.* New York: Pantheon, 2006.

Leeder, Elaine. *The Gentle General: Rose Pesotta, Anarchist and Labor Organizer.* Albany: State University of New York Press, 1993.

Pernicone, Nunzio. *Carlo Tresca: Portrait of a Rebel.* New York: Palgrave Macmillan, 2005.

Anderson, Sherwood (1876–1941)

Sherwood Anderson was an American novelist, short-story writer, and memoirist best known for his collection of interconnected stories, *Winesburg, Ohio* (1919). Anderson sought to portray American life unadulterated by artistic pretense, in the tradition of Walt Whitman, Mark Twain, and Theodore Dreiser. Using the town of Winesburg as a symbol of Middle America, he was able to explore his perception of modern American dilemmas, specifically the loss of regional culture, the disappearance of the pastoral landscape, and the advent of consumerism and homogenized popular culture. Anderson's greatest influence came in the period between the world wars.

Anderson was born on September 13, 1876, in Camden, Ohio, to Erwin and Emma Anderson. The family was forced to move frequently because of the fluctuating business prospects of his father, a Union Army veteran of the American Civil War. They finally settled in Clyde, Ohio, in 1884. Until he was seventeen, Anderson helped support his family as a newsboy, housepainter, stock handler, and stable groom. He was only intermittently educated during these years.

Beginning his adult life as an unskilled laborer, Anderson eventually achieved financial security as a factory owner in the early 1900s. In 1904 he married Cornelia Lane, the daughter of a wealthy Ohio couple, and they had three children. But Anderson was unsatisfied with his success, seeing it as nothing more than a "materialistic existence."

In November 1912, Anderson left his office at midday, disappeared, and was found four days later in Cleveland, having suffered a mental breakdown. (He would later refer to this episode as his break with the bourgeois lifestyle he had thus far led and the beginning of his career as an artist and social critic.) In 1916, Anderson divorced his wife and married an artist named Tennessee Mitchell. Having secured a job as a copywriter in Chicago, Anderson became part of the "Chicago Renaissance" along with newfound friends and fellow writers Floyd Dell, Theodore Dreiser, Ben Hecht, and Carl Sandburg. A loose literary movement prominent until the mid-1920s, the Chicago Renaissance sought to present a realistic portrayal of urban America without the sentimentality popular in the high Victorian fiction of the previous generation. Its body of authors critiqued the capitalist, industrial economy and the seemingly failed American promise that hard work translated into emotional and material success. Anderson's *Winesburg, Ohio* typified this early modernist movement in its exploration of universal themes about the effects of industrialization and modernization on the lives of individuals and the frustrations of small-town life.

Anderson had begun to publish his work in the leftist journal *The Masses* in 1914. These early writings included stories that formed the nucleus of *Winesburg, Ohio,* which, in turn, contains many of the themes important to Anderson's later writings.

The book itself is a collection of twenty-three stories about a small Ohio town that were written over a four-year period (1915–1919) and were frequently reprinted as individual short stories, but Anderson considered the work a cohesive whole. "I felt that, taken together, they made something like a novel, a complete story," he stated in his *Memoirs* (1942). The narrator of the stories speaks with a mocking sentimentality as a means of expressing the author's disillusionment at the materialism of modern society, which engenders a social disintegration and a withering of individual identity.

Anderson's original idea for the title was "The Book of the Grotesque." Although his publisher convinced him to use the name of the fictional town where the stories take place, *Winesburg, Ohio* is nevertheless an exploration of the tragically grotesque in humanity. For example, in "Hands," a disgraced schoolteacher, Wing Biddlebaum, lives on the outskirts of Winesburg and is befriended by a young newspaper reporter, George Willard. Over the course of their conversations, Wing explains to George that his emphatic hand gestures are the only way he knows to express his deeply held emotions. This form of expression cost him his job as a teacher at a boys' school in Pennsylvania, where Wing was falsely accused of molesting his students and forced to flee, finally settling in Winesburg.

Similar themes of inexpressible emotion, the grotesque, and the inability to communicate authentically in a homogenized culture also can be found in the works of other later modernists such as Ernest Hemingway, F. Scott Fitzgerald, and T.S. Eliot, all influenced by the rapid modernization of American life during the 1920s. During this formative period, Anderson also published the novels *Poor White* (1920), *Many Marriages* (1923), *Horses and Men* (1923), and *Dark Laughter* (1925), as well as the short-story collection *The Triumph of the Egg* (1921).

None of Anderson's other works, however, enjoyed nearly the popularity or critical acclaim of the *Winesburg, Ohio* stories. Anderson died in 1941 while traveling in Panama.

By the 1960s, Anderson's work was largely eclipsed by that of such contemporaries as Fitzgerald, Hemingway, and Sinclair Lewis. In the 1970s, literary critics found a new interest in Anderson and established his reputation as one of the earliest American modernists.

Jason Stacy

See also: Fiction; Theater.

Further Reading

Anderson, David, ed. *Critical Essays on Sherwood Anderson.* Boston: G.K. Hall, 1981.

Anderson, Sherwood. *Winesburg, Ohio: A Group of Tales of Ohio Small Town Life.* New York: Dover, 1995.

Papinchak, Robert Allen. *Sherwood Anderson: A Study of the Short Fiction.* New York: Twayne, 1992.

Townsend, Kim. *Sherwood Anderson.* Boston: Houghton Mifflin, 1988.

Anti-Catholicism

In the twentieth century, American anti-Catholicism peaked in the 1920s, though suspicion of Roman Catholics by the Protestant majority had been commonplace since the early nineteenth century. Many Protestants believed that Catholics' first loyalty was to the pope and that the pope was bent on dominating America. They also were suspicious of aspects of Catholic culture, such as the secrecy of the Mass (conducted in Latin), the activities of the Catholic fraternal organization Knights of Columbus, the influence of Catholic schools, and alleged sexual abuses of nuns and monks. Such fears continued into the 1920s with the influx of Catholic immigrants, Catholic opposition to liquor prohibition, and the presidential candidacy of Al Smith, a Roman Catholic and critic of Prohibition, in 1928. Reactions included the passage of immigration restrictions in 1921 and 1924, and a resurgence of the Ku Klux Klan (KKK) in the early 1920s.

Prohibition and Prejudices

Catholic opposition to the prohibition of liquor was well known. Several priests had expressed their support for the antiliquor campaign, but most parishioners opposed it, and the Catholic Church officially promoted voluntary moderation and abstinence over making alcohol illegal.

When the Oklahoma attorney general ruled in 1917 that the sacramental wine used in Mass was not exempt from that state's prohibition laws, Catholics across the nation voiced their outrage, and church officials in Oklahoma challenged the ruling in court. The state supreme court ruled the following year that religious wines were exempt from the ban. Catholics remained opposed to Prohibition, and some supporters of the national liquor ban, which took effect in January 1920, criticized Catholics as subversive. The Reverend W.A. Redburn of the Wesley Methodist Church in Sacramento, California, for example, in 1922 blamed Catholics for both bootlegging and prostitution in that city.

The Ku Klux Klan portrayed itself as a champion of Prohibition and a leading defender against the spread of Roman Catholicism in America. Reorganized in 1915, the Klan expanded its membership after World War I, charging that Catholic voters plotted to turn over control of the nation to the pope. KKK membership in the early 1920s may have reached 5 million nationally and included a number of prominent politicians and Protestant clergy. Klan members served as governors and dominated several state legislatures. In Northern and urban regions, Klan prejudice against Catholics rivaled its racism against blacks.

In Atlanta, Klan leaders urged members to fire Catholic employees and boycott Catholic-owned businesses, and they attempted to coerce the board of education into firing all Catholic teachers. The Michigan Klan organized a nearly successful referendum to close Catholic schools. The Kansas City Klan demonstrated against Catholics at the city's Convention Hall. The New York City Klan counseled its members to bar Catholics from their homes and from employment. And in Portland, Oregon, the Klan told its members that Catholics aimed to destroy the nation's public school system, and it advised members to act Christlike by attacking that city's Roman Catholic church.

But anti-Catholic sentiment reached beyond the Klan. Georgia Congressman Thomas Watson published a booklet purporting to document Catholic efforts to corrupt schoolchildren. Several Oklahoma school districts fired Catholic public schoolteachers. The Evangelical Protestant Society sought to ban the teaching or profession of the Catholic faith in America. In 1922, the Oklahoma Americanization Society sought signatures on a statewide petition to require children to attend public school through the eighth grade. Catholic schools, it was said, taught loyalty to the pope rather than civic responsibility.

Some anti-Catholics made unsubstantiated claims about wrongdoing at convents and monasteries. Klan leaders, for example, accused Catholics of kidnapping Protestant girls and forcing them to become nuns. Between 1912 and 1928, more than 500 anti-Catholic lecturers toured the United States, many falsely claiming to be former nuns or priests. For example, Mrs. Ed C. Alumbaugh and Helen Conroy—who called herself Sister Mary Ethel—related their fictitious experiences as nuns and warned that Catholics intended to murder all Protestants and destroy the American government. They distributed literature asserting that priests and nuns engaged in sexual relations, that Catholic orphanages abused children, and that the Catholic Church ordered the killing of illegitimate children.

Numerous anti-Catholic publications supported their speaking tours. Anti-Catholic newspapers such as *The Menace* (with a circulation of several hundred thousand), *Rail Splitter, Watcher of the Tower, Oklahoma Herald,* and *American Searchlight* all gained wide readership. *The Awful Relations of Maria Monk,* a fabricated story about a former nun originally published in 1836, sold thousands of copies.

The Knights of Columbus, a social organization for male Catholics, also came under sharp criticism.

The Atlanta City Council passed a resolution in 1921 declaring the Knights "un-American." The Klan justified its own secret meetings by noting that the Knights also met in closed session. Klan speakers charged that Catholics intended to seize Washington, D.C., by force, that Knights held military drills at their meetings, and that they stashed guns in churches. In Memphis, Tennessee, the Klan produced phony Knights of Columbus oaths such as the *Fellowship Forum,* an oath that included a vow to hang, boil, or burn alive all Protestant men, women, and children.

Al Smith Campaign

The frequency and virulence of anti-Catholic attacks generally increased after Al Smith became the Democratic Party's nominee for president in 1928. A Roman Catholic, Smith was elected governor of New York in 1918 despite a strong upstate anti-Catholic vote. Smith was the target of recurring anti-Catholic diatribes. The Reverend George W. McDaniel, president of the Southern Baptist Convention, condemned Smith in 1926 for kissing the ring of a Catholic cardinal. A March 1927 *Atlantic Monthly* article argued that no Catholic could fulfill the duties of the presidency, because his loyalty would be divided between the Constitution and Catholic Church teachings. Methodist Bishop James Cannon, head of the Anti-Saloon League, a leading temperance group, campaigned against Smith's candidacy, declaring that the Catholic Church was "the Mother of ignorance, superstition, intolerance and sin."

As the 1928 campaign accelerated, anti-Catholic pamphlets, handbills, and posters proliferated across America. Much of the criticism came from within the Democratic Party itself, under Bishop Cannon's direction, while the Republican Party funded religious attacks against Smith in Alabama and Oklahoma. A Methodist magazine in Atlanta informed readers that it was their right to vote against Smith, because he was Catholic. Scores of anti-Catholic newspapers called for Smith's defeat, and Cannon distributed hundreds of anti-Smith pamphlets.

Much of the campaign was waged in the American South. The *Baptist Courier* of Greenville, South Carolina, reported that one of Smith's close associates had served as private chaplain to the pope. Faculty members at the Southern Baptist Theological Seminary charged that the pope coveted America's wealth and that a Smith presidency would allow him to seize it. The *Baptist and Commoner,* published in Arkansas, described the Catholic Church as spawned in hell and priests as money grabbing. A vote for Smith, it was said, would put the pope in charge of America, destroy the nation's public schools, and stain all Protestant spouses as adulterers and all Protestant children as bastards. The *Texas Baptist Trumpet* stated that a Smith presidency would bring the inquisition to America.

Republican Herbert Hoover easily defeated Smith in the November election. The economy was said to weigh heavily in voters' minds, but a number of politicians and commentators attributed Smith's defeat chiefly to his religion. Privately, Smith agreed.

The immigration restrictions imposed in the 1920s helped reduce Protestant fears of a Catholic majority. In the 1930s, with the Klan discredited in many parts of the country, anti-Catholic sentiment declined. Suspicion of Roman Catholics persisted in some locations, particularly in the South, and flared again in 1960 when John F. Kennedy became the second Catholic to run for the presidency on a major party ticket.

James E. Klein

See also: Americanization; Catholics and Catholicism; Irish Americans; Italian Americans; Ku Klux Klan; Smith, Al.

Further Reading

Finan, Christopher M. *Alfred E. Smith: The Happy Warrior.* New York: Hill and Wang, 2002.

Greeley, Andrew M. *An Ugly Little Secret: Anti-Catholicism in North America.* Kansas City, MO: Sheed Andrews and McMeel, 1977.

Jackson, Kenneth T. *The Ku Klux Klan in the City, 1915–1930.* 2nd ed. Chicago: Ivan R. Dee, 1992.

McDonough, Gay W. "Constructing Christian Hatred: Anti-Catholicism, Diversity, and Identity in Southern Religious Life." In *Religion in the Contemporary South: Diversity, Community, and Identity,* ed. O. Kendall White, Jr., and Daryl White. Athens: University of Georgia Press, 1995.

Anti-Prohibition Movement

The single most important anti-Prohibition organization in the country in the 1920s, the Association Against the Prohibition Amendment (AAPA), lobbied Congress and launched publicity campaigns in its effort to overturn the Eighteenth Amendment to the Constitution.

Captain William T. Stayton, a retired naval officer, lawyer, and businessman, founded the AAPA in 1919, only weeks before the Eighteenth Amendment

went into effect. The politically conservative Stayton made it clear that while he advocated the repeal of Prohibition, he was not a traditional "wet," a term most often associated with liberal big-city Democrats and immigrants. Believing that the consumption of alcohol needed to be moderated, not outlawed, he adopted the slogan "Temperance, not wet." Stayton and the AAPA argued that Prohibition was an unjust extension of federal power into the private lives of Americans and that it deprived citizens and the government of a valued source of revenue.

Stayton found a receptive audience, and the association boasted 100,000 members by the end of 1920. He undertook a campaign of letter writing, pamphlet distribution, and speaking tours that sparked the interest and the support of some of the nation's most prominent businesspeople. Henry Joy, president of the Packard Motor Company and a former member of the Anti-Saloon League, was among the first industrial leaders to support the AAPA. Tired of being harassed by Treasury agents looking for beer, and disheartened by the senseless murder of a duck hunter federal agents assumed was a rumrunner, Joy abandoned his Prohibitionist past and joined the ranks of the repealers by the mid-1920s. He was far from alone. By 1926, the AAPA had 726,000 members, and by the early 1930s, its supporters included DuPont, General Motors, and John D. Rockefeller, Jr. Backed by dozens of millionaire industrialists, the AAPA found little difficulty in expanding its efforts to end Prohibition.

The organization easily gained the support of America's major brewers, but Stayton publicized that financial contributions from beer interests would never be allowed to exceed one-twentieth of the AAPA operating budget. In so doing, he hoped to free the AAPA from the taint of self-interest that had plagued other efforts made by brewers to oppose Prohibition.

The AAPA's success can be attributed in large part to Stayton's decision not to be directly associated with the beer interests or the "wets." The organization's skillful use of anti-Prohibition propaganda was equally effective in gaining popular support. The AAPA published material in all of the major newspapers assessing the dangers and side effects of Prohibition, citing statistics that evoked a visceral response from readers. In 1928, the AAPA reported that approximately 15 million pounds of hops had been sold during the year, enough to make 20 million barrels of illegal beer. The loss of tax revenue alone, the AAPA argued, was reason enough to end Prohibition.

As early as 1922, Molly Pitcher Clubs affiliated themselves with the AAPA. Led by anti-Prohibition activist and Tammany Hall figure M. Louise Gross, the clubs decried the "tendency on the part of our National Government to interfere with the personal habits of the American people." The Molly Pitcher Clubs never grew much beyond their New York City base, but by the early 1930s, the Women's Organization for National Prohibition Reform (WONPR), founded by Pauline Sabin, the wife of AAPA treasurer Charles Sabin, could claim almost 1.5 million members nationwide.

By 1932, the movement to repeal Prohibition had become so widespread that it attracted the attention of presidential candidate Franklin D. Roosevelt, who called for a "wiser plan" to regulate the consumption of alcohol. In February 1933, Congress passed the Twenty-first Amendment to the Constitution, overturning Prohibition, and it went to the states for ratification. On December 4, 1933, the day before final ratification, Roosevelt issued Executive Order No. 6474, creating the Federal Alcohol Control Administration (FACA) to investigate and regulate the sale of alcohol and alcoholic beverages.

Prohibition was officially repealed on December 5, 1933, opening the door to employment for more than 1 million Americans and filling government coffers with tax and licensing revenues that reached $1 billion annually by 1940. The sale of alcohol resumed in most states, but under various restrictions. In many states, vendors could sell only prepackaged liquor. Most states prohibited the sale of liquor on Sundays and enforced mandatory closing times on bars and liquor stores. In many states, the sale of liquor was prohibited on Election Day, Thanksgiving, Memorial Day, Christmas, and other public holidays.

Michael A. Rembis

See also: Anti-Saloon League; Prohibition (1920–1933); Volstead Act (1919).

Further Reading

Kyvig, David E. *Repealing National Prohibition.* 2nd ed. Kent, OH: Kent State University Press, 2000.

Rose, Kenneth D. *American Women and the Repeal of Prohibition.* New York: New York University Press, 1996.

Anti-Saloon League

The national Anti-Saloon League (ASL), later renamed the Anti-Saloon League of America, was a leading temperance group founded on December 18, 1895, in Washington, D.C. The ASL worked to unite prohibitionist sentiment, helped enforce existing temperance laws, and promoted further anti-alcohol legislation. By the 1910s, the league was the leading proponent for national prohibition of liquor, which became a reality under the Eighteenth Amendment, effective January 1920.

The Anti-Saloon League was essentially the brainchild of the Reverend Howard Hyde Russell, a former attorney and Republican politician who had experienced a religious conversion in 1883. Having founded the first local ASL in Ohio in 1893, Russell joined forces with delegates from fifteen other state organizations to form the national Anti-Saloon League in Washington in 1895. Russell's vision for the Anti-Saloon League was novel in the temperance movement. Unlike the Women's Christian Temperance Union (WCTU) and other organizations, the ASL would work within the two-party system and take a nonpartisan approach. The Anti-Saloon League, Russell argued, should work to elect any politician who supported the cause of temperance; it would support any candidate who was dry, regardless of party affiliation.

Russell also advocated that the national organization function as a bureaucracy. The ASL consisted of a network of what one historian has called "local agitators," well versed in temperance politics. Their main links with one another were a semimonthly newspaper and the salaried organizers in Washington. Russell divided the league into specialized departments: finance, which would raise funds; agitation, which would prepare educational and propaganda materials; law enforcement, which would help assist public officials enforce temperance laws; and legislative, which would lobby in statehouses and the nation's capital. Like a modern business firm, the ASL was to be undemocratic, with selected, not elected, national and local governing boards. Russell concluded that by relying on churches, pamphlets, public meetings, and nearly constant pressure on legislators, the ASL could alter public opinion, making antiliquor legislation a reality.

The league struggled during the late 1890s, unable to elect many temperance candidates. In 1905, however, the ASL backed the victor in the contest for governor of Ohio. The incumbent governor, Republican Myron P. Herrick, had rejected legislation that would have allowed localities to ban liquor. In response, the ASL supported Democrat John M. Pattison, a temperance candidate, who won by a substantial margin, largely due to the league's support.

The ASL's success brought it national attention and new recruits. By 1908, only four states did not have local ASL chapters. The number of churches affiliated with the league doubled during the first two decades of the twentieth century.

On December 10, 1913, the ASL began to advocate for national prohibition, staging a parade of more than 4,000 members on Pennsylvania Avenue in Washington, D.C. Supporting passage of the Hobson-Sheppard bill, which would have made the consumption, transportation, and distribution of alcohol illegal, the ASL began to lobby and hold rallies in 1914. But the bill fell short of the required two-thirds majority.

Undaunted, the ASL, the WCTU, and the Prohibition Party all exploited World War I concerns about alcohol's effects on American soldiers and defense workers. Wayne Wheeler, a lobbyist for the ASL, argued that resources used for alcohol production should be used to support the war effort. He also played to wartime nativist fears, pointing out that most brewers were of German extraction and questioning their patriotism.

In early 1918, a bill calling for an Eighteenth Amendment to the Constitution that would make the manufacture and consumption of alcohol illegal was passed; it was ratified by the requisite three-quarters of the states by January 1919. The ASL then attempted to enforce national Prohibition, supported the Volstead Act of 1919, and promoted pledge programs and law enforcement days.

Rifts developed in the organization during the 1920s. Wheeler, for instance, believed that the league should focus on enforcement issues, while Ernest Cherrington, head of the organization's publishing arm, the American Issue Publishing Company, argued for educating Americans about the dangers of alcohol. In addition, charges that officials were embezzling funds tarnished the organization's reputation during this period. With the repeal of the Eighteenth Amendment in 1933, the ASL faded in importance, though it continues to operate as the American Council on Alcohol Problems.

Bruce E. Stewart

See also: Anti-Prohibition Movement; Prohibition (1920–1933); Speakeasies; Volstead Act (1919).

Further Reading

Hamm, Richard F. *Shaping the Eighteenth Amendment: Temperance Reform, Legal Culture, and the Polity, 1880–1920.* Chapel Hill: University of North Carolina Press, 1995.

Kerr, K. Austin. *Organized for Prohibition: A New History of the Anti-Saloon League.* New Haven, CT: Yale University Press, 1985.

Link, William A. *The Paradox of Southern Progressivism, 1880–1930.* Chapel Hill: University of North Carolina Press, 1992.

Anti-Semitism

After World War I, Americans were fearful of Bolshevik subversion and worried that foreigners were attempting to undermine the nation's values and traditions. The old way of life seemed to be disappearing. These anxieties led many Americans to seek scapegoats for the ills, real and imaginary, that plagued the nation. Anti-Semitism was part of this reaction, and an alleged connection between Jews and bolshevism became a staple of anti-Semitic propaganda.

The association of Jews with radicalism and subversion reached its apotheosis in *The Protocols of the Elders of Zion.* First published in Russia in 1905, it soon spread into Europe and was brought to America by Russian émigrés during World War I. *The Protocols of the Elders of Zion* attracted widespread attention when it was published as a series of articles in a London newspaper in 1921. A paranoid fantasy conjured by the czarist Russian secret police at the turn of the twentieth century, the work claimed to show that Jews were masterminding a world revolution to undermine Christian civilization.

On May 20, 1920, *The Dearborn Independent,* a weekly newspaper owned by automobile magnate Henry Ford, published an article drawn from the *Protocols* entitled "The International Jew: The World's Problem." This inaugurated a series of attacks on Jews that ran in the newspaper for several months. Charging American Jews with a plot to subvert traditional American ways, Ford's propaganda found acceptance in rural areas and small towns, despite condemnation by such luminaries as President Woodrow Wilson and former President William Howard Taft. Finally, in 1927, under pressure of several lawsuits and a boycott, Ford issued a public apology and soon shut down the *Independent.*

Certainly the most egregious expression of American nativism during the 1920s was the revival of the Ku Klux Klan (KKK). At its height in 1924, it counted over 4 million members around the country. Although its primary targets in the defense of "one hundred percent Americanism" were Catholics and African Americans, Klan doctrine included Jews as an obstacle to preserving the "real America." The KKK, until its collapse in the late 1920s in the face of scandal and bad press, was the first substantial, organized mass movement in which Jews were the victims of sporadic small-town boycotts and similar anti-Semitic harassments.

Jews were the most upwardly mobile ethnic group in American society during the 1920s, but they were excluded from some hotels, summer resorts, and social clubs. As they began to leave the crowded immigrant quarters of large cities, they came up against residential discrimination. Even wealthier Jews found themselves unwelcome in the fashionable sections of city and suburban developments.

The most troubling form of social discrimination occurred in higher education. Large numbers of the children of immigrant Jews sought college admittance, recognizing this as the key to economic and cultural advancement. Eastern colleges in particular were faced with increasing numbers of Jewish applicants and reacted by establishing a variety of methods to limit the number of acceptances. Once admitted, Jewish students often faced social distancing and resistance, and they responded by forming Jewish fraternities. Educational discrimination became a national issue in June 1922, when Harvard University's president, A. Lawrence Lowell, announced that his college was considering a quota system for Jewish students. Jewish leaders reacted strongly to this form of prejudice, and a Harvard faculty committee rejected Lowell's proposal in April 1923.

Jews also encountered considerable resistance as they attempted to move into white-collar professions. Employers typically specified that Christians were preferred for office, sales, and executive positions. Banking, insurance, and public utility firms were in the forefront of anti-Jewish prejudice. The 1920s witnessed a steady decline in the proportion of Jewish applicants accepted to medical schools, and Jewish doctors had a hard time securing internships and staff positions in hospitals. Law schools did not discriminate against Jewish applicants, but Jewish lawyers were generally not accepted into large, well-established firms. Jews increasingly entered the teaching profession, where open, competitive examinations were required, but they were excluded from many faculty positions in American universities throughout the 1920s and beyond.

Following World War I, there was a strong movement to restrict immigration to the United States. The diffuse fears about foreign radicals created concern that a series of labor strikes in 1919 was a prelude to revolution. One underlying worry stemmed from the exponential increase of Jewish immigrants from Southern and Eastern Europe, areas viewed as hotbeds of revolutionary fervor. Much of the pressure to close America's doors to newcomers came from labor leaders seeking to protect jobs endangered by immigrant labor, as well as from nativists who saw the arrival of 800,000 Russian and Polish Jewish immigrants between 1920 and 1922 as a menace to the American way of life.

The ultimate result of the restrictionist movement—the Immigration Act of 1924—established a national origins quota system, which discriminated against immigrants from Southern and Eastern Europe. Its impact can be seen in the decline of Jewish immigration in this period: 49,729 in 1924; 10,001 in 1925; and 12,290 in 1929.

Leslie Rabkin

See also: Anti-Catholicism; Immigration; Jewish Americans; Ku Klux Klan.

Further Reading

Dinnerstein, Leonard. *Antisemitism in America.* New York: Oxford University Press, 1995.

Katz, Jacob. *From Prejudice to Destruction: Anti-Semitism, 1700–1933.* Cambridge, MA: Harvard University Press, 2005.

Perry, Marvin, and Frederick. M. Schweitzer. *Anti-Semitism: Myth and Hate from Antiquity to the Present.* New York: Palgrave Macmillan, 2005.

Appliances, Household

While many new household appliances were invented before World War I, they truly came into their own in the 1920s. Much-improved versions of refrigerators, vacuum cleaners, toasters, sewing machines, radios, and washing machines began to show up in ever-increasing numbers in American homes. By the end of the decade, however, most American households still could not afford many of the appliances that would become ubiquitous in the post–World War II era.

Several developments led to the increase in household appliances during the Jazz Age. The decade's growing prosperity, coupled with new forms of consumer credit, enabled those with modest incomes to purchase expensive durables. Advertisers contributed to the desirability of household appliances, emphasizing standards of cleanliness and health that the new gadgets promised to deliver.

Manufacturers introduced a host of new household appliances in the 1920s. But conveniences such as telephones and refrigerators remained outside the budget of most American families until after World War II. *(H. Armstrong Roberts/Stringer/Retrofile/Getty Images)*

Most important to the growing use of appliances was the spread of electricity. While some early appliances were powered by gas motors, they were noisy and produced noxious fumes, requiring them to be vented outside. But between 1912 and 1929, the number of American homes wired for electricity soared from less than one in six to more than two in three; in urban areas, the rates were even higher. Roughly 85 percent of nonfarm households had electricity by 1930.

Applications and Uses

Most of the new appliances of the Jazz Age fell into three general categories: entertainment and communication (radio and telephone), food preservation and preparation (refrigerator, toaster, range), and cleaning (vacuum cleaner and washing machine). Two popular new appliances that fell into none of these categories were the incandescent lamp and the electric sewing machine.

Cost often dictated which items a household was likely to own. The most expensive were the refrigerator and the washing machine, although mass produc-

tion brought down their price significantly as the decade progressed. In 1920, the average refrigerator cost about $900—three-quarters of a factory worker's annual income—but by decade's end the price dropped to less than $200, which was still too expensive for most working- and middle-class incomes. Thus, fewer than 10 percent of American households had refrigerators or washing machines in 1929.

Smaller consumer durables such as vacuum cleaners, priced at about $50 in 1928, and toasters, at about $20, were more affordable and hence more widespread. Nevertheless, as late as 1929, just one-fourth of families owned vacuum cleaners and only one in five had a toaster.

The radio, with its promise of news and entertainment, was easily the most popular new appliance of the 1920s. Whereas only a handful of households owned radios in the early 1920s, that number reached nearly 70 percent by 1930. This far outnumbered telephone ownership, which required monthly service payments that did not fit most household budgets.

For those who could afford them, the new appliances changed life dramatically. The refrigerator did away with both the icebox and the need to have it constantly replenished by icemen. Shopping habits changed, as it was no longer necessary to make daily trips for perishable food items such as meat and milk. At the beginning of the 1920s, however, refrigerators were ungainly machines. An insulated wooden cabinet, containing the compressor that cooled the air inside, stood in the kitchen, connected by belts to large and noisy motors in the basement that provided the power. Bulky insulation limited the capacity of most early refrigerators. The switch to metal cabinets helped eliminate that problem by the mid-1920s, and the development of smaller motors made possible the modern, self-contained refrigerator, first introduced by Frigidaire in 1923. Refrigerators with freezer units had to await the introduction of a more efficient cooling gas, Freon, in the early 1930s, and did not become popular until shortly after World War II.

The invention of the electric thermostat in 1923 revolutionized both cooking and home heating. In the kitchen, it meant that cooks no longer had to check oven temperatures by hand, which not only eliminated oven burns, among the most common of household injuries in the pre-thermostat era, but also made for more consistent temperature control, allowing food to be cooked faster and more evenly. Between

1921 and 1927, Americans increased their annual spending on electric ranges from $1.7 million to $12.1 million.

Thermostats also made toasters more efficient; users no longer had to watch the bread to make sure it did not burn. The first automatic pop-up toasters were largely used in restaurants and bakeries. In 1926, the McGraw Electric Company introduced the Toastmaster, the first automatic unit for home use.

In 1922, Maytag introduced the first electric washing machine for the home, employing the still-used process of an agitation cycle in which clothes were cleaned by beating them against rotating central fins. Drying the clothes was another matter, however. Previously, clothes were wrung out by traditional wringers, though electric ones atop the washing machine drum were available on some units. The tumbling-drum electric dryer was not introduced to the household market until after World War II, so clothes still had to be air-dried on clotheslines.

Before World War I, vacuum cleaners required exhausting hand cranking and produced little suction. Electric motors generated a more powerful suction. In 1926, the Hoover Company introduced beater bars, which loosened dirt from carpets so that the vacuum motor could suck it up more effectively. So popular did the company's machines become that the verb "hoover," referring to the vacuum cleaning process, had entered the vocabulary by the late 1920s.

Impact on Households and Society

One development stemming from the new electric appliances was the servantless household. As late as the early 1900s, the vast majority of middle-class households employed domestics to take care of or assist in basic cleaning and cooking. With washing machines and ranges making both tasks physically easier and less time-consuming, homemakers could dispense with regular help, though the wealthy would continue to employ servants. Outside providers of services for households—such as local laundries or ice companies—saw their customer base shrink as more appliances entered American homes.

Although advertisers promised that the new appliances made the tasks of the housewife easier, these devices paradoxically upped the stakes for women. Older standards of cleanliness and healthful food preparation gave way to newer, higher ones, usually bolstered by scientific findings about the dangers of household germs and the importance of a balanced diet. For example, when clothes were washed by hand, people were willing to wear the same garments for several days or weeks before cleaning them. Now, partly because of the influence of advertising, they expected to wear clean clothes every day. Using newly discovered psychological techniques, advertisers played on women's anxieties that they were not doing enough for their families unless they met the new standards. And because these appliances were billed as laborsaving devices, women were now expected to shoulder household duties without servants to help them.

In the 1920s, many of the new inventions were largely confined to the rich and the upper reaches of the middle class. It was not until after World War II that the appliances first introduced on a limited basis in the Jazz Age truly would revolutionize American society across all classes. It would take a more broadly felt and sustained economic boom than that of the 1920s to put them into the hands of working-class and lower-middle-class Americans.

James Ciment and Leigh Kimmel

See also: Air-Conditioning; Electricity Industry; Radio.

Further Reading

Davis, L.J. *Fleet Fire: Thomas Edison and the Pioneers of the Electric Revolution.* New York: Arcade, 2003.

Kyvig, David E. *Daily Life in the United States, 1920–1939: Decades of Promise and Pain.* Westport, CT: Greenwood, 2002.

Rubin, Susan Goldman. *Toilets, Toasters, and Telephones: The How and Why of Everyday Objects.* San Diego, CA: Browndeer, 1998.

Arbuckle (Fatty) Scandal

Fatty Arbuckle was one of the most popular stars of the silent film era until a 1921 sex scandal destroyed his career and led studio heads to crack down on the behavior of their stars in an effort to improve Hollywood's image.

Roscoe Conkling Arbuckle was born on March 24, 1887, in Smith Center, Kansas. He became interested in the theater at an early age and worked at local vaudeville houses. He had a keen understanding of comedy and would delight vaudeville audiences with his polished slapstick routines in which, despite his increasing girth, he would perform agile pratfalls.

In 1912, Arbuckle began working for Mack Sennett, owner of the Keystone Film Company, and became a star through the Keystone Kops comedies.

Arbuckle gained fame for his slapstick skills, including his ability to sling two custard pies in opposite directions with amazing accuracy. He left Sennett's studios in 1916 for the Famous Players-Lasky, a division of Paramount Pictures, and gained complete artistic control over his films. Over the next five years, his popularity continued to grow, and in 1921, Paramount offered him $3 million to direct and star in a series of films over three years, an unheard-of sum at the time.

During the first eight months of 1921, Arbuckle made eight films for Paramount and was in need of a break. On September 3, he and two friends drove to San Francisco and checked into a suite of rooms at the luxurious St. Francis Hotel with plans for a three-day party over the Labor Day weekend. Although Prohibition was in full force, Arbuckle had arranged to have bootleg gin and whiskey delivered. Many people attended the party, including a twenty-six-year-old actress named Virginia Rappe. At one point during the party, Arbuckle was in a room with Rappe, who began screaming. Other guests rushed into the room and saw that Rappe appeared to be in pain. When the hotel doctor arrived, she said that her injuries were the result of an attempted rape by Arbuckle. The doctor, however, believed her problem was caused by intoxication.

Rappe died at a local sanatorium on September 9. The cause of death was listed as peritonitis brought on by a rupture of the bladder. Authorities believed that her bladder might have ruptured due to an attempted sexual assault by Arbuckle. On September 10, Roscoe "Fatty" Arbuckle was charged with murder. Newspapers ran sensational accounts of the incident, littered with falsehoods and exaggerations. William Randolph Hearst's newspapers, in particular, painted Arbuckle as a cold-hearted sexual predator with a debauched private life.

Opening arguments in the *State of California v. Roscoe Arbuckle* began on November 18, 1921. Conflicting testimony by witnesses marked the trial, as did allegations that San Francisco District Attorney Mathew Brady had bribed some of the witnesses to offer damning testimony. Arbuckle took the stand in his own defense and denied that he had sexual contact with Rappe. He said he found her lying in pain on the floor of the bathroom and placed her on the bed.

The jury was deadlocked 10–2 in favor of acquittal. A new trial began on January 9, 1922, which also resulted in a hung jury. A third and final trial in March 1922 ended in a not-guilty verdict.

The series of trials, combined with Paramount's cutting off his funds, left Arbuckle deeply in debt. More important, as a result of the affair, Hollywood considered Arbuckle a bad investment. He was unable to find work as an actor, although it was reported that his friend and fellow comedian Buster Keaton allowed him to direct scenes in one of Keaton's movies. Arbuckle also directed a few films for a minor studio. Near the end of his life, the comedian was signed on by Jack Warner to work on a series of short-subject comedies. Arbuckle died in relative poverty and obscurity on June 29, 1933.

The Arbuckle scandal affected far more than the lives of the comedy star and the aspiring actress. It was the first in a series of scandals—including the unsolved 1922 murder of director William Desmond Taylor and the 1923 drug-related death of director-actor Wallace Reid—that rocked the Hollywood community in the early Jazz Age. Fearing that the incidents would sully Hollywood's image in Middle America and perhaps cut into ticket sales, the studios hired Will Hays—who had gained fame as U.S. postmaster general for his crackdown on the spread of obscene materials through the mail—to head the industry's trade association, the Motion Picture Producers and Distributors Association of America. Hays would impose a strict moral code for films in the early 1930s, limiting the portrayal of sex and violence through the 1960s.

Beth Kattelman and James Ciment

See also: Celebrity Culture; Film Industry.

Further Reading

Edmonds, Andy. *Frame-Up! The Untold Story of Roscoe "Fatty" Arbuckle.* New York: William Morrow, 1991.
Oderman, Stuart. *Roscoe "Fatty" Arbuckle: A Biography of the Silent Film Comedian, 1887–1933.* Jefferson, NC: McFarland, 1994.
Yallop, David A. *The Day the Laughter Stopped: The True Story of Fatty Arbuckle.* New York: St. Martin's, 1976.

Architecture

While most people refer to the 1920s as the Jazz Age, after the musical genre that gained popularity during the decade, architectural critics and historians have another term to describe the two decades that followed World War I: the machine age. Although machines were nothing new in the 1920s, they began to permeate everyday life to an extent they never had before—from the radio that graced people's

Movie Palaces

As motion pictures overtook vaudeville as America's favorite form of entertainment in the years immediately following World War I, theater owners began to replace their small theaters that seated several hundred patrons with larger theaters dedicated to showing films. Some 4,000 movie theaters were built by the end of 1922.

Many movie theaters, particularly those in small towns and suburbs, were small and plain. In downtown shopping and entertainment districts, however, huge edifices began to rise, with seating for thousands. They were grand affairs, with elaborate decoration inside and out. They featured the latest in lighting technology, and some featured huge Wurlitzer organs for live music accompaniment to the silent films shown on the giant screens. These "movie palaces" had become a staple of American social and cultural life by the mid-1920s.

In 1913, Broadway impresario Samuel "Roxy" Rothapfel opened the first of the movie palaces, the Regent Theater just north of New York's theater district. Rothapfel pioneered many of the features that would become hallmarks of the movie palace—unreserved seating and low ticket prices, elaborate fixtures, and fantasy architecture, in the Regent's case inspired by the palaces of Moorish princes. As Rothapfel famously remarked, "Don't give the people what they want . . . give 'em something better." The Regent inspired imitators across the city, including the Strand, the Rialto, and the Rivoli.

Theater chains such as those owned by Marcus Loew and movie mogul William Fox were soon competing across the country to build larger and more elaborate theaters. Among the most elaborate was the baroque Chicago Theater, built by chain owners Abe and Barney Balaban and Sam and Morris Katz at a cost of $4 million (more than a $100 million in today's money).

The movie palaces offered more than a luxurious environment. They also offered working- and middle-class patrons a taste of the aristocratic life, pampered by a huge staff dedicated to serving their every need, including valet parking and ushers who brought snacks to their seats. Some theaters went even further. The Fox and Roxy in San Francisco included fully staffed hospitals to treat patrons who became sick, while Chicago's Avalon Theater included a plush nursery—decorated in the style of a Persian palace—for patrons' babies and children. Loew's 72nd Street Theater in New York offered to board pets while customers enjoyed the show.

As the Great Depression took hold in the early 1930s, however, chain owners and movie companies became hard-pressed to fill the movie palaces they had built in the booming 1920s. The theaters built in the 1930s tended to be smaller and simpler affairs. With the decline of many downtown entertainment districts in the 1950s and 1960s—along with diminished audiences due to competition from television—many of the movie palaces ran into financial trouble. Some were torn down; others were transformed into housing or churches. However, as downtowns began to revive in the late twentieth century, some of the mothballed and decrepit theaters, such as Atlanta's Fox Theater, famous as the venue for the premiere of *Gone with the Wind* in 1939, were renovated and returned to their former glory.

James Ciment and Maria Reynolds

parlors to the automobile that sat in their driveways. While traditionally styled buildings, incorporating classical or Gothic styles continued to be built in large numbers, many architects responded to the new ubiquity of machines and mass production with designs that emphasized the building as machine. The resulting designs were either stripped down and functional, as in the early International style, or the more ornamented machine-as-parts aesthetic, in which the building's various elements incorporated machine-like motifs.

The new machine-age architecture went beyond aesthetics, however, as architects began to realize the possibilities of the steel-frame construction, first employed in the late nineteenth century but reaching a kind of apotheosis in the great skyscrapers built or conceived in the late 1920s. Domestic architecture also reflected the new aesthetic, as American designers began to view houses as machines for living. One particular machine—the automobile—had an even more direct impact on architecture, ushering in a whole new kind of building, the roadside service station.

Machine-as-Parts Aesthetic

Influenced by European antecedents such as the Viennese Secessionist school, with its use of geometric patterns, the machine-as-parts style employed certain older forms, including the tower and dome and the use of ornamentation. But it also represented a significant departure from tradition in its use of setbacks: towers that rose in steps rather than straight columns from base to top. The ornamentation, moreover, had a stripped-down look, flattened and geometrical.

One of the best-known early examples of the machine-as-parts building was the Nebraska state capitol in Lincoln, commissioned in 1920 and finished in 1932. Designed by perhaps the most significant American practitioner of the machine-as-parts style, Bertram Grosvenor Goodhue, the building featured a square tower, an octagonal cupola of several stories, and a golden dome, each set back from the element beneath, and all sitting atop a massive base of several stories. Each component stood out distinctly and featured strong angles and flattened ornamentation. Together they gave the building the appearance of a dynamo, particularly when it was illuminated by electric lights. Indeed, with electricity coming into widespread use, many architects in the 1920s began to design their buildings as structures for round-the-clock public viewing, lit with natural light during the day and with artificial light at night.

While the Nebraska state capitol sat by itself on wide-open ground, many of the stepped-back, machine-as-parts buildings of the 1920s were erected in the constricted confines of major cities. Responding to complaints about the shadows cast by the growing numbers of skyscrapers on its streets, the New York City municipal government passed a law in 1916 setting height limits for the street façades of new buildings. Architects who wanted to maximize the interior space of their buildings—a critical factor, given the high cost of Manhattan real estate—were required to set back the towers above the low-rise, street-front base.

By the end of the 1920s, most major American cities had adopted variations of the New York law, although most of the finest examples of the stepped-back, machine-as-parts style went up in Manhattan, many of them the work of Goodhue's students. One of the most celebrated examples was the Barclay-Vesey tower in downtown Manhattan, designed by Ralph Walker in 1922 and completed four years later, for the New York Telephone Company. The massive base of the building was topped by a stepped series of towers, each culminating in a crenellated roofline that tied the various elements of the building into a whole, even as each part stood out distinctly against the others. Other notable examples are Raymond Hood's 1924 American Radiator Building and Hood, John Mead, and J. André Fouilhoux's Daily News Building, begun in 1929 and finished in 1931.

Many of the new skyscrapers served a nonstructural purpose—that of advertisement for the company whose headquarters they housed. While buildings had long been commissioned as an expression of the owner's wealth and power, the skyscrapers of the 1920s—reflecting the rising significance of advertising—were more explicitly promotional, a celebration of the business ethos that was so much a part of the social mood of the 1920s. Hood's Radiator Building resembled the product made by its owner, while the Daily News headquarters featured the paper's name in huge letters across the top—the billboard as architectural ornament.

Perhaps the most unabashed expression of the building as architectural advertisement was New York's Chrysler Building, designed by William Van Allen and constructed between 1928 and 1931. Built in the stepped-back, machine-as-parts style, the seventy-seven-story tower, at 1,048 feet high, was briefly the tallest building in the world. It featured a

The 1920s brought a burst of skyscraper construction to U.S. cities. New York's iconic Chrysler Building, completed in 1930, would be the world's tallest building, though only briefly. The Empire State Building took away that distinction the following year. *(Stringer/Hulton Archive/Getty Images)*

number of architectural and ornamental elements suggestive of the automobiles manufactured by the company, including gargoyles suggesting hood ornaments and a metal-clad spire.

International Style

By the end of the decade, the machine-as-parts style began to give way to what became known as the International style, which came to dominate architecture in much of the Western world. The International style celebrated the pure functionality of machines and the possibilities of modern materials like steel, glass, and reinforced concrete. It embraced transparency through the extensive use of plate glass, and it eschewed ornamentation, which would detract from the purity of the design and negate the stripped-down functionalism of the structure. Many of the buildings were cantilevered to emphasize the lightness made possible by reinforced concrete and the glass-clad, steel-frame construction.

The International style originated in Europe in the work of France's Le Corbusier and Germany's Walter Gropius, his Bauhaus movement, and Ludwig

Mies van der Rohe, who coined the movement's credo: "Less is more." In America, the most widely celebrated manifestation of the early Internationalist skyscraper was George Howe and William Lescaze's Philadelphia Savings Fund Society Building (1928–1932). Devoid of ornament, the building also eschewed what Howe and Lescaze considered the unfunctionality of the stepped-back design. Instead, the sweeping curved base, with an abundance of glass, was topped by a smaller, rectilinear tower—a minimal form of step-back design that was included to meet city ordinance and no more.

Domestic architecture was also influenced by the International style, largely through the work of two Austrian émigrés—Rudolf Schindler and Richard Neutra, both of whom did their most celebrated work in Los Angeles. Schindler had come to L.A. to finish a number of Frank Lloyd Wright projects, after Wright went to Tokyo in 1920 to design and build the Imperial Hotel. After helping to finish the Hollyhock House, an example of Wright's Mayan-inspired architecture of the early 1920s, Schindler went on to build the 1926 Lovell Beach House in Newport Beach. Constructed in reinforced concrete atop a framework that resembled the rib cage of a whale, the house featured a simple rectangular shape, sweeping use of glass, and an unornamented design that would come to be hallmarks of the International style. Two years later, Neutra built the Lovell Health House for the same client, incorporating many of the same features including sweeps of glass and unornamented reinforced concrete. The cantilevered-frame structure emphasized the house's dramatic setting in the Hollywood Hills.

Although traditional forms continued to hold the interest of American architects during the Jazz Age, many celebrated the machine and the dynamism of the modern. Much of the decade's architecture continued to feature flowery ornamentation and tried-and-true classical and Gothic forms, but architects also incorporated new materials in conventional forms. The decade also witnessed a daring embrace of new forms inspired by the age of machines and mass production.

James Ciment

See also: Design, Industrial; Hood, Raymond.

Further Reading

Fitch, James Marston. *Architecture and the Esthetics of Plenty.* New York: Columbia University Press, 1961.
Roth, Leland M. *American Architecture: A History.* Boulder, CO: Westview, 2001.

Wilson, Richard Guy, Dianne H. Pilgrim, and Dickran Tashjian. *The Machine Age in America, 1918–1941.* New York: Harry N. Abrams, 1986.

Armstrong, Louis (1901–1971)

Before he was eighteen years old, trumpeter and cornetist Louis Armstrong, an icon of jazz and American culture through much of the twentieth century, had established himself as an innovative stylist and popular performer. By the end of the Jazz Age, he was one of America's most successful recording artists.

Armstrong was born in the Uptown district of the city that gave birth to jazz, New Orleans. There is some dispute regarding the date of his birth; although the date of record is August 4, 1901, Armstrong claimed he was born on July 4, and some documents list his birth year as 1900. Born in poverty, Armstrong was raised by his grandmother after his father abandoned the family. Frequently in trouble with the law, he was sent to the New Orleans Home for Colored Waifs, where he learned the cornet and played in the institution's band.

Like other city kids, Armstrong would follow the marching bands of New Orleans as they paraded around the city during festivals and funerals. He learned from popular musicians such as Bunk Johnson, Buddy Petit, and, most significantly, cornet player Joe "King" Oliver, who acted as his mentor. When Armstrong was fifteen years old, Oliver arranged for him to perform with the band of pianist Fate Marable, which played on Mississippi River steamboats. In 1919, when Oliver left New Orleans, Armstrong took his place in Edward "Kid" Ory's band, one of the leading jazz ensembles in the city.

Between 1919 and 1922, Armstrong established himself as one of the most popular jazz musicians in New Orleans. But jazz and African American culture in general had been undergoing significant changes. Hundreds of thousands of African Americans were fleeing Southern poverty and racism for opportunities in the burgeoning cities and manufacturing centers of the North. As African Americans moved North, they brought with them blues and jazz; both musical forms became inflected with the faster pace of urban life.

Armstrong joined the exodus in 1922, moving to Chicago after Oliver invited him to play in his Creole Jazz Band. It was a propitious time for the young and talented musician. Chicago's black population jumped from just over 100,000 in 1920 to nearly a quarter-million by 1930, providing a growing body of musicians with an appreciative and relatively prosperous audience. Jazz and the blues were an integral part of the musical landscape of Chicago, in clubs, on the radio, and on records. In 1923, Armstrong made his first recordings, playing second cornet to Oliver in a series of cuts for the Gennett Company of Richmond, Indiana.

In 1924, Armstrong met and married his second wife (he wedded three women in his lifetime), the pianist of the Creole Jazz Band, Lil Harden, who convinced him to further his career by moving to New York, then the focal point of the Harlem Renaissance. In New York, Armstrong joined the Fletcher Henderson Orchestra, which performed regularly at the famous Roseland Ballroom on Broadway. Armstrong played with Henderson for a little more than a year, making a number of recordings under the band's name. He also recorded as an accompanist for a series of popular blues singers, including Gertrude "Ma" Rainey, Maggie Jones, and Bessie Smith, one of the most popular recording artists of the Jazz Age. With Smith, Armstrong recorded "St. Louis Blues" (1925), regarded by many jazz critics as the most influential blues recording of the decade.

At the end of 1925, again at Harden's insistence, Armstrong moved back to Chicago, to play with the house band at the popular Bill Bottoms Dreamland nightclub. The move became a major turning point in Armstrong's career—and the history of jazz. For it was in Chicago, between November 12, 1925, and December 5, 1928, that Armstrong produced an unparalleled body of recorded work. Contracted by Okeh records, he brought together a studio-only group of noted New Orleans musicians: trombonist Kid Ory, clarinetist Johnny Dodds, banjoist Johnny St. Cyr, and Lil Harden on piano (and later, pianist Earl "Fatha" Hines). Together they made the historic studio recordings of the Hot Five and Hot Seven bands, some sixty in all. Among them were the classics "Gut Bucket Blues" (1925), "Potato Head Blues" (1927), "Cornet Chop Suey" (1927), "Alligator Crawl" (1927), "Don't Jive Me" (1928), and "Basin Street Blues" (1928).

Jazz history was made at the first session when Armstrong provided the vocals for a tune entitled "Heebie Jeebies" (1926). The first time through, he sang the song just as it was written; for the second take, he improvised a series of vocal sounds as if playing an instrument—a technique called "scat." The

New Orleans musicians such as Louis Armstrong, pictured here in 1927, helped spread jazz to the rest of the country as they joined the mass migration of African Americans from the rural South to cities in the North, Midwest, and West. *(Stringer/Hulton Archive/Getty Images)*

become not only the most celebrated jazz musician of the twentieth century and a screen star, but a goodwill ambassador for the United States as well. Armstrong died on July 6, 1971.

Leslie Rabkin and James Ciment

See also: Jazz; Oliver, Joe "King."

Further Reading

Armstrong, Louis, and Thomas Brothers. *Louis Armstrong, in His Own Words: Selected Writings.* New York: Oxford University Press, 2001.

Bergreen, Laurence. *Louis Armstrong.* New York: Broadway, 1998.

Giddins, Gary. *Satchmo: The Genius of Louis Armstrong.* New York: Da Capo, 2001.

The Hot Fives and Sevens. Audio CD, Boxed set. New York: JSP Records, 1999.

Art, Fine

Modern art arrived in the United States with the 1913 Armory Show in New York City, which exposed the American public to the work of European impressionists, neoimpressionists, and cubists for the first time. The exhibition, housed at the 69th Infantry Regimental Armory in Manhattan from February 17 to March 15, sparked a new spirit of experimentation among American artists. Equally important, it encouraged interest among American art patrons in the new styles emanating from Paris, thereby creating a market for modern art produced by Americans.

Also promoting new departures in art in the years leading up to World War I was New York City gallery owner Alfred Stieglitz. At his 291 Gallery, named for its address on Fifth Avenue, Stieglitz not only displayed the work of innovative European artists such as Henri Matisse and Pablo Picasso but also mounted shows of African, pre-Columbian, and Japanese art and artifacts that proved influential in the development of Western modernism. Stieglitz's main contribution to American art, however, came through his patronage of a group of U.S. artists working in the new genres. These included John Marin's impressionist and fauvist paintings, Arthur Dove and Max Weber's cubist creations, and Marsden Hartley's postimpressionist work, reminiscent of the paintings of the Dutch artist Vincent van Gogh.

The 291 artists, as they were called, rejected the classicism of Gilded Age artists such as John Singer Sargent and William Merritt Chase as well as the

recording became a best seller, helped by Armstrong's first performance as a singer and his inimitable gravelly voice.

Sometime in 1927, as he was making a name for himself in the jazz clubs of Chicago, Armstrong made the switch from the cornet to the trumpet. Chicago was changing, too. A crackdown on vice in 1929 closed many clubs, cabarets, dance halls, gambling joints, and brothels, all of which were venues for jazz. Meanwhile, Armstrong's marriage was failing, so in the spring of 1929, he decided to return to New York for an engagement at Harlem's Connie's Inn.

While in New York, Armstrong played in the orchestra of a 1929 Broadway review, *Hot Chocolates,* in which he was featured singing "Ain't Misbehavin'," by Fats Waller. The show marked another turning point in his career, as it brought him to the attention of sophisticated New York theatergoers and opened the way for big-time bookings.

By the 1930s, "Satchmo" (short for "satchelmouth," referring to his large mouth) was a well-known performance artist. He would go on to gritty realism of New York's early twentieth-century Ashcan school, as rendered by artists such as George Bellows and John Sloan. Instead, they emphasized formalistic experimentation—the dappled light of the impressionists, the neoprimitivism and savage coloring of the fauvists and neoimpressionists, and the multiple perspectives and geometric patterning of the cubists.

Before World War I, American artists were still adopting techniques pioneered in Europe, but the 1920s witnessed the first real effort by U.S. artists to develop styles unique to their side of the Atlantic. They were again nurtured by Stieglitz, who opened two influential New York galleries in the 1920s—the Intimate Gallery in 1925 and An American Place in 1929. Another important art patron was the heiress Gertrude Vanderbilt Whitney, whose collection of more than 600 works by contemporary American artists, offered to and rejected by the Metropolitan Museum of Art, would serve as the core collection of the Whitney Museum of American Art, which opened in New York in 1931. Art patrons Lillie Bliss and Abby Rockefeller (wife of the Standard Oil heir) founded the Museum of Modern Art in New York City in 1929. While MoMA focused largely on European art in its early years, it nevertheless helped establish modernist works as "serious" art among patrons and the public, which in turn helped American artists working in the various new idioms.

Precisionism

Three new schools of distinctively modernist American art emerged in the 1920s: precisionism, Southwestern Modernism, and the New Negro movement, also known as the Harlem Renaissance after the predominantly African American neighborhood of New York City where the movement was based. Each of the three schools was a response to distinct aspects of the American nation, landscape, and society.

Precisionism explored the modern industrial and commercial landscape of the country's great metropolises. Charles Sheeler, for example, offered a series of hard-edged, precisely rendered paintings (and photographs) in the mid-1920s inspired by the Ford Motor Company's River Rouge Plant in Detroit, considered the most modern factory of its day. Gerald Murphy depicted the everyday products of the new consumerism in a flattened style of primary colors that evoked the advertising billboards rapidly going up along American roads. Among his most cele-

brated works is *Razor* (1924), a still life consisting of a mass-produced shaving razor, fountain pen, and book of matches. Joseph Stella's early 1920s series *The Voice of the City of New York Interpreted* featured city landscapes rendered in brightly colored and sharply defined geometric shapes, conjuring the imagery of stained-glass windows. The abstract rectilinear shapes in sculptor John Storrs's works of the 1920s evoked the skyscrapers being erected in financial districts across America—physical manifestations of the business ethos dominating American society and politics during the decade.

Perhaps the most famous of the precisionists was Edward Hopper, although much of his most celebrated work dates from the 1930s and 1940s. Best known for his realistic but strangely dreamlike portrayals of urban alienation, Hopper was heavily influenced by the emerging film industry of the 1920s. His depictions of everyday city life have the appearance of being staged for the camera, like a still from a movie. Among his most frequently reproduced works from the Jazz Age is *Automat* (1927), which captured a solitary, pensive young woman poised over a cup of coffee in the eponymous cafeteria.

New Negro Movement and Southwestern Modernist

Even more unique to the American scene than the work of the precisionists—who had their counterpart in the futurist school in Europe—was the art coming out of the New Negro movement. (The term came from an influential 1925 book of essays on the emerging urban black culture edited by philosopher Alain Locke.) Since the early 1900s, rural Southern blacks had been making their way to the great cities of the Northeast and Midwest, partly to escape the intense racism of the South and partly to take advantage of the job opportunities offered in factories. By the early 1920s, Harlem in upper Manhattan had emerged as the largest and most vibrant of the new black urban neighborhoods. There, African American artists such as painter Aaron Douglas and sculptor Sargent Johnson fused modernist styles, like cubism, with traditional African motifs. But perhaps the most popular of the New Negro visual artists was Archibald Motley, Jr., working out of Chicago, home to the second largest black community in the North. Motley captured the urban scene in the city's South Side neighborhood in a flattened, neoprimitivist style of vibrant colors and simple shapes.

Far from the urban centers, the painters of the Southwestern modernist school were influenced by two other cultures unique to the American scene: Native American and Chicano, or Mexican American. The stark and distinctive landscape of the region, the American Southwest, gave the school its name. Southwestern modernists had their patron in Mabel Dodge, a wealthy heiress who, in 1919, moved from New York's Greenwich Village to Taos, New Mexico, where she bought a ranch that she turned into a retreat for writers. The ranch, and the stunning mountain and desert landscape around it, soon attracted numerous visual artists, turning Taos into a major art colony of the 1920s. Another such colony, though less influential, emerged in Carmel, California, around the same time.

Among the artists drawn to Taos were Andrew Dasburg and Raymond Jonson. In paintings such as *New Mexican Village* (1926), Dasburg melded a cubist idiom with distinctive Southwestern tones and light to capture the unadorned, rectilinear shapes of the region's unique adobe architecture. Jonson, coming out of the precisionist school, rendered the New Mexican mountains in simplified, hard-edged sculptural forms in his *Earth Rhythms* series of the mid-1920s.

Art historians generally agree that the most influential artist to emerge from the Southwestern Modernist school was Georgia O'Keeffe. Like Jonson, O'Keeffe began her artistic career in the late 1910s and early 1920s as a New York precisionist painter. In her 1926 painting *The Shelton with Sunspots,* O'Keeffe rendered the skyscraper where she lived (with her husband Stieglitz) in flattened tones and simple shapes, crisply rendered with stylized clouds and a dazzling reflection of sunlight that almost blinds the viewer. O'Keeffe began visiting New Mexico in 1917 but did not move there permanently until 1929. In the intervening years, she brought back numerous artifacts from the Southwest that would feature in a series of iconic paintings, most notably of ghostly cow skulls.

Like Hopper, O'Keeffe produced her most notable work in the 1930s and 1940s. Both artists, however—two of the most important of the twentieth century—first developed their unique style in the vibrant art scene of the 1920s, the first decade in which modernist American artists pioneered their own idioms wholly independent of the prevailing European styles.

James Ciment

See also: Harlem Renaissance; O'Keeffe, Georgia.

Further Reading

Doss, Erika. *Twentieth-Century American Art.* New York: Oxford University Press, 2002.

Hunter, Sam. *American Art of the 20th Century.* New York: Harry N. Abrams, 1973.

Wilson, Richard Guy, Dianne H. Pilgrim, and Dickran Tashjian. *The Machine Age in America, 1918–1941.* New York: Harry N. Abrams, 1986.

Asian Americans

For Asian Americans, the 1920s were marked by discrimination and a series of legal battles over immigration and citizenship rights. While each Asian immigrant group, and each group's American-born descendants, faced unique challenges, all Asian groups faced immigration restrictions and limits on their ability to become U.S. citizens.

Chinese Americans were the first major group of Asians to immigrate in the mid-nineteenth century, but the Chinese Exclusion Act of 1882 barred Chinese laborers from entering the country; the act was renewed in 1892 and in 1902. Agreements in 1907–1908 between U.S. President Theodore Roosevelt and the government of Japan limited immigration from that country but did not prevent the entry of family members of Japanese immigrants already in the United States. Residents of the Philippines, a U.S. territory since shortly after the Spanish-American War of 1898, were permitted to enter the United States but were not allowed American citizenship.

Japanese immigrants faced the greatest animosity in the 1920s, since they were the only group of Asians in America to significantly increase in numbers during the period, not only as a result of immigration, but also through natural increase. Anti-immigrant groups such as the Oriental Exclusion League, the Native Sons of the Golden West, the American Legion, and the American Federation of Labor all lobbied for Japanese exclusion on the grounds that Japanese immigrants were taking jobs away from American workers and that they could never assimilate into American society. Animosity was particularly strong in California because of the concentration of Japanese immigrants there (more than 60 percent of the Japanese living in the United States lived in California) and this group's economic success. While Japanese farmers worked only 1 percent of California's cultivated land, they produced 10 percent of the total value of California crops.

A national fear of Japan's growing power in East Asia, lingering anti-Chinese sentiment, and concerns on the East Coast of massive immigration from Southern and Eastern Europe resulted in a 1921 temporary immigration quota that limited the influx from each country to 3 percent of that country's immigrant population in the United States according to the 1910 U.S. Census. The National Origins Act of 1924 reduced immigration quotas to amounts based on 2 percent of a nation's immigrant population according to the 1890 census and excluded from immigration anyone "ineligible for citizenship," meaning all Asians. Asian immigration would not resume until World War II, when China, allied with America in the struggle against Japan, was granted a quota of 100 immigrants per year.

Asian immigrants were not allowed to become citizens of the United States since antebellum naturalization laws allowed only "free white persons" to become citizens. The Fourteenth Amendment, which had been ratified shortly after the American Civil War, allowed for the naturalization of "persons of African descent," but not Asians.

Between 1887 and 1923, U.S. federal courts heard twenty-five cases regarding the citizenship rights of Asian Americans, culminating in two U.S. Supreme Court decisions, *Takao Ozawa v. United States* (1922) and *United States v. Bhagat Singh Thind* (1923). In *Ozawa,* the Court ruled that Japanese American businessman Takao Ozawa's application for citizenship should not be granted because he was not of the Caucasian race or of African ancestry. The decision meant that Asians in general could not become citizens. Bhagat Thind argued that, as a "high class Hindu" from the strict caste society of India, he could trace his roots back to Europe and was a "pure Aryan." The Court held, however, that while anthropologically he might be white, "in the popular conception of race" he was not white and therefore not eligible for citizenship.

Asian groups also faced discrimination under California's Alien Land Act (1913), which forbade land ownership for those "ineligible for citizenship," and the 1922 Cable Act which stipulated that an American woman who married a man "ineligible for citizenship" would lose her citizenship as long as the marriage continued. For American-born Asian women, who were American citizens by birth, this meant a loss of citizenship and an inability to regain their citizenship should their marriage end.

As just a tiny proportion of the overall U.S. population—persons of Chinese and Japanese ancestry, the two largest groups, represented 0.15 percent of Americans in 1920—Asian Americans struggled in vain to win the basic right to citizenship. Not until after World War II, and especially after the passage of a quota-ending immigration reform law in 1965, would their numbers increase substantially.

Charles J. Shindo

See also: Immigration; Immigration Laws of 1921 and 1924.

Further Reading

Chan, Sucheng. *Asian Americans: An Interpretative History.* Boston: Twayne, 1991.

———, ed. *Entry Denied: Exclusion and the Chinese Community in America, 1882–1943.* Philadelphia: Temple University Press, 1990.

Chuman, Frank F. *The Bamboo People: The Law and Japanese-Americans.* Del Mar, CA: Publisher's, 1976.

Atlas, Charles (1892–1972)

In 1922, for the second year in a row, Charles Atlas was named "the World's Most Perfectly Developed Man." The distinction was conferred by a panel of judges assembled at New York's Madison Square Garden by fitness celebrity Bernarr MacFadden and the staff at his magazine, *Physical Culture.* By winning the competition, Atlas cemented his status among fitness buffs and became a pop culture icon. In the ensuing years, he helped change popular perceptions of male physical fitness and basic ideas about masculinity. In the process, he became the central figure of one of the most successful mail-order businesses of the twentieth century, leaving an enduring legacy for American fitness culture.

Atlas was born Angelo Siciliano in Calabria, Italy, on October 30, 1892. He immigrated to America with his family when he was a child. Charles was his middle name, and he adopted the name Atlas from the titan of Greek myth who held up the heavens. Starting out as a bodybuilder in New York, he went on to perform as the "strong man" in the Coney Island Circus Side Show in the early 1900s.

After winning the World's Most Perfectly Developed Man competition for the second time, Atlas teamed up with a doctor to sell a twelve-week, mail-order fitness course that the two men designed together. Atlas spurned weight lifting and instructed his students to exercise by pitting muscles in resistance to each other, a method now called isometrics. The program thus did not require any equipment or expenses beyond the $30 course fee, an important consideration for young customers with little disposable income.

The Atlas program, however, offered lessons about more than just exercise. Drawing from the contemporary wisdom of doctors, health advisers, and physical culture (bodybuilding) experts, the Atlas program offered guidance on everything from a healthful diet to the importance of habits such as going to bed early, sleeping with a window open for fresh air, and undergoing regular enemas to move closer to physical perfection. For Atlas, fitness was not a hobby but a lifestyle, and one his students had to embrace to truly emulate him.

Success eluded Atlas until a young New York University graduate named Charles Roman bought out the doctor's interest. Roman provided the missing ingredients to turn Charles Atlas, Ltd., the company he incorporated with Atlas in 1929, into a phenomenal success. Linking physical well-being, personal character, and personality, Roman marketed the course as a way for men in their teens to mid-twenties to re-create themselves and become new, better men through fitness. While Atlas used his personal notoriety to promote the company, Roman wrote catchy slogans about manhood and self-improvement, such as the still-trademarked term "Dynamic Tension" for Atlas's isometric method. Together, the two men created a business so successful that it thrived even through the Great Depression, selling millions of courses by 1930.

Atlas's story and larger-than-life persona were important to the company's success. The company's publicity portrayed Atlas as the ideal physical specimen of manhood and an approachable mentor. Atlas, an experienced showman, knew how to portray fitness, himself, and his course. In addition to numerous publicity stunts, Atlas maintained his image by habitually removing his shirt to show off his physique. Atlas considered fitness a cause, and he advocated it with the zeal of a true believer.

Stories of Atlas's journey toward physical perfection enhanced his charisma. For much of his youth, he had been small and unathletic. He described discovering the ideal of male fitness in his teens while contemplating statues of Greek gods (hence his choice of the name Atlas). He recalled coming up with the idea for "Dynamic Tension" while studying the sleek muscles of tigers in motion. As much of the advertising and course literature was written as a message from Atlas to the reader, customers felt a personal connection with Atlas and they could strengthen that feeling of connection by taking his course.

The most famous personal bridge between Atlas and his customers was a print advertisement that has appeared in countless publications, becoming an enduring classic of American advertising. In the ad, Roman's brainchild, a series of panels tell the story of a skinny teenage boy at the beach with a pretty girl. A muscular bully comes over and kicks sand in the teenager's face, humiliating him. Atlas informs the reader that he was once the skinny teenager—a "ninety-seven-pound weakling." He began bodybuilding, he explains, to neutralize the threat of bullies and become a real man. He goes on to say that his course could help others do the same.

Atlas remained muscular and devoted to fitness until his last day. He died of a heart attack in December 1972. He was predeceased by his wife, Margaret, but survived by their two children. He had sold his interest in Charles Atlas, Ltd., to Roman many years before, and the company is still in business.

John Fiorini

See also: Fads and Stunts; Leisure and Recreation.

Further Reading

Bushyeager, Peter. "The World of Atlas." *Men's Health* 6:5 (1991): 56–61.

Charles Atlas, Ltd. http://www.charlesatlas.com.

Gustaitis, Joseph. "Charles Atlas: 'The World's Most Perfectly Developed Man.'" *American History Illustrated* 21 (September 1986): 16–17.

Toon, Elizabeth, and Janet Golden. "'Live Clean, Think Clean, and Don't Go to Burlesque Shows': Charles Atlas as Health Advisor." *Journal of the History of Medicine and Allied Sciences* 57:1 (2002): 39–60.

Automobile Industry

The automobile was by no means a new invention in the 1920s, and full-scale manufacture had been launched by Henry Ford with his Model T in 1908. The first assembly line, which radically increased the speed of production and decreased the cost of the product, had been created in 1913. It was in the 1920s, however, that the automobile achieved widespread market penetration and began to change American culture in significant ways. From 1920 to 1929, U.S. automobile production increased from 2.2 million units annually to 5.3 million, an increase of more than 140 percent.

Diversity of brands and models—including this 1927 Chevrolet—helped General Motors surpass Ford as the world's largest automotive manufacturer in the late 1920s. Styling, market segmentation, and consumer financing further fueled GM's expansion. *(FPG/Hulton Archive/Getty Images)*

At the beginning of the decade, the Ford Motor Company was still the leading American automaker, with General Motors (GM) running second. But smaller companies could survive and even be competitive, particularly in the luxury trade. Such companies as Pierce-Arrow, Duesenberg, and Packard produced handsome, powerful, luxurious vehicles for the wealthy, while Hupmobile, Hudson, Studebaker, and Nash produced midrange cars.

Ford had attained the preeminent position through vigorous exploitation of mass production and economies of scale, which enabled the company to slash the price of a Model T to new lows every year. In 1923, the Model T reached its high-water mark— a total of 1,817,891 produced. Yet the design of the Model T had not changed in years, and it was such a simple, durable car that it did not wear out quickly. The result was a substantial and growing market for used "Tin Lizzies," as the Model T was affectionately called. One could easily buy a used Model T for one-tenth the price of a new one. And as owners became

more prosperous, they wanted to trade up from the bare-bones Model T to something a little fancier, perhaps a Chevrolet from General Motors.

The development of consumer credit, pioneered by GM's creation of the General Motors Acceptance Corporation, further fueled the demise of the Model T. As long as purchasers had to pay the entire cost up front, in cash, the cheapest car was the best buy. Once they could pay for it over time, however, the desire for additional features quickly outstripped the interest in rock-bottom pricing. GM took advantage of the new economic reality by creating a full gamut of makes and models, from the low-end Chevrolet, through midrange Oldsmobiles and Buicks, to the luxurious Cadillac.

General Motors also began introducing mechanical innovations such as hydraulic brakes and electric starters. Typically, such devices would be first introduced on high-end models; as economies of scale lowered production costs, they would be added to progressively lower-tier models. GM executives also realized that customers would be willing to pay a premium for a fully enclosed car that would remain comfortable in all kinds of weather.

Henry Ford resisted the tides of change as long as he could. When company executives presented him with the prototype of an improved car to replace the Model T, Ford literally tore it up. By 1926, sales of the Model T were rapidly declining, and GM's sales were steadily growing. The following year, Ford closed all of his factories for six months to retool, after which he brought out the Model A. More than 300,000 of the new cars were sold before the first one rolled off the assembly line. The half year of downtime had been a critical setback, however, and GM pulled into first place in U.S. car sales. Never again would Ford dominate the world automobile industry, and the company faced competition for second place from a new rival, Chrysler.

By the early 1930s, most of the smaller car manufacturers had been bought out by one of the Big Three or had been killed off by the Great Depression. The oligopoly of the Big Three would remain unchallenged as rulers of the U.S. automobile industry until the rise of foreign imports after World War II.

Leigh Kimmel

See also: Automobiles and Automobile Culture; Federal Highway Act of 1921; Ford, Henry; Sloan, Alfred P.; Technology.

Further Reading

Brinkley, Douglas. *Wheels for the World: Henry Ford, His Company, and a Century of Progress.* New York: Viking, 2003.

Kyvig, David E. *Daily Life in the United States, 1920–1939: Decades of Promise and Pain.* Westport, CT: Greenwood, 2002.

Volti, Rudi. *Cars and Culture: The Life Story of a Technology.* Westport, CT: Greenwood, 2004.

Automobiles and Automobile Culture

The automobile was invented in the late nineteenth century. Henry Ford perfected the mass production of inexpensive automobiles in the first decade of the twentieth century, but the rise of a distinctive mass automobile culture awaited the beginning of Jazz Age prosperity in the United States. In 1919, American automakers produced roughly 1.6 million cars; by the end of the 1920s, that figure had risen to 4.6 million, an increase of nearly 300 percent. Total registration of cars (new and used) topped 23 million by

No technology did more to change the way Americans entertained themselves than the automobile. Here, hundreds of motorists and their families escape city heat for a July Fourth weekend on Nantasket Beach outside Boston in 1925. *(Hirz/Hulton Archive/Getty Images)*

1929. In fact, as the Great Depression set in, humorist Will Rogers noted that Americans would be the first people to drive to the poorhouse, as they were more likely to give up their house and livelihood than their cars. Such was the fascination with and increasing necessity of the auto.

Creating Demand

Several forces drove the automobile culture in the 1920s. One was the automobile industry itself. While Ford had subscribed to the idea that simplicity and cost would attract consumers, other automakers—most notably General Motors (GM)—came to realize that cars were more than mere transportation devices; they were a means by which consumers could establish an identity for themselves. While Ford famously said customers could choose any color as long as it was black, GM began offering a spectrum of colors and styles, meeting almost every budget and lifestyle. The company also pioneered the idea of annual model changes, making it necessary for fashion-conscious consumers to purchase a new auto before their old one wore out.

More fundamental changes in auto design also made the product more attractive in the Jazz Age. By the mid-1920s, the closed body style was the most common, allowing people to drive year-round without additional foul-weather gear. Technical innovations allowed the driver more "creature comforts," such as windshield wiper blades, locking doors, and heaters. The first car radios were introduced by Motorola in the 1920s. Under the hood, engines were less complicated and required less maintenance, enabling more people to drive.

Car companies made it easier to purchase their product. During the 1920s, a number of automakers introduced installment payments, using the car itself as collateral on the loan taken to buy it, a crucial development given that automobiles were the most expensive purchase in any consumer's life other than a home. In addition, more affordably priced used cars became available for purchase from dealers, independent car lots, and private individuals.

Developments in the transportation infrastructure were another factor in the creation of the automobile culture. While America had been knit together by a web of railroad tracks by the early twentieth century, its intercity road system was rudimentary, with almost no paved roads outside urban areas. This inadequacy became apparent to the government shortly after World War I, when an army convoy of ninety vehicles took several months to make its way from the East Coast to San Francisco. At the time, individual states were wholly responsible for highway construction, and interstate road-building was not coordinated. As a result, many highways ended at state lines. In 1921, Congress passed the Federal Highway Act, setting standards for intercity highways and committing $75 million in matching funds for states to build the roads. The tax on gasoline was raised to pay for this expenditure.

Finally, the automobile created its own demand. Like many innovative products, the automobile soon seemed indispensable. As suburbs spread out from the burgeoning cities of the 1920s, the car became essential for commuting to urban centers for work or entertainment, though this form of transportation would remain the preserve of the middle and upper classes until after World War II. Farmers found the automobile critical to ending their isolation from neighbors and to providing access to towns where they could purchase the new goods being made available by American industry.

Impact on the Economy and Government

The automobile industry became increasingly critical to the American economy in the 1920s. A huge employer and a major source of investment and profit, automobile manufacturing created a host of sub-

sidiary industries. Solid tires damaged paved surfaces and made for a very uncomfortable ride. Companies such as Firestone, Goodyear, and Michelin accommodated the need for new pneumatic tires.

AC Delco, Motorcraft, and Champion supplied parts for the various automakers. For people who did not wish to own a car but needed the advantages of one, the Yellow Cab Company and Hertz Rent-a-Car were founded. Insurance companies began offering policies to cover automotive accidents. The use of heavy trucks also increased on the highways of America. Many transport companies saw a niche that trains could not fill, supplying smaller quantities of goods to more locations, and often in better time for short distances. Gasoline stations, repair shops, and road construction companies proliferated.

Automobiles also filled government coffers with licensing fees, traffic fines, parking fees, and gasoline taxes. But cars created problems as well. Regulating traffic required states to form special police or patrol units to set and enforce driving rules and speed limits. By 1929, twenty-two states had established some sort of state highway patrol system to contend with the onslaught of cars, trucks, and other motorized vehicles on the roads. Another aspect of control was the development of a unified system of highway markings, including stop signs and the lane lines painted on road surfaces.

Changes in Lifestyle

Automobiles changed the ways Americans recreated. Teenagers and young adults found in the automobile an escape from home, a place where they could experiment with intimacy away from their parents' gaze. Couples and families soon began vacationing by automobile, creating a new hospitality infrastructure of motels, auto camps, and drive-in restaurants.

Automobiles also gave rise to a new spectator sport. Auto racing, which was growing in popularity before World War I, expanded in the 1920s. In fact, the origins of the NASCAR stock-car racing circuit took hold in the Jazz Age. Bootleggers and law enforcement officers of the time often had the same kind of car; whether rum-runners could escape pursuing authorities was a matter of their own mechanical abilities and the fine tuning of their cars. When the new racing league was formed, it was based on the premise that all cars started out equal but could be tuned for better performance and driver handling.

For all its impact on American life during the Jazz Age, the automobile culture did not fully penetrate many areas of the country, nor had automobile ownership become ubiquitous. It would take the sustained economic boost following World War II to achieve that. Certainly the 1920s offered a preview of how the automobile would dominate life in America in the second half of the twentieth century and beyond.

James Ciment and Cord Scott

See also: Automobile Industry; Federal Highway Act of 1921; Ford, Henry; Leisure and Recreation; Sloan, Alfred P.; Travel and Tourism.

Further Reading

Davies, Pete. *The American Road*. New York: Henry Holt, 2002.

Goddard, Stephen. *Getting There: The Epic Struggle Between Road and Rail in the Twentieth Century*. Chicago: University of Chicago Press, 1996.

Gregory, Ross. *Almanacs of American Life: Modern America 1914 to 1945*. New York: Facts on File, 1995.

Kasczynski, William. *The American Highway*. Jefferson, NC: McFarland, 2000.

McShane, Clay. *The Automobile: A Chronology of Its Antecedents, Development, and Impact*. Westport, CT: Greenwood, 1997.

Aviation

Among all the new technologies that emerged in the United States during the Jazz Age, none stimulated the imagination of the American people more than aviation. And for good reason. The airplane represented the transportation mode of the future, and pilots of both sexes created a whole new genre of celebrity at a time when the burgeoning mass media was helping to create the celebrity culture itself. On the economic and financial side, the foundation of the aviation industry—construction, passenger and freight transport, and military applications—was laid or built upon in the 1920s.

Design Innovation

At the end of World War I, the airplane was barely fifteen years old, but the necessities of warfare had given rise to significant innovations in aircraft design, and the progress continued through the 1920s. Better aerodynamics and engine design gave new planes the ability to carry greater weight, travel longer distances, and fly at greater speeds and higher altitudes. Critical to this last development was the invention by General Electric's Stanford Moss of super-charging technology, which allowed aircraft engines to operate with less oxygen intake, crucial for high-altitude flying.

Innovations in electronics helped as well, including steady improvements in flight instruments. Pilots at the beginning of the decade flew by dead reckoning, landmark observation, and a feel for their aircraft's operation. By 1929, military aviator and innovator James Doolittle—who would earn fame for conducting the first aerial bombing of Tokyo in World War II—had proved that a pilot could fly by instrumentation alone.

Government contracting—particularly by the military—helped push technological innovation, but many inventions were the product of the new aircraft industry itself. Like most new industries in America, this one started out with a number of smaller firms that were gradually bought out by larger ones. By the end of the 1920s, U.S. aircraft construction was dominated by three major players: Boeing, McDonnell-Douglass, and Lockheed. Notably, though, none of these three produced the decade's most popular and versatile aircraft, the Ford Trimotor, whose large, enclosed fuselage revolutionized freight and passenger transport.

As in the case of military aircraft design, the development of the air freight industry was spurred by government contracting. Demand for rapid delivery led the U.S. Post Office to develop airmail and to contract with private companies for its delivery. Mail contracts—especially after passage of the Airmail Act of 1925—helped fledgling companies like Pan American Airways, American Airlines, and Delta Airlines get off the ground in the 1920s. The Post Office also established the first air postal routes, many of which became the standard air routes that would last into the twenty-first century. In 1926, Congress passed the Air Commerce Act, which helped regulate what had been a freewheeling industry by setting federal standards for the licensing of pilots and inspections for the flightworthiness of aircraft.

Despite all the technological innovations, aircraft were largely unable to fly at sufficiently high altitudes to avoid turbulence. Thus, passenger air service was only for the hardiest of travelers. While trains could offer luxury accommodations, air travel remained drafty, bumpy, and even painful. The only seeming advantage of air travel—speed—was undercut by the fact that most planes could not fly safely at

Pan Am

Throughout much of the twentieth century, the blue globe logo of Pan American Airways was the symbol of the new mobility made possible by advances in commercial aviation. Although there were other international carriers, Pan Am epitomized sophisticated travel for millions of Americans, offering those who could afford it the chance to wing their way to exotic locations virtually anywhere in the world.

Pan Am's birth, however, was anything but sophisticated. The airline was the brainchild of Juan Trippe, a former Wall Street broker who turned to the fledgling airline industry in the mid-1920s in search of a more exciting career. He got plenty of excitement when he decided to launch the country's first overseas international airline route. Along with several wealthy investors, Trippe founded the Florida-based Aviation Corporation of America in the summer of 1927 to ferry mail from Key West, Florida, to Havana, Cuba. To secure the federal contract, however, the airline had to begin service by October 19. Unfortunately, Trippe had no planes; the Fokker model he had ordered was still being built. Scrambling, he chartered a plane from the failing West Indian Aerial Express in the Dominican Republic and beat Washington's deadline by a slim twenty-four hours. Three months later, on January 16, 1928, the airline flew seven passengers from Key West to the Cuban capital, launching the first regularly scheduled international airline route in U.S. history.

As the year progressed, Trippe and his fellow investors acquired other local carriers, merging them into a new company, which they dubbed Pan American World Airways, or Pan Am for short. They also moved the company's headquarters to the larger and more lucrative market of Miami, a shift made possible by the airline's purchase of the newly designed, longer-range Fokker F10 Trimotor.

With their own runway—no commercial airport existed in Miami yet—Pan Am's facility, officially known as Dinner Key (as if it were on an island in the Florida Keys), represented a new level of traveling sophistication. Passengers and special guests were served elegant meals in the upper-deck restaurant. While dining, they could watch Pan Am's growing fleet of planes—soon called Pan Am Clippers, after the swift sailing ships of the nineteenth century—arrive from Havana and other exotic locales in the Caribbean and South America. In 1929, Pan Am merged with Grace Airways, which offered flights from Buenos Aires, Argentina, more than 4,000 miles away. By the end of the 1920s, Pan Am was flying mail and passengers to destinations throughout Latin America.

Pan Am would continue to expand in the 1930s and through the 1950s and 1960s, the golden age of high-class jet travel. But airline deregulation and increased competition from low-cost carriers began to cut into Pan Am's profits beginning in the 1970s. In 1991, the great pioneer of American overseas aviation in the Jazz Age was forced to file for bankruptcy. The last Pan Am plane touched down on December 4, 1991.

James Ciment and David A. Serafini

Although still in its infancy in the 1920s, commercial aviation offered well-heeled and intrepid travelers—including these boarding an American Airlines sleeper plane—a faster way to reach their destinations. *(MPI/Hulton Archive/Getty Images)*

night, as instrumentation was not advanced enough even by the end of the decade. To offset this problem, some airlines offered packages of train and air travel, with passengers flying during the day and transferring to trains at night. Not surprisingly, many aviation experts in the 1920s believed that lighter-than-air ships, or dirigibles—far more comfortable, if slower than planes—represented the future of passenger air travel.

More successful were developments in the field of military aviation. World War I had demonstrated the value of aircraft in warfare, especially in providing reconnaissance. In 1922, the U.S. Navy commissioned its first aircraft carrier, the USS *Langley*, and during the Nicaraguan intervention of 1927, aircraft were used to strafe and harass guerrillas fighting the U.S. forces. Airships represented an alternative to heavier-than-air aircraft for reconnaissance and even bombing missions, though their slower speeds made them vulnerable to attack by fighter aircraft first introduced in the middle of World War I.

Stunt Pilots and Record Setters

Throughout the decade, aviation remained largely the preserve of aces, daredevils, and endurance pilots. An abundance of surplus World War I pilots and planes led to the formation of stunt clubs. With such colorful names as the Black Cats or the Flying Circus,

pilot clubs put on shows that amazed the crowds on the ground. Stunts ranged from relatively simple barrel rolls to dangerous maneuvers in which a passenger moved from a speeding car or motorcycle to a low-flying plane. The trick of guiding a plane through an open set of barn doors gave rise to the term for exhibition stunt flying—barnstorming.

As flyers set endurance and speed records, their demands on aircraft helped push technological innovation. In 1926, Robert Byrd became the first person to fly over the North Pole, and in 1929, he was one of the first to fly over the South Pole. To further the pursuit of flight records, newspapers and other companies sponsored trophies such as the Bendix Cup, for the fastest speed recorded on a triangular course, and the Schneider Cup, for nonstop transcontinental travel.

The Orteig Prize, sponsored by French-born New York hotelier Raymond Orteig, inspired the greatest aviation achievement of the decade. Putting up $25,000 in prize money, Orteig challenged any pilot to fly solo across the Atlantic. In May 1927, former airmail pilot Charles Lindbergh became the first to accomplish the feat, flying nonstop from Long Island, New York, to an airstrip just outside Paris, France, in thirty-three and a half hours, making him an instant international celebrity.

Throughout the Jazz Age, flight was mostly the domain of such celebrities and pioneers rather than ordinary Americans. It would take the rapid innovations of World War II, the invention of the jet engine, and the development of pressurized cabins for millions of Americans to take to the air.

James Ciment and Cord Scott

See also: Byrd, Richard E.; Lindbergh Flight (1927); Technology; Travel and Tourism.

Further Reading

Bilstein, Roger. *Flight in America 1900–1983: From the Wrights to the Astronauts.* Baltimore: Johns Hopkins University Press, 1994.

Dwiggins, Don. *The Barnstormers: Flying Daredevils of the Roaring Twenties.* Blue Ridge Summit, PA: TAB Books, 1981.

Edwards, Jim, and Wynette Edwards. *Images of America: Chicago—City of Flight.* Chicago: Arcadia, 2003.

Lomax, Judy. *Women of the Air.* New York: Dodd, Mead, 1987.

Lopez, Donald. *Aviation: A Smithsonian Guide.* New York: Macmillan, 1995.

Bailey v. Drexel Furniture Company (1922)

In its 1922 ruling in the *Bailey v. Drexel Furniture Company* case, the U.S. Supreme Court declared that a federal tax on companies that use child labor was unconstitutional. Although the Constitution grants Congress the right to impose taxes, the Court ruled that this was not a tax per se, intended primarily to raise revenue, but a regulatory fee on commerce within a single state. This, the justices determined, was not a right granted to Congress by the Constitution and was therefore reserved to the states under the Tenth Amendment. In a broader context, the decision—like the 1923 ruling against minimum wage laws in *Adkins v. Children's Hospital*—was part of a conservative, probusiness backlash against progressive legislation during the 1920s.

Child labor had been part of American life since early colonial times, with young people being put to work on family farms and in family workshops. With the advent of the Industrial Revolution in the early nineteenth century, however, child labor moved away from the home and into factories and mines. Many employers preferred children to adult workers because they worked for less pay and were more docile. The hours were often long and the work conditions harsh, to the detriment of the children's health and education. Such concerns led to a consensus by the end of the century that child labor had to be outlawed or heavily regulated. By 1900, laws of varying effectiveness were enacted in most states.

North Carolina, the site of the Drexel Furniture Company, was one state that resisted the trend, as its thriving furniture industry relied on child labor. The federal government, under the progressive President Woodrow Wilson in the 1910s, sought a national ban on most forms of child labor, particularly in industrial settings. The Supreme Court, however, had long since determined that working conditions in individual states were not directly within the purview of the federal government. President Wilson and Congress, therefore, had to find a way around such restrictions.

The first attempt was the Keating-Owen Act of 1916, which banned goods produced by child labor from moving across state lines. Interstate commerce could be regulated by Congress, according to previous Court decisions. Nevertheless, the Supreme Court overturned Keating-Owen in *Hammer v. Dagenhart* (1918), ruling that the Tenth Amendment reserves control of production to the states. In other words, production was not interstate commerce, so Congress could not regulate it. This went against previous rulings regulating the flow of manufactured goods, but the Court dismissed such caveats by saying that its previous decisions had involved dangerous goods, such as adulterated foods.

The progressives in Congress were not easily dissuaded. They knew that the Supreme Court had granted the legislative branch great leeway in the realm of taxation. The one exception had been the progressive income tax, forcing proponents to amend the Constitution with the Sixteenth Amendment. Also, the Supreme Court had upheld a tax on margarine, so Congress decided it was on solid ground in taxing manufactured goods. In 1919, Congress passed the Child Labor Tax Law, which imposed a 10 percent excise tax on the net profits of companies that employed children (under age sixteen in mines and under age fourteen in factories). In September 1921, the Bureau of Internal Revenue (predecessor to the Internal Revenue Service) assessed the Drexel Furniture Company of North Carolina a tax bill of more than $6,000 for employing an underage child. The company paid the tax, demanded a refund, and filed suit to get it.

Writing for the majority in the *Bailey* decision, Chief Justice William Howard Taft expressed concern that if the Court permitted such a tax, it would give Congress a green light to impose restrictions that infringed on the power of states as reserved to them under the Tenth Amendment. After *Bailey*, federal efforts to regulate child labor ended for the rest of the 1920s, since progressives lost control of Congress, and conservative Republicans had little interest in passing legislation opposed by the business community.

With President Franklin D. Roosevelt and the New Deal in the 1930s, the ban on child labor was put back on the national agenda. In 1938, the Fair Labor Standards Act and other legislation banned most forms of child labor. A more liberal Supreme Court declared the measure constitutional in 1941.

Scott Merriman and James Ciment

See also: Child Labor; Labor Movement; Law and the Courts.

Further Reading

Burton, David Henry. *Taft, Holmes, and the 1920s Court: An Appraisal.* Madison, NJ: Fairleigh Dickinson University Press, 1998.

Hindman, Hugh D. *Child Labor: An American History.* Armonk, NY: M.E. Sharpe, 2002.

Hobbs, Sandy, Jim McKechnie, and Michael Lavalette. *Child Labor: A World History Companion.* Santa Barbara, CA: ABC-CLIO, 1999.

Renstrom, Peter G. *The Taft Court: Justices, Rulings, and Legacy.* Santa Barbara, CA: ABC-Clio, 2003.

Baker, Josephine (1906–1975)

Josephine Baker, sometimes referred to as the "Black Venus," was one of the African American entertainers who brought the Jazz Age to Europe, introducing ragtime, the cakewalk, and jazz to a continent exhausted by the barbarities of World War I. Although Baker earned her fame initially from her scanty dance costume, she was a multitalented stage entertainer, singer, and film actress who remained a star for more than half a century.

She was born Freda Josephine McDonald on June 3, 1906, in the slums of St. Louis. Her mother was a washerwoman and sometime dancer, and her father was a vaudeville drummer who abandoned the family soon after her birth. Baker's career began early. By age thirteen, she was dancing professionally in vaudeville and on Broadway. She was fortunate enough to arrive in New York during the Harlem Renaissance, an outpouring of cultural expression by African Americans, and in 1922 she performed in Eubie Blake and Noble Sissle's hit African American musical, *Shuffle Along.* At first just a member of the chorus line, by 1924 she had earned a starring role in Blake and Sissle's *Chocolate Dandies.* While these pro-

The expatriate African American entertainer Josephine Baker became a sensation in Jazz Age Paris with her exotic beauty and sensual stage routines, including her famous "banana dance." *(Walery/Stringer/Hulton Archive/Getty Images)*

ductions transformed Broadway with their infusion of contemporary African American dance and music, other elements of the production were not far removed from minstrelsy, a traditional stage genre in which African Americans acted to white stereotypes.

In Paris, Baker personified *le jazz hot* in *les années folles* (crazy years), as the French called the Jazz Age, making her first European appearance in 1925 as a member of the Revue Nègre, a company of Harlem musicians and dancers. The show was wildly successful because of its dances (especially the Charleston), its music (New Orleans saxophonist Sidney Bechet was one of the players), its references to Africa and the primitive, and its exotic costumes and nudity. In *La Danse Sauvage,* between Baker and an African dancer, Joe Alex, Baker entered virtually nude, carried upside down on Alex's shoulders as his captured prey, then slid sinuously to the ground. Baker's dancing then demonstrated a vitality of the body that audiences had never seen before. Paris went crazy over Baker, who was showered with expensive gifts and marriage proposals.

In 1926, she left the Revue Nègre for star billing at the Folies Bergère, a famed musical theater, where she performed her notorious "banana dance," a sinuous performance where her body was garbed with little more than a string of bananas around her waist. She then opened the first of a series of Parisian night-clubs, all under the name Chez Joséphine. She also toured in Europe and South America. But she failed spectacularly in the Ziegfeld Follies, a leading musical revue of 1936.

Paris and Berlin, however, were particularly receptive to African American performers, and African American performers felt comfortable in those cities after their experience of racism in the United States. Black music and dance were part of the more general movement of primitivism in the avant-garde arts of the period (following Pablo Picasso's discovery of African sculpture around 1906), and Baker was cele-brated by avant-garde sculptors, painters, and writers. Western artists celebrated *l'art nègre* (Negro art) for its supposedly intuitive creative impulses, even while stereotyping black performers and artists as essentially primitive beings. Africans were also seen by Western audiences as more purely sensual and African women as more sexualized than their white counterparts. Baker played to this stereotype in her Folies "banana dance," in which she portrayed a jungle maiden, Fatou, who climbed backward out of a tree and moved seduc-tively toward a sleeping white hunter.

Even as Baker acted the part of the African primitive on stage, she was transforming herself off-stage into an elegant cosmopolitan, a glamorous im-age not then possible for African American performers in the United States. She was also gaining notoriety as a singer. Baker lived lavishly, spending liberally on clothes, jewelry, and exotic pets. She was the most photographed woman in the world in her day, and by 1927, she was earning more money than any other performer in Europe.

Baker continued a larger-than-life existence after the Jazz Age. Married five times, she also had many lovers. During World War II, she worked with the French Red Cross and, after the fall of France in 1940, was an active member of the resistance movement, for which she was much honored. At her estate in the Dordogne, she adopted twelve children from around the world (her "Rainbow Tribe") to prove that chil-dren of different ethnicities and religions could be a

family. Meanwhile, her public stance against racism and discrimination earned her some condemnation in the United States, especially during her infrequent re-turns in the 1950s and 1960s. By the 1970s, however, her native country was beginning to offer her the ac-claim she had long known in Europe. Baker died in Paris on April 12, 1975, just days after starring in a show celebrating her half-century onstage.

Marty Roth

See also: Dance, Performance; Jazz; Theater.

Further Reading

Gates, Henry Louis, Jr., and Karen C.C. Dalton. "Josephine Baker and Paul Colin: African American Dance Seen Through Parisian Eyes." *Critical Enquiry* 24:4 (1998): 903–34.
Hammond, Bryan, and Patrick O'Connor. *Josephine Baker.* London: Jonathan Cape, 1988.
Martin, Wendy. "'Remembering the Jungle': Josephine Baker and Modernist Parody." In *Prehistories of the Future: The Primitivist Project and the Culture of Modernism,* ed. Elazar Barkan and Ronald Bush. Stanford, CA: Stanford University Press, 1995.
Rose, Phyllis. *Jazz Cleopatra: Josephine Baker in Her Time.* New York: Doubleday, 1989.

Baldwin, Roger (1884–1981)

Roger Nash Baldwin was a cofounder, in 1920, and first executive director of the American Civil Liber-ties Union (ACLU). His experiences before and dur-ing World War I convinced him that the rights of minorities would not always be respected, and that only legal public action would enable members of minority groups to exercise their constitutional rights. During the 1920s, he was able to enlist the leading attorneys and philanthropists of the day to bring the public's attention to the need for civil liber-ties.

Early Life

Baldwin was born on January 21, 1884, in Wellesley, Massachusetts. His father was a manufacturer, and both sides of the family could be traced back to the Pilgrims. As a young man, he developed interests in art and nature, and his Unitarian family instilled in him a commitment to public service. After earning bachelor's and master's degrees from Harvard Univer-sity, he moved to St. Louis, Missouri, in 1905 to teach sociology at Washington University and work part-time at a settlement house. Two years later, he was appointed chief probation officer for the juvenile court of St. Louis. His experiences over the next three years enabled him to write *Juvenile Courts and Probation* (1912), a highly regarded text that became a standard in the field for the next half-century. During this time, he adopted two boys, but both died as young men.

In 1909, Baldwin had attended a lecture by the anarchist Emma Goldman that marked a turning point in his life. Until that time, he had been a moderate progressive reformer who believed that American institutions were essentially good and that greater control by the people would improve conditions. Goldman's views, as well as opposition by the majority of Americans to racial equality and birth control, convinced Baldwin that radical change was necessary.

In 1917, Baldwin joined the American Union Against Militarism (AUAM), an organization opposed to U.S. entry into World War I. With the Socialist Norman Thomas, he founded the National Civil Liberties Bureau (NCLB) to defend draft resisters and conscientious objectors. The organization lobbied for alternative service for conscientious objectors and advised them on possible legal actions. The AUAM leadership was uncomfortable with Baldwin's activities, however, and later that year he reestablished the NCLB as an independent organization. Baldwin widened the NCLB's focus to include freedom of speech and the press and the defense of citizens against the 1917 Espionage Act. The government came to regard the NCLB as a dangerous radical organization.

When Baldwin was called upon to register for the draft in September 1918, he refused. Arrested, tried, and convicted, he was sentenced to a year in prison. His response at trial, a statement defending civil liberties, was a model of the philosophy he supported throughout his adult life. While in prison, Baldwin kept active by writing to his friends and organizing the prisoners into a cooperative league.

Baldwin was released in July 1919 and shortly thereafter married Madeleine Doty, a pacifist and feminist. With her encouragement, Baldwin spent six months roaming the United States and experiencing life as an unskilled worker. He joined the International Workers of the World (IWW, or Wobblies) and served as a union spy in a steel strike in Pittsburgh.

American Civil Liberties Union

In January 1920, while living in New York, Baldwin joined with other civil libertarians in reconstituting the NCLB as the American Civil Liberties Union. He would serve as the ACLU's executive director and driving force for the next thirty years. Especially during the organization's early years, he concentrated on the constitutional rights he valued most—racial equality and the freedoms of speech, press, and assembly.

During the 1920s most Americans regarded the ACLU as a radical organization that threatened the existing order. The Ku Klux Klan was on the rise, federal agents were rounding up suspected leftist radicals and subversives in the Red Scare, and nativist sentiment was reflected in popular and governmental opposition to immigration. Following Baldwin's principle that speech should never be censored for its content, the ACLU represented labor, immigrants, Klan members, and political leftists.

Without Baldwin, according to many historians, the ALCU might not have survived the antithetical nature of the 1920s. The organization's survival can be credited to Baldwin's energy, personal charisma, dedication to the cause, and extensive network of acquaintances. The board of directors consisted mostly of notables that he recruited, including Helen Keller, Norman Thomas, Felix Frankfurter, and Jane Addams. He was also able to recruit top lawyers to work for the ACLU cause, and most did so without pay. His passion and high principles also succeeded in raising funds among wealthy patrons. Baldwin accepted a salary of only $2,500 and donated funds from his writings to the organization.

At first, Baldwin hesitated to use litigation to pursue his goals, doubting that the courts would sympathize with the unpopular minorities he represented. During the 1920s the courts were almost uniformly antagonistic to expanding civil liberties. Instead, the ACLU relied on direct action—mostly demonstrations and political action by groups. Baldwin participated in many demonstrations in favor of free speech. He was arrested in 1924 during a demonstration in Paterson, New Jersey, in which he was attempting to read the Declaration of Independence. In 1927, the New Jersey Supreme Court reversed Baldwin's conviction, one of the few victories for freedom of assembly during this time.

The ACLU offered legal assistance in some of the most famous cases of the 1920s. At the ACLU's urging, Clarence Darrow represented John Scopes, a teacher in Tennessee, in the famous 1925 "Monkey" trial, for teaching the theory of evolution. ACLU lawyers also filed legal challenges to the roundup and deportation of radicals, and provided assistance to the anarchists Sacco and Vanzetti when they were tried for murder in 1921. Other notable ACLU clients during the 1920s included the author James Joyce, labor unions, the Ku Klux Klan, and Jehovah's Witnesses. Although Baldwin personally disagreed with some of their positions, he supported their right to free speech and full legal representation.

Baldwin continued his support of political radicals into the 1930s but became increasingly more moderate during the course of that decade. The success of the New Deal convinced him that government institutions could be used to help the poor and minorities. He became disillusioned with communism as the evils of the Stalin regime in the Soviet Union came to light. In 1940, he pushed through a measure to keep supporters of totalitarian regimes off the board of the ACLU. Elizabeth Gurley Flynn, a founding member of the ACLU and a close friend of Baldwin, was ejected.

In 1942, Baldwin helped establish the International League for the Rights of Man, later redesignated the International League for Human Rights. During World War II, he objected to the forced relocation of Japanese Americans but did not protest other limits on civil rights. Baldwin supported government measures during the Cold War and became a lifelong supporter of FBI director J. Edgar Hoover after Hoover promised to refrain from domestic surveillance.

Baldwin retired from the ACLU in 1950, but he remained active in the campaign for civil liberties. He was awarded the Presidential Medal of Freedom by President Jimmy Carter in January 1981. Baldwin died in Oakland, New Jersey, on August 26, 1981.

Tim J. Watts

See also: American Civil Liberties Union; *Gitlow v. New York* (1925); Law and the Courts; Palmer, A. Mitchell; Red Scare of 1917–1920; *Schenck v. United States* (1919); Scopes Trial (1925).

Further Reading

Carnes, Mark C. *Invisible Giants: Fifty Americans Who Shaped the Nation but Missed the History Books.* New York: Oxford University Press, 2002.
Cottrell, Robert C. *Roger Nash Baldwin and the American Civil Liberties Union.* New York: Columbia University Press, 2000.
Klein, Woody, and Roger Nash Baldwin. *Liberties Lost: The Endangered Legacy of the ACLU.* Westport, CT: Praeger, 2006.
Lamson, Peggy. *Roger Baldwin, Founder of the American Civil Liberties Union.* Boston: Houghton Mifflin, 1976.
Walker, Samuel. *In Defense of American Liberties: A History of the ACLU.* New York: Oxford University Press, 1990.

Baseball

The Jazz Age began with the darkest scandal in baseball history, a conspiracy by members of the Chicago White Sox to throw the 1919 World Series. But baseball also witnessed a golden age, when newsreels and radio broadcasts, a new free-swinging style of play, and the emergence of stars like Babe Ruth and Lou Gehrig made baseball, already America's favorite spectator sport, even more popular and profitable. And though the era's pervasive racism kept African American players out of the major leagues, black businessmen stepped up to the plate in 1920 to form a popular alternative, the Negro leagues.

The origins of baseball as a spectator sport date back to the mid-nineteenth century and the formation of the first amateur and semiprofessional baseball clubs in New York and other East Coast cities. By the late nineteenth century, many of the clubs had turned professional and were part of the National League, founded in 1876. Twenty-five years later, the American League was created, and in 1903, the team with the best record from each league began playing a yearly championship known as the World Series. During the first two decades of the twentieth century, baseball grew in popularity. New stadiums were built in New York, Chicago, Boston, Philadelphia, and other cities as the average number of spectators for a game increased from thousands to tens of thousands.

End of the Dead Ball Era

The era preceding World War I was a heyday of great pitchers such as Grover Cleveland Alexander, Walter Johnson, and Cy Young. One of the reasons for this was the ball itself. Because baseballs were expensive—about $70 each in 2007 dollars—owners generally kept the same ball in play through a whole game. By the end of nine innings, the ball was usually soft and dirty, hard to see and hard to hit. Thus, despite a few great early twentieth-century hitters like Ty Cobb and Honus Wagner, games were usually low-scoring, defensive matches, with outcomes often hinging on bunts, singles, and stolen bases.

In 1920, two rules were introduced that ended this "dead ball" era in major league baseball. First, tampering with the ball was prohibited, ending a practice whereby pitchers rubbed spit and other substances on the ball's surface to make it harder for batters to hit. Second, umpires were told to put a new ball in play when the existing one got scuffed or dirty. A cleaner ball was easier for the batter to see and once hit, a firmer ball traveled a longer distance. This made the game safer—a dirty, hard-to-see ball was blamed for the 1920 hit-by-pitch death of Cleveland Indian shortstop Ray Chapman—and potentially more exciting.

These changes were part of an array of reforms that the major leagues undertook in the wake of the Black Sox scandal, in which a number of Chicago White Sox players allegedly took payoffs from professional gamblers to throw the 1919 World Series to the Cincinnati Reds. In 1920, fearing that the scandal would keep fans away from the game, team owners agreed to discard the game's weak oversight

committee and replace it with a new, more powerful presiding officer, or commissioner. Kenesaw Mountain Landis, a federal judge with a reputation for honesty and toughness, was hired as the game's first commissioner. Landis immediately barred eight of the offending White Sox players from the game, and in his twenty-four years as commissioner, he made the office independent of the owners. While Landis had frequently ruled against organized labor as a judge, he now sought to rein in the kind of exploitive labor practices engaged in by owners like Charles Comiskey of the White Sox. According to many observers of the game, the Black Sox scandal had its origins in Comiskey's low pay scale and mean-spirited treatment of players.

Babe Ruth and the New Media

New equipment and a strong commissioner helped revive the sport, but it was a single player—a hard-living, bandy-legged, reform-school graduate named George Herman "Babe" Ruth—who set the stage for baseball's emergence as a truly mass spectator sport in the 1920s. Ruth's career paralleled the changes in the game. Signed by the Boston Red Sox as a pitcher in 1914, Ruth began playing first base and outfield in 1918, becoming a leading home-run hitter. In 1920, he was traded to the New York Yankees. Now playing in America's largest city, and the nation's media capital, Ruth became an instant star with his extraordinary long-ball hitting. Permanently shifted to the outfield, he slugged fifty-four home runs in his first full season with the Yankees, fifty-nine in his second, and sixty in 1927—a record that would stand for thirty-four years.

Ruth's power hitting drew millions of new fans to the sport and changed the way baseball was played. It also brought great fortunes to the owners and high salaries to a select few stars. Ruth earned as much as $100,000 in a season, an extraordinary sum for the day. By the end of the 1920s, a host of new hitting stars—including the Yankees' Gehrig, the Philadelphia Athletics' Jimmie Foxx, and Hack Wilson of the New York Giants and Chicago Cubs—had emerged as the stars of the game, replacing the pitching heroes of the pre–World War I era. Yet it was the Yankees and their "murderers row" of long-ball hitters who dominated the sport during the 1920s, winning six American League pennants and three World Series titles. Many baseball historians and fans consider the 1927 Yankees—with their 110 wins and 44

Major League Baseball's first commissioner, Judge Kenesaw Mountain Landis, helped restore the game's image after the 1919 Black Sox scandal, in which members of the Chicago White Sox conspired with organized crime figures to throw the World Series. *(National Baseball Hall of Fame Library/Major League Baseball/Getty Images)*

losses, a .714 winning percentage—the greatest team in the history of the sport.

Enhancing the renown of these larger-than-life players was a new larger-than-life stage. At a time when there were no major league teams west of St. Louis or south of Washington, D.C., the new media of the 1920s brought the sport home to millions, even if they lived hundreds of miles from a stadium. Newsreels, first introduced in the late 1910s but gaining in popularity with the advent of sound in 1927, offered highlights of the week's games to movie audiences across the country. Improvements in photography and the introduction of tabloids like the New York *Daily News* led to expanded baseball coverage, with plenty of fast-action photos. But it was radio—with its ability to allow distant fans to listen to games in real time—that had the greatest potential to expand baseball's popularity. While some team owners, notably Chicago Cubs' William Wrigley, Jr., embraced the new medium, others feared that it would cut into ticket sales, as fans would stay home and listen to the game rather than come to the stadium to watch it.

Negro Leagues

In the late nineteenth century, a number of African American baseball players competed on integrated professional squads. But beginning in the 1870s, various leagues moved to ban them from play. By the 1890s, there were no integrated clubs left. In response, a number of all-black teams were established, beginning with the New York Cuban Giants in 1885. Early efforts to organize the teams into a league failed, however, due to lack of money and leadership. In 1920, Rube Foster, a former player with various black teams, brought together several African American businessmen and team owners, and together they established the Negro National League (NNL). The new all-black professional circuit consisted of eight teams in the Midwest and was governed by the National Association of Colored Professional Base Ball Clubs.

In 1923, two NNL team owners in Philadelphia, Pennsylvania, and Atlantic City, New Jersey, broke with the league to form the rival Eastern Colored League (ECL). Animosity and player-raiding gave way, by the end of 1924, to cooperation and the establishment of the first Negro World Series. But disputes over player contracts and a lack of money led to the disbanding of the ECL in the middle of the

1928 season. The ECL was replaced by the American League in 1929, but both leagues ultimately succumbed to the harsh economic times of the Great Depression. New leagues would not emerge until the late 1930s. These African American leagues would end for good when integration came to major-league teams in the late 1940s and early 1950s.

Baseball continued to gain in popularity through the Great Depression and World War II, experiencing a second golden age in the 1950s and early 1960s. Most serious fans of the game and sports historians agree that, regardless of the level of talent—and great baseball players have emerged in every era of the game—the sport reached its pinnacle of popularity in that first great age of spectator sports, the 1920s.

James Ciment

See also: Black Sox Scandal; Landis, Kenesaw Mountain; Leisure and Recreation; Radio; Ruth, Babe.

Further Reading

Rader, Benjamin G. *Baseball: A History of America's Game.* Urbana: University of Illinois Press, 2002.

Seymour, Harold. *Baseball.* New York: Oxford University Press, 1960.

Wallop, Douglass. *Baseball: An Informal History.* New York: W.W. Norton, 1969.

Beauty Industry and Culture

Like many other consumer-oriented businesses in the United States, the beauty industry—cosmetics and hair and nail products—underwent a dramatic transformation during the 1920s. This was closely related to a variety of economic and social trends, including a shift away from local production toward nationally recognized brands, and the increased reliance on advertising to promote the products. In addition, the rise of chain stores offered lower prices and wider distribution, making previously expensive items more affordable.

Also at work were modernizing forces that strongly impacted the growing beauty industry. One was the women's rights movement and the social liberation that followed the successful crusade for women's suffrage, achieved with ratification of the Nineteenth Amendment in 1920. Women felt freer to experiment with new ideals of beauty, including more daring fashions and a more liberal use of cosmetics. The Jazz Age was marked by a new explicitness in the public display

The Miss America Pageant

It was the summer of 1921. Conrad Eckhold, owner of Atlantic City's Monticello Hotel, had a problem—how to keep tourists in the southern New Jersey beach resort town, and at his hotel, after the traditional Labor Day end to the summer holiday season. Meeting with other members of the city's Hotelmen's Association, Eckhold suggested a festival of entertainment and activities that would include a two-day beauty pageant called "Atlantic City's Inter-City Beauty Pageant." The winner would be awarded a three-foot-high Golden Mermaid trophy.

The organizers brought other cities into the contest by having newspapers throughout the Northeast sponsor local beauty contests and inviting the winners to Atlantic City for the finals. Eight contestants participated in the first pageant, held September 7–8. The winner was sixteen-year-old Margaret Gorman from Washington, D.C., whose long hair and Cupid's bow mouth gave her a striking resemblance to Hollywood star Mary Pickford. Having drawn some 150,000 attendees to the festival, the organizers realized they had struck tourist gold. They also knew that, hands down, the beauty pageant was the highlight of the festival.

The following year, the contest was a significantly bigger affair. It was stretched to three days in order to present the fifty-seven contestants and to allow for an evening gown segment as well as the original bathing suit competition. As the event had become a truly national affair—contestants came from as far away as Los Angeles and Seattle—it was fitting that the winner be known as "Miss America." The crowd was bigger too, with no fewer than 250,000 watching the crowning of fifteen-year-old Mary Catherine Campbell of Ohio.

In an age of headline-grabbing publicity stunts and media events, the Atlantic City beauty contest was one of the biggest. Even the august *New York Times* ran extensive coverage of the event in 1923, including contestant pictures, biographies, and detailed descriptions of their outfits. Artist Norman Rockwell joined the panel of judges, which crowned Campbell a winner for the second year in a row. No longer was the pageant just about who looked best in a bathing suit or gown. Now the contestants were judged in several categories, such as form, carriage, health, features, simplicity, training, adaptability, character, and personality. Talent would not be added until 1935.

By 1924, the contest was a national sensation, with the winner that year—Ruth Malcomson of Philadelphia—receiving offers to star in Broadway shows and Hollywood movies. Malcomson, however, turned them all down, preferring to return to her life as a social worker. The 1925 winner, Fay Lanphier of California, was not as humble, accepting a starring role in *The American Venus,* a feature film about the contest.

Still, the Miss America pageant was not without its critics or scandals. There were instances of married women and professional models and actresses competing. Conservatives and Evangelical Christians complained about its effects on the morals of America's youth. But such carping could not halt the popularity of the contest, which continued to attract national attention long after the Jazz Age.

Abigail B. Feely

of the female body, and the new openness was a radical departure from the ideals of Victorian times.

All of the changes were promoted not just by advertising but also by a popular new mass entertainment medium: movies. Now, women and men in big cities and small towns alike were exposed to the latest fashions and cosmetics, up close and larger than life on the silver screen.

Products and Brands

Beauty products represented a high-growth industry. Revenues climbed from about $14 million in 1909 to more than $140 million in 1929, with much of the growth coming in the last ten-year span. Key to the increase was the rise of national chain stores. By 1929, Woolworth's, the largest chain store in America, enjoyed annual sales of roughly a quarter-billion dollars.

Chain stores operated in urban centers, small towns, and the newly emerging suburbs around major cities. They used economies of scale and efficient distribution systems to bring costs down and make beauty products, among other items, affordable to more women. They also offered greater choice and a new democratic atmosphere to buying. Before World War I, most beauty goods were sold in salons, where working women often felt intimidated and unwelcome. Chain stores, by contrast, afforded buyers relative anonymity. The stores were mostly self-service, and women could try on different and more daring applications of cosmetics without risking the disapproval of salon patrons and owners.

One product in particular illustrated the new trends in cosmetics buying: lipstick. Prior to World War I, rouge and face powder were the most popular makeup items, but they were relatively expensive, and women usually had to apply them carefully, in the home. In 1915, however, American entrepreneur Maurice Levy invented a metal sheath for lip rouge, allowing women to carry it with them in a purse or pocket. The innovative design also facilitated mass production and distribution of the new product. Lipstick, cheap and portable, came in a wide array of colors, offering a quick and easy way for women to personalize their look. By the end of the Jazz Age, lipstick was the most widely sold cosmetic product in America.

With sales of cosmetics and other beauty products growing rapidly, new entrepreneurs moved to exploit the expanding market. The beauty industry represented one of the few commercial arenas in which women played a significant role. Two immigrant women, Elizabeth Arden from Canada and Helena Rubinstein from Poland, both of whom marketed nationally recognized lines of cosmetics under their own names, were among the most successful beauty product manufacturers of the decade—and beyond.

Nationally distributed brands also guaranteed a certain level of quality. The Food and Drug Act of 1906 had outlawed the use of harmful ingredients and misleading labeling. The creation of national brands further assured consumers that they were getting consistent quality.

Advertising was a major force both in the growth of the cosmetics industry in general and in the establishment of brand loyalty. Between 1915 and 1930, advertising expenditures on beauty products in the top thirty mass-circulation magazines grew from $1.3 million to $16 million annually. Advertising dollars spent on the new medium of radio between 1927 and 1930 soared from $300,000 annually to $3.2 million.

A New Aesthetic

The ideal of feminine beauty changed significantly during the Jazz Age but did not represent a complete break from the past. Makeup was usually applied conservatively, to emphasize chastity and delicacy, a look captured in the virginal, wraith-like film stars of the prewar era, most notably Lillian Gish and Mary Pickford, both of whom used makeup to downplay their features. Eyebrows were carefully plucked, mascara barely applied, and lip rouge used to form the tiniest of Cupid's bow mouths.

Several trends in the 1920s helped to supplant that virginal ideal of feminine beauty with a more sexualized image. Growing urbanization and the political and economic liberation it afforded women freed growing numbers of working women from the constraints of church, family, and community. The birth control movement in the 1920s signaled a new willingness of women to accept their sexuality rather than repress it. The most glaring symbol of this sexual liberation was film star Theda Bara, who flaunted her screen persona as a seductive vamp with revealing outfits and highly stylized cosmetics—kohl-lined eyes, heavy applications of mascara, and reddened lips—applied by makeup artists such as Rubinstein and Max Factor. Films and advertising increasingly emphasized physical attractiveness as an important attribute of a woman's identity.

The result was the sexualized image of the flapper, the young, liberated, hedonistic by-product of the women's rights movement and the carefree Jazz Age. The flapper represented the antithesis of the Victorian ideal of feminine beauty. Her makeup was flashy, with brightly painted lips, and her clothes were revealing. Throughout the 1920s, hemlines steadily rose from just above the ankle to a scandalously short length that left the knees exposed. Stockings tended to be sheer. Sleeves disappeared, leaving arms and shoulders bare.

The flapper also presented a notably androgynous look. Women cropped their hair short, wearing it bobbed, with straight bangs across the forehead and tight curls around the temples. Rather than corseting the waist, which pushed the breasts up to form the classic hourglass figure, women often used undergarments to flatten their breasts. While at first glance this androgynous look seemed to deemphasize female sexuality, it in fact enhanced it by making women appear free and independent.

The androgynous effect also applied to the male aesthetic of the 1920s. Both men's and women's fashions emphasized the lithe, tapered look, and men's hairstyles emphasized a highly stylized cut, similar to the bob, with a sleekness achieved through beauty products. The new men's style was personified by Hollywood's first male sex symbol, Rudolph Valentino. Again, advertising and the silver screen helped establish the new aesthetic.

Historians often cite the 1920s as the birth of modern American society, with its mass forms of entertainment, its liberated sexuality, and its nationally advertised consumer culture. Nowhere was this more evident than in the growing beauty industry and the newly sexualized ideal of feminine beauty, established by Madison Avenue and Hollywood, and taken to heart by increasing numbers of urbanized and liberated women.

Leslie Rabkin and James Ciment

See also: Advertising; Fashion, Women's; Retail and Chain Stores.

Further Reading

Dotson, Edisol Wayne. *Behold the Man: The Hype and Selling of Male Beauty in Media and Culture.* New York: Haworth, 1999.
Peiss, Kathy. *Hope in a Jar: The Making of America's Beauty Culture.* New York: Metropolitan, 1998.
Scanlon, Jennifer. *Inarticulate Longings.* New York: Routledge, 1995.
Sivulka, Juliann. *Soap, Sex, and Advertising.* Belmont, CA: Wadsworth, 1998.

Beiderbecke, Bix (1903–1931)

Known for his clear, melodic cornet playing, Leon Bismark "Bix" Beiderbecke was one of the first white jazz musicians to influence black musicians, and the melodic nature of his playing is thought to have had an influence on the development of early jazz. He died young of alcohol-related ill health, quickly becoming synonymous with the Roaring Twenties.

Born in Davenport, Iowa, on March 10, 1903, Beiderbecke had a relatively comfortable, middle-class upbringing. Despite tutoring from a piano teacher, he never learned to read music. In his teens, he often sat on the banks of the Mississippi listening to the jazz bands playing on passing steamboats. After hearing a number of recordings by the Original Dixieland Jass Band in 1919, he was inspired to buy a cornet and teach himself to play. By the end of the year, he was performing at school events and in local groups; by 1921, he was leading his own jazz ensemble, the Bix Beiderbecke Five.

Because of his poor grades, his parents sent him to Lake Forest Academy in September 1921. Its proximity to Chicago resulted in frequent trips to the city that ultimately led to his dismissal from the school in May 1922. He spent the next year traveling back and forth between his home in Davenport and jazz gigs in Chicago. In April 1923, Beiderbecke met Frankie Trumbauer, an alto saxophonist then appearing at the Davenport Coliseum; the two would work together on and off for the rest of Beiderbecke's life. At the end of 1923, Beiderbecke joined Chicago's Wolverine Orchestra (named after the song "Wolverine Blues" by blues great Jelly Roll Morton), and the band enjoyed significant success in the following year. The Wolverine Orchestra recorded several sets for the Gennett Record Company, where Beiderbecke made his first recording. Released in May 1924, "Fidgety Feet" earned him recognition as one of the country's most creative cornet players.

In October 1924, Beiderbecke left the Wolverine Orchestra to join the Jean Goldkette Orchestra, only to quit in December after a frustrating few months. Goldkette's orchestra had a more formal setup requiring band members to use written scores, while the Wolverine had provided a more improvisational structure better suited to the cornetist's talents. In January 1925, Beiderbecke moved to Richmond, Indiana, where, with an ensemble called Bix Beiderbecke and the Rhythm Jugglers, he recorded the first of his own compositions, "Davenport Blues." The Jugglers were a quintet that featured Paul Mertz on piano, Don Murray on clarinet, Tommy Gargano on drums, and future bandleader Tommy Dorsey on trombone.

Under pressure from his parents, Beiderbecke enrolled at the University of Iowa in the spring of 1925. When academics got in the way of his playing, however, he dropped out, moving around the country and sitting in with various groups such as the California Ramblers of New York, the Charlie Straight Orchestra in Chicago, the Breeze Blowers in Michigan, and the Frank Trumbauer orchestra of St. Louis. He stayed with Trumbauer until May 1926, when both musicians joined the Jean Goldkette Orchestra. This time the experience was more positive for Beiderbecke, not least because of Bill Challis, who joined as the band's arranger in September 1926. Challis's arrangements were much more accommodating to Beiderbecke's improvisatory style.

As Beiderbecke toured the Northeast and Midwest in 1927 with the Goldkette Orchestra, recording for radio and the Victor label, his playing became increasingly fluent and inventive. He, Trumbauer, and small groups of musicians from the orchestra and other bands made a series of seminal recordings as either Frankie Trumbauer and His Orchestra or Bix Beiderbecke and His Gang, including such tracks as "Singin' the Blues," "Clarinet Marmalade," and "Goose Pimples." In September, Beiderbecke recorded his second composition, the impressionistic piano solo "In a Mist," for Okeh Records; the piece would become one of his best-known works.

When the Goldkette Orchestra folded because of financial difficulties, Beiderbecke and Trumbauer joined the world-famous Paul Whiteman Orchestra. During the winter of 1927 and throughout 1928, the band toured the country. Beiderbecke also returned to the recording studio, producing his classic "From Monday On." His last recording with Whiteman was in September 1929, "Waiting at the End of the Road," part of a set that he was unable to finish due to illness.

Beiderbecke's health was deteriorating rapidly in these years, owing to excessive consumption of bootleg gin. As a result, his life was punctuated with trips to hospitals and recuperation time in Iowa. His performances became erratic, and though he played with a range of famed musicians, from Hoagy Carmichael to Benny Goodman to Gene Krupa, he did not record much. He briefly led a group in September 1930 but used the years 1930–1931 primarily to work on his piano compositions, resulting in "Candlelights," "Flashes," and "In the Dark." Beiderbecke died on August 6, 1931.

His influence was most apparent among white musicians, but Beiderbecke was one of the first white musicians to be admired by black musicians, particularly trumpet players, including Louis Armstrong, Rex Stewart, and Doc Cheatham. More broadly, his influence on the early development of jazz was in his lyricism, for which he was universally admired. He was one of the first American jazz musicians to integrate elements of European classical music, notably harmonic concepts.

Sam Hitchmough

See also: Jazz.

Further Reading

Berton, Ralph, and Nat Hentoff. *Remembering Bix: A Memoir of the Jazz Age.* New York: Da Capo, 2000.
Lion, Jean Pierre. *Bix: The Definitive Biography of a Jazz Legend.* New York: Continuum International, 2005.

Berger, Victor (1860–1929)

Victor Luitpold Berger was a Socialist leader from Milwaukee, Wisconsin, who served in the U.S. House of Representatives (1911–1913; 1923–1929), edited and published prominent Socialist newspapers, and gained national notoriety when he was refused his seat in Congress and sentenced to prison in 1919 for denouncing U.S. entry into World War I.

Born on February 28, 1860, in Nieder Rebbach in the Austrian Empire, Berger considered himself ethnically German but was also of Jewish heritage. His family emigrated to the United States in 1878 and settled in Milwaukee, where he taught in the public schools and a synagogue, met German Socialists after joining the German immigrant social organization Turnverein, and edited workers' newspapers: the *Arbeiter Zeitung* (Newspaper of the Workers) and *Wisconsin Vorwaerts* (Forward). In 1897, Berger joined Social Democracy of America, an advocacy group for producer cooperatives, and he played a leading role in the formation of the more politically oriented Social Democratic Party in 1898. This group evolved into the Socialist Party of America.

Berger served as leader of the Milwaukee Socialists and what was called the right wing or "sewer Socialists" of the national party. As editor and publisher of the *Social Democratic Herald* from 1901 to 1913 and the *Milwaukee Leader* from 1911 to 1929, Berger pushed his ideas of constructive socialism. Based on the revisionist Marxism of Eduard Bernstein, this type of socialism advocated electoral success, gradual local reform, including building sewers and parks, and gaining support of trade unions. It differed from the left-wing alternative of direct action, revolution, and support from only industrial unions. Berger's ideas led to political success in Milwaukee when he won a seat as alderman in 1910 in an election dominated by Socialists.

Building on his local success, Berger secured his first term in the U.S. House of Representatives in 1911, becoming the first Socialist to serve in that body. From this position, Berger fought for worker and civil rights, such as public ownership of utilities, women's suffrage, and universal health insurance. While a passionate advocate for the average worker, Berger was not always inclusive. He called for immigration restriction to protect jobs and wages of American-born workers from Asians, Latin-Americans, and Africans, who he believed lacked understanding of the Socialist concept of working-class solidarity. Berger faced mounting criticism from the left wing of his own party, who saw his actions in Congress as gradualist reform measures that only delayed the pending working-class revolution.

Divisiveness stemming from World War I gained Berger his most enduring fame. Berger opposed America's entry into the Great War because he desired world peace, and he considered the conflict orchestrated by capitalists and fought by workers. His position was popular with Milwaukee's large German population. With passage of the Espionage Act in 1917, Berger encountered legal difficulties. Restrictions on second-class mailing of subversive materials all but wiped out his *Milwaukee Leader,* while his strident opposition to the war led to federal indictments issued in March 1918. However, Berger won election to the U.S. House of Representatives in November 1918. Judge Kenesaw Mountain Landis found Berger guilty of subversion in 1919 and sentenced him to twenty years in prison, a decision that Berger appealed. But the House refused Berger his seat because of his conviction, his supposed pro-German sympathies inferred from antiwar remarks, and his supposed pro-Bolshevik stance.

In truth, Berger despised the Kaiser's government but defended the right of the people of Germany to protect their sovereignty against what he deemed an aggressive czarist Russia. Berger, along with other members of the right wing of the Socialist Party, condemned the Bolsheviks for their violence and undemocratic nature, a move that ultimately split the party. After Berger was refused his seat in Congress, a special election was held to fill the vacant seat. Berger again won and, in January 1920, again was denied his seat. The seat remained vacant for the term.

In 1921, in *Berger v. United States,* the U.S. Supreme Court reversed Berger's conviction because Landis's strong anti-German prejudice prohibited a fair trial, and recent Supreme Court decisions had added "clear and present danger" to the definition of subversion. All cases against Berger were dropped in 1922.

Berger remained politically active during the 1920s despite the declining importance of American socialism. Like many other postwar Socialists, he endorsed the idea of a labor party that united radicals and reformers. He supported the 1922 campaign of Progressive Republican Robert La Follette for U.S. senator from Wisconsin, despite decades of sniping between the two over the merits of government regulation versus government ownership of business. Berger supported La Follette again in 1924 when he ran for president on the Progressive ticket. Nevertheless, La Follette's insistence that Communists be excluded from the convention of this new coalition of farmers and workers drew sharp criticism from Berger, who preferred that the Communist minority be rebuked on the convention floor by the democratic-minded majority rather than through systematic exclusion.

Berger won elections to the U.S. House of Representatives in 1922, 1924, and 1926. During each term, he continued to fight for the rights of American workers by pushing for public housing, unemployment insurance, and old-age pensions. He lost re-election in 1928 in part because the national party refused to endorse the repeal of Prohibition, an issue of importance to Milwaukeeans because of the brewing industry and large ethnic German population. Nevertheless, socialism remained a vital force in Milwaukee politics into the 1950s in large measure because of Berger's early influence as organizer and propagandist. Berger died on August 7, 1929, after being hit by a streetcar.

Thomas F. Jorsch

See also: Red Scare of 1917–1920; Socialism and the Socialist Party of America.

Further Reading

Judd, Richard W. *Socialist Cities: Explorations into the Grass Roots of American Socialism.* Albany: State University of New York Press, 1990.

Miller, Sally M. *Victor Berger and the Promise of Constructive Socialism, 1910–1920.* Westport, CT: Greenwood, 1973.

Berlin, Irving (1888–1989)

One of the most popular and prolific songwriters in American history—with more than 3,000 songs, sixteen film scores, and numerous Broadway musicals to his credit—Irving Berlin established himself as a major figure in American music, theater, and film during the Jazz Age, even as his personal life included great tragedy. Berlin's life story was the classic rags-to-riches tale of a poor immigrant who attained enormous professional and financial success over the course of a lifetime that spanned most of the twentieth century.

Born Israel Beilin on May 11, 1888, in Tyumen, western Siberia, Russia, he was the youngest of eight children of Moses and Leah Beilin. When he was five, the Beilins immigrated to America, fleeing the persecution of anti-Semitic pogroms in Russia. They arrived at Ellis Island in September 1893, and immigration officials changed the family's name to Baline. The Balines settled into a tenement on New York's Lower East Side, where Moses, a rabbi, found employment certifying kosher poultry. After his father's death in 1901, Israel dropped out of school to sell newspapers while his siblings worked in sweatshops. Ashamed at his meager contributions to the family's earnings, he left home at age thirteen to fend for himself.

At first he made a living singing in saloons. By age fifteen, he was employed as a singing waiter at a restaurant in Pelham, just north of the city, where he taught himself to play piano. In 1907, at the request of his employer, he wrote the lyrics to "Marie from Sunny Italy" as the signature song of the restaurant. He split the seventy-five-cent advance with his collaborator, pianist Nick Nicholson. When his name was misprinted on the sheet music as "I. Berlin," he liked the sound of it and adopted the name Irving Berlin.

Over the course of the next decade, Berlin composed a number of Tin Pan Alley ragtime hits, rollicking show tunes, and dance numbers. He made a brief foray into melancholy waltzes and ballads, including "When I Lost You" (1912), a heartfelt tribute to his young wife, Dorothy Goetz, who had contracted pneumonia and typhoid fever during their honeymoon in Cuba and died just five months after their wedding.

In 1918, Berlin was drafted into the U.S. Army. Stationed at Camp Upton in Yaphank, New York, he staged the musical *Yip! Yip! Yaphank,* casting more than 300 soldiers for the musical extraordinaire. After World War I, Berlin wrote a number of songs with none too subtle lyrics rooted in social and political commentary, such as "That Revolutionary Rag" (1919), about the Russian Revolution; "Prohibition" (1919), a humorous ditty in which bartenders, chorus girls, laborers, and soldiers mourn the death of alcohol with the ratification of the Eighteenth Amendment; and "Leg of Nations" (1920), which spoofed President Woodrow Wilson's League of Nations, proposing instead an international league of beautiful women.

In 1919, theater producer Florenz Ziegfeld hired Berlin to write a number of songs for his Ziegfeld Follies stage show. Berlin's contributions included such songs as "A Pretty Girl Is Like a Melody," "Mandy," and "I'd Rather See a Minstrel Show." Berlin continued to write for Ziegfeld throughout the 1920s.

In 1920, Berlin teamed up with musical producer Sam H. Harris to found and build the Music Box, a New York theater that would feature musical comedies. The theater opened in 1921 and featured Berlin's music in *The Music Box Revue* (1921–1924) and the Marx Brothers comedy *The Cocoanuts* (1925). Berlin's music debuted in Hollywood in the first motion picture with sound, *The Jazz Singer* (1927), featuring Al Jolson singing the hit song "Blue Skies."

Berlin was active in defending the legal rights of songwriters. In 1924, he successfully lobbied Congress to block the passage of a bill that would have exempted radio broadcasters from compensating songwriters. The following month he met and fell in love with a wealthy twenty-one-year-old socialite named Ellin Mackay. Although shunned by her anti-Semitic father and her socialite circle, the two had a happy marriage, until the tragic death of their two-year-old daughter, whose birth had inspired "Blue Skies."

Like many other Broadway actors, directors, and songwriters, Berlin was lured west by the lucrative opportunities of Hollywood, moving to Los Angeles in 1928. There, he wrote songs such as "Let Me Sing and I'm Happy" (1928, for the film *Mammy*), "Swanee Shuffle" (1929, for the film *Hallelujah!*), and "Puttin' on the Ritz" (1929, for the film of the same name) as the burgeoning motion picture industry continued to experiment with sound. While Berlin enjoyed enormous professional success in California, he also experienced more tragedy: on Christmas morning 1928, his infant son died of what would later be called "crib death." The Berlins would have two more children, Linda in 1932 and Elizabeth in 1936.

Berlin's career continued to prosper. He wrote numerous musicals and film scores, including *Face the Music* (1932), *As Thousands Cheer* (1933), *Top Hat* (1935), *Alexander's Ragtime Band* (1938), *Holiday Inn* (1942, winning an Oscar for his song "White Christmas"), *Annie Get Your Gun* (1946), *Easter Parade* (1948), and *White Christmas* (1954). He also wrote Dwight D. Eisenhower's presidential campaign songs of 1952 ("I Like Ike") and 1956 ("Ike for Four More Years"). In spite of ill health in his later years, he lived to be 101 years old. Berlin passed away in his sleep, at home in New York City, on September 22, 1989.

Jennifer Aerts Terry

See also: Jazz; Theater.

Further Reading

Barrett, Mary Ellin. *Irving Berlin: A Daughter's Memoir.* New York: Simon & Schuster, 1994.

Bergreen, Laurence. *As Thousands Cheer: The Life of Irving Berlin.* New York: Viking, 1990.

Freeland, Michael. *A Salute to Irving Berlin.* Santa Barbara, CA: Landmark, 1988.

Furia, Philip. *Irving Berlin: A Life in Song.* New York: Schirmer, 1998.

Jablonski, Edward. *Irving Berlin: American Troubadour.* New York: Henry Holt, 1999.

Bernays, Edward L. (1891–1995)

An innovator in the field of modern public relations, Edward L. Bernays developed tools and practices that enabled him to influence the general public to look favorably upon his clients. Using scientific methods, Bernays counseled his clients and worked behind the scenes to manipulate media coverage to their advantage.

Bernays was born on November 22, 1891, in Vienna, Austria. His father was a wealthy merchant and grain exporter; his mother was a sister of Sigmund Freud. The family moved to the United States when Bernays was one year old. After graduating from Cornell University in 1912, he was briefly employed by a grain merchant on the New York Produce Exchange, but Bernays was more interested in journalism, particularly in its ability to sell the public on ideas. He soon acquired a job as an editor and a promoter for the *Dietetic and Hygienic Gazette* and the *Medical Review of Reviews.*

Bernays saw the journals as a vital source of public information about human sexuality and safe practices. In 1913, he actively supported the production of *Damaged Goods,* a play about venereal disease. To raise public support for the play, he invited liberal, socially prominent individuals to join the Sociological Fund, an organization he created. The membership dues of $4 included a ticket to *Damaged Goods.* Bernays then used the example set by the illustrious citizenry to solicit general support for the project. The play was a success, and Bernays dropped his journalism commitments to work in public relations. Over the next three years, he publicized such stars as opera singer Enrico Caruso and the Ballets Russes.

When the United States entered World War I, Bernays became a member of newspaper publisher George Creel's Committee on Public Information, the U.S. government agency for propaganda. Bernays was responsible for directing Latin American News, the primary purpose of which was to secure popular and government support for U.S. policies in that part of the world. He later helped encourage employers to hire returning veterans.

Bernays's experience with the Creel Committee convinced him that there were new opportunities to exert influence on what was known then as the "mass mind." In 1919, he was part of the American delegation to the Paris Peace Conference. That same year, he opened an office to provide counsel on public relations to government, businesses, and individuals. In 1922, he married Doris Fleischman, one of his partners.

Bernays was careful to explain the distinction between his work and that of a press agent. While press agents merely got publicity for a client, public relations mediated between the client and the public, interpreting each to the other. As many corporations were interested in fostering a favorable image with the public, his firm soon prospered. His client list during the 1920s included General Motors, Liggett & Myers, Philco, Procter & Gamble, and the United Fruit Company.

Bernays, historians note, was not the first person to create and carry out a public relations campaign, but he was the first to use rigorous, scientific methods. He believed public relations should be based on social science methods, especially those of psychology. He taught the first college course on public relations, in 1923, at New York University, and wrote extensively on the subject. His book *Crystallizing Public Opinion* (1923) was highly regarded, and he followed it up five years later with *Propaganda.*

In his writings, Bernays went against the grain of generally accepted wisdom in the field of public relations—that a company's public image was best served through a full disclosure of all aspects of its business and that a public relations specialist's main job was to get a company's message across in as many possible forums as possible. Instead, he asserted, effective public relations was about shaping a company's message, promoting the positive and downplaying the negative. It also required an understanding of mass psychology. The public, Bernays argued, was essentially rational and typically made decisions and reached conclusions shaped by preconceived stereotypes.

One of his first clients was the Venida Hair Net Company, which faced ruin in the early 1920s because changing hairstyles did not require hairnets. Bernays undertook a campaign to publicize accidents that occurred when loose hair got tangled in machinery. He also supplied information about possible contamination in restaurants and bakeries if hair was not contained. Venida's business rebounded, and local governments passed ordinances requiring certain workers to wear hairnets.

When the luggage industry hired him to reverse a trend toward traveling light, especially among women, Bernays persuaded newspapers to print items in which social trendsetters advocated multiple changes of clothing for women who traveled. Luggage sales shot up. Procter & Gamble hired Bernays to increase sales of Ivory Soap. He responded with national contests for the best carvings from soap bars. Panels of noted artists judged the winners, and newspapers covered the stories. Again, sales increased.

In 1929, Bernays directed a celebration in Dearborn, Michigan, called Light's Golden Jubilee, held to honor Thomas Edison for his invention of the light bulb in 1879. Attended by such famous Americans as Henry Ford, John D. Rockefeller, Jr., and President Herbert Hoover, the celebration was covered in the national press, and the U.S. Post Office issued a special stamp. Bernays's role in the event, however, was mercenary, as he had been hired by the electric power industry to promote the installation of electricity in American homes.

Throughout his life, Bernays was assisted in his work by his wife, Doris, who made many contributions to their company's success and to the field of public relations. One of the most important was the development of *Contact,* a quarterly newsletter sent to media people around the country. The publication promoted their firm's work and helped attract new clients.

Bernays supported many liberal causes. During the 1920s, he handled publicity for the National Association for the Advancement of Colored People, and President Hoover appointed him to the Emergency Committee for Employment in 1930. During World War II, Bernays advised several federal agencies about their publications. After the war, he cut back on his public relations work. One of the last campaigns was for the United Fruit Company in the early 1950s, portraying Guatemalan leader Jacobo Arbenz, then threatening to nationalize some of the company's banana plantations, as a Communist sympathizer. The campaign helped generate support for a CIA operation that overthrew Arbenz in 1954.

In 1946, Bernays established the Edward L. Bernays Foundation to advise organizations on international communications and to encourage leadership in public relations, social responsibility within the business sector, and community service. Bernays officially retired in 1962, but he continued to advise clients until he was 100 years old. He died in Cambridge, Massachusetts, on March 9, 1995.

Tim J. Watts

See also: Advertising; Lasker, Albert.

Further Reading

Bernays, Edward L. *Biography of an Idea: Memoirs of Public Relations Counsel.* New York: Simon & Schuster, 1965.

———. *Crystallizing Public Opinion.* New York: Boni and Liveright, 1923.

Larson, Keith A. *Public Relations: The Edward L. Bernayses and the American Scene: A Bibliography.* Westwood, MA: F.W. Faxon, 1978.

Tye, Larry. *The Father of Spin: Edward L. Bernays and the Birth of Public Relations.* New York: Crown, 1998.

Birth Control

Following World War I, public access to birth control information and devices increased. Underlying the trend were a number of legal, social, political, technological, and economic developments. Still a largely taboo subject even in the Jazz Age, birth control nevertheless made major steps toward public acceptance and improved reliability during the 1920s.

Although the Comstock anti-obscenity law passed by Congress in 1873 still prohibited public dissemination of birth control information, two important court cases during the Jazz Age would help undermine some of the restrictions against the distribution of birth control information and devices. The first was *New York v. Sanger* (1918), in which a state appellate court decided that activist Margaret Sanger was not guilty of breaking state obscenity laws for distributing birth control advice and contraceptive devices. This decision allowed Sanger to reopen the birth control clinic that police had closed down in 1916. Sanger would go on to found the National Birth Control League (later known as Planned Parenthood) in 1921 to advocate birth control across the country, though it avoided breaking the Comstock law by not distributing explicit birth control information across state lines.

The second key case was *Young Rubber Corporation, Inc. v. C.I. Lee & Co.* (1930), in which the U.S. Court of Appeals for the Second Circuit decided that it was not against federal law to ship medicines or devices that might have a contraceptive use across states lines, as long as they had some other legitimate medical purpose. While the decision did not legalize the interstate trade in contraceptive devices, it did give manufacturers and distributors of such devices potential legal cover if they were prosecuted for violating the Comstock law.

The courts were responding in part to changing public opinion and a greater openness to discussing sexual issues. For the millions of U.S. soldiers serving overseas in World War I, European laws and customs, which allowed much greater discussion and distribution of birth control devices, were an eye-opener. At the same time, military officials became alarmed at the venereal disease epidemic that swept through the armed forces. The exposure to more liberal attitudes about sex and information about the spread of venereal disease eased the qualms of the medical profession, government officials, and the public at large about

discussing birth control, since the most popular device at the time, the condom, was also an effective prophylactic against the spread of venereal diseases.

The commingling of birth control with public health policy was also seen in the eugenics movement, which promoted improving the human race by preventing supposedly inferior people from breeding. Using "public health" as justification, a number of states passed forced sterilization laws aimed at "unfit" members of society, including mentally impaired persons and habitual criminals; in some Southern states, most of those sterilized were African Americans. In 1927, the U.S. Supreme Court upheld the constitutionality of such laws in its *Buck v. Bell* decision, upholding a Virginia statute calling for the forced sterilization of the "feeble-minded."

Technology and business also helped promote birth control in the 1920s. As states eased the legal restrictions, various companies entered the business of producing birth control devices. In 1925, J. Noah Slee, owner of the Three-in-One Oil Company and a supporter of Sanger's efforts, founded the Holland Rantos Company in Philadelphia to make diaphragms according to Sanger's specifications. Using ambiguous advertising that portrayed the diaphragm as a new feminine hygiene product—similar to the Kotex feminine napkin, introduced in 1921, and widely advertised by its maker, the Kimberly-Clark Corporation—Holland Rantos and other diaphragm makers were able to promote the use of contraceptives while skirting restrictive federal laws about the distribution of such devices.

Condom manufacturing also soared in the 1920s. The development of the disposable condom, the introduction of assembly-line manufacturing techniques, and better condom testing—through the use of electrical charges—helped reduce the cost of condoms and increase their availability and effectiveness. By 1930, U.S. manufacturers were producing nearly 1.5 million condoms a day.

While law, business, and technology contributed to the proliferation of birth control devices, ultimately it was changing attitudes about sexuality that helped gain greater acceptance for birth control. Premarital sex was still widely frowned upon in the Jazz Age, but increasing numbers of people were subscribing to the views of psychologists that sexuality was about more than procreation; it was a key ingredient to a healthy marriage and for mental health in general.

The result of such thinking and the increased social acceptance of birth control was the declining birth rate throughout the 1920s. Fertility rates, which had begun to fall in the early nineteenth century, now experienced a sharper decline. For women aged twenty to forty-four, the number of children under age five per 1,000 women dropped from 604 in 1920 to 511 in 1930, the greatest single-decade percentage drop in U.S. history other than the 1970s.

Still, it would take the law some time to catch up with the change in public attitudes. With *Griswold v. Connecticut* in 1965, the U.S. Supreme Court held that restrictions against the use of contraceptive devices by married couples were unconstitutional.

James Ciment and Kevin Kern

See also: Health and Medicine; Marriage, Divorce, and Family; Population and Demographics; Sanger, Margaret; Sex and Sexuality; Sheppard-Towner Act (1921).

Further Reading

McCann, Carole R. *Birth Control Politics in the United States, 1916–1945.* Ithaca, NY: Cornell University Press, 1994.

Meyer, Jimmy Elaine Wilkinson. *Any Friend of the Movement: Networking for Birth Control 1920–1940.* Columbus: Ohio State University Press, 2001.

Tone, Andrea. *Devices and Desires: A History of Contraceptives in America.* New York: Hill and Wang, 2001.

Black Sox Scandal

In 1920, eight members of the Chicago White Sox baseball team were accused of conspiring with gamblers to accept a cash payoff in exchange for deliberately losing the 1919 World Series against the Cincinnati Reds. Although a jury found them innocent of conspiracy charges, the players were permanently banned from professional baseball. This controversy, baseball's most notorious to date, was dubbed the "Black Sox Scandal."

The White Sox had won the 1917 World Series and were widely expected to win again in 1919. Throughout the season, however, dissension brewed in the locker room, with two factions—the more polished, college-educated players and their rougher teammates with little formal schooling—dividing the team and undermining morale and unity. Moreover, there was widespread dissatisfaction with team owner Charles Comiskey, chiefly for his unwillingness to pay his players competitive wages. Ironically, the nickname "Black Sox" was in vogue before the gambling scandal emerged; its original meaning arose when the players decided to stop washing their uniforms to protest Comiskey's mandatory laundry fee.

Arnold "Chick" Gandil, the Sox first baseman, is believed to have been the first of the team members to forge ties with a gambler, most likely Joseph "Sport" Sullivan of Boston. The proposed scheme was that Gandil would try to win the cooperation of several teammates, including pitchers Claude "Lefty" Williams and Eddie Cicotte, shortstop Charles "Swede" Risberg, third baseman George "Buck" Weaver, and outfielders Oscar "Happy" Felsch and "Shoeless" Joe Jackson. Sullivan would provide $80,000 to pay these players for their assistance in throwing enough games to ensure a Reds victory in the World Series. Meanwhile, a small-time gambler and former baseball player named "Sleepy" Bill Burns independently offered Gandil $100,000 to throw the series. Gandil agreed, mostly likely intending to accept both sets of bribes.

Gandil was able to get Williams, Cicotte, Risberg, Jackson, and Felsch to go along with the scheme. Another player, infielder Fred McMullin, overhearing talk of the deal, insisted on joining the conspiracy. Weaver refused to participate. For their part, gamblers Sullivan and Burns separately approached Arnold Rothstein, the gambling kingpin of New York, for financial backing. Rothstein apparently refused Burns, but he did grant Sullivan $80,000 seed money, giving him half before the series began and promising the remainder after the Sox lost.

But the gamblers' greed soon complicated things. Sullivan reneged on his agreement with Gandil, forwarding the player only $10,000, far less than the $100,000 he had promised. Then Rothstein's bodyguard, Abe Attell, who wanted to get in on the scam, contacted Burns and told him that Rothstein had changed his mind and would fully back his plan. Attell began searching for funds to back up his claim that Rothstein was now in on the deal with Burns.

As the series approached, and sports writers and fans expected the Sox to win, gambling odds ran heavily in their favor. Thus, gamblers with knowledge of the "fix," who were intending to bet on the underdog Cincinnati Reds, stood to win significant sums. But as more and more people became involved, it was harder to keep the secret; bets on the Reds rose and the odds against them sank dramatically, partially undermining the original bribery scheme.

Throughout the series, the gamblers made— and broke—several finance-related promises to the players. Burns and Attell never raised the money they had promised and, after the third game, dropped out of the scheme. Sullivan persevered longer, but he also fulfilled only part of his promises. Near the end of the series, the White Sox players decided to abandon the whole scheme and play to win, but a visit from Rothstein's thug, who threatened bodily harm against them, put an end to that idea.

Although rumors of the fix had surfaced, it was not until December 15, 1919, that news broke in the press. After that, Cicotte and Jackson were persuaded to speak to a grand jury, and Williams quickly followed suit. The trial against the gamblers and the players had to be delayed when depositions mysteriously disappeared. At the time, it was not illegal in Illinois for players to gamble on their own teams, nor was it illegal to deliberately lose a ball game. Accordingly, prosecutors charged Cicotte, Felsch, Gandil, Jackson, Risberg, Weaver, and Williams (charges against McMullin had been dropped) with several counts of conspiracy, including one stating that they had conspired to damage Comiskey's business. However, the team owner actually made significantly more money in 1920 than in 1919, undermining the case. The players were cleared of all charges, but their baseball careers were over.

In the wake of the scandal, team owners hired a tough federal judge named Kenesaw Mountain Landis in 1920 to serve as professional baseball's first commissioner and to help restore the image of the game. Landis then banned eight players implicated in the scandal: Cicotte, Felsch, Gandil, Jackson, McMullin, Risberg, Weaver, and Williams. As Landis noted, "Regardless of the verdict of juries, no player who throws a ball game, no player who undertakes or promises to throw a ball game, no player who sits in confidence with a bunch of crooked players and does not promptly tell his club about it, will ever play professional baseball."

Most sports historians agree that Landis's tough stance on the scandal helped baseball out of the worst public relations crisis in its history. During the rest of the Jazz Age, professional baseball would reach new heights of popularity.

Kelly Boyer Sagert

See also: Baseball; Landis, Kenesaw Mountain.

Further Reading

Asinof, Eliot. *Eight Men Out: The Black Sox and the 1919 World Series.* New York: Henry Holt, 1963.
Sagert, Kelly Boyer. *Baseball's All-Time Greatest Hitters: Joe Jackson.* Westport, CT: Greenwood, 2004.

Blues

During the Jazz Age, American audiences developed an appreciation for authentic musical forms such as the blues, which reached them through performances by traditional folk musicians, vaudeville revues, and concert orchestras, and in recordings and radio broadcasts. The blues had been recognized as a distinctive genre during the three decades before World War I, when the legacy of nineteenth-century minstrel shows and field hollers from the rural South established its lyric and musical patterns. At that time, the blues was a part of the general repertoire of "songster" performers, who entertained their audiences with a variety of popular songs.

African American composer and musician W.C. Handy was the most well-known interpreter of the blues during the Jazz Age. Having heard the basic twelve-bar, "AAB" lyrics of folk blues street performers in the South while traveling with his minstrel orchestra during the 1890s, Handy was composing his own version of blues music by the early 1900s, most famously in "Memphis Blues" (1912) and "St. Louis Blues" (1914).

After World War I, he became increasingly viewed as a society concert performer, and although his version was not considered authentic, Handy's music, along with that of bandleader Paul Whiteman, was the style of the blues that became most familiar to white audiences in America and Europe. They performed the blues as a simple form of jazz or gospel stylings that illustrated the humor and tragedy of black American culture. In the 1920s, professional voice teachers included the blues in their formal instruction. For example, Louis Aschenfelder, a New York City teacher in the mid-1920s, offered "interpretation of popular songs, jazz, and blues" to his students, along with the standard operatic training.

However, it was the vaudeville version of the blues that led to its visibility among the middle and lower-middle classes, and to its viability as a recorded product. Its favorable reception by mass audiences followed the paths of Tin Pan Alley sheet music and of traveling revues that featured song-and-dance numbers and a star performer. Ma Rainey, a blues singer who traveled with minstrel shows in the years leading up to World War I, was one of the earliest recognized vaudeville singers of the blues. She also had a direct influence on the emergence of Bessie Smith as a blues and jazz performer in the 1920s. Billed on tour as the "Empress of the Blues," Smith became the most successful blues singer in the vaudeville tradition, with such songs as "Down-Hearted Blues" and Handy's "St. Louis Blues."

The "race records" of the era resulted from the increased economic prosperity of both African Americans and whites following World War I, and from the improvement in sound-recording equipment. Jazz and blues recordings became available in 1917 and initially were aimed at white audiences. By 1920, however, the record-buying public had broadened to include African Americans who were bridging the gap between rural and urban life. In that year, a Cincinnati vaudeville blues singer named Mamie Smith traveled to New York and recorded "Crazy Blues" for Okeh Records, setting in motion a marketing push at African Americans. Columbia Records signed Bessie Smith, who recorded "Down-Hearted Blues" in 1923, and more than 180 songs in the next several years. These commercial successes led recording executives to seek out the traditional folk blues singers of the juke joints and crossroads of the South, such as Charley Patton of Mississippi and Blind Lemon Jefferson of Texas, and barrelhouse piano players in urban areas.

In 1928, Handy presented a Carnegie Hall concert of blues and ragtime with a cast of fifty musicians and singers, a performance before a mostly white, well-dressed audience that viewed the blues as part of the pageant of Americana. By this time, however, the popularity of blues was waning. Through the Great Depression, folklorists John and Alan Lomax recorded the folk blues of the South for the Library of Congress. This work and later research by African American scholars John W. Work and Lewis Wade Jones were the foundation for the folk blues revival of the post–World War II era, including the urban electric blues.

Kevin Grace

See also: Armstrong, Louis; Jazz; Migration, Great; Smith, Bessie.

Further Reading

Davis, Francis. *The History of the Blues: The Roots, the Music, the People from Charley Patton to Robert Cray.* New York: Hyperion, 1995.

Handy, W.C. *Blues: An Anthology.* New York: Da Capo, 1990.

Oliver, Paul. *The Story of the Blues.* Philadelphia: Chilton, 1973.

Bohemianism

Bohemianism refers to the tendencies, behaviors, and attitudes associated with certain counterculture groups, especially artists, writers, actors, students, and others who have seceded from the middle class. The term "bohemian" was used in fifteenth-century France to refer to gypsies, who were mistakenly thought to have been natives of the Czech province of Bohemia.

Ideas and Trends

American bohemianism, initially personified by the writers Edgar Allan Poe and Walt Whitman, emerged in the United States during the nineteenth century and peaked in the years just prior to the nation's entry into World War I. Among intellectuals and artists of the time, bohemianism was inseparable from the same reforming impulse that inspired early feminism, socialism, and even anarchism. Bohemians believed in personal liberation and were in rebellion against politics as usual, patriarchy, organized religion, militarism, capitalism, and middle-class values. Many bohemians and their reform-minded peers convinced themselves that a new age would be ushered in by virtue of their rebellious example.

Prewar bohemians generally drew no distinction between aesthetics and rebellion. They sought liberation through creativity. They favored the primitivism of French painter Paul Gauguin, the shocking realism of the Ashcan school, startling avant-garde works such as Marcel Duchamps's *Nude Descending a Staircase* (1912), and other revolutionary paintings exhibited at the Sixty-Ninth Regiment Armory in February 1913. They favored modernism, epitomized by the writing of James Joyce, T.S. Eliot, Ezra Pound, William Faulkner, and others. These new movements challenged conventional notions of art, literature, and reality. They also offended many in the middle class, thereby exposing the alleged philistinism of the bourgeoisie.

Beyond their admiration for iconoclastic art and radical ideas, bohemians showed their disdain for middle-class expectations by their openly decadent lifestyles. They did not value steady jobs, comfortable dwellings, or fashionable furnishings. Indeed, they romanticized the poor and made a virtue of poverty, even though many were from well-to-do families, had attended elite universities, and traveled in Europe. They advocated free love, they drank, and a few

Greenwich Village

Like most American communities, Greenwich Village—a low-rise section of Lower Manhattan in New York City—has undergone considerable change over the course of its history. In the early eighteenth century, it was a farming village isolated from Manhattan's commercial and population centers. It remained a bucolic suburb until the 1820s, when elegant Federal-style townhouses began to replace farms, particularly in the vicinity of Washington Square Park. The establishment of New York University in 1831 attracted art galleries, theaters, and other cultural institutions, as well as commercial enterprises.

The character of the district changed once again during the late nineteenth century with the arrival of immigrants from Germany, Italy, and Ireland. Many were laborers who found jobs at nearby breweries, warehouses, and docks. Some settled in houses that had formerly accommodated single families of the wealthy class but had since been converted into rooming houses and small apartments. Landlords and real-estate speculators created cheap housing by razing older residences and putting up tenements.

In the years between 1900 and World War I, Greenwich Village emerged as the symbolic center of bohemianism in the United States. For creative and unconventional people who sought an alternative to middle-class lifestyles, the Village provided a congenial setting. It was quaint and picturesque, with secluded side streets. Rents were low, cafés plentiful, and restaurants inexpensive. Manhattan's many art galleries, publishing houses, and cultural institutions were readily accessible. The Village also offered the stimulation of ethnic, cultural, and intellectual diversity, though class and ethnic differences sometimes generated conflicting expectations about public behavior. Because the Village's population was constantly in flux and the middle class outnumbered, no group was in a position to impose any kind of social orthodoxy. Bohemians and others could presume to live as they pleased, free of bourgeois constraints.

The Jazz Age brought significant change to Greenwich Village. The opening of the West Side subway and extension of Seventh Avenue through the district made it less self-contained. Industry moved out, and new residents, mostly professionals and businesspeople, flowed in. Zoning decisions to preserve the residential and architectural character of key blocks also had the effect of raising property values and stimulating residential construction. In addition, many landlords improved existing buildings and raised the rents. The net effect of these changes was to reduce population density, increase the proportion of native-born Americans in relation to immigrants and aliens, raise the average age, and increase the number of middle-class residents. Under the circumstances, many poor laborers and impoverished bohemians could no longer afford to live there.

During the 1920s and after, the Village's reputation for offbeat lifestyles and entertainments made it a tourist attraction, even though bohemianism waned significantly between 1917 and 1945. After World War II, the Village once again became a hotbed of counterculture, drawing the Beat Generation of the late 1940s and 1950s, the hippies of the 1960s and 1970s, and the gay, lesbian, and transsexual movement in the 1970s and 1980s.

William Hughes

experimented with drugs. They slept through the morning and lived for the night. They adopted modes of dress that made them instantly distinguishable from the more respectable elements of society. Women wore sandals and shapeless dresses made of coarse cloth; some smoked in public, a behavior much frowned upon in polite society. Men went ungroomed and wore rough flannel shirts.

Bohemianism was not confined to any single location, though its communities were based predominantly in cities. There were bohemias in San Francisco, Los Angeles, New Orleans, Charleston, Boston, Philadelphia, and even Lincoln, Nebraska, and Oklahoma City, all attracting bohemians from small towns and other regional backwaters. Bohemians seeking a temporary break from city life often gathered at such summer retreats as Provincetown, on Massachusetts's Cape Cod, or in Taos, New Mexico, or Carmel, California. But the most influential concentrations of bohemianism in the United States immediately before and after World War I were to be found in Chicago and New York City, particularly Greenwich Village.

Chicago bohemians included the unorthodox economist Thorstein Veblen, journalists Floyd Dell and Ben Hecht, novelists Theodore Dreiser and Sherwood Anderson, and poets Witter Bynner and Carl Sandburg. It was in Chicago that Harriet Monroe launched the famous little magazine *Poetry,* which promoted imagism and other avant-garde poetry. Like many others, Dreiser and Dell soon relocated to Greenwich Village, the true mecca of bohemianism. There Dreiser wrote his highly controversial, naturalistic novel *An American Tragedy* (1925), while Dell, in addition to writing novels, served as an associate editor of *The Masses,* a short-lived but vital journal of socialism and contemporary culture.

In its heyday, the Village attracted a number of people who, individually and collectively, made noteworthy contributions to art and thought in America. Among them were the arts patron Mabel Dodge, Socialist commentator Max Eastman, journalist John Reed, poet Edna St. Vincent Millay, and dramatist Eugene O'Neill. Dodge, sometimes labeled the "Queen of Bohemia," was a noted hostess and enthusiast for innovative thinkers, artists, and writers. Her well-publicized social gatherings attracted luminaries from all over the city, including the political philosopher Walter Lippmann, labor organizer Big Bill Haywood, radical journalist Lincoln Steffens, anarchist Emma Goldman, and birth control advocate Margaret Sanger, along with an assortment of bohemian writers, artists, and eccentrics. These events had the effect of both advancing progressive social and intellectual causes and promoting new directions in literature and the arts.

Eastman, the former academic who founded and edited *The Masses* and *The Liberator,* was equally influential, for he was in a position to encourage new writing, publicize innovations in the arts, and publish radical social and economic commentary. Reed was the leading foreign correspondent of his day, famed for his sympathetic firsthand accounts of the Mexican and Russian revolutions. Like Mabel Dodge, his sometime lover, Reed was at the center of a social circle that brought together bohemians and political radicals.

Millay, in her personal behavior as well as her poems, celebrated the sexual emancipation of women. She also wrote short plays for the Provincetown Players, a theatrical group named for the Cape Cod resort favored by East Coast bohemians. The Players later opened a theater in Greenwich Village, where they mounted inexpensive productions of new plays by American dramatists, including those of O'Neill, the most important American playwright of the first half of the twentieth century.

Inspired by the modern theater movement in Europe, personified by Strindberg, Ibsen, Shaw, Stanislavski, and Reinhardt, O'Neill employed expressionism, symbolism, and interior monologues in his plays, along with heavy infusions of Freudianism. Applying these modernist elements to American settings and circumstances, he forged the kind of drama that must have seemed revolutionary compared to the formulaic plays being offered on Broadway. Certainly the experimental works presented in the Village by the Provincetown Players could not have found a home in the commercial theaters of the period.

Decline in the Jazz Age

Bohemianism remained at the center of the cultural scene during the Jazz Age but it had lost much of its rebellious spirit. During World War I and after, political radicals came to view bohemianism as politically irresponsible and self-indulgent. Many bohemians, faced with a choice between art and politics, opted for art. Also, bohemianism no longer had a monopoly on youthful rebellion. The Jazz Age provided the young with a variety of avenues for self-expression and personal liberation without the bother of poverty (real or pretend) or the expectation of creativity associated with bohemianism. In addition, the bohemian impulse tends to diminish with the arrival of maturity or success, for bohemianism is typically a phase of life that occurs during youth. Many of those who had invigorated bohemianism simply grew up and moved on. Those who came after them did not have the same sense of breaking new ground.

Indeed, by the late 1920s, many of the battles for personal liberation had already been fought and won, while bohemianism had developed its own set of prescribed behaviors. The unconventional had become conventional; to affect bohemianism was to run the risk of being not a nonconformist but a stereotype. The most authentic American bohemians of the period were most likely abroad, among the expatriates who had flocked to Paris after World War I.

Three other factors contributed to the attenuation of American bohemianism during the 1920s: its commercialization, its selective acceptance by many in the middle class, and the impact of the Great Depression. Thanks in part to the public's fascination with *la vie de bohème,* a cagey entrepreneur such as Guido Bruno could profit by installing "poets" and "painters" in a Greenwich Village attic and selling tickets to tourists who wanted to observe bohemians in their natural setting.

Commercialization sanitized bohemianism, making it more widely acceptable, especially to those in the middle class for whom the work ethic and materialism no longer seemed sufficient. Like bohemians, they began to value leisure, personal creativity, and self-realization. Bohemianism had penetrated middle-class culture, but in the process it lost some of its decadence and much of its authenticity. Such was the appeal of this new mainstream bohemianism that Greenwich Village and other quaint bohemian haunts attracted real-estate investors, who acquired and improved properties, then raised the rents. Businesspeople and professionals moved in; artists and writers departed.

The collapse of the national economy after 1929 was the final blow to Jazz Age bohemianism. When so many were under duress, it would have been ridiculous—and unspeakably cruel—to glamorize or feign poverty, or demean what was left of a dwindling and insecure middle class. For the duration of the Great Depression, and then World War II, survival took precedence over the bohemian ideals of self-expression and personal liberation, just as in the arts

the experimental or avant-garde styles favored by bohemians gave way to social realism.

William Hughes

See also: Art, Fine; Jazz.

Further Reading

Aaron, Daniel. *Writers on the Left.* New York: Avon, 1965.

Douglas, Ann. *Terrible Honesty: Mongrel Manhattan in the 1920s.* New York: Noonday, 1995.

Hurewitz, Daniel. *Bohemian Los Angeles and the Making of Modern Politics.* Berkeley: University of California Press, 2007.

Parry, Albert. *Garrets and Pretenders: A History of Bohemianism in America.* New York: Dover, 1960.

Stansell, Christine. *American Moderns: Bohemian New York and the Creation of a New Century.* New York: Henry Holt, 2001.

Wetzsteon, Ross. *Republic of Dreams: Greenwich Village: The American Bohemia, 1910–1960.* New York: Simon & Schuster, 2002.

Borah, William (1865–1940)

A powerful Republican from the progressive wing of the party, Senator William Edgar Borah of Idaho—who served from 1907 to 1940—advocated government aid to farmers during the 1920s. He is best known, however, for his work as chair of the Senate Foreign Relations Committee, in which capacity he advocated a pacifist foreign policy.

Born on June 29, 1865, on a farm near Fairfield, Illinois, Borah was the seventh child and third son of William and Elizabeth West Borah. He studied at the Cumberland Presbyterian Academy before moving to Lyons, Kansas, to study law under his brother-in-law and attend the University of Kansas. He passed the Kansas bar in 1887, but bored with his prospects in small-town Kansas, and possibly in the face of a scandal, he left the state three years later and headed west. Short on funds, he got off the train in Boise, Idaho, established a law practice in the raucous boomtown, and began his career by defending the murderer of a Chinese man on racist grounds.

In 1892, Borah became the secretary to Idaho Governor William McConnell, whose daughter, Mary, he married in April 1895. Thereby established as a respectable citizen, Borah made his reputation as a corporate lawyer and state's attorney, prosecuting the 1899 trial of Paul Corcoran for a murder committed during the Bunker Hill mine strike. Rising in the Republican ranks, Borah was elected to the U.S. Senate for the first time in 1906 by the Idaho legislature. Before leaving for Washington, D.C., he prosecuted William "Big Bill" Heywood and Harry Orchard for an alleged International Workers of the World conspiracy to assassinate former Idaho Governor Frank Steunenberg. Although unsuccessful, his arguments made Borah a trial lawyer of national stature.

In the Senate, Borah championed the proposed Seventeenth Amendment to the Constitution requiring the direct election of senators. Despite his progressive beliefs and great admiration for Theodore Roosevelt, who was running as a third-party candidate in the 1912 presidential election, Borah remained loyal to the Republican Party and backed William Howard Taft. Yet Borah defied the party line time after time, voting for war preparedness as World War I drew in nations around the globe, but ferociously opposing curtailment of civil liberties and conscription. In 1918, he joined Henry Cabot Lodge in working to defeat Senate ratification of the Treaty of Versailles, denouncing it for entangling foreign alliances and the punitive reparations placed on Germany. Such stands made Borah popular with immigrant groups, especially German and Irish voters. He also opposed interventions in Russia and Latin America.

Although he campaigned halfheartedly for Republican presidential candidate Warren G. Harding in 1920, Borah voted increasingly for his own ideas rather than the party line. In 1920, he demanded that the Republican National Committee return a large contribution from oil baron Harry Sinclair. Borah found a patron in antiwar philanthropist Salmon Levinson and in 1921–1922 sponsored the Washington Naval Disarmament Conference—only to denounce the "balance of power" that would constrain American armaments by linking them to those allowed to other nations. President Calvin Coolidge sought to contain Borah by making him a confidant, but the maverick senator broke openly with the president over participation in a world court and pressed relentlessly for diplomatic recognition of Soviet Russia. Borah positioned himself as the leader of the "Farm Bloc" of agricultural states, demanding sweeping programs of national commodities marketing and high tariffs, but he never followed through on the proposals.

While other Republican leaders avoided the politically scorching issue of military bonus pay, Borah was openly against the proposal. He was a staunch prohibitionist and opposed women's suffrage, eccentrically preferring to leave alcohol regulation to the federal government and female voting to the states.

From 1924 until the election of 1932, Borah served as chair of the Senate Foreign Relations Committee, making him one of the most powerful figures in the government. In that position, he advocated developing international institutions that would use enlightened public opinion to prevent nations from going to war. In the interest of peace, he supported the Locarno Treaty, easing tensions in Europe by resolving territorial disputes, and urged the United States to back the Kuomintang government of China. In 1927, he discussed with French foreign minister Aristide Briand the formation of a multilateral peace treaty that became the Kellogg-Briand Pact (1928), which sought to ban war as an instrument of national policy.

Borah campaigned for Republican presidential candidate Herbert Hoover in 1928, but he publicly broke with the new president over farm relief and the Hawley-Smoot tariff. After the stock market crash of 1929, Borah broke with the administration by advocating government intervention in the form of relief and a world economic conference to revise the Treaty of Versailles. In 1933, now in the political minority party and removed from his powerful chair, Borah became the immediate antagonist of President Franklin D. Roosevelt and the New Deal. To the shock of his progressive supporters, in 1935 he voted against the Costigan-Wagner anti-lynching bill on constitutional grounds. He participated in the 1935 Republican presidential primaries but pulled out early in the campaign.

Although Borah denounced Japanese aggression in Asia and fascism in Europe, he staunchly refused to vote for "cash and carry" supplies to England and announced that the 1939 "Phony War" would remain just that—a European family affair in which Americans had no part. An isolationist and political renegade to the last, Borah died in his apartment in Washington, D.C., on January 16, 1940.

Margaret Sankey

See also: Kellogg-Briand Pact (1928); Locarno Treaties (1925); Progressivism; Republican Party; Washington Naval Conference (1921–1922).

Further Reading

Ashby, LeRoy. *Spearless Leader: Senator Borah and the Progressive Movement in the 1920s.* Urbana: University of Illinois Press, 1972.

McKenna, Marian. *Borah.* Ann Arbor: University of Michigan Press, 1961.

Miller, Karen A.J. *Republican Insurgency and American Foreign Policy Making, 1918–1925*. Westport, CT: Greenwood, 1999.

Boston Police Strike of 1919

When most of Boston's police walked off the job at 5:45 P.M. on September 9, 1919, striking against what they said were inadequate wages and poor working conditions, chaos ensued. Many Bostonians, particularly in the city's Irish and working-class neighborhoods, took advantage of the walkout to vandalize and loot stores that evening and the following day. In a stern response, Mayor Andrew J. Peters called out local militia units, who fired into rioting mobs, killing nine and wounding twenty-three. This only temporarily halted the rioting, which continued for several days.

Meanwhile, Governor Calvin Coolidge, declaring that public servants had no right to strike and jeopardize public order, dispatched the entire Massachusetts National Guard to the city in a show of force. Government officials refused to negotiate with the strikers or their union. With the nation in the midst of a strike wave and gripped by post–World War I fears of radical subversion, public opinion rallied around Coolidge, turning him into a national political figure and propelling him onto the Republican Party ticket the following year as the candidate for vice president and, after the death of President Warren G. Harding in 1923, into the White House.

The Boston police strike was the result of several grievances. Police officers earned an average of twenty-nine cents an hour less than most of the city's skilled workers. New recruits were paid just two dollars per day, a figure that had not been raised in more than sixty years, and they were not paid at all for time spent testifying in court (a routine part of the job). Normal workdays ranged from ten to thirteen hours, and most officers worked thirteen days out of every two weeks. Working conditions were often appalling, and officers complained of bug- and rodent-infested stations. While the city provided coats and hats, police officers were expected to pay for their own uniforms and boots. Complaints to the police commissioners were ignored or dismissed. Out of frustration, the police decided in August 1919 to join the American Federation of Labor.

Police officers were not the only workers complaining of low pay, long hours, and poor working conditions in Boston and around the country in the year or so following the end of World War I. Labor militancy was on the rise. Seattle had been hit by a general strike in February, and the nation's steelworkers would walk out a month after the Boston police. Massachusetts was hit with nearly 400 strikes in 1919 alone.

The Boston police strike, however, was also related to the unique ethnic politics of the city. Like all big cities in the Northeast, Boston had seen a massive influx of immigrants from Southern and Eastern Europe during the late nineteenth and early twentieth centuries. Moreover, it continued to attract large numbers of Irish immigrants, who had been pouring into the city since the mid-nineteenth century. Most of the immigrants tended to join the Democratic Party, but the state government had been dominated by the Republicans since the Civil War. In 1885, the Republican-controlled state legislature took the power to appoint the police commissioner away from the mayor, who was usually a Democrat, and turned it over to the governor, who was usually a Republican.

Edwin Curtis was typical of the police commissioners appointed by the Massachusetts governors. A member of the old patrician elite of Boston, and a Republican, he saw the Democrat- and immigrant-dominated police as little better than the poor inhabitants of the city's ghettos. He treated the police with disdain, while the legislature starved the force of funds. The conservative Curtis was also an opponent of trade unions. After the police formed theirs in August, he issued a ruling that prohibited officers from joining unions. This gave him the legal pretext to refuse to negotiate with the union and to fire union leaders from the force.

On September 9, the patrol officers' union voted 1,134–2 to go on strike. The ensuing riots were triggered by many of the same tensions that plagued the force. Poor and immigrant Bostonians, many of them unemployed by postwar layoffs, expended their pent-up rage at the city's elite by attacking not only stores downtown but also the mansions in Boston's wealthier neighborhoods.

America in 1919 was in the grip of a Red Scare, triggered not only by a wave of strikes but also by fears of a Socialist revolution; just two years earlier, the Russian government had been toppled by Bolshevik radicals. State and federal officials in

America responded with massive raids against leftist organizations and the deportation of hundreds of radicals to the Soviet Union. In Boston, Curtis quickly replaced the striking police, a harsh measure that proved popular with city residents. Most Bostonians agreed with government authorities and blamed the rioting not on the city's immigrant poor but on the striking police. Ironically, several months later, government officials were to offer the replacement police virtually all the things—better pay, shorter hours, free uniforms, and better working conditions—for which the original officers had struck.

James Ciment and Bruce E. Stewart

See also: Coolidge, Calvin; Labor Movement.

Further Reading

Connolly, James J. *The Triumph of Ethnic Progressivism: Urban Political Culture in Boston, 1900–1925.* Cambridge, MA: Harvard University Press, 1998.

Tager, Jack. *Boston Riots: Three Centuries of Social Violence.* Boston: Northeastern University Press, 2001.

Thernstrom, Stephen. *The Other Bostonians: Poverty and Progress in the American Metropolis, 1880–1970.* Cambridge, MA: Harvard University Press, 1973.

Bow, Clara (1905–1965)

Clara Bow reigned as the greatest female sex symbol and the biggest Hollywood star of the late 1920s. Known for playing spirited, lovestruck young women who drank, danced, smoked, and flirted, and always got their men, she appeared in fifty-seven films from 1922 to 1933. With her curly red hair, translucent skin, and full scarlet lips, she embodied the glamorous, sexually liberated flapper of the Jazz Age. Indeed, her flapper roles, especially the seductive salesgirl in Paramount's box-office hit *It* (1927), made her a sex symbol. She would forever be remembered as the "It Girl."

Clara Gordon Bow was born on July 29, 1905, in Brooklyn, New York. Her father was a Coney Island busboy; her mother was schizophrenic and epileptic. An unwanted child, she grew up in an impoverished, working-class family plagued by alcoholism, severe mental illness, and physical abuse. Bow escaped by immersing herself in the exciting new medium of motion pictures, and from an early age she longed to become a movie star.

She received her big break in 1921 when, at the age of sixteen, she won first prize in a national Fame

Known as Hollywood's "It Girl," Clara Bow was one of the most popular stars of the burgeoning film industry—and the quintessential flapper. *(Otto Dyar/Hulton Archive/Getty Images)*

and Fortune beauty contest sponsored by Brewster Publications, the Brooklyn-based publisher of *Motion Picture, Motion Picture Classic,* and *Shadowland* magazines. With the company's assistance, Bow received a studio screen test and made her cinematic debut in *Beyond the Rainbow* (1922), although all her scenes were eventually cut from the film. She soon landed a supporting role in a successful film about nineteenth-century New England whaling, *Down to the Sea in Ships* (1922).

In 1923, Bow signed a $50-a-week contract with Preferred Pictures in Hollywood. Under studio chief B.P. Schulberg, who was notorious for leasing out his roster of overworked, underpaid actors to other studios, Bow appeared in twenty-six silent feature films from 1923 to 1925, including *Daughters of Pleasure* (1924), *The Adventurous Sex* (1925), *Eve's Lover* (1925), *The Lawful Cheater* (1925), *Parisian Love* (1925), and *Free to Love* (1925), sometimes working on as many as three at once.

Bow attracted the attention of critics and filmgoers alike. In 1924, the Western Associated Motion Picture Advertisers named her a Baby Star, an award bestowed on up-and-coming actresses who demonstrated a potential for stardom. Bow's enchanting performance as a "hotsy-totsy" flapper in a 1925 box-office hit about college life, *The Plastic Age,* enhanced her growing reputation as, in the words of studio publicists, "the hottest jazz baby in films." In 1926, she signed a contract with Paramount Pictures and had leading roles in such films as *Dancing Mothers* (1926), *The Runaway* (1926), *Mantrap* (1926), and *Kid Boots* (1926), opposite Eddie Cantor.

Bow's breakthrough performance came in Paramount's 1927 blockbuster *It,* a romantic comedy loosely adapted from British writer Elinor Glyn's best-selling novella. "It" was a euphemism for sexual appeal and magnetism, and in the film Bow displayed plenty of both as Betty Lou Spence, a plucky department store clerk who pursues and eventually wins over the handsome, debonair store heir. The film grossed more than $1 million and transformed Bow into a national sensation.

A string of popular movies followed, including *Rough House Rosie* (1927), *Hula* (1927), *Get Your Man* (1927), *Wings* (1927; first Academy Award for Best Picture), *Red Hair* (1928), *Ladies of the Mob* (1928), and *The Fleet's In* (1929). Most of these were formulaic comedies designed to capitalize on Bow's stardom as the "It Girl." Although these thinly scripted films allowed her to demonstrate only a limited acting range, Bow entranced moviegoers with her ravishing beauty, outrageous flirtatiousness, and alluring sex appeal. By 1929, she was the most popular actress in Hollywood, but the terms of her Paramount contract (under which she earned $5,000 a week) made her one of the lowest-paid female leads in the industry.

Bow became as well known for her flamboyant lifestyle and off-screen escapades as for her screen roles. Rumors of her gambling, carousing, and wild all-night parties abounded in Hollywood, and studio publicists filled the gossip columns with stories of her love affairs and broken engagements to actors Gilbert Roland and Gary Cooper, director Victor Fleming, and entertainer Harry Richman. Although Bow had a long parade of wealthy, famous suitors, her déclassé Brooklyn background and dreadful manners prompted the Hollywood film community to ostracize her, and she actually led a solitary life with only a handful of close friends. "A sex symbol," she once remarked, "is always a heavy load to carry when one is tired, hurt, and bewildered."

Terrified of delivering dialogue, and plagued by a strong Brooklyn accent and nervous stammer, Bow made her talking film debut in *The Wild Party* (1929) and went on to appear in eight more pictures over the next two years, including *Dangerous Curves* (1929), *Love Among the Millionaires* (1930), and *Her Wedding Night* (1930). In May 1931, however, a combination of shattered nerves and three highly publicized sex and gambling scandals forced her to retire from films. She staged a brief comeback in *Call Her Savage* (1932) and *Hoop-La* (1933) for Fox before her acting career came to a permanent end in 1933. She was twenty-eight years old.

In December 1931, Bow married cowboy actor and longtime beau Rex Bell, and the couple moved to Rancho Clarita, a 300,000-acre cattle ranch near Searchlight, Nevada, where they raised two sons. But Bow struggled with schizophrenia, severe depression, chronic insomnia, and barbiturate dependency. Much of her post-Hollywood life was spent recuperating in sanitariums or living in seclusion on her Nevada ranch and, after separating from her husband in 1950, in a modest home in Culver City, California. She died of a heart attack on September 27, 1965, at the age of sixty, and is buried alongside her husband in the Forest Lawn Memorial Park Cemetery in Los Angeles.

Patrick Huber

See also: Beauty Industry and Culture; Celebrity Culture; Film; Film Industry.

Further Reading

Basinger, Jeanine. *Silent Stars.* New York: Alfred A. Knopf, 1999.

Morella, Joe, and Edward Z. Epstein. *The "It" Girl: The Incredible Story of Clara Bow.* New York: Delacorte, 1976.

Stenn, David. *Clara Bow: Runnin' Wild.* New York: Cooper Square, 2000.

Boxing

The growing popularity of boxing during the Jazz Age was part of the public's fascination with spectator sports, a result of new media outlets like radio, film, and tabloid newspapers, and the rise of popular sports heroes. Millions of people attended or followed a host of sporting matches, from baseball and college football to amateur and professional golf and tennis. As spectator sports became increasingly popular, efforts were launched to make them more legitimate in the eyes of the public, usually through the creation of

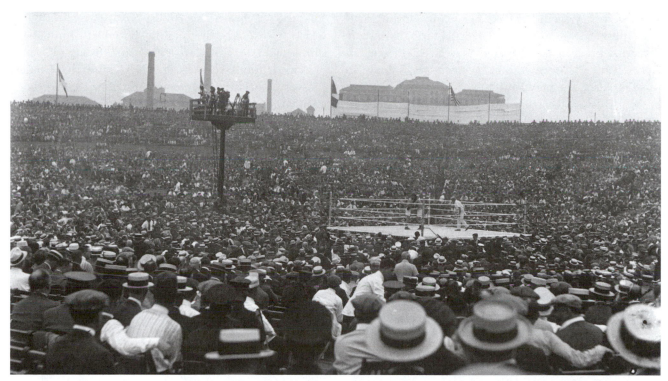

Spectator sports such as boxing became big business in the 1920s. The heavyweight title fight between Jack Dempsey and challenger Georges Carpentier in July 1921 represented the sport's first million-dollar gate. Dempsey won the bout in a fourth-round knockout. *(Topical Press Agency/Stringer/Hulton Archive/Getty Images)*

governing institutions. In professional boxing, that effort produced the National Boxing Association (NBA, later the World Boxing Association, WBA) in 1921, the first "sanctioning body" in the history of the sport. The NBA ranked fighters and arranged matches between champions and those it deemed the most deserving challengers, charging fees to promoters for these services.

Professional boxing's appeal with the public was greatly enhanced by a single charismatic star, Jack Dempsey. The son of a poor Colorado rancher, Dempsey had learned to fight in brawling, bare-knuckle matches in Western mining towns before catching the eye of boxing promoter Tex Rickard. In 1919, Rickard pitted Dempsey against the reigning champion, another son of the ranching West named Jess Willard—at six feet, seven and a half inches, the second tallest heavyweight champion in boxing history. While Willard was expected to dispatch Dempsey easily, the outspoken underdog's insistence that he would destroy Willard caught the public's fancy. And indeed, Dempsey unleashed one of the most brutal attacks in boxing history, knocking Willard to the mat seven times in the first round. Willard had never been knocked down before and by

the time he threw in the towel between the third and fourth rounds, Willard had suffered a broken jaw, broken ribs, and a partial loss of hearing.

Dempsey took to the road, on the vaudeville circuit, demonstrating the methods he had used to defeat Willard and helping to spread boxing's popularity. In 1921, Rickard set up a match between Dempsey and French champion Georges Carpentier, using the recently established medium of radio to promote the bout as a showdown between European sophistication and Western grit. The 80,000-plus fans who attended the Jersey City fight brought in more than $1.8 million, the first time a fight had broken the million-dollar mark. The fight made history not because it was a financial success or because Dempsey won with a knockout in the fourth round, but because it attracted more than 300,000 radio listeners across the Northeast—the first demonstration of the electronic medium's capacity to bring entertainment to masses of people. Throughout the 1920s, boxing became an increasingly lucrative sport. Receipts at New York City's Madison Square Garden, America's premier boxing arena in the 1920s, ran to nearly $8 million from 1924 to 1926.

Dempsey would defend his championship title two more times, both in 1923, before taking an extended break. In 1926, Dempsey faced off against Gene Tunney, a former Marine from New York. It was Dempsey the brawler—and accused draft dodger in World War I—against a clean-cut, well-spoken opponent. Dempsey's hard living in the years since his 1923 fights undermined his effectiveness in the ring, however, and he was defeated in ten rounds in front of more than 120,000 fans in Philadelphia. A year later, Dempsey was again defeated by Tunney, at Chicago's Soldier Field. The bout was famed for its "long count," in which the referee postponed the count against Tunney after Dempsey knocked him to the mat in the seventh round but refused to return to his corner. The delay allowed the champion to return to his feet and go on to defeat Dempsey after ten rounds.

Just as cities were becoming the focal point of American life and culture in the Jazz Age—the 1920 U.S. Census recorded more people in urban than rural areas for the first time in the nation's history—so boxing was becoming an increasingly urban sport. Small clubs and settlement houses, set up by philanthropists and activists to provide the urban immigrant masses with welfare, education, and social activities, offered amateur boxing to immigrant youth as a way to get them off the streets and keep them out of crime.

The spread of amateur boxing led to the Golden Gloves tournament. First established in Chicago in 1923, it lasted only one year before boxing was banned by the state of Illinois, both because of its inherent brutality and because it was believed to attract gambling and organized crime elements. In 1927, however, the legislature reversed itself, partly in order to host the second Dempsey–Tunney match. Chicago officials were also aware that boxing brought in major tax revenues. (Madison Square Garden alone produced more than $100,000 a year in taxes for the city and state of New York in the 1920s.) The Golden Gloves tournament soon spread to New York and other cities across the country.

Amateur urban boxing also produced contenders for the professional ring. One of these ethnic, urban boxers was light heavyweight champion Benny Leonard, one of a crop of Jewish and Italian fighters who emerged out of New York's teeming immigrant neighborhoods in the 1920s. Known as the "ghetto wizard," Leonard is regarded by many boxing historians as the finest nonheavyweight boxer of the Jazz Age.

By the end of the 1920s, boxing's reputation as a dangerous and disreputable sport had diminished, and it had established its legitimacy through governing institutions such as the NBA and the Golden Gloves association. Moreover, the sport's ability to earn millions of dollars in gate receipts, as well as hundreds of thousands in taxes for city and state coffers, helped convince many municipalities and states to revise laws that restricted or prohibited the sport.

James Ciment and Kevin Grace

See also: Dempsey, Jack; Leisure and Recreation; Radio.

Further Reading

Bodner, Allen. *When Boxing Was a Jewish Sport.* Westport, CT: Praeger, 1997.

Evensen, Bruce J. *When Dempsey Fought Tunney: Heroes, Hokum, and Storytelling in the Jazz Age.* Knoxville: University of Tennessee Press, 1996.

Sammons, Jeffrey T. *Beyond the Ring: The Role of Boxing in American Society.* Champaign: University of Illinois Press, 1988.

Brandeis, Louis (1856–1941)

A liberal Supreme Court justice from 1916 through 1939, Louis Dembitz Brandeis was often in the minority on a Court dominated by conservatives in the 1920s. Nevertheless, his progressive ideas about civil liberties, limitations on the power of government, and the rights of workers—as well as his legal writings, which emphasized economic and social issues as well as points of law—would prove influential as the Court shifted to the left in the 1930s.

Brandeis was born on November 13, 1856, in Louisville, Kentucky. His parents were nonpracticing Jews who had emigrated from Austria. Raised in a well-to-do household, Brandeis showed remarkable intelligence, graduating from high school at the age of fourteen. He attended a private academy in Dresden, Germany, while his family lived in Europe, enrolling at Harvard Law School upon his return to America in 1875. Brandeis not only finished at the head of his class but received the highest marks in the school's history, all before he was twenty years old.

After practicing law in St. Louis for a year, Brandeis returned to Boston and, with former classmate Samuel Warren, formed a law partnership specializing in business and corporate cases. Warren's social connections brought in wealthy clients, but it was Brandeis's legal acumen that helped make the firm one of the city's most prosperous. At the same time, Brandeis became one of the first attorneys in America to offer his services, free of charge, to poor clients. In the early 1900s, Brandeis, a strong believer in the rights of consumers and workers, organized a local consumers league to persuade Boston utilities to reduce their rates and provide better service. He established a savings bank that enabled low-income families to secure life insurance at reasonable rates, and fought the local streetcar monopoly over fares and service.

In 1908, Brandeis was asked by the government of Oregon to act as cocounsel in a Supreme Court case—*Muller v. Oregon*—testing the state's law limiting the working hours of women. His voluminous brief was a landmark of legal writing. Rather than focus on legal precedent, Brandeis provided copious statistics and lengthy discussions of the sociological, economic, and psychological aspects of the case. Such documents, referred to as "Brandeis briefs," established the norm in legal writing in cases involving social welfare and environmental issues.

Brandeis's successful work on the *Muller* case, as well as his arbitration of a 1910 New York garment workers' strike that helped to establish minimum wages and maximum hours, earned him a national reputation as a liberal thinker and activist. Brought to the attention of progressive politicians, he was hired as a legal adviser to Wisconsin Senator Robert La Follette and President Woodrow Wilson. In 1914, Brandeis was elected head of the Provisional Executive Committee for Zionist Affairs, the leading American organization supporting a Jewish homeland in Palestine. That same year, he wrote a book called *Other People's Money—and How the Bankers Use It,* a scathing attack on antidemocratic trusts and investment banks.

In 1916, when Wilson nominated Brandeis for the Supreme Court, a fierce political battle developed. Not only was Brandeis the first Jew to be nominated, but his prolabor, antitrust background made him anathema to business interests. Nevertheless, Brandeis was confirmed after four months of hearings.

On the Court, the new associate justice put his clerks to work amassing the sociological and economic data he needed to back up his decisions, particularly those involving labor and social welfare issues. Brandeis believed it was important, whether he was in the minority or the majority on a decision, to educate the public as to his reasoning.

While Brandeis had already made a name for himself exploring the legal ramifications of economic issues, on the Supreme Court he is best remembered for the Jazz Age opinions he wrote concerning civil liberties. In 1919, he voted with the majority in *Schenck v. United States,* upholding the World War I–era Espionage Act and the government's right to imprison individuals for actively opposing the military draft in wartime. Before the year was out, however, Brandeis was modifying his support of the "clear and present danger" doctrine limiting free speech. In *Abrams v. United States* (1919), Brandeis and Oliver Wendell Holmes, Jr., author of the *Schenck* decision, dissented from the majority, arguing that anarchists opposing U.S. intervention in the Russian Revolution were not in violation of the Sedition Act, another World War I–era law that made it a crime to use "disloyal, profane, scurrilous, or abusive language" against the U.S. government. In 1921, writing the minority opinion in *Schaefer v. United States,* Brandeis rejected using different criteria for what constituted free speech in wartime and peacetime.

Ironically, Brandeis's greatest defense of free speech came in *Whitney v. California* (1927), in which he joined in a unanimous decision upholding the government's right to limit speech deemed "inimical to the public welfare." His concurring opinion is considered by many legal scholars one of the finest defenses of free speech in American legal annals. In it, Brandeis argued that the free exchange of ideas is critical to democracy. Thus, the government has to go beyond proving a "clear and present danger" in order to limit free speech; it must show that the danger from such speech is immediate, with no time to rebut it. In effect, Brandeis argued that unpopular speech should be combated by more speech, in what Holmes called the "marketplace of ideas," rather than by government repression.

Brandeis's last major decision of the Jazz Age concerned privacy, an issue he had been exploring for decades. In 1928, the Court heard arguments in *Olmstead v. United States.* At issue was whether government phone wiretaps violated the Fourth and Fifth Amendments to the U.S. Constitution, protecting citizens against unreasonable searches and self-incrimination, respectively. In his dissenting opinion in the 5–4 ruling, Brandeis argued that the law had to take into account new technological means for invading a person's privacy.

Brandeis's reasoning would be extensively cited in the 1967 *Katz v. United States* decision that effectively overturned *Olmstead.* Moreover, his expansive interpretation of what constitutes the right of citizens to privacy would lay the foundation for other landmark decisions of the late twentieth century, including *Griswold v. Connecticut* (1967), concerning the right to birth control, and the 1973 *Roe v. Wade* decision giving women the right to choose an abortion.

Brandeis defended many of President Franklin D. Roosevelt's New Deal programs, until ill health forced him to retire in 1939. He died in Washington on October 5, 1941.

James Ciment and Tim J. Watts

See also: Law and the Courts; *Schenck v. United States* (1919).

Further Reading

Baker, Leonard. *Brandeis and Frankfurter: A Dual Biography.* New York: Harper & Row, 1984.

Mason, Alpheus Thomas. *Brandeis: A Free Man's Life.* New York: Viking, 1946.

McCraw, Thomas K. *Prophets of Regulation: Charles Francis Adams, Louis D. Brandeis, James M. Landis, Alfred E. Kahn.* Cambridge, MA: Belknap Press, 1984.

Strum, Philippa. *Louis D. Brandeis: Justice for the People.* Cambridge, MA: Harvard University Press, 1984.

Urofsky, Melvin I., and Oscar Handlin. *Louis D. Brandeis and the Progressive Tradition.* Boston: Little, Brown, 1981.

Bureau of Investigation

The Bureau of Investigation, later renamed the Federal Bureau of Investigation, was established in 1908 by Attorney General Charles Bonaparte, who complained that he was forced to borrow detectives from other federal agencies whenever he needed them for official Justice Department duties and investigations. Bonaparte insisted that a dedicated federal police agency was needed. Opponents contended that such a force could be abused by an ambitious president, who might use it to harass political opponents. Bonaparte allayed these fears by promising that the Bureau of Investigation would be restricted to investigating interstate crime, and that it would never be used to look into the political or religious beliefs of individuals.

Despite Bonaparte's hopes, the Bureau of Investigation languished for nearly a decade, operating on a meager budget. Moreover, many of its agents lacked the professional training Bonaparte had envisioned. But World War I and its aftermath changed the situation drastically. Attacks by German-hired saboteurs, especially the heavily publicized destruction of an arsenal on Black Tom Island in New York

Harbor, increased pressure to strengthen the Bureau of Investigation. And the 1917 revolution in Russia raised concerns that radical elements in the United States might attempt a similar takeover of the U.S. government. These fears led to the Red Scare of 1919 and to the politicization of the bureau's activities.

On June 2, 1919, bombs went off in twelve different cities across the United States. One destroyed the home of Attorney General A. Mitchell Palmer, who took decisive action. On January 2, 1920, agents of the Bureau of Investigation joined forces with state and local police agencies to raid meeting halls known to be gathering places for radicals and anarchists, with the intent of arresting and deporting those who were not U.S. citizens. They captured more than 10,000 persons in thirty-three cities, but their sometimes heavy-handed tactics aroused civil libertarians and significant segments of the public, who saw in the raids evidence that the Bureau of Investigation had become the political police of the executive branch. In the end, just a few hundred of the arrestees were actually deported, and the National Civil Liberties Bureau (the future American Civil Liberties Union) protested what they said was the arbitrary and brutal way in which police had handled individuals under detention.

As fears of subversions dissipated in the early 1920s—and in response to the political uproar against the Palmer Raids—chief William Flynn began steering the department away from cracking down on political subversives and more toward what Bonaparte had originally envisioned as the bureau's main activity—investigating interstate crime.

In 1924, Flynn was replaced by J. Edgar Hoover, who had led the bureau's actions against subversives under Palmer. Hoover, who would later devote significant resources to not only investigating radicals but also harassing civil rights and antiwar leaders in the 1950s and 1960s, moved to professionalize a force that had been compromised by politics and even corruption. He wrote new rules that ended patronage appointments, and he purged the staff of agents with criminal records. The regular civil service examination was replaced by a more rigorous one, and salaries and benefits were increased, resulting in an increase in agents' social prestige. Agents received extensive training that covered every aspect of their future duties, from marksmanship and the care of firearms to the proper collection and handling of evidence and questioning witnesses.

Although the Jazz Age was marked by a major upsurge in organized crime, largely as a result of Prohibition, the bureau remained relatively aloof from the battles against the mob. Instead, agents concentrated on apprehending solitary bank robbers and killers who were prowling the Midwest, their crimes made possible by the mobility the automobile lent them. Such notorious criminals as "Pretty Boy" Floyd, "Baby Face" Nelson, and "Ma" Barker's gang could rob a bank in one state, then flee a hundred miles to take refuge in another state, thus stymieing the attempts of pursuing state police to bring them to justice. But the Bureau of Investigation, with its nationwide jurisdiction, could chase them down. Capturing such notorious individuals brought more public recognition to the bureau and its director than any number of busts of illegal distilleries.

Leigh Kimmel

See also: Crime, Organized; Hoover, J. Edgar; Palmer, A. Mitchell; Red Scare of 1917–1920.

Further Reading

Breuer, William B. *J. Edgar Hoover and His G-Men.* Westport, CT: Praeger, 1995.
Potter, Claire Bond. *War on Crime Bandits, G-Men, and the Politics of Mass Culture.* New Brunswick, NJ: Rutgers University Press, 1998.

Burroughs, Edgar Rice (1875–1950)

The author of more than seventy novels, published beginning in 1912, Edgar Rice Burroughs is best known as the creator of the jungle hero Tarzan. His books have sold hundreds of millions of copies in more than fifty languages, and film adaptations of the Tarzan novels have turned his characters into pop culture icons. Burroughs was also the author of scores of science fiction, western, and other novels—most of them heroic adventure fantasies. At the height of his success, Burroughs presided over a multimedia empire, licensing Tarzan statuettes, ice cream, and bread, and spinning off Tarzan comic strips, radio shows, and movies. He was the founder of the suburban Los Angeles community of Tarzana, and in 1931, he became the first American author to incorporate himself. While critics have dismissed Burroughs as a writer-for-hire of the pulp trade and his stories for their racist and sexist overtones, his characters endure as seemingly permanent fixtures on the cultural landscape.

Early Failures

Edgar Rice Burroughs was born in Chicago on September 1, 1875, to George Tyler Burroughs, a Union major during the Civil War, and Mary Evaline Zieger, of Pennsylvania Dutch heritage. Burroughs attended the Harvard School in Chicago but withdrew for health reasons in 1891. His parents sent him to Idaho to join two of his older brothers on their ranch. During a brief stay, he developed what was to become a lifelong interest in animals and riding. After a stint at the Phillips Academy in Andover, Massachusetts, Burroughs enrolled in the Orchard Lake, Michigan, Military Academy, where he stayed for a year to teach geology after failing the entrance exam to West Point.

Burroughs's infatuation with the military persisted, and he enlisted in the regular army in 1896, only to request a discharge for health reasons ten months later. He rejoined his brothers for a brief period as a rancher in Idaho, bought and sold a stationery store, then worked for a time at the American Battery Company, the family business in Chicago. He married his childhood sweetheart, Emma Hulbert, in January 1900 and returned to Idaho with her in 1903 to dredge for gold. This and a succession of other mining ventures failed, and, after a short period in Salt Lake City working as a railway cop, Burroughs returned to Chicago in 1905.

For the next several years, he pursued a number of occupations. He achieved moderate success as a salesman for Sears, Roebuck but quit to start his own business selling entrepreneurship courses. The venture soon failed. By this time, the family included two children, and money was short. It occurred to Burroughs, an avid reader of short-story magazines, that he might be able to write and sell similar adventures. His first story, "Under the Moon of Mars" (later published in book form as *A Princess of Mars*), was serialized by *All-Story* magazine in early 1912, earning its author $400. That same year, *All-Story* published *Tarzan of the Apes* in its entirety in its October issue. The story was an immediate success, and Burroughs's literary career was under way.

Tarzan, Mars, and Venus

The hero of the Tarzan series is John Clayton, Lord Greystoke, an English aristocrat who is raised by apes after his mother and father meet an untimely death in a remote African jungle. Tarzan, young Lord

Greystoke's name in "ape-speak," quickly rises to a position of leadership in his ape tribe by virtue of his superior intelligence and dexterity with tools.

Over the course of twenty-four novels, Tarzan falls in love with a lively and intelligent American, Jane Porter, raises a family, regains his title, discovers lost cities and tribes, foils the plots of treacherous villains, and rescues countless damsels in distress. Throughout his adventures, he never fails to display courage, strength, justice, and good breeding. An innately noble and larger-than-life hero, Tarzan has been compared to such other American creations as Leatherstocking and Superman.

Burroughs also penned three series of science fiction adventures set on Mars and Venus, and in Pellucidar, a lost world at the center of the Earth. The Martian novels feature an intricately imagined world, down to descriptions of architecture and discussions of Martian eating habits. Like the Tarzan series, the Martian novels feature a strong central character, John Carter, whose adventures as warrior and lover reprise themes common through all Burroughs's works. Indeed, Burroughs's introduction of a romantic element into his science fiction stories constituted a first for the genre. Other works include *The Land That Time Forgot* (1917–1918), part of the Caspak trilogy, as well as movie scripts and journalistic pieces.

Criticism and Disappointment

Burroughs's stories have been criticized for their negative stereotyping of different peoples, including Africans and Germans, their sexist overtones, and their blatant themes of racial and social hierarchy. During World War I, his patriotism verged on propaganda, and anti-German sentiment in *Tarzan the Untamed* (1918–1919) and *The Land That Time Forgot* cost him readers. In his books and characters, Burroughs placed great emphasis on heredity: by dint of his aristocratic stock, for instance, Tarzan is able to transcend his ape upbringing and teach himself to read and write English. In 1927, writing about an actual murder trial, Burroughs advocated the death penalty for the express purpose of preventing the accused, a "moral imbecile," from procreating. Even on purely literary grounds, Burroughs did not escape criticism. His stories were dismissed by serious critics as pulp.

Burroughs often stated, however, that the main purpose of his fiction was to entertain. And in that

goal, he met with overwhelming success. His books were wildly popular. In some years his income surpassed $100,000, a large sum for a writer in the Jazz Age, yet his expenditures always seemed to exceed his available cash. Lawsuits over permissions and royalties also took their toll, and the estate that he purchased in California—later to be named Tarzana—operated at a perennial loss. At one point, he saw great potential in Hollywood and the film adaptations of his stories, but he was soon disillusioned by his lack of creative control over their production.

Edgar Rice Burroughs died on March 19, 1950, of heart disease. He was unquestionably one of the most popular authors of the twentieth century, and many of his books are still in print today.

Eric Paras and Jenifer Paras

See also: Fiction; Weissmuller, Johnny.

Further Reading

Fenton, Robert W. *Edgar Rice Burroughs and Tarzan: A Biography of the Author and His Creation.* Jefferson, NC: McFarland, 2003.

Holtsmark, Erling B. *Edgar Rice Burroughs.* Boston: Twayne, 1986.

Porges, Irwin. *Edgar Rice Burroughs: The Man Who Created Tarzan.* Provo, UT: Brigham Young University Press, 1975.

Taliaferro, John. *Tarzan Forever: The Life of Edgar Rice Burroughs, Creator of Tarzan.* New York: Scribner's, 1999.

Byrd, Richard E. (1888–1957)

In an age of aviation firsts, Richard Evelyn Byrd stands out for his daring and pioneering polar flights in the late 1920s, including the first successful air journey to the South Pole. These exploits made the former U.S. Navy pilot the second most famous aviator in America during the Jazz Age, after Charles Lindbergh, against whom Byrd unsuccessfully competed to become the first to fly solo across the Atlantic Ocean.

Born in Winchester, Virginia, on October 25, 1888, Byrd was a member of one of the state's oldest and most prestigious families, though it had fallen on hard times after the Civil War. From a young age, Byrd showed a penchant for adventure and the self-promotion needed to finance his expeditions. At the age of eleven, he traveled to the Philippines by himself to visit relatives, sending back dispatches that

Richard E. Byrd, America's most celebrated explorer of the twentieth century, became the first person to fly to the South Pole in 1929. However, his claim to have reached the North Pole three years earlier is now widely discredited. *(Imagno/Hulton Archive/Getty Images)*

were printed in local papers. Byrd attended the University of Virginia but soon decided on a military career, transferring to the Virginia Military Institute and then the U.S. Naval Academy, graduating in 1912. In the navy, Byrd was trained as an aviator and commanded the service's air division in Canada during World War I. By 1919, Byrd had pioneered key technical developments and methods for over-ocean navigation. As a result, the navy placed him in charge of the flight plan for the first transatlantic crossing in 1919.

But it was polar exploration, the last great frontier in the early twentieth century, that truly fascinated Byrd. During World War I, he had been part of a naval reconnaissance mission to Greenland. During the early 1920s, Byrd was a member of several unsuccessful U.S. Navy attempts to reach the North Pole by air. In the summer of 1925, he organized his own private expedition, fearing that Norwegian explorer Roald Amundsen, the first to reach the South Pole by land, would beat him to the North Pole by air. But Byrd's expedition was aborted when the landing skis of a plane collapsed on takeoff.

The fear of being bested also led to the most controversial event in Byrd's life. On May 9, 1926, the aviator, joined by former navy pilot Floyd Bennett, took off from an airfield on the Norwegian island of Spitsbergen, about 1,000 miles from the pole. According to both Byrd and Bennett, the two reached the North Pole despite an oil leak, but their return to Spitsbergen was well ahead of schedule, leaving experts skeptical. (The 1997 discovery of Byrd's diary, with partially erased navigation readings, fueled suspicion that the pair never made it to the North Pole and that Byrd may have tried to cover up the fact.) Nevertheless, the American public lionized Byrd's achievements, and he became the country's newest aviation hero.

Byrd's attempt to organize the first solo transatlantic flight (and claim the Orteig Prize of $25,000), with Bennett at the helm, failed in 1927, when the Fokker Trimotor aircraft they were testing crashed during a practice flight. Bennett was severely injured. That May, as the pilot was healing and the aircraft was being repaired, Charles Lindbergh completed his triumphant flight.

Partly to regain his status as hero and partly to accomplish the next logical feat in his aviation career, Byrd organized a major expedition to Antarctica. The goal was to become the first person to fly over the South Pole. With a crew of forty-two men and ninety-five dogs, along with 650 tons of supplies, including three aircraft, Byrd set sail for the southern polar region in the fall of 1928 (spring below the equator). Landing in November, Byrd christened his base Little America, which would eventually become the first permanent U.S. scientific base in Antarctica. On November 29, Byrd achieved his goal without dispute or controversy, making the first successful flight over the South Pole. After fourteen more months of scientific and exploration work in the Antarctic, Byrd returned to America, once again a national hero. He was showered with acclaim, and the navy promoted him to admiral, leading to his popular title of "Admiral of the Antarctic."

Byrd made a second expedition to Antarctica in 1933, sponsored by companies such as the CBS radio network and General Foods. He decided to build upon his reputation by flying to the continent's interior and wintering there alone, but the effort nearly killed him. Fumes from his generator poisoned him with carbon monoxide, and he had to be rescued by a team sent overland from Little America. Byrd went on to make four more expeditions to Antarctica under U.S. government auspices, but none captured the public's imagination like his efforts in the 1920s and early 1930s. Byrd died on March 11, 1957.

James Ciment

See also: Aviation.

Further Reading

Byrd, Richard E. *Alone: The Classic Polar Adventure.* New York: Kodansha International, 1995.

Hoyt, Edwin P. *The Last Explorer: The Adventures of Admiral Byrd.* New York: John Day, 1968.

Rodgers, Eugene. *Beyond the Barrier: The Story of Byrd's First Expedition to Antarctica.* Annapolis, MD: Naval Institute Press, 1990.

Canada

In a number of ways, the 1920s marked a decade of transition for Canada. The nation had begun somewhat tenuously with four provinces under the British North America Act of 1867 and had matured considerably in the last half of the nineteenth century. A great railroad united Canada from east to west; large cities developed as centers of industry, population, and culture; vast agricultural regions became spectacularly productive and, along with manufacturing and extractive industries, helped define a large, export-driven economy. By the turn of the twentieth century, Canada had become a second, fully mature, largely English-speaking society in North America. Indeed, it was a significant contributor to the Allied effort in World War I and had emerged as an important "middle power."

Challenges

During the 1920s, Canada's economy expanded and contracted rapidly, in part owing to Canada's dependence on trade (especially the export of raw material and finished goods) and as a result of its increasing connection to the United States and decreasing connection to Great Britain and the Commonwealth. Economic growth helped usher in an era of conveniences, including automobiles and paved roads, electricity and central heating systems, telephones, radios, movies, and ready-made clothes.

The economy also presented challenges for particular regions and peoples, and helped strengthen certain reform and protest movements, especially in the Maritime and Prairie Provinces. Reform movements on behalf of women's rights and French-speaking Canada continued. This led to a lively political scene, which brought the rise of William Lyon Mackenzie King, who would serve as prime minister from 1921 to 1930 and again from 1935 to 1948.

The overriding challenge for Canada during the 1920s was to chart an independent course, apart from and equal to Great Britain, the former mother country, and the United States, the colossus to the south, while continuing to develop a distinctly Canadian polity, economy, and society respectful of the differences between its Anglophone and Francophone regions. With respect to economics and culture, the United States posed a huge, perhaps insurmountable threat.

When Great Britain declared war against Germany in August 1914, Canada supported the Allied effort. More than 50,000 Canadians died in the fighting, and many times that number were wounded, but the war also brought prosperity. Great Britain and France needed Canadian foodstuffs, raw materials, and manufactured goods. Domestically, the war exacerbated tensions between Anglophone and Francophone peoples, as French Canadians increasingly viewed the costly conflict as one of British imperial aspirations and not for the benefit of Canada.

The war-inflated economy helped further the movement of peoples from rural to urban areas and from the Maritime and Prairie Provinces to Ontario and Quebec. By 1920, more Canadians lived in urban than rural areas. Retailing changed with the rise of chain stores such as Safeway, A&P, Eaton's, and Loblaws. U.S. companies and capital replaced British companies and capital as the largest source of foreign investment.

When war-related orders ended, a deep economic depression hit the Prairie agricultural sector and the Maritime Provinces. Indeed, the economy of the 1920s centered on recovery from the war. Initially, as European armies disbanded and veterans returned home, the Allies no longer needed to import large quantities of food. Within a few years, however, Canadian grain exports to Europe recovered, and wheat agriculture moved into the semi-arid regions of Saskatchewan and Alberta. Similarly, war-inflated manufacturing orders gradually returned to a more normal, peacetime cycle.

Economic Revival

By the start of the 1920s, Canada was reviving. Its export-driven economy had suffered as Europe

Winnipeg General Strike of 1919

At midday on May 15, 1919, more than 22,000 union and nonunion employees in and around Winnipeg, western Canada's largest city, walked off their jobs in a general strike authorized in an overwhelming vote by the city's union members. The strikers included manufacturing and service workers, everybody from the men who loaded grain onto trains to the women who ushered theatergoers to their seats. Government workers also struck. The walkout brought most economic activity in the city, except for essential public services, to an immediate halt. The job action continued for nearly six weeks—making it the longest general strike in North American history—but it achieved none of its goals.

The Winnipeg strike of 1919 was an exercise in political and economic muscle-flexing and a test of the general strike as a negotiating technique. A simple frontier town until the 1880s, Winnipeg by 1919 was a center of railway traffic, international grain trading, grain storage, manufacturing, and commerce, with a growing number of unionized employees. The number of small local strikes had been increasing, particularly during the later years of World War I, and Winnipeg voters had increasingly supported prolabor political candidates.

For many of the workers, the action was a sympathy strike. They were not seeking anything immediate for their own unions or themselves. Rather, they walked out to support the demands of others, specifically employees in Winnipeg's building and metal trades, whose demands included a shorter workweek, higher pay, and recognition of their union.

The initial exhilaration of Winnipeg's general strikers disappeared by early June. They had not expected the resistance of government and business leaders, who feared that general strikes might become a viable bargaining tool in Canada. Government and private-sector employees lost their jobs and were replaced by strikebreakers. Strike leaders were arrested.

On June 21, thereafter known as Bloody Saturday, a group of frustrated strikers, demoralized by the arrests of other strikers and strike supporters and the diminishing numbers in their ranks, burned a city streetcar during a demonstration in front of Winnipeg's city hall. Armed Royal North West Mounted Police charged the crowd, sticks and stones were thrown, shots were fired into the crowd, and two demonstrators were killed. Soon after, the Winnipeg general strike petered out. Some strikers returned to work; others, replaced by strikebreakers, took new jobs or moved elsewhere.

Debate still rages over the Winnipeg general strike's ultimate impact. Its conspicuous failure ushered in an era of more moderate actions, as well as more successful efforts at economic and political reform that lasted throughout the Jazz Age. Canadian workers came to see British-style labor politics—working within the political system to achieve gains for the working class—as a more feasible and attractive alternative than such disruptive strikes. The rhetoric of reform replaced some of the rhetoric of revolution. Winnipeg's employers continued to bargain with each of the individual locals representing their employees, unless they chose to bargain with coalitions of all of their employees' unions. Industry-wide bargaining eventually came to Canada, but not until long after the Jazz Age had ended.

Steven B. Jacobson

recovered from the ravages of war, then stabilized. Equally important, however, was a dramatic shift in foreign trade. The United States had moved from a debtor nation to the world's greatest creditor nation during the war, and Canada's trade triangle tilted more toward the United States than to Great Britain. Canada's trade surplus with Britain was more than canceled out by its trade deficit with the United States. American companies began to dominate segments of the economy through Canadian subsidiaries.

The locus of the economy moved from the Maritime Provinces, which suffered as industries shifted from burning coal to oil, to the provinces of Ontario and Quebec. Mining increased, and Canada continued heavy exports of vegetable products, wood products (especially pulp for American newspapers), and animal products. The regional shift in prosperity also affected Canada in cultural as well as economic terms. The central government ended its large and effective campaign to encourage immigration from overseas and terminated its free land grants program, making it necessary for immigrants wishing to farm to possess sufficient capital to purchase land, seed, animals, and equipment. Consequently, a majority of the 1 million immigrants to Canada during the 1920s settled in cities, furthering the urbanization of the country.

One of the biggest changes in the economy—the rise of the automobile—also brought changes in culture, lifestyle, and the physical landscape. The number of cars, motorcycles, trucks, and buses in Canada tripled during the 1920s. The mass-produced internal combustion engine not only spawned a new industry but also brought a dramatic increase in paved roads, along with traffic lights, sidewalks, and all the other attributes of automobile society. Trucks competed with railroads to transport heavy freight.

Automobiles, improved roads, telephones, indoor electricity, and hydroelectric power all helped create an urban culture that favored Ontario and Quebec over the other provinces. The city of Toronto, in particular, grew rapidly, and what had been farming areas outside the city soon became suburbs, served by streetcars, paved roads, electric lights, and a housing boom. Cheaper, more available electricity spurred an increase in manufacturing, which in turn sparked population growth. Immigrants from other countries and Canadians moving from rural areas helped fuel the expansion of cities. Hamilton, London, and Windsor flourished. Ottawa nearly tripled in population during the decade.

Politics

Politics in Canada underwent a transformation after World War I. In 1919, William L.M. King succeeded Wilfrid Laurier as leader of the Liberal Party, beginning a domination of national politics that would last nearly three decades. King had lived in the United States, worked in settlement houses, gained experience in dealing with labor issues, and served in the Canadian House of Commons and as a Labor minister. He favored a highly progressive platform, though few of the measures would win passage in the Canadian Parliament.

The Conservative Party was led by Arthur Meighen, who, during the war, had been responsible for government policies that upset a number of interests, including French Canadians, Prairie farmers, recent immigrants, Montreal business interests, and organized labor. Meighen became prime minister in July 1920, upon the resignation of Conservative leader Robert Borden. But in the national elections of December 1921, the Liberals won a majority and King succeeded Meighen as prime minister. King and the Liberals retained power throughout most of the decade.

At the same time, there was significant regional opposition. Economic changes hit the Maritime Provinces hard. The eastern shipbuilding industry was in decline, as was the shipping of Nova Scotia coal; more trade was moving south to the United States than by sea to Great Britain; and companies relocated factories to the larger cities of Montreal and Toronto. Economic decline led to a loss of population in the Maritime Provinces, which meant fewer seats in Parliament and declining political influence. A.P. Paterson, a grocer, argued for maritime rights, maintaining that all of Canada should provide support for any region that was economically disadvantaged. E.N. Rhodes of the Conservative Party in Nova Scotia joined the movement and helped end four decades of Liberal control in that province. Maritimers switched votes from the Liberal Party to the Conservative Party in various elections, but they lacked the political power to achieve their goal.

In the Prairie Provinces, farmers were disenchanted with the two major parties and with government's unwillingness to lower tariff barriers. Lower tariffs would have aided Canadian agriculture exports, since many countries responded to Canadian tariffs by raising their tariffs on Canadian exports, principally agriculture. Ten members of Parliament left the Union Party, established as a coalition government during the war, and in 1920 formed the National Progressive Party. In Alberta, rural Ontario, Manitoba, New Brunswick, and Nova Scotia, Progressive Party candidates generally fared well. The election of 1921 showed the differences, with the Liberals winning 116 seats, almost all of them east of the Ottawa River; the Conservatives won 50 seats, mostly from Ontario; and the Progressives won 64 seats, mostly in the West. The Progressives could not unite on major issues, however, and King was able to siphon away support. By 1930, the party had largely disappeared from Canadian politics, though Prairie discontent would continue.

By 1929, meanwhile, the American-based white supremacist Ku Klux Klan, which had reemerged in the 1920s, had spread north into Canada with 125 local chapters in Saskatchewan alone. The success of the Klan in the late 1920s reflected the fear of some older-stock Canadians about change and the future.

But challenges to the established order also came from several reform movements. Women's suffrage was secured in British Columbia, Alberta, Saskatchewan, and Manitoba in 1916, Ontario in 1917, Nova Scotia in 1918, New Brunswick in 1919, and Prince Edward Island in 1922. Women gained the right to vote in federal elections in January 1919, and Agnes MacPhail became the first woman elected to the Canadian House of Commons in 1921. Quebec held out on granting women's suffrage until 1940.

The normal role for most Canadian women in the 1920s was that of mother to a large family. With little access to effective birth control, Canadian women were faced with considerable housework and child-rearing responsibilities. Many women, especially in rural areas, faced backbreaking work and, often, an early death.

In Quebec, a movement championed by the writings of Abbé Groulx identified Francophone Canada, Catholic Canada, and rural Canada as largely the same and sought to distance Quebec from the changes taking place, particularly to the west. It feared secularization and Americanization and fought the advance of popular culture. The movement wanted to preserve the village, small farm, and rural life.

Perhaps the greatest challenge of the decade came from the United States. New labor-saving devices invented in America increased the amount of leisure time and brought major changes to Canadian society. A growth in public education along with greater leisure time led to a more secular and less church-based culture. Some bemoaned what they perceived as a decline in morals and rise in hedonism.

Culture

The 1920s marked the rise of popular culture in America, and the changes quickly crossed the border. As Canada became increasingly reliant on the automobile, American-owned companies made some three-quarters of cars sold in Canada. In 1914, there were 69,598 cars registered in Canada; by 1919, the number had increased to 341,316.

American radio also crossed into Canada; approximately four out of five Canadians regularly listened to American radio. Canadian stations, reflecting the smaller towns in which they were located and less income from advertising, were lower wattage and lacked a strong signal. Given that most Canadians lived within seventy-five miles of the border, the weak Canadian radio signals were no match for the strength of stations from larger American cities along the border. Meanwhile, mass-circulation magazines from America, such as *Ladies Home Journal* and *The Saturday Evening Post,* became staples in Canadian homes. Service clubs such as Kiwanis, Rotary, and Lions, which had become popular in the United States, established chapters in Canadian cities.

The 1920s also marked the rise of popular spectator sports in Canada. While ice hockey had originated north of the border, several franchises in the National Hockey League, with the notable exceptions of teams in Toronto and Montreal, had relocated to U.S. cities. Still, Canadians participated in recreational sports and attended professional sporting events in great numbers. Amateurs played hockey, football, baseball, and lacrosse, while professional teams drew fans in hockey, football, and baseball. The 1920s were also a golden age for women in sport. The legendary Edmonton (Alberta) Grads, a high school squad that stayed together after graduation and compiled an astonishing record of 512–20, dominated women's basketball in Canada and internationally.

Perhaps most important, movies came to symbolize popular culture as the decade progressed, with American films dominating Canadian movie theaters. Canada lacked the capital to create a strong, domestic movie industry, and Hollywood had the great advantages of natural landscape, climate, and lower labor costs. Eventually the threat of being overwhelmed by American culture would lead Canada to pass content laws to protect and nurture a distinctive Canadian popular culture in film, television, magazines, and other media.

On the eve of the Great Depression, Canada and Canadians had changed greatly since the end of World War I. The nation and its people had become less British and less European, more oriented toward America, more diverse, and more concerned about their rightful place in the world.

Charles M. Dobbs

See also: Immigration.

Further Reading

Allen, Richard. *The Social Passion: Religion and Social Reform in Canada, 1914–1928.* Toronto: University of Toronto Press, 1971.

Bondy, Robert J. *The Confident Years: Canada in the 1920s.* Scarborough, Ontario: Prentice-Hall, 1978.

Bothwell, Robert, Ian Drummond, and John English. *Canada, 1900–1945.* Toronto: University of Toronto Press, 1987.

Hunt, C.W. *Booze, Boats, and Billions: Smuggling Liquid Gold.* Toronto: McClelland & Stewart, 1988.

Riddell, Walter Alexander, ed. *Documents on Canadian Foreign Policy, 1917–1939.* Toronto: Oxford University Press, 1962.

Robin, Martin. *Shades of Right: Nativist and Fascist Politics in Canada, 1920–1940.* Toronto: University of Toronto Press, 1992.

Thompson, John Herd, and Allen Seager. *Canada, 1922–1939: Decades of Discord.* Toronto: McClelland & Stewart, 1990.

Trofimenkoff, S.M. *Action Française: French Canadian Nationalism in the Twenties.* Toronto: University of Toronto Press, 1975.

————, ed. *The Twenties in Western Canada.* Ottawa: National Museums of Canada, 1972.

Capone, Al
(1899–1947)

Al Capone was one of the most notorious organized crime figures of the Jazz Age. Based in Chicago, Capone's nationwide organization grossed an estimated $100 million a year during the late 1920s, largely through the production, smuggling, and selling of alcohol, illegal under the decade's Prohibition laws. An extraordinarily violent man—the 1929 St. Valentine's Day Massacre of seven members of a rival gang, which Capone allegedly orchestrated, represents one of the most brutal episodes in the history of American organized crime—Capone was ultimately convicted and imprisoned on one of the most banal of charges: tax evasion.

Alphonse Gabriel Capone was born on January 17, 1899, in Brooklyn, the fourth son of immigrants from southern Italy. He quit school at age fourteen after assaulting a teacher, then took odd jobs and drifted in and out of youth gangs that engaged in petty crime.

By the time he was eighteen, Capone had joined the powerful Five Points Gang in Lower Manhattan, led by the organized crime figure Frankie Yale. Capone worked as a bouncer and bartender at Yale's tavern, the seedy Harvard Inn. There, he got into a knife fight with another gangster that left him with a wound to his right cheek and the nickname he would carry with him—and resent—for the rest of his life: Scarface. Around the same time, Capone married Mae Josephine Coughlin, who soon gave birth to a son.

Quick-witted, fearless, and violent, Capone soon proved useful to Yale, performing at least two murders

The head of Chicago's largest organized crime syndicate in the 1920s, Al Capone made a fortune circumventing the Jazz Age prohibition on the manufacture, distribution, and sale of alcohol. The source of his nickname, Scarface, can be seen on his left cheek. *(Hulton Archive/Getty Images)*

for him by 1919, but he was also troublesome. After Capone got into a fight with a rival gang, Yale dispatched him to Chicago.

Settling in the suburb of Cicero, west of Chicago, Capone went to work for a local mob leader named Johnny Torrio. At first, he served as a bouncer at illegal bars, or speakeasies, and as a capper, the man who stood outside houses of prostitution enticing customers to come in. To give himself the appearance of a legitimate businessman, Capone also set himself up as a dealer in secondhand furniture. Torrio, who was trying to turn his various ventures into a well-oiled organized crime operation, was impressed by Capone's enterprise and good sense. By 1922, Capone was Torrio's second in command, responsible for the two most lucrative criminal activities: prostitution and alcohol.

The following year, the Torrio-Capone gang faced a setback with the election of Chicago reform mayor William Dever, who launched a major crackdown on organized crime in the city. Under Capone's leadership, Torrio moved his operations to Cicero, where Capone used an army of thugs in 1924 to intimidate voters into electing a mayor and council beholden to Torrio. So confident was Capone of his power that he actually assaulted the mayor on the steps of city hall to show the public who was really in charge.

Despite Dever's best efforts, organized crime flourished in Chicago, with rival gangs controlling gambling, prostitution, and bootlegging operations in various parts of the city. When the Torrio-Capone gang began to move into the lucrative Gold Coast neighborhood controlled by the North Side Gang, a mobster war broke out, leading to attempted assassinations against both Torrio and Capone in 1925. Torrio nearly died from his wounds; after recuperating and then serving a year in prison for probation violations, he retired and moved to Italy. Capone was now in charge of what had become the biggest organized crime operation in Chicago.

Capone was both a brilliant executive and a ruthless executioner. He helped streamline criminal enterprise in the city by using the managerial techniques of big business, while expanding his operations across the Midwest and into the Northeast. At the same time, he launched a brutal series of attacks on rival gangs, triggering a wave of murderous violence that engulfed Chicago in the second half of the 1920s, culminating in the St. Valentine's Day Massacre of 1929.

Two years before the massacre, to escape state investigators, Capone had moved to Palm Island, Florida, and had continued to run his operations by long-distance telephone and courier. In the February 14 attack, allegedly ordered by Capone from his Florida estate, seven members of a gang led by George "Bugs" Moran were lured to a warehouse on North Clark Street under the pretext of a bootleg alcohol sale and then gunned down.

As in many of the murders attributed to Capone, he was able to escape prosecution through bribery of public officials and through witness and jury intimidation. Capone was allegedly responsible for several dozen murders in Chicago in the late 1920s but was never successfully prosecuted for a single one. Still, the St. Valentine's Day Massacre would prove his downfall. Capone, who had cultivated public opinion through conspicuous acts of charity, such as milk programs for poor children, saw himself vilified, even among his fellow Italian Americans, for the murders. In addition, the attack was simply too brazen for law enforcement officials to ignore.

An incorruptible former Bureau of Investigation agent named Eliot Ness was in charge of the Treasury Department's Bureau of Prohibition in Chicago. Ness made Capone his highest priority target and, with the help of the Internal Revenue Service, indicted Capone on tax evasion violations in 1931.

This time, the charges stuck. Capone was sentenced to federal prison for eleven years, but released in 1939, after serving seven and one-half years. Historians dispute the cause of Capone's death, with some arguing it was heart attacks, others saying it was a stroke and pneumonia, and still others stating that it was brought on by complications caused by syphilis. All can agree, however, that Al Capone died at his Florida estate on January 25, 1947.

James Ciment and Leigh Kimmel

See also: Crime, Organized; Ness, Eliot; Prohibition (1920–1933).

Further Reading

Helmer, William J. *The St. Valentine's Day Massacre: The Untold Story of the Gangland Bloodbath That Brought Down Al Capone.* Nashville, TN: Cumberland House, 2004.

Kobler, John. *Capone: The Life and World of Al Capone.* New York: Da Capo, 1992.

Schoenberg, Robert J. *Mr. Capone.* New York: Morrow, 1992.

Catholics and Catholicism

American Catholicism during the Jazz Age experienced some of its greatest progress, despite prejudices within the mainstream culture. Catholics expanded, centralized, and consolidated their dioceses and educational institutions. A number of prominent cardinals, bishops, and priests emerged to restructure urban dioceses and lead nationwide movements for Catholics. Lay people expanded their role in the church. And a Catholic—Al Smith—won the Democratic nomination for president in 1928, although he was defeated in the general election. By the end of the 1920s, Catholics could reflect on the beginnings of a renaissance, of an increased respectability, that would reach full flower in the next decade.

Roman Relevance and Theology

Pope Benedict XV led the Roman Catholic Church from 1914 to 1922, and Pope Pius XI served from 1922 to 1939. The two pontiffs deserve mention in relation to American Catholicism because of several of their encyclicals—open letters from a pope to priests and laity about current issues. In the Jazz Age, papal encyclicals addressed postwar reconciliation (*Pacem* and *Dei munus pucherrimum,* 1919), missionary activities (*Maximum illud,* 1919, and *Rerum Ecclesiae,* 1926), laity participation (*Ubi arcano Dei consilio,* 1922), and a condemnation of ecumenism (*Mortalium animos,* 1928). These encyclicals directed the church hierarchy's energies. For instance, Pius XI's *Ubi arcano* encyclical inspired the international Catholic Action movement, partially represented with groups such as the Sodality of Our Lady—organized by Daniel A. Lord, S.J., in the United States in 1926.

In terms of theological currents, the Catholic Church escaped the modernist versus fundamentalist controversies that split Protestant churches in the 1920s. Pope Leo XIII had condemned "Americanism" in an 1899 letter (*Testem Benevolentiae*) to an American bishop, which many interpret as a condemnation of theological modernism, a movement that favored individualism and practicality over contemplation and obedience to the hierarchy. In 1907, Pope Pius X explicitly and vigorously denigrated theological modernism in an encyclical (*Pascendi Dominici Gregis*). Both documents, as well as the new Code of Canon Law in 1917, prevented any real development of liberal Catholic theology in the Jazz Age.

Moreover, these papal condemnations reinforced the encouragement given in 1879, with Leo XIII's encyclical *Aeterni Patris,* to revive scholastic theology and philosophy—namely, the study of Thomas Aquinas's *Summa Theologica* and other works. This relatively conservative new movement, called neoscholasticism, dominated Catholic intellectual life in the first half of the twentieth century. Catholic theology in the 1920s, therefore, was strongly conservative in relation to earlier, turn-of-the-century Catholic theology—and especially in relation to the spirit of progressivism and the Protestant Social Gospel movement.

Figures in the American Hierarchy

In the Jazz Age and afterward, several American-born bishops, trained in Rome, became leaders of the most populous, urban dioceses in the Midwest and Northeast. John Cardinal Glennon served in St. Louis, William Cardinal O'Connell in Boston, Dennis Cardinal Dougherty in Philadelphia, Francis Cardinal Spellman in New York City, and George Cardinal Mundelein in Chicago. Other well-known bishops, such as James Cardinal Gibbons of Baltimore, finished long terms of service around the beginning of the Jazz Age. These leaders adapted the Catholic Church to an American setting by promoting assimilation; building or expanding diocesan seminaries; centralizing their administrations; fundraising for the pope, missions, and local charities; and exerting public and private influence over local and national politics. These "consolidating" bishops set the tone for less visible Catholics in the South and West.

Cardinal Mundelein, for example, in leading Chicago's diocese from 1916 to 1939, brought Catholicism from a premodern organization to prominence as perhaps the best-run diocese in America. One of Mundelein's earliest acts was to restrict ethnic-language parishes in the city, thereby forcing American assimilation on the diocese. Construction projects were fundamental to his program, as he directed the building of Quigley Preparatory Seminary and the massive Saint Mary of the Lake Seminary, which he hoped would serve as the nation's most important Catholic university in the West. (In honor of the project, the town of Area voted to rename itself Mundelein.)

Chicago's hosting of the Twenty-eighth International Eucharistic Congress in June 1926 introduced Cardinal Mundelein's influence to the world's Catholics. This hugely successful, week-long devotional gathering served as a pilgrimage event for thousands of priests and laypeople. Conducted in parish churches and at Soldier Field during the week, the events culminated at Saint Mary of the Lake Seminary, where an estimated 500,000 attended.

Mundelein earned a reputation as a first-rate fund-raiser when his staff pioneered the use of Catholic Bishop of Chicago (CBC) bonds. These instruments, sold on the open market, helped foster a centralized credit scheme for the diocese. Mundelein's influence in national politics came later, during the New Deal, when he came to see President Roosevelt's program as a way to implement two papal encyclicals on social justice (*Rerum novarum*, 1891, and *Quadragesimo Anno*, 1931).

Growing Public Presence

An increasingly more organized and active Catholic laity began to emerge in church affairs in the 1920s. This activity arose from the increasing presence of Irish Catholics in the middle class: they could afford to do more. In the Jazz Age, groups such as the International Federation of Catholic Alumnae and the National Catholic Welfare Conference were on the rise. Catholic educational institutions, such as primary and secondary schools, as well as colleges and universities, also grew throughout the course of the decade. Meanwhile, laity enthusiasm helped make weekly periodicals such as *America* and *Commonweal* (founded in 1924) popular Jazz Age reading for Catholics. In politics, Al Smith, a Catholic Democrat who became governor of New York and was a presidential candidate in 1928, represented the larger public presence of Catholicism in the period.

The International Federation of Catholic Alumnae (IFCA) was organized in 1915 by college-educated women whose primary interest lay in promoting education. The group received ecclesial approval from Benedict XV and Pius XI; Monsignor Edward A. Pace of the Catholic University of America acted as the organization's first director. Headquartered in New York City, the IFCA expanded to approximately 80,000 members by 1930, its growth supported by the increasing number of Catholic women's colleges in the 1920s. The IFCA's activities included providing scholarships for nuns, protesting

religious persecution in Mexico, and establishing a board of review for motion pictures. The last, according to *Commonweal*, would "fight the salacious and meretricious" in film.

Christened the Motion Picture Bureau in 1922, this group reviewed films for approximately a dozen years before the creation of its more infamous descendant, the Legion of Decency. In the late 1920s, the bureau's first director, IFCA member and lawyer Rita McGoldrick, LLD, initiated radio broadcasts of their film reviews. When the Legion of Decency floundered in the early 1930s, its leaders moved their headquarters to New York City and used IFCA reviewers, allowing female Catholic laity to influence film censorship until the early 1960s.

The National Catholic Welfare Conference (NCWC) began in 1917 as the National Catholic War Council. Conceived in coordination with the Knights of Columbus, the War Council helped organize Catholic support for America's efforts in World War I. The next year, the organization came under the control of the American bishops, and it became the NCWC in 1922. One of the NCWC's first big battles was the Smith-Towner bill, first introduced in 1918, which sought monetary aid for education and the creation of a national department of education. Catholics feared that state-funded, inherently Protestant schools would monopolize America's educational system. The Jesuit weekly *America* argued that the bill would create a "Prussianized" or Bolshevist education system. With the already existing Catholic Education Association (CEA), the NCWC fought passage of the bill. By 1929, the CEA would be fully subsumed by the NCWC as its department of education.

Meanwhile, Catholic schools and institutions of higher education continued their maturation process in the 1920s. Many Catholic institutions referring to themselves as "colleges" at the turn of the twentieth century served large numbers of secondary students. By the second half of the Jazz Age, however, these students were primarily served by diocesan Catholic high schools. Whereas secondary students constituted half the population of Catholic colleges in 1916, they no longer counted as college students by 1926.

Catholic higher education continued to expand its programs and institutions in the Jazz Age. It should be noted that Jesuits controlled most of America's largest Catholic men's colleges of the mid-1920s, as well as Catholic universities with professional and graduate students. Professional programs in business, education, engineering, law, and medicine, first established in 1900, continued through the Jazz Age. Catholic women's colleges had likewise been growing since 1899. By 1926, they educated about one-third of the nation's total Catholic undergraduate population. In 1930, there were forty-five accredited women's colleges, with another twenty-nine awaiting accreditation. In that year, the Sisters of Charity of the Blessed Virgin Mary (or BVMs), opened the famous "skyscraper" Mundelein College in Chicago—named after the same cardinal who had invited them to the city and helped raise funds for the college's construction.

Further progress of Catholicism in the Jazz Age and Catholics' uneasy integration into American society and culture is demonstrated in Al Smith's political career. As the offspring of Irish Catholic immigrants and the Tammany Hall political machine, Smith first emerged as a national political figure at the 1924 Democratic National Convention. As New York's governor, he campaigned for the Democratic presidential nomination as an anti-Prohibition and anti-Klan candidate. Smith did not gain the nomination that year, but he did in 1928—when he faced Republican Herbert Hoover in the election. The national campaign featured charges of Smith's purported papal allegiance, the most prominent political criticism made by anti-Catholics in the decade. For this and because of the nation's economic prosperity at the time, Smith lost to Hoover by 6.4 million votes. Despite Catholics' increasing integration into the American political and education systems, the charge of "popery" still resonated with the American public. A significant proportion of the electorate feared that Catholicism, with its hierarchical, international structure, was an antidemocratic religion. At the same time, the bigotry that accompanied the 1928 election also stirred sympathy among more liberal Americans—a positive backlash that resulted in greater respect for Catholics in subsequent decades.

Tim Lacy

See also: Anti-Catholicism; Irish Americans; Italian Americans.

Further Reading

Ellis, John Tracy. *American Catholicism.* 2nd ed. Chicago: University of Chicago Press, 1969.

Gleason, Philip. *Contending with Modernity: Catholic Higher Education in the Twentieth Century.* New York: Oxford University Press, 1995.

Kantowicz, Edward R. *Corporation Sole: Cardinal Mundelein and Chicago Catholicism.* Notre Dame, IN: Notre Dame University Press, 1983.

McBrien, Richard P. *Lives of the Popes: The Pontiffs from St. Peter to John Paul II.* New York: HarperCollins, 1997.

Skerrett, Ellen, Edward Kantowicz, and Steven M. Avella. *Catholicism, Chicago Style.* Chicago: Loyola University Press, 1993.

Skinner, James M. *The Cross and the Cinema: The Legion of Decency and the National Catholic Office for Motion Pictures, 1933–1970.* Westport, CT: Greenwood, 1993.

Celebrity Culture

Celebrities have been part of American culture from early colonial days. Benjamin Franklin, for example, was celebrated up and down the Atlantic seaboard for his statesmanship, inventiveness, and writing. In the late nineteenth century, author Mark Twain and inventor Thomas Edison were nationally renowned for their accomplishments. All three of these Americans assumed larger-than-life personas in the public imagination, yet many people could identify with them on a personal level. Although such celebrity existed long before the Jazz Age, it was during the 1920s that a full-blown celebrity culture arose. An industry developed to promote certain individuals as celebrities for a mass audience hungry for gossip and information about the lives and accomplishments of famous people.

Several factors contributed to the growth of a celebrity culture in the 1920s. Mass media—film, tabloid journalism, radio, and newsreels—and the emergence of mass public spectacles like professional sports contests were the most important developments. But the advent of the public relations profession and increasingly sophisticated advertising agencies contributed to the celebrity culture as well. In addition, many Americans, particularly urban residents, were earning more money than they had in the past and could afford to buy a radio, a movie ticket, or a copy of the photo-laden, gossip-filled tabloid papers like New York's *Daily News,* launched in 1919. Urban Americans were also developing new psychological needs. No longer tied to the web of relationships and institutions that characterized rural and small-town life, they longed for connection to larger communities. Fandom—whether for a sports team or a movie star—offered a new form of community and social connection.

The 1920s also witnessed the growth of what might be called democratic celebrity, the possibility

Three of Hollywood's leading lights—left to right: swash-buckling hero Douglas Fairbanks, child star Jackie Coogan, and romantic leading man Rudolph Valentino—pose together in 1925. The birth of modern celebrity culture coincided with the golden age of movies. *(Topical Press Agency/Stringer/Hulton Archive/Getty Images)*

first time, people could see the face of an actor or actress in detail, creating a psychological connection with a performer. Film projected these celebrities in a glowing light on a vast screen, often in an ornate movie palace dedicated to the art form and its stars. Film was also a mass medium, with the same movie playing in hundreds of communities across the country. The movie star, therefore, was both intimate and distant, familiar and larger than life, contradictory aspects that enhanced audience fascination.

Hollywood studios and the stars themselves became increasingly adept at shaping a public persona through careful selection of film roles and well-oiled publicity machines. Mary Pickford, "America's Sweetheart," cultivated an image of innocence through roles that portrayed her as the girl-next-door. Her husband, Douglas Fairbanks, established himself as the swashbuckling hero in such films as *The Mark of Zorro* (1920) and *The Thief of Baghdad* (1924). Although both had divorced other partners—still a matter of scandal at the time—when they married in 1920, they became the most celebrated couple in Hollywood. Indeed, scandal plagued Hollywood celebrities during the 1920s, until studio heads cracked down on the flamboyant lifestyles of their stars through blacklisting and establishing codes of conduct. But while some of the public was offended by Hollywood behavior, the sexual goings-on in the film community were trumpeted in popular tabloids and in a whole new genre of journalism, the film magazine.

Sports stars also had their scandals. Babe Ruth, the Yankee slugger and perhaps the greatest sports celebrity of the decade, was known for his womanizing and heavy drinking at a time when alcohol consumption was illegal. But for the most part, sports stars such as Olympic swimmer Johnny Weissmuller and football hero Red Grange generally enjoyed a more wholesome reputation. Still, celebrity-generating forces were at work in sports no less than in film. First, there was a new mass audience that could view sports heroes in newsreels or listen to their achievements on radio. And while ornate movie palaces were the showcases for Hollywood celebrities, sports stars performed in huge new stadiums. More money and leisure time allowed more people to attend baseball and football games, and even to participate in tennis and golf in greater numbers, thereby enhancing the celebrity status of top golfers like Bobby Jones and tennis stars like Bill Tilden.

Finally, the rising publicity and media industries of the 1920s created celebrities out of people in

that anyone, no matter how obscure, might rise to national celebrity status. There were stories of pretty young women from the Midwest being discovered by Hollywood movie producers, and of young immigrants winning slots on professional baseball teams. Or, at its most democratic, celebrity could be won by a person sitting atop a flagpole longer than anyone had before.

Aside from such stunt celebrities, who faded in and out of public consciousness with the next day's news, the celebrities of the 1920s fall into three categories: film, sports, and news, the latter category encompassing those whose achievements or notoriety earned them lasting attention in the press and the public imagination.

Theater actors and opera stars had long been celebrities in America, but film offered something different to the public. Movies were at once larger than life and more intimate than the stage. For the

Death of Valentino

He was one of the most popular stars of the silent film era, and certainly the first male sex symbol to come out of the movie industry. Women swooned at his image, and his nickname, the "Great Lover," only added to his popularity among female moviegoers. When Rudolph Valentino died suddenly in August 1926—of peritonitis following surgery—the nation erupted in grief usually reserved for presidents and national heroes.

He was born Rodolfo Alfonso Raffaello Piero Filiberto Guglielmi Rudolph Valentino on May 6, 1895, in Castellaneta, Italy. He was well educated, but he apparently lacked ambition. In 1913, he came to the United States and took odd jobs as a gardener, busboy, and exhibition dancer. He traveled to California in 1917 and became a dance instructor, finally finding his way to Hollywood. After several bit parts and uncredited supporting roles, his big break came in 1921 in the movie *The Four Horsemen of the Apocalypse*. The film was a huge success, and Valentino was a star. His roles in such subsequent features as *The Sheik* (1921), *The Young Rajah* (1922), *The Eagle* (1925), and *Son of the Sheik* (1926) sealed his status as a romantic lead. Although some of his roles would showcase his dancing and comedic skills, he became known for his swarthy good looks, hypnotic eyes, and killing smile.

The details of Valentino's personal life became as popular as his movies. His two failed marriages, his purported affair with actress Pola Negri, and even a temporary beard were the subjects of fan gossip. Many men failed to see why he was so popular, and questions arose about his masculinity and the effect of his image on the self-identity of the average American male.

On the evening of August 14, 1926, Valentino became violently ill after spending the night with friends in New York City. The next afternoon, he underwent emergency surgery to remove his appendix and repair a perforated ulcer. He showed signs of improvement at first, but a high fever and infection set in. Without antibiotics, which had yet to be invented, the infection raced throughout his body. When Valentino died on August 23, 1926, he was only thirty-one years old.

Newspapers around the world published the first-ever "Extra" editions for the death of a movie star. His passing caused an outpouring of grief the nation had rarely seen. At least two women committed suicide when they heard the news. Up to 100,000 people jammed the street in front of the funeral home, hoping to view his body. Waiting crowds grew impatient and tried to storm the building. In the chaos that ensued, windows were broken, cars overturned, and several people injured. Police strained to control the crowds, and it took a full day for order to be restored.

After a funeral mass at Saint Malachy's Catholic Church in Manhattan, Valentino's body was transported across the country for burial at the Hollywood Forever Cemetery in Hollywood, California. Rumors surrounding his death persist to this day, although claims that he was poisoned or committed suicide have been largely discredited. Memorial services are still held at his grave every year on the anniversary of his death, and Valentino—who had no wish to grow old—remains forever an American cultural icon.

David A. Serafini

the news—some heroic, some notorious. The most famous celebrity of the Jazz Age to emerge from news coverage was probably Charles Lindbergh, whose solo flight across the Atlantic in 1927 made him an international hero. However, the American public was equally fascinated by people they feared or loathed. Chicago gangster Al Capone became a national celebrity, featured in newsreels and tabloids, for a brutal mob war that left dozens of people dead in the late 1920s.

Despite the hard times that followed the onset of the Great Depression in the early 1930s, the celebrity culture that arose in the Jazz Age remained strong. While the names may have changed, film, sports, and the daily headlines provided new figures for public curiosity and adoration throughout the 1930s. Historians theorize that many Americans followed the lives of celebrities as a way to forget their own straitened economic circumstances. The celebrity culture that emerged in America in the Jazz Age was to become a permanent part of popular culture.

James Ciment

See also: Beauty Industry and Culture; Bow, Clara; Chaplin, Charlie; Ederle, Gertrude; Fairbanks, Douglas; Film; Fitzgerald, F. Scott, and Zelda Fitzgerald; Gish, Lillian; Grange, Red; Jones, Bobby; Pickford, Mary; Radio; Rogers, Will; Ruth, Babe; Swanson, Gloria; Tilden, Bill; Weissmuller, Johnny.

Further Reading

Boorstin, Daniel. *The Image: A Guide to Pseudo Events in America.* New York: Vintage Books, 1961.

Ponce de Leon, Charles L. *Self Exposure: Human Interest Journalism and the Emergence of Celebrity in America, 1890–1940.* Chapel Hill: University of North Carolina Press, 2002.

Chamber of Commerce, U.S.

Chambers of commerce are business networks organized to improve the commercial environment of a specific geographical area through shared information, cooperative ventures, and political lobbying. During the strongly probusiness political and cultural climate of the Jazz Age, chambers of commerce thrived in the United States. The national U.S. Chamber of Commerce grew dramatically during the 1920s, as local chambers were founded in many smaller cities and towns. By the end of the decade, the organization claimed more than 16,000 member affiliates nationwide.

Originating in seventeenth-century France, chambers of commerce were founded in various European cities during the Enlightenment and spread to North America with the establishment of the first American chamber in New York City in 1768. By 1870, more than forty chambers of commerce, also known as boards of trade, were operating in American cities.

Fueled by a dramatic increase in the number of young, middle-class professionals resulting from a growth of the corporate and financial sectors of the American economy, chambers of commerce proliferated during the late nineteenth and early twentieth centuries. Local chambers were organized nationally under the U.S. Chamber of Commerce, founded in 1912 at the behest of President William Howard Taft as a means of strengthening ties between business and government.

From its inception, the U.S. Chamber of Commerce exercised formidable political power, lobbying Congress for passage of the Federal Reserve Act in 1913 and for the repeal of wartime economic regulations following the end of World War I. The organization was also instrumental in convincing the federal government to strengthen the U.S. Merchant Marine. The product of a Progressive Era trend toward the formation of civic and professional organizations that also produced the American Bar Association, the National Municipal League, and the National Association for the Advancement of Colored People (NAACP), the U.S. Chamber of Commerce nevertheless joined the backlash against progressivism in the 1920s, advocating a return to the laissez-faire business environment of the late nineteenth century.

With the support of the conservative, probusiness presidents of the 1920s, chambers of commerce advanced a political agenda that included support for government promotion of foreign trade, less government regulation of business, and less support for labor unions. Opposition to the growing labor movement was of particular concern, and local chambers and the national organization lobbied state and local governments to prevent legislation and other policy actions that would legitimize organized labor. Seizing upon the anti-immigrant sentiments of the 1920s, the U.S. Chamber of Commerce promoted an "Americanization" program that cast labor unions as extensions of the Socialist and Communist movements of contemporary Europe. Yet, unlike the National Association of Manufacturers, which advocated a similar political agenda, the U.S. Chamber of Commerce periodically encouraged its members to seek compromises with organized labor to minimize market disruptions and negative publicity, and to adapt to regulatory and other policy changes. The U.S. Chamber of Commerce was a strong advocate of employee representation plans, also known as "company unions," organized by employers as alternatives to conventional labor unions.

The U.S. Chamber of Commerce enjoyed a particularly close relationship with the Hoover administration. In the late 1920s, Julius Barnes, a friend and former business partner of Hoover, was elected chair of the organization. Following the stock market crash of October 1929, the U.S. Chamber of Commerce worked with Hoover's Department of Commerce to establish voluntary standards for controlling wages, prices, and unfair business practices. Consistent with his belief in laissez-faire economics, Hoover had encouraged the cooperation as an alternative to government intervention in the economic crisis that would become known as the Great Depression.

The U.S. Chamber of Commerce initially supported the policies of Hoover's successor, Franklin D. Roosevelt. But as Roosevelt adopted an increasingly interventionist stance toward American business, cooperation between his administration and the chamber began to wane, reaching a low point following the enactment of the Wagner Act and Social Security Act in 1935. The U.S. Chamber of Commerce resumed a cooperative relationship with the Roosevelt administration during World War II but strongly opposed the expansion of government during the latter half of the twentieth century. It remains one of the most powerful probusiness lobbying groups in America.

Michael H. Burchett

See also: Commerce Department, U.S.; National Association of Manufacturers.

Further Reading

Issel, William. "Business Power and Political Culture in San Francisco, 1900–1940." *Journal of Urban History* 16:1 (1989): 52–77.

Mack, Charles S. *Business, Politics, and the Practice of Government Relations.* Westport, CT: Quorum, 1997.

Werking, Richard Hume. "Bureaucrats, Businessmen, and Foreign Trade: The Origins of the United States Chamber of Commerce." *Business History Review* 52:3 (1978): 321–41.

Chaplin, Charlie (1889–1977)

The film comedian and director Charlie Chaplin was the first global star of the mass media age. A cultural icon, he fundamentally influenced the silent era of film. Chaplin was one of the first film "auteurs": directors whose vision shaped every aspect of a film, from story to cinematography to music. He handled almost every facet of film production, even learning to read music so he could write the scores. He was also notable for working independently of the studio system for most of his career. Chaplin's Little Tramp character enjoyed phenomenal success, but his life was plagued by controversy that led to his exile from America in 1952.

Charles Spencer Chaplin was born on April 16, 1889, in London, England. Both of his parents were music hall artists, but his father's alcoholism and mother's mental illness, which led to her institutionalization, left young Chaplin abandoned and forced to spend time in workhouse orphanages. These experiences of Victorian London street life would inform many of his films.

Chaplin first acted on the stage at the age of nine, then joined theater impresario Fred Karno's sketch comedy troupe, which brought him to the United States in 1910. In 1913, Chaplin signed with producer Mack Sennett at the Keystone Film Company, and he acted in his first Hollywood short film, *Making a Living,* in 1914.

While moving from one studio to another in the late 1910s—from Essanay (1915) to Mutual (1916–1917) to First National (1918)—Chaplin was establishing himself as a national and international film star. America was gripped by "Chaplinitis," and his Little Tramp—a character he introduced in his second film *Kid's Auto Races* (1914) and developed in subsequent films—had matured into a character that blended physical comedy and pathos with social commentary, appealing to a wide audience at many levels. The Tramp, with his bowler hat, tight coat, baggy trousers, twirling cane, toothbrush moustache, and waddle-like walk became an international film icon.

By 1919, Chaplin was a global figure, his distinctive on-screen character a commentary on the inequities and absurdities of the modern age. Over the next decade, he continued to explore themes of poverty and alienation in the city, siding with the un-

Arguably the most popular film star of America's Jazz Age, British-born actor and director Charlie Chaplin contemplates a knee-high model of his most famous screen persona, the "Little Tramp." *(General Photographic Agency/ Stringer/Hulton Archive/Getty Images)*

derdog and pointing out the dangers and oppression facing many factory workers.

The year 1919 marked a significant shift in Chaplin's career, as he moved from short films to longer pieces of work. This coincided with his joining three of the other most powerful figures in film— celebrated director D.W. Griffith and movie stars Douglas Fairbanks and Mary Pickford—in the creation of United Artists, a film distribution company that signaled their intent to be independent from the existing Hollywood studio system. The films that Chaplin made for United showcased his creativity, but they often employed anticapitalist imagery and stories pitting the working-class Tramp against sinister business figures out to exploit him. As a result, conservative groups in America thought his work rested on themes of subversion and socialism.

The creation of United Artists overlapped with Chaplin's contractual ties with First National, which required eight films. Through the multimillion-dollar First National contract, Chaplin became an independent producer and had the creative space to

make longer films. Chaplin built his own studio facilities in Los Angeles, which produced *A Dog's Life* (1918), *Shoulder Arms* (1918), *Sunnyside* (1919), and *A Day's Pleasure* (1919). His desire to make longer features resulted in *The Kid* (1921), a film that costarred the child actor Jackie Coogan and broke new ground with its style. Much of the material for the film drew heavily on Chaplin's childhood memories, while its combination of pathos and comedy won the film popular and critical acclaim.

Chaplin was mobbed by fans on his visits to London and Paris for the premieres, but he faced an increasingly unsettled time as he waited to fulfill his contractual obligations at First National, and as his marriage to Lita Grey broke down. His final films for First National were *The Idle Class* (1921), *Pay Day* (1922), and *The Pilgrim* (1923).

The contractual obligations with First National, combined with the divorce, delayed Chaplin's getting started at United Artists. *A Woman of Paris* was not released until 1923, four years after the studio was founded. The film received critical acclaim but proved unpopular, as Chaplin did not feature in it. His second release, *Gold Rush* (1925), became Chaplin's most successful silent film, grossing $4 million within the first few years. *The Circus* (1928) was also successful, despite negative publicity in 1927 when details of his divorce were leaked to the press. Many women's groups criticized Chaplin for not supporting his young wife and two children, and there were boycotts of his films across the country.

Chaplin suffered a nervous breakdown in 1928. His next film was *City Lights* (1931), which, along with *Modern Times* (1936), was successful even though it was silent in the new era of talkies. Chaplin's first talkie, *The Great Dictator,* would not be released until 1940.

Controversy plagued Chaplin. He was shadowed by British claims that he avoided military service during World War I, and in America his films were labeled subversive and even vulgar in their depictions of the underside of life. The FBI opened a file on Chaplin in 1922, as its director, J. Edgar Hoover, was concerned that Chaplin's themes undermined capitalist ideals. This suspicion would persist and ultimately lead to the star's exile in 1952. That year, his support for a second front in Russia during World War II contributed to House Un-American Activities Committee hearings and the revocation of his visa while he traveled to London. Chaplin lived out his exile in Vevey, Switzerland.

His private life was also scrutinized. He married four times and had eleven children. He married Mildred Harris in 1918, divorced in 1920, married Lita Grey in 1924, and divorced in 1928. Both women were sixteen years old when he married them; both of these marriages ended in sordid divorce cases, the second culminating in a record $825,000 settlement. Criticisms about vulgarity and morals that had been leveled at his films were now being reflected in his private life, including his 1922–1923 relationship with the actress Pola Negri. His third marriage, to Paulette Goddard in 1936, ended in 1942. In 1943, at the age of fifty-three, he married eighteen-year-old Oona O'Neill (the daughter of American playwright Eugene O'Neill), again rankling those who criticized his personal life.

At the first Academy Awards celebration, in 1929, Chaplin won a special award for *The Circus*, for "versatility and genius in writing, acting, directing and producing." He was awarded an honorary Oscar in 1972 and was made a Knight of the British Empire by Queen Elizabeth II in 1975. Charlie Chaplin died in Switzerland on December 25, 1977.

Sam Hitchmough

See also: Celebrity Culture; Film; Film Industry.

Further Reading

Chaplin, Charles. *My Autobiography.* Reprint. New York: Plume, 1992.

Hayes, Kevin. *Charlie Chaplin: Interviews.* Conversations with Filmmakers Series. Oxford: University Press of Mississippi, 2005.

Maland, Charles J. *Chaplin and American Culture.* 1989. Reprint. Princeton, NJ: Princeton University Press, 2001.

Chicago Race Riot of 1919

The deadliest and most destructive of the twenty-six major race riots that took place in the United States during the Red Summer of 1919—so-called because of the anticommunist agitation of the day—happened in Chicago. It began on a 96-degree Sunday afternoon, July 27, on the South Side's Twenty-ninth Street beach on Lake Michigan.

The immediate cause of the outbreak was the deliberate drowning of a black youth, Eugene Williams, by a white youth, George Stauber, who hit him with a brickbat, knocking Williams off a large raft and sending him under. The raft was said to have floated beyond the invisible boundary separating the "black beach" from the "white beach," prompting white beachgoers to throw stones at the raft. When black onlookers demanded that police arrest the perpetrator, the white officers arrested one of the boisterous complainants instead.

The frustrated blacks took matters into their own hands and sought retribution, attacking whites who were seen in black neighborhoods. White citizens quickly seized the initiative, however, marching en masse into black areas of the city, attacking residents, and setting fire to black homes and businesses. A fourteen-day conflagration ensued, in which twenty-three blacks and fifteen whites were killed and more than 500 people were injured.

Racial tensions had been building in Chicago throughout the years of World War I. Housing and unemployment were dire problems. The black population of Chicago had increased from 44,000 to 109,000 since 1910, as Southern sharecroppers left the fields and traveled north in search of better-paid industrial work—a mass exodus known as the Great Migration. Most of the migrants were unaccustomed to life in the city and Northern folkways. Blacks were forced into the poorest section of the city, on the South Side, where gambling, prostitution, saloons, and the criminal element were rampant and where the stench of the nearby stockyards hung heavily in the air. Those who sought to integrate upscale white neighborhoods met stiff resistance from white real estate agents and residents. Employment for blacks was available, but competition with white ethnic immigrants and their offspring proved intense.

The black vote, consistently Republican at the time, made African Americans the enemies of the Democratic political machine and gave racist whites yet another reason to resent the black presence in Chicago. Greatly exacerbating racial tensions were the "athletic clubs," a guise for territorial gangs of white youths who worked for corrupt political bosses in exchange for immunity from prosecution for their own criminal activities. These gangs rigidly enforced the unwritten rules of racial segregation as just another aspect of their territorialism.

The police force was firmly under the control of white political bosses who, whether Republican or Democrat, were equally prejudiced against blacks in racial disputes. The Chicago media also was biased against blacks, generally giving whites the benefit of the doubt and assuming the guilt of blacks in their coverage. Newspaper editors, usually through subtle innuendos, but openly once the riot started in 1919, encouraged whites to defend themselves and their neighborhoods from black assailants.

Although black voters had given Republican Mayor William Hale Thompson his winning margin in the previous election, he maintained an antiblack attitude throughout the riot. He refused to call in the National Guard to restore order until the riot's fourth day, by which time most of the damage had been done.

After starting at the beach that Sunday afternoon, the riot spread to the stockyards during the workweek and into the black neighborhoods during the weeknights. A rainstorm put a damper on the efforts of arsonists, otherwise much of Chicago might have gone up in flames. When more than 6,000 National Guard troops finally arrived, they were instructed to treat black and white rioters equally, and their efforts brought relative calm to the city by dispersing the white mobs.

The mayor dismissed the Guard on August 8, declaring the riot over, and appointed a commission to study what had happened. The commission's report recommended that the city ameliorate the social and economic conditions that had led to the riots, including providing better educational, housing, and recreational facilities in black neighborhoods. The report also recommended more effective policing.

Racial tension in Chicago continued, however. Within a year, another racial altercation left four people dead. Throughout the 1920s, Chicago would continue to experience racial tension, with occasional flare-ups of violence but without full-scale rioting.

Thomas Adams Upchurch

See also: African Americans; Rosewood Massacre (1923); Tulsa Race Riots of 1921.

Further Reading

Chicago Commission on Race Relations. *The Negro in Chicago: A Study of Race Relations and a Race Riot.* Chicago: University of Chicago Press, 1922.

Spear, Allan H. *Black Chicago: The Making of a Negro Ghetto, 1890–1920.* Chicago: University of Chicago Press, 1967.

Tuttle, William M., Jr. *Race Riot: Chicago in the Red Summer of 1919.* New York: Atheneum, 1970.

Child Labor

The 1920 U.S. Census revealed that child labor in America, while generally on the decline, persisted in all states. Congress stepped up its efforts to regulate employment of children, but neither the courts nor the states would support such federal control.

The U.S. labor force included just over 1 million children between the ages of ten and fifteen in 1920, a nearly 50 percent drop from the 2 million reported in 1910, despite a 15.5 percent increase in total population in that age group. Of the 1 million reported at work, 61 percent were employed in agricultural jobs. Nearly 90 percent lived in southeastern and south central states, though every state had child agricultural laborers.

The 413,549 children who toiled in nonagricultural labor—for example, in shops, factories, offices, and restaurants—represented a 26 percent decline from ten years earlier. Cotton mills employed the most children; other large employers included shoe and cigarette factories, silk and knitting mills, and offices. Many boys worked on the street as bootblacks or "newsies" (newspaper vendors) and in offices as messengers and errand boys, while thousands of girls were employed as mill workers, waitresses, typists, and telephone operators.

The reported decrease in child laborers steeled opponents of regulation. Journalists and other skeptics, however, pointed out that the 1920 census was taken in January, when many child agricultural laborers were out of work, while the 1910 census was taken during the planting season. Some also argued that the 1920 figures did not accurately reflect the population of child laborers after 1922, when the U.S. Supreme Court overturned the second of two national child labor laws.

Working conditions for children were the subject of numerous novels and investigative reports, and, by the 1920s, the application of scientific and industrial innovations had led to improvements in this area. Nevertheless, a subcommittee of the White House Conference on Child Health and Protection reported in 1932 that, "now as in the past, almost all working children are employed in jobs that are absolutely unskilled, mechanical and monotonous in the extreme." The group's nearly 600-page report on child labor included detailed analysis of trends throughout the last decade. Citing as an example the children working in Pennsylvania's glass industry during the mid-1920s, the subcommittee wrote that "many children, even when their tasks are light, are employed in or in connection with machinery that offers a high degree of hazard, and others are in occupations in which dusty or lint-laden air, fumes and poisonous substances, create conditions favorable to tuberculosis and industrial poisoning, to which children and young persons are especially susceptible."

States had begun limiting the number of hours that children could work, and boosting the minimum age at which they could begin working. By 1929, thirty-six states had set an eight-hour maximum workday in factories for children under age sixteen, and thirty-nine had passed laws preventing children from working in factories before age fourteen.

Congress had tried in 1916 to impose federal oversight, but the U.S. Supreme Court had found that such regulation overstepped the federal government's power to regulate interstate commerce. In *Bailey v. Drexel Furniture Co.* (1922), the Court declared unconstitutional a federal tax on the profits of any employer that violated national child labor laws. Grace Abbott, chief of the U.S. Children's Bureau, reported the following January that only thirteen states had passed child labor laws equivalent in force to the federal statutes invalidated by the Court's opinions.

Child labor opponent and American Federation of Labor (AFL) head Samuel Gompers called a conference in 1922 at the Washington, D.C., headquarters of the AFL, where it was agreed that a constitutional amendment would be the only legal means of regulating child labor at the federal level. In 1924, the House and Senate adopted such an amendment in the form of a joint resolution introduced by Representative Israel Moore Foster (R-OH). The proposal's scope was broad, extending federal legislation to employment of children under the age of eighteen.

The amendment required not only congressional approval but also ratification by three-fourths, or thirty-six, of the forty-eight states. Opponents such as the National Association of Manufacturers and the Farmers' States' Rights League waged a propaganda war in newspapers, magazines, and leaflets, arguing that the measure was unnecessary and unfairly expanded federal powers. Some argued it was a Communist plot. Proponents of the amendment counterattacked, forming the Organizations Associated for Ratification of the Child Labor Amendment and distributing pamphlets of their own. Ultimately, however, only twenty-eight states ratified the amendment, which remains pending in Congress today.

Overall, the 1920s saw much progress on the child labor issue, with declines in the use of underaged workers in virtually every industry, though significant numbers continued to be employed in the agricultural sector. Much of this decline was due to the generally prosperous economy of the Jazz Age.

With higher employment and better wages among the adult population, there was less need for families to put children to work to supplement incomes. However, the generally probusiness climate of the era prevented the enactment of any serious legislation, or constitutional amendment, to limit or ban the use of child workers. With unemployment on the rise again in the 1930s, the United States would see a slight resurgence of child labor during the Great Depression.

Catherine W. Dolinski

See also: *Bailey v. Drexel Furniture Company* (1922); Children and Child Rearing; Labor Movement.

Further Reading

Samuel, Howard D. "Troubled Passage: The Labor Movement and the Fair Labor Standards Act." *Monthly Labor Review* (December 2000): 32–37.

Trattner, Walter I. *Crusade for the Children: A History of the National Child Labor Committee and Child Labor Reform in America.* Chicago: Quadrangle, 1970.

White House Conference on Child Health and Protection. *Child Labor: Report of the Subcommittee on Child Labor.* New York: Century, 1932.

Children and Child Rearing

During the 1920s, a change took place in American society that altered the lives of more than 43 million children and their families: For the first time in the nation's history, more Americans resided in urban settings than on farms. This shift had a major impact on the family. According to the U.S. Census, the proportion of children living in two-parent farm families soon dropped to 30 percent, while 55 percent of children now lived in nonfarm families By 1921, farm earnings had decreased by 40 percent; between 1922 and 1929, an average of nearly 2 million people left farms and small towns each year, relocating to more urban areas.

Rural life, with its close family ties and strict morals, was being replaced by an urban culture that many thought consisted of anonymous crowds dedicated to moneymaking and pleasure. In rural societies, many family members worked side by side to sustain themselves in small communities. But in many urban families, fathers spent their workdays away from home, earning the income required to support the family, while mothers remained at home to care for the children and household.

The new living arrangements were accompanied by a substantial decline in large families. By the 1920s, the median number of siblings in families with adolescents had dropped by two-thirds, to only 2.6 from its nineteenth-century peak of 7.3. By the end of the decade, nearly 60 percent of American children were the family's only child or had only one or two siblings. It had become common to put off marriage and having children, and the birth rate sank to the lowest point in American history.

Increased education was another noteworthy change in children's lives. Between 1919 and the end of the 1920s, enrollment in elementary and secondary schools grew by more than 4 million students, an increase from 78.3 percent to 81.7 percent of children five to seventeen years old. High school enrollment (grades 9–12) jumped from 10.2 percent to 17.1 percent, while college enrollment rose from close to 600,000 to more than 1.1 million.

At the same time, 31 percent of white children and 57 percent of African American children lived at least part of their lives with one or no parent. African American children in the rural South saw few changes in their lives before the civil rights movement. Pervasive prejudice and racism confined black youth to the lowest rungs of society and denied them access to the emerging middle class of urban America. As for Native American children, the 1928 Meriam Report cited the failure of U.S. Indian policy, pervasive poverty, and the desperate plight of Indian youth—but little was done to improve the situation.

Changes in Parental Roles

The traditional American family had been a multifunctional institution, entrusted with a variety of tasks, including economic support, education, religious training, recreation, and health and welfare responsibilities. In the America of the 1920s, these functions were gradually being taken over by social institutions, which some sociologists believe weakened the family institution. City families appeared to be adrift in a sea of urbanization, materialism, individualism, changing gender relationships, and self-promotion. Family bonds were further challenged by the desire or necessity of married women to work outside the home, children's immersion in the new youth culture, and the diminished family role of fathers.

The ideal became the "companionate family," focused on close emotional bonds and more democratic in roles and responsibilities. Tolerant parents

were to act as friends and guides to their children. The modern father was no longer viewed as the main source of authority and maker of important decisions. The good father of the 1920s was to be understanding and sympathetic, playing with and listening to his children. His main family obligations were to be kind and a good provider. Mothers retained their traditional role as the dominant force in the affective dimensions of family life. But much of children's play, schooling, and social life took place outside the home and away from both parents.

Lives of City Youth

Urban children in the Jazz Age spent an increasing amount of their free time on city streets and at public amusements. Movies, for example, doubled in attendance during the second half of the 1920s, from 40 million visits to 100 million. The street offered American youth opportunities for making money, meeting friends, playing games, and socializing.

The novelty of the city, the apparently unlimited possibilities for the future, and the end of old restraints and social customs combined to make the 1920s a golden age for American youth. It was a good time to be young and optimistic. In the streets, children were able to shape their own notions of right and wrong and fair play, often at variance with prevailing social norms. For example, children learned in school and at home that gambling was wasteful and sinful, stealing was a crime, money was for saving, and that citizens avowed allegiance to the law and the officials who enforced it. In rough urban streets, however, they might observe that kids shot craps or pitched pennies, that stealing an orange from a grocer was as common as stickball, that money was for spending, and that one's primary loyalty was to friends, family, and fellow gang members, not the law or the police who enforced it.

Reformers perceived an increasingly anarchic behavior among America's youth exposed to the rough democracy of the streets. Educators, psychologists, psychiatrists, and social workers had their own conceptions of what being a child should mean. They believed children needed to be protected, not only from abuse and neglect but also from the seamy aspects of life. The 1920s were home to an army of such experts, all offering volumes of advice—much of it confusing and contradictory, all of it aimed at parents perceived as inadequate and failing to bring up their children properly.

Most of the reformers were middle-class in outlook, while the children they wanted to change were of the urban working class. The parents of these children, however, had their own concerns. They worried less about the dangers their children faced in their urban environment than the danger they, as breadwinners, were exposed to in trying to make a living in the city. In addition, they resented the assumed superiority of the reformers.

Yet, some reformers accomplished a great deal for children. They helped to make schooling universal, to reduce infant mortality by 19 percent, and to promote greater access to health care. They worked to eliminate child labor and ultimately succeeded in ending some of the exploitation of children by large factories.

The Science of Child Rearing

The parenting style espoused by child-rearing experts in the 1920s was in step with the business models of the day. Americans became increasingly convinced that science, with its systematic observations and efficient methods, could successfully organize a whole range of human activities, including child rearing.

Many mothers welcomed the experts' ideas of child rearing. For one thing, amid the demographic shift to urban living and the influx of immigrants from abroad, many women were isolated from the network of mothers, aunts, and grandmothers who had handed down their wisdom about child care. In addition, growing affluence in the middle class provided some mothers with more time to obsess about their children.

Experts also appealed to the public's fascination with being "modern." An eager audience of increasingly better-educated women embraced the idea that they were rearing their children in partnership with up-to-date professionals. The advice, however, could be dubious or contradictory. For example, some experts advised mothers that babies should cry fifteen to thirty minutes a day for exercise, that they should never play with a baby younger than four months, and that they should not lavish too much love on their infants. Some experts advised fathers to keep their distance and act as disciplinarians when necessary, while others encouraged fathers to be emotionally close and playful companions.

In general, the 1920s witnessed a national focus on improving health care for children. Public policies were shaped by a new expertise about children and child care. Child guidance clinics proliferated, and parent education expanded.

Leslie Rabkin

See also: Birth Control; Child Labor; Health and Medicine; Marriage, Divorce, and Family; Sheppard-Towner Act (1921); Women and Gender; Youth.

Further Reading

Fass, Paula S., and Mary Ann Mason. *Childhood in America.* New York: New York University Press, 2000.
Illick, Joseph E. *American Childhoods.* Philadelphia: University of Pennsylvania Press, 2002.
Miller, Nathan. *New World Coming: The 1920s and the Making of Modern America.* New York: Scribner's, 2003.
Nasaw, David. *Children of the City.* New York: Oxford University Press, 1986.
Zelizer, Viviana A. *Pricing the Priceless Child: The Changing Value of Children.* Princeton, NJ: Princeton University Press, 1994.

China, Relations with

The 1920s were not especially active years in formal Sino-American relations—a lull before the storm of the 1930s and the world war that followed. The absence of close interaction between the Chinese and U.S. governments reflected the lack of a strong central authority in China at the time, as well as isolationist sentiments within the various Republican administrations in the United States.

The decade began with the Washington Naval Conference of 1921–1922, which dealt with more than naval affairs. One of the treaties that came out of the conference, the Five-Power Treaty, set limits on the navies of various powers; another, the Four-Power Treaty, sought ways to resolve international disputes in East Asia and Pacific regions. The third treaty, the Nine-Power Treaty, dealt specifically with China, guaranteeing that country's independence, sovereignty, and territorial integrity. All three treaties sought to limit Japan's growing power, and as Japan represented the greatest threat to China in the 1920s, the treaties all served Chinese interests.

The Nine-Power Treaty, which most directly related to China, offended virtually all parties in that vast and divided Asian country, including the republican government, the increasingly powerful Communist Party, and the various warlords who held sway over vast stretches of Chinese territory in the 1920s. While the treaty spoke of guarantees of Chinese independence, it did little to end the decades-old "unequal treaty" system, whereby various European powers and Japan imposed their own spheres of influence on the country. In some areas, European traders were given tariff advantages, and Chinese laws did not apply to European residents.

Still, as the only world power without a sphere of influence in China, the United States was seen as an honest broker by Chinese government authorities. Washington's successful push at the conference for the "open door" trading policy—whereby all foreign traders would be granted equal access to all parts of China, thereby guaranteeing competitiveness, lower prices for imported goods, and higher prices for exports—was much appreciated in China.

Given China's lack of a strong central government, however, there was little the United States could do for or with the country during the 1920s. American diplomats were largely reduced to observing China's gradual descent into a three-way civil war involving the warlords, Communist forces under Mao Zedong, and the republican government. Following the death of Sun Yat-sen, founder of the republic, the government had come under the sway of Sun's former military chief Jiang Jieshi (Chiang Kai-shek).

U.S. diplomats hoped to act as brokers in renegotiating the various "unequal treaties" between China and various European powers and Japan. Time and again, they were stymied by a Chinese government not strong enough to assume the powers that would be surrendered by European governments once the old treaties were renegotiated or abandoned. Even after Jiang launched a major offensive against warlords in the north of the country, it was not clear that his government in Nanjing had enough authority to negotiate with the United States.

The lack of a strong central government created a power vacuum that Japan, the great power of Asia, was more than ready to exploit. When Tokyo began to act more aggressively toward China in the 1930s, there was little the United States could do. Japan occupied Manchuria in 1931, launching a full invasion of China in 1937.

Charles M. Dobbs and James Ciment

See also: Four-Power Treaty (1921); Japan, Relations with; Washington Naval Conference (1921–1922).

Further Reading

Cohen, Warren I. *Empire Without Tears: American Foreign Relations, 1921–1933.* Philadelphia: Temple University Press, 1987.

Ellis, L. Ethan. *Republican Foreign Policy, 1921–1933.* New Brunswick, NJ: Rutgers University Press, 1995.

Iriye, Akira. *After Imperialism: The Search for a New Order in the Far East, 1921–1931.* Cambridge, MA: Harvard University Press, 1965.

Pollard, Robert T. *China's Foreign Relations, 1917–1931.* 1933. Reprint. New York: Arno, 1970.

Cigarettes and Tobacco

By the end of World War I, the popular image of cigarettes and tobacco in American society had taken a dramatic shift from that of previous decades. Before the war, particularly since the 1870s, the use of tobacco had fallen under strong criticism from health advocates, social reformers, and corporate employers. In particular, smoking was viewed as a cause and symptom of degeneracy in moral, mental, and physical health, and was generally perceived as a habit of the lower classes, of immigrants, and of artistic people outside mainstream society.

After the United States entered the war in 1916, however, former antismoking organizations such as the Red Cross, the Salvation Army, and the Young Men's Christian Association (YMCA) developed morale-boosting programs to send cigarettes to American soldiers overseas. The YMCA distributed more than 2 billion cigarettes to the troops in Europe. While smoking remained a prominent public health issue during the 1920s, the respectability it gained during the war led to increased cigarette consumption throughout the decade.

Cigarettes were prominent in national magazine and billboard advertising campaigns. Popular actors smoked cigarettes in motion pictures, and cigarette smoking was featured in the events portrayed in newspapers and novels. Smoking was viewed by consumers as a symbol of sophistication, as well as a form of liberation from society's strictures. The number of women smokers more than doubled during the decade, in part a reflection of their efforts to redefine their traditional roles in society and establish economic and political parity with men. Anticigarette activists pressed Will Hayes, the powerful head of the Motion Picture Producers and Distributors of America, to eliminate film scenes of women smoking cigarettes because they believed this portrayal threatened the future of American womanhood.

Lucy Page Gaston, who coined the term "coffin nail" to describe cigarettes, helped found several anticigarette leagues, continuing her fight against tobacco until her death in 1924. After Prohibition went into effect in 1920, Gaston was joined in her efforts by the popular evangelist Billy Sunday, a former professional baseball player who often used stories from his baseball past to dramatize the dangers of smoking cigarettes and to illustrate how cigarettes could lead to mental decline and even insanity.

Schools and universities also went on the attack. In 1922, the State of Nebraska refused to let any students in its state normal colleges to do any of their coursework at Columbia University in New York, the University of Chicago, or Northwestern University in Evanston, Illinois, because it was reported that those universities permitted women to smoke. Hope College in Michigan declared that no student who smoked would be recommended for a teaching position in high schools or academies.

Even in this climate, cigarette sales continued to climb. In 1926, U.S. cigarette consumption reached 85 billion for the year. By the end of the decade, consumption of cigarettes continued to rise. But throughout the decade, medical researchers reported the dangers associated with inhaling and the absorption of nicotine, and high mortality rates for infants born of smoking mothers. Opponents to cigarettes, such as Senator Reed Smoot of Utah, attempted to regulate tobacco advertising by including tobacco under the auspices of the Pure Food and Drug Administration. Smoot stated that his concern was not with tobacco use by adults, but advertising aimed at children. He was joined by the Women's Christian Temperance Union, which sought to control advertising and institute campaigns to educate children against smoking. The dramatic increase in smoking, however, was reflected in federal tax revenues from cigarette sales, which in 1927 soared more than $28 million above the total in 1925. Smoking cigarettes had become a common part of everyday life.

Kevin Grace

See also: Advertising; Food and Diet; Health and Medicine.

Further Reading

Gately, Iain. *Tobacco: A Cultural History of How an Exotic Plant Seduced Civilization.* New York: Grove, 2001.

Sobel, Robert. *They Satisfy: The Cigarette in American Life.* New York: Anchor/Doubleday, 1978.

Tate, Cassandra. *Cigarette Wars: The Triumph of "The Little White Slaver."* New York: Oxford University Press, 1999.

Coal Industry

Coal supplied 70 percent of America's energy needs during the first two decades of the twentieth century. Production increased dramatically, from approximately 270 million tons in 1900 to about 501 million tons in 1910. World War I further accelerated demand for coal in the United States, fueling an increase in production to a peak of more than 678 million tons in 1918. After the war, demand fell sharply, sending bituminous coal production to a low of 458 million tons in 1919 and resulting in a decrease in total production to just over 545 million tons in 1920.

Coal production rebounded during the 1920s, reflecting an ongoing increase in demand, even as coal supplied an ever-smaller percentage of total energy use during the decade due to the increasing reliance of utilities and industries on oil and natural gas. Advances in coal-mining technology in the 1920s—such as improved drilling and blasting techniques, and new machinery to assist in the cutting and loading of coal—increased safety as well as productivity, allowing coal mines to keep pace with growing demand. The trend toward mechanization, particularly the development of machinery that reduced the need for miners to hand-load coal, rendered mining less labor-intensive, offsetting increases in demand for unskilled labor as the mining industry grew in response to the increase in coal demand. The effect of mechanization on the labor market was one of numerous forces that led to the nation's many coal strikes during the 1920s.

The post–World War I drop in coal demand occurred just as organized labor, represented by the United Mine Workers of America (UMWA), began to increase pressure on the industry to raise wages and reduce working hours. The wartime increases in demand for coal had been a boon to mine owners, who profited greatly; at the same time, the real wages of miners remained low or actually declined. The increases in coal production and owner profits thus drove miners to seek higher wages and shorter working hours.

The coal strike of 1919, ultimately halted by federal injunction in July, was a harbinger of the future of the coal industry in the 1920s, as the power of the UMWA, under its new president, John L. Lewis, grew and the labor forces of more mines became unionized. A series of violent clashes between strikers and armed guards in Matewan, West Virginia, in 1920 and 1921, which resulted in dozens of deaths and the deployment of state police and militia, further illustrated the growing power of the UMWA and increased the resentment of mine owners toward organized labor. Lesser strikes in various regions of the country occurred in 1922, 1925, and 1931.

The coal strikes of the 1920s, combined with natural market forces, produced dramatic but short-lived fluctuations in coal production. Yet the general upward trend in both demand and production continued until the Great Depression at the end of the decade brought about a steady decline in the American coal industry. By the mid-1930s, coal accounted for approximately 45 percent of the country's total energy consumption, with the balance supplied by oil, natural gas, and hydroelectric power. Coal exports, always a small percentage of total coal production, also declined, as economic depression spread worldwide. The outbreak of World War II created a sharp increase in demand, but the general downward trend in demand for coal continued through the remainder of the twentieth century, rebounding slightly toward the end of the century, as oil and natural gas prices increased.

Michael H. Burchett

See also: Coal Strike of 1919; Electricity Industry; Lewis, John L.; Railroads and Railroad Industry; Technology.

Further Reading

Alm, Alvin L. *Coal Myths and Environmental Realities: Industrial Fuel-Use Decisions in a Time of Change.* Boulder, CO: Westview, 1984.

Gordon, Richard L. *World Coal: Economics, Policies, and Prospects.* New York: Cambridge University Press, 1987.

Long, Priscilla. *Where the Sun Never Shines: A History of America's Bloody Coal Industry.* New York: Paragon, 1989.

Coal Strike of 1919

On November 1, 1919, more than 400,000 of America's coal miners went on strike, seeking primarily a 60 percent wage hike. The increase was demanded largely as compensation for a loss in real wages resulting from inflation during World War I and its immediate aftermath.

During World War I, in order to maximize production, the War Production Board of the federal government had become heavily involved in the coal industry. The board helped coordinate railroads and shipping to move coal more efficiently and, under the 1917 Smith-Lever Act, gave President Woodrow Wilson authority over the distribution of food and fuel. The Wilson administration established the U.S. Fuel Administration (USFA) in 1917 to promote price stability and cooperation among producers, workers, and government regulators.

Under its chief administrator, Harry Garfield, the son of assassinated president James Garfield, the USFA permitted wages to rise modestly. Garfield also helped negotiate the Washington Agreement of 1917, which encouraged unionism but prohibited strikes for the duration of the war or until April 1, 1920, whichever came first. As inflation rapidly overtook wage increases, however, worker frustration and anger grew. When the war ended in November 1918, many workers saw no reason to hold to their no-strike pledge.

Further contributing to the unrest was John L. Lewis's need to prove his leadership as vice president of the United Mine Workers of America (UMWA). Along with securing higher wages, Lewis wanted to end the strike penalty of a dollar a day for each worker, which had been imposed by the federal government under wartime rules. Lewis also demanded a thirty-hour workweek, citing the industry's unhealthy, exhausting, and debilitating labor conditions. To achieve these ends, Lewis called the workers out on strike roughly one year after the armistice ending World War I.

But Lewis and the striking coal workers had misread the public climate. A series of major strikes across the country earlier in the year—including the Seattle general strike, the Boston police strike, and the national steel industry strike—had inflamed public opinion against militant labor activity. Adding to the anti-union atmosphere was the anticommunist Red Scare gripping the nation. The 1917 Russian Revolution had triggered a panic in America that led to antileftist raids and deportations under U.S. Attorney General A. Mitchell Palmer.

President Wilson immediately denounced the 1919 coal strike, and the federal judiciary determined that, because the United States had yet to sign a formal peace treaty, the country was still at war and the Smith-Lever Act was still in effect. An injunction was issued by Indiana State Judge Jonathan Langham against the union and its members, the newly formed Bureau of Investigation sent out agents to arrest workers, and U.S. troops were deployed by the Wilson administration to mining areas.

The injunction kept union organizers away from the mines, and some workers returned to work rather than face the dollar-a-day fine (daily wages for unskilled workers were generally $2 to $3 per day). Mine operators, sensing that public sentiment was on their side, stood firm, refused the workers' demands, and forced them out of company housing; they argued that the miners were willing to let ordinary Americans freeze, so there was nothing wrong with forcing the strikers out into freezing temperatures in retaliation.

The impact of the strike was felt throughout American society. Store and factory hours were reduced, the public was encouraged to lower the temperatures in their homes, and, by December, the nation's trains were running on restricted schedules. As a result, further attempts were made to force the miners back to work. Strikebreakers were employed, and the governors of Oklahoma and Pennsylvania sent in the militia to protect them against attacks from striking miners. President Wilson threatened to send in troops to mine the coal, and Palmer won injunctions against the miners in the courts, which threatened union officials with jail time and the unions with crippling fines. There was also a major campaign in the press, spearheaded by the Wilson administration and mine owners, to paint the strikers in the worst possible light. It was not a hard sell, as most of the nation's major newspapers were hostile to unions generally and the UMWA specifically.

Union moderates at the national level tried to persuade more radical local leaders to accept a compromise deal that fell far short of the 60 percent increase initially demanded. The rank and file finally conceded, agreeing in mid-December to go back to work with a 14 percent wage increase and no change in working hours or strike penalties.

The impact of the strike would be felt throughout the 1920s and into the 1930s. Lewis battled radicals for control of the union, becoming its president in 1920. Still, radicals remained in control of many of the locals, and Lewis was unable to stop a number of wildcat strikes in the 1920s. Ultimately, Lewis and his supporters were able to purge many of the more radical local leaders by tarring them with charges of Communist sympathies.

By maintaining his leadership at the national level, Lewis succeeded in laying the groundwork for the accommodations reached among the union, coal industry management, and the administration of Franklin D. Roosevelt during the great wave of industrial labor organizing in the 1930s. Lewis would ultimately take the UMWA out of the American Federation of Labor in 1935 to form the more industrially based Congress of Industrial Organizations.

But that was more than a decade in the future. During the early 1920s, the immediate result of the strike was tense relations between organized labor and management. Operators, facing increased competition

from oil, sought to cut the wage differential between organized and nonorganized mines, usually by lowering wages at the former.

John Barnhill and James Ciment

See also: Coal Industry; Demobilization, Industrial; Labor Movement; Lewis, John L.

Further Reading

Bernstein, Irving. *The Lean Years: A History of the American Worker, 1920–1933.* Boston: Houghton Mifflin, 1960.

Fox, Maier B. *United We Stand: the United Mine Workers of America, 1890–1990.* Washington, DC: United Mine Workers of America, 1990.

Levy, Elizabeth, and Tad Richards. *Struggle and Lose, Struggle and Win: The United Mine Workers.* New York: Four Winds, 1977.

Commerce Department, U.S.

The U.S. Commerce Department played an important role during World War I in mobilizing the nation's resources for the war effort. Following the war, the department was transformed and expanded as a result of the energy and vision of the new secretary, Herbert Hoover. The Commerce Department became a central agency for collecting and disseminating information about American business and for activities designed to encourage the growth of the economy. Regulations for new technologies were developed that remained in force for most of the twentieth century.

The Department of Commerce and Labor, an executive-branch department, originated in 1903. On March 5, 1913, the two functions were divided, and the Department of Commerce was established. It was responsible for conducting the national census every ten years and maintaining lighthouses and other aids to commerce. During World War I, the Commerce Department also played an important role in providing information about draft-eligible men and the manufacturing capabilities of the nation. Even so, its activities were limited. When Herbert Hoover was nominated by Warren G. Harding to head the department, a former secretary of commerce told him that no more than a few hours of work would be required each day.

Hoover, known as the "Great Engineer" for his experiences in international mining and his work in providing relief to Belgium during the war, was determined to have the department contribute more directly to the growth of American prosperity. His goal was to promote a rational economy that would effectively end poverty in the United States. After taking office in March 1921, he realized that the department could collect and provide more information to businesses to help them make better decisions. In July 1921, the Bureau of the Census began a monthly publication, *Survey of Current Business,* with statistics on industrial production and inventories. This was followed by *Commerce Reports,* which compiled information from trade data. Both newsletters were helpful to managers who wanted to track trends and competition.

Secretary Hoover attracted national headlines when he organized the President's Conference on Unemployment in August 1921. At the time, in the midst of the recession following World War I, up to 5 million American men were unemployed. Hoover believed that the government should finance public works to help create economic stability. He especially favored the construction and improvement of roads, which he regarded as a boost to commerce throughout the nation.

Hoover also supported agricultural cooperatives as a way to enhance prosperity in the farming sector. As secretary, he lobbied Congress to fund credits for cooperatives and other organizations that could reduce waste and promote efficiency. He especially favored credits to foreign buyers for the purchase of American agricultural products. Hoover believed this would reduce surpluses and keep farm income high, with minimal federal government involvement. By 1925, Hoover's initiatives had helped increase foreign trade by one-third over what it had been in 1913.

The department's Bureau of Foreign and Domestic Commerce actively helped to connect producers with foreign markets. Widely publicized examples of the Commerce Department's successes included a program to sell surplus rice from California to Japan. Perhaps inevitably, Hoover's involvement in agriculture brought him into conflict with the secretary of agriculture, Henry Wallace.

Hoover's plans for the Department of Commerce brought him into conflict with other departments as well. He convinced Congress and the president to transfer the Geological Survey and the Bureau of Mines from the Interior Department to the Commerce Department. Recognizing the importance of new technologies and the need to regulate them, in 1922, Hoover organized the first annual conference on radio. This led to Congress passing legislation in 1927 to establish a Radio Division in the Department of Commerce, with the job of assigning and regulating the public airwaves. Hoover also recommended federal support for and regulation of a civil aviation industry. The Aeronautics Division, forerunner of the Federal Aviation Administration, became part of the Commerce Department in 1926.

Under Hoover's stewardship, the Commerce Department also helped establish national standards. The Bureau of Standards expanded its role from testing material used by the government to testing a broader variety of materials used by industry. Thanks to the bureau's research, national standards were established for products ranging from automobile brakes and elevators to electrical equipment and safety equipment for workers. As a result of these standard sizes and practices, both consumers and manufacturers saved money and effort.

A measure of Hoover's success and importance at the Commerce Department is the increase in its budget. When he assumed control of the department in 1921, the annual budget was $860,000. By the time he left at the beginning of 1929, the budget had grown to $38 million.

Tim J. Watts

See also: Economic Policy; Hoover, Herbert.

Further Reading

Barber, William J. *From New Era to New Deal: Herbert Hoover, the Economists, and American Economic Policy, 1921–1933.* Cambridge, UK: Cambridge University Press, 1985.

Burner, David. *Herbert Hoover: A Public Life.* New York: Alfred A. Knopf, 1979.

Hawley, Ellis W., ed. *Herbert Hoover as Secretary of Commerce: Studies in New Era Thought and Practice.* Iowa City: University of Iowa Press, 1981.

Bowers, Helen, ed. *From Lighthouses to Laserbeams: A History of the U.S. Department of Commerce.* Washington, DC: U.S. Department of Commerce, Office of the Secretary, 1995.

Communist Party

The early years of the American Communist Party were hardly auspicious. Founded in 1919, the party reached the height of its influence only in the late 1930s and 1940s, amid the crises of economic depression and world war. Emerging from within the Socialist movement, and inspired by the Bolshevik takeover in Russia, American Communists in the 1920s were hampered by a number of factors, including government repression, internal factionalism, and the party's subordination to a foreign power, the Soviet Union.

Moreover, the party's leadership and many of its members were concentrated in immigrant communities at a time of rising nativism in the United States.

Although the creation of the party had been precipitated by the Bolshevik takeover of the Russian government in October 1917 and the founding of the Communist International (Comintern) in March 1919, the roots of American communism lay in the fertile soil of indigenous Socialist and radical politics. In the months following the end of World War I, a left-wing majority within the declining Socialist Party seemed poised to take control of the organization. The left-wing members—mostly from the party's foreign-language federations, many of them immigrants from Eastern Europe and sympathetic to the Bolsheviks—disdained party moderates who sought to renew prewar political reform efforts. The left wing instead advocated revolutionary "mass action" in concert with aroused workers, then part of an unprecedented wave of postwar strikes. Thus, conditions were ripe for the left wing to heed the call of the Comintern, which urged all Socialists to foment revolutions in capitalist countries. The left wing, once it openly embraced this program, was soon expelled by the Socialist Party leaders.

By the end of 1919, two separate Communist parties had emerged. The larger of the two, the Communist Party of America, was dominated by members organized into foreign-language groups. The smaller Communist Labor Party was composed of mostly English-speaking and native-born members.

The early years were marked by intense factionalism between and within the two Communist parties, as well as raids, surveillance, and infiltration at the hands of the U.S. government, which pushed both parties underground. These obstacles, compounded by a conservative shift in public sentiment, caused the parties to lose members. The combined membership of the two Communist parties dropped from roughly 40,000 in 1919 to 12,000 in 1922. At the behest of the Comintern, the competing parties merged in 1922, resurfaced as the Workers' Party, and began to engage openly in political and trade union activities.

The story of Louis Fraina illustrates the tragic character of these early years. Born in Italy in 1895, he moved in and out of the Socialist Party, working as a journalist, and helped lead the revolutionary left wing to break away from the party. Fraina was the foremost promoter of the Bolshevik revolution, publishing and editing numerous political and theoretical papers. In 1918, he introduced the first English-language work on the Bolsheviks, *The Proletarian Revolution in Russia,* an anthology of writings by Vladimir Lenin and Leon Trotsky. Although he was a talented propagandist and incisive thinker, Fraina's meteoric rise succumbed to the merciless factionalism of the party's first years, a divisiveness exacerbated by the pressures of postwar repression and jockeying for Comintern approval. Wrongfully accused by his comrades of being a government spy, Fraina left the party and, under the name Lewis Corey, became well known as an economist and anticommunist.

In the middle and late 1920s, American Communists engaged in a variety of political and trade union efforts that established the party as a formidable organization on the Left. Prodded by the Comintern's moderating United Front policy promulgated in 1921, the Communists set aside immediate revolutionary hopes and began to work with mass organizations and institutions. Early efforts included participation in forming the Farmer-Labor Party (F-LP); however, condemnation from the conservative American Federation of Labor (AFL) and the opportunistic maneuvers of the Communists soon destroyed the F-LP. The Communists were isolated from Robert M. La Follette's Progressive Party campaign in 1924, and Communist candidates in later elections usually fared poorly.

The Communists' work within various unions proved more substantial. William Z. Foster, already noted for leading the 1919 steel strike, joined the Communists in the early 1920s while heading the Trade Union Educational League. Through the league, Foster helped coordinate Communists and other activists within the AFL's member unions and became the most influential Communist in the labor movement during this period.

Communists enjoyed some success in leading several unions, including the Garment and Fur and Leather workers, and led the landmark 1926 textile strike in Passaic, New Jersey. Further political missteps and rejection by AFL leaders, however, caused the Communists to abandon work within the unions by 1929, when they began to establish industrial unions outside the AFL under the rubric of the Trade Union Unity League. In many ways, these efforts prefigured the far more successful unions of the Congress of Industrial Organizations in the 1930s.

Justin F. Jackson

See also: Anarchism; Red Scare of 1917–1920; Socialism and the Socialist Party of America.

Further Reading

Barrett, James R. *William Z. Foster and the Tragedy of American Radicalism.* Urbana: University of Illinois Press, 1999.

Buhle, Paul M. *A Dreamer's Paradise Lost: Louis C. Fraina / Lewis Corey (1892–1953) and the Decline of Radicalism in the United States.* Atlantic Highlands, NJ: Humanities Press, 1995.

Communist Party USA. http://www.cpusa.org.

Fried, Albert. *Communism in America: A History in Documents.* New York: Columbia University Press, 1997.

Coolidge, Calvin (1872–1933)

A conservative Republican who assumed the presidency upon the death of Warren G. Harding in 1923, the quiet and morally upstanding Calvin Coolidge helped restore the integrity of the presidency after the many scandals that had engulfed the administration of his predecessor. Coolidge then went on to win a full term of his own, presiding over one of the nation's great economic booms.

Rise in Politics

Calvin Coolidge was born on July 4, 1872, at Plymouth Notch, Vermont. His famous personality traits were apparent early, namely a dry wit, shyness, and a tendency toward silence. Coolidge worked on the family farm and in his father's general store, and he attended public and private schools in Vermont. He won a national college writing competition, graduated *cum laude* from Amherst College in 1895, and studied law in the firm of Hammond and Field in Northampton, Massachusetts. He was admitted to the bar in 1897.

Coolidge would hold more public offices than any other president. Among his political positions were city solicitor, clerk of courts, and mayor of Northampton. He advanced steadily through the ranks of Massachusetts state government, serving as a member of the general assembly, president of the state senate, lieutenant governor, and finally governor from 1919 to 1920. His 1914 speech "Have Faith in Massachusetts," delivered when he became senate president, is considered his masterpiece of public speaking, summarizing his conservative philosophy and arguing against the progressive, proregulation wing of his own party.

As governor, Coolidge reduced and reorganized state departments, and his forceful handling of the

Massachusetts Governor Calvin Coolidge inspects National Guardsmen he called in to restore order during the Boston police strike of 1919. His tough stance against the police earned him a national reputation and a place on the 1920 Republican ticket as the candidate for vice president. *(Keystone/Stringer/Hulton Archive/Getty Images)*

1919 Boston police strike—mobilizing the state guard and sending a telegram to Samuel Gompers that declared, "There is no right to strike against the public safety by anybody, anywhere, anytime"—catapulted Coolidge to national prominence. Against the directive of party bosses, delegates to the 1920 Republican National Convention nominated Coolidge for the vice presidency on the ticket with Warren G. Harding.

Given the relative powerlessness of the office, Coolidge had little to do as vice president. Notably, he was not tainted by the numerous scandals that came to plague the Harding administration, the most notorious being the Teapot Dome bribery scandal.

Presidency

With the unexpected death of President Harding, Coolidge became president on August 3, 1923. By the light of a kerosene lamp, Coolidge's father, Colonel John Coolidge, a notary public, administered the oath of office at the family homestead at Plymouth

Notch, Vermont. The newly installed president then went upstairs, said a prayer, and went to bed. The next morning, after visiting his mother's grave, he set out for Washington, D.C.

The drama and simplicity of the transition of power captivated the nation, creating a groundswell of support for the hardworking chief executive. From the outset, his aura of honesty and old-fashioned values stood in sharp contrast to the corruptions of the Harding administration. Coolidge purged the remnants of the discredited Harding clique, ensured the prosecution of wrongdoers, and took firm control of the party apparatus. Most Republicans surrendered readily to the dominance of the "Puritan in Babylon"—referring to his socially conservative mien in an age of perceived moral license—since many believed that he was all that stood between the GOP and oblivion in the aftermath of the Harding administration scandals.

Coolidge's skillful use of the press—through regular press conferences, colorful photo opportunities, and frequent radio addresses—made "Silent Cal" a media favorite. He effectively crafted his image to become the personification of integrity; in his silence, he seemed to rise above the turmoil of petty politics. Coolidge would be the last American president not to use a speechwriter, and many historians have cited him as one of the best writers to occupy the White House.

Adding to the president's political fortune was the popularity of his wife, Grace Goodhue Coolidge, a vivacious and outspoken woman who became involved in a number of charitable causes. She and her husband received the nation's sympathies when their son Calvin, Jr., died of blood poisoning at age sixteen in the summer of 1924.

In the run-up to the 1924 election, the taciturn and reserved Coolidge campaigned little, partly because of the recent death of Calvin, Jr. The American people, heeding his campaign slogan to "Keep Cool with Coolidge," gave the president a decisive victory over Democratic candidate John Davis: 382 electoral votes to 136.

Coolidge advocated probusiness policies, frugality in government, debt reduction, and tax cuts. The national debt declined from $22.3 billion in 1923 to $16.9 billion by 1929, federal expenditures were reduced from $5.1 billion in 1921 to $3.3 billion by 1929, and taxes were cut in four of the six years of the Coolidge presidency. The effective tax rate on the wealthy was reduced to 20 percent, and

many Americans paid no income tax. As the gross national product and real earnings increased dramatically, the strong economic performance came to be referred to as "Coolidge prosperity."

With Coolidge's support, Congress passed a number of major judicial reforms. Coolidge took extraordinary interest in court appointments but had the opportunity to nominate only one justice to the Supreme Court: Harlan Fiske Stone, a conservative. At the same time, Coolidge was determined to defend presidential power against encroachments by Congress and the judiciary.

Another conservative act was his 1924 veto—overridden by Congress—of the veterans' Bonus Bill, a measure to extend payments to World War I veterans. He signed into law the highly restrictive Immigration Act of 1924, which set strict quotas on arrivals from Southern and Eastern Europe.

Progressivism

As president, Coolidge supported a number of progressive measures. He signed legislation in 1924 that granted citizenship to Native Americans, and allowed for the creation in 1927 of the Federal Radio Commission (later the Federal Communications Commission) to regulate the airwaves. He signed the Jones-White Act in 1928, calling for the construction of merchant ships; designated $250 million for the construction of public buildings in Washington, D.C.; and called for more funding for aviation and the construction of the Saint Lawrence Seaway.

Coolidge repeatedly expressed concern for the civil and economic rights of African Americans. He criticized the Ku Klux Klan, ended discrimination against black Justice Department employees, and called for federal anti-lynching laws and medical school scholarships for black students.

In addition, Coolidge released the remaining Sedition Act violators convicted during the Wilson administration. These were radical and leftist politicians, such as Socialist Party leader Eugene V. Debs, who had violated the harsh wartime Sedition Act by opposing U.S. entry into World War I and advocating resistance to the draft.

In foreign policy, Coolidge was surprisingly activist. He sent 5,000 Marines to Nicaragua in 1926 to protect American interests, signed the Kellogg-Briand Pact of 1928 outlawing war as an instrument of national policy, and supported American participation in the World Court but not the League of

Nations. His administration negotiated the Five-Power Treaty of 1923, reducing the size of the great powers' naval forces, and the Dawes Plan for Reparations of 1928, which helped stabilize the international financial system by extending loans to an economically troubled Germany. Good relations were restored with Mexico, and the president attended the International Conference of American States in Havana, Cuba, in 1928.

Throughout his administration, Coolidge sought to portray himself as a humble New Englander called to serve his country. He surprised the nation in 1927 when he released a statement that read, simply, "I do not choose to run for President in 1928." Silent Cal left office in March 1929 amid great popularity and published his autobiography later that year. He kept his distance from the administration of his successor, Herbert Hoover, who soon was grappling with the effects of the Great Depression.

Coolidge died of a heart attack at his Northampton home on January 5, 1933, at the age of sixty. He was buried at Plymouth Notch.

Russell Fowler

See also: Boston Police Strike of 1919; Election of 1924; Republican Party.

Further Reading

Coolidge, Calvin. *The Autobiography of Calvin Coolidge.* New York: Cosmopolitan, 1929.

Ferrell, Robert H. *The Presidency of Calvin Coolidge.* Lawrence: University Press of Kansas, 1998.

Fuess, Claude Moore. *Calvin Coolidge: The Man from Vermont.* Hamden, CT: Archon, 1965.

Sobel, Robert. *Coolidge: An American Enigma.* Washington, DC: Regnery, 1998.

Country Music

Rural and isolated American communities, especially in the Appalachian South and the ranching West, had a strong music tradition. Handmade music was shared on front porches and in backyard parties, and the songs were handed down through time, played on fiddle, banjo, and guitar for friends and family. Story songs and dance tunes were popular, as were songs of faith and work songs.

Country music told of the familiar, of home. During the Jazz Age, as people moved from country to city, came in contact with people from different backgrounds, and coped with changes in technology and in the structure of society, they longed for that touch of home. Technological advances in recording and broadcasting paved the way for many to find that touch in music. As the 1920s unfolded, this music of the rural South and West became the foundation of a music industry that continues to the present day.

Most radio stations were city based in the 1920s. Their signals reached rural listeners, though, as well as those urban transplants who missed the sounds of home. Between 1923 and 1925, stations in Dallas, Chicago, and Nashville began featuring live "old-time" music on regular weekly programs known as barn dances. Nashville's version would become Tennessee's Grand Ole Opry, a country music institution and cultural icon.

Record companies took notice of this niche, too. In 1922, the Victor Talking Machine Company recorded Texas fiddle player Eck Robertson, accompanied by American Civil War veteran and fellow fiddler Henry Gilliland, playing the upbeat traditional tune "Sally Goodin," backed with the equally lively old-time standard "Arkansas Traveler." This was the first time Southern white rural musicians were featured on a record. In 1924, fellow Texan Vernon Dalhart made the two-sided Victor recording of "The Prisoner's Song" and "The Wreck of the Old '97," the first country music record to sell 1 million copies. In 1925, real-life ranch hand Carl T. Sprague, the first singing cowboy, recorded "When the Work's All Done This Fall," which sold about 900,000 copies.

With the availability of record players and radio, artists began to be known outside their own areas. Gospel music and Cajun music were also first recorded during this time. Recording companies such as Victor, Okeh, and Columbia sent agents through the rural South and West with mobile recording outfits, looking for the next big country music artist.

In late summer 1927, in Bristol, Virginia, Ralph Peer of Victor Records found two acts that would sell records not only during the Jazz Age but for decades to come. The first was Mississippi native Jimmie Rodgers, at the time living nearby in North Carolina. Rodgers had an easygoing presence, a distinct style that gave a contemporary sound to traditional music, an ability to mix genres from blues to old time, and a batch of his own songs, as well as a signature yodel. The songs he recorded that first day in Bristol were not big hits, but they did well enough to get him another chance. The next sessions produced "T for Texas" and "Blue Yodel." Other enduring music from Rodgers includes "Miss the Mississippi and

You," "My Rough and Rowdy Ways," "Waiting for a Train," and "Somewhere Down Below the Dixie Line."

Peer also recorded a local group, the Carter Family: A.P. Carter; his wife, Sara; and his sister-in-law, Maybelle Carter. Like Rodgers, the trio had a unique way of making old songs seem new, and new songs seem timeless. Their mountain-born family harmonies, along with Maybelle's guitar style and their varied song selection, marked them as truly original artists. The Carters' work had a wide appeal in the Jazz Age, and they continued to influence artists in many genres from that time to the present. They sold tens of thousands of records even during the hard times of the Great Depression. Carter Family songs include such country classics as "I'm Thinking Tonight of My Blue Eyes," "Will the Circle Be Unbroken," "Wildwood Flower," "Little Darlin' Pal o' Mine," and "Keep on the Sunny Side."

Country music experienced many of the changes that affected other forms of mass culture in the 1920s. Once largely a form of folk music with distinctive traditions in various parts of the nation, country music became more homogenized and commercialized through radio and record production.

Kerry Dexter

See also: Blues.

Further Reading

The Bristol Sessions. Sound recording. Nashville: Country Music Hall of Fame, 1991.

The Carter Family: Their Complete Victor Recordings. Sound recording. Cambridge, MA: Rounder Records, 1993–1998.

Oermann, Robert K. *A Century of Country.* New York: TV Books, 1999.

Credit and Debt, Consumer

Prior to the twentieth century, consumer credit was a virtually alien concept for most Americans. Ordinary citizens borrowed money primarily for purchases essential to their livelihoods, such as seed or land, or in cases of emergency. Middle- and working-class borrowers relied primarily on local merchants or family members for loans. In most cases, bank loans were available only to the wealthy and were used for capital investment. Although a few manufacturers, such as the Singer Sewing Machine Company and the International Harvester Corporation, extended credit to consumers to purchase their products, consumer credit remained unavailable to the majority of Americans. Moreover, social taboos regarding debt continued to restrict the demand for loans to purchase consumer goods.

Attitudes toward consumer credit and debt began to change during the early twentieth century as American society became more urbanized and mass production made more consumer goods available to the public. Realizing that few consumers would be able to pay cash for these goods, more manufacturers began to extend installment plans as an option for purchasing their products. The success of the Singer and International Harvester credit plans had demonstrated that even consumers of modest means could be trusted to pay their debts on time.

The creation of the Federal Reserve System in 1913 provided the financial sector with a measure of security against severe economic instability. As a result, banks and other financial institutions began to regard the extension of consumer credit as a more viable option. Ordinary Americans, lured by new labor-saving and technological devices such as radios, washing machines, and automobiles, and the potential of these devices to enhance their lives, became more accepting of consumer debt.

Automobiles in particular fueled the growth of consumer credit in the 1920s. As better roads and more reliable mass-produced vehicles made automobile travel more practical, demand for them grew among middle- and working-class Americans. The creation of the General Motors Acceptance Corporation (GMAC) in 1919 started a trend toward manufacturer-financed automobile purchases, and Ford and other automobile manufacturers followed suit. Loans for automobile purchases were soon a sizable portion of the credit issued by banks, savings and loans, and consumer finance companies, which flourished as a result of the credit boom. By the mid-1920s, approximately 75 percent of all new automobiles in the United States were purchased on credit.

The purchase of homes through long-term mortgages also began in the 1920s. Prior to World War I, most consumers purchased homes with cash or short-term mortgages of five years or less. Following the war, banks began offering twenty-year mortgages, providing many middle-class consumers with the opportunity to become homeowners. The resulting boom in real estate purchases was rapid and dramatic; by the end of the 1920s, nearly two-thirds of new home purchases in the United States were financed by credit, up from 47 percent in 1912 and 55 percent in the early 1920s.

Although consumer credit in the 1920s consisted primarily of installment plans for the purchase of specific items, other forms of credit that would become more popular in subsequent decades also emerged. Some hotels and department stores began issuing credit cards to favored customers, and oil companies offered charge cards to automobile owners and businesses for gasoline purchases, ushering in the concept of revolving consumer credit. Layaway plans, which allowed store patrons to pay for items over time while stores held the items in safekeeping, were used more frequently during the 1920s. Purchasing stock on credit, known as "margin" investment, also became popular.

The dramatic growth of consumer credit in the 1920s has been cited as a factor contributing to the stock market crash of 1929. This practice fueled an overexpanded economy supported by an unsustainable level of debt, and exacerbated the subsequent economic depression as an explosion of defaults on loans, mortgages, and installment plans led to the widespread failure of banks and businesses. Yet the establishment of consumer credit as an acceptable and practical feature of the nation's economy set a precedent for future growth of the credit industry during the latter half of the twentieth century. As a result of consumer credit, the average American enjoyed a higher standard of living but also accumulated increased levels of debt, raising concerns about the long-term financial well-being of a large segment of the population.

Michael H. Burchett

See also: Advertising; Appliances, Household; Automobile Industry; Automobiles and Automobile Culture; Housing; Real Estate; Retail and Chain Stores; Stock Market.

Further Reading

Calder, Lindol. *Financing the American Dream.* Princeton, NJ: Princeton University Press, 1999.

Olney, Martha L. "Credit as a Production-Smoothing Device: The Case of Automobiles, 1913–1938." *Journal of Economic History* 49:2 (1989): 377–91.

Crime, Organized

Con operations and urban gangs had long been part of the American scene. What was different about organized crime in the Jazz Age was its scale and so-phistication, a response to the opportunities made available by the national prohibition on alcohol in 1920. As operations expanded to embrace citywide and even regional areas, criminal syndicates adopted the managerial and organizational models developed by legitimate big businesses—albeit with certain modifications, such as murdering rivals and breaking the bones of overdue debtors. As *New Yorker* magazine writer Alva Johnston commented in the 1920s about the illegal alcohol trade, "beer has lifted the gangster from a local leader of roughs and gunmen to a great executive controlling a big interstate and international organization."

Contributing Factors

A host of long-term factors explain the evolution of organized crime in the 1920s. One was urbanization. The growth of major cities allowed the main business of organized crime—vice—to flourish. Large urban centers concentrated enough people in a small area to make the provision of prostitution, gambling, or illicit drugs a profitable enterprise. Urban anonymity and freedom from social constraints of family, church, and community also allowed vice to flourish.

Large-scale immigration, another factor, contributed to the growth of cities and brought in large numbers of people from cultures where underground and illegal economies flourished. Moreover, many of the new immigrants were impoverished, discriminated against by mainstream American society, and ambitious—a combination that led some to seek illegitimate paths to the American dream of social mobility and economic success.

Finally, the same innovations in communication and transportation that helped legitimate businesses grow into national enterprises also contributed to the expansion of organized crime.

There was also one overarching short-term cause behind the growth of organized crime in the Jazz Age: Prohibition. In 1919, the efforts of social reformers were realized with the ratification of the Eighteenth Amendment to the U.S. Constitution prohibiting "the manufacture, sale, or transportation of intoxicating liquors" within one year. Prohibition, however, was never popular in America's immigrant-filled, heavily Catholic cities. A popular and addictive but now illegal vice, a vast customer base, and a general contempt among much of the public for Prohibition created the ideal setting for the growth of organized crime.

Urban areas were already rife with organized crime when the provisions of the Eighteenth Amendment and its enabling legislation, the Volstead Act, went into effect on January 16, 1920. During the Progressive Era, local, state, and federal officials cracked down on gambling (by 1909, every state in America had banned casinos), drugs (the Harrison Narcotics Tax Act of 1914 placed tight regulations on the sale of opiates and cocaine), and prostitution (most cities and states had banned the practice by the early 1900s), ironically creating the conditions in which organized crime flourished. Thus, when alcohol was made illegal, there was already a rudimentary infrastructure for its illicit importation, distribution, and sales. Moreover, because twenty-six states had banned alcohol before national Prohibition went into effect, there were already thousands of illegal bootleggers—unregulated and illicit manufacturers of alcohol—throughout the country. The major organized crime rings then set to work creating interstate and even international distribution networks to access illegally produced alcohol, smuggle it into the country, and sell the product to speakeasies (illegal bars) and other customers.

One of the most powerful figures in organized crime, New York gambling kingpin and bootlegger Arnold Rothstein was alleged to have been the mastermind of the Black Sox scandal, in which eight Chicago White Sox players conspired to throw the 1919 World Series. *(Jack Benton/Hulton Archive/Getty Images)*

Operations

Organized crime rings were adept at protecting their turf and operations, both from rival gangs and from law enforcement. Crime gangs had long engaged in violent attacks on one another. The notorious Chicago crime boss of the 1920s, Al Capone, had gotten his start in organized crime in New York's Five Points Gang. He was known for his ruthless use of violence against other gangs that attempted to move into the Five Points territory. But too much violence could be bad for business, not only causing the loss of key personnel but also stirring up public outrage that might lead to crackdowns by law enforcement. Thus, urban gangs negotiated treaties to divide up neighborhoods and business.

Powerful crime bosses had influence not only over all of the gangs in a given urban area but over key politicians and law enforcement officials as well. New York City crime boss Arnold Rothstein, for example, had a citywide organization specializing in illegal gambling and loan-sharking (the practice of lending money at high interest, with severe physical penalties for those who failed to make their payments on time). By 1920, Rothstein had become the person other organized crime figures turned to for financing, resolving conflict with other gangsters, and smoothing over problems with politicians and law enforcement officials.

Having built a citywide operation, Rothstein had the managerial skills—as well as the ruthlessness—to take advantage of the opportunities opened up by Prohibition. In spring 1920, a bootlegger named Max "Big Maxey" Greenberg, who had been transporting scotch from Canada across the Detroit River, approached Rothstein with a business proposition. Greenberg was looking to expand his operations and needed a loan of $175,000. Rothstein agreed to back him but decided they would get their liquor straight from the source in England and Scotland. Rothstein would finance the operation and give Greenberg and his associates a share of the profits.

Over the next twelve months, Rothstein's ships made eleven voyages across the Atlantic. Greenberg and his associates acted as the U.S. distributor, supplying trucks and warehouses that Rothstein held as collateral. Following a close call with law enforcement, Rothstein ended his partnership with Greenberg in 1921 but continued quietly to finance bootlegging operations, reaping enormous profits.

St. Valentine's Day Massacre

The explosive increase in organized crime in major American cities during Prohibition led to a number of violent clashes between rival mobs for control of territory. Such a struggle ensued between the Irish and German gangs controlling Chicago's North Side and the Italian gang, led by Al Capone, controlling the South Side. During the 1920s, Capone managed to eliminate much of the leadership of the North Side gang, which had come under the control of George "Bugs" Moran.

On the morning of February 14, 1929, as several members of the North Side gang awaited a shipment of bootleg liquor at a garage in the Lincoln Park neighborhood, five men—three of them dressed as police officers—burst into the building brandishing Thompson submachine guns, ordered those present against a wall, and opened fire, killing all seven of Moran's men. Moran appears to have been the primary target of the ambush, but he was not present. Having arrived late for the meeting, he fled when he saw men dressed as police entering the building.

Although the audacity and brutality of the massacre bore the mark of Capone, none of its perpetrators was ever prosecuted. Many believed that Chicago police—many members of the force were allegedly on Capone's payroll—had planned and carried out the massacre. A subsequent investigation by the internal affairs division of the force, however, cleared the police.

The one victim still living when police arrived, Frank "Tight Lips" Gusenberg, refused to identify the assailants, and he died shortly thereafter. Capone was in Florida at the time of the killings, providing him with an alibi. With most of Moran's top henchmen killed in the attack and the effectiveness of the North Side gang diminished, Capone was able to assume control over much of their territory during the following months.

After years of unsuccessful efforts by local and state authorities to prosecute Capone for murder and racketeering, federal authorities refocused their attention on Capone in the wake of the massacre. Although they were unsuccessful in arresting him for his many violent pursuits, in 1931 they finally managed to convict him on charges of tax evasion.

The "St. Valentine's Day massacre" captured public attention, simultaneously inspiring public outrage against organized criminal activity and stirring Americans' fascination with the gangsters of the Roaring Twenties. In the days following the massacre, lurid photographs of the murder scene, showing the corpses lying where they fell, appeared in newspapers across the United States. The massacre—and fictional ones modeled after it—continued to be a popular subject in books and movies for decades after the incident.

Michael H. Burchett

Greenberg and his associates also became extremely wealthy through bootlegging. By the end of the decade, Greenberg owned blocks of real estate in New York City and Philadelphia.

In Chicago, meanwhile, Capone was expanding his operations throughout the Midwest and as far away as Florida through the systematic elimination of his rivals. It is estimated that the gang wars instigated by Capone and his syndicate were responsible for the deaths of more than 800 people between 1924 and 1928.

Capone was in charge of a highly successful organization, developing smuggling operations and links to bootleggers, creating his own manufacturing facilities, and opening his own speakeasies in Chicago and other Midwestern cities. Capone's gang also perfected the art of "protection," requiring owners of independent speakeasies to pay extortion money to keep their bars open and prevent being injured or killed. By the end of the 1920s, Capone's operations employed an estimated 6,000 people and brought in revenues of roughly $2 million per week.

Law Enforcement

Once established, a crime organization's success depended on finding ways to prevent politicians, police, and prosecutors from interfering with operations. This was often accomplished through bribery and entertainment, allowing politicians free and easy access to the speakeasies and houses of prostitution run by organized crime syndicates. Rothstein, for example, enjoyed a close relationship with New York City's Mayor Jimmy Walker, while Al Capone was said to own the government of Cicero, a city on Chicago's outskirts where he moved his operations after reformer William Dever was elected Chicago's mayor in 1923. Later in the 1920s, Chicago's Mayor William Hale Thompson was said to profit personally from organized crime.

Interference by law enforcement was handled not only through bribery but also by infiltration. Police officers were paid to ignore the comings and goings at speakeasies, while higher-ups in the force could tip off gangsters about coming raids on their operations.

Most big-city mayors held "wet" views, meaning they opposed the very concept of Prohibition. While they deplored the violence of organized crime wars, mayors feared that vigorous law enforcement was likely to exacerbate the problem by disturbing the gangs' territorial and revenue-sharing agreements. Thus, most mayors resigned themselves to a major organized crime presence in their cities.

Even reformers might give up after a time. In 1924, Philadelphia Mayor W. Freeland Kendrick appointed a former U.S. Marine Corps general, Smedley Butler, as police commissioner, specifically to root out organized crime's influence in the police force and shut down the operations of crime boss Max "Booboo" Hoff. After two years, Butler gave up, explaining that the job was a "waste of time."

Nor was the federal government especially active in cracking down on organized crime. Congressional appropriations to enforce Prohibition laws never amounted to more than a few million dollars annually, a sum ridiculously small given the scope of the problem. Moreover, the Prohibition Bureau, Washington's enforcement agency, was entrusted to the Treasury Department, which gave it a low priority. Bureaucratic struggles in Washington prevented the bureau from being transferred to the Justice Department, where it probably belonged. As for the Bureau of Investigation (precursor to the Federal Bureau of Investigation), it was an understaffed, unprofessional outfit until reformed by newly appointed head J. Edgar Hoover in 1925. Even then, it was given no formal jurisdiction over organized crime. In the end, it was the Internal Revenue Service that brought about the most publicized organized crime prosecution of the Jazz Age, the indictment and conviction of Al Capone on tax evasion charges in 1931.

The Gangster Image

Some participants in organized crime viewed themselves as Robin Hood figures. However, rather than stealing from the rich and giving to the poor, they might take from the vice addicted and give to the law abiding. Al Capone cultivated his image as a philanthropist to Chicago's working people, conspicuously providing daily milk rations to Chicago's underprivileged schoolchildren.

While charity represented a conscious effort to gain acceptance, the gangster also appealed to the darker side of the public soul. Many ordinary people indulged in the occasional visit to a speakeasy or a bet on the numbers (illegal lotteries), making it more difficult for them to condemn those who provided such illicit pleasures. Moreover, the gangster image—tough-talking, well-dressed, easy with money, and popular with women—appealed to many young men, helping to recruit them into the business.

The Roaring Twenties are often thought of as a golden age of the gangster. Prohibition provided unprecedented opportunities to make a fortune by satisfying illegal vices, and crime bosses like Capone and Rothstein led powerful operations across whole regions of the country. But while the Eighteenth Amendment and the Twenty-first Amendment repealing it in 1933 provide historical bookends to Prohibition, the gangster era was already coming to a close before Prohibition ended. The onset of the Great Depression in 1929 lessened the public's tolerance for flashy crime figures. And some of the key figures were disappearing from the scene: Rothstein was murdered in 1928, and Capone was put on trial and sent to a federal penitentiary in 1931–1932.

Legacy

The golden age was over, but the legacy of the gangster era lived on. Many mid- and upper-level operatives went on to carve out their own organized crime operations in the 1930s and beyond. The extremely violent Dutch Schultz, a former truck driver for Rothstein, branched out into the numbers and protection rackets in Harlem in the 1930s. Charles "Lucky" Luciano, Frank Costello, Benjamin "Bugsy" Siegel, and Meyer Lansky—major figures in the expansion of organized crime into a national enterprise after World War II—all got their start or had their careers enhanced through affiliations with Rothstein's operations in the 1920s. Indeed, the organizational ideas and ruthless violence of the 1920s would serve them well as they moved into illegal drugs and casino gambling in a new age of organized crime that began in the late 1940s. Even new federal laws and enforcement activity in the late twentieth century could not shut down organized crime operations that had their start in the Jazz Age.

James Ciment, Leigh Kimmel,
and Michael A. Rembis

See also: Bureau of Investigation; Capone, Al; Criminal Punishment; Hoover, J. Edgar; Ness, Eliot; Prohibition (1920–1933); Schultz, Dutch; Speakeasies; Volstead Act (1919).

Further Reading

Balsamo, William, and George Carpozi, Jr. *Crime Incorporated: The Inside Story of the Mafia's First 100 Years.* Far Hills, NJ: New Horizon, 1996.

Reppetto, Thomas. *American Mafia: A History of Its Rise to Power.* New York: Henry Holt, 2004.

Ruth, David E. *Inventing the Public Enemy: The Gangster in American Culture, 1918–1934.* Chicago: University of Chicago Press, 1996.

Criminal Punishment

The Jazz Age was a time of rapidly growing crime and rapidly rising incarceration rates. In response to these trends, government officials instituted a number of innovations, including the construction of new prisons, restrictions on the use of convict labor, and most significantly, new methods of classifying prisoners. At the same time, however, a host of earlier Progressive Era reforms, including educational programs, were set back by overcrowded conditions in many of the nation's prisons.

Despite the relative prosperity and low unemployment of the decade, ordinary crimes against persons and property grew dramatically from the end of World War I in late 1918 to the onset of the Great Depression in late 1929, rising by 50 to 100 percent in most categories. With the passing of tough new anticrime ordinances at the state and federal levels, as well as a host of laws passed with the onset of Prohibition, prison populations increased dramatically as well, from 50 to 100 percent in most states. The federal prison population grew from roughly 3,900 in 1915 to more than 13,000 in 1930.

Decades before the U.S. Supreme Court issued decisions protecting the rights of criminal suspects, policing methods in the Jazz Age often bordered on brutality. Criminals were rarely informed of their rights, and coerced confessions, while technically unconstitutional, were permitted in many courts of law. Indeed, the 1920s saw the introduction of the term "third degree" into the popular lexicon: the first degree of pressure on a suspect was arrest, the second was being thrown in jail, and the third was administered at the police station, where officers used verbal and physical assault to get a suspect to confess to a crime.

Still, there were improvements in arrest and conviction procedures. The 1920s saw the wholesale abandonment of the Bertillon system for identifying suspects, named after its inventor, French criminologist Alphonse Bertillon, who developed it in the late nineteenth century. This unwieldy system of photographs and anatomical measurements gave way to the simpler and more reliable method of fingerprinting.

Psychological Methods of Evaluation

New psychology-based methods for classifying types of criminals began to be employed during the 1920s. Earlier approaches had been based on the assumption of inbred criminality—the view that some members of society are biologically predisposed to deviate from social norms. This propensity, it was believed, could be ascertained through phrenology, or measurements of the skull to determine which parts of the brain are more or less developed than others. However, several extensive studies of prisoners conducted in Britain and the United States in the early twentieth century largely disproved such assumptions.

In 1916, New York State's Sing Sing prison opened the nation's first criminology clinic, under the direction of psychologist Bernard Glueck. Rather than classify prisoners by biological type, Glueck used psychological evaluation. Roughly one-fifth were classified as psychopathic, about one-third were classified as mentally retarded, and about one-tenth were classified as mentally ill. Glueck recommended that Sing Sing be transformed into an intake institution where prisoners would be classified before being sent to regular prisons or to asylums for treatment. Glueck's recommendations went largely unheeded, but the idea that psychological methods of evaluation should become part of the prison system gained widespread acceptance. Across the country, penitentiaries hired psychologists, and clinics were set up for the treatment of some criminals.

The real potential of Glueck's findings lay not so much in criminal punishment as in criminal justice. Criminals could be judged by their personal psychology and their ability to take responsibility for their crimes. Thus, a psychopathic individual should be incarcerated for a longer period and in a different institution than a mentally retarded criminal. While psychologists called for the individualization of criminal justice and the classification of causes, the legal system remained based on categories of crime, despite the fact that in the American justice system, all individuals are equal before the law.

Nevertheless, some changes began to be seen in criminal law and punishment. A few states continued the Progressive Era trend toward incarcerating juveniles in reformatories and those guilty of lesser crimes on work farms. Massachusetts and New Jersey led the nation in using psychologists to determine which criminals belonged in high- and low-security prisons, as well as which ones should be granted parole. Indeed, both probation and parole rates rose significantly in the 1920s.

Prisoner Populations and New Prison Regimes

Higher probation and parole rates aside, a soaring prison population led to major overcrowding across the country. The doubling and tripling up of prisoners in cells designed for one person became commonplace. A study of Ohio prisons in 1925, for example, found that the state's 2,500 long-term prisoners were jammed into just 900 cells, and Missouri's 2,800 convicts were crowded into 970 cells. The overcrowding came despite a wave of prison construction, which included new penitentiaries, new cellblocks, and new nontraditional institutions like work farms and camps.

Correctional regimes were also changing, though not necessarily for the better. In the early nineteenth century, many prisons had instituted what was known as the Auburn system, after the New York prison of that name, under which prisoners were isolated from one another in order to reduce bad influences. Left in their cells, criminals were expected to reflect on their moral failings, with the goal of achieving penitence (hence the term "penitentiary"). Early methods of punishment were based on the idea that criminal behavior is a moral failing.

Much of this thinking was overturned during the Progressive Era, as criminologists came to accept that criminal behavior is based largely on social and environmental factors, such as poverty or broken families. Thus, early twentieth-century reforms did away with isolation on the assumption that it could do little for prisoners. Instead, it was believed that prisoners should be resocialized, made fit for productive citizenship and a return to society through education programs and indoctrination. Moreover, prisoners had to learn to get along with others, leading to a new emphasis on allowing prisoners to mingle with one another.

The overcrowded conditions of America's prisons during the 1920s served to undo many of these reforms. Indeed, the mixing of prisoners was found to lead to more acts of violence and rioting; prison officials responded by isolating those considered incorrigible—a determination sometimes based on psychological testing and sometimes as a response to violent behavior.

Many of the programs of the Progressive Era suffered from a reduction in prison revenues. Responding to pressure from organized labor and working-class voters, many states had passed laws limiting the use of convict labor by private contractors. Between 1923 and 1930, the number of convicts working in prison fell from roughly two-thirds to one-half. Meanwhile, the number of those working for the state—making license plates or growing food for state institutions, for example—doubled from one-third of those working to roughly two-thirds. Thus, American prisons during the 1920s were being cut off from a major source of income, production for private contractors. Adding to the reductions in prison revenues was the conservative fiscal politics of the era.

A number of events began to bring the problems of the nation's prisons to light in the late 1920s, including a series of exposés written by prisoners and a string of riots at state and federal prisons from New York to Colorado. In 1929, President Herbert Hoover responded to the problem by establishing the U.S. Bureau of Prisons, which exposed the failures of the federal prison system and advocated a number of reforms to ease overcrowding, end the physical abuse of prisoners, and institute new educational and other social programs. However, the effects of the Great Depression in the early 1930s and the attending crisis in government finances aborted many of these reforms before they could get started.

James Ciment

See also: Bureau of Investigation; Capone, Al; Crime, Organized; Hoover, J. Edgar; Ness, Eliot.

Further Reading

Martin, John B. *Break Down the Walls: American Prisons, Present, Past, and Future.* New York: Ballantine, 1954.

McKelvey, Blake. *American Prisons: A History of Good Intentions.* Montclair, NJ: Patterson Smith, 1977.

Cummings, E.E. (1894–1962)

E.E. Cummings was an American poet, novelist, playwright, essayist, and artist. He is best known for the unorthodox style of his poetry, which is characterized by creative use of punctuation and sentence structure. Cummings was part of the twentieth-century movement away from traditional poetic meter and rhyme scheme, as well as from late Victorian poetic themes. A close reading of his poetry, however, reveals a dedication to classical forms such as the sonnet and to pastoral themes.

Edward Estlin Cummings was born in Cambridge, Massachusetts, on October 14, 1894, to Edward and Rebecca Haswell Clarke Cummings, affluent, liberal parents who encouraged him to pursue his artistic interests. Cummings's father was a Harvard professor of political science and later became a Unitarian minister. The future poet began writing verse at age ten. Cummings attended Cambridge Latin High School and published poems and fiction in the school paper.

As an undergraduate at Harvard, Cummings befriended future novelist John Dos Passos, poet and critic S. Foster Damon, poet Robert Hillyer, poet John Brooks Wheelwright, and novelist and critic

Malcolm Cowley. These writers formed a circle known to their peers as the Harvard Aesthetes. Cowley described Cummings in these years as in revolt against "cleanliness, godliness, decorum, public spirit . . . , [and] chastity." According to Cowley, the only thing Cummings respected was personal integrity. In 1915, upon graduating from Harvard *magna cum laude,* Cummings spoke to his peers at the undergraduate commencement about the innovations in modern literature. A year later, he took an M.A. in English and classical studies at Harvard.

During World War I, Cummings volunteered for a French ambulance corps. On his way to France, however, Cummings met William Slater Brown, an avowed anarchist, pacifist, and acquaintance of anarchist theorist Emma Goldman. Both men were appalled at the conditions of trench warfare and touched by the war-weariness of the French soldiers. After expressing their pacifist sentiments in letters home, Cummings and Brown were reported by a French censor and were falsely arrested for espionage. Cumming spent three months in a French detention camp. Cummings's father used his political connections to get his son released.

The deceptively innocent style for which Cummings is famous appeared early in his work. Both *The Enormous Room* (1922), a novel based on his experiences in the French prison, and *Tulips and Chimneys* (1923), his first collection of poems, were influenced by early modernists Gertrude Stein and Amy Lowell. Cummings, however, shaped the modernist sensibility of each to his own style, using modifiers as nouns, for example, or constructing an overtly simplistic voice to portray the superiority of the spontaneous and innocent over the rational and hierarchical.

After studying art in Paris from 1918 to 1924, Cummings returned to New York. His friend Dos Passos had found publishers for *The Enormous Room* and *Tulips and Chimneys,* and both works met with some popular success. Cummings's father was killed in 1926 in an automobile accident, and his poem "my father moved through dooms of love" pays homage to his memory.

Also in 1926, Cummings secured a job as an essayist and portrait artist for *Vanity Fair* magazine, a position that allowed him time to travel and pursue painting and writing. His work as a visual artist was exhibited in two New York Society of Independent Artists shows in the early 1920s. He published his first collection, *CIOPW* (an acronym for the materials he used—charcoal, ink, oil, pencil, watercolor), in 1931.

Cummings's many books of poetry—*ViVa* (1931), *No Thanks* (1935), *50 Poems* (1940), *95 Poems* (1958), *73 Poems* (1963), and *Fairy Tales* (1965), to name just a few—met with both critical as well as popular success. Some literary critics called his work naive and simplistic and charged Cummings with being artistically static. Still, Cummings received many awards, including the Dial Award (1925) and two Guggenheim Fellowships (1933 and 1951). He was also named the Charles Eliot Norton Professor at Harvard for 1952–1953.

Beneath Cummings's playful tone was a constant war with the conventional. He was especially harsh toward anything he perceived as upholding Victorian standards of decorum. In *Tulips and Chimneys*, for example, he included sonnets to prostitutes he had known from his days at Harvard and listed them proudly by name. Cummings's work often had a timeless quality, employing the past tense to evoke a nondescript and perfect "then."

He celebrated outcasts and the downtrodden, lifting them to a heroic status. These portrayals, however, often were laced with an irony that called into question the nature of hero worship itself. In "i sing of Olaf glad and big," Cummings describes the arrest, torture, and death of a conscientious objector and ends the poem with the lines "unless statistics lie he was / more brave than me:more blond than you."

A pronounced anti-intellectual strain also runs through Cummings's work. Scientists, philosophers, politicians, and moralists were subject to scorn. In their stead, he celebrates the intuitive sense of the child who can see the world as "puddle-wonderful" and "mud-luscious."

Cummings spent the last years of his life traveling, lecturing, and vacationing at his summer home, Joy Farm, in New Hampshire. He died there on September 3, 1962.

Jason Stacy

See also: Poetry.

Further Reading

Cummings, E.E. *Complete Poems, 1904–1962.* Ed. George J. Firmage. New York: Liveright, 1991.

Friedman, Norman. *E.E. Cummings: A Collection of Critical Essays.* New York: Prentice Hall, 1972.

———. *E.E. Cummings: The Art of His Poetry.* Baltimore: Johns Hopkins University Press, 1967.

Kennedy, Richard S. *Dreams in the Mirror: A Biography of E.E. Cummings.* New York: Liveright, 1994.

Sawyer-Laucanno, Christopher. *E.E. Cummings: A Biography.* New York: Sourcebooks, 2004.

Dance, Performance

The Jazz Age was remarkably fruitful for dance innovation, stylistic variety, and performer diversity. The
varied influences of European émigré dancers and cho-
reographers, vaudeville and Broadway shows, African
American culture and music, and emerging modernist aesthetics flourished. The artistic creativity of
this period laid the foundations for the 1930s Hollywood musical, launched the careers of many professional dancers, and influenced dance for the rest of the
twentieth century.

Ballet performances by European émigrés took
the nation by storm between 1916 and 1929. Serge
Diaghilev's *Ballets Russes* opened in New York in
1916, popularizing the dance form. Russian dancer
and choreographer Mikhail Fokine established a
school in New York in 1921 and choreographed for
Florenz Ziegfeld's Follies and American stars such as
Gilda Grey. Despite Folkine's efforts and the popularity of ballerina Anna Pavlova, who performed in the
United States between 1910 and 1925, an American
ballet company was not formed until after World
War II.

Influenced by performances at the Folies
Bergère music hall in Paris, chorus lines flourished in
America under the direction of John Tiller's military-
inspired "precision style" choreography. The Missouri
Rockets, later known as the Radio City Rockettes,
was formed in 1925. Ziegfeld's Follies (1907–1932)
incorporated chorus lines into various acts. Before
leaving for Paris to perform at the Folies Bergère
in 1926, African American dancer Josephine Baker
joined Florence Mills's *Shuffle Along* (1921) chorus.
With her outrageous costumes and unique personality, Baker became a sensation, epitomizing the exotic
style of the increasingly popular black musical revue.

Other stage productions by Florence Mills,
Plantation Revue (1922), *Dixie to Broadway* (1924),
and *Blackbirds* (1926), relied heavily on the historical
influence of minstrel shows and African American
dances. The new sounds of jazz bands, particularly

those popularized at Harlem's Savoy Club, made a
lasting mark on performance dance in the 1920s.
Flournoy Miller and Aubrey Mills combined jazz and
dance performance in the show *Runnin' Wild* (1925).
The production popularized the dance most associated with the Jazz Age, the Charleston. Miller and
Mills's shows borrowed African American dance
forms, including the black bottom, which would
later be co-opted by white performers and audiences
as the Lindy Hop and the jitterbug in the 1930s and
1940s.

The African American tradition of tap dancing
reached new heights in the 1920s. The legendary Bill
"Bojangles" Robinson performed first on the stage,
then on screen. He debuted his trademark "stair
dance" in the Broadway show *Blackbirds* (1928).
Robinson would survive the transition from the im-
provisation of vaudeville shows to musical films.
Other stage dancers, including Fred Astaire, Jack
Donahue, Eleanor Powell, Ruby Keeler, and Ginger
Rogers, also made the transition to film stardom in
Hollywood.

A significant development in Jazz Age dance
performance was partners "breaking" with each other.
This mid-dance shift from couples' steps to solo performance enabled greater individual expression, a
trend that continued in the 1920s. Innovator Ruth
St. Denis and husband Ted Shawn left vaudeville and
Broadway to form Denishawn, a dance company that
furthered the modern aesthetic begun by Isadora
Duncan and Loie Fuller a decade before. Experiment-
ing with lighting and stage effects, ethnic dances,
natural inspirations, free-style movement, and flowing costumes, the partners founded a school in Los
Angeles in 1915 and raised a generation of modern
dancers. In 1919, dancer Martha Graham joined
Denishawn and soon epitomized the modernism that
would elevate dance above entertainment into an expressive and communicative art form.

Graham continued to develop her own modern,
uniquely American style while working two seasons
with the Greenwich Village Follies and later teaching dance in Rochester, New York. The "Graham

technique" involved barefoot dancing with a strong relationship to the ground and movement from the center of the body. Her use of plain costumes and backdrops accentuated the central role of movement as a form of communication. Graham had her first solo recital in New York in 1926, performing *Three Gopi Maidens* and *A Study in Lacquer.* She continued to impress audiences with her ability to express abstract ideas through movement and her distinctive solo performances in *Dance* (1929) and *Heretic* (1929). In 1929, Graham founded her own dance company and worked to bring the full force of modern dance to the twentieth century.

Abigail B. Feely

See also: Baker, Josephine; Jazz; Music, Classical; Theater.

Further Reading

Anderson, Jack. *Ballet and Modern Dance: A Concise History.* Princeton, NJ: Princeton, 1986.

Dodd, Craig. *Ballet and Modern Dance.* Hong Kong: Elsevier-Dutton, 1980.

Driver, Ian. *A Century of Dance: A Hundred Years of Movement from Waltz to Hip Hop.* London: Cooper Square, 2001.

Reynolds, Nancy, and Malcolm McCormick. *No Fixed Points: Dance in the Twentieth Century.* New Haven, CT: Yale University Press, 2003.

Dance, Popular

Abandoning decorum for the sensual, the sexual, and the energetic, popular dance in the 1920s merged with the liberation of women, the daring atmosphere of the speakeasy, a new affluence—especially among the young—and the flash and excitement of newly popular urban ballrooms. This confluence contributed to a wave of new dance fads, including the shimmy, the Charleston, the black bottom, the varsity drag, and the Lindy Hop. All were danced to the syncopated beats of modern jazz and swing.

Some dances of the ragtime era before World War I—particularly the tango and the fox-trot—continued, but the fox-trot was updated to reflect the quicker tempos of jazz and became known as the quickstep.

Jazz Dances

The origins of jazz dances are often difficult to trace. Many seem to have been around in some form for many years before they became popular in the 1920s. Almost all of them had their genesis in Southern

Nothing captured the carefree atmosphere of the Jazz Age better than the Charleston, a popular dance step demonstrated here by two contestants at a national competition held in Chicago's Trianon Ballroom. *(Hulton Archive/Getty Images)*

black culture and gained popularity in society at large during the 1920s through stage productions and film. The shimmy, more a movement than a dance—a shaking of the body from top to bottom—became popular just after World War I. Its roots were in black dance halls, but it was the white actress Mae West who first created a sensation with it on Broadway in the show *Sometime* (1919). In 1922, Polish émigré actress and dancer Gilda Gray (born Marianna Winchalaska) performed it in the Ziegfeld Follies, a popular Broadway series.

In 1923, the Ziegfeld Follies featured the show *Runnin' Wild,* with an all-black cast and a dance called the Charleston, which became the most popular dance of the Jazz Age. Dance historians believe that its characteristic body movements—involving rapidly moving feet and swaying upper torso—led to the description of women dancers as "flappers," which became a popular term for liberated young women in the 1920s. A contemporary article in *The New York Times* described the Charleston's popularity as reaching from the chic homes of the rich to the crowded tenements of the poor.

The black bottom, another dance craze, was popularized in the Broadway show *Dinah* in 1924. In its simplified form, the dancers hopped forward and backward and slapped their buttocks. Its name came from its likely origins in the predominantly African American Black Bottom neighborhood of Nashville. In 1927, the hit Broadway show *Good News* featured a song that some historians say became an anthem of the Jazz Age: the "Varsity Drag." In the show, the tune was accompanied by a Charleston-like dance step, performed by popular stage star Don Tomkins. The varsity drag soon spread across America as a dance craze.

The Lindy Hop, named after aviator Charles Lindberg's "hop" across the Atlantic, was among the most vigorous of the many athletic dances of the 1920s. The Lindy Hop started in a club rather than on stage—at the famous Savoy Ballroom in Harlem—and had acrobatic elements, most notably when male dancers tossed and spun their female partners. Eventually, the Lindy Hop would morph into the jitterbug, the East Coast swing, and the West Coast swing—all still popular among ballroom dancers today.

Older Dances

Although much of the Jazz Age was a break from the decorum of earlier decades, the past—including older dances—did not disappear altogether. The tango, sensual and sultry, originated in Argentina in the 1890s and gained popularity in the United States during the ragtime era at the turn of the twentieth century. The year 1921 brought a comeback, however, with the release of the movie *The Four Horsemen of the Apocalypse,* in which Rudolph Valentino and Beatrice Dominguez danced a sexy tango to the delight of audiences.

The fox-trot was created by stage star Harry Fox in 1914 for the vaudeville-style shows he performed in a New York cinema theater. Fox provided entertainment between silent movies by dancing and telling jokes. His signature dance became known as the fox-trot and remained popular during the Jazz Age. As people danced the fox-trot to the faster beat of jazz music, the dance became fused with the Charleston. By the late 1920s, the two synthesized into the quickstep.

Many of the dances of the 1920s—especially the jazz dances—exist today as cultural icons of the Jazz Age. Dances like the Charleston, the Lindy Hop, and the varsity drag (with the associated megaphone

and raccoon coat) have created a lasting image of the Jazz Age and remain a reflection of the energy and exuberance of that unique decade.

William Toth

See also: Blues; Jazz; Leisure and Recreation; Radio.

Further Reading

Emery, Lynne Fauley. *Black Dance from 1619 to Today.* 2nd ed. Princeton, NJ: Princeton, 1988.

McDonagh, Don. *Dance Fever.* New York: Random House, 1979.

Thorpe, Edward. *Black Dance.* Woodstock, NY: Overlook, 1990.

Darrow, Clarence (1857–1938)

Through his role in the highly publicized Leopold and Loeb murder case and the Scopes "Monkey" trial, Clarence Darrow enhanced his reputation as the most prominent attorney of the 1920s. Willing to risk his reputation on behalf of unpopular causes, Darrow consistently advocated on behalf of organized labor, the poor, and the defenseless and for the cause of civil liberties.

Clarence Seward Darrow was born on April 18, 1857, in Kinsman, Ohio, the son of a self-educated woodworker and casket maker. His mother was free-thinking, and both parents were avid readers who held unconventional religious views. Fervent abolitionists, they gave Darrow a middle name honoring the abolitionist senator William Seward. Given these influences, Darrow developed his lifelong passion for reading and a willingness to embrace unpopular causes. After attending the University of Michigan's law school for one year, he passed the Ohio bar exam in 1878. Darrow moved to Chicago in 1886 and there established his legal reputation. He fought against capital punishment and for workers and the poor. He participated in the defense of American Railway Workers Union President Eugene V. Debs after the Pullman strike of 1895, and of International Workers of the World President William Heywood in Idaho in 1905.

During the 1920s, Darrow served as a defense attorney in three of the most notorious cases of the decade. The Leopold and Loeb murder trial was one of the most highly publicized and controversial trials in the nation's history. Nathan Leopold and Richard Loeb, young men from wealthy Chicago families, kidnapped and killed fourteen-year-old Robert Franks on May 21, 1924, for a thrill. Upon their arrest, the two confessed to the crime, and the state's attorney, Robert E. Crowe, announced he would seek the death penalty. Darrow accepted the case because of his opposition to capital punishment. In a risky maneuver, Darrow convinced his clients to plead guilty to the charges of kidnapping and murder so as to advance directly to the sentencing phase of the trial and concentrate his efforts on avoiding execution. The risk paid off, as Darrow convinced Judge John Caverly that, although the two men were clearly guilty, capital punishment was itself a crime against humanity. Caverly sentenced the young men to life in prison plus ninety-nine years.

Darrow is probably best known for his participation in the Scopes trial of 1925. An agnostic, he took up the defense of biology teacher John Scopes for teaching evolution (in violation of a Tennessee state statute). Former presidential candidate and fundamentalist Christian William Jennings Bryan had already volunteered to assist the prosecution. When the presiding judge refused to allow the defense to call any prominent scientists and Bible scholars to testify as experts, Darrow called Bryan to the stand and questioned him for two hours as an expert on the Bible. Although Scopes was ultimately convicted, Darrow's cross-examination of Bryan provided a highly publicized counterpoint to religious fundamentalism.

A less well-known case, but one with a great impact on American jurisprudence, concerned Ossian Sweet, a successful African American physician from Detroit. Sweet had purchased a house in an all-white section of the city in May 1925, shortly after three other black families in similar neighborhoods in the city had been driven out of their homes by Ku Klux Klan mobs. The Sweet family moved into their house on September 8. That night, several hundred whites surrounded the Sweet house, throwing rocks and threatening violence. The mob returned the following night and resumed stoning the house. A shot was fired from a second-story window; one member of the mob, Leon Breiner, was killed and another one wounded. Eleven members of the Sweet family who were in the house were charged with first-degree murder.

At the request of the National Association for the Advancement of Colored People, Darrow took the case. He centered his defense on the issue of racism, accusing the state's witnesses of lying in their testimony in order to deprive the Sweets of their right to live where they wished. After a month-long trial, the all-white jury failed to reach a verdict.

In April 1926, the state put Sweet's brother Henry—alleged to have fired the fatal shot—on trial for a second time. After another month-long trial, culminating in a seven-hour summation by Darrow in which he reviewed and condemned the history of American racism, the jury acquitted Henry Sweet. Charges against the rest of the family were dismissed by Judge Frank Murphy, who described Darrow's summation as "the greatest experience" of his life.

Despite age and declining health, Darrow spent the last years of his life continuing to battle against capital punishment and for the rights of the ordinary person. In 1932, he convinced Illinois Governor Henry Horner to commute the death sentence of a seventeen-year-old convicted of murdering a streetcar operator on the grounds that the young man's actions were a direct result of an impoverished upbringing. In 1937, an ailing Darrow appeared before the Michigan state legislature to argue successfully against the re-establishment of capital punishment in the state. Darrow died on March 13, 1938.

Richard M. Filipink, Jr.

See also: American Civil Liberties Union; Criminal Punishment; Leopold and Loeb Case (1924); Scopes Trial (1925).

Further Reading

Darrow, Clarence. *The Story of My Life.* New York: Scribner's, 1932.
Jensen, Richard J. *Clarence Darrow: The Creation of an American Myth.* New York: Greenwood, 1992.
Stone, Irving. *Clarence Darrow for the Defense.* Garden City, NY: Doubleday, 1941.
Weinberg, Arthur, and Lila Weinberg. *Clarence Darrow: A Sentimental Rebel.* New York: G.P. Putnam, 1980.

Daugherty, Harry M. (1860–1941)

Harry M. Daugherty was a member of the "Ohio Gang," a group of Republican politicians who used their positions in the administration of President Warren G. Harding for personal gain. In 1921, Daugherty was appointed U.S. attorney general in return for helping Harding get elected. During his three years in office, Daugherty was accused of several forms of wrongdoing, including accepting payoffs from those who profited from property seized during World War I and from those who violated Prohibition. His failure to prosecute officials indicted in the

Teapot Dome scandal led President Calvin Coolidge to demand his resignation in 1924.

Harry Micajah Daugherty was born on January 26, 1860, in Washington Court House, Ohio. His father died when Daugherty was only four. The family struggled financially and, as a boy, he was forced to work at a series of odd jobs. Ambitious and intelligent, he graduated from the University of Michigan Law School at age twenty. Daugherty waited a year to be eligible to take the bar exam, passed the exam, and returned to Washington Court House to start a law practice. After turning from criminal to corporate law, he became active in local Republican politics and was elected town clerk in 1882 and city councilman in 1886. In 1891, he was elected to the state House of Representatives and served until 1895.

Opponents saw him as a grasping politician more interested in personal gain than in serving his constituents. Daugherty was accused of selling his vote for U.S. senator in 1893, and although the allegations were never proved, they negatively impacted his ability to win another elected office. His campaigns for state attorney general, governor of Ohio, and the U.S. Congress all failed.

Daugherty displayed a knack for organization, however, and became an important power broker in the Ohio Republican Party. Important Ohio politicians turned to him for assistance with their campaigns; he was chair of William Howard Taft's unsuccessful reelection campaign in Ohio in 1912. When Harding announced his intention to run for president in 1920, Daugherty was one of his first supporters. Harding seemed to have little chance, but Daugherty predicted before the Republican convention that Harding would emerge as the Republicans' compromise candidate.

After Harding's nomination, Daugherty served as the campaign manager. He helped formulate the strategy of keeping Harding from saying much of importance, focusing instead on likeability. After winning the general election that November, Harding rewarded Daugherty by appointing him attorney general.

Observers soon realized that Daugherty was a poor choice for that responsibility, as he began appointing cronies and friends from Ohio to important positions in the Justice Department despite their lack of qualifications. He appointed as his assistant Jesse Smith, a friend from Ohio with whom he currently shared an apartment. Smith, while not officially a government employee, began peddling jobs, protection, and pardons from the Justice Department.

One of the most lucrative rackets derived from the attorney general's control of property seized from enemy aliens during World War I. Smith arranged for payments to individuals with claims against the property; in return, payoffs were deposited into accounts for Smith and Daugherty in a bank run by Daugherty's brother Mal. Other payoffs came from those seeking protection from arrest for violating Prohibition statutes. When evidence of the corruption became public knowledge in 1923, Smith committed suicide. Daugherty and his brother destroyed the records that implicated the attorney general.

Daugherty also used his office to protect his friends and settle personal grudges. In 1923, when congressional hearings brought the Teapot Dome scandal to light, Daugherty refused to investigate or prosecute those implicated. When criticized by senators for this failure, Daugherty ordered the head of the Federal Bureau of Investigation, William J. Burns, to harass the senators and their families.

His malfeasance notwithstanding, Daugherty could point to certain accomplishments as attorney general. He created a division in the Department of Justice to investigate fraud in war contracts from World War I, and he established the first federal prison for criminal offenders with no prior convictions. In 1922, when railroad workers went on strike across the nation, Daugherty convinced President Harding that Communists were behind the action and obtained a court injunction forcing the strikers back to work. It was the first time this tactic had been employed by the attorney general's office. The move backfired, however, as public sentiment was squarely with the strikers and no firm evidence surfaced to show Communist backing. Daugherty's injunction became a political liability for Harding. A resolution in Congress called for the attorney general's impeachment in September 1922, but he was cleared of charges the following month.

When Harding died in 1923, Daugherty stayed on as attorney general under President Calvin Coolidge. As the scandals of the Harding administration became clear, however, Coolidge recognized that Daugherty was a political liability. He asked for the attorney general's resignation, and Daugherty complied on March 28, 1924. He returned to Ohio to practice law.

In 1927, Daugherty was indicted by a federal grand jury on charges of defrauding the U.S. government. He was tried twice for corruption, and both times the trials ended in hung juries. He continued to practice law until his retirement in 1932, and he worked to clear his name for the remainder of his life. His memoirs, *The Inside Story of the Harding Tragedy* (1932), failed to convince most Americans that he was innocent of the various corruption charges brought against him. Daugherty died in Columbus, Ohio, on October 12, 1941.

Tim J. Watts

See also: Alien Property Custodian Scandal; Harding, Warren G.

Further Reading

Daugherty, Harry M., and Thomas Dixon. *The Inside Story of the Harding Tragedy.* New York: Churchill, 1932.

Giglio, James N. *H.M. Daugherty and the Politics of Expediency.* Kent, OH: Kent State University Press, 1978.

Mee, Charles L. *The Ohio Gang: The World of Warren G. Harding.* New York: M. Evans, 1981.

United States Congress. Senate Select Committee on Investigation of the Attorney General. *Investigation of Hon. Harry M. Daugherty, Formerly Attorney General of the United States.* Washington, DC: Government Printing Office, 1924.

Davis, John W. (1873–1955)

John W. Davis, perhaps best known among contemporaries for his skills as a lawyer, was the Democratic nominee for president in the election of 1924. His campaign was badly run and probably doomed from the start. After a resounding defeat by Republican Calvin Coolidge, Davis returned to his private law practice, in which he became identified with business and conservative clients.

John William Davis was born in Clarksburg, West Virginia, on April 13, 1873. His father was an attorney and former member of Congress. Davis attended Washington and Lee University, receiving his A.B. in 1892 and his LL.B. in 1895. The university hired him to teach law, which he did for one year, but Davis soon returned to Clarksburg to join his father's practice, where he displayed exceptional skills. His clients included the major mining, railroad, and other business interests of the region.

Davis was also willing to argue on behalf of liberal causes. When he defended a group of miners who had been arrested for violating an injunction against a protest march, his eloquent courtroom arguments won the miners only light sentences. Later in his career, as a member of the Judiciary Committee, he would help to write the Clayton Anti-Trust Act (1914), which included an anti-injunction clause that helped labor unions against businesses.

Davis was not naturally drawn to politics. Nevertheless, he accepted nomination to the state legislature in 1898 and won easily. His next political office came in 1910, when he won a seat in the U.S. House of Representatives. In 1912, as Woodrow Wilson was elected president, Davis was returned to Congress for a second term.

At first, Davis supported many of Wilson's New Freedom initiatives, although he opposed liberal ideas such as equality for women and the expansion of federal power. In 1913, Wilson appointed Davis U.S. solicitor general, charged with arguing federal government cases before the Supreme Court. Despite personal objections to some of the cases, Davis proved to be a superior litigator. He persuaded the Court to overturn an Oklahoma statute intended to prevent African Americans from voting, and he succeeded in getting an Alabama law allowing convicts to be "leased" by businesses overturned as involuntary servitude. He won forty-eight of the sixty-seven cases he argued before the Court. Most of the justices appreciated his demeanor and legal arguments and openly encouraged President Wilson to appoint Davis to the bench. Instead, Wilson appointed him ambassador to Great Britain in 1918, where he charmed the British government and people.

In 1920, Davis was mentioned as a possible Democratic candidate for president. He left government in 1921 to join a prestigious Wall Street law firm that later became Davis Polk Wardwell. He specialized in work for large corporations, such as J.P. Morgan. Davis's business relationship with his clients encouraged him to take a more conservative view.

In 1924, Davis was again considered a candidate for the Democratic nomination. The party was deeply split along regional and religious grounds. Western and Southern Democrats generally favored Prohibition, accepted nativism, and urged federal relief for farmers. Eastern Democrats wanted to modify Prohibition, favored equal rights for immigrants and minority groups, and called for urban assistance. When the delegates met in New York City on June 24, there was no consensus on the party nominee. For seventeen days, none of the candidates received the two-thirds majority required for the nomination. After ninety-nine ballots, the delegates were released from their obligations, and on the 103rd ballot, they finally selected Davis as a compromise candidate. His silence on the issues did not alienate anyone.

Davis offered the position of vice president to several men, but all of them refused. Charles W. Bryan, the governor of Nebraska, eventually accepted the role. Bryan was the younger brother of former Democratic nominee and populist William Jennings Bryan, and his choice represented an attempt to balance the ticket. However, his acceptance of Ku Klux Klan support alienated many Democrats. The Klan issue became central to the campaign; an anti-Klan plank in the party's platform was defeated by just one vote after extended debate.

Davis's presidential campaign was poorly run, perhaps because he believed that he had no chance of winning. His candidacy was harmed by a strong third party, the Progressives, who nominated Robert La Follette as their candidate. Many liberal Democrats, disillusioned by the failure to condemn the Ku Klux Klan, joined the Progressive bandwagon. Davis also stumbled by picking an inexperienced campaign manager. In his speeches, Davis adopted a probusiness attitude, making him sound more like Coolidge than most Democratic candidates. Davis's past association with J.P. Morgan also damaged his credibility as a Democrat. In addition, his speeches, widely broadcast on radio, were flat and uninspiring; their failure to convince listeners had national impact.

In the end, most American voters decided that, given the existing prosperity, there was no reason to end Republican control of the White House. Coolidge won reelection with 15.7 million votes; Davis garnered 8.4 million, and La Follette received 4.8 million.

After his loss, Davis turned away from politics, but he spoke out in support of New York Democrat Al Smith in the 1928 presidential race. In 1932, he supported Franklin D. Roosevelt but became a critic when Roosevelt unveiled his New Deal. In his law practice, Davis continued to work with big business and on conservative issues.

His two most famous cases before the U.S. Supreme Court came toward the end of his life. In 1952, he successfully argued in *Youngstown Sheet & Tube Co. v. Sawyer* that President Harry Truman had exceeded his constitutional authority by seizing steel factories needed for war manufacturing. And in 1954, he was counsel in *Briggs v. Elliott,* one of five cases involving school desegregation (the most famous of which was *Brown v. Board of Education*). In *Briggs,* Davis argued unsuccessfully that judicial precedent favored "separate but equal" facilities for black and white children. By the time of his death on March 24, 1955, he had argued 141 cases before the Supreme Court, the most by any lawyer to that time.

Tim J. Watts

See also: Democratic Party; Election of 1920; Election of 1924.

Further Reading

Davis, John W. *The Ambassadorial Diary of John W. Davis: The Court of St. James, 1918–1921.* Morgantown: West Virginia University Press, 1993.

———. *The Reminiscences of John W. Davis.* Oral history. Columbia University, 1954.

Harbaugh, William Henry. *Lawyer's Lawyer: The Life of John W. Davis.* New York: Oxford University Press, 1973.

Huntley, Theodore A., and Horace Green. *The Life of John W. Davis.* New York: Duffield, 1924.

Dawes, Charles (1865–1951)

A successful businessman and banker who became a leading figure in the Republican Party, rising to the position of U.S. vice president in 1925, Charles Gates Dawes is best known for the plan he negotiated in 1924 to reorganize European finances in the wake of World War I.

Born on August 27, 1865, in Marietta, Ohio, he was the son of Brigadier General Rufus and Mary Burman Gates Dawes. Inspired by the excitement of his father's 1880–1882 term in the U.S. House of Representatives, Dawes excelled at Marietta University and graduated from the Cincinnati Law School in 1885 at age twenty, too young to be licensed as a lawyer. Two years later, he began a private practice in Lincoln, Nebraska, but he made his name prosecuting railroads for unfair freight charges as head of the Lincoln Board of Trade.

While in Lincoln, Dawes became lifelong friends with future Democratic presidential candidate William Jennings Bryan and John J. Pershing, who would lead U.S. forces in Europe during World War I. On January 24, 1889, Dawes married Caro Blymyer, the daughter of a Cincinnati industrialist, with whom he had a son, Rufus, and a daughter, Carolyn. Rufus died in a drowning accident in 1912, and the couple later adopted two daughters, Dana and Virginia.

A successful businessman and banker, Dawes relocated to Chicago after the economic depression of 1893, buying the LaCrosse Gaslight and Coke Company and the Northwestern Gaslight and Coke Company in 1895. Long interested in banking and finance, he published *Banking System of the United States and Its Relationship to the Money and Business of the Country* (1894), which advocated deposit insurance and stricter regulation. Dawes became involved in the 1896 presidential campaign of William McKinley, assisting campaign manager Mark Hanna to fight machine politics in Illinois, and delivering the state at the Republican convention in St. Louis. From 1897 to McKinley's assassination in 1901, Dawes served as comptroller of the currency, focusing on currency reform and antitrust regulation.

Although active in Republican politics, Dawes was not an intimate of Theodore Roosevelt and held no further official appointments until the United States entered World War I in 1917. He was a pillar of Chicago society, undertaking such charitable works as the establishment of inexpensive hotels and bread wagons for the hungry, as well as funding the Chicago Grand Opera. With Pershing's help, he sought a commission as a major in the Seventeenth Engineers but was quickly drafted for administrative work. Heading the General Purchasing Board as a lieutenant colonel, he organized labor corps and produced plans for pooling war materiel and regulating motor traffic in the war zone. In 1919, he was named head of the U.S. Liquidation Commission, selling off war surplus in Europe. After his return to the United States, he served on the Decorations Board and the Veterans' Bureau. His colorful and expletive-laden testimony justifying military spending before the House Committee on War Expenditure catapulted him to national prominence.

President Warren G. Harding offered him a cabinet position as secretary of the treasury in 1921, but Dawes preferred the directorship of the budget. In that capacity, he reorganized government procurement and cut waste, saving $1 billion in his first year. Dawes's reforms were adapted by the British in 1931 and remained in place in the United States until the New Deal. In 1923, Dawes formed the Minute Men of the Constitution, organizing more than 42,000 Illinois members to stand up to organized crime and racist violence. With Radio Corporation of America (RCA) founder and president of the General Electric Company Owen D. Young, Dawes traveled to Europe in 1924 as part of the Reparations Commission to adjust German postwar economic sanctions. The result, the Dawes Plan, earned him and Austen Chamberlain of Great Britain the Nobel Peace Prize in 1925. Dawes donated his half of the prize money to the Walter Hines Page School of International Business at Johns Hopkins University in Baltimore.

In 1924, the Republican Party nominated Dawes as vice president, to run on the ticket with Calvin Coolidge. With Coolidge mourning the death of his son, Dawes did most of the active campaigning, bucking the advice of party leaders by speaking out vehemently against the Klan and union corruption, and for political reform, all contentious issues in Republican states. Although Dawes's high-pitched voice and long speeches were ill suited to the medium of radio, his sincerity and knowledge won over many independent voters. At his inauguration, Dawes delivered a blistering speech to the Senate, castigating the body for its filibustering and deadlock tactics, which upstaged President Coolidge's own inaugural address. Dawes proved active in presiding over the Senate, forcing cloture on the Pepper-McFadden banking reform bill in 1927 and helping to secure Senate approval of the Kellogg-Briand Pact in 1928.

From 1929 to 1931, during the administration of President Herbert Hoover, Dawes served as U.S. ambassador to Great Britain, negotiating naval arms reduction and arranging the Five-Power Naval Conference in 1930, as well as stabilizing the Bank of England with a massive American loan and seeking to mediate the 1931 Japanese invasion of Manchuria. In January 1932, Dawes resigned his ambassadorship to preside over the Reconstruction Finance Corporation (RFC), infusing funds into banks made unstable by the 1929 stock market crash. In June 1932, he resigned that position to take over the board of directors of the Central Republic Bank and Trust in Chicago, saving it from collapse through an RFC loan, which was paid back within ten years.

Dawes spent the rest of his life as a private businessman and underwriter of charitable projects, such as archeological explorations in southern France and Central America. A tune he wrote in 1911 as an amateur pianist, "Melody in A Major," became highly popular and surfaced again in 1951 as the standard "It's All in the Game." Dawes died at his home in Evanston, Illinois, on April 23, 1951.

Margaret Sankey

See also: Coolidge, Calvin; Dawes Plan (1924); Election of 1924; Reparations and War Debts; Republican Party.

Further Reading

Leach, Paul Roscoe. *That Man Dawes*. Chicago: Reilly & Lee, 1930.

Pixton, John. *American Pilgrim: A Biography of Charles Gates Dawes*. Ogontz: Pennsylvania State University Press, 1970.

Timmons, Bascom N. *Portrait of an American: Charles G. Dawes*. New York: Henry Holt, 1953.

Dawes Plan (1924)

Named for Charles G. Dawes, the financier and diplomat (and later vice president of the United States) chiefly responsible for devising and negotiating it, the 1924 Dawes Plan provided for a reduction in the amount of reparations an economically overburdened Germany had to pay its former enemies from World War I. The plan also called for American loans to the German government to help it pay the reduced reparations.

The Dawes Plan was designed to undo some of the harsher terms of the Versailles peace treaty imposed by the Allies after World War I. Under the 1919 Versailles agreement, Germany was officially blamed for the war and ordered to pay huge reparations to Great Britain, France, and other powers, a total later set at $33 billion. Although U.S. President Woodrow Wilson worried that heavy reparations might cripple the German economy and undermine peace in Europe, he was overruled by Britain and France, the latter country having suffered the bulk of the fighting on its soil.

As Wilson predicted, Germany found the reparations extremely burdensome. Although the country made an initial installment payment in 1921, severe economic conditions, including high inflation, led Germany into default in 1922. In response, in January of the following year, French and Belgian troops occupied Germany's Ruhr Valley, a coveted industrial region, further destabilizing the German economy. In hopes of finding a long-term solution to the problem, an international committee on reparations was formed early in 1924 consisting of ten members, two each from Britain, France, Belgium, Italy, and the United States. The American delegation included banker Charles G. Dawes, who would lead the committee, and Owen D. Young, founder of Radio Corporation of America (RCA) and president of the General Electric Company.

After several months of negotiations, the committee issued a report in April 1924 that all parties accepted, and the Dawes Plan went into effect in September 1924. Under the plan, France and Belgium removed their troops from the Ruhr Valley; German reparation payments were relaxed; the German Reichsbank (central bank) was reorganized; a series of financial reforms were put in place to stabilize the German currency; new taxes were introduced in Germany to raise revenues; and a series of international loans, many originating from the United States, were made available to the German government. Implementation of the Dawes Plan averted what could have become a significant international crisis, and its chief proponents, Dawes and his British counterpart, Austen Chamberlain, were awarded the 1925 Nobel Peace Prize.

The Dawes Plan offered only temporary relief to Germany. Although it lightened the burden of reparations, helped stabilize the currency, and encouraged foreign investment in the nation's economic infrastructure, it also left the German economy overly dependent on foreign influence, especially large amounts of capital from the United States. Hence, Germany would suffer from the collapse of the U.S. economy at the end of the decade. Despite the settlement, Germany still could not afford to make consistent reparation payments and in 1929, the Dawes Plan was superseded by the Young Plan, named for committee head Owen D. Young. The Young Plan lowered the total amount of reparations to just over $26 billion and gave Germany nearly sixty years to pay them. The rise to power of the Nazis, who stridently opposed any reparations, and the outbreak of World War II ended the payments.

Ben Wynne

See also: Dawes, Charles; Europe, Relations with; Reparations and War Debts; Young Plan (1929–1930).

Further Reading

Auld, George P. *The Dawes Plan and the New Economics.* New York: Doubleday, Page, 1927.

McKercher, B.J.C. *Anglo-American Relations in the 1920s: The Struggle for Supremacy.* Edmonton, Canada: University of Alberta Press, 1991.

Timmons, Bascom N. *Portrait of an American: Charles G. Dawes.* New York: Henry Holt, 1953.

DeMille, Cecil B. (1881–1959)

A visionary but tyrannical movie director, Cecil B. DeMille is credited by film historians as the inventor of the Hollywood blockbuster. His two biblical epics—*The Ten Commandments* (1923) and *The King of Kings* (1927)—employed casts of thousands and vast sets. They proved extremely popular with audiences and, despite huge budgets, highly profitable for the studios that produced them.

Cecil Blount DeMille was born on August 12, 1881, in Ashfield, Massachusetts, the son of an impoverished teacher. After attending military school in Pennsylvania and the American Academy of Dramatic Arts in New York City, DeMille had a marginally successful career as an actor and playwright in the early 1900s, largely in collaboration with vaudeville producer Jesse Lasky.

Theater was largely in a slump during the early 1910s, as the rising entertainment of movies was stealing audiences. So in 1913, DeMille switched to moving pictures. DeMille and Lasky joined with Lasky's brother-in-law, Samuel Goldfish—later Samuel Goldwyn, cofounder of Paramount Pictures and Metro-Goldwyn-Mayer (MGM)—to start the Jesse L. Lasky Feature Play Company and produce feature-length films.

In 1913, DeMille went to Arizona to shoot a film adaptation of the play *The Squaw Man* but found the location unsuitable. DeMille moved on to Los Angeles, where he found the climate perfect for year-round shooting, helping to launch the nearby community of Hollywood as the center of the American movie industry. Despite cost overruns, *The Squaw Man* (1914) proved profitable, and DeMille went on to direct dozens of films—both dramatic and comedic—during the late 1910s and early 1920s, the golden era of silent film.

DeMille also experimented during this period with a film genre for which he would become renowned in later years, the historical epic. But *Joan the Woman* (1917), based on the life of Joan of Arc, was a box-office disaster. After several more unsuccessful attempts at historical filmmaking, DeMille gave up on the idea and turned to more popular genres: social comedies and westerns. Perhaps the most successful of these was the 1919 comedy *Don't Change Your Husband*.

In 1923, DeMille thought of recasting the biblical story of Exodus in the narrative style of a western. From this grew *The Ten Commandments*, the most expensive movie made up to that time, and Paramount studio head Adolph Zuker nearly pulled it lest it bankrupt the company. Its mix of piety and titillating displays of sin proved a popular draw, and the film was a huge success.

His reputation secured by that triumph, DeMille parted ways with Paramount and set up his own studio. In 1927, he produced *The King of Kings*, about the life of Jesus. In Mary Magdalene he found just the character to provide the element of sin that would draw in audiences, and he wove a story of a secret tryst with Judas, the betrayer of Christ.

While DeMille always avoided being too sexually explicit, other Hollywood directors were not so careful. Fearing a backlash against Hollywood and its products if the sexuality was not toned down, DeMille took a notable role in the creation of the Hays Office, which set restrictions on what could be shown in a movie. He was concerned that if the movie industry did not police itself, Congress would be forced to step in and legislate censorship.

DeMille weathered the lean years of the Depression and World War II but became an increasingly controversial figure in Hollywood after the war. Politically conservative, he became involved in Senator Joseph McCarthy's blacklists against suspected Communists in Hollywood during the 1950s. Many people would long regard him as having betrayed his colleagues, since a large number of the people blacklisted were innocent of any Communist ties.

In 1956, DeMille undertook a remake of *The Ten Commandments,* with Charlton Heston as Moses. This proved to be DeMille's last film, as he suffered a heart attack while filming on location in Egypt. After a second heart attack, he died on January 21, 1959.

Leigh Kimmel

See also: Film; Film Industry; Swanson, Gloria.

Further Reading

DeMille, Cecil B. *The Autobiography of Cecil B. DeMille.* Ed. Donald Hayne. Englewood Cliffs, NJ: Prentice Hall, 1959.

Edwards, Anne. *The DeMilles: An American Family.* New York: Abrams, 1988.

Higashi, Sumiko. *Cecil B. DeMille and American Culture: The Silent Era.* Berkeley: University of California Press, 1994.

Koury, Phil. *Yes, Mr. DeMille.* New York: Putnam, 1959.

Demobilization, Industrial

Like other major wars in American history, World War I saw a major increase in government spending, as well as an expansion of the government's role in regulating and directing the economy for the purposes of supplying defense needs. When the fighting ended in November 1918, the United States faced the problem of releasing the economy from governmental control and demobilizing millions of men and a few hundred thousand women to civilian life. While it achieved some of its aims with relatively little disruption to the economy—particularly in the gradual way it released key industries from government controls—the federal government's sudden canceling of hundreds of millions of dollars in war contracts threatened to plunge the economy into depression.

Federal spending in the early 1910s was roughly $700 million annually. Over the course of the roughly nineteen months of U.S. participation in World War I, the government spent $33 billion. To pay for the war, the government in 1916 instituted new taxes on the incomes of wealthier Americans. In 1918, an excess profits tax was established to tap some of the vast revenues businesses were accruing through government contracts, sales to other nations in the war, and a wartime inflation of prices that exceeded gains in wages and salaries. Despite these new sources of revenue, however, the federal debt rose from $1 billion in 1915 to $20 billion in 1920.

The Wilson administration, along with Congress, had created a host of new agencies to regulate the economy for defense purposes. The Fuel Administration allocated coal resources to factories and railroads; the Railroad War Board took over management of the nation's railroads, guaranteeing a steady return to the companies equal to the average revenues they had earned between 1915 and the beginning of the war, in April 1917; the Food Administration stimulated increased farm production through guaranteed prices for crops; and the National War Labor Board wrote standards for working conditions in defense plants and arbitrated more than 1,200 labor disputes during the war. Most powerful of all was the War Industries Board, which took over the allocation of scarce resources and ordered factories to convert from civilian to wartime production.

All of this regulation went against the grain of traditional laissez-faire ideology. But it was accepted by the nation's business community on patriotic grounds—many top business leaders went to work in Washington at nominal salaries for the duration of the war—and because the legislation creating these agencies stipulated that they would be disbanded once the fighting was over. Railroads, for example, would revert to private control no later than twenty-one months after the armistice, while Wilson disbanded the War Industries Board within sixty days after the war ended, despite economists' warnings that such a precipitous removal of controls could disrupt production and lead to inflation or even economic recession. But Wilson, like most Americans of his day,

was a firm supporter of the free market, believing that excessive government regulation of the economy was counterproductive.

As in the Civil War and World War II, the ranks of the U.S. armed forces shrank relatively quickly once World War I ended. From a high of 3.7 million in late 1918, with 2 million serving in Europe, troops dropped to 2.7 million by June 1919. By the end of that year, the number fell to less than a million. The National Defense Act of 1920 authorized a total force of fewer than 300,000; legislation in 1922 brought the number down to 136,000.

Demobilized soldiers were sent home with their transportation paid for and a $60 bonus. With millions being demobilized, there was great fear of a recession, but it did not appear, partly because many soldiers and civilians cashed in war bonds and spent the money on consumer goods, such as new clothes, appliances, and cars. But the absence of a postwar economic crash was primarily because government continued to spend heavily—far above the revenues it was taking in. Part of that spending included loans to wartime allies so that they could continue to buy American goods while they rebuilt or converted their own domestic industries. This also kept demand high, warding off recession. The government also assisted a variety of industries—including steel, coal, and textiles—as well as the agricultural sector by not dumping surplus food and materiel onto the market.

By the end of 1919, virtually all the wartime regulations had been lifted, and the various agencies charged with running the economy had wound up their activities. The exception was the Railroad War Board, which had essentially been renting the nation's railways for the duration of the conflict and running them under a unified management. Under the Transportation Act of 1920, Congress reinstated private management and offered compensation to the railroads for the cost of the transition. Railroads would have to reimburse the government for improvements made to their track and rolling stock, but at low interest and over ten years. By the early 1920s, demobilization was largely complete but some of the mistakes that had been made would serve as lessons for the much bigger demobilization effort that followed World War II.

James Ciment

See also: Military Affairs; Recession of 1921–1922; War Finance Corporation.

Further Reading

Asinov, Eliot. *1919: America's Loss of Innocence.* New York: Donald I. Fine, 1990.

Hicks, John D. *Republican Ascendancy, 1921–1933.* New York: Harper, 1960.

Noggle, Burl. *Into the Twenties: The United States from Armistice to Normalcy.* Urbana: University of Illinois Press, 1974.

Democratic Party

As the 1920s began, the Democratic Party was divided over several issues, blamed for various elements of economic and social disorder, and seemed on the verge of irrelevance. Indeed, the election of 1920 brought not only the resounding defeat of the party's presidential candidate, James M. Cox of Ohio, but the loss of all but 100 seats in the House of Representatives and several senatorial contests. It would take the better part of the decade and the Great Depression to rebuild the party and bring it back to a position of prominence.

Out of World War I

An early sign that rough times were ahead for the party came as early as the 1918 off-year elections. The Democrats lost several House seats that year, mainly in the West as a reaction to the 1917 Smith-Lever Act (a wartime measure that set limits on crop prices), and lost their majority in the Senate. Still, it was only after World War I that the American people truly began to show their dissatisfaction with the party and turn away in large numbers. Farmers were angry that they had lost their protected domestic market at the end of the war and that prices had fallen. Progressives felt betrayed when President Woodrow Wilson agreed to the harsh measures imposed on Germany by the Allies at the Paris Peace Conference in 1919. Further, Wilson's insistence on U.S. membership in the League of Nations was a burden to many Democrats running for office in 1920. In addition, Wilson's stroke in October 1919 had rendered him incapable of governing effectively in the face of inflation, economic recession, growing labor and racial tension, and the Red Scare.

The election of 1920 saw Ohio Governor James Cox run for the presidency, with Assistant Secretary of the Navy Franklin D. Roosevelt as his running mate. Cox made the League of Nations the central issue of his campaign, and he ran with enthusiasm. However, the Republicans outspent and outmaneu-

vered Cox, running the first modern media campaign. In the last weeks before election day, Cox reluctantly called for changes to the League charter, but it was too late. Warren G. Harding, also from Ohio, won the election decisively.

Many ethnic groups, specifically German, Irish, and Italian, turned away from the Democratic Party over the League and the Treaty of Versailles, believing that their native lands had been slighted in one way or another. Furthermore, growing tension between Catholics and Protestants, as well as anti-immigrant nativists upset over what they perceived as a loss of American identity, prompted much of that base to leave the party for the GOP.

The Democrats would make something of a comeback in 1922, a recession year. High interest rates and taxes were hurting farmers, who took out their frustration on Republicans. Democrats made gains in Congress, holding on to all of their contested seats and driving seventy-eight members of the opposition out of office. Republicans would retain control of the House, but by a smaller margin. The Democratic comeback was largely attributable to urban dwellers and immigrants, who came back to the party after Harding's 1920 landslide. This, however, led to divisions with Southerners and Westerners, who were typically Protestant and had supported Prohibition, more of a Republican cause. Furthermore, the resurgence of the Ku Klux Klan, whose objects of hate included Roman Catholics (hence most urban voters and immigrant groups), greatly influenced national and regional politics. This only further divided the party with the election of 1924 on the horizon.

Two major figures of the Democratic Party at that time were William McAdoo and Al Smith, both of New York. McAdoo, Wilson's son-in-law and the natural successor to populist William Jennings Bryan, supported Prohibition and was ambivalent about the Ku Klux Klan. McAdoo was seen as the champion of rural Democrats in the West and South. Smith, the governor of New York and a product of the Tammany Hall political machine, opposed Prohibition and the Klan and appealed to city dwellers and immigrants. This rivalry paved the way to the 1924 Democratic National Convention, which saw 103 ballots cast before both leading candidates withdrew their names. Chosen as a compromise candidate was former Congressman John W. Davis of West Virginia, who would lose the November election by a huge margin to Calvin Coolidge. The Democrats faired better in local and

Tammany Hall, New York City's century-old political machine, began to lose its grip on power during the 1920s. Here, its headquarters on Manhattan's Union Square is festooned with flags and banners for the 1924 election. *(Jack Benton/Hulton Archive/Getty Images)*

congressional races, however, with the Republicans making only slight gains.

The biggest issue following the 1924 election was the disorganization of the national party apparatus. The Democratic National Committee had been in existence in name only, and Franklin D. Roosevelt, then recovering in Warm Springs, Georgia, from the onset of polio, realized that the reorganization of the committee was vital if the party was to succeed at the national level. Infighting, regional division, Prohibition, and Klan issues had torn the committee apart. Roosevelt called for a conference in Washington in order to reunify and reinvigorate the organization. His calls went unheeded, and the national party apparatus continued to lack focus and direction until 1930.

Coolidge Era

Following the 1924 elections, congressional Democrats showed bipartisan support for several Republican measures, including tax reform and farm relief. But progressives and conservatives in the party remained divided, primarily due to the emergence of Smith as

the nominal leader of the party. He would be reelected governor of New York in 1926, a year that saw Democrats further reducing the Republican majority in Congress but again failing to gain clear control.

Smith was proud of his Catholicism and unabashedly opposed to Prohibition. This endeared him to voters in the cities, who identified with his unpolished New York City accent. Those in the rural South and the West, however, remained disenchanted with Smith and the direction the party was taking. To secure the presidential nomination in 1928, Smith emphasized his conservative leanings in order to win back these constituencies. He was opposed to women's suffrage, still a contentious issue among many, and warned against what he called "the dangerous overcentralization of federal power."

Smith won the nomination but faced long odds as a Catholic candidate in a country of Protestants, many of whom held strong anti-Catholic biases. Many voters also resented his Tammany roots. Finally, a resurging economy and a popular Republican candidate, Commerce Secretary Herbert Hoover, spelled his defeat. Still, Smith had registered the largest popular vote ever by a Democratic candidate and carried every large city that had voted Republican four years earlier. The urban vote in particular proved to be a strong base for the Democrats, but at the cost of the South.

Many urban residents came back to the Democratic fold, thanks to the efforts of local political machines, seen as the protectors of the poor and the newly arrived immigrant. These organizations had been in existence since the nineteenth century, and their influence was still being felt during the 1920s. Even progressive efforts to reform the civil service, which would take away the machine's patronage, would not totally dismantle them for some years to come, and the Democratic Party benefited more than did the Republicans. Democratic mayors such as James Curley of Boston, Martin Behrman of New Orleans, Frank Hague of Jersey City, and Tom Pendergast of Kansas City provided jobs and enrolled voters into the party. These efforts would be key to victory on the local level, and for the Democrats nationally, during the 1930s.

The year 1928 would also see the emergence of Franklin D. Roosevelt as the new leader of the party, following his victory in the New York race for governor. Roosevelt had maintained his party contacts in the years following his polio attack and had the support of Smith, who urged him to run as his replacement.

Onset of the Depression

In October 1929, security prices in the New York Stock Exchange dropped sharply, and financial panic quickly set in on Wall Street and throughout the country. Earlier in the year, President Hoover had refused to call on Congress to stop rampant stock speculation, even as prices for commodities fell and production lagged. When the market crashed, he called for wages and prices to be maintained at existing levels but did little else, believing that the economy would eventually correct itself.

The Democrats at first rallied around the president in this crisis. As time went on, however, they became more and more critical of him and the Republicans. In the elections of 1930, just weeks after the crash, the Democrats regained control of the House, and missed a majority in the Senate by just one vote. It was the first of four consecutive Senate elections in which the Democrats would make major gains. Institutionally, this was largely due to the revival of the Democratic National Committee, which finally came together in the context of economic crisis and the weakening of Hoover and the GOP. In addition, farmers came back to the party, and their votes were key in electing governors and other local officials. The national party began to lay the groundwork for placing blame on Hoover directly, which in turn would lead to the recapture of the White House in 1932, when Roosevelt gained the presidency.

While the 1920s may have seen numerous failures for the Democrats, signs of what the party would become were apparent. A growing progressive faction, later defined as liberal, would help identify the party with its causes and ideals. Farmers and Southerners, in the midst of an agricultural depression, felt betrayed by the Republicans and returned to the party they thought had abandoned them only a decade earlier. Finally, the urban-industrial segment of the population proved to be solidly Democratic, as indicated by the success of Al Smith in cities in 1928 and his support from organized labor. These elements would be crucial to the success of the party not only for the election of 1932, but for the three decades that would follow.

David A. Serafini

See also: Davis, John W.; Election of 1918; Election of 1920; Election of 1922; Election of 1924; Election of 1926; Election of 1928; Kennedy, Joseph; McAdoo, William G.; Republican Party; Walker, Jimmy; Wheeler, Burton K.; Wilson, Woodrow.

Further Reading

Burner, David. "The Democratic Party, 1910–1932." In *History of U.S. Political Parties, 1910–1945.* Vol. 3. Ed. Arthur M. Schlesinger, Jr. New York: Chelsea House, 1973.

———. *The Politics of Provincialism: The Democratic Party in Transition, 1918–1932.* New York: Alfred A. Knopf, 1968.

Craig, Douglas B. *After Wilson: The Struggle for the Democratic Party, 1920–1934.* Chapel Hill: University of North Carolina Press, 1992.

Witcover, Jules. *Party of the People: A History of the Democrats.* New York: Random House, 2003.

Dempsey, Jack (1895–1983)

Legendary heavyweight boxing champion Jack Dempsey helped define the 1920s as a golden age in American athletics, when sports became a highly lucrative business, and intense newspaper and radio coverage made athletes national celebrities. From 1919, when he won the heavyweight crown by defeating champion Jess Willard, to 1927, when he lost the title to Gene Tunney, Dempsey was the most renowned fighter and one of the most popular celebrities in America. The first boxer to attract $1 million in gate receipts for a single fight, Dempsey was known for his bobbing and weaving, straight-ahead ring style, which relied less on finesse than on power and stamina, characteristics that prompted sportswriter Damon Runyon to nickname him the "Manassa Mauler."

Jack Dempsey was born William Harrison Dempsey on June 24, 1895, in Manassa, Colorado, the son of a poor rancher who had migrated from West Virginia. Dempsey's early life was marked by frequent moves throughout Colorado and Utah as his father struggled to earn a living. Leaving school following the eighth grade, he traveled as a hobo from mining town to mining town, often earning money as a saloon fighter, issuing a challenge and then passing a hat if he won the bout. By 1914, he was fighting professionally in scheduled matches, and he took the name "Jack" after the nineteenth-century boxer Nonpareil Jack Dempsey. In the rough-and-tumble frontier camps and small arenas of the West, Dempsey earned a reputation as a fearless, hard-hitting fighter who often knocked out his opponents. He fought three bouts in New York City in 1916 and then returned to the West to build up his record.

By 1919, Dempsey attracted the attention of boxing promoter Tex Rickard, who signed him for a title fight against the champion, Willard. On July 4 in Toledo, Ohio, Dempsey and Willard battled for the crown. Dempsey's unrelenting fierceness led to seven knockdowns of Willard in the first three rounds. With his face pummeled and cut, several teeth knocked out, and suffering a broken jaw, Willard was unable to come out of his corner for the fourth round, and Dempsey became the new world's heavyweight champion.

In the weeks following the match, Dempsey traveled the vaudeville circuit throughout the country, appearing before theater audiences to recount his title fight and demonstrate his boxing style.

The publicity he garnered from these performances brought him widespread public attention and established him as one of the premier sports figures of the decade. Dempsey successfully defended his title twice in 1920, but his image became tarnished when he was indicted on charges of draft evasion during World War I. During his trial in June 1920, he maintained that he was the sole support of his mother, siblings, and first wife, a prostitute who, after their divorce, had publicly accused him of avoiding military service. Although the jury acquitted him, Dempsey would carry the label of "slacker" for many years.

In 1921, Rickard set up a title defense against Georges Carpentier, a French war hero who was portrayed in the media as handsome, witty, and sophisticated—in stark contrast to Dempsey's rough-hewn frontier manner. Held in Jersey City, New Jersey, on July 2, the "Fight of the Century" brought 80,000 fans to a massive wooden stadium built especially for the bout. Carpentier was knocked out in the fourth round. Gate receipts of more than $1.7 million, and the hundreds of thousands of listeners to the radio broadcast, demonstrated that boxing in America had indeed become big business.

Inactive in 1922, Dempsey returned to the ring in 1923 for two title matches. In the first, he took on Tommy Gibbons in Shelby, Montana, on July 4, winning a fifteen-round decision. On September 14 in New York City, Dempsey fought Argentine heavyweight Luis Firpo. The challenger was knocked down seven times in the first round but succeeded in punching Dempsey through the ropes before the bell. The champion made it back into the ring just before the ten-count and, in the next round, knocked out Firpo with a left hook. Gate receipts totaled more than $1 million.

For the next two years, Dempsey continued to build his popularity by appearing in motion pictures, endorsing commercial products, and traveling throughout the United States and Europe. His most notable fights came in 1926 and 1927 against Gene Tunney, the "Fighting Marine." His long layoff, however, cost him the heavyweight crown when Tunney beat him on September 23, 1926, in Philadelphia. A year later in Chicago, Dempsey and Tunney fought a rematch that became famous for its controversial "long count." In the seventh round, Dempsey knocked Tunney to the canvas but neglected to go to his own corner right away. The referee delayed his count until Dempsey went to his corner, which allowed Tunney to rise to his feet and recover. Tunney won the bout in ten rounds, and it was Dempsey's last fight.

Dempsey stayed active in the sport by promoting bouts, managing a few fighters, and acting as a referee for boxing and wrestling matches. He lost most of his savings when the stock market crashed in 1929, but he was able to capitalize on his celebrity status, making personal appearances and opening a restaurant in New York. In World War II, Dempsey served as a commander in the U.S. Coast Guard, overseeing its physical fitness program and touring the war's Pacific theater to boost morale among the troops.

Considered one of the greatest boxers in history, and certainly one of the most famous athletes of the twentieth century, Dempsey was relatively light for a heavyweight, fighting at only 185–190 pounds. But he overcame any disadvantage he may have had in weight with his brutally efficient punching. Jack Dempsey died on May 31, 1983, at the age of eighty-seven.

Kevin Grace

See also: Boxing; Celebrity Culture.

Further Reading

Dempsey, Jack, with Barbara Piatelli Dempsey. *Dempsey.* New York: Harper & Row, 1977.

Kahn, Roger. *A Flame of Pure Fire: Jack Dempsey and the Roaring '20s.* New York: Harcourt Brace, 1999.

Roberts, Randy. *Jack Dempsey: The Manassa Mauler.* Baton Rouge: Louisiana State University Press, 1979.

Sammons, Jeffrey T. *Beyond the Ring: The Role of Boxing in American Society.* Champaign: University of Illinois Press, 1988.

DePriest, Oscar (1871–1951)

The first African American to be elected to Congress in the twentieth century was Oscar Stanton DePriest. A Republican from the First Illinois District, he was elected in 1928 and served three terms (1929–1934). The only African American member of Congress at the time, he represented a rapidly growing black population on Chicago's South Side and attempted to introduce a series of antidiscrimination bills.

DePriest was born to former slaves in Florence, Alabama, on March 9, 1871. He migrated north to Chicago in 1889 and set up successful painting and contracting businesses before establishing himself in real estate. Embraced by Republican Party leaders, he served as a Cook County commissioner for two terms in the first decade of the twentieth century. As the city's black population increased and the second ward became more than 50 percent black, Republican leaders promoted DePriest for the board of aldermen, Chicago's city council. He won the election, becoming Chicago's first African American alderman in 1915. With about 80 percent of black Chicagoans living on the city's South Side, the potential for establishing strong black communities and institutions was growing.

Having worked initially with white Republicans who controlled the city's black wards, DePriest ran again in 1919 on the People's Movement Club ticket, an independent party he founded. The party was one of a growing number of black political groups in northern cities, brought about by the large numbers of African Americans who moved from the rural South to the urban North in the 1910s and 1920s.

After losing in his first attempt in 1926, DePriest won election to the U.S. House of Representatives in 1928, becoming the first African American in Congress since Reconstruction, the first Northern black congressman, and a national reflection of black pride and progress. Among the groups that campaigned for him was the Alpha Suffrage Club, established by the activist Ida B. Wells-Barnett, who had cofounded the National Association of Colored Women.

DePriest's name became nationally known when his wife, Jesse, was invited to tea at the White House as part of a contingent of congressional wives—a visit both hailed and criticized in the nation's press. Jesse DePriest's attendance at the tea marked the first official visit of a black person to the White House since Theodore Roosevelt met with educator Booker T. Washington in 1901.

DePriest did not get many measures passed but was able to raise black issues to the national stage. Both the House and Senate passed his amendment to the bill establishing the Civilian Conservation Corps in 1933, ensuring that the agency could not discriminate on the basis of race, color, or creed. He also introduced anti-lynching legislation on several occasions, for which the National Association for the Advancement of Colored People (NAACP) had lobbied fiercely, but was unsuccessful in getting it passed. He argued unsuccessfully for the transfer of jurisdiction in cases where defendants believe they are unable to get a fair trial because of race; however, a measure would be passed by Congress at a later date. He also proposed that states that persistently discriminate against blacks should be docked congressional seats, and that former slaves over the age of seventy-five should be awarded a monthly pension. His commitment to civil rights issues was reflected in an eclectic range of campaigns, including efforts to have African Americans appointed to the U.S. Naval Academy.

The practically wholesale transfer of African American voting allegiance to the Democratic Party during the New Deal years left DePriest, as a black Republican, on shifting ground. Established black leaders such as editor W.E.B. Du Bois and labor organizer A. Philip Randolph strongly criticized the Republicans and questioned the largely unrewarded allegiance that blacks had shown them. DePriest began to encourage Southern blacks to adopt tactical and strategic voting to protect their position, including voting Democratic and maintaining a politically independent identity.

In December 1931, he organized a nonpartisan conference in Washington, D.C., to discuss future black political strategy and ideology. Attended by some 300 delegates from twenty-six states, the conference signaled the need of African Americans to adopt a unified, politically pragmatic position. But DePriest's conservative attitude toward federal relief programs and other economic issues was unpopular, and he lost his seat to Arthur W. Mitchell, a black New Deal Democrat, in 1934. One of his Chicago protégés, William Dawson, was elected to Congress in 1942, a position he retained until 1970.

DePriest remained active in public life, serving again as a Chicago alderman from 1943 to 1947, before returning to his real estate business. He died on May 12, 1951.

Sam Hitchmough

See also: African Americans; Republican Party.

Further Reading

Drake, St. Clair, and Horace Cayton. *Black Metropolis: A Study of Negro Life in a Northern City.* Chicago: University of Chicago, 1993.

Grossman, James R. *Land of Hope: Chicago, Black Southerners, and the Great Migration.* Chicago: University of Chicago Press, 1989.

Design, Industrial

American industrial design—the design of everyday products for home, business, and industry—came into its own in the 1920s. Practitioners began to move away from the mere ornamentation of products toward a more holistic approach to design, where the overall aesthetic of a product became an integral part of the design and manufacturing process. By the end of the decade, appliances, architectural interiors, automobiles, and the graphic arts all began to evince what art historians call a modernist aesthetic, influenced by the streamlined look of machines and simplified forms borrowed from abstract art.

A variety of factors led to the new emphasis on design in the industrial process. The first was the prosperity of the era, particularly among the rising urban and suburban middle classes. With more disposable income, these consumers were attracted to products that went beyond the merely functional. Second was the role of advertising, as manufacturers competed for consumer dollars by highlighting the attractiveness of their products. Third was the introduction not only of the automobile but also of new household appliances such as the radio, refrigerator, toaster, and other labor-saving devices—all of which offered a new canvas on which designers could ply their craft.

The Profession

Developments within the design profession also contributed to a new emphasis on industrial design in the Jazz Age. By the end of World War I, America had emerged as the wealthiest society in history, the economic powerhouse of the planet, and a creditor nation to the world. Drawn by the opportunities created by this wealth, a host of foreign designers—Germany's Kem Weber; France's Raymond Loewy, William Lescaze, and George Sakier; Austria's Paul Frankl and Joseph Urban; Greece's John Vassos; and New Zealand's Joseph Sinel—and homegrown American designers such as Walter Teague and Egmont Arens joined in advancing new ideas about the importance of design in mass production.

At the same time, professional organizations such as the National Alliance of Art and Industry, art schools such as the Cleveland School of Art and Chicago Art Institute, and museums such as the Metropolitan Museum of Art in New York, the Cleveland Museum of Art, and the Chicago Art Institute all began to promote the idea of industrial design to man-

ufacturers and the consuming public. To promote their ideas they tried to entice fine artists and art students to apply their talents to the realm of industrial design.

While the origins of the new emphasis predated World War I, a key development was the 1920 release of a comprehensive study on the state of industrial design conducted by Charles Richards, the director of New York's Cooper Union, a leading art, architecture, and engineering school. Commissioned by the National Society of Vocational Education, the Richards study noted that manufacturers lacked an understanding of the importance of industrial design. Most industrialists, the study observed, were simply interested in the efficiency and cost of their products, failing to take into account how a more attractively designed product would improve their bottom line and enhance the enjoyment of their products by the consumer.

The Richards study also observed that industrial design suffered from a second-class status in the minds of artists, art students, and art school administrators, all of whom emphasized the superiority of the fine arts of sculpture and painting. Given the lack of respect for industrial design in both industry and the educational sector, the report advocated "not only higher material rewards for designers but a more recognized and dignified status." In America, the report noted, "the designer has practically no status other than that of a worker in the industries. In Europe he is regarded as an artist and occupies a dignified position in the community." In America fine artists who also worked in industrial design often sought anonymity for fear that having their names associated with manufactured

Geometric shapes and sweeping lines marked the art deco aesthetic of Jazz Age industrial and interior design, as seen in this 1929 film set. *(General Photographic Agency/Stringer/ Hulton Archive/Getty Images)*

products would undermine their reputations as serious artists. The report pointed out that manufacturers did not recognize that value might be added to products associated with a particular designer.

Machine Aesthetic

At the beginning of the Jazz Age, the design elements of most mass-produced products were peripheral: a sculpted leg on a washing machine, for instance, or curlicues on the door latch of a refrigerator. While Richards called for a new emphasis on design elements to address the dearth of serious industrial design in America, other designers and critics were arguing that the age of machines and mass production called for a whole new approach to design. Machines, they claimed, should be embraced as aesthetic objects rather than a negation of natural beauty. As an anonymous writer in the *Literary Digest* noted in 1924, "the machine, for all its services to mankind, is so often represented in the role of Beast in its relation to Beauty in the life of the world that it has come to stand as a symbol of ugliness." Or, as ceramicist Leon Volkmar noted two years earlier in *The New York Times,* "if you must have the machine, evolve a new type of beauty that will express the machine plus intelligent direction."

Designers and critics believed that a machine-made product should emphasize the process that created it. "A good pattern in terms of this mechanized industrialism," noted art critic Lewis Mumford in 1923, "is one that fulfills the bare essentials of an object; the 'chairishness' of a chair, the 'washiness' of a basin; and any superfluity that may be added by way of ornament is in essence a perversion of the machine process."

By the mid-1920s, the call for a new emphasis on industrial design, along with the growing embrace of mass production and mechanization by designers, had resulted in what art critics referred to as the "machine aesthetic," which would come to dominate industrial design from the 1920s through the 1940s. This aesthetic took several forms. One was "art moderne," a design style that embraced the complexity of the machine. Products designed in the art moderne style included complex and abstract decorative elements that were intended to mimic the interplay of parts in complicated machinery.

By the late 1920s and 1930s, however, art moderne was giving way to a new aesthetic known as "machine purity," which downplayed the complexity of the machine in order to focus on the simplicity and purity of the machining process. Products designed

in the machine purity style emphasized simple lines, shapes, and forms. If the product was a machine itself, the actual parts were kept hidden behind a façade that highlighted the speed, repetition, and single-minded purpose of the machine. As the lines emphasizing the speed and simplicity of the machine became increasingly exaggerated, the machine purity aesthetic would give way to the streamlined style that would dominate industrial design in America through the 1930s and 1940s.

James Ciment

See also: Appliances, Household; Architecture; Art, Fine; Automobiles and Automobile Culture; Hood, Raymond; Technology.

Further Reading

Pulos, Arthur. *American Design Ethic: A History of Industrial Design to 1940.* Cambridge, MA: MIT Press, 1983.
Wilson, Richard Guy, Dianne H. Pilgrim, and Dickran Tashjian. *The Machine Age in America, 1918–1941.* New York: Harry N. Abrams, 1986.

Dewey, John (1859–1952)

John Dewey was one of the founders of a distinctly American school of philosophy known as pragmatism, though Dewey preferred to call it "instrumentalism" or "experimentalism." Pragmatists dispensed with the Hegelian notion that beliefs represent a higher reality or an absolute truth, arguing instead that beliefs were merely ways of looking at the world and that they should be retained or discarded depending on how useful they were in helping the believer achieve concrete goals.

Dewey was born in Burlington, Vermont, on October 20, 1859, to parents of modest means. After attending public schools, he majored in philosophy at the University of Vermont. Upon graduation in 1879, he taught high school for two years in Oil City, Pennsylvania. He obtained a Ph.D. in philosophy at Johns Hopkins University in 1884 and taught at the universities of Michigan, Minnesota, and Chicago, and at Columbia University.

Pragmatism and Education

Like many progressives at the beginning of the twentieth century, Dewey advocated the scientific method of experimentation to get to truth and believed that this method should be applied to philosophy, psychology, and political science. Healthy mental development, he maintained, comes from a person's efforts to adjust to the environment through experimentation, trying out different ways of looking at and interacting with the world until finding a belief system that provides happiness and fulfillment. Dewey also advocated democracy, believing that it was not only a system of government but a means of association that allowed the maximum space for people to experiment and achieve personal growth.

Dewey's main focus, however, was educational. From his work in philosophy and psychology, Dewey argued that education should be a process that brings the child from a state of doubt and uncertainty to an understanding of the world through the process of finding practical solutions to problems. Thus, older pedagogical methods emphasizing rote learning were inadequate to prepare children for their future roles as citizens, as productive agents in a modern industrial society, and as psychologically adjusted adults. Instead, Dewey argued that education should emphasize practical problem solving through the interplay of thinking and doing, and thinking about the results of doing.

While some of his most seminal work on educational theory was completed long before the Jazz Age—his two most important works, *The School and Society* and *The Child and the Curriculum,* were published in 1899 and 1902, respectively—many of his theories began to be implemented in the nation's schools during the 1920s. In this period, Dewey became an international ambassador of ideas and a proponent of democratic structures of education, as well as a commentator on political and social institutions.

International Recognition

What separated Dewey from many contemporary and past philosophers is his view of philosophy as a means to resolve the great problems of humankind and society. Between 1919 and 1934, Dewey was invited to give lectures and conduct analysis of the social institutions of Japan, China, Turkey, Mexico, the Soviet Union, Scotland, and South Africa. The trips produced voluminous writings and several influential books, including *The Quest for Certainty* (1929), which summed up Dewey's anti-Hegelian ideas that beliefs and ideas are tools for understanding reality and solving problems, rather than immutable truths in and of themselves.

In 1918, Dewey, on sabbatical from Columbia University, was a visiting professor at both the University of California at Berkeley and Stanford University. In California, Dewey gave a series of lectures that became the basis for *Human Nature and Conduct* (1922), which explored the role of habit in human behavior. In 1919, Dewey arrived in Japan to give formal lectures at Tokyo Imperial University and informal lectures around the country, resulting in the highly regarded *Reconstruction in Philosophy* (1919), which used the experiences of historical figures to teach people how to use their past experiences to improve their thought processes. In China from 1919 to 1921, Dewey gave some 133 lectures and wrote nearly forty articles for such publications as the *New Republic,* many concerning the developing social institutions of China.

In 1924, the president of Turkey, who was in the midst of reforming and secularizing Turkey's political and social institutions, invited Dewey to play a role in the reconstruction of the nation's educational system. Dewey obliged, advocating democratic, progressive education and working to end illiteracy and improve human capital for economic development. At the request of Mexican authorities, Dewey was invited to lecture in the nation's capital, visit other cities, investigate the educational system, and provide an analysis and recommendations. In both Turkey and Mexico, where religious sentiments ran strong, Dewey helped to provide a rationale for public secularism.

In 1928, Dewey traveled with an American cultural exchange group to the Soviet Union to examine the educational system and found many of his theories already being implemented. Although Dewey's social philosophy is sometimes conflated with Marxian ideology—both Marx and Dewey were concerned with the absorption of the individual into the collective—Dewey's sentiments and methods were much different from those of Marx and certainly different from those of Lenin and Stalin. And for Dewey, education more than radical shifts in the means of production would be the key to the Soviet experiment.

Dewey was invited to give the prestigious Gifford Lectures in natural theology at the University of Edinburgh in 1929. His lectures were transposed into perhaps his most effective philosophical work, *The Quest for Certainty* (1929).

Dewey died on June 1, 1952, at the age of ninety-two, having published about 1,000 works in philosophy, psychology, social and educational theory and practice, economics, and social criticism. He also participated in the founding of important social organizations such as the National Association for the Advancement of Colored People and the American Association of University Professors.

Steven R. Loomis and James Ciment

See also: Education, Elementary and Secondary; Education, Higher.

Further Reading

Martin, Jay. *The Education of John Dewey.* New York: Columbia University Press, 2002.

McDermott, John, ed. *The Philosophy of John Dewey.* Vols. 1 and 2. Chicago: University of Chicago Press, 1981.

Rockefeller, Steven. *John Dewey: Religious Faith and Democratic Humanism.* New York: Columbia University Press, 1991.

Ryan, Alan. *John Dewey and the High Tide of American Liberalism.* New York: W.W. Norton, 1995.

Dominican Republic, Intervention in

From 1916 through 1924, thousands of U.S. troops occupied the Caribbean island nation of the Dominican Republic. As in its occupation of neighboring Haiti from 1915 to 1934, the United States deployed troops in response to the collapse of the country's government that threatened U.S. business and strategic interests. Although U.S. occupation forces helped build the nation's infrastructure, create a modern police force, and introduce American culture to the island, they were also accused of abusing their authority and treating Dominicans as second-class citizens in their own land.

The Dominican Republic—whose population is a mix of black former slaves, mixed African European peasants, and a small minority of rich and influential whites—gained its independence from Spain in 1821 but was ruled for much of the first two decades of its history by Haiti. Taking advantage of a civil war in Haiti, Dominican rebels won control of the country in 1844. Through the end of the nineteenth century, the country was ruled by a series of military strongmen known as *caudillos.* A brief exception was 1861–1865, when Spain was invited back in to rule the country. From 1882 to 1899, the republic was governed by a reform-minded caudillo, Ulises Heureaux, who helped modernize the country. His assassination led to a return of political chaos.

American interests in the Dominican Republic can be traced back to the years just after the U.S. Civil War, when the administration of President Ulysses S.

Grant contemplated annexing the country. Although that never came to pass, the United States replaced various European nations as the dominant foreign power in the Dominican economy, with U.S. business interests heavily investing in infrastructure and agriculture. Despite this infusion of capital, Dominican finances continued to deteriorate, and in order to get the country to pay off its foreign debt, the United States seized control of the Dominican customs department—the main source of public revenues—in 1905.

U.S. supervision could not prevent further chaos. Following the collapse of the government of President Juan Isidro Jimenez in early 1916, the country plummeted into political turmoil once again. On May 16, 1916, several hundred U.S. Marines landed in the capital of Santo Domingo, just a year after a similar contingent had moved in to occupy the Haitian capital of Port-au-Prince.

The occupation forces immediately declared martial law, and the occupation government launched several initiatives. Public works projects built roads, hospitals, and schools. A national police force was created to fight crime and establish order. U.S. Marines introduced aspects of American culture to the island, most notably the game of baseball, which would become a national passion.

The U.S. military presence also had its dark side. The occupation government offered little opportunity for Dominicans to play a role in their own affairs. Many of the American troops were racist toward the Dominicans, abusing and insulting the largely dark-skinned population. Such racist attitudes and practices, in the face of traditional Dominican nationalism, triggered a rebellion in the eastern reaches of the republic. To combat the rebels, or *gavilleros,* the United States sent additional troops. Despite commanding much greater firepower, however, it took U.S. Marines five years to put down the rebellion. As in the roughly contemporary counterinsurgency campaign in Haiti, U.S. occupation forces were guilty of committing numerous atrocities.

Back in Washington, Republican presidential candidate Warren G. Harding made ending the occupations of the Dominican Republic and Haiti an important element of his foreign policy platform. Once elected, he insisted that the U.S. occupation forces speed the return to Dominican sovereignty. To that end, a provisional president was appointed in 1922 and national elections held in 1924. With the victory of pro-U.S. candidate Horacio Vásquez, the United States withdrew its troops before the year was over.

The effects of the U.S. occupation were lasting. With the onset of the Great Depression in 1930, the Dominican economy collapsed, leading to antigovernment violence. Rafael Trujillo Molina, the head of the U.S. established police force, did not intervene. He allowed the government to collapse—then seized power himself. One of the most brutal and corrupt dictators in twentieth-century Caribbean history, Trujillo ruled the Dominican Republic until 1961. The chaos that followed his assassination in May of that year ultimately would lead to another, much bigger invasion by U.S. Marines in 1965.

James Ciment

See also: Haiti, Intervention in; Havana Conference of 1928; Latin America, Relations with; Military Affairs.

Further Reading

Calder, Bruce J. *The Impact of Intervention: The Dominican Republic During the U.S. Occupation of 1916–1924.* Princeton, NJ: M. Wiener, 2006.
Knight, Melvin. *The Americans in Santo Domingo.* New York: Arno, 1970.

Dos Passos, John (1896–1970)

The American modernist writer John Dos Passos is best known for his fictional trilogy *U.S.A.,* made up of *The 42nd Parallel* (1930), *1919* (1932), and *The Big Money* (1936). Dos Passos's writing is characterized by a social realism that incorporates newspaper clippings, biography, autobiography, and his own imagination to capture American culture through its disjointed pieces.

Born John Rodrigo Dos Passos on January 14, 1896, he was the son of a wealthy Chicago lawyer of Portuguese lineage. Although his parents did not marry until he was in high school, Dos Passos's father provided him financial support and an excellent education. For the first sixteen years of his life, however, he was not allowed to use his father's surname. His mother, the daughter of a wealthy and socially prominent Virginia family, spent much of her time outside the country with her son for fear of scandal. After attending the Choate School in Wallingford, Connecticut, Dos Passos toured France, England, Italy, Greece, and the Middle East for six months with a private tutor. He later described his youth as that of a "hotel child." He was taunted because of his ambiguous nationality, his combination of English and

French accents, and his eyeglasses and slight build. Some critics have conjectured that his uncertain family status and national identity influenced his literary search for an overarching American character.

As an undergraduate at Harvard University, Dos Passos thought of becoming an architect but soon joined the editorial staff of the *Harvard Monthly,* for which he wrote reviews and articles. In 1916, he wrote a piece for the magazine titled "A Humble Protest," which decried the advent of an industrial society, an early example of his concern about the dehumanizing effects of modernization and capitalism on the human spirit, a concern that would become a hallmark of his later fiction. At Harvard, Dos Passos was part of a circle known as the "Harvard Aesthetes," with E.E. Cummings, S. Foster Damon, Robert Hillyer, John Brooks Wheelwright, and Malcolm Cowley, all of whom would play a vital role in the advent of American modernism.

Like Cummings, Dos Passos graduated from Harvard in 1916 and, along with the future poet and Harvard professor Robert Hillyer, joined the French volunteer ambulance corps. He would stay on in Paris after the war, joining a celebrated group of expatriate American artists and writers known as the Lost Generation. Many of them were influenced by experimental artistic and literary trends on the continent and were eager to escape what they saw as a puritanical and provincial culture back home in the United States. The war had created a sense of disillusionment with the world and a willingness to depart from prewar social and artistic convention. World War I transformed Dos Passos's interest in modernist literature into a desire to unite the literary avantgarde with radical politics. His first novels, *One Man's Initiation: 1917* (1920) and *Three Soldiers* (1921), expressed his idea that World War I represented the final madness of a capitalist economy and culture that ultimately treated its citizens as expendable commodities.

The American trends toward consumerism and conservative politics during the 1920s further confirmed Dos Passos's view that social and literary activism were the only means by which society could be reformed. In addition to his activism in support of pacifist and Socialist causes, he wrote the novel *Manhattan Transfer* (1925) in a stream-of-consciousness style that provided an acute attack on the corrosive effects of modern consumer capitalism on the individual. The commercial success of this novel marked the beginning of Dos Passos's popularity.

The controversial Sacco and Vanzetti trial in 1921 was a lightning rod for Dos Passos's radicalism. The prosecution's attack on the two men's radical politics signaled, for Dos Passos, the ultimate example of American capitalism at war with the nation's democratic principles. Like other defenders of the two Italian American anarchists, Dos Passos believed they were being railroaded because of their anticapitalist politics and immigrant, working-class status. Their execution in 1927 marked for Dos Passos the final degradation of American politics into oppressive capitalist oligarchy.

In 1928, Dos Passos visited the Soviet Union to study an alternative to American capitalism. During the late 1920s, he also wrote the first installment of what would be the *U.S.A.* trilogy, *The 42nd Parallel*. In *U.S.A.,* Dos Passos follows the lives of twelve fictional characters, surrounding them in nonfictional details of American culture. These details include biographies of historical figures, "newsreels" to let the outside world into the narrative account, and autobiographical sketches. The effect of the novels was to present a sense of steady American decline as the country moved into and out of World War I. In this coming-of-age tale, the various protagonists find themselves dehumanized by militarism until a sense of outrage fires them to take political action against an unjust and undemocratic social order.

U.S.A. marked the high tide of Dos Passos's political radicalism. By the mid-1930s, he came to the conclusion that the American Communist Party was primarily interested in political power rather than the plight of the worker. As he changed his views on communism, Dos Passos wrote a series of articles in the mid-1930s critical of American Communists' rigid adherence to orthodox Marxist economic theory. When his friend José Robles was executed by Communist forces during the Spanish Civil War (1935–1939), Dos Passos officially broke with international communism. Throughout the rest of the 1930s, he questioned the viability of mass movements and feared their susceptibility to tyrants. In the 1940s, Dos Passos claimed that dictators such as Stalin and Hitler were equally a product of this susceptibility.

Dos Passos's move to libertarianism in the 1940s was confusing to many of his literary supporters, for whom such a shift smacked of reactionary politics. However, Dos Passos's political shifts during these years reflected his individualism and suspicion of monolithic culture and society, sympathies he had held since the 1920s.

Elected to the American Academy of Arts and Letters in 1947, Dos Passos continued to write until his death on September 28, 1970.

Jason Stacy

See also: Fiction; Journalism.

Further Reading

Brantley, John. *The Fiction of John Dos Passos.* New York: Moulton, 1968.

Dos Passos, John. *The Best Times: An Informal Memoir.* New York: New American Library, 1966.

Ludington, Townsend. *John Dos Passos: A Twentieth-Century Odyssey.* New York: Carroll and Graf, 1998.

Rohrkember, John. *John Dos Passos: A Reference Guide.* New York: G.K. Hall, 1980.

Dreiser, Theodore (1871–1945)

A pioneer of naturalism, a literary movement influential in the late nineteenth and early twentieth centuries, Theodore Dreiser is best known for novels that explore the underside of American life—especially *Sister Carrie* (1900) and the critically acclaimed Jazz Age best seller *An American Tragedy* (1925). The naturalist school was marked by a journalistic attention to detail; characters driven by their baser instincts; themes of crime, vice, and social conflict; and story lines that emphasized how larger social and historical forces often overwhelm individual will in a fatalistic view of modern life.

Herman Theodore Dreiser was born in Terre Haute, Indiana, on August 27, 1871. His father, John Paul Dreiser, was a German Catholic who had come to America to make his fortune. Dreiser's mother, Sarah Schanab, was a Mennonite from Ohio who had met and married John Paul when she was only sixteen years old. At the age of fifteen, Theodore Dreiser boarded a train and moved to Chicago, where he eventually became a feature reporter for a local newspaper called the *Globe.*

Dreiser's managing editor at the *Globe,* John T. McEnnis, recognized potential in Dreiser's writing and helped him secure a position at a more reputable newspaper in St. Louis, where he met and became engaged to Sara Osborne White. In 1894, Dreiser left St. Louis and went to work for newspapers in Ohio, Buffalo, and Pittsburgh. He ultimately ended up in New York City, which would become his primary residence for more than forty years. Dreiser married Sara Osborne White in December 1898.

His experiences as an urban reporter provided the material for his first novel, *Sister Carrie.* Although modern critics consider *Sister Carrie* a masterpiece of American naturalism, early-twentieth-century readers objected to its gritty, realistic portrayal of the vagaries of urban life and Dreiser's nonmoralizing account of a young woman who goes unpunished for transgressing conventional sexual morality. The book's publisher had cut a number of passages before publication and gave it only limited circulation. Until the publication of his second novel, *Jennie Gerhardt* (1911), which received a much more positive response, Dreiser often distributed copies of *Sister Carrie* himself. An uncensored version of *Sister Carrie* was not published until 1982. Although his writing is usually not acclaimed for its style, Dreiser is generally considered an important figure because his work introduced a new realism and sexual candor into American fiction.

After 1911, Dreiser's writing took on a more explicitly political tone, in part because of the censorship he faced when publishing *Sister Carrie* and *Jennie Gerhardt,* another story of seduction, this time of a young woman who bears the illicit child of a U.S. senator. In his third novel, *The Financier* (1912), Dreiser began to focus more specifically on American social and economic institutions. Dreiser's realism and his increasing politicization made everything he wrote between 1900 and 1925 a target for censors, including his account of his adventures in Europe, *A Traveler at Forty* (1913). Upon his return from Europe, Dreiser moved into New York City's Greenwich Village. He separated from Sara and began associating with leading political radicals, such as Max Eastman, Daniel DeLeon, and Floyd Dell. He supported Margaret Sanger and the birth control movement, and he befriended the anarchist Emma Goldman. He also began writing for more radical journals, such as *The Masses* and *Seven Arts.*

Dreiser once again faced censorship issues with his next two novels. Because of its focus on the seamy side of modern life, Harper and Brothers refused to publish his fourth novel, *The Titan* (1914), a sequel to *The Financier,* forcing Dreiser to take his manuscript to the English publisher John Lane Company. On the eve of World War I, the New York Society for the Suppression of Vice persuaded government officials to order the removal of *The "genius"* (1915), an autobiographical novel with explicit sexual content, from bookshelves, resulting in a protracted legal battle. The book was finally reissued in 1923. Dreiser's experiences with censorship, as well as attacks against his "barbaric naturalism" and his unconventional writing style, led him to become an outspoken critic of those who would suppress literature for the sake of propriety.

Although Dreiser enjoyed critical acclaim for his work, his early books did not sell well, and his constant battles with publishers over censorship left him mentally and financially spent. He was at a low point in 1919 when he met Helen Patges Richardson, a young aspiring actress. Dreiser and Richardson moved to Hollywood in 1919, beginning a tumultuous twenty-five-year relationship.

Dreiser's only commercially successful novel, *An American Tragedy,* was based on an actual murder that occurred in 1906. *An American Tragedy* tells the story of Clyde Griffiths, a young man whose desire for wealth and status overwhelms his moral sense and ultimately compels him to plan the murder of his pregnant girlfriend, a factory worker named Roberta. Griffiths takes Roberta on a boating trip on isolated Big Bittern Lake, where he intends to drown her and make it appear to be an accident. After having made all the preparations, Griffiths finds that he cannot bring himself to harm Roberta, but she accidentally falls into the water and drowns. Following a lengthy trial, Griffiths is found guilty of murder and is executed. Dreiser's publisher, Horace Liveright, cut the huge manuscript nearly in half and published *An American Tragedy* in two volumes in 1925.

In 1927, the Watch and Ward Society of Boston sought to ban distribution of the novel, leading to a trial and an appeal that dragged on in the courts for years. Nevertheless, the novel was both a critical and commercial success selling more than 25,000 copies in the first six months and garnering Dreiser further income from the sale of the movie rights. The first film version appeared in 1931, followed in 1951 by a popular remake entitled *A Place in the Sun.* Dreiser was finally able to live the lifestyle that he had dreamed of all his life.

Like other left-leaning Americans, Dreiser was interested in the social revolution in Russia, and he visited there in 1927, publishing a memoir of his travels called *Dreiser Looks at Russia* (1928). The visit also led to a renewed focus on politics. Much of his energy and writing in subsequent years focused on politics, as well as his other passion, scientific and philosophical study. He wrote little fiction in the late 1920s and 1930s. By the end of the 1920s, Dreiser had become famous as a champion of literary freedom in America. He would continue his activism, on a number of fronts, until his death on December 28, 1945.

Michael A. Rembis

See also: Fiction.

Further Reading

Elias, Robert H. *Theodore Dreiser: Apostle of Nature.* Ithaca, NY: Cornell University Press, 1970.

Lundquist, James. *Theodore Dreiser.* New York: Frederick Ungar, 1974.

Matthiessen, F.O. *Theodore Dreiser.* New York: William Sloane, 1951.

Shapiro, Charles. *Theodore Dreiser: Our Bitter Patriot.* Carbondale: Southern Illinois University Press, 1965.

Drugs, Illicit and Illegal

The decade after World War I saw a significant shift in the use of illicit, mind-altering drugs in the United States. Consumption of cocaine, heroin, and marijuana remained a problem throughout the decade, despite growing efforts by local, state, and national authorities to restrict access to these drugs. Nationally, cocaine, opium, and its derivative heroin produced the greatest alarm. Concern over marijuana initially was most acute in Southwestern states, though all state governments had banned it by the mid-1930s. The increased attention on drug enforcement during the 1920s relegated those involved in the drug trade to the fringe of society.

As the twentieth century began, public health officials estimated that 250,000 Americans were opium addicts and 200,000 were addicted to cocaine, much of which reached the public through legal patented medicines. In 1914, Congress passed the Harrison Drug Control Act, which banned the use of opiates without a medical prescription and required doctors and druggists to prove the medical necessity of all prescriptions. The law incorrectly included cocaine (a stimulant) as an opiate, as did several subsequent state laws.

These restrictions altered the demographics of drug consumption. Before 1900, most opiate users were middle-class women; by 1919, men and women used these substances equally. Social attitudes toward drug users shifted from pity to fear as Congressman Richmond Pearson Hobson (D-AL) and others cultivated the image of drug fiends preying on others.

Following World War I and the adoption of national liquor prohibition, alarm over drug use escalated. In 1919, the narcotics division of the Treasury Department estimated that a million drug addicts resided in America, served by an illegal national drug cartel. Hobson, formerly a vocal advocate of the liquor ban, now focused his ire on heroin use, claiming that there were 4 million addicts in the United States. Although he had little evidence to support his assertions, the National Broadcasting Company granted him free airtime on 400 radio affiliates as a public service. The Woman's Christian Temperance Union, the Elks, the Masons, and the Kiwanis Club all supported his crusade against the drug menace. A 1923 study by the Public Health Service, which revised the national drug use figures to 110,000, did little to quell the growing alarm over America's perceived drug problem.

Effects of Illegalization

The government addressed drug use as a criminal rather than a medical issue. The U.S. Supreme Court, in *United States v. Doremus* (1919), ruled that the Harrison Act did not exceed constitutional boundaries, a reversal of earlier rulings. The Court also ruled in *Webb v. United States* (1919) that doctors have no right to maintain addicts by supplying them with drugs. The Treasury Department, charged with enforcing Prohibition, created the Narcotics Division under the direction of Levi G. Nutt. The group urged the creation of federal drug detoxification centers, but Congress did not act on the proposal until 1935 because of budget constraints. In 1920, federal drug enforcement officials began a campaign to close locally funded drug treatment centers; forty-four of these had opened since the war, most in New York and Connecticut and a few in Louisiana, California, Ohio, Texas, and Tennessee.

In 1922, the Supreme Court ruled in *United States v. Behrman* that prescribing even diminishing amounts of an illegal drug to wean an addict is illegal. That same year Congress passed the Narcotic Drug Import and Export Act (the Jones-Miller Act), which created a Narcotic Control Board to monitor the manufacture of drugs and banned the export of illegal drugs from America except for legitimate medical purposes. The legislation also shifted the legal burden from the prosecutor to the defendant to prove that his or her possession of drugs was legitimate. Elizabeth Washburn Wright, widow of one of the authors of the 1914 Harrison Act, lobbied the federal government to limit the production of drugs for legal purposes, fearing that addicts were obtaining these substances. In 1924, Congressman Steven G. Porter (R-PA) held hearings on drug use and concluded that approximately half of the inmates at the federal prison in Leavenworth, Kansas, were drug offenders and that many of them were addicts. In reaction, Congress passed the Heroin Act, which banned all importation of that substance regardless of its intended use.

Porter, Wright, and Episcopal Bishop Charles Henry Brent, another prominent antidrug crusader, represented the nation at the Second Geneva Conference on international drug policy in 1924–1925. Together they shaped the American platform, which called for reducing agricultural production of drug plants such as poppies. The European delegates, by contrast, wanted treatment centers for drug users to reduce the international demand for illegal drugs. The United States therefore refused to ratify the 1925 International Opium Convention, and Porter continued to dominate America's international drug policy through the rest of the decade.

The number of drug addicts who had become addicted while hospitalized declined in America during the 1920s. By 1930, most addicts were pleasure addicts. Many of these were lower-class young men in Northern cities who used heroin, the drug of choice because it was cheaper than morphine and was perceived to be safer than cocaine. Most addicts were intravenous users, injecting the drug to achieve a better high than was possible from sniffing it. Addicts tended to live in run-down areas and held menial jobs, often in speakeasies where their drug use was viewed as less objectionable. In pool halls, brothels, and gambling dens, they created their own community of buyers and sellers, generally rejecting traditional values of family and hard work for the instant gratification of a drug high. Drug use also brought people into contact with organized crime, an increasing problem during the 1920s. Prominent New York mobster Arnold Rothstein became a leading drug trafficker during the decade, although his criminal dealings did not become public until after he was killed in 1928.

Marijuana

Marijuana smoking became commonplace in the 1920s. The drug laws generally did not include marijuana, or cannabis, as a banned substance. In fact, U.S. federal law said little about marijuana before 1937. Several states took the lead in banning the substance, a difficult task because marijuana was a common, uncultivated plant in many parts of America. Texas, Utah, and California outlawed cannabis in 1915, and politicians from the southwestern United States pressured the Treasury Department to ban marijuana imports for all but medical purposes. In 1923, Louisiana, Nevada, Oregon, and Washington banned cannabis; New York and Colorado followed suit in 1927 and 1929, respectively.

Sensationalized reports circulated. New Orleans newspapers in 1926 reported that marijuana shipments from Cuba and Mexico passed through that city to customers as distant as Cleveland, Ohio, and that schoolchildren were smoking the evil weed. Denver, Colorado, newspaper reports on marijuana smoking by Mexican migrant laborers who could not afford bootleg liquor spurred that state to ban cannabis. The federal government demonstrated its growing concern over marijuana use in 1929, when it classified cannabis as an addictive narcotic and made addiction centers available to prisoners who smoked it.

In 1930, the federal government charged several narcotics bureau officers in New York City with accepting bribes from drug traffickers. The investigation uncovered ties between Rothstein and the family of Levi G. Nutt, chief of the Treasury Department's narcotics division. Although Nutt was exonerated, the hearings led to a shake-up in the structure of federal narcotics enforcement. The Prohibition Reorganization Act of 1930 (the Porter Act) established the Federal Bureau of Narcotics (FBN), independent of liquor enforcement agencies. Harry J. Anslinger became the first commissioner of the FBN, a post he would hold for more than thirty years. Anslinger focused on ending marijuana use, although he had no legal jurisdiction in this area.

Improvements in the international reporting of legitimate drug production aided enforcement officers, who implemented large drug busts in late 1930 and early 1931. Several American drug traffickers were arrested in Europe. The burgeoning drug trade of the 1920s declined, though enforcement fell off by the mid-1930s as traffickers improved their ability to disguise their activities. The antidrug crusaders left an indelible impression on drug enforcement and the drug culture in the United States. Drug policy in the 1920s—emphasizing interruption of supply rather than treatment to reduce demand—became the enforcement model in subsequent decades and helped to drive the drug culture to the margins of American society.

James E. Klein

See also: Crime, Organized; Criminal Punishment; Health and Medicine; Prohibition (1920–1933).

Further Reading

Brecher, Edward M., and the Editors of Consumer Reports. *Licit and Illicit Drugs: The Consumers Union Report on Narcotics, Stimulants, Depressants, Inhalants, Hallucinogens, and Marijuana—Including Caffeine, Nicotine, and Alcohol.* Boston: Little, Brown, 1972.

Gray, Mike. *Drug Crazy: How We Got Into This Mess and How We Can Get Out.* New York: Random House, 1998.

Jonnes, Jill. *Hep-cats, Narcs, and Pipe Dreams: A History of America's Romance with Illegal Drugs.* New York: Scribner's, 1996.

Musto, David R. *The American Disease: Origins of Narcotics Control.* New Haven, CT: Yale University Press, 1973.

Du Bois, W.E.B. (1868–1963)

The historian, sociologist, novelist, and editor W.E.B. Du Bois was the preeminent African American intellectual and civil rights activist of the Jazz Age. Born William Edward Burghardt Du Bois on February 23, 1868, in Great Barrington, Massachusetts, he was reared by his mother, Mary, after his father abandoned the family. Du Bois took a B.A. at Fisk University in 1888 and earned another B.A. and a Ph.D. in history from Harvard University in 1890 and 1895; he was the first black person ever to receive a doctorate from Harvard.

In 1897, after brief stints as a professor and researcher at Wilberforce University and the University of Pennsylvania, Du Bois accepted a professorship in sociology at Atlanta University, where he wrote his most famous work, *The Souls of Black Folk* (1903). In 1905, Du Bois joined with Boston editor William Monroe Trotter to found the Niagara movement, a short-lived effort to win civil and political rights for African Americans. Five years later, Du Bois left academia to take the post of director of research and publicity at the newly formed National Association for the Advancement of Colored People (NAACP).

In the following years, using his position as the editor of the NAACP's widely read magazine *The Crisis,* he forcefully denounced white racism and demanded full equality for African Americans. Disappointed that the service of black soldiers during World War I was not rewarded with more rights for African Americans, Du Bois angrily declared in a May 1919 editorial that black veterans would not only "return from fighting" but would "return fighting." The militant editor expressed his disgust at the race riots that rocked American cities during the summer of 1919 and applauded the efforts of an increasing number of blacks to repel white attacks. Du Bois's semi-autobiographical *Dark Water: Voices from Within the Veil* (1920) reflected his growing bitterness about U.S. race relations.

Although Du Bois praised the militancy of the "New Negro," he continued to support interracial activism for an integrated American society. Hence, he became increasingly concerned about the widespread appeal of the separatist program of black nationalist Marcus Garvey and his all-black Universal Negro Improvement Association (UNIA). Between 1919 and 1921, Garvey repeatedly ridiculed the NAACP's program and belittled Du Bois's idea that a small black elite, the "Talented Tenth," would be able to lead African Americans to full equality. The two men engaged in a vicious exchange of insults in *The Crisis* and the UNIA's *Negro World.* Du Bois, the NAACP, and other African American leaders initiated

The leading African American intellectual and civil rights activist of his generation, W.E.B. Du Bois advanced his increasingly radical views in the pages of *The Crisis,* the official NAACP journal he edited from its founding in 1910 to 1934. *(C.M. Battey/Stringer/Hulton Archive/Getty Images)*

a concerted "Garvey Must Go" campaign to undermine the Jamaican's appeal.

What Garvey and Du Bois shared, however, was their advocacy of Pan-Africanism, an ideology emphasizing the need for the social, political, economic, and cultural unity of all African peoples, both on the continent and in the diaspora. In the aftermath of World War I, Du Bois organized several Pan-African congresses to discuss the problem of European colonialism. Du Bois's first trip to the African continent in December 1923 further intensified his interest in the region.

In 1924, Du Bois and the NAACP began to support a cultural movement of black writers, artists, and musicians that came to be known as the Harlem Renaissance. As early as 1923, *The Crisis* had begun to introduce its readers to the literary works of young black writers such as Langston Hughes, Zora Neale Hurston, and Countee Cullen. In *The Gift of Black Folk: The Negro in the Making of America* (1924), Du Bois maintained that blacks were gifted with a special sense of beauty, which could be seen in their artistic accomplishments. Du Bois, like black intellectual Alaine Locke, spoke of a "Negro Art Renaissance" and encouraged black writers and artists to submit their work to prize competitions organized by the NAACP. Along with the Urban League's *Opportunity, The Crisis* became one of the most important forums for black writers of the 1920s.

By mid-1926, however, Du Bois was disenchanted with the Harlem Renaissance, which he accused of neglecting the political role of black art in the struggle for racial equality. In his essay "Criteria of Negro Art" (1926), he insisted that all art ought to be regarded as propaganda. According to Du Bois, blacks could not afford to produce art for art's sake and should refrain from producing descriptions of the immoral life of the black ghetto to satisfy white people's curiosity. He believed that the realistic depictions of black life in the works of Wallace Thurman, Claude McKay, white writer Carl Van Vechten, and others were an affront to the entire African American community. In his novel *Dark Princess: A Romance* (1928), which criticized European colonialism, Du Bois attempted to demonstrate that fiction could be infused with a political message.

Du Bois's visit to the Soviet Union in September 1926 marked the beginning of his interest in so-cialism. In the early 1920s, he had dismissed Marxist class analysis as an inadequate approach to solving the problems faced by black Americans. By 1927, however, Du Bois had become highly critical of capitalism. That year, he organized a Pan-African congress in New York City. The unresponsiveness of Republican presidential candidate Herbert Hoover to issues of race during the presidential election of 1928 and the onset of the Great Depression in 1929 pushed Du Bois even farther to the left.

In 1934, because of his differences with the NAACP leadership, Du Bois left the organization and rejoined the faculty at Atlanta University. Before the end of the 1930s, he wrote three more monographs, including *Black Reconstruction in America* (1935) and his first autobiography, *Dusk of Dawn: An Autobiography of a Concept of Race* (1940). The NAACP rehired Du Bois in 1944, but he was dismissed four years later because of his public advocacy of socialism and his support for the Progressive Party in the 1948 presidential election. His work with various Communist organizations in subsequent years led the U.S. government to temporarily confiscate his passport, and he was harassed by federal authorities and shunned by many black leaders during the Red Scare of the 1950s.

Du Bois married Socialist writer Shirley Lola Graham in 1951 (his first wife, Nina Gomer, had died one year earlier) and produced three more works of fiction before the end of the decade. In 1961, he became a member of the Communist Party and emigrated from the United States to Ghana. Two years later, at age ninety-five, he became a citizen of Ghana. W.E.B. Du Bois died on August 27, 1963, in Accra, Ghana.

Simon Wendt

See also: African Americans; Harlem Renaissance; Lynching; National Association for the Advancement of Colored People.

Further Reading

Du Bois, W.E.B. *The Autobiography of W.E.B. Du Bois.* New York: International Publishers, 1968.

Lewis, David Levering. *W.E.B. Du Bois: Biography of a Race, 1868–1919.* New York: Henry Holt, 1993.

———. *W.E.B. Du Bois: The Fight for Equality and the American Century, 1919–1963.* New York: Henry Holt, 2000.

Rampersad, Arnold. *The Art and Imagination of W.E.B. Du Bois.* New York: Schocken, 1976.

Economic Policy

Historians, economists, and other commentators continue to debate the role of economic policy in the 1920s and its impact on the Great Depression, beginning with the stock market crash of October 1929. On the one hand, the American economy was generally strong during the 1920s, and the federal government and its policies were responsible in some measure. On the other hand, the Great Depression reflected some of the economic problems of the 1920s, and perhaps more farsighted policies could have helped ease the impact.

In his 1921 inaugural address, Republican President Warren G. Harding stated that, with the war over, it was time to put "our public household in order," to end "government's experiment in business," and to restore "lightened tax burdens." Harding's approach did not greatly differ from that of his Democratic predecessor, Woodrow Wilson. It would not be until the New Deal era that the Keynesian idea of an activist government smoothing out the business cycle would take hold.

Republican Policy

While there was no overarching economic policy, successive Republican presidents, aided by a GOP-controlled Congress, favored reducing taxes, government expenditures, and the national debt; they also supported foreign repayment of American war loans and higher U.S. tariffs on imported goods. The Federal Reserve System, meanwhile, did not fully understand the tools at its disposal to help guide the economy. Indeed, this was a decade before the great British economist John Maynard Keynes published *The General Theory of Employment, Interest, and Money* (1936), ushering in the concept of Keynesian economics and the onset of more active government management of economic cycles.

Andrew Mellon, who served as secretary of the treasury from 1921 to 1933, was strongly committed to reducing government expenditures, paying down the national debt, and lowering taxes. Mellon believed that high income tax rates would "tend to destroy individual initiative and enterprise, and seriously impede the development of productive business." During the 1920s, he achieved his goal. Although a coalition of Democrats and progressives in Congress resisted Mellon's effort to secure significant reductions in income tax rates, the top bracket fell during the course of the decade, from 73 percent in 1920 to 56 percent in 1922, 46 percent in 1924, and 24 percent in 1929; the lower income brackets declined proportionately. Government expenditures, as reflected in the annual federal budget, declined from $5 billion in 1921 to $3.1 billion in 1929 despite some inflation. The total federal debt also decreased, from $24 billion in 1921 to $17 billion in 1929.

The commitment to reducing expenditures and lowering taxes helped bring about the Washington Naval Conference of 1921–1922. At the time, spending on the U.S. Navy accounted for more than 40 percent of America's postwar federal budget. Seeking to end the wartime naval building boom and thereby help reduce U.S. federal expenditures, Secretary of State Charles Evans Hughes organized the conference of naval powers. Among them, in addition to the United States, were France, Great Britain, Japan, and Italy. The conference, held in Washington, D.C., began in November 1921 and concluded with the signing of the last of several agreements in February 1922.

The conference resulted in three major treaties. The Four-Power Treaty, signed on December 13, 1921, sought to lower tensions among the major Pacific Ocean naval powers by renouncing further territorial expansion. The Five-Power Treaty, signed on the last day of the conference, February 6, 1922, sought to halt the naval building boom yet preserve the relative strengths of major navies. The United States, Great Britain, Japan, France, and Italy all agreed to a ten-year moratorium on battleship and aircraft carrier production and a reduction of their gross ship tonnage. The Nine-Power Treaty, also signed the day the conference adjourned, guaranteed China's independence, sovereignty, and territorial integrity.

Loan Repayments and Tariffs

Successive presidential administrations and the U.S. Congress insisted that the Allies repay their wartime loans. This was a complicated matter. World War I had brought devastation throughout Europe, destroying farms, homes, factories, transportation facilities, and communication lines. The European victors, led by France and Belgium, wanted the vanquished Central Powers, principally Germany, to pay for the damage. Germany and its allies, however, had also suffered and could not make such payments easily. A three-sided international system ensued, whereby the U.S. government and private agencies would lend Germany and Austria money to make reparation payments to the Allies, who in turn would repay their war debts to the United States. This system continued, albeit with modifications, through the 1920s, until the onset of the Great Depression shook the world economic and financial order to its core.

High postwar tariffs (import levies) added to the negative economic impact of debt repayment and war reparations. Elected officials agreed with corporate America that higher tariffs benefited the U.S. economy, and Congress passed the Emergency Tariff of 1921 to provide temporary protection for twenty-eight agricultural commodities, including corn, wheat, meat, sugar, and wool. This was followed by the Fordney-McCumber Tariff of 1922, named for Representative Joseph W. Fordney (R-MI) and Senator Porter J. McCumber (R-ND). The measure increased tariffs on a long list of goods by 27–35 percent.

The United States, however, did not need such protection at the time, as it had emerged from the war as a great creditor nation. The U.S. tariffs prompted foreign governments to seek protection for their own markets and producers by raising their own national tariffs. Moreover, the threat to international trade limited the ability of other countries to increase trade and capital holdings, whether to pay off war debts to the United States or reparations to the other Allied nations.

Immigration Restrictions

In the 1920s, the U.S. government moved to limit the free flow of immigration into the country. While the impetus was certainly cultural—seeking to freeze the ethnic composition of American society as it was before the third great wave of immigration from Southern and Eastern Europe—immigration restriction also was an important economic policy. In May 1921, Congress passed the Emergency Quota Act, which limited annual immigration from any country to 3 percent of the total number of persons of that nationality living in the United States at the time of the 1910 census—a total of no more than 357,000. In May 1924, Congress passed the National Origins Act, which limited immigration to only 2 percent of each nationality based on the 1890 census—reducing total annual immigration to only 164,000.

By reducing immigration, these measures cut down on the supply of labor in the United States, a goal of craft unions. Cutting off the flow of cheap labor from abroad contributed to the rise in real wages during the 1920s but also to a decline in the rate of growth of the U.S. economy, since there were fewer new Americans to purchase and consume goods, housing, and services.

Agriculture

The 1920s also brought a crisis in America's agricultural sector. Farmers were growing more food but were unable to significantly reduce costs, faced increased international competition in basic commodities, and saw prices for basic commodities drop substantially and remain low throughout the decade. The result was an economic depression in farm communities long before the stock market crash of 1929. Farm-state politicians sought to legislate a solution, the McNary-Haugen bills, whereby the federal government would help protect home markets and purchase surplus production to sell abroad.

Senator Charles McNary (R-OR) and Representative Gilbert Haugen (R-WI) had adopted the idea of George Peck, president of the Moline Plow Company, to legislate a two-tiered system of prices—higher at home, where tariffs lessened competition, and lower abroad to meet the market. It was a complicated concept. The government would pass protective tariffs to guarantee high U.S. prices for basic commodities. Since there were no requirements for reduced production, farmers would likely overproduce. Consequently, a government-chartered corporation would purchase surplus production at the high, tariff-protected domestic price and would seek to market it abroad, where surplus production from other countries was also flooding the international market. If the corporation had to sell agricultural commodities abroad for less than it paid at home, farmers—at least in theory—would compensate for the losses. The initial bill proposed to cover corn and wheat with no requirements to reduce production, although such a reduction would have helped to increase demand or the prices paid by the public.

The legislation failed in 1924 for lack of Southern support, as it did not provide support for staple Southern crops. Another attempt in 1926 failed for similar reasons. In 1927, the bill's sponsors added price supports for tobacco and cotton, thereby gaining enough Southern support to pass the measure, which was then vetoed by President Calvin Coolidge. In 1928, in part to make it an issue in the national election campaign, the coalition succeeded in pushing the measure through Congress, and Coolidge vetoed it again.

Coolidge rejected the McNary-Haugen bills for a number of reasons. He agreed with Secretary of Commerce Herbert Hoover that the bills had flaws: there were no production limits, farmers would be encouraged to overproduce, and prices would be further dampened. The president also opposed outright federal interference in the marketplace, though he would have welcomed farmers banding together voluntarily to reduce production. And if the government gave assistance to one sector of the economy, he reasoned, there would be pressure to act in other sectors as well. The ultimate result of this approach would be a planned economy, closer to the Socialist ideal, rather than the free-market system so valued by Coolidge and most Republicans in the 1920s. But without legislation and without a change in conditions in which farmers produced and marketed crops, the agricultural economy remained poor throughout the 1920s.

The Stock Market Crash

Correctly or not, historians tend to view economic policy and perhaps the entire decade of the 1920s through the prism of the great stock market crash of 1929. In the 1920s, the stock market allowed investors to purchase stock "on the margin," putting up little cash and borrowing the rest on the assumption that stock prices would always rise and stock holdings would always be worth more. Margin buying drove the market to dizzying heights, and to the inevitable economic correction—the bursting of the bubble—on Black Thursday, October 29, 1929. As the market plum-

meted, nervous brokers made "margin calls," or demands for the difference between the amount invested in the stock and the new lower price of the stock; many clients were forced to sell their holdings to meet the calls, putting even greater downward pressure on the market. Although relatively few Americans actually owned stock, the crash of 1929 marked the end of the era of easy money and rampant speculation.

Contrary to popular myth, the crash did not inevitably lead to the Great Depression. It did, however, reflect the weaknesses in the economy of the 1920s and the government's capacity to guide the economy through this unsettling event. There was too much concentration of wealth and too small a middle class. There was virtually no regulation of financial markets, and the Federal Reserve System did not yet recognize the power of the tools it possessed. Economic theory had yet to advance much beyond laissez-faire, and government was reluctant to interfere directly in the economic cycle.

Yet U.S. economic policy during the 1920s seemed to meet the needs of the nation. Per capita annual income increased from $517 to $618, and with prices declining, real income increased by about 30 percent. For many Americans, ownership of a home, automobile, radio, record player, and other conveniences became part of daily life, and new diversions became part of the regular routine.

Charles M. Dobbs

See also: *Adkins v. Children's Hospital* (1923); Agricultural Marketing Act of 1929; Agriculture; *Bailey v. Drexel Furniture Company* (1922); Dawes Plan (1924); Demobilization, Industrial; Federal Power Commission; Federal Radio Commission; Fordney-McCumber Tariff of 1922; Hoover, Herbert; Mellon, Andrew; Progressivism; Railway Labor Act (1926); Recession of 1921–1922; Sheppard-Towner Act (1921); War Finance Corporation.

Further Reading

Best, Gary Dean. *The Dollar Decade: Mammon and the Machine in the 1920s.* Westport, CT: Praeger, 2003.

Leuchtenburg, William E. *The Perils of Prosperity, 1914–1932.* 2nd ed. Chicago: University of Chicago Press, 1993.

McCoy, Donald R. *Coming of Age: The United States During the 1920s and 1930s.* Baltimore: Penguin, 1973.

Perrett, Geoffrey. *America in the Twenties: A History.* New York: Simon & Schuster, 1982.

Potter, Jim. *The American Economy Between the World Wars.* New York: John Wiley and Sons, 1974.

Shaffer, Butler D. *In Restraint of Trade: The Business Campaign Against Competition, 1918–1938.* Lewisburg, PA: Bucknell University Press, 1997.

Soule, George H. *Prosperity Decade: From War to Depression, 1917–1929.* New York: Harper & Row, 1947.

Ederle, Gertrude (1906–2003)

When Gertrude Ederle swam across the English Channel in August 1926, she rose to international celebrity as the first woman to accomplish the feat. Ederle held several world records for women swimmers, and she had won three medals at the 1924 Olympic Games in Paris, but her crossing of the Channel, done in record time for a man or woman, was celebrated with a ticker tape parade, film roles, and the adoration of the American people.

Gertrude Caroline Ederle was born on October 23, 1906, in New York City. Her parents were German immigrants who owned a delicatessen. At the family's lake cottage in New Jersey, Ederle showed early promise as a swimmer. When she was thirteen, she joined

Covered in grease to protect her from the frigid waters, Gertrude Ederle enters the ocean at Cape Gris-Nez, France, on August 6, 1927, on her way to becoming the first woman to swim the English Channel. *(General Photographic Agency/Stringer/Hulton Archive/Getty Images)*

the Women's Swimming Association on New York's Lower East Side, an organization founded by Charlotte Epstein to promote women's participation in sports. Epstein recognized Ederle's ability as a swimmer and encouraged her to participate in swim meets. Ederle, who suffered from a lack of self-esteem and eventually dropped out of school, found success in swimming.

By 1920, Ederle dominated women's swimming in the United States. She won national championships for amateurs in both the 220-yard and 440-yard freestyle. In 1922, she entered the Joseph P. Day Cup race—three and one-half miles across New York Bay—against fifty other women, including British champion Hilda James. Although it was Ederle's first long-distance competition, she finished first. Later that year, she won the 500-meter freestyle at the Amateur Athletic Union Outdoor Championships, and, between 1922 and 1924, she set nine amateur world records in distances between 100 and 500 meters. Ederle's successes won her an invitation to join the U.S. women's swim team for the 1924 Olympics. In Paris, she won a gold medal in the 4x100-meter freestyle relay and bronze medals in the 100-meter and 400-meter freestyle.

The 1920s was a time of great public interest in sports. Newspapers reported sports accomplishments under banner headlines, radio brought a new air of excitement to coverage, and staged events of various kinds had become highly popular. In this environment of increased excitement and exposure, Ederle hoped to parlay her fame and success into additional opportunities. She decided to find long-distance swimming records she could break.

On June 15, 1925, she set a record by swimming twenty-one miles from Manhattan to Sandy Hook, New Jersey, in just over seven hours. That feat was a mere warm-up for Ederle's main goal—swimming the English Channel. She had attempted to swim the Channel earlier in 1925 but, suffering from cramps, had to be pulled from the water and was disqualified only six miles from completion.

Ederle was determined to try again. Five men had swum the Channel before her, including Thomas W. Burgess, who agreed to be her coach for the 1926 attempt. On August 6, Ederle set out at 7:09 A.M. from Cape Gris-Nez, France, for the opposite shore in Dover, England. Her father, sister, and coach followed in the tugboat *Alsace*, shouting encouragement to her and reading radiograms sent by her mother, who was following her progress. Her body was coated with sheep grease to help keep her warm, and she ate small meals—chicken broth, chocolate, slices of pineapple, and periodic sugar cubes—to keep up her strength.

The weather conditions were bad. Strong winds and rain hampered Ederle's progress. Burgess urged her to give up twice, but she refused. Despite being blown off course, which forced her to swim thirty-five miles instead of the nominal twenty-one miles across the Channel, she arrived at Dover in the dark of night, having taken fourteen hours and thirty-one minutes to make the crossing. Her time was two hours less than the best time by a man. Her record remained until 1964.

Two million admirers turned out for Ederle's ticker tape parade in New York City. President Calvin Coolidge called her "America's Best Girl," and she was invited to appear at special events throughout the country. But fame proved fleeting. After appearing in a movie (*Swim, Girl, Swim,* 1927), touring with Billy Rose's Aquacade, and making the vaudeville circuit, Ederle and her agent found entertainment opportunities harder to come by as other events captured the public's attention.

Ederle suffered from a nervous breakdown in 1928, and subsequently faced a series of physical ailments. The many hours she had spent in the water aggravated a hearing problem she had had since childhood, finally leading to partial deafness. Despite a back injury in 1933 that put her in a cast or brace for four years, Ederle thrilled visitors at the 1939 New York World's Fair by swimming the full length of the Aquacade. She spent most of her final years as a swimming instructor of deaf children.

Ederle was elected to the International Swimming Hall of Fame in 1965, and she was inducted into the Women's Sports Hall of Fame in 1980. She died at a nursing home in Wyckoff, New Jersey, on November 30, 2003.

Tim J. Watts

See also: Celebrity Culture; Leisure and Recreation.

Further Reading

Adler, David A., and Terry Widener. *America's Champion Swimmer: Gertrude Ederle.* San Diego, CA: Harcourt, 2000.

Besford, Pat. *Encyclopedia of Swimming.* New York: St. Martin's, 1971.

Condon, Robert J. *Great Women Athletes of the 20th Century.* Jefferson, NC: McFarland, 1991.

Guttmann, Allen. *Women's Sports: A History.* New York: Columbia University Press, 1991.

Woolum, Janet. *Outstanding Women Athletes: Who They Are and How They Influenced Sports in America.* Phoenix, AZ: Oryx, 1992.

Education, Elementary and Secondary

From 1918 to 1929, education in America underwent changes that would prove influential for decades to come. Both the student population and the teacher workforce changed dramatically after World War I, with an influx of immigrants and the urbanization and industrialization of the nation as a whole. Progressive educational thinking in this era gave rise to two lasting developments: the comprehensive high school and the junior high school.

Societal Changes

By the beginning of the twentieth century, elementary education had become an established norm for the majority of Americans. In 1900, nearly 17 million students were attending elementary school, well over 70 percent of the age-group. At the same time, only 600,000 were attending secondary school. From 1900 to 1930, the percentage of seventeen-year-olds attending high school rose from 6 percent to almost 30 percent, the latter representing almost 5 million students.

In the early part of the century, 25 percent of Americans lived in the nation's seven largest cities, immigration had increased dramatically, and the industrial economy had expanded, as had American power in the world. These societal changes led to concerns about the ability of American workers to be successful in the new economy, the role of citizens in an urbanized society, and the place of American power in the world. One response was the modern K–12 school system, which would educate citizens to be part of a modern workforce.

This system would have less effect on blacks, Hispanics, and Native Americans, whose schools tended to suffer from shorter terms, fewer supplies, and lower teacher pay. During the 1920s, fewer than 5 percent of high school–aged blacks attended school. Young women attended in much higher numbers than in the past, however: 60 percent of public high school graduates in the 1920s were female.

Teacher Workforce

Women increasingly dominated the teaching profession. Whereas 30 percent of teachers had been men in 1900, that figure dropped to approximately 15 percent in the 1920s. At the same time, the sheer number of teachers increased rapidly—more than doubling from approximately 423,000 teachers in the first decade of the 1900s to 854,000 by the end of the 1920s. Teacher salaries also grew dramatically during this period (even adjusted for inflation). The average annual salary for a teacher was $325 in 1900, rising to $1,420 by the end of the 1920s.

The need for teachers in the new junior and senior high schools, the growth of the national economy, and the expansion of teacher unions all contributed to the increased number of teachers and higher teacher salaries. Because the new school system was based on the hierarchical model of organization, unions were a natural outcome, as teachers, like industrial workers, came to see the need for a collective voice in bargaining for their own interests. In addition, teachers began to recognize their increasing power and influence in the educational system. During the course of the 1920s, the American Federation of Teachers (AFT) and the National Education Association (NEA) solidified their positions as the nation's two largest teacher organizations.

Progressive Movement

In 1892, a group of ten college presidents met to consider the preparation for students entering American colleges and made two recommendations. First, the Committee of Ten recommended that schools focus on teaching basic learning skills rather than students' rote recitation of facts. Second, the committee recommended that all high school students complete a standard curriculum including Greek, Latin, English, a modern language, mathematics, science, natural history, history, and geography. These two recommendations helped solidify the curriculum of the modern American comprehensive high school, whereby all students follow a standardized, college-preparatory set of courses.

Over time, the thinking changed about what high schools should provide. In 1918, educator Clarence Kingsley and the NEA, which he headed, published a report titled *The Cardinal Principles of Secondary Education,* which established a number of essential goals for American secondary education: teaching students health, basic academic skills, how to develop and live worthy home lives, a vocation, citizenship, how to use leisure time, and character development. These goals were set to prepare students for a productive adult life as workers within the new economy, as members of a family and larger community, and as citizens within the larger social order. John Dewey, a leading educational theorist and professor at Columbia Teachers College in New York, articulated a progressive philosophy, arguing that the student's needs and experience should be the focus of education in order to prepare the student to be a productive member of society.

Prior to 1918, the focus of American education policy had been on the development of an elementary system spanning the early portions of a student's education, from kindergarten through the eighth grade. In 1920, the average American completed 8.2 grades of education. But the new approach focused on the development of a high school system that could provide all Americans with a general education, prepare the majority of students for a vocation, prepare a minority of students for college, and act as an agency of civic, social, and personal development. In short, the modern comprehensive high school resulted from a combination of the *Cardinal Principles* and the philosophy of progressivism.

Comprehensive High School and Junior High School

The trend toward comprehensive high schools was primarily a grassroots movement in American education. Urbanization and industrialization required specialization of occupations, professions, and careers, and the high school was the main institution to provide the basic educational foundation on which specialized skills could be built. Between 1900 and 1930, a new secondary school was built on the average of nearly one per day, while local communities continued to finance well over 80 percent of all educational costs. In 1920, total expenditures for public schools were approximately $1 billion; by 1930, expenditures had more than doubled, to $2.3 billion, while state and federal funding remained consistently near 17 percent.

Attendance at the high school level grew from 1.7 million before World War I, to 2.4 million after the war, to 4.4 million by the stock market crash in 1929. The majority of the growth took place in public education. In 1920, some 231,000 high school graduates were from public schools, and 80,000 were from private institutions. By 1929, the total number of public high school graduates had risen to 592,000, while the number of graduates from private high schools had fallen to 75,000.

Another enduring legacy of the period was the use of educational testing. During World War I, the American military had used intelligence testing to identify capable candidates for officer training school.

After the war, testing companies began to focus on identifying promising students. On the basis of test scores, schools could place students in tracks that would allow them to maximize their talents and aptitudes—an approach very much in keeping with the philosophy of progressivism. Industrialists especially endorsed the testing movement, as they wanted schools to be more successful at producing the skilled workers and managers needed in a diverse industrial economy. Nearly 75 percent of high school graduates moved directly from the tracks they followed in school into corresponding fields of employment.

In an effort to assist students in making educational and employment choices, schools began to provide guidance counselors, vocational training, and a nonclassical curriculum. Using students' test results, guidance counselors helped students choose the best educational track for their aptitudes and interests. Vocational training grew dramatically with the Smith-Hughes Act of 1918, the first piece of educational legislation in America with a specific focus on job training.

The emergence of the comprehensive high school also made the immediately preceding grades more crucial. Industrialists and progressives proposed another level of vocational training that would take place in the seventh and eighth grades. Many educators also encouraged the creation of junior high schools in order to better prepare students for entry into high school. College administrators argued that elementary schools focused on adolescent development while lowering academic standards for students throughout the system. They proposed a separation of children and adolescents around the age of twelve, at which point they would graduate them from elementary school to junior high school. By the end of the 1920s, there were 1,842 junior high schools and 3,227 junior-senior high school combinations.

Erik P. Ellefsen and Jon M. Eckert

See also: Children and Child Rearing; Dewey, John; Education, Higher.

Further Reading

Edwards, Virginia B., ed. *Lessons of a Century: A Nation's Schools Come of Age.* Bethesda, MD: Editorial Projects in Education, 2000.

Gutek, Gerald L. *Education and Schooling in America.* 2nd ed. Englewood Cliffs, NJ: Prentice Hall, 1988.

Rury, John L. *Education and Social Change: Themes in the History of American Schooling.* 2nd ed. Mahwah, NJ: Lawrence Erlbaum, 2005.

Snyder, Thomas D. *120 Years of American Education: A Statistical Portrait.* Washington, DC: Center for Education Statistics, 1993.

Tyack, David. *The One Best System: A History of American Urban Education.* Cambridge, MA: Harvard University Press, 1974.

Urban, Wayne, and Jennings Wagoner, Jr. *American Education: A History.* Boston: McGraw-Hill, 1996.

Education, Higher

While the popular image of college life in the Jazz Age is that of carefree students bundled in raccoon coats and rooting for their alma mater's football team, the era was actually a critical period in the development of modern America's system of higher education. Colleges continued the shift, begun in the early 1900s, away from a traditional curriculum based on the classics to one more oriented toward the needs of business, the professions, and government. Parents, educators, the business community, and students themselves tended to see college as less a retreat from society than a way to prepare for a professional career. The Jazz Age also witnessed a dramatic expansion in American higher education, both in the faculty and number of departments at colleges and universities and in their overall enrollment. Approximately 600,000 undergraduates attended college and university in the 1919–1920 academic year, rising to 900,000 by 1925–1926, and 1.1 million by decade's end.

Impact of World War I

World War I was a catalyst of change in higher education. Its immediate effect was to lower enrollment, as young men of college age either entered the military or took jobs in the full-employment economy produced by war orders from Europe and the U.S. government. Enrollment declined from roughly 500,000 in 1914 to about 400,000 in 1917. However, the war nurtured the idea of the importance of higher education, spurring enrollment in the postwar era.

World War I created a proliferation of government agencies that required trained professionals and managers, thereby increasing both the need and the perceived value of a college education. As Dartmouth College president Ernest M. Hopkins argued in 1917, "There ought to be a conviction aroused which should amount to propaganda that every man who is qualified to enter an institution of higher education should do so, and that the young men and women of the country should understand that a stronger argument exists for such a course this year than ever before." With the end of the war came the recognition that higher education would also play a major role in fashioning the peace. For example, some 2,000 studies, largely the work of professors and other scholars, were produced for the Paris Peace Conference.

Impact of Big Business

American society in the 1920s reinforced the ideas that higher education was critical to economic development, that a college degree represented the single most important asset a young person could have in establishing a career, and that the curriculum and focus of higher education had to become more professionally oriented. As in so many other aspects of American life during the Jazz Age, business was a driving force behind these new ideas. As corporations got bigger—an unprecedented wave of business mergers took place in the 1920s—the need for a professional managerial class became more evident. The businesses in the late nineteenth century, which had been run as the owners' personal enterprises, gave way to multifaceted organizations overseen by more professionally oriented boards of directors.

Nowhere was this more evident than in the automobile industry. At the Ford Motor Company, founder Henry Ford continued to hold the reins of power, believing that administration, marketing, and research could be kept to a minimum. But at rival General Motors, president Alfred Sloan developed a sophisticated managerial system that emphasized strategic and long-term planning. Partly as a result of this managerial revolution, GM's market share rose from 19 percent in 1924 to 43 percent by 1929, overtaking Ford as the nation's leading automaker.

As economists looked to the postwar economy in 1919, they estimated that there would be a need for no less than 600,000 new managers in the coming decade. This triggered a demand for business education. Between 1919 and 1924, 117 new business programs were set up at American colleges and universities; the number of business degrees granted rose from less than 800 in 1916 to nearly 1,400 in 1920 and nearly 5,500 in 1928.

Business also produced a growing need for professionally trained engineers and scientists, as the number of industrial laboratories in the United States

increased from about 300 in 1918 to 2,300 in 1940; the ranks of those doing research in the business sector soared from about 1,200 to 27,000. To fill these positions, businesses increasingly turned to colleges and universities. Whereas just fifty companies asked to be listed with Stanford University's vocational guidance committee before the war, the figure rose to 400 by 1922. College placement services became an increasingly important part of what institutions of higher education could offer students and businesses. While virtually no colleges or universities had placement programs in 1900, nearly 50 percent of large universities had them a quarter-century later.

Changing Curricula

Colleges and universities responded to the changing needs of American society by altering their curricula. Programs became more diverse, requiring all students to take classes in the sciences, the arts, the humanities, and especially the social sciences. This broadening of the traditional liberal arts programs was partly inspired by pedagogical theorist and philosopher John Dewey, who argued that institutions of higher learning should combine both practical and cultural education, so as to avoid strictly vocational training as well as the genteel dilettantism of nineteenth-century higher education. This, Dewey contended, would meet not only the needs of students, who would become fulfilled human beings, but also society at large, which would gain a well-rounded citizenry.

Not all social critics, however, were optimistic about the direction of higher education in the 1920s. Particularly on the Left, critics worried that big business was having too much influence in the shaping of a utilitarian curriculum designed to fill professional and managerial ranks. The title of Upton Sinclair's 1923 critique of modern education, *The Goose Step,* captured this concern.

Even as higher education was becoming more practically oriented and enrollment was expanding, elitism continued to plague many American colleges and universities. Most college students in the 1920s were the sons of the middle and upper classes. A survey of colleges in the 1923–1924 academic year found that more than half of all students were the offspring of managers, professionals, or businesspeople, while these represented less than 20 percent of the working population. And while women represented roughly 40 percent of undergraduate enrollment in the 1920s, few were represented in professional schools outside of education and nursing.

At many colleges, ethnic and racial minorities were subject to discrimination and even quotas that limited their enrollment. While Jews made up 80 percent of the student body at egalitarian City College of New York in 1919, they constituted just 20 percent at private Columbia University down the street. This was only partly due to discrimination, however. At a time when most first-generation Jewish immigrant families remained in the working class, public schools charged an affordable $60 tuition a year on average in the 1920s, while private schools asked a more prohibitive $400 and offered little in the way of financial aid. African Americans were virtually unseen on most campuses. Only about 1,000 attended integrated colleges and universities over the course of the 1920s. Enrollment at black colleges, meanwhile, increased from just over 2,100 in 1917 to nearly 14,000 in 1927.

Despite these flaws, the Jazz Age was a time of increasing professionalization and democratization in America's system of higher education. Less focused on the classics, modern curricula included a broad array of courses in the social and hard sciences. A college education was considered a key ingredient to economic and social advancement for hundreds of thousands of young Americans, an idea that would be realized on a vastly expanded scale in the wake of World War II.

James Ciment

See also: Dewey, John; Education, Elementary and Secondary; Youth.

Further Reading

Levine, David O. *The American College and the Culture of Aspiration, 1915–1940.* Ithaca, NY: Cornell University Press, 1986.

Thompson, Jo Ann Gerdeman. *The Modern Idea of the University.* New York: P. Lang, 1984.

Election of 1918

Woodrow Wilson and the Democrats had gained control of the presidency and Congress in the election of 1912, and Wilson had retained control in 1916 by running on a platform of peace and progressivism. In the fall of 1918, as the United States neared its midterm congressional elections, Wilson was heading to Paris to negotiate the treaties to end World War I. The foundation of the peace would be his Fourteen Points, the centerpiece of which was a League of Nations to help prevent future conflicts.

Wilson himself was to head the delegation and he did not invite any notable Republicans from the Senate or House to join the group. As he was leaving for Paris in October, he made an appeal to voters in the upcoming election: "If you have approved of my leadership and wish me to continue to be your unembarrassed spokesman in affairs at home and abroad, I earnestly beg that you will express yourself unmistakenly to that effect by returning a Democratic majority to both the Senate and House of Representatives."

Wilson threw down the gauntlet, and the Republicans picked it up. They especially attacked the idea of a League of Nations, arguing that it might compromise America's sovereignty. Wilson envisioned an international body with enforcement powers, which the Republicans contended would mean ongoing involvement in world affairs and the possibility of League leadership forcing America to fight a war. Both prospects were causes of concern to many Americans. While the GOP attacked Wilson and his agenda and the voting public expressed increasing concern, the president was in Paris involved in difficult negotiations to secure the peace and the League organization he so badly wanted.

There were, to be sure, other issues. The electoral coalition established by Wilson in 1912 had slipped in 1916 and continued to decline thereafter. The administration had agreed to legislation that favored Southern cotton over Midwestern wheat and paid for it at the polls. In heavy wheat-farming areas, where the price per bushel had fallen from $3.40 in spring 1917 to the legislated price of $2.20, the Democrats lost twenty-three districts to Republicans. And there were issues as well with wool farmers, cattle ranchers, and railroad rates for shipping grain. Thus, in addition to the matter of the League, the Midwest voted its displeasure with Southern control of agricultural policy. Indeed, Wilson had initially appointed five cabinet members from the South and four from the rest of the country.

Typically, the party not holding the presidency gains in off-year elections (when there is no presidential election), and true to form, the Republicans regained control of the Senate in 1918 by 49–47, a pickup of six seats, and strengthened their control of the House of Representatives by 240–190, gaining twenty-one seats. These results, more dramatic than usual, were an explicit and resounding defeat for

Wilson, for the last vestiges of progressivism operating abroad ("to make the world safe for democracy"), and for American participation in a League of Nations. They also represented a sectional defeat for a Southern-dominated Democratic Party in the Midwest, although Democratic candidates ran well in the Northeast, South, and West.

Given the outcome of the 1918 election, Republicans looked forward eagerly and Democrats somewhat glumly to the national elections in 1920. The Democratic coalition appeared to be collapsing, and the Republican Party was constructing a new coalition of business and social conservatives that would let it retain power for many years.

Charles M. Dobbs

See also: Democratic Party; Republican Party; Socialism and the Socialist Party of America; Wilson, Woodrow.

Further Reading

Burner, David. *The Politics of Provincialism: The Democratic Party in Transition, 1918–1932.* New York: Alfred A. Knopf, 1968.

Clements, Kendrick A. *The Presidency of Woodrow Wilson.* Lawrence: University Press of Kansas, 1992.

Cooper, John Milton. *Breaking the Heart of the World: Woodrow Wilson and the Fight for the League of Nations.* New York: Cambridge University Press, 2001.

Ferrell, Robert H. *Woodrow Wilson and World War I, 1917–1921.* New York: Harper & Row, 1985.

Election of 1920

The election of 1920 was a referendum on the worldview of outgoing President Woodrow Wilson. The Democratic candidate nominated to succeed Wilson was Governor James Cox of Ohio. Wilson, who had suffered both a debilitating stroke the previous October and the refusal of Congress to endorse the Treaty of Versailles in November, wanted the campaign to be a national referendum on his internationalist views and cherished League of Nations. Instead, voters overwhelmingly opted for the "return to normalcy" proposed by the Republican candidate, Senator Warren G. Harding of Ohio. It was the promise of a vague Americanism and a return to an isolationism that likely never existed, but it struck the right chord with traditional mainstream voting blocs.

The Republicans had held their nominating convention in Chicago in early June. There were eleven serious candidates at the outset, and after eight ballots, none of the three front-runners—General Leonard Wood, Senator Hiram Johnson of California,

A suffragist holds a sign urging women to participate in the 1920 national election, the first in which all American women could vote. *(APA/Hulton Archive/Getty Images)*

and Governor Frank Lowden of Illinois—could gain a majority. Harding emerged as the front-runner on the next ballot and won a majority on the tenth ballot to become the Republican standard-bearer. Although Harding had not authored any significant legislation in the Senate and had made few waves in national politics, GOP bosses finally selected him because he looked like a president and promised that there were no scandals in his background. (Harding had failed to disclose his extramarital affairs and a child born outside of marriage.) It also seemed that Harding might appeal to women, a newly enfranchised class of voters. As his running mate, the Republicans selected the well-regarded Massachusetts Governor Calvin Coolidge, who had gained national recognition for his firm intervention in the Boston police strike of 1919.

At the Democratic convention in San Francisco in late June, fourteen candidates initially were in the running, and another seven entered once the balloting began. For thirty-seven ballots, none of the three front-runners—former Treasury Secretary William Gibbs McAdoo, Attorney General A. Mitchell Palmer, and Ohio Governor James Cox—could distance himself from the others. All three represented key factions in the Democratic Party as well as fault lines. On the thirty-eighth ballot, Palmer finally released his delegates, most of whom gravitated to Cox. The Ohio governor gained a majority of votes on the forty-third ballot and officially won the nomination on the forty-fourth. To help assuage supporters of President Wilson, Cox selected Franklin D. Roosevelt of New York, a Wilsonian progressive and assistant secretary of the navy, as his running mate.

Cox held positions that were not that different from those held by Harding. Cox was mildly in favor of the League of Nations, mildly against prohibiting the consumption of alcohol, and mildly for reform. He and Roosevelt campaigned vigorously, calling for government help in the development of natural resources and education, and in assistance for farmers and industrial workers. But Cox was running too soon, before many recent working-class immigrants, such as Italian Americans and Polish Americans (who were a natural constituency of the Democratic Party and would become the bulwark of Roosevelt's New Deal coalition in the 1930s) began voting in large numbers. Cox was also hampered by the shadow of Woodrow Wilson and his insistence on making the election a referendum on joining the League of Nations.

Harding ran in an older style. He was well financed and chose to campaign almost exclusively from the front porch of his home in Marion, Ohio, where various groups of Republican voters came out to see him. He spoke in a soothing tone to older-stock Americans, who identified with his view of life, work, religion, and politics. He promised no new progressive crusades at home and no entangling commitments abroad; instead, he pledged a "return to normalcy."

Harding won a resounding victory, with 16 million votes to 9 million for Cox. In the electoral college, Harding won 404 votes to Cox's 127. In Congress, Republican candidates replicated the Harding victory, winding up with 301 seats in the House of Representatives and 59 seats in the Senate. Indeed, Cox and Roosevelt ran well only in the South, a long-standing Democratic stronghold.

Harding's victory signaled, at least for a time, the end of the Progressive movement in American politics and a rejection of international entanglements. The Republican coalition was to prove shaky, however, and the Democratic Party would gradually begin finding a voice that appealed to ethnic groups and working-class people in burgeoning cities of the North while holding on to the "Solid South."

Charles M. Dobbs

See also: Democratic Party; Harding, Warren G.; League of Nations; McAdoo, William G.; Republican Party; Socialism and the Socialist Party of America.

Further Reading

Burner, David. *The Politics of Provincialism: The Democratic Party in Transition, 1918–1932.* New York: Alfred A. Knopf, 1967.

Carter, Paul A. *The Twenties in America.* Arlington Heights, IL: Harlan Davidson, 1975.

Goldberg, David J. *Discontented America: The United States in the 1920s.* Baltimore: Johns Hopkins University Press, 1999.

Hicks, John D. *Republican Ascendancy, 1921–1933.* New York: Harper & Row, 1960.

McCoy, Donald R. *Coming of Age: The United States During the 1920s and 1930s.* Baltimore: Penguin, 1973.

Election of 1922

As in many midterm elections when one party controls both the White House and Capitol Hill, the 1922 congressional election offered voters a chance to express their disapproval with the party in power. And the electorate did just that, though not enough to entirely undo the large majorities the Republicans had won in both houses in the pivotal election of 1920. There was a widespread feeling that Congress had done little to address the nation's problems, most especially concerning the brief but sharp recession of 1921–1922. But the election was also about something bigger and more long-term. The gains the Democrats made in 1922 demonstrated that they were winning a new base in urban America, especially among the growing numbers of immigrants and their offspring, who were just beginning to vote in large numbers.

Republican strength in Congress following the 1920 election belied very real weaknesses. The Republican-Democratic split was 59–37 in the Senate and 301–131 in the House, giving Republicans control of the legislative agenda. President Warren G. Harding was a passive executive, believing that legislation should originate in Congress. But the Republicans in Congress were neither unified nor well led, and they could point to few successes beyond tax cuts for the wealthy and corporations and higher tariffs on imported goods. While manufacturers loved the latter, many Americans—both urban and rural—resented the higher prices on foreign goods (as well as higher prices on American goods that faced less foreign competition). Farmers had their own concerns, as foreign countries retaliated with their own tariffs on American farm exports, reducing U.S. farmers' access to foreign markets and thus depressing crop prices, which had already declined significantly from their World War I highs.

The Republican landslide of 1920 had, paradoxically, made Republicans more vulnerable. In the electorate's resounding rejection of President Woodrow Wilson's policies in 1920, many Republican congressional candidates had won office in districts that were traditionally Democratic. In 1922, these Republicans had nothing to run on—neither legislative accomplishment nor party loyalty.

More important, perhaps, though not as obvious at first glance, was the increasing Democratic control of big cities (with populations greater than 150,000) and the party's ability to build successful coalitions among union members, ethnic minorities, and others. Since 1894, most big-city districts had gone to Republican candidates in congressional elections. But that long era of dominance appeared to be coming to an end. The 1922 election was the first step toward building a new and lasting coalition to replace the one that Wilson had built largely on progressivism and peace, a process that would be completed with the Great Depression election of 1932.

In the Midwest and West, some districts that had gone Republican in the great tide of 1920 returned to the Democratic fold. The Republican-Democratic split in the House narrowed to 225–207 (five seats went to third-party candidates). This reduction in Republican numbers was a major turnaround just two years after one of the greatest Republican landslides in American history. In the Senate, Democrats gained six seats, also a major shift given that, in any election, only one-third of all Senate seats are contested. As a result, the Republican-Democratic split was whittled down to 53–42 seats (one seat went to a third-party candidate).

What made the Democratic gains more impressive was that they were garnered despite electoral odds that favored their opponents. Many Republican-controlled state legislatures had refused to redraw districts based on new population figures from the 1920 census, although redistricting is traditionally done in American politics every ten years. If the legislatures had redrawn districts, urban districts would have been

allocated greater weight. And because Democrats were making gains in urban areas, they would have had greater electoral strength and greater numbers in the Congress that convened in 1923. However, the congressional district maps drawn in 1911 after the 1910 census would remain in effect until 1932, when districts were finally redrawn to reflect the broad shift of population from rural areas to big cities.

Charles M. Dobbs and James Ciment

See also: Democratic Party; Republican Party.

Further Reading

Allen, Frederick Lewis. *Only Yesterday: An Informal History of the 1920s.* New York: John Wiley, 1931.

Burner, David. *The Politics of Provincialism: The Democratic Party in Transition, 1918–1932.* New York: Alfred A. Knopf, 1968.

Hicks, John D. *Republican Ascendancy, 1921–1933.* New York: Harper & Row, 1960.

McCoy, Donald R. *Coming of Age: The United States During the 1920s and 1930s.* Baltimore: Penguin, 1973.

Election of 1924

President Calvin Coolidge had been in office only fifteen months when the 1924 election was held. Formerly the vice president, he had come to power upon the death of President Warren G. Harding in August 1923. Although Harding was popular at his death, his administration was mired in a series of scandals referred to as "Teapot Dome," after a naval oil reserve in Wyoming that was sold off to friends of Secretary of the Interior Albert Fall in exchange for unsecured, interest-free loans.

A taciturn New Englander with a reputation for personal integrity, Coolidge was never implicated in Teapot Dome or the other Harding administration scandals being investigated in the months leading up to the election. Also to his credit, Coolidge was presiding over a nation that was enjoying a thriving economy. Outside the agricultural sector, which remained depressed throughout the decade, the nation's economy was booming, unemployment was low, and real wages were rising across the board.

Coolidge used his advantages skillfully. His campaign staff perfected the art of photo opportunities and press conferences to put the popular Coolidge before the American people as much as possible. There was no question that he would be the nominee, and he won on the first ballot at the Republican Party convention in Cleveland by an overwhelming 1,209 to 44 votes. He then pushed to make sure that his own political beliefs, including fiscal probity, mild internationalism—he advocated U.S. participation in the new world court—and limited social reforms, such as a federal anti-lynching law, were incorporated into the party platform. The flamboyant Charles G. Dawes—Chicago lawyer, banker, first director of the Bureau of the Budget, and author of the Dawes Plan to restructure Europe's World War I debt to American financial institutions—was nominated for vice president, after the former governor of Illinois, Frank Lowden, declined.

The unity of the Republicans was especially striking in comparison to what went on at the Democratic convention in New York City's Madison Square Garden, a contentious gathering where delegates were divided over the role of the racist and anti-immigrant Ku Klux Klan in the party. In 1924, the Klan was at the height of its popularity, with as many as 5 million members throughout the country. At the convention, anti-Klan delegates were opposed by Klan supporters and delegates who did not particularly like the Klan but wanted to avoid the divisive issue of Klan influence. The party platform that was eventually agreed upon did not expressly condemn the Klan. Instead, it placed a major focus on Republican scandals and called for a stronger internationalism than that offered by the Republicans, including the old Wilsonian idea of U.S. participation in the League of Nations.

But the Klan issue could not be put to rest. Anti-Klan delegates united behind Governor Alfred E. Smith of New York, and pro-Klan forces supported William Gibbs McAdoo, a former secretary of the treasury who was the son-in-law of former President Woodrow Wilson. When it became clear after 102 ballots that neither candidate could secure the necessary two-thirds majority, the convention nominated John W. Davis, a New York lawyer who had served as a West Virginia congressman, solicitor general, and ambassador to Great Britain. Many Democratic leaders hoped that the conservative Davis could draw probusiness votes away from the business-friendly Coolidge. Governor Charles W. Bryan of Nebraska, the brother of former populist Democratic presidential candidate William Jennings Bryan, was nominated for vice president. The exhausted Democrats finally adjourned after sixteen days of infighting.

Meanwhile, the Progressive Party, a powerful third party in the previous decade, persuaded an aging Senator Robert M. La Follette of Wisconsin to accept its presidential nomination on a ticket with Senator Burton Wheeler of Montana. Despite his advanced years, La Follette found the energy to mount an aggressive campaign and condemned the administration's conservative labor and farm policies. He also called for the nationalization of the railroads and urged judicial reforms. Angered over court injunctions against strikers and conservative Supreme Court decisions finding prolabor laws unconstitutional, La Follette called for the direct election of federal judges, the barring of lower federal courts from finding acts of Congress unconstitutional, and the empowering of Congress to overrule rulings of the Supreme Court.

As for the campaign, the taciturn Coolidge mostly stayed in Washington; he was expected to win an easy victory, and he and his wife were in mourning over the recent death of their sixteen-year-old son. Eventually the president defended the federal court system against La Follette's proposed judicial reforms in speeches delivered in nearby Baltimore. He also spoke at Howard University in Washington, D.C., and denounced the Klan's "propaganda of prejudice and hatred." Editorial pages and cartoons presented the president as a champion of the rule of law and La Follette as an advocate of anarchy. Yet the most important issue in Coolidge's favor was the strong economy, or "Coolidge prosperity," as it was called. The Democratic Davis's Wall Street connections alienated many farm and labor organizations, and his attacks on Harding-era scandals and administration policies benefiting "the privileged classes" failed to draw much interest. Most voters seemed to want to follow the advice of the comforting Republican slogan "Keep Cool with Coolidge."

The size of the president's landslide in the election surprised even his most enthusiastic supporters. Coolidge garnered roughly 15 million votes to Davis's 8 million and La Follette's 4 million. As for the electoral college, Coolidge received 382 votes, Davis 136. La Follette won the 13 electoral votes of his home state of Wisconsin. Republican candidates for Congress benefited significantly from Coolidge's strong showing, gaining twenty-two seats in the House for a majority of 247–183 (five seats were held by third-party candidates) and five seats in the Senate for a majority of 54–41 (with one third-party member), thereby reversing Democratic gains in the 1922 midterm election.

Russell Fowler and James Ciment

See also: Coolidge, Calvin; Davis, John W.; Democratic Party; La Follette, Robert; Progressivism; Republican Party.

Further Reading

Boller, Paul F., Jr. *Presidential Campaigns.* New York: Oxford University Press, 1984.

Eaton, Herbert. *Presidential Timber: A History of Nominating Conventions, 1868–1960.* New York: Free Press of Glencoe, 1964.

Lorant, Stefan. *The Glorious Burden: The History of the Presidency and Presidential Elections from George Washington to James Earl Carter, Jr.* Lenox, MA: Authors Edition, 1976.

Election of 1926

The election of 1926 marked an important transition between the Republican dominance of the early 1920s and the rise of Franklin D. Roosevelt's Democratic base in the 1932 elections. Although the GOP retained control of both the Senate and the House in this off-year election, the Democrats made key gains, indicating the party's growing new appeal to urban and white ethnic voters.

In the Senate, Republicans held control by the slimmest of majorities: 48 Republicans, 47 Democrats, and 1 Farmer-Labor Party member, who frequently would vote with the Democrats. Tied votes would be broken by Vice President Charles Dawes, who served as president of the Senate. This closely divided outcome reflected, in part, the significant swing of the pendulum from the election of 1920, when Warren G. Harding's coattails helped bring many Republicans into the Senate from states that traditionally had elected Democrats.

Six years later, these first-termers were running for reelection, and the issues that had helped propel Harding—against the League of Nations, for Prohibition and a return to "normalcy"—had receded into the background. Moreover, of thirty-four Senate seats being contested, Republicans held twenty-seven, Democrats held seven, and all seven were from Southern states that, in the 1920s, were solidly Democratic. Political experts at the time noted that at least eighteen of the twenty-seven Republican-held Senate seats were vulnerable, and that the states these senators represented had a long history of electing Democrats.

Other outcomes were more mixed. The Republicans retained control of the House of Representatives by 238–194 (three seats went to third-party candidates), a considerably smaller majority than the GOP had enjoyed after the election of 1920. Moreover, the Democrats made gains in big cities. As more and more immigrants from East-ern and Southeastern Europe became citizens and as their children reached voting age, it appeared that Democratic candidates would fare increasingly well in America's big cities, reversing Republican control that had lasted many decades. Finally, Republicans held twenty-six governorships and Democrats twenty-two.

What were the national issues that determined the outcome? Republicans generally campaigned on "Coolidge prosperity." The nation was at peace, the economy appeared strong, and Republicans claimed credit for all that had turned out well. President Calvin Coolidge noted that prosperity was the only issue of consequence, and other issues such as Prohibition and the influence of the weakened Ku Klux Klan were in the past. Republican candidates claimed they had kept wages up and prices down and that high protective tariffs had helped farmers and manufacturers and increased American trade overseas.

Democrats were moving to new issues. Many campaigned for lower taxes, to maintain the high tariffs, and in support of relief for farmers. But with steadily increasing fervor, many began to campaign in support of worker unions, which, in the decade before the New Deal, had tenuous legal standing. Democratic candidates in urban areas also campaigned on cultural values—addressing the complex views on Prohibition and drinking, religion, and the role of government in helping the less fortunate. Democrats also attacked the administration as "morally and intellectually bankrupt," subservient to big business, indifferent to farmers' woes, and unfair in overtaxing small incomes. It would take the onset of the Great Depression to convince voters that such a platform was necessary for America.

Charles M. Dobbs

See also: Democratic Party; Republican Party.

Further Reading

Burner, David. *The Politics of Provincialism: The Democratic Party in Transition, 1918–1932.* New York: Alfred A. Knopf, 1968.

Carter, Paul Allen. *The Twenties in America.* Arlington Heights, IL: Harlan Davidson, 1975.

Goldberg, Ronald Allen. *America in the Twenties.* Syracuse, NY: Syracuse University Press, 2003.

Hicks, John D. *Republican Ascendancy, 1921–1933.* New York: Harper & Row, 1960.

McCoy, Donald R. *Coming of Age: The United States Through the 1920s and 1930s.* Baltimore: Penguin, 1973.

Election of 1928

With the Wall Street crash of October 1929 still nearly a year in the future, the landslide 1928 election victory of Republican presidential candidate Herbert Hoover and the continuing Republican majorities in both houses of Congress seemed to portend the ongoing dominance of the party and its conservative probusiness principles. To historians, the election portended the shift to a Democratic majority that would last from the early years of the Great Depression through the end of the 1970s. Not only did the Democrats continue to make gains in urban areas and among white ethnic voters—as they had done since the early 1920s—but, for the first time, they elected just such an urban white ethnic—Governor Alfred Smith of New York—as their presidential standard-bearer. And though they failed to win the presidency or take back Congress, the Democrats continued to build a new coalition of Southern voters and big-city ethnics, union members, and religious minorities.

In August 1927, President Coolidge announced that he did "not choose to run for president in 1928," but it was several months before national Republican figures took the president seriously. Once they did, however, there was little question who their nominee would be. When the Republicans gathered at their national convention in Kansas City in June 1928, they selected Herbert Hoover on the first ballot. A successful businessman and self-made millionaire, Hoover had served as secretary of commerce through both the Harding and Coolidge administrations, making the department an active shaper of federal economic policy. And, if there was one man with whom Americans credited the booming 1920s economy, it was Hoover. At the same time, Hoover was different from his probusiness Republican predecessors, more willing to experiment with progressive ideas on government having a role in directing the economy and providing better lives for ordinary people. Hoover was also viewed as a great humanitarian who, as head of America's relief efforts, helped to feed starving millions in Europe during and after World War I.

The Democrats met in Houston and selected the governor of New York, Al Smith, as the party's presidential nominee. Governor Smith was an effective and experienced politician, but he had several political liabilities. He favored an end to Prohibition even though a majority of Americans wanted it continued,

and he had emerged out of the immigrant neighborhoods of New York City, which many rural and small-town Americans equated with dangerous foreign political ideas, sinful lifestyles, and rampant corruption. Most of all, Smith was the first Roman Catholic to head a major party ticket, and this at a time of resurgent fundamentalism and anti-Catholic prejudice. To help allay voter fears about Smith's religion and urban background—particularly in the critical but heavily Protestant South—the Democrats chose Senator Joseph T. Robinson of Arkansas as the vice-presidential nominee.

Despite their very different backgrounds, Hoover and Smith ran on fundamentally similar platforms on the economy and the role of government. Both the Republican and Democratic parties were committed to reducing national debt and taxes and maintaining high tariffs. The only significant difference was their position on labor: Democrats opposed the anti-union policies of the Republicans, including their support of injunctions to break strikes. Still, the two parties were so similar on basic economic policy that Democrats raised substantial campaign funds from business interests, nearly equaling those raised by Republicans.

The differences between the two presidential candidates had more to do with cultural values. Smith was a New Yorker, and his accent, religion, background as a machine politician, and opposition to Prohibition all strongly affected the race. Fear of the unfamiliar and unknown led many traditional Democratic voters to temporarily switch their party alliance and support Hoover and the Republicans.

Indeed, Hoover won a great victory, with more than 21 million popular votes to Smith's 15 million, and 444 electoral college votes to Smith's 87. Minor parties barely figured in the total for the first time since the early 1900s. Hoover also received more urban votes than any previous Republican presidential candidate, although Smith still won the majority. Hoover's coattails helped Republicans win a 270–164 majority in the House (with one third-party seat), their widest margin since 1920, and a solid majority in the Senate of 56–39 (one seat went to a third-party candidate).

Republican gains were short-lived, however. Most of the voters would return to the Democratic fold in future elections. More important, the Smith candidacy helped build the new Democratic coalition in cities. The party carried the twelve largest cities in the United States, which it had never done previously, and won in 122 Northeastern counties that previously had voted Republican. If a Democratic presidential nominee could build on the gains that Smith made in major cities and regain the South, that individual would likely win the presidential election, especially if the economic prosperity upon which the Republicans built their majorities should disappear.

Charles M. Dobbs

See also: Democratic Party; Hoover, Herbert; Republican Party; Smith, Al.

Further Reading

Burner, David. *The Politics of Provincialism: The Democratic Party in Transition, 1918–1932.* New York: Alfred A. Knopf, 1967.

Fausold, Martin L. *The Presidency of Herbert C. Hoover.* Lawrence: University Press of Kansas, 1985.

Hicks, John D. *Republican Ascendancy, 1921–1933.* New York: Harper & Row, 1960.

Lichtman, Allan J. *Prejudice and the Old Politics: The Presidential Election of 1928.* Chapel Hill: University of North Carolina Press, 1979.

Silva, Ruth C. *Rum, Religion, and Votes: 1928 Reexamined.* University Park: Pennsylvania State University Press, 1962.

Electricity Industry

For the U.S. utilities industries, the Jazz Age represented a period of major growth and transition. After a brief drop in the early 1920s—a result of postwar demobilization and a sharp economic slump—both production and consumption increased dramatically between the end of World War I and the onset of the Great Depression. At the same time, in a period of dramatic consolidation, thousands of local, often municipally owned utilities were privatized or bought out by large national holding companies, some of them little more than speculative ventures.

Expansion

Access to electricity in America more than doubled during the Jazz Age, from fewer than one in three households in 1920 to more than two out of three households by 1930. In urban areas, the percentage was even higher; roughly 85 percent of nonfarm households were wired by the end of the 1920s. In addition, per household use of electricity also went up, requiring large increases in production. The demand for industrial electricity rose as well, as factories continued the conversion from coal- and steam-powered equipment to cleaner, more compact, more efficient

electric motors. In 1914, approximately one-third of all power equipment in U.S. factories was run by electricity; by 1923, the figure had climbed to 60 percent, and by 1927 to 70 percent.

All of this growth required vast increases in electricity production. Between 1919 and 1929, total annual electrical production in the country climbed from 38.9 million kilowatt hours to 97.4 million. Demand for both of the major sources for the production of electric power—water and fossil fuels (coal, oil, and natural gas)—grew significantly. In 1919, hydroelectric power generated 14.6 million kilowatts; in 1929, after a surge of dam building in virtually every part of the country, the figure stood at 34.6 million. For fossil fuels, total power generation shot from 24.3 million kilowatts in 1919 to 62.7 million kilowatts in 1929. Natural gas came into its own as a source of power during the 1920s. While the output from coal climbed modestly from 35.1 million kilowatts in 1919 to 44.9 million in 1929, and as output from fuel oil actually dropped from 11.1 million to 10.1 million kilowatts, the power generated from natural gas soared from 21.4 million kilowatts to 112.7 million.

The increase in production and consumption was made possible in part by technological advances, including more efficient generator designs and more effective means of long-distance electricity transmission. However, what truly made the growth possible were huge investments in infrastructure, up to $750 million annually by the mid-1920s. Given the enormous costs of building this infrastructure—and the inevitable efficiencies of scale in such a capital-intensive industry—corporate consolidation was inevitable.

Holding Companies

From the 1880s through World War I, most electricity in America was generated by local firms. By the early 1920s, however, larger utility companies began to swallow up the smaller ones, and by the middle years of the decade, the consolidation trend was in full swing. This trend coincided with a move toward privatization. During the Progressive Era, public opinion favored government ownership of critical industries and natural monopolies like utilities. But that thinking was reversed in the probusiness climate of the 1920s, which saw hundreds of municipally owned utilities privatized and bought out by major utility companies.

The preferred legal form of ownership for utilities was the holding company, a parent corporation that owned smaller utility concerns in various states. The large holding companies offered advantages: more capital for infrastructure development, more engineering experience, and more expert management. By the end of the decade, the ten largest utility holding companies in America generated roughly three-quarters of the nation's electricity. As the electricity industry became more efficient, the holding companies were able to reduce prices to consumers. Although rates varied by locale, the overall trend in household electricity prices was slightly downward over the course of the 1920s. The big holding companies offered even bigger breaks to major industries, partly out of concern that large factory owners might build their own generating capacity.

Some holding companies were less concerned with efficiency and service and more concerned with sheer size. Many purchased companies in far-flung regions of the country, making it impossible to integrate the systems into a single transmission network. The largest of the holding companies, Insull Industries, owned utilities in twenty-one states. In addition, some of the holding companies, including Insull, were little more than pyramid schemes: the head holding company owned other holding companies, which owned more holding companies, with the levels of ownership sometimes four or five deep.

This allowed for enormous gains to those who owned stock in the companies. As natural monopolies, most utilities were tightly regulated and limited to a specific rate of return, often 7–8 percent. Through sophisticated and sometimes illegal bookkeeping practices, holding companies were able to get around these limits, earning profits of 20, 30, and even 40 percent. Given these potential gains, speculators flocked into the market, creating ever more intricate holding companies. The complicated, sometimes impenetrable corporate structures allowed disreputable owners to make their companies seem more profitable than they were, causing stock prices to rise.

Nobody was more celebrated on Wall Street in the 1920s for making a fortune at this game than Samuel Insull, the man behind Insull Industries. And nobody was more vilified in the 1930s when the holding company pyramids collapsed, costing investors billions. An immigrant from England, Insull went to work in the London office of inventor and electricity magnate Thomas Edison. With Edison, he

founded the Commonwealth Edison electrical utility company in Chicago in the 1880s. Gradually, Insull began to buy out other utilities, creating holding companies on top of holding companies and borrowing heavily to make the next purchase. As the economy was expanding during the 1920s, Insull could take profits from his holding companies to make more purchases. When the economy contracted after the stock market crash of 1929, Insull was unable to pay his creditors, and his empire collapsed. Insull was ultimately found innocent of securities laws violations, but the type of utility holding company pioneered by Insull was outlawed by the Public Utilities Holding Act of 1935.

James Ciment

See also: Appliances, Household; Coal Industry; General Electric; Oil and Oil Industry; Technology.

Further Reading

McDonald, Forrest. *Insull.* Chicago: University of Chicago Press, 1962.
White, W.S., Jr. *American Electric Power: 75 Years of Meeting the Challenge.* New York: Newcomen Society in North America, 1982.

Eliot, T.S. (1888–1965)

An American-born poet, playwright, and literary critic, T.S. Eliot is best known for his poetry—including "The Love Song of J. Alfred Prufrock" (1915), "The Waste Land" (1922), "The Hollow Men" (1925), and *The Four Quartets* (1936–1942). He is considered one of the most important figures in literary modernism.

Thomas Stearns Eliot was born into a prominent St. Louis family on September 26, 1888. His father was a successful businessman. His mother, a teacher, social volunteer, and poet, introduced him to the work of such American intellectuals and literary figures as Ralph Waldo Emerson and Henry David Thoreau. While raised Protestant, Eliot was frequently taken to Catholic Mass by his Irish nanny, his first exposure to a religion he would convert to at the age of thirty-nine.

Eliot attended Smith Academy, a preparatory school connected to St. Louis's Washington University, and later the prestigious Milton Academy outside Boston. Both schools emphasized a classical education, which exposed Eliot to ancient and modern languages. He would later make use of this education in his frequent allusions to classical literature and his use of French and German in his poetry. Eliot earned a B.A. degree from Harvard University, publishing a few of his earliest poems in the college's literary magazine, the *Harvard Advocate*. After attending Merton College, Oxford, in 1914–1915, Eliot studied philosophy as a graduate student at Harvard. Although he finished his dissertation in 1916, he failed to return from Britain to defend it and so never earned his doctoral degree. The dissertation would be published one year before his death as *Knowledge and Experience in the Philosophy of F.H. Bradley* (1965).

By the late 1910s, Eliot was settled into life in London and married to Vivienne Haigh-Wood, an Englishwoman who had been a dancer and governess (the couple would later separate). Like other expatriate American literary and artistic figures, Eliot spent a good deal of time in Paris during the 1920s. While most of the Americans of the Lost Generation eventually returned to the United States, Eliot stayed on in Europe, becoming a British citizen and converting to Catholicism in 1927.

Long before he moved among the literary set in Paris of the 1920s, Eliot had established himself as an acclaimed but provocative literary figure. Most critics consider "The Love Song of J. Alfred Prufrock" from 1915 the first of his many poetic masterpieces. From its first startling line, comparing the evening sky to a "patient etherised upon a table," Eliot distanced himself from the prevailing historicism and romanticism of the English poetry of the day. Rather than rhapsodizing on the sublime beauty of nature, Eliot focused on the boredom and disillusionment of modern civilized life. In the poem, Eliot enters the mind of the eponymous protagonist as he bemoans his own apathy, lack of energy, lost opportunities, and spiritual emptiness. Like other practitioners of the modernist school of literature, Eliot used the stream-of-consciousness technique to capture the thoughts of his protagonist, and he included images of the banalities of modern urban life set against biblical allusions and classical literature.

In 1922, Eliot published his most famous work, "The Waste Land," in the premiere issue of *Criterion*, a small but influential literary quarterly Eliot had launched with his wife. Once again, Eliot returned to the theme of the disillusionment and entropy of modern civilization. Instead of offering a monologue from the mind of a single protagonist, however, "The Waste Land" is told in various voices and literary styles, borrowed from such diverse sources as classical Greek philosophy, conversation overheard on the street, bits of journalistic reportage, Anglican prayers, and music-hall lyrics. Lines of French, German, and Greek are mixed into this modernist tour de force that, in its broken syntax, captures the cacophony of contemporary urban life and, in its wide-ranging and seemingly random literary and cultural allusions, the lack of a defining and unifying culture in modern European civilization.

The disillusioned spirit of "The Waste Land," in lines about a people and society adrift, unanchored from their own past, is thought to be Eliot's response to the horrors of World War I, a common theme in modernist literature. In any case, "The Waste Land" is cited by literary scholars as the defining poem of the modernist sensibility, the lyric counterpart to James Joyce's masterpiece novel, *Ulysses,* also published in 1922.

Eliot's last universally acclaimed masterpiece of the Jazz Age was "The Hollow Men" (1925), another poem about post–World War disillusionment and the spiritual emptiness of modern civilized life, rendered in brutal imagery of decay, destruction, and death. Its closing stanza, an apocalyptic message told in nursery-rhyme doggerel, provides one of the most shocking juxtapositions in English poetry: "This is the way the world ends / This is the way the world ends / This is the way the world ends / Not with a bang but a whimper."

Eliot also stands as one of the most important literary theorists of the twentieth century, helping forge what became known as the "New Criticism," the dominant trend in literary criticism from the 1920s through the 1960s. New Criticism insisted on "close reading" of literary works, focusing on short passages of works in question, analyzing their vocabulary, syntax, and punctuation for deeper meaning, as if each passage were under a microscope. New Criticism also closed out the larger world in which a work had been written, eschewing attempts to understand a work through the author's biography or historical context. Eliot's New Criticism analysis of the seventeenth-century metaphysical poets, such as John Donne, brought them out of the obscurity into which they had fallen by the early twentieth century.

While Eliot's language seemed shocking to many contemporaries and was harshly attacked by critics, he soon became recognized as one of the most influential twentieth-century poets in any language and was awarded the Nobel Prize in Literature in 1948. He died in London on January 4, 1965.

James Ciment

See also: Poetry.

Further Reading

Eliot, T.S. *The Complete Poems and Plays of T.S. Eliot.* New York: Faber, 1969.

Gordon, Lyndall. *T.S. Eliot: An Imperfect Life.* New York: W.W. Norton, 2000.

Williamson, George. *A Reader's Guide to T.S. Eliot: A Poem-by-Poem Analysis.* Syracuse, NY: Syracuse University Press, 1998.

Eugenics

The term *eugenics* (from Greek roots meaning "good birth") was coined in 1883 by the English anthropologist and explorer Francis Galton. A cousin of Charles Darwin, Galton undertook statistical studies to demonstrate the hereditary nature of particular human traits. The eugenics movement in the United States was fed by multiple streams: European thought about heredity, the emerging field of genetics, and progressive health and social legislation. It enjoyed its headiest success in the two decades following World War I but later fell into discredit because of the horrors unleashed by Nazi Germany's massive eugenics campaign.

Large-scale immigration from Eastern and Southern Europe gave rise to widespread fear in the United States of the degeneration of "native" racial stock by the beginning of the twentieth century. Under the influence of the Progressive movement, many states were taking proactive steps to ensure the general health and well-being of their populations; in this context, legislative efforts to protect "racial health" seemed a natural step. In 1896, Connecticut passed laws forbidding marriage with the "feeble-minded," and similar statutes spread throughout the nation.

A major proponent of these measures was biologist Charles B. Davenport, founder of the Station of Experimental Evolution at Cold Spring Harbor, New York. Davenport sought to guide the evolution of flora and fauna through calculated intervention. In 1910, he and partner Henry H. Laughlin launched the Eugenics Record Office, a private research and advocacy center with the goals of assembling information on human genetic traits and promoting the eugenics movement. Davenport and Laughlin argued vigorously for public intervention to protect the

American gene pool from the weak and unfit. Testifying before the House Committee on Immigration and Naturalization in 1920, Laughlin warned of the dangers to American genetic health posed by degenerate elements from abroad.

The Immigration Act of 1924 demonstrated the willingness of Congress to act on the expert testimony of eugenicists. The act's provisions drastically reduced the overall flow of foreigners into the United States and established a hierarchy of those who were able to obtain admission. Asians were excluded outright, and undesirable European groups were limited by a simple formula: annual immigration for a given nationality could not exceed 2 percent of the total number of people from that nation who had been residents of the United States in 1890. Because Northern and Western European groups had dominated immigration before then, the 1924 legislation disproportionately limited immigrants from Eastern and Southern Europe. Their numbers plummeted accordingly.

Some states found these protective measures insufficient. From the beginning of the century, numerous states had practiced the sterilization of "imbeciles" and others considered unfit to reproduce. The 1927 U.S. Supreme Court decision in *Buck v. Bell,* which upheld a Virginia law making sterilization mandatory for the mentally retarded, lent judicial approval to this conduct. In that ruling, Justice Oliver Wendell Holmes, Jr., declared that it was far better for society to "prevent those who are manifestly unfit from continuing their kind" than to execute their "degenerate offspring" for crime, or allow them to starve in their imbecility. In all, some 64,000 Americans would be sterilized through the operation of such laws.

Eric Paras

See also: Americanization; Birth Control; Immigration.

Further Reading

Kevles, Daniel J. *In the Name of Eugenics.* Cambridge, MA: Harvard University Press, 1985.

Schiller, F.C.S. *Social Decay and Eugenical Reform.* London: Constable, 1932.

Europe, Relations with

During the Jazz Age, America's relationship with Europe was complicated: intimate and close, yet distant and suspicious. Politically and strategically, the two were as far apart as their respective shores. In the wake of World War I and the Paris Peace Conference in 1919, the American people and their elected representatives turned away from active involvement in the continent's age-old intrigues and retreated into isolationism. Economically, however, the United States was bound up with Europe in a web of finances, largely concerning the vast debt to American financial institutions accrued by Britain and France during World War I. On the positive side of the ledger, American trade with Europe grew significantly, though not as fast as with other parts of the world. U.S. business also reversed the trend of the previous 150 years by investing more funds in Europe than Europe invested in the United States.

Cultural exchanges between the United States and Europe also tended to flow east rather than west. Jazz Age American culture—largely its popular manifestations, such as films and music—began to have a major impact on European culture and life. At the same time, the traditional flow of people from Europe to America slowed significantly as a result of restrictive U.S. immigration legislation in the first half of the decade. Conversely, there was a new flow of Americans to Europe. A small but significant number of American artists, writers, and musicians established temporary or even permanent residence in Europe—especially in what Americans still considered the cultural capital of the world, Paris.

Background

The United States has always been a nation of nations: peoples and the offspring of peoples from Europe, Africa, Asia, and the Americas. But European culture predominated from the colonial period. Not only do the vast majority of Americans trace their ancestry to Europe, but the nation's political, legal, and economic systems—along with many cultural and social norms—were also largely influenced by the "Old World."

Yet the United States has always had an uneasy relationship with Europe. It broke with Britain in a bloody revolution. And while it got caught up in the European wars of the French Revolution and Napoleonic era, it sought, after 1815, to keep aloof from diplomatic and military entanglements. But European investment in America and purchases of American agricultural products—like cotton—provided critically needed capital that helped the United States develop into the industrial giant it became by the late nineteenth century.

The constant influx of European peoples infused American culture and society with new influences, from foods to political theories. And while Americans began to develop their own literary and musical voices by the mid-nineteenth century, the visual arts in the United States remained largely beholden to Europe until well into the twentieth century.

War and Peace

It can be argued that the reversal of Europe's traditional dominance in its relationship with America began on a single day—April 6, 1917—when the U.S. Congress responded to the pleas of President Woodrow Wilson and declared war on Germany. Albeit reluctantly, the United States entered World War I. It would take nearly a year for the United States to bring its full military and industrial weight to bear in the conflict, but once it did, the country's participation was pivotal, forcing Germany and its Austro-Hungarian and Ottoman allies to sue for peace in November 1918. But even before America entered the war militarily, it had been supplying vast amounts of food and war materiel to the Allies. With their economies crippled by war, Britain and France in particular were forced to borrow $2.3 billion from American financial institutions between 1914 and 1916, an enormous sum for the day.

When the war ended, Britain, France, and other Allies were not shy in expressing their gratitude to America. France, for one, showered medals and honors on U.S. officers and soldiers for saving the country from German occupation. When President Wilson arrived in the French capital for the postwar peace conference in January 1919, he was greeted as a hero by thousands of cheering Parisians. Less warm was his reception from some of Europe's leaders. Wilson had a plan for the postwar world, his famous Fourteen Points. Among other things, they called for arms restrictions, free trade, freedom of the seas, and self-determination for subject peoples. In addition, Wilson urged a nonvindictive settlement with Germany, believing that there would be no peace unless continental Europe's most powerful state was both prosperous and politically integrated with other powers. All of these goals, he hoped, would be realized by a new international institution, the League of Nations.

The Allied leaders at Versailles shared some of Wilson's goals, notably for a League of Nations. They were, however, less enamored with those points that called for a dissolution of empire (particularly upsetting to Britain) and a forgiving attitude toward Germany. France in particular had seen much of its productive northeastern factories and farms destroyed by the fighting and was especially reluctant to accept this proposal. Moreover, Wilson was self-righteous and unbending, lacking flexibility and tact. "How can I talk to a fellow who thinks himself the first man in two thousand years who has known anything about peace on Earth," remarked French Premier Georges Clemenceau. "Wilson imagines that he is a second Messiah."

The American president was forced to compromise. Although he feared that harsh treatment of Germany might turn that nation toward the same radical bolshevism that engulfed Russia, he reluctantly agreed to Allied demands for enormous German reparation payments and a humiliating clause in the peace agreement that blamed Germany for the war. He was also forced to give way on the matter of empire and self-determination, allowing for a system of League of Nations "mandates" by which former German and Ottoman possessions would be turned over to Britain, France, and Japan, with only vague promises of eventual independence. Wilson did all this to secure the linchpin of his vision for the postwar order: the League of Nations. Here he got his way, including Article 10, establishing the principle of collective security of all member states.

Back home, however, most Americans were suspicious of European politics and reluctant to continue America's involvement in world affairs, especially given the compromises Wilson was forced to accept at Versailles. He had originally explained the war to the American public as a crusade for democracy, but the peace treaties seemed like the same old European power politics. The Senate blocked U.S. membership in the League of Nations.

The rejection of League membership was one of several key developments in America's return to isolationism regarding European affairs. Another was Republican Warren G. Harding's overwhelming victory in the 1920 presidential election. A Midwesterner who held to that region's traditional wariness of foreign entanglements, Harding ran on a platform with a strong isolationist plank.

Radicalism and Immigration

America's postwar turning away from Europe was about more than just foreign affairs. If the maneu-

verings at Versailles inspired American disgust at traditional European power politics, the 1917 Bolshevik takeover in Russia had inspired fear of radical European ideologies. The Communists who seized power in Russia denounced capitalism, private property, religion, and what they called "bourgeois democracy." The United States immediately severed ties with the new Soviet Union and, for a time, sent troops in support of anticommunist forces there. At home, communism triggered the Red Scare, a fear that political radicals, largely of European birth, were seeking to foment a revolution in the United States. In response, the federal government launched raids on radical political organizations, arresting thousands of people and deporting several hundred European-born resident aliens and citizens to the Soviet Union in 1919.

The Red Scare contributed to an upsurge in anti-immigrant nativism in the early 1920s, leading to restrictive immigration legislation in 1921 and 1924. The quota system at the heart of the legislation allowed immigration from Northern and Western Europe to continue at roughly the same pace of about 100,000 to 150,000 per year. But newcomers from Southern and Eastern Europe—where most of the foreign radicals were believed to come from—dropped from about 500,000 per year in the 1910s to about 130,000 per year in the 1920s and fewer than 10,000 per year in the 1930s.

Economic Ties

Despite the isolationist trend, business and financial leaders were only too eager to establish closer relations with Europe. General Motors expanded by buying up auto manufacturing firms in Europe, while the fledgling International Telephone and Telegraph Corporation employed tens of thousands of Europeans to run the phone systems it owned there. By the end of the 1920s, U.S. corporations had invested nearly $10 billion in Europe.

Trade between the United States and Europe expanded alongside direct investment, though not as dramatically. Excluding the war years, when American food and materiel poured into Europe at the rate of nearly $5 billion annually, U.S. exports to the continent climbed from $1.48 billion in 1913—the last full year before the war—to $2.34 billion in 1929. Significant as that growth was, it paled next to the increase in U.S. exports to the rest of the world, which climbed from just under $1 billion in 1913 to $2.9 billion in 1929. Whereas Europe took roughly 60 percent of America's exports in 1913, it bought less than 45 percent by 1929. Similarly, imports from Europe climbed from about $900 million in 1913 to $1.3 billion in 1929; however, the overall portion of European products among U.S. imports fell from roughly 50 percent in the former year to less than 33 percent in the latter.

In the 1920s, the United States consistently ran a trade surplus with Europe, which climbed from about $600 million in 1913 to just over $1 billion in 1929. There were several market reasons for this. American industry was highly efficient and competitive, and American products—from Singer sewing machines to Ford automobiles—were quite popular in Europe. But there was a political factor at work as well. Republicans, who had a virtual lock on the federal government in the 1920s, controlling the White House and both houses of Congress, were traditionally the party of protectionism; they favored high tariffs on imported manufactured goods. In 1922, the Fordney-McCumber tariff legislation established some of the highest tariffs in American history. Then, with the coming of the Great Depression, the Republicans passed the even more restrictive Hawley-Smoot Tariff of 1930.

In the nineteenth century, tariffs had served to protect infant American industries from tough foreign competition, particularly from the United Kingdom. By the 1920s, however, the United States was an industrial juggernaut, with highly competitive industries and a large trade surplus. It was also the world's largest creditor nation, with European countries in especially heavy debt to U.S. financial institutions. To pay back these debts, Europe needed to sell products to the United States, but high tariffs made that difficult.

Economic relations between Europe and America in the 1920s were a game of financial musical chairs. France and Britain used German reparations to help them meet their own debt payments to America. But those reparations—combined with French occupation of some of Germany's most productive coal-producing and industrial regions—led to a collapse of the German economy in 1923. To keep German reparations flowing to England and France—allowing them to make payments on their own debts to U.S. financial institutions—the United States extended loans to Germany. In the wake of the Wall Street crash of 1929, however, the outflow of U.S. capital slowed to a trickle, and European economies were dragged down as well.

Cultural Exchange

The millions of American soldiers who descended on Europe during World War I brought more than their guns and a willingness to fight. They came with an optimism that three years of war had sucked out of European society. "America was a good idea," wrote German author Hans Joachim, "it was the land of the future.... In America technology was at the service of human life. Our interest in elevators, radio towers and jazz was expressive of the wish to beat the sword into a plowshare . . . convert the flame thrower into a vacuum cleaner."

Europeans became enamored of American culture in the 1920s, whether in the form of jazz dancer Josephine Baker or the movies produced in Hollywood. As Edward Windsor, the Prince of Wales, remarked, "The film is to America what the flag once was to Britain. By its means Uncle Sam may hope some day, if he be not checked in time, to Americanize the world." Indeed, 95 percent of all films shown in Britain, 70 percent in France, and 60 percent in Germany came from the United States.

While the flood of American cultural output to Europe was new, traditional American deference to European control did not disappear entirely. Drawn by its art and architecture, its café life and food, American tourists traveled to Europe in unprecedented numbers, from an annual flow of about 15,000 immediately following World War I to roughly a quarter of a million by the end of the 1920s. Not only did their $300 million annual spending help alleviate the balance of trade deficit, but it also introduced the latest in European fashion, ideas, and culture throughout America. Although significantly smaller in number, American expatriates—drawn to Europe by its culture as well as its undervalued currency and its legal alcohol—proved an equally important conduit for European ideas and culture into America's consciousness. In Europe, especially Paris, authors such as Ernest Hemingway, Gertrude Stein, and Langston Hughes fused European and American literary traditions into a new modernist sensibility.

It is important to remember that no era stands apart from the flow of history, and that continuities matter as much as change. While America attempted to pull away from Europe in the wake of

World War I, Europe remained more important to the American economy than any other region in the world, just as the politics of Europe could not be entirely ignored by U.S. policy makers. At the same time, European art, music, and literature still held a predominant place in American culture. What made the Jazz Age so pivotal was not that European influences ceased but that the flow of ideas, goods, money, and political influence began to be reversed, with America slowly emerging as the dominant partner in U.S.-European relations.

James Ciment and Rachel Gillett

See also: Dawes Plan (1924); Food Administration, U.S.; Fordney-McCumber Tariff of 1922; Four-Power Treaty (1921); Fourteen Points; Geneva Arms Convention of 1925; Kellogg-Briand Pact (1928); League of Nations; Locarno Treaties (1925); Paris Peace Conference of 1919; Reparations and War Debts; Siberian Intervention; Versailles, Treaty of (1919); Washington Naval Conference (1921–1922); Wilson, Woodrow; Young Plan (1929–1930).

Further Reading

Burk, Kathleen. "The Lineaments of Foreign Policy: The United States and a 'New World Order,' 1919–1939." *Journal of American Studies* 26 (1992): 377–91.

Cohrs, Patrick O. *The Unfinished Peace After World War I: America, Britain and the Stabilisation of Europe, 1919–1932.* Cambridge, UK: Cambridge University Press, 2006.

Costigliola, Frank. *Awkward Dominion: American Political, Economic, and Cultural Relations with Europe, 1919–1933.* Ithaca, NY: Cornell University Press, 1984.

Eckes, Alfred E., Jr., and Thomas W. Zeiler. *Globalization and the American Century.* Cambridge, UK: Cambridge University Press, 2003.

Evangelicals and Evangelical Christianity

Evangelical Christianity in the Jazz Age consisted of ecumenical, somewhat conservative members of mainstream Protestantism. Evangelicals were less conservative than Fundamentalists (enthusiasts of Lyman and Milton Stewart's 1909 text *The Fundamentals*). As theologian Harry Emerson Fosdick noted, "All Fundamentalists are conservatives, but not all conservatives are Fundamentalists."

Some Evangelicals, such as those following the tradition of religious publisher and Moody Bible Institute founder Dwight L. Moody, could exhibit characteristics of modernists in terms of theology. Insofar as they are an identifiable group, the story of Evangelicals in the 1920s is that of Protestants navigating the tempest between the liberal Social Gospel and Fundamentalism.

To Be an Evangelical

In many ways, "Evangelical" is synonymous with "Protestant." Martin Luther saw his separatist movement as an *evangelische Kirke* (evangelical church). The historian Mark Noll asserts that Evangelicals were "an American brand of Protestant Christianity." Another historian, Martin Marty, notes Josiah Strong's 1913 observation of a major split in American Protestantism and argues that the term Evangelical came to denote the private, or individual, Protestantism, in contrast with the public, Social Gospel theology dominant in the Progressive Era.

Evangelicals in the Jazz Age came from nearly all Protestant denominations, including Lutherans, Presbyterians, and Southern Baptists. Despite the absence of any central, authoritative institutional structure for Evangelicals, the historian David Bebbington argues for four common theological traits of the group: (1) *conversionism,* the belief that lives need to be changed [in a personal, private way]; (2) *activism,* the expression of the gospel in effort; (3) *biblicism,* a particular regard for the Bible; and (4) *crucicentrism,* a stress on the sacrifice of Christ on the cross." Evangelicals also tend toward literal interpretations of the Bible, a degree of anti-intellectualism, a focus more on piety than on politics, and premillennialism, or in some cases, dispensational premillennialism (also called dispensationalism).

Premillennialism and dispensationalism both hold that social change ought to be deemphasized in favor of preparing for Jesus Christ's miraculous second coming and thousand-year reign. The world is a "wrecked vessel," the premillennialist Moody once said, and since Christ's reappearance is imminent, the believer ought to concentrate on personal holiness. Moreover, immorality, war, and political disturbances—the upheavals of World War I and modernity—served as proof that the decline was under way and that the second coming was near.

Moody popularized premillennialism in the late nineteenth century. Around the same time, the theologian John Nelson Darby systematized dispensationalism. Darby's system of biblical ages of the world, or dispensations, included a final dispensation that included Moody's premillennial beliefs. Both Moody's and Darby's thinking increasingly influenced conservative Protestants in the early twentieth century.

Billy Sunday

A few well-known celebrity preachers ranked among Evangelicals in this period. One of the most prominent, Billy Sunday, proved adept at evangelizing in the United States. A former professional baseball player, Sunday reached popular heights as a revivalist preacher well before World War I, and he maintained visibility well into the 1920s. In 1914, he tied for eighth place (with Andrew Carnegie) in an *American Magazine* poll that asked "Who is the greatest man in the United States?" In June 1917, nearly 75,000 people listened to Sunday's preaching on the last day of a revival in New York City. In addition to converting people to the "old-time religion," Sunday opposed advocates of the liberal Social Gospel such as theologians Washington Gladden, Francis Peabody, and Walter Rauschenbusch.

Like other Evangelicals, Sunday was a staunch advocate of Prohibition, having preached his famous "Booze Sermon" (formally titled "Get on the Water Wagon") since beginning his speaking career in the mid-1890s. He celebrated the onset of Prohibition in January 1920 by parading a coffin containing "John Barleycorn" through the streets of Norfolk, Virginia. The same year, Sunday entertained the notion of being the Prohibition Party's vice-presidential candidate, sharing a ticket with potential presidential candidate William Jennings Bryan. Sunday was not nominated, and he ended up supporting the Republican nominee, Warren G. Harding.

Even after celebrating his sixtieth birthday in 1922, Sunday remained a formidable Protestant presence, as he continued his preaching crusades. In the Jazz Age, he favored fundamentalism as opposed to modernism, thus favoring the position of William Jennings Bryan in the Scopes trial.

By the end of the 1920s, however, the popularity of Sunday's revivalist evangelism had diminished. In the early 1930s, he used radio broadcasts to bring his revivalist preaching to larger audiences. Yet Sunday's conservative, even fundamentalist positions, as well as his mass appeal, foreshadowed a mix that would make Evangelical television preachers popular in the latter half of the twentieth century.

Evangelical Institutions

Chicago's ecumenical, pan-Protestant Young Men's Christian Association (YMCA) offers an example of an Evangelical institution in the Jazz Age. The Chicago

Old-time religion and newfangled technology came together in the career of Billy Sunday, one of the most popular Evangelical radio preachers of the Jazz Age. *(Pictorial Parade/Hulton Archive/Getty Images)*

YMCA required new members to submit to the "Evangelical Test" (also known as the "Portland Test," established in 1869), which held adherents to beliefs such as biblical infallibility. Billy Sunday, for instance, would have submitted to it when he served as the Chicago YMCA's religious director at the turn of the century.

The Evangelical Test lasted into the middle of the 1920s, when the theologically moderate L. Wilbur Messer served as the Chicago YMCA's general secretary. Messer had already earned his reputation as a moderate when he negotiated the delicate task of separating the YMCA from the conservative Moody Bible Institute before the 1920s, while maintaining the Evangelical Test.

In 1924, the more religiously liberal William J. Parker succeeded Messer. Parker served as an example of Josiah Strong's private Protestantism. During Parker's term, the Chicago YMCA moved away from its religious focus toward a focus on character development. The organization liberalized and secularized in a decade when fundamentalism gained followers, but it also publicly distanced itself from prominent national YMCA member Sherwood Eddy, who supported Socialist teachings. By the end of the 1920s, the Chicago YMCA—perhaps not unlike the nation's other urban YMCAs—essentially became a social service agency for both men and women that only nominally promoted an Evangelical, Protestant Christian message.

Although Evangelical Christianity was not an explicitly organized movement or theology, the category of Evangelical as it is thought of today existed during the Jazz Age. In 1943, Evangelicals would officially set themselves apart from other Protestant denominations at the first meeting of the National Association of Evangelicals in Chicago.

Tim Lacy

See also: Fundamentalism, Christian; McPherson, Aimee Semple; Norris, J. Frank; Protestantism, Mainstream.

Further Reading

Bebbington, David. *Evangelicalism in Modern Britain: A History from the 1730s to the 1980s.* London: Unwin Hyman, 1989.

Bruns, Roger A. *Preacher: Billy Sunday and Big-Time American Evangelism.* New York: W.W. Norton, 1992.

Marsden, George M. *Fundamentalism and American Culture.* 2nd ed. New York: Oxford University Press, 2006.

Marty, Martin E., ed. *Modern American Protestantism and Its World: Historical Articles on Protestantism in American Religious Life.* Vol. 10, *Fundamentalism and Evangelicalism.* New York: K.G. Saur, 1993.

———. *Protestantism in the United States: Righteous Empire.* 2nd ed. New York: Scribner's, 1986.

Expatriates

See Lost Generation

Fads and Stunts

Among the aspects of American life that typified the carefree and exuberant nature of the Jazz Age was the seemingly endless parade of highly publicized fads and crazes during the 1920s. Dozens of amusements and pastimes enjoyed a spectacular but short-lived burst of national popularity before fading from public interest; perhaps hundreds of others gained popularity in particular regions of the country. Meanwhile, Madison Avenue advertising agents and Hollywood studio publicists employed novel, attention-getting publicity stunts to market name-brand products or the latest motion pictures. Millions of Americans during this "Age of Play" eagerly embraced fads and stunts as a way to participate in the nation's vibrant mass culture.

Fads were entertaining to be sure, but participating in them also offered people a forum for public self-expression. Even some of the most ridiculous fads attracted thousands of adherents. Ironically, mass participation enabled ordinary people to conform to the social behavior of others and, at the same time, to distinguish themselves from the crowd. In the new age of bureaucracies, assembly-line labor, and standardized products, during which institutions and machines seemed to be eroding the very possibility of individual accomplishment, fads and stunts offered people opportunities to demonstrate their creativity, talent, and uniqueness. During the 1920s, radio broadcasts, mass-circulation magazines, daily newspapers, and motion picture newsreels glorified these fad participants and marathon record-breakers as icons of robust American individualism.

Daredevils

Several of the most memorable stunts of the 1920s were daredevil feats of courage and stamina. Pilots barnstormed the country in discarded World War I biplanes, thrilling air-show audiences with breathtaking maneuvers such as upside-down flying and barrel rolling. Even more spectacular were the death-defying feats of "wing-walkers," who balanced on the wings of a plane in flight while driving golf balls, turning cartwheels, or juggling balls. Other aerial stunts were specifically designed to generate publicity for particular consumer products. In 1923, for example, the Curtiss Candy Company hired a pilot to scatter thousands of its new Baby Ruth candy bars, each attached to a tiny parachute, over Pittsburgh and other major cities.

Perhaps the most outrageous publicity stunt of the 1920s was flagpole sitting, in which a person perched atop a flagpole for days or even weeks on end. The most famous Jazz Age flagpole sitter was Alvin "Shipwreck" Kelly, a professional stuntman who ignited this national craze in 1924 when he spent thirteen hours and thirteen minutes atop a flagpole to attract crowds to a Hollywood theater. Kelly, who balanced on flagpoles as a paid publicity stunt for hotels, theaters, car dealerships, amusement parks, and other businesses, remained perched above the boardwalk in Atlantic City, New Jersey, for an astonishing forty-nine days in 1930.

Flagpole sitting also appealed to teens and college students who craved a moment of fame. In 1929, more than twenty Baltimore teenagers broke the juvenile flagpole-sitting record. Fifteen-year-old Avon "Azie" Foreman outlasted the others, perching on an eighteen-foot pole for ten days and ten hours.

Recreational Fads

Several fads of the 1920s revolved around mass-produced consumer products. The Chinese parlor game mah-jongg, introduced to the United States in 1922, enchanted middle-class Americans. In 1923, mah-jongg sets reportedly outsold radio receivers, and an estimated 15 million people, mostly women, played regularly. Crossword puzzles became a fad after the 1924 publication of Simon & Schuster's *Cross Word Puzzle Book,* the first collection of its kind. In the midst of that craze, enthusiasts competed in crossword puzzle tournaments across the country, and the University of Kentucky offered a course on crossword

Crossword Puzzles

Although they appeared in American newspapers just before World War I, it was not until the 1920s that crossword puzzles became a popular pastime in the United States. Their origins have been traced to ancient Rome, but the person credited with inventing the modern crossword puzzle is Arthur Wynne, an English immigrant. Assigned the task of coming up with a new game for the "Fun" section of the *New York World* by his editors, Wynne adapted elements of existing games in the section—word squares, word jumbles, rebuses, anagrams, and connect-the-dot drawings—to fashion the unique puzzles of clues and grids of interconnected words. He called the game a "word-cross," and the first one appeared in the December 21, 1913, edition of the *World*, then one of the city's leading dailies.

The pastime quickly gathered a devoted following, and readers began sending in their own puzzles, which the *World* began publishing the following year. When typesetting errors led the paper to cancel the word-cross in 1914, the outcry from readers was so immediate and so impassioned that the publisher restored the puzzles within a week. Wynne reversed the name of the game to cross-word and then dropped the hyphen.

Crossword puzzles appeared exclusively in the *World* from 1913 to 1924, until two Columbia University graduates, Dick Simon and Lincoln Schuster, established the Simon & Schuster publishing house in New York. One of the first books they chose to produce was a volume of crossword puzzles. The book was a colossal success and propelled the crossword craze to a nationwide audience.

People did crossword puzzles at work, on the train, at the beach, and in their homes. The puzzle's distinctive grid was featured in everything from high-fashion clothing to jewelry and architecture. Newspaper and book publishers across the country hired poets, writers, and just plain crossword aficionados to develop puzzles for their own publications. To make their creations unique, puzzle makers soon introduced themes, colors, and geometric patterns. New forms of crossword puzzles were introduced, including "free-form" or "skeleton" styles, with no black squares, to challenge the public's increasing skills. By 1930, "crossword" had entered standard dictionaries.

Ironically, the newspaper that has become most closely associated with crossword puzzles in the United States—*The New York Times*—was one of the last to add them to its lineup of features. The "old gray lady" of journalism did not run its first crossword puzzle until 1942.

Matthew Drumheller and James Ciment

---

puzzles. The mass marketing of inexpensive pogo sticks and yo-yos also spawned national crazes.

Tennis, golf, and miniature golf became all-consuming pastimes during the 1920s, as did social dancing, particularly among teens and college students, who danced the jazzy new steps in hotel ballrooms, nightclubs, dance halls, speakeasies, and fraternities. The most famous dance of the Jazz Age, the Charleston, swept the nation after being introduced to theatergoers in James P. Johnson and Cecil Mack's 1923 all-black musical revue *Runnin' Wild*. Other dance crazes followed, including the black bottom, varsity drag, collegiate, and raccoon.

The popularity of dancing led to an endurance fad called marathon dancing. In 1923, Alma Cummings set an international record of twenty-seven hours of nonstop dancing at an Audubon Ballroom contest in New York City. Soon, contestants in New

York, Boston, Chicago, Dallas, and other cities were fox-trotting and Charlestoning in quest of a new world's record. By 1924, dance marathons had escalated into mass public spectacles, with professional promoters, large cash prizes, dozens of contestants, paying audiences, and extensive coverage in the nation's mass media. The contests, which featured couples dancing continuously except for fifteen-minute breaks each hour, dragged on for days or even weeks. The most famous dance marathon of the Jazz Age occurred in 1928, when Milton Crandall, a Hollywood press agent, staged a contest dubbed "The Dance Derby of the Century" at New York's Madison Square Garden. After 428 hours, the State Board of Health commissioner stopped the competition when one contestant collapsed and had to be hospitalized.

Beyond dance marathons, Americans' search for self-expression and fleeting fame also spawned other endurance fads. In 1928, *The New York Times* reported that an "endurance epidemic" had seized the nation. Tens of thousands of Americans competed in rocking-chair derbies, milk-drinking marathons, egg-eating races, gum-chewing contests, marathon eating bouts, and "noun and verb rodeos" (nonstop talking contests). In 1928, promoter Charles C. "Cash and Carry" Pyle organized a grueling cross-country footrace from Los Angles to New York City that inventive sportswriters billed as the "Bunion Derby." Out of a field of almost 200 runners, nineteen-year-old Andrew Payne

won the $25,000 first prize with a time of 573 hours. Even children and teenagers got swept up in the endurance craze, competing in rope-skipping contests, ball-bouncing marathons, roof-sitting feats, yo-yo competitions, pogo-stick marathons, kite-flying contests, and long-distance bicycle races.

Self-Improvement Fads

A number of fads during the 1920s were born of the urge for self-improvement. Weight-conscious Americans, particularly young women, began counting calories and dieting, or "reducing," as it was known, to maintain good health and, more significantly, to achieve the slender figure of the flapper so idealized in women's magazines, films, and advertising. Dieting manuals, such as Lulu Hunt Peters's best-selling *Diet and Health, with Key to the Calories* (1918), along with commercial dieting programs, reducing creams, exercise records, and other weight-loss products, flooded the market.

Concerns about health and fitness fueled a body-building and physical fitness craze among men. Bodybuilders such as Charles Atlas, who won the 1922 title of Most Perfectly Developed Man, inspired tens of thousands of men to take up weight-lifting and fitness regimens. In 1924, Atlas began marketing mail-order instructions for his Dynamic Tension program, which he claimed had transformed him from a ninety-seven-pound weakling into a physically perfect Adonis.

Other self-improvement fads focused on the psychological. Tens of thousands of middle-class Americans sought self-fulfillment and happiness in the teachings of Émile Coué, a French psychotherapist whose best-selling *Self-Mastery Through Conscious Auto-suggestion* (1922) recommended a self-hypnosis program based in part on daily repetition of the affirmation "Every day, in every way, I am getting better and better." The writings of Sigmund Freud, particularly *The Interpretation of Dreams* (1900), generated such interest that psychoanalytic terms such as *repression, sublimation,* and *complex* became part of everyday vocabulary.

The Exotic

Some fads reflected a national obsession with the exotic and foreign. An Egyptian craze, spawned by archeologist Howard Carter's 1922 discovery of the pharaoh Tutankhamen's tomb, had a strong influence on American architecture, fashion, and music. Other foreign cultures, particularly Asian and Middle East-

Among the most popular crazes in a decade famous for fads and stunts was the crossword puzzle. Here, a bather in Palm Beach, Florida, draws a crossword puzzle on her beach parasol. *(General Photographic Agency/Hulton Archive/Getty Images)*

ern, likewise inspired styles and fads. With its ornate oriental architecture and decor, Grauman's Chinese Theater, which opened in Hollywood in 1927, was constructed to resemble a giant red pagoda. Rudolph Valentino's 1921 box-office hit *The Sheik,* and its 1926 sequel *The Son of the Sheik*, helped fuel the national craze for Middle Eastern exoticism.

Hawaiian music became enormously popular during the Jazz Age, and Tin Pan Alley songwriters churned out dozens of novelty numbers about Hawaiian life—among them "Hula Hula Dream Girl" (1924) and "That Aloha Waltz" (1928). This craze in turn inspired a ukulele fad. Musicians formed ukulele clubs, music schools offered ukulele lessons, and music companies published ukulele instruction booklets and song collections.

Fads flourished during the Jazz Age for several reasons. The 1920s witnessed a gradual shortening of the standard workweek, increases in wages and salaries, and a comparatively steady cost of living. As a result, ordinary Americans enjoyed both more leisure time and more disposable income with which to participate in recreational pastimes. Although zany fads and stunts contributed to a popular mythology that obscures some of the more serious and complex trends of a pivotal American decade, they were indeed an element of the 1920s that helped make it unique.

Patrick Huber

See also: Atlas, Charles; Dance, Popular; King Tut's Tomb; Leisure and Recreation.

Further Reading

Furhman, Candice Jacobson. *Publicity Stunt! Great Staged Events That Made the News.* San Francisco: Chronicle, 1989.

Hoffmann, Frank W., and William G. Bailey. *Arts and Entertainment Fads.* New York: Haworth, 1990.

———. *Mind and Society Fads.* New York: Haworth, 1992.

———. *Sports and Recreation Fads.* New York: Haworth, 1991.

Martin, Carol. *Dance Marathons: Performing American Culture in the 1920s and 1930s.* Jackson: University Press of Mississippi, 1994.

Marum, Andrew, and Frank Parise. *Follies and Foibles: A View of 20th Century Fads.* New York: Facts on File, 1984.

Sann, Paul. *Fads, Follies, and Delusions of the American People.* New York: Bonanza, 1967.

Fairbanks, Douglas (1883–1939)

Dashing, dynamic, and versatile in the new medium of motion pictures, Douglas Fairbanks was the first action star of the big screen. He also directed every detail of his films, wrote screenplays, designed sets, and helped create the distribution company United Artists.

Born Douglas Elton Thomas Ullman on May 23, 1883, in Denver, Colorado, to an upper-middle-class family, Fairbanks showed an early talent for performing. His father, a prominent attorney who would abandon the family when Douglas was five years old, taught his young son to recite Shakespeare. As a teenager, Fairbanks began appearing in local theater productions, then national ones, making his Broadway debut in 1902. *Man of the Hour* (1906) marked his emergence as a star of the stage. In 1907, he married Anna Beth Sully, the daughter of a wealthy businessman. Despite his critical success, Fairbanks was having trouble supporting his wife in the style to which she had been accustomed, and he considered going into a more lucrative line of work.

Like many stage actors of the time, Fairbanks had little respect for motion picture performers. The new medium was proving increasingly lucrative, however, and the financial temptation of screen acting became too hard to resist. His father-in-law had gone bankrupt and was now coming to Fairbanks for financial help. In 1915, the actor moved his family (which now included Douglas Fairbanks, Jr., who would follow in his father's footsteps and become a star in his own right) to Hollywood and signed with Triangle Pictures for $2,000 a week. Assigned to the unit of pioneering director D.W. Griffith, Fairbanks made his film debut in *The Lamb* (1915). Griffith, however, whose strength was melodramas, did not quite know what to do with Fairbanks's exuberance.

The screenwriter Anita Loos, however, recognizing his particular talents, wrote a number of social comedies that showcased Fairbanks's athleticism. Among them were the 1916 films *The Habit of Happiness, Manhattan Madness,* and *The Good Bad Man.* These films made Fairbanks a star. After he formed his own production company, his streak of hits continued with *In Again, Out Again* (1917), *The Man from Painted Post* (1917), and *The Knickerbocker Buckaroo* (1919).

Fairbanks, Charlie Chaplin, and Mary Pickford, the three highest-paid actors of the period, joined with D.W. Griffith to found United Artists (UA) in 1919, which gave them control over the distribution as well as the production of their films, thereby cutting them in for a larger share of the profits and granting them creative autonomy. *His Majesty the American* (1919) and *The Mollycoddle* (1920) were Fairbanks's first films under the UA banner. A year later, after divorcing their respective spouses, Fairbanks and Pickford—two of the greatest film stars of their time—were married.

From that point on, Fairbanks became even more of a fan favorite and more powerful in the industry. From their hillside estate, Pickfair, he and Pickford reigned over Hollywood society. Fairbanks achieved his greatest success with such costume adventures as *The Mark of Zorro* (1920), *The Three Musketeers* (1921), *Robin Hood* (1922), *The Thief of Baghdad* (1924), and *The Black Pirate* (1926). Even as his roles became less about acting and more about performing elaborate stunts, Fairbanks carried out diverse creative duties and took them all seriously. In addition to keeping a close eye on budgets, he did production design, worked closely with directors, and made sure the historical details of the films were accurate.

In films, Fairbanks was robust, energetic, optimistic, and always smiling. Offscreen, he tried to convey the same persona. Newspapers and magazines praised him for being a clean-living role model for America's youth. Fairbanks also took a prominent leadership role in the film industry. He became the first president of the Motion Picture Academy of Arts and Sciences in 1927, hosted the first Academy Awards in 1929, and was one of the first stars to immortalize his handprints in cement on the Hollywood Walk of Fame. In 1929 he helped create the film program at the University of Southern California, which eventually became one of the most important film schools in the country.

By decade's end, however, Fairbanks's star had begun to fade. In 1929, he and Pickford starred in *The Taming of the Shrew,* his first talking picture. The film did not do well at the box office, and the marriage of "America's Sweethearts" broke up. Some critics cite Fairbanks's speaking voice as the reason for his decline in popularity, claiming it lacked authority. Others point to his age. Fairbanks was already in his thirties when he had become a movie star (playing juveniles), and he was in his mid-forties during the leaping and swordplay of *The Black Pirate* (1926). After more sedentary roles in films such as *Reaching for the Moon* (1930) and *Mr. Robinson Crusoe* (1932), Fairbanks retired, making his last screen appearance as an aging bon vivant in the 1934 British film *The Private Life of Don Juan.*

In 1936, Fairbanks married the model and socialite Lady Sylvia Ashley. Three years later, at age fifty-six, Fairbanks died of a heart attack at his home in Santa Monica, California.

Tom Cerasulo

See also: Film; Film Industry; Pickford, Mary.

Further Reading

Carey, Gary. *Doug and Mary.* New York: E.P. Dutton, 1977.

Cooke, Alistair. *Douglas Fairbanks: The Making of a Screen Character.* New York: Museum of Modern Art, 2002.

Schickel, Richard. *Douglas Fairbanks: The First Celebrity.* London: Elm Tree, 1976.

Tibbets, John. *His Majesty the American: The Cinema of Douglas Fairbanks, Sr.* New York: A.S. Barnes, 1977.

Farmer-Labor Party

The Farmer-Labor Party (FLP) represents one of the few concerted attempts by leftists and progressives in the 1920s to wrest political control from the two major parties. Born of the hopes and frustrations of farmers, labor leaders, and progressives in the months after the end of World War I, the Farmer-Labor Party briefly seemed to be the best instrument for advancing civil liberties, industrial regulation, and the rights of unions and workers in America. However, postwar conservatism, competition with other third-party and reform efforts, and fickle support from labor unions combined with other factors to consign the party to irrelevance within only a few years.

The patriotic and antiradical mood in the country during World War I had fatally weakened the Socialist Party and hobbled the newly formed Communist Party. Yet a painful postwar recession caused widespread unrest among farmers and workers, generating interest in a new political party in various regions, including the upper Midwest, the Northwest, and the industrial Northeast. In December 1918, the Chicago Federation of Labor, led by the radical but nonsocialist John Fitzpatrick, issued a call for a convention to found a national party modeled after the successful British Labour Party. Labor leaders who resented the increasingly antilabor stance of federal, state, and local governments welcomed the call, and within months local labor parties formed in nearly fifty cities across the country.

In 1919, delegates formed the National Labor Party, a move supported at the time by farmers in the Midwest and Northwest who were active in the Nonpartisan League. The new party also drew crucial support from unions within the American Federation of Labor that represented up to one-half of the AFL's entire voting power. By July 1920, however, when Fitzpatrick led a Chicago convention in transforming the earlier group into the Farmer-Labor Party, AFL president Samuel Gompers had withdrawn much of labor's support, crippling the party's viability in the 1920 elections.

At the 1920 Chicago convention, labor leaders argued about the platform with political activists from the Committee of Forty-Eight, a reform group composed of Socialists, progressives, and liberal intellectuals. Many of these "48ers" had supported Teddy Roosevelt's failed "Bull Moose" Progressive candidacy in 1912 and Democratic President Woodrow Wilson, until the latter retreated from wartime government intervention in the economy. Committee of Forty-Eight leaders attempted to reconcile the more radical program of FLP laborites, which called for democratic control of industry, with a more moderate platform supported by potential presidential candidate and well-known progressive Senator Robert La Follette of Wisconsin. When this attempt failed, the labor-dominated convention nominated Parley P. Christensen, a relatively unknown radical lawyer from Salt Lake City.

With limited funds and few staff, Christensen nevertheless ran a vigorous campaign calling for nationalization of large-scale industries, recognition of the Soviet Union, amnesty for wartime political prisoners, and expanded civil liberties and civil rights for African Americans. Christensen ultimately gained 290,000 votes, even less than Socialist Eugene V. Debs's 915,000, against the victorious Republican candidate, Warren G. Harding.

FLP groups dissolved rapidly after 1920. Undeterred, Fitzpatrick maintained the national FLP in Chicago and called for a party convention in 1923, after leaders from major railroad unions aborted initial efforts to establish an independent political movement. By this time, American Communists, pressured by the Comintern in Moscow to abandon their attempts to build the party through their own electoral campaigns, turned to mass organizations. The Communist Party, sensing an opportunity in a revitalized Farmer-Labor Party, had some of its members attend the July 1923 convention in Chicago as delegates from other organizations.

Fitzpatrick, a longtime friend of labor leader and Communist William Z. Foster, initially welcomed participation by the Communists. However, when Fitzpatrick and other Chicago labor leaders at the convention realized how few actual unions and non-Communist-dominated organizations were present, they attempted to delay the re-formation of the FLP until they could gain a wider base of support. Nevertheless, well-organized Communist delegates, eager to launch a political effort under their influence, disregarded Fitzpatrick and persuaded the majority of delegates to form the Federated Farmer-Labor Party (FF-LP). Many union leaders at the convention, including Fitzpatrick, denounced the Communists and returned to the traditional politics of the AFL. The FF-LP quickly withered away, and many former Farmer-Laborites supported Robert La Follette's Progressive Party bid for the presidency in 1924.

Several unaffiliated state Farmer-Labor parties, the most famous of which was the Minnesota FLP, ran candidates with some success well into the 1930s. In Minnesota, the FLP continues through its merger with the Democratic Party, which formed the Democratic-Farmer-Labor Party.

Justin F. Jackson

See also: Agriculture; American Farm Bureau Federation; Nonpartisan League; Progressivism.

Further Reading

Shapiro, Stanley. "'Hand and Brain': The Farmer-Labor Party of 1920." *Labor History* 26:3 (1985): 405–22.
Tobin, Eugene M. *Organize or Perish: America's Independent Progressives, 1913–1933.* Westport, CT: Greenwood, 1986.
Weinstein, James. *The Decline of Socialism in America, 1912–1925.* Piscataway, NJ: Rutgers University Press, 1984.

Fashion, Men's

American men's fashion during the Jazz Age was characterized by a sweeping transition from the conventional to the avant-garde. Longing for a carefree existence after the horrors of World War I, Americans in the 1920s celebrated life, youth, and activity. Clothing became comfortable, colorful, less restrictive, and more accommodating to an active lifestyle filled with travel, sports, and leisure. As advances in mass production techniques made fashion more affordable and available, advertisers increased men's desire for the latest fashions.

In the years after World War I, men traded in their narrow-shouldered, high-waisted, Edwardian-style suits for the more relaxed, broad-shouldered, double-breasted suits of the early 1920s. Formal eveningwear consisted of a black or midnight blue tuxedo jacket with matching pants, a white, wing-collared shirt, and a black or white tie. Silk gloves, spats, and a top hat commonly accompanied this ensemble. The white dress shirt became a symbol of masculinity in the 1920s. The handsome, square-jawed "Arrow Shirt Man," the creation of illustrator J.C. Leyendecker, advertised dress shirts and collars that declared the wearer "a hunk of male magnificence." Wildly popular among women, the Arrow Shirt Man became a 1920s sex symbol, receiving more than 17,000 fan letters and a few marriage proposals.

One controversial change in men's fashion concerned shirt collars. For generations, men had worn detachable stiff, white, upright collars that fastened to their dress shirts. By the early 1900s, designers introduced a folding "soft collar." Dubbed the "American collar," it was derided by Europeans as slovenly and sloppy.

Athleticism influenced fashion designers to modify casual clothing for comfort and durability. The tweed Norfolk jacket, knickerbockers (knee-length golf pants), hiking breeches, and riding suits supported the sporting lifestyle associated with youth and healthy, outdoor living. Light-colored flannel trousers worn with a two-inch-wide belt, paired with a white, open-necked shirt, white shoes, a straw boater hat, and a navy blue blazer epitomized prosperity and leisure. Wool sweaters with shawl collars and pullovers were popular with the artistic and athletic community alike. American tennis champion Bill Tilden popularized the tennis sweater, a light-colored, V-neck, cable-knit pullover. In 1929, international tennis champion René Lacoste liberated tennis players from their tie and starched collars when he donned a white, ribbed-collar shirt with short, banded sleeves. Lacoste, dubbed "le crocodile" by the press because of his tenacity on the court, had a small crocodile embroidered on his shirt; the trademark polo shirt continues to be a fashion favorite.

Wide-legged Oxford trousers, embraced by American college students, originated at Oxford University in 1925. Young student athletes, rebelling against a university "no knickers in class" policy, defiantly slipped baggy pants over their knickers and attended class without changing clothes. In New York, Wanamaker's department store advertised Oxfords as "the trousers that have created a furore in England." Concurrently, "plus-fours," fuller versions of knicker-bockers, began replacing the tighter-fitting golf pants and were worn as "sporty" travel and casual wear.

Jazz Age men expected comfort at every level. Underwear and sleepwear fabrics became lighter and more supple. Silk and cotton sleeveless undershirts and "athletic" boxer shorts replaced woolen and flannel union suits. Crepe, silk, and percale pajamas replaced "old-fashioned" flannel nightshirts. After a long day at work, men slipped into luxurious silk, velvet, or brocade smoking jackets or dressing gowns. Advertisers promoted lines of loungewear with images of wealthy businessmen and Hollywood stars, equating leisure time with success.

Fashion accessories became status symbols. Neckties, once simply black, were offered in a wide variety of styles, textures, colors, and patterns. In 1924, *Men's Wear* magazine commented on the "patterns and colors unthinkable previously" as drab socks gave way to bold displays of color and design. Hard-crowned felt hats with round brims, such as the homburg, fedora, bowler, and derby, denoted respectability, while men wore lightweight straw boaters and panamas in warmer weather. Sporty tweed golf caps in check or plaid, once a sign of the working class, and later dubbed houndstooth, became popular among the upper class. Hollywood westerns popularized the ten-gallon, Stetson, and cowboy hats.

The proliferation of department stores and haberdasheries sparked fierce competition among retailers that led many to offer payment plans and special sales. Live mannequins and innovative window displays encouraged shoppers to enter and browse. Mail-order firms such as Sears, Roebuck, and Company and Montgomery Ward encouraged patronage through sales, discounted shipping, and the ease of shopping from home. Colorful magazine ads depicting "jazzy," "smart," and "correctly attired" gentlemen enticed men to spend hard-earned cash on the latest trends. But perhaps *Vogue* described the best incentive for being a "snappy" dresser: "get pretty . . . if you want to be loved by one of today's fair maidens."

Jennifer Aerts Terry

See also: Advertising; Fashion, Women's.

Further Reading

Blum, Stella, ed. *Everyday Fashions of the Twenties: As Pictured in the Sears and Other Catalogs.* New York: Dover, 1981.

Constantino, Maria. *Men's Fashion in the Twentieth Century: From Frock Coats to Intelligent Fibres.* New York: Costume and Fashion, 1997.

Langley, Susan. *Roaring '20s Fashions: Jazz.* Atglen, PA: Schiffer, 2005.

Schoeffler, O.E., and William Gale. *Esquire's Encyclopedia of Twentieth Century Men's Fashion.* New York: McGraw-Hill, 1973.

Fashion, Women's

In his 1928 study *Economics of Fashion,* Columbia University marketing professor Paul H. Nystrom declared: "Fashion is one of the greatest forces in present-day life. It pervades every field and reaches every class. . . . To be out of fashion is to be out of the world." Nystrom's observation captures the dramatically enhanced interest in fashion, particularly women's fashion, during the 1920s. With the dramatic rise of consumer culture and the culture of celebrity, fashion became a pursuit for more and more American women—even those of more limited economic means. American women saw new fashions displayed in films, posters, and magazines. Catalogues, standardized sizes, department stores, and bargain sales made the "flapper" styles available to women of all classes and tempted many to follow the changing fashions from season to season.

Changes in women's clothing during the Jazz Age were more dramatic than in any previous era. Hemlines rose to the knee, some women's hair styles were shorter than men's by mid-decade, and the use of cosmetics was seen as an everyday practice for ordinary women, rather than something confined to the worlds of prostitution or the theater. Ready-made clothing in standard sizes became widely available. As the ideal female figure was boyish and angular, dresses were styled with a flattened bustline and dropped waist. All of these trends represented a dramatic departure from the staid fashions of the Victorian era.

Many of these changes began as a result of World War I. Fabric was rationed during the war, and women, who took over men's jobs, needed clothing that allowed them to move freely. This meant less fabric was used in clothes, hemlines rose, and lighter slips were worn, giving women's dresses a more streamlined look. The changes stuck when the war was over, especially as the influence of innovative Parisian couturier Coco Chanel spread to America.

By 1925, when skirt hems were just above the knee, some Americans thought the short hemline scandalous. A Utah law called for a fine and imprisonment for those who wore "skirts higher than three inches above the ankle," and a similar bill was introduced but not passed in Ohio. Hemlines began to drop again after 1925, but they became more elaborate, with scalloped or floating edges. By 1930, the widespread adoption of the "bias cut" pioneered by Madeleine Vionnet meant that skirts clung more closely to the body.

Women's shoes became increasingly important fashion items, featuring elaborate buckles and details. Flesh-colored stockings were introduced to emphasize shoes and the daring expanse of leg afforded by knee-length skirts. To be especially provocative, some flappers rolled their stockings down to the knee.

Accompanying the rising hem was the dropped waist. At mid-decade, the waistline of any fashionable skirt or dress was hip level. Lines were very angular and most dresses and virtually all coats and jackets were square-shouldered. Some women resorted to "bust-flatteners" or bound their breasts for a stylish effect.

The boyish look was emphasized by the "bob" haircut, which appeared in 1920. As the decade progressed, women's hair was cut so short that one style was dubbed the "Eton Cut," after the famous English boy's school. Hat styles adapted to the new hairstyles. The cloche—the hat of the decade—was bell-shaped, brimless, close-fitting, and worn low over the forehead.

The lighter and looser women's clothing of the 1920s represented a major departure from the heavy, form-fitting fashions of the Victorian and Edwardian eras. *(Luigi Diaz/ Hulton Archive/Getty Images)*

Faces were adorned with powder, lipstick, rouge, mascara, and eyebrow pencil. With the cosmetic industry booming, makeup "compacts"—travel-size containers of compressed face powder—became fashion items in their own right. Trendy young women would apply makeup in public, and celebrity aviators Ruth Elder and Phoebe Omlie were happy to be pictured reapplying their face powder after difficult flights.

Looser-fitting clothes and the emphasis on an active, athletic figure made it acceptable for women to take part in a variety of sports and leisure activities. The rejection of corsets and bustles meant women's fashions were less damaging to the body than in previous centuries, when tight corsets pressed in and injured internal organs. At the same time, however, the ideal of slenderness and the practice of extreme dieting became integral to fashion during the Jazz Age.

The fashions of the 1920s presented African Americans with new challenges and opportunities. They faced pressure to whiten their skin and straighten their hair in accordance with fashion, but many resisted the pressure and waged "antiwhitening" campaigns. Middle-class black Americans avoided "scandalous" modern dress styles to gain respectability in the eyes of white society. Black entrepreneurs, women and men alike, flourished providing fashion and beauty products to an African American clientele.

Many American women saw the advances in fashion as a political expression of freedom and individual choice, a sequel to the political success they had won with the ratification in 1920 of the Nineteenth Amendment, which granted them the vote. In her classic 1930 *Lessons of Loveliness,* beauty writer Nell Vinick proclaimed that clothes and cosmetics were "symbols of the social revolution" and the "forces that women have used to break away from conventions." Fashion was more than frivolity in Jazz Age America. Film stars, socialites, and salesgirls alike viewed it as central to the liberated lifestyle of the New Woman.

Rachel Gillett

See also: Advertising; Beauty Industry and Culture; Celebrity Culture; Fashion, Men's.

Further Reading

Laver, James. *Costume and Fashion.* 3rd ed. London: Thames & Hudson, 1995.

Nystrom, Paul H. *Economics of Fashion.* New York: Ronald, 1928.

Peacock, John. *The 1920s: Fashion Sourcebook.* New York: Thames & Hudson, 1997.

Peiss, Kathy. *Hope in a Jar: The Making of America's Beauty Culture.* New York: Metropolitan, 1998.

Vinick, Nell. *Lessons in Loveliness.* New York: Longmans, Green, 1930.

White, Shane, and Graham White. *Stylin': African-American Expressive Culture from Its Beginnings to the Zoot Suit.* Ithaca, NY: Cornell University Press, 1998.

Federal Bureau of Investigation

See Bureau of Investigation

Federal Highway Act of 1921

In response to the significant growth in popularity of the automobile, ushered in by the appearance and mass production of the Model T in preceding years, the U.S. Congress passed and President Warren G. Harding signed into law the Federal Highway Act of 1921. The measure updated and modified the Federal Road Act of 1916, the first piece of legislation to mandate federal funds for the construction, improvement, and expansion of roads and highways.

The 1921 act called for the construction of an interconnected, federal interstate highway system. Any state that did not devote 7 percent of its roads to the national highway system would not receive any revenues raised by the new system. In addition, three-sevenths of a state's highways had to be for the purpose of interstate travel. For those states that met the legislation's requirements, the Federal Highway Act matched state funds with federal monies, derived from an increase in the national gasoline tax. The newly established federal highway system would be managed by both the Bureau of Public Roads and the National Highway System.

The changes called for by the Federal Highway Act of 1921 significantly expanded American interstate transportation. Specific elements of the legislation included the following:

- Creating a National Highway System (eventually designated Route 66);
- funding a system of two-lane interstate highways;
- mandating that paved federal roads be at least eighteen feet wide;
- establishing Forest Development Roads for the management of national forests;
- constructing Forest Highways, serving communities within and adjacent to national forests;

- allocating $75 million in matching federal funds to states that meet the law's requirements;
- establishing direct state control over road and bridge construction;
- authorizing states to collect the gasoline tax; and
- designating the Boston Post Road, running the length of the eastern seaboard, as U.S. Route 1.

The new national system consisted of new state highways and 250 improved, modernized, and expanded marked trails. Interstate travel became significantly easier, and the western part of the country, from Chicago to Los Angeles, was connected by a new transcontinental road, designated Route 66 in 1927. In addition, funds from the 1921 legislation enhanced scenic travel in the United States. Finances were provided to turn dirt tracks into concrete roads, and New York City's Bronx River Parkway was designated the nation's first scenic highway.

As the network of roads expanded and improved following the Federal Highway Act of 1921, the use of automobiles continued to skyrocket. Vehicle registrations in the United States increased from 10.4 million in 1921 to 26 million just ten years later. To continue funding the growth and construction of federal highways, the gasoline tax was increased from one cent in 1919 to four cents in 1929.

Adam Shprintzen

See also: Automobile Industry; Automobiles and Automobile Culture; Economic Policy; Railroads and Railroad Industry.

Further Reading

McNichol, Dan. *The Roads That Built America: The Incredible Story of the U.S. Interstate System.* New York: Sterling, 2006.

Rose, Albert C. *Historic American Roads: From Frontier Trails to Superhighways.* New York: Crown, 1976.

Seeley, Bruce E. *Building the American Highway System: Engineers as Policy Makers.* Philadelphia: Temple University Press, 1987.

Teaford, Jon C. *The Rise of the States: Evolution of American State Government.* Baltimore: Johns Hopkins University Press, 2002.

Wik, Reynold M. *Henry Ford and Grass Roots America.* Ann Arbor: University of Michigan Press, 1972.

Federal Power Commission

The Federal Power Commission was established in 1920 as an independent agency of the U.S. government to encourage and regulate the production of hydroelectric power. Prior to that time, control over navigable rivers and water resources on federal lands had been divided among various federal agencies and departments. As a result of the Federal Water Power Act, which created the power commission, the U.S. government took a more direct role in encouraging and determining the sites of hydroelectric power plants, foreshadowing the expansion of control under President Franklin D. Roosevelt's New Deal.

The increased use of electricity during the late nineteenth century led to its production through the harnessing of rivers and streams. Early power plants produced relatively small amounts of electricity, which could not be transmitted any great distance. By the early twentieth century, improved technology made the creation of larger power plants possible. Only a limited number of sites were suitable for hydroelectric plants, however, since production depended on water flow.

Federal statutes before 1920 required anyone who wanted to build a hydroelectric plant to approach different federal bodies. Dams and plants on a navigable river required congressional approval. Projects located on federal lands had to be licensed by the secretary of the interior, while projects on federal forest reserves had to be authorized by the secretary of agriculture. The need to streamline the licensing process was made apparent by experiences in World War I, when the demands of wartime production led to shortages of coal and oil. The power shortfall was made more critical during the winter of 1918, when strikes reduced the amount of coal available. Power plants servicing some eastern cities were forced to shut down because they had no coal on which to run their generators. By 1919, some authorities were predicting that domestic supplies of oil would be exhausted by the end of the 1920s.

Given these fears, many people in government and private industry looked to hydroelectric power to meet the energy needs of the future. Water energy was virtually inexhaustible and could provide cheap power for industry and homes. By 1920, hydroelectric plants supplied 40 percent of the nation's electrical power.

A bill was introduced in Congress in 1916 to create a federal bureau to regulate the licensing of hydroelectric projects, and after a series of hearings, the measure was passed by both houses in May 1920. President Woodrow Wilson signed the bill into law on June 10, 1920, establishing the Federal Power Commission. The new body included the secretaries of war, agriculture, and the interior, an executive secretary, and about thirty other people on loan from the departments of war, agriculture, and the interior. The commission was charged with licensing nonfederal hydropower projects that affected navigable rivers, were located on federal land, used water or water power at a federal dam, or affected interstate commerce. Although the projects had to be licensed by the federal government, the legislation intended that funding would come from private resources.

The commission was also required to approve only those projects that complied with a comprehensive plan to improve or develop a waterway. Conservationists regarded the creation of the commission as a great victory, since it confirmed rivers and waterways as national resources controlled by the federal government, not individual states.

The Federal Power Commission began its work early in 1921, studying proposals and granting licenses. The licenses were good for no less than thirty nor more than fifty years. The long terms were intended to reassure private developers that they would have time to amortize the initial costs of a project and make a profit. The commission was swamped with licensing requests, many of them for renewals to existing hydroelectric projects. Congress intended for the commission to determine if these older plants still made sense and if they met the requirements outlined by newer laws and regulations.

In the first two years of its existence, the Federal Power Commission received 321 applications for licenses. The total power generated by these new plants exceeded 15,000 megawatts and accounted for more than three times the capacity of existing hydroelectric plants. With its small staff overwhelmed by the requests, the commission, in 1928, ordered a halt to processing new applications except in cases of emergency.

Congress recognized the need for more resources and passed legislation transforming the Federal Power Commission into an independent agency. It was reconstituted in 1930 with five members appointed by the president and approved by Congress. In 1935, Congress further amended the commission's authority to regulate interstate aspects of the electrical power industry. The Federal Power Commission was abolished on October 1, 1977, when Congress created the Federal Energy Regulatory Commission as part of the Department of Energy.

Tim J. Watts

See also: Economic Policy; Electricity Industry.

Further Reading

Breyer, Stephen G., and Paul W. MacAvoy. *Energy Regulation by the Federal Power Commission.* Washington, D.C.: Brookings Institution, 1974.

Conover, Milton. *The Federal Power Commission: Its History, Activities, and Organization.* Baltimore: Johns Hopkins University Press, 1923.

Schwartz, Bernard, ed. *The Economic Regulation of Business and Industry: A Legislative History of U.S. Regulatory Agencies.* New York: Chelsea House, 1973.

Swidler, Joseph C., and A. Scott Henderson. *Power and the Public Interest: The Memoirs of Joseph C. Swidler.* Knoxville: University of Tennessee Press, 2002.

Federal Radio Commission

The Federal Radio Commission was an outgrowth of the explosion in radio broadcasting during the 1920s. The first commercial radio station (KDKA in Pittsburgh) went on the air in 1920; just two years later, there were more than 500 commercial radio stations, and by 1930, more than 600. With the growth of the radio industry, stations were impinging on one another's signals, and it was essential to bring order to the resulting chaos. The Federal Radio Commission was created in 1927 to fulfill this need.

When radio was in its infancy, there was little concern about the way in which transmitters sent out their signals. In fact, the earliest transmitter technology, the spark-gap, or space between conductors, could not even be tuned or modulated. The only way to broadcast a signal was to turn it on and off in a pattern corresponding to the dots and dashes of Morse code, useful for transmitting messages to ships at sea and other places that could not be reached by wire, but useless for transmitting speech or music.

The invention in the 1910s of tunable radio transmitters allowed for the transmission of a signal on a tightly defined frequency. In addition, the contemporary development of a system of modulation, which made it possible to transmit voices and music, made radio broadcasting possible. Once the idea of broadcasting music, news, and sports to the general public proved itself in the marketplace, stations began to spring up all across the country.

The rise of commercial radio broadcasting caught government regulators by surprise. The only legislation in effect in the early 1920s, the 1912 Federal Radio Act, had been drafted under the assumption that radio technology would be used primarily by government, the military, and corporations to send brief messages to their people in the field. Legislators had also assumed that radio would remain essentially a wireless version of the telegraph, and thus had mandated that all stations operate on a single assigned frequency.

What had worked for wireless telegraphy was a disaster for broadcast entertainment. Radio stations broadcast almost continuously, which meant that two stations within range of each other would interfere with each other's signals. In some areas, stations developed agreements to alternate hours of operation to avoid such interference. Other stations simply increased their power output until they overwhelmed the interfering station's signal. Some stations went as high as 100,000 watts (modern clear-channel stations are restricted to 50,000 watts), enabling people in the transmitter's immediate vicinity to pick up the station's broadcasts on random metal objects.

In 1922, the federal government allocated a second frequency for broadcast radio, but it only slightly improved the situation. Many stations solved the problem for themselves by moving to unauthorized frequencies. When radio preacher Aimee Semple McPherson was warned against doing so in 1925, she sent Commerce Secretary Herbert Hoover a colorful telegram, claiming that her frequency choices were determined by God and that attempts to force her to broadcast on a set frequency were the work of Satan.

As it became increasingly obvious that market forces would not resolve the issues, broadcasters began to call for federal regulation to sort out the chaos. Since the airwaves were a limited resource and broadcasts crossed state lines with impunity, it was not hard to make a constitutional argument for the establishment of a federal agency to govern the operation of radio stations. Congress adopted the 1927 Radio Act, which created the Federal Radio Commission to manage the use of the airwaves in the public interest.

The Federal Radio Commission defined the frequency bands in which radio stations were to confine their signals and the power levels at which they could transmit, and established standards of good practice. The new regulations were met with mixed reactions. Although the large commercial broadcasters such as NBC's Red and Blue networks welcomed the end of signal interference, many smaller stations complained of getting short shrift. Educational stations in particular were often confined to poor frequencies that were susceptible to interference from natural sources such as lightning and solar flares, and often were permitted to broadcast only during the day. By the end of the 1920s, four out of five small educational stations had gone off the air, a loss that would not be remedied until after World War II, with the movement to revive educational broadcasting.

Leigh Kimmel

See also: Economic Policy; Radio.

Further Reading

Kyvig, David E. *Daily Life in the United States, 1920–1939: Decades of Promise and Pain.* Westport, CT: Greenwood, 2002.

Leinwoll, Stanley. *From Spark to Satellite: A History of Radio Communication.* New York: Scribner's, 1979.

Lewis, Tom. *Empire of the Air: The Men Who Made Radio.* New York: E. Burlingame, 1991.

Fiction

The 1920s are widely considered one of the great decades of American literature. A host of new writers, disillusioned by the carnage of World War I, sought to break with the past and develop new styles and new narrative structures, while exploring themes relevant to a rapidly changing America. The major American writers of the Jazz Age attained their reputations in large part because they explored the era's social and cultural transformations with insight and originality, and in so doing created indelible (but somewhat selective) images of their time and place.

Among the highly regarded writers to emerge during the period were Sherwood Anderson, Sinclair Lewis, F. Scott Fitzgerald, John Dos Passos, Ernest Hemingway, and William Faulkner. Together they marked the arrival of a new literary generation whose unique experiences and perspectives, not to mention their special talents, invigorated American fiction. They were the writers who individually and collectively defined their era, both for contemporaries and later generations, and whose work left a lasting imprint on the nation's culture.

War and Disillusionment

The Great War was a catalyst for some of the most penetrating fiction of the Jazz Age. The war also proved to be a setup for disillusionment, due in large part to the excesses of the Committee on Public Information, or Creel Commission, named after its chair, George Creel. The propaganda agency was

Book-of-the-Month Club

The Jazz Age was an age of commerce and innovation, and modern American literature was, among other things, a commodity. Although writers, publishers, and booksellers needed to be conscious of the marketplace and attuned to potential consumers of their work, the market for books was limited largely to major cities until the mid-1920s. Few small towns, rural areas, or even small cities had bookstores or lending libraries, and local newspapers rarely carried book reviews. It was in response to the problems of publicizing and distributing books nationwide that Harry Schermer, a New York advertising executive, founded the Book-of-the-Month Club, the country's first book club, in 1926.

An early advertisement set out the conditions and benefits of membership. Members were required to purchase a monthly selection at the retail price, plus postage, and were promised top-quality titles at a reasonable price. To choose the books for his new enterprise, Schermer enlisted a panel of well-regarded writers and critics: Dorothy Canfield, Henry Seidel Canby, Heywood Broun, Christopher Morley, and William Allen White. Their initial selection in April 1926 was *Lolly Willowes,* a novel by Sylvia Townsend Warner.

In return for their commitment to purchase twelve books annually, members would receive, at monthly intervals, the *Book-of-the-Month Club News,* in which one of the panel members offered advance commentary on the Book-of-the-Month selection. The *News* also listed alternative titles for members who did not want a particular month's offering. Members would enjoy the convenience of purchasing books from home. Never again, the advertisements promised, would readers miss worthwhile books simply out of carelessness or lack of information.

All booksellers in the United States, including the Book-of-the-Month Club, faced competition from recent technological innovations for readers' attention. However, while the tradition of reading aloud in the family parlor had given way to the phonograph, radio, and the movies as entertainment alternatives, other developments promised to broaden the potential market for literature. In the mid-1920s, more Americans than ever before were completing high school, and national prosperity meant that more people could afford to purchase books—if only they knew which authors or titles might interest them.

Schermer, it appears, had judged the marketplace well. By the end of its first year, the Book-of-the-Month Club had enrolled 40,000 members. The total reached 100,000 before the end of the decade, virtually guaranteeing that monthly selections would qualify as best sellers.

Critics worried that the club's panel would impose its tastes on naive readers and promote conformity in American literature by influencing publishers to promote books similar to the club's typical choices. Highbrows complained that the Book-of-the-Month Club offered only middlebrow fare. But its defenders pointed to the Pulitzer Prize winners that the club had selected. Over time, the Book-of-the-Month Club distributed books by Nobel laureates Thomas Mann, John Galsworthy, Ernest Hemingway, William Faulkner, Sinclair Lewis, and Sigrid Undset.

The Book-of-the-Month Club achieved its founder's principal objectives, revolutionizing the marketing of books in the United States and making literature more readily available nationwide. In its first twenty-five years of operation, the Book-of-the-Month Club distributed more than 100 million books.

William Hughes

created by the Wilson administration in 1917 to promote national solidarity on U.S. intervention in the war. The committee demonized the enemy, proscribed dissent, idealized America's war aims, exaggerated the glory of war, and censored negative news from the battlefield. Young Americans went to war full of unrealistic expectations and largely ignorant of the horrors of war. It was not long, however, before many of them became aware of the gap between official rhetoric and the realities of combat. The early novels of Dos Passos, Hemingway, Faulkner, and even Fitzgerald conveyed a sense of the immediate and lasting effects of war on their generation. All four writers were in uniform in some capacity during the war, though only Hemingway, who was seriously wounded, and Dos Passos actually experienced combat.

One Man's Initiation: 1917 (1919) and *Three Soldiers* (1921) by John Dos Passos were among the earliest major American novels about World War I. Strewn with corpses and maimed soldiers, they were scathing attacks on the hypocrisy and stupidity that had incited the war. Dos Passos depicted battle as an impersonal killing machine and advanced the idea that only radical social change could put an end to the insanity.

Ernest Hemingway's fictional accounts of the Great War depict the panic and confusion of men in battle, the pervasiveness of violence, and the randomness and ugliness of death. The writer's taut, objective prose communicated with clarity and intensity the experience of modern warfare. Readers could well understand why Hemingway's battle-scarred protagonists Nick Adams (*In Our Time,* 1925) and Frederick Henry (*A Farewell to Arms,* 1929) could lose faith in ideals such as "courage" and "honor." Hemingway advanced no collective solution for the problem of war. The most his men and women could do was withdraw from the destruction. After the war, many of the young men and women who had experienced it firsthand could not bring themselves to return to their homes in the United States to live as they had before. Some settled in Europe as expatriates. One of these was Hemingway, who based his novel *The Sun Also Rises* (1926) on the experiences of American expatriates in Paris during the 1920s. Hemingway's narrator is Jake Barnes, a cynical journalist whose war wounds have left him sexually impotent. He compensates by indulging his remaining appetites. He lives for food and wine (in excessive quantities), the café scene in Paris, fishing, and bullfights in Spain. The fictional expatriates of *The Sun Also Rises* seem aimless in

their movements, purposeless in their work, and pointless in their talk. Their love is invariably misdirected; their coupling is passionless and indiscriminate. Small wonder, then, that author and bohemian Gertrude Stein would say of their real-life counterparts that they were all "a lost generation."

As for those who came home from the war, they were—as depicted by the novelists of their generation—ruined for civilian and family life. Scarred by war, they turned cynical, restless, fatalistic, and wary, cutting themselves off from others. In "The Big Two-Hearted River," Hemingway's alter ego, Nick Adams, seeks the solitude of the backwoods. We know from related stories that Nick has been damaged by the war. A solitary fishing trip is his way of shutting out the past, if only for a while. Nick needs the ritualized distractions of fishing and camping to keep him occupied so he does not have to think about the war or experience the emotional pain elicited by such thoughts.

William Faulkner, in *Soldiers' Pay* (1926), tells the story of Donald Mahon, who returns from the fighting disfigured and partially blind. Donald feels estranged from his former life, and the townspeople do not know how to relate to the damaged veteran. Some are morbidly curious about his wounds; others simply pity him or avoid him. Only a war widow seems capable of accepting him as he is. They marry, but soon Donald perishes from his injuries. In *Sartoris* (1929), Bayard Sartoris is an aviator back from the war where he witnessed his twin brother's death in aerial combat. He cannot adjust to postwar life. He is restless and reckless, though he finds some solace in hunting, an escape that briefly reconnects him to nature and the ways of his youth. Eventually he marries but does not truly settle down. He abandons his wife and child to become a test pilot and finally satisfies his apparent death wish by crashing an experimental aircraft.

Another veteran in *Sartoris* is a young African American named Caspey Strother, whose family has served the aristocratic Sartorises for generations. Strother returns from the war with a newfound insolence. He has seen something of the world beyond Mississippi, and he has learned that Negroes are treated differently outside the Deep South. He assumes that his military service entitles him to a degree of respect not usually extended to Southern blacks. To further his case, he resorts to exaggerating his exploits in the war, but no one takes him seriously. Hoping to convince others that he is no longer the subservient young farmhand he was before the war, Strother ignores directives and evades chores. But he soon finds that he is still dependent upon the Sartorises. With some prodding from his relatives, he falls back into subservience. The Great War has not altered his standing in the regional caste system, but it has radically altered his view of his condition. As with the white veterans, it has left him at odds with his time and place.

Cosmopolitanism Versus Provincialism

Another fruitful source for Jazz Age fiction was the cultural divide between cosmopolitanism and provincialism, or between modernity and nostalgia. This division expressed itself in certain distinct differences between the city and the small town in American life. Artists, intellectuals, bohemians, professors, and journalists saw cities as centers of progress, places where individuals enjoyed greater personal freedom and where culture thrived. To them, American small towns were havens of conformity and small-mindedness, dominated by religious fundamentalism, petty businessmen, and Prohibition. But most small-town Americans cherished their way of life. They perceived themselves as the beleaguered guardians of traditional American values, which were threatened by the social, cultural, and moral innovations they associated with modernity and the decadent cities. That small-town America remained predominantly Anglo-Saxon and Protestant, while Catholic and Jewish immigrants from Southern and Eastern Europe had gathered in cities, no doubt added to the climate of mutual suspicion.

If in politics the small town still prevailed, the culture wars were a different matter. Three of the period's most influential works of fiction heaped scorn on American provincialism and virtually everything it represented. In the loosely connected stories of *Winesburg, Ohio* (1919), Sherwood Anderson showed how small-town life inhibited the instinctual needs and natural longings of its fictional inhabitants. Those who cannot or will not conform to the community's narrow standards are rejected, unhappy, lost, or warped for life. Anderson's approach was primarily psychological. Sinclair Lewis's attacks on provincial America were more broadly social in scope and satirical in method. His novel *Main Street* (1920) exposed the shallow cultural pretensions, crass commercialism, and sheer unpleasantness of a fictional

small town, Gopher Prairie, Minnesota. Lewis's *Babbitt* (1922) satirized the booster mentality of the small-business types who set the tone for such places. In both novels, the leading character aspires to a more satisfying way of life but is thwarted by the cultural or social limitations inherent in small-town existence.

On balance, Jazz Age fiction was not so hard on city life. *Manhattan Transfer* (1925) by John Dos Passos was a major exception. Although Dos Passos was no defender of the small town and its values, his novel is a devastating panorama of life in the big city between the 1890s and the mid-1920s. Although the city provides some of his characters with opportunities for upward social mobility, even wealth and fame, most of its inhabitants are forced to lead sordid lives. Like the protagonists of the writer's war novels, the people of *Manhattan Transfer* are caught up in a great impersonal mechanism that controls their fortunes and frustrates their hopes. Even those few who achieve material success fail to attain happiness or satisfaction in their relationships. As Dos Passos describes it, the city seems no less repressive than the small towns in the works of Sherwood Anderson and Sinclair Lewis.

William Faulkner and F. Scott Fitzgerald were ambivalent about the cultural divide that separated city and small town. In 1929, Faulkner launched his unique fictional chronicle of rural Yoknapatawpha County and its county seat, Jefferson. *Sartoris* was the first of several novels in which Faulkner sets out the history and character of a land and people far removed from America's cultural centers. His complex portrait of rural and small-town life is unflattering. Modernity has bypassed Jefferson, which is bound by regressive social and racial codes. But Faulkner's small-town characters, black and white, have a sense of self that is lacking in the people of Winesburg or Gopher Prairie. Their identities are grounded in social tradition, regional history, and family connections. Such qualities, Faulkner seems to suggest, make for a richer existence than can be found in the cosmopolitan cities of the North and East.

F. Scott Fitzgerald also found in regionalism a basis for questioning the supposed superiority of the metropolis. Nick Carraway, who narrates *The Great Gatsby* (1925), is a Midwesterner who goes East to attend college, after which he takes a job on Wall Street. To him, the East initially seems preferable to what he left behind, "the bored, sprawling, swollen towns beyond the Ohio . . . with their interminable inquisitions." Nick can hardly believe his good fortune at being drawn into the dazzling social milieu of his mysterious Long Island neighbor, Jay Gatsby, who has placed himself at the very center of a world of wealth and glamour. To Nick, these qualities exist in the East on a scale unimaginable to most Midwesterners. Eventually disillusioned, Nick turns away from New York and goes home to Minnesota. He is left with only "unaffected scorn" for the privileged but self-absorbed, uncaring, and amoral people he has known on Long Island—though he retains some affection and admiration for Gatsby, who turns out to have been, like Nick, a transplanted Midwesterner.

Before *Gatsby* elevated him to the upper echelon of American authors, Fitzgerald was best known for glamorizing the new lifestyles of young middle-class women. The emergence of the "New Woman" was a major social development of the period, and Fitzgerald was among the first to exploit it as a subject for fiction. The flapper appeared prominently in his early novels (*This Side of Paradise*, 1920; *The Beautiful and the Damned*, 1922) and short stories (*Flappers and Philosophers*, 1920; *Tales of the Jazz Age*, 1922). His fictional flappers are typically good-looking, sporty, flirtatious, fashionable, outspoken, and in open rebellion against Victorian morality. Ernest Hemingway's Brett Ashley of *The Sun Also Rises* added to the literary mystique of the New Woman. An expatriate, Brett generally does as she pleases, answers to no one, and asserts a degree of sexual freedom typically accorded only to men. Indeed, she calls herself "a chap," wears a man's hat, and has her hair cut in a boyish style. (Jake Barnes says it is Brett who started the twenties fashion for bobbed hair.)

For Fitzgerald and Hemingway, the New Woman ultimately came to personify social breakdown. Their young heroines, for all the newfound freedom and excitement in their lives, usually are unfulfilled and purposeless. Hemingway's Brett Ashley, for instance, is incapable of love and remains dependent on men for money and self-esteem. And a closer look at Fitzgerald's early fiction reveals that, aside from their youthful high spirits, his flappers are self-absorbed, immature, materialistic, and shallow. Neither author chose to write about other liberated young women of the Jazz Age, the idealistic ones who tried to advance broad social reforms, including economic and political equality for women. It was left to popular female novelists, such as Zona Gale and Fannie Hurst, to provide fuller renderings of the New Woman.

Styles, Techniques, and Narrative Structures

The greatest novels and stories of the Jazz Age continue to interest readers today, not simply as social documents but also because of their literary qualities. Hemingway, Faulkner, and others introduced new styles, techniques, and psychological insights to the writing of fiction. Together with the leading poets of their era, they modernized American literature.

Hemingway's style typically features simple sentence structure and journalistic objectivity, as well as repetition and rhythm, all painstakingly worked out to put the focus on precisely those circumstances and details that would re-create in the reader the emotions that they had first triggered in the writer. That technique is what enabled Hemingway to write about war, bullfights, hunting, and fishing with such immediacy. Faulkner, on the other hand, often confounded readers, writing almost endless run-on sentences that often were unclear on first reading. His narrative structures could be as dense and convoluted as his sentences, and Faulkner was a determined subjectivist. In *The Sound and the Fury* (1929), for instance, he used modernist techniques such as stream of consciousness, fragmentary flashbacks, and multiple perspectives to take readers into the minds of his characters. Faulkner was also a regionalist. His ear for Mississippi dialects and his preoccupation with local knowledge enabled Faulkner to create a rich fictional chronicle of his small corner of America.

Sherwood Anderson alternated lyrical passages with bland understatement and limited but effective symbolism to achieve his effects. As in much of the period's writing, there is a trace of Freudianism—the ideas of Sigmund Freud, the Viennese psychiatrist, were just then becoming fashionable among American intellectuals and writers. Fitzgerald employed no such intellectual doctrines. Neither did he fall back on the advanced literary techniques associated with modernism. His style reflected the author's unique capacity for social observation, his unerring feel for the spirit of Jazz Age youth, and his gift for phrase making (as when Gatsby says of Daisy Buchanan that "her voice is full of money").

Dos Passos was a method writer, though in his case it was a method of his own invention. He constructed the narrative of *Manhattan Transfer* the way a documentary film editor combines disparate images and incidents to create an overall impression.

This technique enabled Dos Passos to present a fictional cross-section of contemporary New York City. In his *U.S.A.* trilogy, Dos Passos expanded this method to encompass elements of the entire nation from the Great War through the domestic crises of the 1930s.

Other Leading Lights

Only Sinclair Lewis, the most conventional of the decade's major writers, appeared on the annual lists of best-selling authors, a reminder that a cultural epoch is not defined exclusively by its principal innovators. Other Jazz Age writers also provide a useful overview of the literary scene between 1918 and 1929.

There were, for instance, established writers who had made their reputations prior to 1918 but continued to create noteworthy fiction during the interwar years. Among these were Edith Wharton (*The Age of Innocence,* 1920; *Old New York,* 1924), Willa Cather (*A Lost Lady,* 1923; *The Professor's House,* 1925; *Death Comes for the Archbishop,* 1927), Ellen Glasgow (*Barren Ground,* 1925; *The Romantic Comedians,* 1926), James Branch Cabell (the Poictesme novels, 1927–1930), Booth Tarkington (*The Magnificent Ambersons,* 1918; *Alice Adams,* 1921), and Theodore Dreiser (*An American Tragedy,* 1925). They might well be thought of as the "old order" of American novelists. Although their talents had not diminished, their work during the Jazz Age was essentially traditional in style and generally, but not always, retrospective in content. They did not greatly influence the emerging generation of American writers.

Dreiser's powerful *An American Tragedy,* which caused a sensation in the 1920s and is now considered a classic of modern American literature, would seem to be an exception to these observations. But Dreiser broke no new ground stylistically, and his novel, which is based on events that occurred in 1906, is infused with the naturalistic view of life that had been a hallmark of American fiction since the 1890s.

At the end of the 1920s and just beyond, the work of Thomas Wolfe was published. His heartfelt coming-of-age novel *Look Homeward Angel* (1929) launched a notable career that came to fruition during the next decade. All these works, from Wharton's to Wolfe's, suggest that Jazz Age fiction cannot be totally isolated from what went before and what came after.

Gertrude Stein (*The Making of Americans,* 1925), Djuna Barnes (*Ryder,* 1928), and Carl Van Vechten (*The Blind Bow-Boy,* 1923; *Nigger Heaven,* 1926) constitute a category of distinctive writers who were marginalized because of their difficult prose, offbeat subject matter, or possibly even their bohemianism. Also at the margin of the literary scene were the leading African American novelists Jean Toomer (*Cane,* 1923) and Claude McKay (*Home to Harlem,* 1928). Their grim subject matter (uprootedness, oppression, deprivation, loneliness, and thwarted hopes) was outside the experience of most white readers, who constituted the core of the reading public.

During the Jazz Age, however, black writers were just beginning to receive some recognition from the majority culture. This was the period of the Harlem Renaissance, when an appreciation for negritude was fashionable among cosmopolitan whites. Even so, writers of white Anglo-Saxon Protestant descent dominated American literature during the Jazz Age, as they had since the days of the Puritans. A variety of obstructions, including immigration policies, the pace of assimilation and acculturation, nativism, anti-Semitism, anti-Catholicism, and restricted access to higher education, kept immigrant and Native American writers, with very few exceptions, from making their presence much felt during the Jazz Age.

Popular Fiction

The most widely read writers of the period were the creators of middlebrow and popular, mass-market fiction intended for educated readers with no taste for ultramodern or experimental literature. The artistic roots of these writers were in the "Genteel Tradition" of American writing, which they kept alive into the Jazz Age. Their style was undemanding but not overly simple. They used familiar narrative strategies and wrote well-crafted, serious fiction for and about thoughtful, earnest people. Occasionally they set a story in a colorful location or historical time period, as if to compensate for a mode of presentation that was otherwise markedly conventional.

Their social views were generally enlightened, rarely radical or ironic. Their novels and stories sometimes questioned existing institutions and ideas, but—except for feminist fiction—they seldom advanced bold alternatives. In general, they simply trusted that reasonable people with good intentions would prevail, if given a chance. Among the leading middlebrow novelists of the Jazz Age were Louis Bromfield (*The Green Bay Tree,* 1924; *Early Autumn,*

1926; *A Good Woman,* 1927), Thornton Wilder (*The Cabala,* 1926; *The Bridge of San Luis Rey,* 1927), Dorothy Canfield Fisher (*The Brimming Cup,* 1921; *Rough Hewn,* 1922; *Her Son's Wife,* 1926), Zona Gale (*Birth,* 1918; *Miss Lulu Bett,* 1920), and Edna Ferber (*The Girls,* 1921; *So Big,* 1924; *Show Boat,* 1926).

Popular writing was not synonymous with middlebrow writing, nor with the best-seller lists, for even highbrow and middlebrow works sometimes reached a mass audience. Sinclair Lewis, Edith Wharton, Booth Tarkington, Dorothy Canfield Fisher, Thornton Wilder, and Edna Ferber all had best-selling books during the 1920s. Most popular writing of the Jazz Age was generic in nature, predictable, and followed the conventions of their respective forms. It included westerns, detective stories, romances, tales of suspense and adventure, historical fiction, humor, and so on—stories in which the reader usually knows what to expect.

The emergence of Dashiell Hammett, who reinvented the crime story, was perhaps the most notable development in popular fiction during the Jazz Age. Hammett introduced a new kind of detective hero—the tough-as-nails private eye, typified by the unnamed "Continental Op." This character first appeared in a story by Hammett for *Black Mask* magazine in 1923, and then in his novels *The Red Harvest* (1929) and *The Dain Curse* (1929). The Continental Op was the forerunner of Hammett's most notable creation, Sam Spade (*The Maltese Falcon,* 1930). Hammett wrote gritty crime tales in a lean style that owed much to Hemingway. He relied heavily on rough dialogue that exploited the slang of street criminals. All this was new to detective fiction. Other popular genres remained relatively unchanged and were dominated by well-established best-selling authors such as Zane Grey (westerns), Dorothy Roberts Rinehart (traditional detective novels), and Kenneth Roberts (historical fiction).

Thanks to Ring Lardner, Dorothy Parker, and Anita Loos, humor deserves special consideration in any survey of Jazz Age writing. All were true originals, and they were very much attuned to the fads, follies, and fashions of their period. Lardner (*How to Write Short Stories,* 1924; *The Love Nest and Other Stories,* 1926) specialized in the sort of low-life characters found in vaudeville houses, racetracks, baseball parks, boxing arenas, and speakeasies. His crude boxers, Tin Pan Alley hustlers, and semiliterate bush-league baseball players speak in the peculiar slang of their circumscribed worlds; the more they talk, the more they unwittingly show themselves to be narrow, self-centered, and self-deceived fools. Parker skewered more fashionable types. Her short stories for *The New Yorker* chronicled with sardonic wit the hypocrisies and insecurities of the mating game as played by shallow Manhattanites. Loos became famous for *Gentlemen Prefer Blondes* (1925), her best-selling tale of Lorelei Lee, a gold-digging flapper. It was said that young working-class women read the novel hoping to learn how to land rich husbands. As it happened, by decade's end there would be fewer wealthy men to snag.

End of an Era

The stock market crash of 1929 ended an age of prosperity; it also ended a literary epoch. The Great Depression did not finish the careers of Jazz Age writers—Faulkner, Hemingway, Dos Passos, and Fitzgerald, for instance, continued to produce important fiction. But the economic and social upheavals that rocked the nation between 1929 and World War II pointed American literature in new directions and brought to the fore writers who were preoccupied with the political and economic aspects of the national experience, particularly as they affected workers and the poor. As Marx supplanted Freud in intellectual circles, social realism and class consciousness superseded literary experimentation and aestheticism in contemporary fiction. In this emergent climate of opinion, John Steinbeck's dispossessed Okies and itinerant farm laborers seemed more authentic and pertinent than Anderson's repressed provincials, Dos Passos's aesthetes, Lewis's boosters, Hemingway's stoics, Fitzgerald's flappers, and Faulkner's self-destructive aristocrats.

William Hughes

See also: *American Mercury*; Anderson, Sherwood; Burroughs, Edgar Rice; Cummings, E.E.; Dos Passos, John; Dreiser, Theodore; Fitzgerald, F. Scott, and Zelda Fitzgerald; Harlem Renaissance; Hemingway, Ernest; Lewis, Sinclair; Lost Generation; Parker, Dorothy; Poetry; Stein, Gertrude; Theater.

Further Reading

Blake, Nelson Manfred. *Novelists' America: Fiction as History, 1910–1940.* Syracuse, NY: Syracuse University Press, 1969.

Botshon, Lisa, and Meredith Goldsmith, eds. *Middlebrow Moderns: Popular American Women Writers of the 1920s.* Boston: Northeastern University Press, 2003.

Cowley, Malcolm. *A Second Flowering: Works and Days of the Lost Generation*. New York: Viking, 1973.

Davis, Simone Weil. *Ad Work: Gender Fictions of the 1920s*. Durham, NC: Duke University Press, 2000.

Dumenil, Lynn. *The Modern Temper: American Culture and Society in the 1920s*. New York: Hill and Wang, 1995.

Elias, Robert H. *Entangling Alliances with None: An Essay on the Individual in the American Twenties*. New York: W.W. Norton, 1973.

Hoffman, Frederick J. *The Twenties: American Writing in the Postwar Decade*. New York: Collier, 1962.

Kenner, Hugh. *A Homemade World: The American Modernist Writers*. New York: Alfred A. Knopf, 1975.

McCormick, John. *The Middle Distance: A Comparative History of American Imaginative Literature, 1919–1932*. New York: Free Press, 1971.

Nash, Roderick. *The Nervous Generation: American Thought, 1917–1930*. Chicago: Rand McNally, 1970.

Raub, Patricia. *Yesterday's Stories: Popular Women's Novels of the Twenties and Thirties*. Westport, CT: Greenwood, 1994.

Rhodes, Chip. *Structures of the Jazz Age*. London: Verso, 1998.

Wilson, Edmund. *The Shores of Light: A Literary Chronicle of the Twenties and Thirties*. New York: Farrar, Straus, and Young, 1952.

———. *The Wound and the Bow: Seven Studies in Literature*. London: Methuen University Paperbacks, 1952.

Film

The 1920s saw film emerge as a respectable artistic medium as well as a celebrated and financially successful industry. This process began with the highly successful epic *Birth of a Nation* by director D.W. Griffith in 1914. It was not until the movie palaces of the 1920s, and the creation of a consistently better product from Hollywood, that American films gained widespread acceptance.

Major Studios

Much of the acceptance of American films had to do with the phenomenal success of the motion picture industry and the million-dollar contracts offered to stars like Mary Pickford and Charlie Chaplin. Those two stars, along with Douglas Fairbanks and D.W. Griffith, formed United Artists in 1919, producing their own films rather than working through the major studios.

Major studios had ways of controlling the industry. Paramount Pictures was the empire of Adolf Zukor, who had bought up smaller competitors and then forced theaters to "block book" all the studio's films, not just the ones with popular stars. First National, a theater chain, began to offer stars direct contracts to make films for their movie houses, granting a star greater independence in choosing projects while ensuring that First National had films to screen. The most dominant player in Hollywood was Metro-Goldwyn-Mayer (MGM), which combined theaters, a production studio, and a distribution company to control all aspects of the film industry.

Together, these studios and stars created motion pictures that appealed not just to the masses but also to an upper-class audience through the use of famous Broadway actors and serious subject matter, such as historical and biblical epics.

Theaters

As a working-class amusement around the turn of the century, movie viewing took place primarily in storefront nickelodeons. Not only were movies inexpensive at five cents, but silent films were easily adapted to non-English-speaking immigrant audiences; title cards could be translated, either by the theater operators providing their own cards, or by an interpreter serving as narrator for the audience. But nickelodeons were small (the largest could accommodate perhaps 400 people), located in marginal neighborhoods, and attended by a mostly male audience. Over the course of the 1910s and 1920s, as the popularity of films increased, movie theaters began to resemble stage theaters, especially in the use of classic architectural elements like columns and pillars around the screen and classic façades on the exteriors. Films attracted more women and children, as well as a more educated and prosperous audience.

Theater owners saw the benefit of creating luxurious environments in which audiences experienced the movies. Samuel L. Rothafel, nicknamed "Roxy," opened a string of lavish theaters in New York, culminating with Radio City Music Hall. These movie palaces gave audience, the sense that they, too, led a glamorous Hollywood life. On the West Coast, Sid Grauman created exotically themed theaters such as the Egyptian and Chinese Theaters, transporting audiences to the exotic locales featured in many of the films. Grauman's Chinese Theater, on Hollywood Boulevard, featured a courtyard where movie stars were invited to imprint their hands or feet in wet concrete, leaving a permanent and tangible reminder of their stardom for audiences.

Most major cities, and smaller ones as well, had at least one movie palace seating over a thousand pa-

The great cinematic innovation of the 1920s was the introduction of sound. In this 1927 photograph, director Alan Crosland gives orders to cast members of *The Jazz Singer,* the first full-length feature with a synchronized sound track. *(Stringer/Hulton Archive/Getty Images)*

trons. Movie palaces not only increased the respectability of the movies but made them more democratic as well; most did not sell different-priced tickets for different sections of the theater (a common Broadway theater practice), and even when they did charge more for boxes or gallery seats, tickets were still within the range of most middle-class Americans. Most theaters, however, relegated African Americans to the balcony.

Scandals

Film's new respectability did not come easily, especially in the wake of scandals in the personal lives of movie stars. In 1920, "America's Sweetheart," Mary Pickford, divorced her husband and three weeks later married screen swashbuckler Douglas Fairbanks, who had also recently divorced his wife. Once married, however, Pickford and Fairbanks reigned over Hollywood from their estate, "Pickfair," setting themselves up as examples of the wholesome lives of movie actors. In 1921, film comedian Rosco "Fatty" Arbuckle hosted a party at a San Francisco hotel. One of his guests, a young actress, Virginia Rappe, was found in one of the rooms and later died under suspicious circumstances, implicating Arbuckle. The film star was tried for involuntary manslaughter and found not guilty, but Hollywood producers, fearing the wrath of religious and culturally conservative groups, blackballed Arbuckle. He quietly continued his career as a director under the name "Will B. Good." Then, in 1922, director William Desmond Taylor

was found dead in his apartment, apparently murdered. Although the case was never solved, speculation in the press ended the careers of actresses Mabel Norman and Mary Miles Minter.

All the media attention brought the industry to the verge of federal censorship, a move producers blocked by imposing self-regulation. In 1922, industry leaders hired Will H. Hays, President Warren G. Harding's former campaign manager, former postmaster general of the United States, and Presbyterian elder, to preside over the newly formed Motion Picture Producers and Distributors Association of America (MPPDA). Known as the "Hays office," the organization did not censor as much as it tried to limit bad publicity for the film industry. While attempts to limit "improper" content were only voluntary and ineffective, the Hays office did forestall government intervention in the film industry.

The Art of Film

The film industry gained artistic respectability by showing how the medium could move and educate audiences, not just entertain them. Cecil B. DeMille's 1927 religious epic *King of Kings* showed that film could complement the sacred, as opposed to leading churchgoers down the wrong path. Documentarian Robert Flaherty illustrated the educational potential of film with his portrait of Eskimo life in *Nanook of the North* (1922) and his depiction of a South Seas island in *Moana* (1926).

The era's greatest motion picture artist was director Erich von Stroheim, who created a string of powerful and artistic films during the decade, beginning with *Blind Husbands* (1919), *Foolish Wives* (1922), *The Merry-Go-Round* (1923), and *The Merry Widow* (1925). Von Stroheim's masterpiece was *Greed* (1924), a faithful adaptation of Frank Norris's novel *McTeague* (1916). In an era when most big films were made in studios, the director's desire for realism led him to film *Greed* on location in San Francisco and Death Valley (in the scorching heat of summer), and to create a film that ran almost nine hours. The studio, however, reduced the film to about two hours, and destroyed the discarded negatives before releasing it. Despite the ruthless editing, many consider *Greed* the greatest silent film of all time.

Most moviegoers did not seek the artistic potential of film so much as its entertainment quality. They flocked to swashbuckling films by Douglas

Fairbanks such as *The Mark of Zorro* (1920), *The Three Musketeers* (1921), *Robin Hood* (1922), and *The Thief of Baghdad* (1924); family dramas with Mary Pickford such as *Pollyanna* (1920), *Tess of the Storm Country* (1922), and *My Best Gal* (1927); and romantic adventures with Rudolph Valentino such as *Four Horsemen of the Apocalypse* (1921), *The Sheik* (1921), and *Son of the Sheik* (1926). Comedy was supplied by Charlie Chaplin in *The Kid* (1921), *The Idle Class* (1921), and *The Gold Rush* (1925), and by Buster Keaton in *Go West* (1925), *The General* (1926), and *Steamboat Bill* (1927), as well as in short films by Laurel and Hardy. Most representative of the 1920s are the films of the "It Girl," Clara Bow, such as *The Plastic Age* (1925), *Mantrap* (1926), and *It* (1927).

The most significant film of the decade was *The Jazz Singer* (1927), as it started the transition to sound film and marked the death of silent film (only Chaplin would be successful with silent films after 1927). *The Jazz Singer* combined silent film with several synchronized sound scenes, primarily when the protagonist, Jackie Rabinowitz (a.k.a. Jack Robin), sang. The transition to sound also allowed Walt Disney to create a talking, singing, and dancing mouse named Mickey, who made his first feature appearance in the animated *Steamboat Willie* (1928).

Charles J. Shindo

See also: Arbuckle (Fatty) Scandal; Bow, Clara; Celebrity Culture; Chaplin, Charlie; DeMille, Cecil B.; Fairbanks, Douglas; Film Industry; Gish, Lillian; Keaton, Buster; Mayer, Louis B.; Pickford, Mary; Rogers, Will; Swanson, Gloria; Theater; Vaudeville; Weissmuller, Johnny.

Further Reading

Brownlow, Kevin. *The Parade's Gone By.* Berkeley: University of California Press, 1976.

Everson, William K. *American Silent Film.* New York: Oxford University Press, 1978.

MacCann, Richard Dyer. *Films of the 1920s.* Lanham, MD: Scarecrow, 1996.

May, Lary. *Screening Out the Past: The Birth of Mass Culture and the Motion Picture Industry.* Chicago: University of Chicago Press, 1980.

Sklar, Robert. *Movie-Made America: A Cultural History of American Movies.* New York: Vintage Books, 1975.

Film Industry

The American film industry underwent dramatic growth during the Jazz Age. In 1920, roughly 30 million tickets were being sold weekly in America; by 1930, the figure had climbed to 100 million, at a time when the total U.S. population was about 120 million. In 1927, filmmaking experienced a technological advance with the introduction of the "talkie," a film with a synchronized soundtrack. The industry underwent a structural change at roughly the same time, with the rise of the studio system.

Like other businesses in the booming corporate economy of the 1920s, the film business experienced consolidation as well as growth. The studio system was Hollywood's version of the vertical integration that had been sweeping American business since the late nineteenth century. With vertical integration, a single corporation controls every aspect of production, from raw materials to manufacturing to distribution and marketing. Raw materials in the movie business meant talent, and under the studio system, the big companies signed long-term and exclusive contracts with budding actors, top directors, and popular stars. The studios also came to control production, owning their own back lots and equipment. Finally, the big studios also developed distribution arms and even owned movie theater chains.

The American film business largely began in and around New York City at the turn of the twentieth century. New York was the center of American theater, so there was abundant acting and production talent. The business end of early filmmaking was dominated by members of the New York immigrant community or their offspring, many of whom had been involved in vaudeville, theater, and entertainment arcades. Some came from the garment business.

About 1910, production began to move west, to the rapidly growing city of Los Angeles and in particular its small northwestern suburb of Hollywood. Moviemakers were drawn there by cheaper labor costs and abundant sunshine, which made it possible to produce movies year-round in an era when primitive lighting made it difficult to film indoors.

Early Hollywood was dominated by small independent film studios and by stars such as Charlie Chaplin and Lillian Gish, whose popularity gave them the power to dictate terms to the relatively weak studio heads. However, even during this talent-dominated, competitive period in the industry, the big studios, led by charismatic and often dictatorial businessmen, were emerging. These included Paramount Pictures, founded in 1914 by Hungarian immigrant Adolph Zukor, who got his start in the fur business; Warner Brothers, started by Polish immigrant brothers Harry, Albert, Sam, and Jack Warner in 1918; and Goldwyn Pictures (later Metro-Goldwyn-Mayer, or MGM), founded in 1916 by the quintessential Hollywood mogul and Polish immigrant Samuel Goldwyn.

Two other major studios rounded out the "big five" of the early studio era: Fox (later 20th Century Fox), started in 1915, and RKO (Radio-Keith-Orpheum), begun in 1928. Two other "majors," as the big studios were called, had a significant role in production but owned few theaters. These were Universal Pictures and Columbia Pictures. The final major was United Artists, founded in 1919 by Chaplin, actors Douglas Fairbanks and Mary Pickford, and director D.W. Griffith. But United, which owned few theaters, was largely a financier and distributor, backing independent producers and distributing their films.

Even as the studios were consolidating their control of production, entrepreneurs such as Sid Grauman and Marcus Loew were building large and ornate theaters—"movie palaces"—across America. And while some of the big studios would eventually move into the movie theater business, Loew traveled in the other direction, using revenues from his theater chain to purchase Metro Pictures in the early 1920s, then buying out Goldwyn and producer Louis B. Mayer to form MGM in 1924.

The 1927 release of the first feature talkie—*The Jazz Singer,* starring Al Jolson—was a key moment for the industry. That film, and several talkie blockbusters that followed, made an enormous amount of money for Paramount Pictures, and in turn caught the interest of East Coast financiers. By the late 1920s, the studios were able to borrow greater and greater sums of money, allowing them to expand their production facilities, buy existing movie theater chains, cultivate talent by signing new actors and directors to long-term contracts, and pay big salaries to keep established stars working exclusively for one studio.

Film historians refer to the studio-system period from the late 1920s through the late 1940s as the "golden age" of Hollywood. The Academy of Motion Picture Arts and Sciences, founded in 1927, was dedicated to advancing the technological and artistic aspects of the motion picture industry. In 1929, the organization hosted its first awards ceremony, the Academy Awards, or Oscars.

The 1920s were not referred to as Hollywood's golden age because of the high quality of films the studios released. Then as now, the industry produced both memorable and forgettable films. But Hollywood at this time, with no competition yet from television, dominated the entertainment world. Moreover, the film community was flush with money, allowing its members to live the well-publicized, glamorous lifestyle with which it became associated in the public imagination.

The studio system and the golden age ended for two reasons. One was a landmark Supreme Court decision, the Paramount decree of 1948, an antitrust ruling forcing studios to sell off their distribution arms. The other blow was the advent of television, which would even more forcefully affect ticket sales in the early 1950s.

James Ciment

See also: Arbuckle (Fatty) Scandal; Celebrity Culture; Chaplin, Charlie; DeMille, Cecil B.; Fairbanks, Douglas; Film; Keaton, Buster; Mayer, Louis B.; Pickford, Mary.

Further Reading

Brown, Gene. *Movie Time: A Chronology of Hollywood and the Movie Industry from Its Beginnings to the Present.* New York: Macmillan, 1995.

Earley, Steven C. *An Introduction to American Movies.* New York: New American Library, 1978.

Koszarski, Richard. *An Evening's Entertainment: The Age of the Silent Feature Picture, 1915–1928.* Berkeley: University of California Press, 1994.

Robinson, David. *Hollywood in the Twenties.* New York: A.S. Barnes, 1968.

Sklar, Robert. *Movie-Made America: A Cultural History of American Movies.* Revised and updated. New York: Vintage Books, 1994.

Fisher, Carl (1874–1939)

Carl Graham Fisher was a pioneering automotive, highway, and land developer known for his skills in sales and promotion. He played a central role in the development of Miami Beach, Florida, as a resort city.

Fisher was born in Greensburg, Indiana, on January 12, 1874. He grew up in poverty and dropped out of school at the age of twelve, when his alcoholic father abandoned the family. Entrepreneurial, athletic, and mechanically inclined, he opened a bicycle shop at the age of seventeen. In his twenties, he opened a garage in Indianapolis and built it into one of the country's leading automobile dealerships. He was a colorful character known for publicity stunts such as suspending a car from a hot-air balloon.

In 1904, Fisher entered into a partnership with Percy Avery, who owned a patent for a compressed gas cylinder filled with acetylene gas and an arc lamp. Avery saw its potential as a replacement for the poor-quality automobile headlights then in use, but he had been unable to obtain financial backing. Fisher provided Avery with the money for the manufacture of what became known as Prest-O-Lite automobile headlights. The headlights were popular, and in 1910, the partners sold out to Union Carbide, making them both multimillionaires.

In 1909, thirty-five-year-old Carl Fisher married fifteen-year-old Jane Watts. The same year, he helped fund and design the famed Indianapolis Motor Speedway, launching the Indianapolis 500 race to attract publicity and spectators. In 1913, he also conceived and helped develop the first modern transcontinental road, the Lincoln Highway, linking New York City and San Francisco. He also envisioned and lobbied the federal government for the Dixie Highway, which ran from Indianapolis south to Miami Beach. In Miami Beach, Fisher would find his greatest success and biggest misfortune.

Fisher and his wife bought a winter home in Miami in 1910. When he first laid eyes on the barrier island adjacent to Miami, between Biscayne Bay and the Atlantic Ocean, he immediately conceived of a plan to develop it into a thriving resort. John S. Collins, a Quaker from New Jersey, had begun developing Miami Beach from mangrove swamps and salt marshes in the 1910s. Fisher lent Collins $50,000 to finish building a wooden bridge from the barrier island to the mainland. In exchange, Fisher received prime land in Miami Beach. He proceeded to dredge the bay and replace the swamps with land held in place by grasses, Australian pines, and other shrubbery.

Miami Beach was incorporated on March 26, 1915. Fisher and his wife moved into their newly constructed estate, The Shadows, that same year. Fisher offered free beachfront property to any settler, but few took his offer. The first lots were sold at auction in 1919, and Fisher used publicity stunts to promote the area, including bands, speedboat regattas, parties, yachts, and appearances by celebrities such as Will Rogers and Irving Berlin. He also appealed to wealthy individuals to build homes there. His most famous stunts included placing photos of beautiful young women in bathing suits in Northern newspapers during winter, and using baby elephants as caddies on his golf courses. One elephant, Rosie,

achieved national fame when newspapers across the country carried photos of her caddying for president-elect Warren G. Harding in late 1920.

Fisher's promotion of his Miami Beach paradise helped spark the great Florida land boom of the era. By 1925, Miami Beach boasted hotels, apartment buildings, polo fields, golf courses, and churches. At the height of the land boom in 1925, Fisher's total worth was an estimated $50 million. Because most of it was in the form of paper assets such as binders, mortgages, tax certifications, and warranty deeds, however, he paid for current projects with estimated future profits. Meanwhile, Fisher was having marital problems. The couple had lost their infant son in 1921, and Jane Fisher adopted a two-year-old boy the following year, but Fisher refused to take part in the adoption. The Fishers divorced in 1926, and he later married Margaret Collier.

Fisher attempted to duplicate his Miami Beach success by creating a northern resort in Montauk on Long Island, New York. The area was just hours from New York City and was already known as a fishing and hunting retreat. In 1925, he purchased the entire 10,000-acre peninsula of virtually undeveloped land for $2.5 million. Outdoor activities for the vacationing wealthy would include yachting, fishing, golfing, shooting, tennis, polo, and swimming. The next several years saw the development of roads, churches, a downtown area, a harbor area, a golf course, civic and commercial buildings, and homes. Fisher reconfigured the landlocked Lake Montauk by cutting a channel to connect it to the sea. This offered the necessary deepwater port for the yachts and other large vessels of wealthy visitors.

As Fisher was developing Montauk, the Florida real estate market was in decline. By 1926, with sellers having replaced buyers, hotels and apartments stood empty. Negative press reports of shady land deals began to spread just as a major hurricane struck in September 1926, doing extensive damage and causing more negative publicity and tourism losses. In 1928, Fisher tried to revive Miami Beach through a nationwide publicity blitz, but a brief upsurge of lot sales and building was cut short by the 1929 stock market crash.

Fisher was forced to sell many of his personal and business assets, including the Indianapolis Motor Speedway, Miami Beach properties, personal homes, yachts, and land. Creditors sold his Miami Beach property to gangsters such as Al Capone; casinos, bookie joints, and nightclubs soon sprang up. Fisher had borrowed heavily against his Miami Beach properties to finance Montauk, and now much of Montauk fell into decay. By 1932, his empire was bankrupt; by 1934, he had declared personal bankruptcy. Fisher spent his remaining years alone in a small cottage in Miami Beach, where he battled alcoholism and cirrhosis. He died on July 15, 1939, at the age of sixty-five.

Marcella Bush Treviño

See also: Florida Land Boom; Real Estate.

Further Reading

Armbruster, Ann. *The Life and Times of Miami Beach.* New York: Alfred A. Knopf, 1995.

Fisher, Jerry M. *The Untold Story of Carl G. Fisher.* Fort Bragg, CA: Lost Coast, 1998.

Foster, Mark S. *Castles in the Sand: The Life and Times of Carl Graham Fisher.* Florida History and Culture Series. Gainesville: University Press of Florida, 2000.

Fitzgerald, F. Scott (1896–1940), and Zelda Fitzgerald (1900–1948)

More than any other author of his generation, F. Scott Fitzgerald shaped American perceptions about the burgeoning youth culture of the early twentieth century. He portrayed an effervescent time of "flappers and philosophers" and coined the term that captured its spirit: the Jazz Age. The immense popular appeal of Fitzgerald and his wife, Zelda, derived not least from the fact that they seemed to be characters out of one of his novels. They were young and glamorous, the quintessential literary couple of the Roaring Twenties, and their public lives embodied almost too perfectly the reckless, breathless ethos of the author's fictional partygoers. Americans watched the giddy ascent of the Fitzgeralds with rapt attention. Fifteen years later, they were already relics of a bygone age, and their dismal descent was largely ignored.

Romantic Egotists

Francis Scott Key Fitzgerald was born in St. Paul, Minnesota, on September 24, 1896; Zelda Sayre Fitzgerald was born in Montgomery, Alabama, on July 24, 1900. Scott published his first work of fiction, a story titled "The Mystery of Raymond Mortgage," at the age of thirteen and continued to generate plays and stories throughout his school years. In 1913, he entered Princeton University, encountering a world of privilege and sophistication to which he fervently

desired admittance. When he failed to make the Princeton football team, Fitzgerald redirected his energies toward literary pursuits, producing theatricals for the Princeton Triangle Club while writing for the *Nassau Literary Magazine* and the campus humor review, the *Princeton Tiger*. While these efforts earned Fitzgerald a name as a talented young writer, they also damaged his grades—to the point that he withdrew from the university in 1915.

The author's return to Princeton in 1916 was cut short by the outbreak of World War I. Fitzgerald enlisted as an officer in late 1917, and while the cessation of hostilities meant that he never had to take up arms, his time in the army did produce an enormous change in his life. In 1918, while stationed in Alabama, Fitzgerald met and fell in love with the beautiful Zelda Sayre, daughter of an Alabama supreme court justice. Discharged in 1919, Fitzgerald abandoned any thought of finishing Princeton, traveling instead to New York City with Zelda as his fiancée.

F. Scott Fitzgerald's novels and short stories chronicled the excesses of the Jazz Age, even as the opulent lifestyle of the writer and his wife, Zelda, shown here in 1921, epitomized its flamboyance. *(Stringer/Hulton Archive/Getty Images)*

Only months later, Zelda broke off the engagement, claiming that Scott's work with an advertising agency was unlikely to afford them the material comforts she desired. Fitzgerald returned to St. Paul, where he edited and resubmitted his twice-rejected book manuscript *The Romantic Egotist*. The book was accepted for publication by Scribner's under a new title, *This Side of Paradise*. Upon its release in 1920, the novel catapulted Fitzgerald to almost instant fame. The twenty-four-year-old writer was hailed as the voice of the rising generation. His short stories were sought after by large-circulation magazines. In April 1920, Scott and Zelda married at New York's St. Patrick's Cathedral.

The Great Fitzgerald

Flappers and Philosophers (1920), a collection of short stories, followed fast on the heels of Fitzgerald's successful novel. Sparkling reviews and brisk sales carried the author—unknown just a few months before—to dizzying heights of celebrity. He and Zelda lived lavishly, taking an apartment in New York and traveling through Europe. Wherever the pair went, they surprised the people around them— by dancing on tables or dipping in fountains—and attracted the attention of newspaper reporters. In later years, Fitzgerald looked back on this period as the happiest he had experienced, a time "when life was literally a dream."

His second full-length work, *The Beautiful and Damned* (1922), earned only lukewarm reviews, but his next collection of stories, *Tales of the Jazz Age* (1922), was touted even more enthusiastically than the first. The Fitzgeralds set themselves up in a spacious house in suburban Great Neck, New York. Yet a lifestyle of free spending and lavish parties burned through money faster than Fitzgerald could earn it. The author wrote short stories to meet his debts, establishing a pattern that would endure for the rest of his career.

Shaken by the failure of Scott's play *The Vegetable* (1923), the Fitzgeralds escaped to Europe in 1924. Shuttling between Paris and the French Riviera, he and Zelda enjoyed the company of other literary giants in exile, including Gertrude Stein, James Joyce, and an as-yet-to-be-discovered Ernest Hemingway. The attractions of the Continent, however, could not undo the damage of the revelation that Zelda had formed a liaison with a French aviator.

A wounded Fitzgerald buried himself in work and produced, in *The Great Gatsby* (1925), his most powerful and original novel. The character Jay Gatsby's quest for something beautiful and transcendent is bounded by a culture that knows no values outside of the starkly material. While the author would always consider *Gatsby* his great achievement, its barren soulscapes failed to move critics. One reviewer referred to its "green oases in an all too arid desert of waste paper," while another opined that "Mr. Scott Fitzgerald deserves a good shaking." A third collection of short stories, *All the Sad Young Men* (1926), generated greater enthusiasm.

Crack-Up

Fitzgerald produced no major publications during the rest of the decade, though he did work assiduously at his lucrative story writing. In 1930, while the Fitzgeralds were once again living in Paris, Zelda experienced a nervous breakdown. Although it was far from evident at the time, this was the beginning of a mental decline that would eventually lead to her institutionalization, and to the effective end of the Fitzgeralds' marriage.

In 1932, during a period of relative stability, Zelda published a first novel, *Save Me the Waltz*. A transparently autobiographical and inescapably mediocre book, it had the added effect of alienating her husband, who resented being portrayed as a "nonentity." Meanwhile, his *Tender Is the Night* (1934)— the last novel he would publish in his lifetime—was greeted with indifference. Worse, it earned him little more than he was accustomed to making on a short story. *The Crack-Up*, a collection of autobiographical essays that Fitzgerald published in 1936, dealt forthrightly with the personal and professional failures that had befallen him since his early success in the 1920s.

More in need of money than ever, Fitzgerald in 1937 accepted an offer to write under contract for Metro-Goldwyn-Mayer (MGM). Hollywood proved a difficult fit, however, and after 1938, he and the studio parted ways. Now far removed from the public eye, Fitzgerald was still at work on *The Last Tycoon*, a novel set in the filmmaking world, when he died of a heart attack on December 21, 1940. Five years after his death, *The New York Times* would still berate him for "squandering the last scraps of his ability in Grade B movies and magazines." Zelda Fitzgerald died in a hospital fire on March 10, 1948.

Eric Paras

See also: Celebrity Culture; Fiction; Lost Generation.

Further Reading

Bruccoli, Matthew J. *Some Sort of Epic Grandeur.* New York: Harcourt Brace Jovanovich, 1981.

Bruccoli, Matthew J., and Jackson R. Bryer, eds. *F. Scott Fitzgerald in His Own Time: A Miscellany.* Kent, OH: Kent State University Press, 1971.

Milford, Nancy. *Zelda.* New York: Harper & Row, 1970.

Mizener, Arthur. *The Far Side of Paradise.* Boston: Houghton Mifflin, 1949.

Prigozy, Ruth. *F. Scott Fitzgerald.* London: Penguin, 2001.

Florida Land Boom

The spectacular Florida land boom of the 1920s revolved around a dramatic rise in real estate transactions and land development that was a part of the decade's wide-ranging speculation fever. At the height of the boom, from 1923 to 1925, an estimated 300,000 new residents settled in Florida.

The land boom, like other consumer phenomena of the Jazz Age, was triggered by major economic and social changes in the country after World War I. Increasing numbers of Americans were enjoying paid vacations, as well as wealth, pensions, and easy credit with which to purchase real estate. Mass production and easy credit made automobiles an affordable and popular choice of transportation. Florida's inexpensive undeveloped land and semitropical climate made it an ideal destination for tourists and new residents. Land speculators and developers rushed to cash in on the boom, which began at Miami Beach in southeastern Florida and spread throughout the state, especially along the east and west coasts.

Many developers planned communities with exotic landscaping. Promoters such as Miami Beach developer Carl Fisher used "cheesecake" photos of bathing beauties on warm sunny beaches, running them in Northern newspapers during winter. Real estate advertising columns swelled so large that Miami boasted one of the country's heaviest newspapers. Publications across the country printed success stories of the quick fortunes made in Florida.

Chambers of commerce also promoted their cities and launched beautification projects, as public-lot auctions attracted large crowds. The state government enacted laws to further the boom and improved transportation and public services to meet the needs of new residents. Among the measures to attract home buyers and new residents were relaxed regulations on realtors and an amendment to the state con-

The Flamingo Hotel on Biscayne Bay was built in 1920 by developer Carl Fisher, the man most responsible for the growth of Miami Beach as one of America's premier resort destinations. *(Hulton Archive/Getty Images)*

stitution prohibiting state income and inheritance taxes.

The range of development ran the gamut from towns and homes of conspicuous splendor to filled swampland with dirt-road outlines and fancy gateways to nonexistent subdivisions. Some never developed, while others became world-renowned vacation spots and cities. Dave Davis created the Davis Islands in the Tampa Bay area; Barron Collier developed Naples and Marco Island on Florida's west coast. On the east coast, Carl Fisher and John Collins developed Miami Beach, George Merrick developed Coral Gables, Joseph Young created Hollywood, and the renowned architect Addison Mizner created Boca Raton. The "Florida lifestyle" that emerged along this "American Riviera" featured Mediterranean Revival architecture, pastel colors, palm trees, beaches, wide avenues, and golf courses.

The speculation was fueled by quick turnover of property. Many of the actual buyers and sellers never visited Florida. Two-thirds of the land was sold by mail. Real estate companies hired a large freelance sales force known as "Binder Boys," who purchased land lots for a 10 percent binder (down payment) that held the land for thirty days. The company then resold the binder to other land speculators at a profit, and the "Binder Boy" would receive a commission. Many lots changed hands several times, and land values rose rapidly—so rapidly that many middle-class buyers were soon priced out of the market. The profits existed only on paper, however, and were realized only if a subsequent buyer could be found.

Lax banking regulations meant that the fast-growing financial services industry often made risky loans and investments and kept little capital on hand. Rents rose dramatically because of the high demand for housing. Railroads could not keep up with the demand for building materials flowing into the state.

Like all speculative bubbles, the Florida land boom was destined to burst. Even as it expanded, newspapers around the country were printing stories of people who had been the victims of land scams. By 1926, all the signs of a bust were in evidence: land prices dropped precipitously, and there were many more sellers than buyers. A series of natural disasters, including severe winter freezes and a devastating hurricane in September 1926, hastened the decline. Many newcomers, realtors, and developers left the state. A banking crisis developed when people began defaulting on loans, and a bond-market slump hurt cities that had borrowed money to finance growth and improvements.

A short-lived phenomenon, the Florida land boom nevertheless had major long-term consequences for the state. Population growth and the rate of urbanization remained on the rise. Thirteen new counties were formed, nine of them located in south Florida. Above all, Florida became internationally known as a vacation, easy-living, and retirement spot—an image it has held ever since.

Marcella Bush Treviño

See also: Fisher, Carl; Real Estate.

Further Reading

Frazer, William Johnson, and John J. Guthrie, Jr. *The Florida Land Boom: Speculation, Money, and the Banks.* Westport, CT: Quorum, 1995.

Nolan, David. *Fifty Feet in Paradise: The Booming of Florida.* New York: Harcourt, Brace, Jovanovich, 1984.

Rogers, William W. "Fortune and Misfortune: The Paradoxical Twenties." In *The New History of Florida,* ed. Michael Gannon. Gainesville: University Press of Florida, 1996.

Flu Pandemic (1918)

Influenza is a regular visitor to the United States, only rarely mutating into a large-scale, deadly disease. In early spring 1918, however, a dangerous flu virus emerged in the Midwest, possibly through the chance combination of avian, porcine, and human flu viruses, though most epidemiologists believe the virus bypassed swine altogether. The earliest form appeared in soldiers at Fort Riley, Kansas, on March 11, 1918, resulting in the deaths of forty-eight strong young men, unlikely victims for a disease of this kind. At first, the new strain appeared in army camps, prisons, and factories but the population at large remained unaffected. Through U.S. military personnel, it spread to Europe, swept the warfront in April 1918, and infiltrated European cities. Already a serious infection, the virus increased in scope and severity in August 1918, mutating into a "superflu" of the H1N1 family and appearing at three crucial port cities: Brest in France, Freetown in Sierra Leone, and Boston in the United States.

Erroneously known as "Spanish Flu," the new strain spread rapidly from the ports along railroad lines and automobile routes. By September 25, the highly contagious flu reached Seattle and San Francisco, spreading by means of sneezes, coughs, and physical contact. The U.S. government, in the middle of the Fourth Liberty Loan Drive and conscripting for the military, had not only little public health authority to organize a quarantine but also little desire to do so.

In the seventeen weeks of the main flu outbreak, more than 25 million Americans were infected, overwhelming a medical system already stretched thin by the deployment of doctors and nurses to the battlefront. The casualties mounted quickly. People died only days after contact with the virus, and their corpses created a critical public health problem in areas that lacked the means to bury them. Also demoralizing was the fact that the most affected populations were young and healthy people, ages fifteen to forty, whose immune systems were the strongest. The elderly generally survived. Scientists later theorized that the toxins released by the immune system to destroy pathogens also damaged the patient's lungs.

Volunteer organizations that had been formed for war work, including the Red Cross, were joined by fraternal and social clubs, medical professionals, and private volunteers to deal with the crisis and set up makeshift hospitals, soup kitchens, orphanages, and laundries in public buildings. As social services broke down, with police, fire, and ambulance personnel out sick, amateurs and retirees took up the jobs under horrific conditions, often falling ill themselves. Encouraged by U.S. Surgeon General Rupert Blue, mayors and governors closed schools, movie theaters, churches, and public transportation facilities. Businesses also suffered. Particularly hard hit were life insurance companies that

Seattle police don masks to ward off infection during the great flu pandemic of 1918, which ultimately claimed half a million lives in the United States and 20 million around the world. *(Stringer/Time & Life Pictures/Getty Images)*

buckled under claims arising from 670,000 American deaths.

Governments and health organizations sought various ways to check the spread of the disease. Attempts to sanitize public fountains, phone booths, and streets with disinfectant failed. Cloth masks, many manufactured by the Levi Strauss company, were required by law but did little to prevent infection.

Efforts to find a medical antidote led to experiments on volunteers from a naval prison in Massachusetts and mass vaccination with known bacilli, but had no effect on the virus. In desperation, people tried home remedies. Some succumbed to depression or suicidal panic. Some who survived the flu were so weak that they died of starvation, hypothermia, or neglect.

In Philadelphia, seminary students roamed the streets, collecting the dead from the sidewalks. Newspaper columns were filled with the names of the dead. Rumors spread that the flu was a German biological weapon, and some blamed German brewers for distributing it or turned their anger on immigrant populations living in slums. Evangelist Billy Sunday declared that the flu was God's punishment of a sinful nation.

Particularly hard hit by the disease were Native Americans, who died at four times the national average, devastating their communities. Even at its worst, however, the flu failed to break down American society entirely, as people from every stratum of society worked together to care for the sick, take on farm chores, distribute food, and look after abandoned children.

In Europe, the influenza pandemic seriously hampered operations on the battlefield and weakened the German population. An estimated 225,000 Germans died from the disease, along with 228,000 British subjects, 375,000 Italians, and 450,000 Russians. The scourge crippled the attempts of new nations like Poland and Hungary to begin the work of government and hindered the Paris Peace Conference of 1919. Spreading to Asia, the flu devastated India, killing some 12–20 million people, and collapsed the infrastructure of numerous Chinese cities.

Kansas: Ground Zero of the Pandemic

Although it was called the Spanish flu, medical historians and epidemiologists believe that the great flu pandemic of 1918 actually began in rural southwestern Kansas. Haskell County in the early twentieth century seems an unlikely locale for the origin of the worst single disease event in human history. It was about as far away from the nation's ports and great cities as anyplace in America could be. Situated on the flat prairie, Haskell County was home to cattle ranches, wheat fields, and most significantly, poultry farms. Epidemiologists now believe that the H1N1 subtype of the species influenza A virus—the one responsible for the pandemic—made its genetic cross-species drift directly from poultry to humans, bypassing the usual path from chickens to swine to humans.

Sometime in late January 1918, a county physician noted a cluster of virulent flu cases in the area. So severe were the symptoms that the *Santa Fe Monitor*, the county's main newspaper, reported the outbreak as pneumonia. By early March, the disease had shown up at Camp Funston, a U.S. Army base near Fort Riley, Kansas; by the middle of that month, more than 1,000 soldiers were ill and forty-eight dead.

The epidemic then seemed to quiet for a while, at least in Kansas, with few new cases reported. The reason, however, was that the soldiers were being sent to Europe to fight in World War I. The great offensives of spring and summer that broke the back of German defenses also hastened the spread of the flu. With demobilization, soldiers carried the disease across Europe and America. Merchant ships serving an increasingly interconnected world economy brought the disease to Latin America, Asia, and Africa.

Back at Camp Funston, the flu returned with a vengeance. By mid-October, some 26,000 people at the facility lay ill. As one soldier wrote home, "it is some such a thing as pneumonia, and [the authorities] think it is pretty bad. . . . They are keeping our beds filled with new patients as fast as we send the old ones 'home well' or to the hospital half-dead. . . . We are getting real short-handed."

The disease could not be confined to the base. In nearby Topeka, hospitals overflowed and morgues could not keep up with the dead. Schools and hotels were converted into emergency infirmaries. State health officials did their best to slow the spread, closing theaters and enforcing strict limits on how many people could ride local streetcars. The young and those usually in good health were the first to fall ill and suffered the worst. Their immune systems produced toxins that attacked not only the virus but the patients' lungs as well.

By early 1919, the worst of the pandemic had run its course in America, though it was still exacting a toll in Asia and other far-flung parts of the globe. Some of its effects were lasting: in the United States, the influenza pandemic temporarily lowered life expectancy by a full decade. And in Kansas, where it all began, an estimated 10,000 died in the outbreak.

James Ciment

The weeks surrounding the armistice of November 11, 1918, saw a decline in cases and allowed for better care of recovering victims, who suffered from shock, pneumonia, heart damage, and brain damage from high fevers. Returning soldiers spread fresh waves of the flu until 1920, but never again at the same level. Slowly the country began to pick up the pieces, reopening public venues, restoring order, and attempting to reconstruct records of death and burial. Some survivors, like the writer Katherine Anne Porter, recorded their experiences in stories like "Pale Horse, Pale Rider." For some who had seen parents, siblings, and friends die horrifically and disappear without funerals or closure, the psychological damage lasted decades. For many adults in the Jazz Age, their most vivid memories were of a seventeen-week struggle with horror and death.

In the aftermath of the pandemic, nations organized powerful public health bureaucracies, including the League of Nations Health Organization, and demanded more stringent public hygiene standards. Research related to the flu led to the development of a vaccine for canine distemper in 1929 and the isolation of swine flu in 1930. Overall, the 1918 flu epidemic was responsible for an estimated 40–60 million deaths worldwide.

Margaret Sankey

See also: Health and Medicine.

Further Reading

Barry, John M. *The Great Influenza: The Epic Story of the Deadliest Plague in History.* New York: Viking, 2004.

Crosby, Alfred. *America's Forgotten Pandemic: The Influenza of 1918.* 2nd ed. New York: Cambridge University Press, 2003.

Kolata, Gina. *The Story of the Great Influenza Pandemic and the Search for the Virus That Caused It.* New York: Farrar, Straus and Giroux, 1999.

Flynn, Elizabeth Gurley (1890–1964)

A labor activist for the Industrial Workers of the World (IWW), a vocal civil libertarian, and the first woman to head the American Communist Party, Elizabeth Gurley Flynn led landmark textile strikes in Lawrence, Massachusetts, in 1912 and Paterson, New Jersey, in 1913. She was born on August 7, 1890, in Concord, New Hampshire, to second-generation Irish Catholics. Her father, a civil engineer, later joined the Socialist Party. Her mother promoted Irish nationalism and woman suffrage. Flynn's parents instilled in young Elizabeth the tireless social advocacy that became her trademark.

After a short stay in Ohio, the family moved in 1900 to the Bronx, New York, where Elizabeth began her long career as a labor leader. At age fifteen, she delivered her first public speech, "What Socialism Will Do for Women," at the Harlem Socialist Club in New York City. She dropped out of high school in 1906 and joined the IWW, or "Wobblies," for which her early activities included speaking out against the alleged frame-up of three IWW leaders who were charged with the murder of the former Idaho governor.

While attending the 1907 IWW convention in Chicago, Flynn met Jack Jones, a labor organizer from Minnesota. Flynn accepted Jones's invitation to speak to miners at the Mesabi Iron Range in northern Minnesota. They fell in love and married in January 1908. Their first child, John Vincent, died shortly after birth in December 1908. Their second child, Fred, was born in May 1910. Between births, Flynn worked on free-speech campaigns in the West, going to jail for her efforts in Missoula, Montana, and Spokane, Washington. These events put a strain on the couple's marriage, as Jack desired a more traditional wife. But as Elizabeth noted in her 1955 autobiography, *The Rebel Girl,* "I saw no reason why I, as a woman, should give up my life for his. I knew by now I could make more of a contribution to the labor movement than he could." The couple split in 1910 and officially divorced in 1926.

Flynn contributed significantly to famous labor struggles. In 1912, she addressed striking textile workers in Lawrence, Massachusetts, and organized the evacuation of the children of strikers by train to Philadelphia. It was in Lawrence that she met the Italian anarchist Carlo Tresca; the pair lived together until 1925. In 1913, Flynn joined the fray at the violent silk weavers' strike in Paterson, New Jersey. The following year, she took up the plight of Joe Hill, an IWW songwriter she believed had been framed for murder by state and federal law enforcement. Before the state of Utah executed him in 1915, Hill wrote the song "The Rebel Girl" in Flynn's honor.

In 1917, Flynn began to focus more on civil liberty issues as the U.S. government cracked down on supposed subversives. In September, she was arrested for vagrancy in Duluth, Minnesota, where she attended a rally for striking IWW miners. Later that month, Flynn was the only woman among 166 radicals arrested for sedition and subversion in Chicago. She and a few others won the right to have their cases tried separately, but they were never brought to trial. Others, however, were tried in federal court and found guilty. Judge Kenesaw Mountain Landis sentenced them to between five and twenty years in prison plus fines. This defeat marked the end of the IWW as a powerful force in the struggle of American laborers.

As a result of the way she and her comrades were treated by the authorities during World War I, Flynn became actively involved in amnesty for political prisoners. She began work for the Workers Liberty Defense Union, a postwar agency that carried on the work of the wartime National Civil Liberties Bureau. Under the slogan "Free Your Fellow-Workers," Flynn sought amnesty for industrial and political prisoners held for activities prior to and during World War I. She published leaflets and wrote newspaper articles demonstrating the plight of workers she believed had been wrongly detained for nothing more than belonging to a union. One such cause involved the IWW members arrested in connection with the Centralia Massacre of November 1919 in Washington.

Flynn also worked for the release of those apprehended during the Palmer Raids, conducted against alleged radicals and subversives during the Red Scare, and for the victims of criminal syndicalist laws—state legislation that made wartime sedition laws permanent. From 1920 to 1925, Flynn worked on behalf of Nicola Sacco and Bartolomeo Vanzetti, anarchists she believed the government framed for a murder in Massachusetts. Flynn viewed them as political prisoners who were arrested and charged for what they believed in rather than for anything they did. Their immigrant backgrounds, Flynn and many others contended, resulted in prejudicial trials. In 1926, in the midst of the appeals process, Flynn became chair of the year-old International Labor Defense. She toured the country making popular appeals for Sacco and Vanzetti. While on this tour, she became ill and dropped out of public life for the next decade.

Flynn reemerged in the late 1930s, working for human rights, free speech, and the Communist Party. A founding member of the American Civil Liberties Union, she remained active in that group until 1940, when it expelled her for being a member of the Communist Party. She had officially joined the party in 1936, although she had considered herself a member since the mid-1920s and had supported the group since its founding in the United States in 1919.

She ran unsuccessfully for Congress in New York in 1942 and again in 1951, after being arrested under the Smith Act during the height of McCarthyism. She was found guilty of disloyalty and spent nearly two and one-half years in prison. Flynn died on September 5, 1964, while visiting Moscow as chair of the American Communist Party.

Thomas F. Jorsch

See also: Industrial Workers of the World; Labor Movement; Sacco and Vanzetti Case (1920–1921).

Further Reading

Camp, Helen C. *Iron in Her Soul: Elizabeth Gurley Flynn and the American Left.* Pullman: Washington State University Press, 1995.

Flynn, Elizabeth Gurley. *The Rebel Girl: An Autobiography, My First Life (1906–1926).* New York: International Publishers, 1986.

Food Administration, U.S.

The outbreak of World War I in Europe in August 1914 left the tiny nation of Belgium, which imported approximately 80 percent of its foodstuffs, in a precarious position. With the nation's occupation by Germany, and the naval blockade by Great Britain effectively cutting off imports from the United States, famine loomed. But Herbert Hoover, a wealthy American businessman living in London, together with a group of mining engineer colleagues, determined that something must be done. As the unpaid head of the Committee to Relieve Belgium, Hoover persuaded Belgians that cornmeal was fit for more than cattle fodder. He also arranged for the purchase of American wheat, meat, and fats and the acquisition of rice from Burma and corn from Argentina. With a budget cobbled together almost entirely from donations, Hoover averaged $12 million per month in expenditures as he purchased food, arranged for its transportation, and negotiated with the British and the Germans to allow its entry into Belgium. The Committee to Relieve Belgium, it has been estimated, kept 10 million people from starvation.

When the United States entered the war in April 1917, President Woodrow Wilson named Hoover the U.S. Food Administrator. While some feared the coercive power of the federal government in wartime, the structure imposed on the economy not only aided in the winning of the war but dramatically altered Americans' relationship with their government. Administrations, commissions, and bureaus became commonplace terms in the nation's lexicon.

Hoover determined that the way to keep American citizens and the Allied forces properly fed was to initiate a campaign of self-sacrifice and self-denial, as opposed to imposing rationing or coercive actions. Americans were told on a daily basis that "Food Will Win the War!" Bright, bold posters encouraged Americans to eat less, conserve more, and plan their menus around wheatless Mondays, meatless Tuesdays, and porkless Saturdays. Home demonstration agents provided lessons in canning, preserving, and menu preparation. County demonstration agents stressed agricultural production on both large and small scales. Farmers were encouraged to raise more wheat, corn, and hogs, and gardeners learned how to gain the most from their victory gardens. Even President Wilson cooperated, with sheep brought in to graze on the White House lawn.

As U.S. involvement in the war deepened, Hoover feared that the demand for foodstuffs would result in inflationary food prices, which in turn could spread to the rest of the economy. Of particular concern to the war effort was the price of wheat. The foreign demand for wheat doubled between August 1914 and May 1917, and a poor crop in 1916 pushed the price of wheat from $1.15 to $3.24 a bushel. With the price of a loaf of bread doubling and some Americans calling for an embargo on wheat sales abroad, Hoover needed to act quickly to ensure a constant, affordable supply of bread products, both in the United States and in Europe.

Hoover's solution was probably the most controversial element of the entire Food Administration. Working with a team of economic advisers, he determined that the appropriate price for a bushel of wheat was $2.20 per bushel. While the move guaranteed that the price of bread would remain within reach of the average American, it also angered farmers. Seeing that the manufacturers of products made with price-controlled wheat could charge inflationary prices for breads, pastas, baked goods, and the like, many of the nation's agriculturalists felt that Hoover and the Food Administration had taken advantage of them. As a result, many farmers became ardently anti-Hoover; others organized into what ultimately would become the American Farm Bureau Federation.

Following the war, Wilson terminated the Food Administration by executive order in August 1920. But its impact continued. The Food Administration and related agencies altered Americans' perceptions of their government, laid the groundwork for expanding federal government, and changed relationships among government, citizens, and producers.

Kimberly K. Porter

See also: Europe, Relations with; Hoover, Herbert.

Further Reading

Clements, Kendrick A. *The Presidency of Woodrow Wilson.* Lawrence: University Press of Kansas, 1992.

Kennedy, David M. *Over Here: The First World War and American Society.* New York: Oxford University Press, 1980.

Nash, George. *The Life of Herbert Hoover: Master of Emergencies, 1917–1918.* New York: W.W. Norton, 1996.

Food and Diet

The Jazz Age marked the advent of modern cooking and eating habits in America. In the course of a decade, the mass marketing of brand-name foods, the modernization of kitchens, the growing influence of scientific nutrition, and the rise of chain restaurants helped to transform how and what Americans cooked and ate. Moreover, these national trends contributed to the emergence of a standardized American food culture that was widely shared and recognizably modern.

During the 1920s, as in prior decades, Americans ate most of their meals at home. Cooking, however, occupied a far less important role in homemakers' daily lives than it did for previous generations. Many middle-class women spent less time in the kitchen because of their involvement in women's clubs, bridge groups, and other social activities. Women in the workforce had fewer hours to prepare meals for their families (more than 3 million married women worked outside the home by 1930). Consequently, the 1920s witnessed a trend toward simpler meals that could be prepared using packaged, commercially processed foods, such as gelatin desserts, condensed soups, and canned vegetables, often purchased at increasingly popular chain grocery stores such as A&P, Kroger's, and Piggly Wiggly.

The Jazz Age also saw the evolution of modern kitchens, complete with gas stoves, electric refrigerators, and a host of other labor-saving appliances that revolutionized American cooking. In 1912, only 16 percent of American homes were wired for electricity; by 1928, more than 63 percent (an estimated 17.6

Broader availability of fresh produce and national advertising campaigns were among the notable developments in the American food industry during the 1920s. California citrus growers, like the Bradford Brothers, marketed their oranges as a magical health food. *(Hulton Archive/Getty Images)*

million homes) had electric power. Electric refrigerators replaced iceboxes, and modern kitchen appliances such as electric mixers, toasters, coffee percolators, and waffle irons became common. Gas ranges had replaced wood- and coal-burning stoves in approximately half of all American homes by 1930. Even though commercially prepared foods and new appliances simplified cooking, meal preparation still consumed approximately nineteen hours per week for urban homemakers and twenty-four hours per week for rural homemakers revealing that, regardless of location, most American households in the 1920s still could not afford many of the new laborsaving appliances.

Rise of Processed Foods

The rise of giant food conglomerates, along with technological innovations in food processing, packaging, and preservation, meant that American households could choose from an unprecedented assortment of foods. By 1920, food processing ranked as the largest manufacturing industry in the nation in terms of both earnings and employees. Giant food corporations, such as General Mills (formed in 1928) and General Foods (1929), spent millions of dollars to develop new products and more efficient forms of packaging and preservation. Bulk foods such as sugar and flour now came packaged in bags, and cardboard milk cartons replaced glass bottles. Advances in can-

ning technology allowed fruits, vegetables, tuna, and cheese to be efficiently preserved and packaged in tin cans. The technique of flash-freezing, first used to preserve fish, was widely used on fruits and vegetables by 1930.

These new manufacturing and packaging processes allowed companies to market a wide range of food products across the nation. Familiar processed foods such as Wonder Bread (1921), Welch's grape jelly (1923), Land O' Lakes butter (1924), Wheaties cereal (1924), Kellogg's Rice Krispies cereal (1928), Peter Pan peanut butter (1928), Velveeta cheese (1928), and Oscar Mayer wieners (1929) all emerged during the 1920s and were available in grocery stores nationwide.

Technological advancements in food production and distribution during the Jazz Age led to an unprecedented variety of foods in American homes. Farmers produced larger crop yields with the assistance of gas-powered tractors and scientific farming strategies. Refrigerated railcars and trucks distributed fresh meats, fruits, vegetables, dairy products, and grains to grocery stores and restaurants across the nation. As a result, homemakers were able to purchase oranges, grapefruits, bananas, lettuce, and broccoli even during the winter months. Overall, food prices declined significantly during the 1920s, which allowed working- and middle-class families to enjoy a greater variety of foods than in previous generations.

Meal Time

During the 1920s, middle-class Americans began to eat meals consisting of relatively light, healthy dishes. Green, leafy salads became particularly popular in middle-class homes, and several well-known salads were invented during the Jazz Age: the Green Goddess salad (1923), the Caesar salad (1924), and the Cobb salad (1926). Popular dinner entrees and side dishes included broiled steaks and chops, casseroles, Swiss steak, meat loaf, spaghetti and meatballs, and chilled fruit and gelatin molded salads. The increased use of reliable gas and electric ovens made cakes a popular dessert.

Cookbooks and promotional recipe booklets, such as *Good Housekeeping's Book of Menus, Recipes, and Household Discoveries* (1924), strongly influenced American cooking during the Jazz Age. Radio cooking shows also provided homemakers with helpful advice about meal planning and cooking. In 1921, the Washburn-Crosby Company's advertising department invented a fictional spokesperson named Betty Crocker, and three years later the company sponsored *The Betty Crocker School of the Air,* the nation's first radio cooking show. Another popular radio homemaker program was *Aunt Sammy,* first broadcast in 1926 and sponsored by the U.S. Department of Agriculture.

Working-Class and Ethnic Diets

While the diets of most middle-class American families became more standardized, those of working-class and immigrant families remained more eclectic and traditional. During the 1920s, urban working-class families ate meals primarily consisting of meat, bread, potatoes, cabbage, and onions, although even these families enjoyed a more balanced diet as a result of relatively lower food prices and greater access to fresh produce. The diets of rural families varied widely according to region, race, ethnicity, and household income. Poorer Southern families, especially sharecroppers and textile workers, subsisted largely on pork and cornmeal, especially during the winter. As a result of their limited diet, the poor often suffered from pellagra, a debilitating and sometimes deadly disease caused by protein deficiency.

With many foreign-born homemakers maintaining the traditional foodways of their homelands, slow-cooked stews, goulashes, and other ethnic specialties remained popular with immigrant families from Eastern and Southern Europe. But during the Jazz Age, Old World cooking and eating customs eroded as the children and grandchildren of immigrants embraced American cooking and eating habits. Ethnic cuisine persisted, but in many cases it was relegated to special occasions such as Sunday dinners, holidays, and family celebrations.

Eating Out

Jazz Age Americans dined out in restaurants and other eating establishments more often than earlier generations had. Between 1919 and 1929, the total number of restaurants in the United States tripled. The advent of National Prohibition in 1920, however, dramatically affected the American restaurant industry, bankrupting expensive restaurants that had relied heavily on liquor sales and eliminating many cheap saloons where factory workers had gathered for inexpensive lunches. With the disappearance of working-class saloons, quick-service restaurants—

automats, cafés, lunchrooms, diners, cafeterias, and sandwich shops—flourished as a source of convenient and affordable meals.

As the number of automobiles in the nation soared from 8 million in 1920 to 23 million in 1930, a booming roadside restaurant industry emerged. Tens of thousands of diners, hot dog stands, barbecue restaurants, and ice cream stands sprang up alongside the nation's roads catering to motorists, business travelers, and vacationers. Curbside service was invented in 1921 when the Pig Stand, the nation's first drive-in sandwich restaurant, opened outside of Dallas, Texas. J.G. Kirby, one of the owners, believed that curbside service would succeed because, as he remarked, "People with cars are so lazy they don't want to get out of them to eat." In 1922, Roy W. Allen and Frank Wright opened three A&W root beer stands in California, and their firm soon became one of the nation's first chains of franchise roadside restaurants, with 171 outlets by 1933.

The 1920s also marked the advent of fast-food hamburger chains. In 1921, Walter Anderson and Edgar W. "Billy" Ingram opened a quick-serve hamburger restaurant in Wichita, Kansas, called White Castle. They soon transformed their business into a chain of restaurants, and by 1931, there were 115 White Castles across the Midwest and East Coast. A host of imitator hamburger chains quickly sprang up, and by 1929, the hamburger had surpassed the hot dog as Americans' favorite fast food.

Treats

Jazz Age Americans ate far more candy and ice cream than had previous generations. During World War I, the Hershey Company supplied the U.S. government with 20-pound blocks of chocolate for distribution to American soldiers. After the war, returning veterans who had acquired a taste for Hershey's chocolate boosted candy bar sales in the United States. During the 1920s, an estimated 30,000 different candy bars—selling for about a nickel apiece—appeared on the market. In 1920, the Curtiss Company introduced the Baby Ruth, followed in 1926 by the Butterfinger. Other candy bars introduced during the 1920s that remain popular today include Mounds (1922), Milky Way (1923), and Reese's Peanut Butter Cup (1923). With the widespread availability of refrigeration, ice cream and a variety of other frozen treats became popular during the 1920s; among these new products were the Good Humor Bar (1920), the

Eskimo Pie (1921), the Klondike Bar (1922), and the Popsicle (1924).

During the 1920s, Americans began to consume soft drinks at an unprecedented rate. In 1929, Americans drank almost 273 million cases of soda, or an average of 53 bottles per person. Most soft drinks were only marketed regionally, and Coca-Cola and Pepsi-Cola, with their aggressive advertising campaigns, were among the few soft drinks to achieve national distribution. Other soft drinks that appeared on the market during the 1920s were Yoo Hoo, Kool-Aid, and 7-Up.

Nutrition and Diet Fads

Throughout the Jazz Age, home economists and nutrition experts continued their attempts to educate Americans about food science and proper nutrition. As late as the 1890s, fruits and vegetables had been considered unnecessary for a well-balanced diet, but by the 1920s, as a result of a series of breakthroughs in food science (including the discovery of vitamins A, C, D, and E), they were known to be crucial for maintaining proper health. At the same time, food companies began tapping into consumers' growing awareness of nutrition by fortifying their cereals, breads, milk, and other processed foods with vitamins and minerals.

Along with a new awareness of scientific nutrition came a wave of calorie-counting and diet fads for men and women. Lulu Hunt Peters's *Diet and Health, with Key to the Calories* (1918), one of the first diet books to promote calorie counting, remained a national best seller throughout the 1920s. Young women in particular felt pressure to achieve the slim, boyish figure popularized by the flapper, and many of them dieted aggressively. Some women resorted to diet regimens, pills, creams, and other commercial weight-loss products. Others smoked cigarettes to curb their appetites. In fact, Lucky Strike cigarettes launched a highly effective ad campaign in 1927 that encouraged women to "Reach for a Lucky instead of a sweet." Men also felt pressure to conform to a slim, muscular body image, and tens of thousands of them participated in muscle-building programs, including champion bodybuilder Charles Atlas's "Dynamic Tension" mail-order regimen, which was regularly advertised in pulp magazines.

Historians often refer to the Jazz Age as the beginning of the modern era in the country's history, and nowhere is this more evident than in the eating, cooking, and dietary practices of the American people, particularly the middle class. New household appliances, processed foods, and a switch to more simplified meals reduced the amount of time spent in the kitchen preparing meals. At the same time, meals became more healthful and dietary information more widespread. The modern eating habits of the 1920s also resulted in the growth of the restaurant industry and the propensity of families to eat out.

Kathleen Drowne

See also: Cigarettes and Tobacco; Health and Medicine; Technology.

Further Reading

Gabaccia, Donna R. *We Are What We Eat: Ethnic Food and the Making of Americans*. Cambridge, MA: Harvard University Press, 1998.

Heimann, Jim. *Car Hops and Curb Service: A History of American Drive-In Restaurants, 1920–1960*. San Francisco: Chronicle, 1996.

Hogan, David Gerard. *Selling 'em by the Sack: White Castle and the Creation of American Food*. New York: New York University Press, 1997.

Inness, Sherrie A. *Dinner Roles: American Women and Culinary Culture*. Iowa City: University of Iowa Press, 2001.

Jakle, John A., and Keith A. Sculle, *Fast Food: Roadside Restaurants in the Automobile Age*. Baltimore: Johns Hopkins University Press, 1999.

Levenstein, Harvey A. *Revolution at the Table: The Transformation of the American Diet*. New York: Oxford University Press, 1988.

Mariani, John. *America Eats Out: An Illustrated History of Restaurants, Taverns, Coffee Shops, Speakeasies, and Other Establishments That Have Fed Us for 350 Years*. New York: William Morrow, 1991.

McIntosh, Elaine. *American Food Habits in Historical Perspective*. Westport, CT: Praeger, 1995.

Pillsbury, Richard. *From Boarding House to Bistro: The American Restaurant Then and Now*. Boston: Unwin Hyman, 1990.

Schwartz, Hillel. *Never Satisfied: A Cultural History of Diets, Fantasies, and Fat*. New York: Free Press, 1986.

Football

Although the American Professional Football Association (later the National Football League) had been founded in 1920, football in the 1920s was still predominantly a college game. Having developed as an extracurricular activity in the Ivy League, primarily at Harvard, Yale, and Princeton universities, football had a connection with college life that even the national pastime, baseball, did not enjoy. The association of football with elite education institutions—even after its spread to state universities and religious schools—

and with young men in a transitional period of their lives reinforced its image as an amateur sport.

Although the games were presented as young scholars testing their mettle on the field of play, by the 1920s, some universities had made a name for themselves through their football teams, most notably the University of Notre Dame, but also Southern Methodist University, the Georgia Institute of Technology (Georgia Tech), and the University of Southern California.

Massive stadiums were constructed to house the crowds and showcase all facets of the sport. Fifty-five concrete stadiums were built in the 1920s, with some seating more than 70,000 spectators. Sprawling new facilities in cities (such as Los Angeles's Memorial Coliseum, Pasadena's Rose Bowl, and Chicago's Soldier Field) as well as on university campuses (such as the University of Illinois's Memorial Stadium and the University of Michigan's Michigan Stadium) provided grounds for the staging of high-profile football games and all the incumbent pageantry. In 1927, Soldier Field was the scene of the second annual meeting between the football teams of the University of Notre Dame and the University of Southern California, attended by what some claim to be the largest crowd ever for a college football game, approximately 120,000 spectators.

Adding to the game's popularity was radio. In 1924, pioneering commercial station WWJ of Detroit set up a microphone in the end zone at a University of Michigan game to provide the first broadcast of a college football game. By the end of the decade, many major games were being aired on the radio, though it would not be until the early 1930s that professional games came to be broadcast.

Knute Rockne of Notre Dame was one of the best-known college football coaches in the 1920s, in part due to Notre Dame's national Catholic following, and in part due to Rockne's use of the press to promote himself, his team, and Notre Dame. From the early 1920s, Rockne wrote articles and columns, ran several summer schools for college and high school coaches, wrote an instructional manual, organized and ran Camp Rockne for boys, and had an endorsement deal with the Wilson Athletic Equipment Company that netted him, by the end of the decade, about $10,000—all this in addition to his main job as head football coach and athletic director.

Notre Dame was often held up as the model of a successful athletic program, not only because it won games but also because the university benefited financially from the program, and many of the young men who participated in it went on to become successful coaches themselves. The financial gains from football could be plowed back into other programs, enhancing the school's academics.

Most athletic programs, however, did not contribute to the academic mission of their universities, and in many cases they drained resources from academics. But favorable publicity was reinforced by sportswriters such as Grantland Rice, Heywood Broun, Paul Gallico, and others who developed a dramatic prose style that turned college football games into mythic life-and-death battles. Rice is best known for writing what many claimed to be the greatest lead in sports journalism history when he described the 1924 Notre Dame backfield as the Four Horsemen of the Apocalypse.

A number of reformers in the 1920s tried to de-emphasize college athletics. In 1924, the Carnegie Foundation for the Advancement of Teaching issued a report denouncing the "commercialism," "excessive expenditure of money," and "too great an insistence on turning out a winning team" in college sports. Much of the blame, the report stated, should be placed on the coach, who "sets the standards of the whole system of intercollegiate sports and is responsible for many of its most demoralizing features." The foundation followed up its report with a five-year study into the problems of big-time college sports, but its final report did little to reform college football; rather, it served as an observation on an emerging system of subsidized college athletes and college football as an industry in which players were a raw material, packaged and sold by the coach and university.

The failure of the reformers illustrated the declining ideal of amateur athletics in a society that increasingly celebrated professionalism, expertise, and specialization. Although college football was packaged for the public by the press, universities, and even Hollywood as an integral part of college life, it was instead dominating the academic mission of many universities.

Despite fans' overwhelming preference for college football, organized professional football made important strides in the Jazz Age. While the earliest professional football games dated back to the last decade of the nineteenth century, it was not until 1920 that the first organization to sponsor professional football was established, as several college football coaches came together to offer opportunities for graduating players. Initially, the American Professional

Football Association (AFPA) sold eleven team franchises, each for $100.

In its first two years, the organization sponsored few games, attracted few fans, and appeared to be heading for extinction. After the 1921 season, however, the league hired a well-known sports promoter named Joe Carr as its president. Carr immediately reorganized the league and changed its name to the National Football League (NFL).

A major step forward in the fortunes of the NFL came in 1925, when the renowned running back of the University of Illinois, Red Grange, signed with the Chicago Bears, prompting the team to go on a national road tour, and helping to sow greater interest in the game. Still, through the end of the 1920s, games remained few, the organization and individual teams struggled financially, and the fan base remained much smaller than that for college football. Only after World War II would the fan base for professional football rival that for the college game.

Charles J. Shindo

See also: Education, Higher; Grange, Red; Leisure and Recreation; Radio.

Further Reading

Oriard, Michael. *King Football: Sport and Spectacle in the Golden Age of Radio and Newsreels, Movies and Magazines, the Weekly and the Daily Press.* Chapel Hill: University of North Carolina Press, 2001.
Sperber, Murray. *Shake Down the Thunder: The Creation of Notre Dame Football.* New York: Henry Holt, 1993.
Watterson, John Sayle. *College Football: History, Spectacle, Controversy.* Baltimore: Johns Hopkins University Press, 2000.

Ford, Henry (1863–1947)

An engineer, an entrepreneur, and a peace activist, Henry Ford was already a celebrated figure at the onset of the Jazz Age. Not only had he introduced the assembly-line technique to the automobile industry and built the first affordable, mass-produced car, but he had also gained international renown for his efforts to negotiate a peaceful resolution to World War I. In the 1920s, however, Ford's reputation suffered serious blows as he failed to respond to competitors' new products and became embroiled in controversy over his anti-Semitic views.

Ford was born on July 30, 1863, on a farm near Dearborn, Michigan. More interested in mechanics

than agriculture, he left home at the age of sixteen to find work in nearby Detroit. (Ironically, Ford would extol the charms of rural living when, in 1929, he opened Greenfield Village museum and park, an idealistic re-creation of a nineteenth-century American agricultural community.) An admirer of inventor Thomas Edison, Ford went to work as an engineer for the Edison Illuminating Company in 1891; within two years, he was chief engineer. However, it was the new technology of the automobile that truly fascinated him and, in his spare time, he built his first car in 1896.

Seven years later, with his own funds as well as money from eleven other investors, he founded the Ford Motor Company. A populist at heart, Ford sought to transform the automobile from a luxury item for the rich into an affordable means of transportation for farmers and workers. Toward that end, he introduced his iconic Model T in 1908. Using mass-production techniques, Ford was selling nearly half a million cars annually by the onset of World War I, at a cost of less than $400 each.

Celebrated in America and abroad for his engineering feats, Ford tried to use his prestige and fame in the cause of world peace, traveling to Europe in 1915 at the head of a delegation of peace activists seeking to negotiate an end to the war. But Ford's conspiracy theory—that secret forces were at work to get America to enter the war—was ridiculed in Europe, and his peace efforts came to naught. Following the war, Ford became a strong advocate of President Woodrow Wilson's efforts to create the League of Nations as an international conflict-resolution organization. While Ford devoted his time and energy to promoting the League, he temporarily assigned his son, Edsel, to the day-to-day operations of the Ford Motor Company. But Ford's efforts were in vain, as the Senate, with the wide backing of the American people, voted against joining the League.

In business, Ford emerged from World War I as perhaps America's leading industrialist. Few products dominated their market like the Model T, which by 1918 represented over half of all car sales in the United States. Such predominance was not to last long, however, and much of the fault for this decline lay with Ford himself. Shortly after the war, Ford took the helm of his company again, though he left day-to-day operations in the hands of his son, Edsel, and then bought back all shares not in his family's hands. With a populist's distrust of banks as parasitic institutions thriving on the enterprise of others, Ford refused to go to the big New York banks to get financing. Instead he cut back on costs at the company, including forcing dealers to pay cash for the cars. This proved difficult and unpopular, and many dealers switched over to selling rivals' cars, undermining Ford sales.

Other aspects of his character also hurt the company. An engineer at heart, rather than a marketer, Ford often seemed reluctant to accept the idea that an automobile was more than just a means of transportation; it was a form of personal identification as well. Ford was disdainful when rival General Motors (GM) introduced the new model year to spur sales, and he also refused to allow customers to personalize their cars with different features and colors. Gradually, however, and under pressure from Edsel and other executives, Ford agreed to introduce the new Model A in 1927. It was a hit, selling 4 million units by 1931. Moreover, Ford agreed to the annual model change that had proved so lucrative for GM.

Ford had already purchased the upscale Lincoln Motor Company, accepting the idea that his company should produce various types of cars to appeal to different budgets. At the same time, Ford held to small-town America's traditional notions of thrift and distrust of debt. While GM was boosting car sales through credit financing—which also turned into a lucrative income stream—Ford refused to set up a similar credit arm for his company until the 1930s.

Following an age-old stereotype, Ford associated Jews with the financial community he so distrusted and loathed. In 1920, he used part of his fortune to publish 500,000 English-language copies of *The Protocols of the Elders of Zion,* which outlined an alleged conspiracy by Jewish leaders to achieve world dominance. Even when *The Times* of London exposed the *Protocols* as a forgery of the old czarist regime in Russia, Ford continued to adhere to its basic thesis. Between 1920 and 1922, *The Dearborn Independent*—a small weekly paper Ford had purchased as an outlet for his increasingly right-wing views on Jews, liberals, immigrants, and trade unionists—published a series of articles titled "The International Jew, the World's Foremost Problem," which Ford later paid to have published as a four-volume book set.

Ford's anti-Semitic beliefs, along with his erratic decisions at the Ford Motor Company, undermined his credibility. In 1920, he had been touted as a possible presidential candidate; by 1930, few took his ruminations on society and politics seriously.

During the 1930s, Ford would become even more isolated, publicly expressing his admiration for Adolph Hitler. After suffering a stroke in 1938, he gave control of the Ford Motor Company to Edsel. Henry Ford died on April 7, 1947.

James Ciment and Leigh Kimmel

See also: Anti-Semitism; Automobile Industry; Automobiles and Automobile Culture; Ford Motor Company.

Further Reading

Bak, Richard. *Henry and Edsel: The Creation of the Ford Empire.* Hoboken, NJ: Wiley, 2003.

Brinkley, Douglas. *Wheels for the World: Henry Ford, His Company, and a Century of Progress.* New York: Viking, 2003.

McCarthy, Pat. *Henry Ford: Building Cars for Everyone.* Berkeley Heights, NJ: Enslow, 2002.

Tilton, Rafael. *Henry Ford.* San Diego, CA: Lucent, 2003.

Ford Motor Company

The Ford Motor Company entered the Jazz Age as one of the great industrial enterprises in the United States. In 1919, it accounted for more than half of the 1.3 million cars sold in the country. And while the Ford remained the top-selling model in 1929, with sales of 1.5 million, its share of overall automobile sales had fallen to just over one-third, overtaken by General Motors as the largest automobile-manufacturing company in the country and the world. It was not the company's engineering that faltered in the Jazz Age, say automobile historians, but the unwillingness of its president, company founder Henry Ford, to embrace new advertising, marketing, and financing ideas.

The Ford Motor Company was founded in 1903 by Ford and eleven other investors. The company was innovative from the start, with its goal of turning the automobile from a luxury for the rich to an accessibly priced necessity for farmers, workers, and the middle class. Ford said that he had wanted to create an automobile that would allow isolated farmers to get to town. His goal was realized in the Model T, introduced in 1908.

To make the car affordable, Ford adopted the assembly-line technique that had been perfected in the meatpacking industry. But whereas meatpackers moved a cow carcass along a line to be disassembled, Ford moved the chassis along a line where workers could quickly attach parts to build a complete automobile. To further cut costs, Ford integrated vertically, securing its own sources of raw materials such as iron and coal, buying ships to transport the iron, and building a vast production plant at River Rouge, near Detroit, to turn those raw materials into finished automobiles, all under one roof.

By 1913, Ford had shortened the time it took to build a car from more than twelve hours to less than three. By 1918, the company had cut the price of the Model T from more than $800 to less than $400, putting it in reach of skilled workers and many farmers.

The Ford Motor Company was also a labor innovator. Arguing that it made economic sense to pay its workers enough to buy the product of their own labor, the company introduced the $5-a-day wage in 1914, an unheard level in the pre–World War I era for what were essentially unskilled and semiskilled workers.

Although Henry Ford was a pacifist, he supported America's defense efforts during World War I. The company, responding to prodding from the federal government, began to manufacture trucks for the military and tractors to increase wartime agricultural output. Still, Henry Ford resented outside influence in his company and, in 1919, moved to buy back all shares not owned by himself or members of his family, though he did give up daily control of the company to his son Edsel. Because he detested debt and distrusted bankers, however, Henry decided to finance the buyback by cutting back on costs, rather than borrowing money. While he successfully took control of all of the company's stock, he sacrificed research and innovation and alienated dealers by forcing them to pay up front and in cash for all cars they took delivery of. Unable or unwilling to do so, many of the dealers decided to drop Ford products for those of other companies.

Although Henry Ford's stubbornness would continue to hurt the company through the 1920s, there were also innovations during that period. In 1922, the company purchased the Lincoln Motor Company, a struggling luxury automaker, in order to market products to more upscale consumers. And, with sales of the increasingly dated Model T sliding, Ford introduced the Model A in 1927. With its hydraulic shock absorbers, automatic windshield wipers, safety glass, gas gauge, and speedometer, the Model A incorporated or introduced a host of innovations. Moreover, the Ford buyer could pick from a variety of colors and options for the first time. But this had been a long time coming. Rival General Motors (GM) had introduced many of these engineering and marketing innovations immediately after World War I and, by 1927, had overtaken Ford as the top seller of automobiles in the American market.

Under the leadership of Alfred Sloan, GM had introduced the model-year change, which helped convince consumers to buy new cars every few years. Ford held to the idea that the best product was one that lasted a lifetime. GM was also quicker to introduce a host of products and product lines for every budget so that consumers who were moving up the social ladder and wanted their cars to make a statement about their new status could stay within the GM family. GM was also innovative in the financing of cars. In 1919, GM launched the General Motors Acceptance Corporation (GMAC), a feature that allowed dealers to help their customers purchase cars on credit. Henry Ford disdained the idea of debt, thus his company refused to go along with the new trend of financing, even though GMAC increased car sales and proved to be a successful revenue earner in its own right.

Ford emerged from the 1920s a highly successful company despite the fact that it had fallen behind GM. But the 1930s would put the company through some of its roughest trials. Weak consumer demand forced Henry Ford to swallow his contempt for credit and permit his company to launch its own financing arm. And while the company had been a labor innovator with its $5-a-day wage in 1914, by the 1930s it proved to be the most resistant to the unionism sweeping America. Long after other manufacturers accepted unions in their plants, Ford held out. It was not until 1941 that the company acquiesced and only then because of pressure from a federal government gearing up for World War II.

James Ciment

See also: Automobile Industry; Automobiles and Automobile Culture; Ford, Henry; General Motors.

Further Reading

Bak, Richard. *Henry and Edsel: The Creation of the Ford Empire.* Hoboken, NJ: Wiley, 2003.

Collier, Peter, and David Horowitz. *The Fords: An American Epic.* New York: Summit, 1987.

Lewis, David Lanier, Mike McCarville, and Lorin Sorensen. *Ford, 1903–1984.* New York: Beekman House, 1983.

Fordney-McCumber Tariff of 1922

The Fordney-McCumber Tariff of 1922—named after its sponsors, Representative Joseph W. Fordney of

Michigan and Senator Porter J. McCumber of North Dakota, both Republicans—dramatically increased tariffs on a host of imported manufactured goods. While widely supported by manufacturers, the tariff, according to most economic historians, proved disastrous for the world economy. Many European countries were deeply in debt to the United States because of loans taken out during World War I. By making it more difficult to sell goods to the United States and thereby raise the dollars needed to meet those debts, the Fordney-McCumber Tariff put enormous strain on international finances.

If the Fordney-McCumber Tariff did not make good economic sense, it was, however, a political winner. The election of 1920 had returned control of Congress and the White House to the Republican Party, and elected officials agreed with corporate America that higher tariffs benefited the national economy by protecting key market segments from foreign imports. They did not seem as concerned about, or as understanding of, the potential challenges to American exports if major trading partners retaliated with their own higher tariffs against American products.

Congress had passed the Emergency Tariff of 1921 to provide temporary protection for twenty-eight agricultural commodities, including corn, wheat, meat, sugar, and wool, given the quick downturn in foreign purchases now that the war had ended. Congress followed this with the Fordney-McCumber Tariff of 1922, which increased tariffs on a long list of imported goods from 27 percent to 35 percent, pushing up the prices consumers paid for those goods by an average of 25 percent. The measure also gave the U.S. Tariff Commission the authority to raise or lower rates by as much as 50 percent without congressional approval.

Fordney had taken the lead in the U.S. House of Representatives in securing passage of the bill, by a margin of 288–177, mostly along party lines. In the Senate, McCumber helped secure passage by a vote of 48–25, again mostly along party lines, after senators added more than 2,000 amendments, each of which was designed to protect a favored industry, company, or plant. The bill eventually went to President Warren G. Harding, who signed it on September 21, 1922.

This Fordney-McCumber Tariff harkened back to the Payne-Aldrich Tariff of 1909 and presaged the disastrous Smoot-Hawley Tariff in 1930. It was the wrong policy at the wrong time. Although the United States had entered World War I as a debtor nation, it emerged as a great creditor nation, with the world's biggest economy and perhaps the world's most efficient agriculture and industry. Essential to reviving the economies of victor and vanquished alike, the United States needed to promote trade, not limit it. Opening America's ports to foreign goods would have encouraged industrial nations to open their ports to American exports, increasing international trade and domestic economies. Instead, the 1922 legislation raised the tariff on imported manufactured goods to levels higher than those created by the Payne-Aldrich Tariff of 1909. In response, foreign governments naturally raised their respective national tariffs.

The Fordney-McCumber Tariff, many historians argue, violated basic economic rules. Traditionally, countries impose tariffs either to protect infant industries against tough foreign competition or to effect balance-of-trade deficits when a country is in debt to foreign creditors. By lowering imports, the country keeps more money at home, which it can use to pay off those debts. But, in the 1920s, America's modern, highly developed industrial sector was among the most competitive in the world, and the country was the top creditor nation. The effect of the tariff on the international financial system was catastrophic, since the European countries that could not sell goods to the United States could not raise the dollars needed to pay off their debts to the United States.

The failure to negotiate lower tariffs, the demand by the Allies that the defeated Central Powers pay the high war reparations, and America's insistence that countries to which it had made loans had to repay their debt produced an untenable situation. Finally, in 1924, the United States agreed to make loans to the Central Powers so that they could make their reparations payments to the Allies, who could then pay back their loans to the United States. In effect, the U.S. government was loaning money so that U.S. financial institutions could get paid back.

In 1930, the even more restrictive Smoot-Hawley Tariff would worsen the situation. Some economists believe that favorable congressional committee action prior to the bill's passage helped to bring about the stock market crash of 1929, as investors recognized the chilling effect that higher and higher tariffs had on international trade and world economic prosperity.

The Fordney-McCumber and Smoot-Hawley tariffs provided some lessons for the future. Attempting to build a new financial order in the wake of World War II, U.S. policy makers pushed for a more open trading system, one that sought to limit restrictive tariffs through such institutions as the General Agreement on Tariffs and Trade (GATT) and, later, the World Trade Organization.

Charles M. Dobbs

See also: Economic Policy; Europe, Relations with.

Further Reading

McCoy, Donald R. *Coming of Age: The United States During the 1920s and 1930s.* Baltimore: Penguin, 1973.

Murray, Robert K. *The Politics of Normalcy: Governmental Theory and Practice in the Harding-Coolidge Era.* New York: W.W. Norton, 1973.

Schattschneider, E.E. *Politics, Pressures, and the Tariff.* New York: Arno, 1974.

Trani, Eugene P., and David L. Wilson. *The Presidency of Warren G. Harding.* Lawrence: Regents Press of Kansas, 1977.

Fosdick, Harry Emerson (1878–1969)

A Baptist minister who served as pastor of New York City's prestigious First Presbyterian Church in the early 1920s and of Park Avenue Baptist Church in the latter part of the decade, Harry Emerson Fosdick was the most prominent religious voice against the resurgent Christian Fundamentalism of his day. A liberal theologian, Fosdick argued that the Bible is not to be taken as the literal word of God but as a chronicle of God's will, telling of his unfolding plan for humanity and the world. This interpretation made Fosdick anathema to Protestant Fundamentalists across America.

Fosdick was born on May 24, 1878, in Buffalo, New York. Both his parents suffered from mental illness. His mother had a nervous breakdown while he was a child, and his father's mental instability interrupted Fosdick's studies at Colgate University. Fosdick was not immune to mental illness either. While studying at Union Theological Seminary in New York City in the early 1900s, he suffered a nervous breakdown. While at the seminary, Fosdick began to form his ideas about the need for the church to address the world's social ills. His ministry to the poor and transients of New York's vice-ridden Bowery district convinced him that the church had to do more than merely cater to people's spiritual needs.

Fosdick was ordained a Baptist minister in 1903 and took up his first pastorate, the First Baptist Church in Montclair, New Jersey. Beginning in 1908, he also taught part-time at Union. But in 1915, he devoted himself full-time to teaching at the seminary,

becoming the Morris K. Jesup Professor of Practical Theology. In that position, Fosdick lectured future pastors on the need to integrate their ministerial duties with practical measures to alleviate social ills.

Fosdick was not alone in preaching such a message, but he was one of the best-known theorists of the Social Gospel, a movement that arose in the late nineteenth century and prevailed among liberal churchgoers into the 1930s. The Social Gospel applied Christian principles to solving the nation's social ills.

Like many other liberals, Fosdick was a strong supporter of America's entry into World War I, seeing it as a crusade to spread democracy to the rest of the world. A visiting minister at several churches in New York, he defended the war in his sermons and, in 1917, published a tract called *The Challenge of the Present Crisis* to express his views. Later, once he had visited the war-ravaged regions of Europe, Fosdick became a pacifist, refusing to support America's entry into World War II.

In 1918, despite his ordination as a Baptist minister, Fosdick was selected as the new pastor at New York City's First Presbyterian Church, where he would serve through 1924. Here he gained national fame as an opponent of Fundamentalism, the conservative Christian movement that preached the infallibility and historical accuracy of the Hebrew Bible and New Testament. Fundamentalism arose in part, say social historians, as a reaction to a rapidly changing America, where science and popular culture seemed to be undermining traditional morals and Christian doctrine.

By the 1920s, Fundamentalists had become a powerful force in American Protestantism. Along with their condemnation of certain aspects of contemporary culture and scientific principles such as evolution, Fundamentalists argued that liberal Protestants, that is, those who embraced modern science and culture, were not true Christians. In perhaps his most famous sermon, "Shall the Fundamentalists Win?" (1922), Fosdick challenged one of the bedrock principles of Fundamentalism—the literal, unchanging, and unyielding truth of the Bible. He proposed that Christianity evolved as society moved forward. Fosdick also published his ideas in popular magazines such as *Harper's, The Atlantic Monthly,* and *Ladies' Home Journal.* He was featured on the cover of *Time* magazine in 1925 and again in 1930.

To the Fundamentalists, Fosdick's ideas renunciated certain facets of Christian faith, and they attacked him relentlessly from the pulpit and in church publications. Leaders of the Presbyterian Church in America found themselves under pressure to condemn Fosdick for his beliefs. Seeking to avoid a damaging fight with conservatives within Presbyterianism, Fosdick resigned from the pulpit of the First Presbyterian Church in 1924, taking up the pastorate at the prestigious and influential Park Avenue Baptist Church, also in New York City. Among its congregants was oil magnate John D. Rockefeller. Together, Rockefeller and Fosdick decided to create an interdenominational church—the American Baptist and United Church of Christ—that would reflect modernist ideas and liberal values. Using Rockefeller's vast funds, land was purchased on Manhattan's Upper West Side and, in 1927, construction began on a vast, Gothic-style cathedral.

In 1930, the Riverside Church opened for services. Fosdick would serve as pastor there until his retirement in 1946. Under his leadership, Riverside Church emerged as one of the nation's preeminent liberal Christian institutions and a center for social work and activism in New York City. In later years, the church would serve as a meeting place and forum for civil rights advocates, antiwar groups, and others supporting liberal and progressive causes. Fosdick died on October 5, 1969.

James Ciment and David Malone

See also: Fundamentalism, Christian; Protestantism, Mainstream.

Further Reading

Fosdick, Harry Emerson. *The Living of These Days: An Autobiography.* New York: Harper, 1956.

Miller, Robert Moats. *Harry Emerson Fosdick: Preacher, Pastor, Prophet.* New York: Oxford University Press, 1985.

Ryan, Halford R. *Harry Emerson Fosdick: Persuasive Preacher.* Great American Orators, no. 2. Ed. Bernard K. Duffy and Halford R. Ryan. Westport, CT: Greenwood, 1989.

Four-Power Treaty (1921)

The Four-Power Treaty, concluded at the Washington Naval Conference of 1921–1922 (officially the Conference on Limitation of Armaments), committed its four signatories—the United States, Great Britain, France, and Japan—to respect the agreements that each had already secured with China. The agreements had been reached in the late nineteenth and early twentieth centuries between the powerful European states, Japan, and a weak Chinese government, granting special trading rights and legal protections in various parts of China. The Four-Power Treaty also guaranteed that various European countries, the United States, and Japan would keep their colonies in the Pacific and East Asia. Finally, the treaty called on all signatories to consult with one another should there be disagreements, thereby avoiding war.

In November 1921, the world's naval powers met in Washington, D.C., to discuss the naval arms race that had begun during World War I, as well as the fluid situation in the Pacific and East Asia. U.S. Secretary of State Charles Evans Hughes had organized the conference to end a naval building boom and thereby reduce federal expenditures, of which the U.S. Navy accounted for some 40 percent. The conference concluded with the signing of the last of three agreements in February 1922.

The Four-Power Treaty, the first to be concluded, was signed on December 13, 1921. A key outcome of the treaty was a weakening of the Anglo-Japanese Alliance of 1902, which had guaranteed mutual defense between Japan and Britain. The alliance had put longtime allies Britain and the United States on a potential path to war, as tensions mounted between Japan and the United States in the western Pacific and East Asia.

The treaty also stipulated that signatories would consult with each other in the event of a controversy between two of them over "any Pacific question"—that is, maritime rights, trade, or colonies. An accompanying agreement stated that the signatories would respect one another's rights regarding the various Pacific islands and mandates they held. This benefited Japan in particular, since it had the most possessions in the Pacific, having gained Germany's former holdings in the Marshall and Caroline Islands. Finally, the agreements set up conflict-resolution processes to prevent the outbreak of war.

The treaty, and the American delegation's support for it, reflected the 1908 Root-Takahira Agreement between the United States and Japan. Secretary of State Elihu Root and Japan's ambassador in Washington, Takahira Kogoro, had agreed to maintain the status quo in East Asia, to recognize China's sovereignty and territorial integrity, to express support for the Open Door policy of the United States—which called for free trade between China and other countries—and to agree to consult when a crisis threatened relations.

Japan believed the agreement meant that America supported Japan's takeover of Korea and thus its general goals in Northeast Asia, and such ambiguity remained in the Four-Power Treaty. Committed to reducing naval spending, the Harding administration had few "sticks" to control Japan, and so it offered "carrots" instead—including an expanded navy and the right to keep its Pacific colonies taken from Germany after World War I. Despite its expansionist tendencies, the Japanese imperialist government operated within the treaty's constraints for its ten-year life.

The relatively quick agreement on this treaty paved the way for the two additional treaties that resulted from this conference. The Five-Power Treaty, perhaps the conference's most famous outcome, limited tonnage of capital ships for the five major naval powers (including Italy). And signatories to the Nine-Power Treaty pledged to respect China's "sovereignty, independence, and territorial and administrative integrity." Furthermore, they would act in accordance with the Open Door Notes proposed by U.S. Secretary of State John Hay in 1899 and 1900 that sought to prevent imperial powers from carving China into closed trading empires, while preserving an open door for American business.

Charles M. Dobbs

See also: China, Relations with; Europe, Relations with; Japan, Relations with; Military Affairs; Washington Naval Conference (1921–1922).

Further Reading

Buckley, Thomas H. *The United States and the Washington Conference, 1921–1922.* Knoxville: University of Tennessee Press, 1970.

Cohen, Warren I. *Empire Without Tears: American Foreign Relations, 1921–1933.* Philadelphia: Temple University Press, 1987.

Ellis, L. Ethan. *Republican Foreign Policy, 1921–1933.* New Brunswick, NJ: Rutgers University Press, 1968.

Iriye, Akira. *After Imperialism: The Search for a New Order in the Far East, 1921–1931.* Cambridge, MA: Harvard University Press, 1965.

Fourteen Points

The Fourteen Points were a list of political goals for the international order in the wake of World War I, as outlined by President Woodrow Wilson in a speech to a joint session of Congress on January 8, 1918. Throughout the war, there had been calls in Congress, the media, and the American public for a just peace without the secret agreements that had contributed to the outbreak of hostilities.

In his Fourteen Points speech, Wilson enumerated his vision of a new international order for postwar Europe, which ranged from specific issues of World War I to a new mechanism for preventing war itself:

- Open agreements between nations;
- freedom of the seas during peace and war;
- a global economic system based on free trade;
- a drastic reduction in armaments among nations;
- a call to govern colonies in the best interests of the indigenous populations;
- the end of German occupation of Russian territory;
- the restoration of Belgium's sovereignty;
- the return of largely French-speaking Alsace-Lorraine from Germany to France;
- a readjustment of Italy's borders based on nationality;
- autonomy for the peoples of the Austro-Hungarian Empire;
- independence for the Balkan states;
- sovereignty for the Turkish portion of the Ottoman Empire, independence for the non-Turkish populations of the Ottoman Empire, and neutralization of the Dardanelles;
- the restoration of Poland as an independent state; and
- the creation of what would become the League of Nations, an international organization in which nations could resolve their conflicts peacefully.

The Fourteen Points were based on Wilson's belief that a just and lasting peace could be possible in an international order based on liberal democracy and where nation-states formed the basis of sovereignty, as opposed to the multiethnic empires of the Hapsburgs and the Romanovs. Wilson believed that the nationalistic aspirations of the various ethnic groups within these empires were among the causes of World War I. Crucial to the success of the implementation of the Fourteen Points was the cooperation of the other three members of the Council of Four at the 1919 Paris Peace Conference: Great Britain, France, and Italy.

The three leaders of those nations did not react warmly to Wilson's proposals. France's Prime Minister Georges Clemenceau expressed exasperation at Wilson's "fourteen commandments"; God gave only ten, he quipped. Britain's Prime Minister David Lloyd George expressed similar criticisms of the idealism of the Fourteen Points. Specifically, both the British and the French balked at the provision regarding open agreements because it went against centuries of tradition in European diplomacy, often conducted secretly. Ironically, the proceedings of the Paris Peace Conference were closed off to reporters, and Wilson himself was uncomfortable around journalists. The provision on the freedom of the seas, meanwhile, appeared to be a specific challenge to British naval supremacy. And the British and French opposed the provisions regarding colonies and national self-determination, since they controlled the world's largest colonial empires. Italy had similar concerns about its smaller imperial holdings and also balked at the provision that called for a readjustment of its borders.

Wilson's Fourteen Points also encountered opposition within the United States, particularly in the Senate, regarding the League of Nations. A faction known as the "irreconcilables" believed that Wilson was going against the advice of the founders of the republic to steer the United States away from entangling alliances. Another faction, the "reservationists," would allow membership but only under certain conditions. Under the leadership of Senator Henry Cabot Lodge (R-MA), they drafted fourteen reservations to counter the Fourteen Points. Among these were that the United States had the right to withdraw from the League of Nations; that the United States would not be obligated to defend any member of the League; that the United States maintain the Monroe Doctrine; and that the United States not accept any decision in which any member cast more than one vote through one of its colonies. The result of these reservations was the nullification of Article X of the League of Nations Covenant, which held that all members were obligated to defend a member if attacked.

The ideals of the Fourteen Points were steadily compromised, in both letter and spirit, during the negotiations at the Paris Peace Conference. Before the war even ended, Britain and France made secret agreements for the acquisition of territories in the Middle East, Africa, and Asia from the defeated powers. Wilson compromised on many of the Fourteen Points in order to ensure the success of what he regarded as the most important one—the League of Nations. Ultimately, the Senate rejected the League of Nations covenant as a repudiation of Wilson's Fourteen Points.

Although the United States did not join the League of Nations, the Fourteen Points continued to serve as a source of inspiration during the 1920s. Its calls for disarmament were echoed during the Wash-

ington Naval Conference of 1921–1922, in which the United States, Great Britain, France, and Japan accepted limits on naval construction. Germany's war reparations were renegotiated through the Dawes Plan in 1924. The Treaty of Locarno in 1925 reaffirmed Germany's borders with France and Belgium. The Kellogg-Briand Pact, signed by the United States, Europe, and Japan in 1928, officially renounced war as national policy. And despite the failure of the League of Nations, the United Nations stands as testimony to Wilson's belief in a world where nations follow international law and in an international organization where disputes may be resolved peacefully.

Dino E. Buenviaje

See also: Europe, Relations with; League of Nations; Paris Peace Conference of 1919; Versailles, Treaty of (1919); Wilson, Woodrow.

Further Reading

Powaski, Ronald E. *Toward an Entangling Alliance: American Isolationism, Internationalism, and Europe, 1901–1950.* Westport, CT: Greenwood, 1991.

Rhodes, Benjamin D. *United States Foreign Policy in the Interwar Period, 1918–1941: The Golden Age of American Diplomatic and Military Complacency.* Westport, CT: Praeger, 2001.

Tilchin, William N., and Charles E. Neu, eds. *Artists of Power: Theodore Roosevelt, Woodrow Wilson, and Their Enduring Impact on U.S. Foreign Policy.* Westport, CT: Praeger, 2006.

Walworth, Arthur. *Wilson and His Peacemakers: American Diplomacy at the Paris Peace Conference, 1919.* New York: W.W. Norton, 1986.

Fundamentalism, Christian

A subset of the Protestant evangelical revivalist tradition, Christian Fundamentalism militantly opposed theological liberalism and the intellectual and cultural foundations of modernism. Initially, Fundamentalists were a loose confederation of people who emerged from the patchwork of American Protestantism to gradually form a coherent movement at the beginning of the Jazz Age. The core ideas of Fundamentalism included evangelism (the call to the lost for salvation through the repentance of sin and the acceptance of Jesus) and inerrancy (a view of the Bible as the infallible word of God). Fundamentalists, however, shared some of these and other views with many conservative Christian groups. Perhaps early Fundamentalism's signature ingredient was its aggressive desire to purify churches and other institutions of perceived error.

Theological Underpinnings

Fundamentalism, as an American religious movement, emerged in response to significant changes in Christian belief that occurred in the late nineteenth and early twentieth centuries. Fundamentalists viewed themselves as guardians of Protestant Christian orthodoxy, particularly in their defense of the authority of scripture, miracles, the virgin birth of Jesus, his divinity, his literal death and resurrection, and his imminent return to earth. Adherents of this belief system derived their name from a series of essays written from 1910 to 1915 titled "The Fundamentals." This collection, penned by American and British conservative religious scholars and popular writers, represented what proponents considered key areas of theological beliefs or "fundamentals of the faith," which required aggressive defense against rising "heresies." Despite the distribution of 3 million copies, the treatise initially received a lukewarm reception from religious periodicals and theological journals. But the publication symbolized the birth of a movement that Curtis Lee Laws, editor of the Northern Baptist Convention's *Watchmen Examiner,* first called "Fundamentalism" in 1920.

The rise of Fundamentalism reflected changes within Protestantism that had been building for decades. As the nineteenth century waned, two groups emerged within the various Protestant denominations: those who attempted to reconcile modern scientific thought and values with Christianity, and those who viewed this resolution as problematic or even heretical. Fundamentalist Christians particularly stressed the authenticity and reliability of the Bible, advocating that it be read as literal truth. They questioned the implications of Darwinism and viewed rationalistic humanist thought as antithetical to their beliefs.

Response to Modern Culture

A number of social and cultural events of the late 1910s and early 1920s radicalized some religious conservatives and spawned the full-blown Fundamentalist movement. The devastation of World War I, the Red Scare and labor strikes, and the continuing erosion of conventional Victorian social norms all heightened religious conservatives' distrust of modern values. Thus, as many Americans gleefully welcomed the fresh rhythms of the Jazz Age, others recoiled from these modern expressions.

Beginning in 1917, the simmering discord within Protestantism erupted into full-blown theological conflicts. Two areas of dispute were the Fundamentalist doctrines of dispensationalism and premillennialism. According to dispensationalism, history is proceeding through periods called "dispensations," which began with innocence in the garden of Eden and will end with Christ's return to earth and establishment of a millennial (thousand year) reign. Premillennialism is the belief that the return of Jesus Christ is imminent. A related concept is the rapture, when believers will be drawn up to meet Jesus and thus escape years of tribulation to be faced by the nonbelievers who have been left behind.

Christians with more liberal views disagreed with the theological underpinnings of these theories as well as their social implications. Perhaps the most controversial element was dispensationalism's negative view of human nature and its rejection of the idea of society's gradual but continual perfectability. Liberals saw the progress of Western civilization as the natural working out of God's kingdom.

Some of the most public quarrels took place in Chicago between the liberal University of Chicago Divinity School and the conservative Moody Bible Institute. Shirley Jackson Case and Shailer Mathews, professors at the University of Chicago, attacked dispensationalism as intellectually untenable and socially dangerous, regarding the theology not only as doctrinal error but a rejection of social progress. They viewed dispensationalism's pessimistic social outlook as undermining America's fight for democracy and progress in Europe. Moody Bible Institute President James M. Gray defended dispensationalists' patriotism and the biblical accuracy of their beliefs, saying that liberals had adopted godless German rationalism and evolutionary naturalism in place of plain biblical truths.

Struggle for Institutional Control

Following these initial fights, Fundamentalists became more aggressive in their struggle for doctrinal purity. William Bell Riley, pastor of the First Baptist Church in Minneapolis, led the organization of the World's Christian Fundamentals Association, which held conferences in various cities beginning in 1919. From 1920 to 1925, the philosophical and theological divergence pushed once unified denominations and educational institutions toward ecclesiastical separation. Church struggles occurred in almost all of the Protestant denominations, but the largest battles took place in the Northern Presbyterian and the Northern Baptist denominations. Baptists, for example, organized institutions such as the Fundamentalist Fellowship (1921), the National Federation of the Fundamentalists of the Northern Baptists (1921), and the Baptist Bible Union (1923). Fundamentalists attempted to remove liberal Christians from seats of power in the churches, seminaries, and mission boards. After initial successes in the early 1920s, Fundamentalists ultimately failed to gain control in the northern United States. Fundamentalists in the South, however, tended to find more success. The Southern Baptist convention, for example, gained nearly 1.5 million new members between 1920 and 1935.

Perhaps the seminal moment of early Fundamentalism was the 1925 Scopes trial, in which Clarence Darrow defended Tennessee schoolteacher John T. Scopes for teaching evolution in a high school although it was prohibited by a state law. Before the trial, Fundamentalist leader William Bell Riley contacted former presidential candidate William Jennings Bryan and encouraged him to act as prosecutor. Although Bryan won the case, the public's perception of the incident irrevocably altered the course of Fundamentalism in America. Fundamentalists increasingly were viewed as uneducated, old-fashioned, and Southern, even though their most important leaders had been pastors and educators from urban centers in the North. After 1925, Fundamentalism lost respectability as a worldview, and its leaders forfeited some of their credibility.

Increasingly, the term "Fundamentalist" applied less to those who simply believed the traditional doctrines of the faith and instead became synonymous with those who promoted a strategy of separation. Having lost their fight for the control of denominations, Fundamentalists retreated from the larger public eye and formed their own independent churches and institutions. Fundamentalism would not regain the broad cultural respect it carried during the Jazz Age until late in the twentieth century, when its critique of modern thought and its defense of biblical authority would become increasingly influential once again among Pentecostals and Evangelicals.

Justin H. Pettegrew

See also: Anti-Catholicism; Catholics and Catholicism; Evangelicals and Evangelical Christianity; Norris, J. Frank; Protestantism, Mainstream.

Further Reading

Beale, David O. *In Pursuit of Purity.* Greenville, SC: Unusual Publications, 1986.

Marsden, George M. *Fundamentalism and American Culture.* New York: Oxford University Press, 1980.

Marty, Martin E., ed. *Modern American Protestantism and Its World: Historical Articles on Protestantism in American Religious Life.* Vol. 10, *Fundamentalism and Evangelicalism.* New York: K.G. Saur, 1993.

———. *Modern American Religion.* Chicago: University of Chicago Press, 1986.

Sandeen, Ernest R. *The Roots of Fundamentalism: British and American Millenarianism, 1800–1930.* Chicago: University of Chicago Press, 1970.

Garvey, Marcus (1887–1940)

The black nationalist leader and president of the Universal Negro Improvement Association (UNIA), which boasted millions of African American members during the Jazz Age, Marcus Mosiah Garvey was born on August 17, 1887, in the seaport town of St. Ann's Bay, Jamaica. The son of a mason, he left school at age fourteen to work as a printer's apprentice. In 1910, Garvey left the island to travel and work in Latin America and Europe. Appalled at the racist treatment and exploitation that confronted non-whites in Latin America and the West Indies, he returned to Jamaica in 1914 to found the UNIA, which advocated black unity, race pride, and black self-reliance.

Garvey traveled to the United States in 1916, establishing a UNIA branch in New York City in 1917. He subsequently organized numerous other branches in the United States, West Indies, Latin America, and Africa.

Message

By the time of his marriage to Jamaican Amy Ashwood in 1919, Garvey had established himself as a well-known radical in Harlem, the black section of New York City. At times, thousands of African Americans turned out to hear his eloquent oratory, which helped him recruit hundreds of thousands of blacks in the following years. The appeal of Garvey's organization stemmed primarily from its emphasis on race pride and economic self-improvement.

Intending to make being black "a virtue," Garvey taught his followers about the glorious past of blacks and declared Jesus to be black. In UNIA auxiliaries such as the African Legion, the Black Cross Nurses, and the black boy scouts, members proudly wore uniforms and bore titles that white Americans traditionally denied them. On the pages of the organization's newspaper, *The Negro World,* Garvey praised black accomplishments and challenged white stereotypes of African Americans. By the early 1920s, circulation of *The Negro World* had reached 200,000. In many ways, the UNIA exemplified the "New Negro" militancy associated with the Harlem Renaissance.

As part of his plan to achieve complete black self-reliance, Garvey also founded various business enterprises, an idea that he had adopted from African American leader Booker T. Washington. The UNIA operated numerous businesses, including a publishing house, cooperative grocery stores, a restaurant, a doll factory, and a steam laundry. In 1919, Garvey founded the Black Star Line, an all-black-operated steamship company that he hoped would enable his organization to establish trade relations with black people around the world.

One year later, the UNIA's first international convention was held in New York City, where delegates from dozens of countries passed a declaration that demanded an end to discrimination and disenfranchisement in the United States and denounced white colonialism in Africa. During the convention, Garvey was elected UNIA president and "provisional president of Africa," a ceremonial title. After long days of debate, large parades of the uniformed African Legion and other UNIA auxiliaries marched through Harlem, where thousands of black onlookers lined the streets to see the pageantry.

Delegates also discussed Garvey's Back to Africa movement, which sought to establish a UNIA base in Liberia to achieve the organization's longtime goal to free Africa from colonial rule and establish an independent black nation. In 1920, Garvey sent a UNIA delegation to Liberia seeking the country's assistance to put his plan into action. Ultimately, however, these negotiations proved unsuccessful.

By the time of the UNIA's second convention in 1921, the organization boasted several million members in 859 branches throughout the world, 500 of which were in the United States. Garvey's militancy, however, earned him numerous enemies who made concerted efforts to destroy his movement. European governments, fearing that the UNIA would destabilize

Jamaican-born Marcus Garvey, the founder of the Universal Negro Improvement Association, advocated a black nationalist response to white American racism, urging followers to found their own businesses and even move to Africa. *(MPI/Stringer/Hulton Archive/Getty Images)*

their colonies in Africa and the Caribbean, banned *The Negro World* in many parts of these regions. The U.S. government similarly branded his aggressive criticism of white racism as subversive and monitored the UNIA's activities.

When federal authorities arrested Garvey for alleged mail fraud in January 1922, integrationist African American leaders such as James Weldon Johnson, W.E.B. Du Bois, and A. Philip Randolph rejoiced, as they strongly objected to his message of black separatism. Many blacks were also disturbed to hear that Garvey had secretly met with Ku Klux Klan leaders in June 1922 to discuss how to maintain racial purity. To make matters worse, Garvey's Black Star Line proved a financial disaster. Amid this wave of controversies, Garvey, now divorced, married his private secretary, Amy Jacques, in July 1922.

Conviction and Imprisonment

In 1923, Garvey was convicted of mail fraud in connection with the Black Star Line but continued to recruit new UNIA members while his appeal was pending. One year later, he launched yet another unsuccessful steamship line and organized the Negro Political Union, which was intended to use black voting blocks to influence U.S. elections. In February 1925, Garvey's appeal was rejected, and he began a five-year sentence at the federal penitentiary in Atlanta, Georgia. Despite his incarceration, Garvey retained control of the UNIA, which had grown to 996 branches worldwide by 1926.

Throughout 1925 and 1926, thousands of Garvey's supporters demonstrated and petitioned for his release, which compelled President Calvin Coolidge to commute his sentence in January 1927. Since the commutation also ordered Garvey's deportation, however, the militant leader was forced to return to Jamaica in November 1927. After traveling to England in 1928, Garvey organized the UNIA's sixth international convention in Kingston, Jamaica, in 1929, but he was unable to prevent the emergence of several rival factions in the organization. That same year, he formed the People's Political Party and ran for a seat in Jamaica's legislative council. Although this political campaign failed, Garvey was elected to the Kingston and St. Andrew Corporation (KSAC) council in late 1929.

In the following years, Garvey continued to serve on the KSAC council and occasionally acted as a trade union leader, but his political aspirations were repeatedly dashed and risky real estate ventures left him bankrupt. In 1934, Garvey held another UNIA convention in Jamaica before relocating to England. One year later, the invasion of Ethiopia by Italy provided the UNIA leader with an opportunity to revive his Pan-Africanist cause, but his attempts to save the flagging movement in the following years were unsuccessful. In August 1938, Garvey organized a last UNIA convention in Toronto, Canada, though by that time the organization was largely defunct. Garvey died on June 10, 1940, in London.

Simon Wendt

See also: African Americans; Du Bois, W.E.B.; Universal Negro Improvement Association.

Further Reading

Cronon, Edmund David. *Black Moses: The Story of Marcus Garvey and the Universal Negro Improvement Association.* Madison: University of Wisconsin Press, 1955.

Martin, Tony. *Race First: The Ideological and Organizational Struggles of Marcus Garvey and the Universal Negro Improvement Association.* Westport, CT: Greenwood, 1976.

Stein, Judith. *The World of Marcus Garvey: Race and Class in Modern Society.* Baton Rouge: Louisiana State University Press, 1986.

Vincent, Theodore G. *Black Power and the Garvey Movement.* Berkeley, CA: Ramparts, 1971.

Gary, Elbert H. (1846–1927)

As president of U.S. Steel, America's largest corporation during the Jazz Age, Elbert H. Gary, a managerial innovator, is best known for his firm stand in the great steel strike of 1919–1920, helping to block the industry's efforts to organize labor. Trained as a lawyer, and an expert in the fledgling field of corporate law, he also served as a county judge in Illinois and president of the Chicago Bar Association.

Born on October 8, 1846, on a farm near Warrenville, Illinois, Elbert Henry Gary would become one of the founders of American big business. As a child, he was stirred by Harriet Beecher Stowe's *Uncle Tom's Cabin* (1852) and Charles Dickens's *Barnaby Rudge* (1841). To help him communicate with immigrant farmhands, his parents, Erastus and Susan Vallette Gary, read aloud from a German Bible. Gary later enrolled at Wheaton College, where he studied Latin.

When the Civil War began, Gary wanted to join the Union army, but he was denied because of his young age. He eventually ran away with a DuPage County regiment, only to be recalled home two months later to care for his ailing mother. He reenrolled at Wheaton but never completed his program of study.

In 1865, following in the footsteps of his idol, Abraham Lincoln, Gary joined his uncle's Chicago law firm as a clerk and studied law—a decision that would shape the remainder of his life. A year later, he enrolled in the Law Department of Chicago University (later Union College of Law, then Northwestern University School of Law) and graduated first in his class in 1867. Gary had grown up in a devoutly Christian home, and at law school he learned to partake of the ways of the world. He began to smoke, though he quit after learning of his mother's disapproval, and he acquired a love for fine clothes.

After graduation, Gary returned to his uncle's firm, but in 1871, he began his own law practice, specializing in insurance and business law. Within a decade he was admitted to the bar of the U.S. Supreme Court and ran for a DuPage County judgeship. He won handily and was reelected four years later, but he declined a third run. Judge Gary, as he was known thereafter, made a name for himself with his reserved nature and legal precision. He was elected president of the Chicago Bar Association in 1893.

Gary had assisted DuPage native John "Bet a Million" Gates in forming the Consolidated Steel and Wire Company. In 1897, Gates again sought Gary's legal acumen to help him acquire the massive amounts of capital needed to join forty steel-wire plants. Despite uncertainties about Gates's role, financier J. P. Morgan agreed to back the new Federal Steel Company because of his respect for Gary's intellect and honesty. Adding the steel holdings of Andrew Carnegie, Gary incorporated the United States Steel Corporation in 1901 and created a national holding company that was capitalized at more than $1 billion and vertically controlled ten companies with more than 200 steel mills, roughly 40 mines, and a fleet of more than 100 barges. Gary would serve as the new company's chairman of the board from its founding until his death in 1927. During its first year of operation, U.S. Steel manufactured more than 65 percent of all steel produced in America. Completed in 1906, the corporation's largest facility and its parent city in Indiana were named in Gary's honor.

With a biblical sense of morality, Gary could be seen as rigid and without a sense of humor. As a guide for young business leaders, he proposed the "Gary Principles" of honesty, education, ambition, loyalty, stability, and adherence to the Golden Rule ("do unto others as you would have them do unto you"). The social commentator H.L. Mencken, among others, found his righteousness overbearing; Mencken called him the "Christian hired man." Gary's devotion to truth and honesty, however, were revolutionary in steel industry management and corporate ethics. Regarding business as a public trust with responsibilities to shareholders, he would respond to any business proposal with the question "Is it right?" To better communicate with shareholders and give all of them a voice, he began the now common custom of holding an annual meeting. U.S. Steel also began to issue highly detailed annual reports that included charts and down-to-the-penny revenue, earnings, and expense reports, a previously unknown practice.

In late 1907 through 1908, Gary brought another innovation to big business when he gathered the leaders of rival steel companies at a series of meetings at the Waldorf-Astoria Hotel in New York City. The purpose of the meetings was to discuss industry policy and draft informal agreements to ward off destructive competition and price-slashing. These discussions led to the formation of the American Iron and Steel Institute in 1908 (Gary served as its first president). These meetings were discontinued after the Supreme Court ruled in the company's favor in the 1920 antitrust case of *United States v. U.S. Steel.*

The greatest test of Gary's mettle was the steel strike of 1919–1920. World War I had greatly benefited the American steel industry but took its toll on the labor force. With past efforts to unionize the steel industry having been unsuccessful, the War Board strongly urged employers to negotiate with unions. Gary, among other industry leaders, did not look favorably upon unions and collective bargaining, believing that they had their own interests, not those of the employees, foremost in mind. Naively, Gary declared that he and mill leadership could work through grievances with individual employees, without dealing through the union. After union requests for meetings with him were declined and a personal request from President Woodrow Wilson to negotiate was rebuffed, an industry-wide walkout was called on September 22.

The strike was bitter and violent, with the city of Gary put under martial law in early October. Eighteen workers were killed, but Gary stood firm. Ultimately, public opinion and even labor leaders turned against the strikers. The strike was finally called off in early January 1920, and workers returned to the mills having gained nothing. Public opinion, however, eventually influenced Gary and the steel industry to institute an eight-hour workday.

Gary, the force behind U.S. Steel for nearly three decades, died in New York City on August 15, 1927.

David B. Malone

See also: Steel Strike of 1919–1920.

Further Reading

Olds, Irving Sands. *Judge Elbert H. Gary (1846–1927), His Life and Influence upon American Industry.* New York: Newcomen Society, 1947.

Tarbell, Ida M. *The Life of Elbert H. Gary: The Story of Steel.* New York: Appleton, 1925.

Gastonia Strike of 1929

On April 2, 1929, approximately 2,000 workers walked out of the Loray Mill at Gastonia, North Carolina. Owned by the Manville-Jenckes Company of Rhode Island, the Loray Mill was distinctive for several reasons. It was the first textile mill owned by Northerners who took advantage of the poor white labor pool by paying its employees lower wages than those earned by their counterparts in the North. It was also the first mill in the South to undergo Frederick Winslow Taylor's "scientific management" principles to increase production. The 1929 strike at the Loray Mill was unique for the large percentages of women who picketed, and who were attacked and arrested by police.

As in many towns during the Jazz Age, the downtown and residential development of Gastonia reflected a booming economy. Blocks of businesses sprang up, as did public buildings and lavish homes in the uptown area, highlighting the conspicuous consumption of the town's elite and the division between the social classes. The town also housed the largest textile mill in the county. The Loray Mill workers tolerated hard work and unhealthy conditions, but when management instituted the stretch-out—whereby two teams performed the work of seven for the same wage—workers demanded a return to the previous method.

In March 1929, a job action at Elizabethton, Tennessee, spread discontent east to the Carolinas. Labor organizer Fred Beal called for a strike vote at Loray Mill, and workers voted unanimously in favor of it. Beal claimed the walkout in the name of the National Textile Workers Union (NTWU) and presented its demands—improved working conditions, higher wages, and improved living conditions in the mill villages—to mill management. Plant manager J.L. Baugh ignored the demands, and production continued as usual. Striking workers were replaced in the mill and evicted from their homes.

Townspeople were disturbed by the number of young women among the strikers, whose fervent participation challenged traditional gender roles and women's place in the public sphere. Many of the striking women workers were free to roam the county, wearing work clothes and speaking coarsely in public—behaviors considered unbecoming to young ladies. However, the older women involved in the strike lent seriousness to the endeavor. Strike leader Vera Buch's shock at finding children under the age of fourteen working in the mill drove her determination to organize the mill.

The conflict escalated in late March when steel cable was strung across the entrance to the mill to keep picketers back. Governor O. Max Gardner sent in five units of the North Carolina National Guard on April 4. On April 21, female workers announced their decision to maintain the strike until their demands for better working conditions and an end to the stretch-out system were met. Many of the male workers, however, crossed the women's picket lines to return to the mill. This effectively broke the strike, though some of the women persevered.

The women's resolve could be attributed to their domestic situations. While men were able to migrate elsewhere to find work, many of the women were committed to the town because of their children and other obligations. Ella May Wiggins, a spokesperson for the workers, wrote and sang empowering ballads that described the women's experiences in the mills. Along the picket lines, women taunted the National Guard, and several were arrested. Between May 16 and June 7 many others stayed away or were kept away by their husbands or fathers because of the increasing violence.

While raiding union headquarters on June 7, the local sheriff was killed in a gunfight, possibly by friendly fire from one of his subordinates. Sixteen organizers and militant strikers were arrested and tried for his murder in Charlotte on August 26. When the case was declared a mistrial, mob violence ensued in Gastonia. At a union rally held on September 14, Wiggins was shot by vigilantes. During the retrial, the charges were reduced from first-degree murder to second-degree murder, and nine of the sixteen defendants were dismissed. Wiggins's killers were arrested, arraigned, and acquitted of all charges. In the end, the workers won none of their demands from the recalcitrant mill owners.

Rebecca Tolley-Stokes

See also: Labor Movement.

Further Reading

Salmond, John A. *Gastonia, 1929: The Story of the Loray Mill Strike.* Chapel Hill: University of North Carolina Press, 1995.

Weisbord, Vera Buch. "Gastonia, 1929: Strike at the Loray Mill." *Southern Exposure* 1:3/4 (1974): 185–203.

General Electric

The General Electric (GE) Corporation took the lead in developing new products for American homes during the 1920s. With its commitment to research and development, advertising, and advocacy of consumer credit, the company changed the living standards of most urban Americans. By the 1920s, GE dominated

the market in electric lighting and the world market for electronics. It also helped solidify the dominance of big business in America with its acquisition of smaller rivals and the creation of the Radio Corporation of America (RCA) in conjunction with American Telephone and Telegraph (AT&T), American Marconi, and Westinghouse.

GE began in 1890 as the Edison General Electric Company, founded and organized by inventor Thomas Alva Edison. In 1892, financier J.P. Morgan engineered a merger between Edison's firm and one of its major rivals, the Thomson-Houston Company, headed by Charles Coffin. The combination of patents held by the two companies allowed the newly formed General Electric Corporation to emerge from its Schenectady, New York, headquarters as the dominant business in the field of electronics. As electricity became more widely available in urban areas during the first two decades of the twentieth century, the company solidified its position. It was one of twelve corporations whose stock was included in the original Dow Jones Industrial Average in 1896, and it is the only one of the original twelve still on the list.

Perhaps the company's most important innovation of the 1920s was the mass production and mass marketing of radio sets. GE and rival Westinghouse were the two largest producers of radios in the world. To enhance its market share, GE established and retained the controlling interest in RCA, which built radios, transmitters, and phonographs for the consumer market. Both to promote the sale of radios and as a means of advertising its other products, GE also pioneered the production of radio programming. Other companies quickly followed suit, radio stations sprang up everywhere, and the airwaves were filled with popular programming and advertising.

At the same time, GE began to change the face of the American home through the creation of household appliances that are today taken for granted. Among the products manufactured and sold by the company were refrigerators, electric stoves, vacuum cleaners, washing machines, and a variety of other items that improved living standards for increasing numbers of Americans. With the proliferation of consumer credit in the form of installment buying, these appliances were increasingly available to the working class as well as the middle and upper classes.

GE also led the way in marketing products on radio and in popular subscription magazines, emphasizing the way new household appliances would provide relief for housewives from their daily toil. The emphasis on freeing up time for leisure activities co-incided with the increased production of radios and broadcast programming. Company advertising also stressed the implications of product ownership within the community. Owning appliances not only eased housework and created leisure time but also conferred status on the owner.

GE's commitment to both the assembly line and more mechanized production was evident in its in-house publications that emphasized the importance of leisure time for its workforce. GE workers were encouraged to accept the newly created norms of the developing consumer culture as a substitute for pride in craftsmanship and identification with the completed product, two factors that were disappearing in the industrial workplace.

As an emerging pillar of the American industrial economy, GE's leadership played a more prominent role in foreign affairs. Owen D. Young, chair of GE's board from 1922 to 1939, was the primary author of the Young Plan in 1929, which tied the payment of German reparations directly to the payment of Allied war debts to the United States. Young hoped to improve European relations and maintain a stable overseas market for American products, but the onset of the Great Depression would defeat those goals.

Richard M. Filipink, Jr.

See also: Appliances, Household; Electricity Industry; Radio; Radio Corporation of America; Swope, Gerard.

Further Reading

Lynes, Russell. *The Domesticated Americans.* New York: Harper & Row, 1963.

Reich, Leonard S. *The Making of American Industrial Research: Science and Business at GE and Bell, 1876–1926.* Cambridge, UK: Cambridge University Press, 1985.

Schatz, Ronald W. *The Electrical Workers: A History of Labor at General Electric and Westinghouse, 1923–60.* Urbana: University of Illinois Press, 1983.

General Motors

Founded in 1908 by William C. Durant, General Motors (GM) emerged as a major industrial corporation during the 1920s, surpassing even the Ford Motor Company as the largest manufacturer of automobiles. As such, it provides a classic example of the industrial reorganization and corporate domination and consolidation that characterized American business during the Jazz Age.

A former insurance company owner and manufacturer of carriages, Durant assumed control of the floundering Buick Motor Car Company in 1905 and turned it into one of the largest automobile producers in the United States. Unlike Henry Ford, who concentrated on producing one affordable model, Durant believed that to be successful, a carmaker had to offer a wide variety of models at every price level. Acting on that belief, he organized General Motors in 1908 by bringing dozens of automakers together under one management team. The new company included Buick, Cadillac, Oldsmobile, and Oakland (later Pontiac), as well as manufacturers of auto parts such as spark plugs and axles.

In its first year, GM captured one-fifth of American auto sales. There was a downturn in 1910, however, and Durant was ultimately ousted as the leader of GM. Backed by the Du Pont family, which was making enormous profits from the manufacture of explosives during World War I, Durant gained control of Chevrolet and muscled his way back to the top of General Motors in 1916. Over the next five years, he added Chevrolet and Fisher Body, as well as several other small carmakers, to the GM family of companies. He also diversified by buying Frigidaire, a manufacturer of household appliances. At the height of GM's expansion, Durant was acquiring a new company every thirty days. By the early 1920s, GM was one of the top billion-dollar corporations in America.

Perhaps Durant's most significant innovation was to organize the General Motors Acceptance Corporation (GMAC), through which consumers could buy cars on the installment plan. By 1927, two-thirds of American cars were being bought on installment, usually with 25 percent down. GMAC ultimately was worth more than all of GM's carmaking divisions.

Rather than exercise complete control of GM, as Henry Ford did at his company, Durant, who believed that tight controls destroyed initiative and led to abuses of power, allowed the various GM companies to operate with relative autonomy. While Durant's management scheme was successful, it also led some GM divisions to engage in wasteful competition with one another for raw materials and customers.

Although GM continued to take market share away from Ford, a post–World War I economic slump hit GM hard, forcing Durant to attempt to prop up the company's stock with his own money and then turn to bankers. In 1923, Wall Street financiers replaced Durant as president of GM with trained engineer and manager Alfred P. Sloan.

Sloan retained the separate divisions created by Durant but implemented tighter management at the top of the corporation. Division managers continued to control their own production, marketing, purchasing, and engineering, but a new central office directed planning and coordination and exercised overall control of the company. Through the use of the same parts suppliers for different models, Sloan was able to gain a significant economy of scale over Ford. Sloan also employed market researchers to analyze production and sales and set future production goals, costs, and prices. Under his leadership, GM's share of the automobile market rose from 19 percent in 1924 to over 43 percent in 1929.

As cars rolled off the assembly line in record numbers, marketing became as important as production at GM. Excitement, sex appeal, and glamour replaced reliability as selling points during the 1920s. Sloan instituted yearly model changes to create what marketers call "planned obsolescence." Customers in the 1920s were offered stylish, enclosed all-weather cars. The new models had self-starters, wind-up windows, power windshield wipers, powerful six-cylinder engines, balloon tires, sleek new lines, and better finishes. Each year, Sloan launched a massive advertising campaign to extol the benefits of the latest models and to convince consumers that higher prices were the inevitable result of progress.

To make buying a new car easier, GM began allowing customers to trade in their old one. GM's divisions were also differentiated by price, with the idea that as customers earned more money and wanted to drive a superior car, they would not have to leave the GM family. While GM survived the Great Depression, its original organizer, Durant, was ruined by the 1929 stock market crash and forced to declare bankruptcy.

Michael A. Rembis

See also: Automobile Industry; Automobiles and Automobile Culture; Ford Motor Company; Sloan, Alfred P.

Further Reading

Kuhn, Arthur J. *GM Passes Ford, 1918–1938: Designing the General Motors Performance-Control System.* University Park: Pennsylvania State University Press, 1986.

Langworth, Richard M., and Ian P. Norbye. *The Complete History of General Motors, 1908–1986.* Skokie, IL: Publications International, 1986.

Geneva Arms Convention of 1925

Convinced that the international arms trade was a root cause of World War I, many world leaders during the 1920s believed that a lasting peace could be achieved through arms limitation. With this goal in mind, the League of Nations invited major arms-producing powers and nonproducing states to a meeting in Geneva, Switzerland, in May 1925 to discuss limiting the arms trade. All major arms producers with the exception of the Soviet Union attended. Although the Geneva Arms Convention failed to curb the arms trade, it produced a significant agreement, the Geneva Protocol, which prohibited the "use in war of asphyxiating, poisonous or other gases, and of bacteriological methods of warfare." The document was signed in Geneva on June 17, 1925, and formally adopted on February 8, 1928.

Portending the convention's failure to achieve its primary initiative, the larger powers and the smaller states squabbled from the beginning of the conference. The arms-producing powers proposed that weapons exports should be prohibited except to legitimate governments under license from the exporting state. The smaller, nonproducing states maintained that any restriction on the sale of arms would undermine their sovereignty. The proposal would give the arms-producing states the power to freeze arms sales to any country by denying a license; the country denied licensing would be without recourse. The nonproducing states also noted that armaments producers could easily manipulate the proposal to increase arms sales. Nothing in the protocol prevented an arms producer from supplying arms to any insurgency movement that it declared a legitimate government.

Other problems arose. A proposal to publicize arms trading was fiercely resisted by the nonproducing states. Arms importers would be compelled to reveal the amount and types of weapons purchased, whereas arms-producing states were not obligated to disclose the size of their arsenals. Eastern European countries, concerned about possible Soviet expansion, believed that the publication of their armaments imports would compromise national security.

The delegates at the Geneva Arms Convention ultimately drew up an agreement that solved a few key dilemmas. The agreement permitted Eastern European regimes to keep their arms imports confidential, but all other nonproducers were required to publicize their imports. The agreement also left unresolved the nonproducers' concerns regarding sovereignty. As a result, the proposal was never ratified. Faced with this setback, the League of Nations worked in subsequent years on a general disarmament agreement, but Nazi dictator Adolf Hitler's October 1933 withdrawal from a disarmament conference ended all hopes of such an accord.

The delegates at the Geneva Arms Convention, however, reached an important agreement regarding the wartime use of poisonous gases and bacteriological agents. Poison gas had first been used during World War I. Although the actual number of battle deaths due to gas exposure was small, death was often slow and excruciating. As a result, an international outcry emerged against the use of poison gas in future wars. At the convention, the United States proposed prohibiting the export of gases for use in war. France suggested, and the group agreed to, a protocol that completely banned the use of poisonous gases in war. At the urging of Poland, this prohibition was extended to bacteriological agents. The delegates signed the protocol on June 17, 1925.

By World War II, most countries had ratified the protocol. The United States and Japan held out, and other countries declared that the protocol would cease to be binding upon them if their enemies used poison gas or bacteriological weapons against them first. Italy used poison gas in its Ethiopian campaign of 1936, but during World War II, the protocol was observed by all countries except Japan, which used poison gas against the Chinese.

The Geneva Protocol has been breached rarely since World War II. The most notorious instance occurred during the Iran–Iraq War of the 1980s, when both belligerents repeatedly used chemical agents. Led by the United States, the international community condemned Iran's and Iraq's actions and called upon all states that had not done so to ratify the protocol.

To date, more than 130 nations have acceded to the protocol. The United States ratified the treaty in 1975 after concerns over the protocol's application to riot-control agents and herbicides were settled. The Geneva Arms Convention's protocol against wartime use of poisonous gas and bacteriological agents stands as one of the great foreign policy achievements of the Jazz Age.

John Paul Hill

See also: Europe, Relations with; League of Nations; Military Affairs; Washington Naval Conference (1921–1922).

Further Reading

Baxter, R.R., and Thomas Buergenthal. "Legal Aspects of the Geneva Protocol of 1925." *American Journal of International Law* 64 (October 1970): 853–79.

Fanning, Robert M. *Peace and Disarmament: Naval Rivalry and Arms Control, 1922–1933.* Lexington: University Press of Kentucky, 1995.

Stone, David R. "Imperialism and Sovereignty: The League of Nations' Drive to Control the Global Arms Trade." *Journal of Contemporary History* 35 (April 2000): 213–30.

German Americans

Germans began arriving in America in large numbers as early as the colonial era. And while Benjamin Franklin, among others, complained about the stubbornness with which German immigrants clung to their language and culture, they were among the ethnic groups most ready to assimilate. In 1928, German American social commentator H.L. Mencken observed, "The melting pot has swallowed up the German-Americans as no other group, not even the Irish." And the process worked in both directions. Many elements of German culture became so embedded in American culture that they lost their German flavor. German cultural imports, such as foods like sausages and sauerkraut and holiday traditions, including Easter eggs, Christmas trees, and a gift-giving Santa Claus, became part of the American mainstream.

During World War I, many people, businesses, and associations submerged their Germanic heritage following America's entry into the war and chose not to reclaim it when the fighting was over. Many Americans with German-sounding names changed them to more English-sounding ones. The Germania Life Insurance Company, for example, changed its name to the Guardian Life Insurance Company.

German, once spoken widely in America, was relegated to the margins of society and all but eliminated in many areas. Missouri Synod Lutherans, one of the largest and most traditional German Protestant sects, dropped German-language sermons in most locales. Nevertheless, German continued to be the most common non-English language spoken in American homes during the 1920s. By the end of the decade, more than 2 million foreign-born German Americans still used German as their principal language, down just 3 percent from ten years prior. Some German parochial schools continued bilingual education, with instruction in German in the morning and English in the afternoon. However, English emerged as the language of the playground. Despite U.S. Supreme Court decisions that affirmed the legitimacy of parochial education (*Pierce v. Sisters of the Holy Name,* 1925) and German-language schools (*Meyer v. Nebraska,* 1923), both experienced a steady decline during the 1920s.

German Americans constituted one of the largest ethnic groups in the United States during the Jazz Age. Throughout the decade, German American associations reemerged slowly and cautiously, but never with the vigor and vitality of the prewar years. For example, the number of German singing societies in Philadelphia fell from sixty-one in 1911 to thirty-eight in 1933. Cultural and civic groups slowly abandoned their native language in activities, publications, and meeting minutes. Prohibition further damaged the viability of many German social clubs, which included drinking as part of their activities and relied on revenues from selling alcohol.

The 1920s marked a time of political disillusionment for many German Americans. At the beginning of the decade, "secular Germans" continued their support for the Socialist Party, while a good number of "church Germans," dissatisfied with Woodrow Wilson's diplomacy, turned at least temporarily to the Republican Party. But the party of Prohibition and immigration restriction could not hold this constituency. The restrictive immigration laws of the 1920s helped stymie the possibility of a resurgence of German culture in America. Even without restriction, second-, third-, and fourth-generation German Americans far outnumbered recent immigrants.

The increased urbanization of the decade diluted the ethnic character of German Catholic parishes and, to a lesser degree, Lutheran ones. However, most German Americans continued to marry other German Americans. With approximately 80 percent of German Americans living in the Middle Atlantic or North Central states during the 1920s, German pastimes such as bowling, swimming, and gymnastics continued to be popular in these regions.

The advent of mass culture in the 1920s, especially national radio programming and talking pictures, served to homogenize American culture at the expense of non-English languages and subcultures. However, German Americans were among some of the country's most celebrated figures—most notably, baseball legends Babe Ruth and Lou Gehrig, aviator Charles Lindbergh, and Herbert Hoover, who received more popular votes in 1928 than any previous presidential candidate.

Michael Jacobs

See also: Immigration; Red Scare of 1917–1920.

Further Reading

Kazal, Russell A. *Becoming Old Stock: The Paradox of German-American Identity.* Princeton, NJ: Princeton University Press, 2004.

Rippley, La Vern J. "Ameliorated Americanization: The Effect of World War I on German-Americans in the 1920s." In *America and the Germans: An Assessment of a Three-Hundred-Year History,* 2 vols, ed. Frank Trommler and Joseph McVeigh. Philadelphia: University of Pennsylvania Press, 1985.

Gershwin, George (1898–1937)

An iconic figure of the Jazz Age, composer George Gershwin combined elements of popular and classical music with influences from jazz and blues to create a distinctive style that encapsulated the spirit of 1920s urban America. With many of his lyrics provided by his brother Ira, Gershwin composed hundreds of popular songs (many of which have become standards), scores for dozens of Broadway shows, the opera *Porgy and Bess* (1935), and several concert hall pieces, including the classic *Rhapsody in Blue* (1924). Although his career was cut short by illness, the charismatic composer embodied in both his brief life and his music the restless energy of post–World War I America.

The second child of Russian Jewish immigrants, Jacob Gershwine (as his birth certificate reads) was born in Brooklyn, New York, on September 26, 1898. His father, Morris Gershovitz, had been a skilled leather worker in Russia and had little difficulty finding work in America. Nevertheless, he changed jobs frequently, and the family's fortunes and residences changed accordingly. At the insistence of his socially ambitious mother, Gershwin enrolled at the High School of Commerce on Manhattan's Upper West Side, but he took little interest in his schoolwork. He spent the summer of 1913 as a pianist at a Catskills resort, and the $5 weekly salary that he earned (more than many adult factory workers earned at the time) might have helped to silence his parents' objections when he quit school at age fifteen to pursue a career in music.

Tin Pan Alley—the block of West 28th Street between Fifth and Sixth avenues in New York City— was the center of the popular music world in the early twentieth century. There Gershwin perfected his piano technique as a song-plugger—someone who plays songs and tries to sell them—for the Remick publishing firm. He spent his Saturdays recording piano rolls for player pianos. Both experiences contributed to Gershwin's unique piano-playing style, as did the influence of the black musicians then performing in Harlem.

A Remick competitor, the Harry Von Tilzer Company, published Gershwin's first song—"When You Want 'Em, You Can't Get 'Em (When You've Got 'Em, You Don't Want 'Em)"—in March 1916; Gershwin was only eighteen years old. Gershwin left his position with Remick in 1917 to concentrate on writing his own material. After working several odd jobs as a pianist, he met with some success "interpolating" songs into Broadway musicals. This was common practice at the time whereby established composers allowed young songwriters to insert one or two songs in Broadway shows.

Gershwin received his first big break in 1918, when he signed a contract with Max Dreyfus, one of the most powerful men in the music-publishing industry. Dreyfus offered Gershwin a staff position as a composer at a salary of $35 per week, plus a $50 advance and royalties on any of his songs that were published. A second break came early in 1919 when Alex Aarons, the son of Broadway producer Alfred Aarons, hired Gershwin to compose the score for the musical *La-La Lucille*. The show, which included the memorable song "Nobody but You," marked Gershwin's first success as the composer of a full-scale production. Later that year, Gershwin collaborated with lyricist Irving Caesar on "Swanee," the song that—when recorded by Al Jolson in 1920—became a major hit and earned for Gershwin substantial royalties (about $10,000) as well as international recognition. The success of "Swanee" also brought Gershwin to the attention of Broadway producers. For the next five seasons, Gershwin's name was up in lights on Broadway as the composer of more than forty songs for *George White's Scandals*.

The Gershwin piece that perhaps best encapsulated the Jazz Age, *Rhapsody in Blue,* premiered at New York's Aeolian Hall on February 12, 1924. The concert's organizer, Paul Whiteman, had long sought to make jazz music "respectable" enough for the concert hall. Having conducted Gershwin's one-act opera *Blue Monday* in the *Scandals of 1922,* Whiteman approached Gershwin about contributing a concerto-like piece to "An Experiment in Modern Music"—a concert that would be attended by the nation's leading

Pianist and composer George Gershwin collaborated with his brother, lyricist Ira Gershwin, on some of the most popular Broadway musicals of the 1920s. He is best remembered, however, for his jazz-influenced classical compositions, *Rhapsody in Blue* (1924) and *An American in Paris* (1928). *(Evening Standard/Stringer/Hulton Archive/Getty Images)*

music critics. With only five weeks to compose the jazz concerto, Gershwin managed to produce a song that would catapult him to fame in the world of classical concert music as well as Broadway. When Whiteman's band recorded *Rhapsody in Blue* in June 1924, with Gershwin on the piano, the record became an international hit.

Gershwin continued to compose songs for musical theater in both New York and London. He and his brother Ira collaborated on some of the top musicals of the 1920s, including *Lady, Be Good* (1924), *Tip-Toes* (1925), *Oh, Kay!* (1926), and *Funny Face* (1927). Gershwin returned to the concert hall with the December 3, 1925, premier of his Concerto in F at Carnegie Hall in New York. Meanwhile, he lived the life of a star, his name or picture appearing in the society columns and arts pages of every major newspaper. He traveled throughout Europe in the spring of 1928, gathering inspiration for what would become *An American in Paris,* which debuted that December. At about the same time, he began dabbling in art as both a painter and a collector.

Gershwin escaped relatively unscathed from the stock market crash of October 1929, having already signed contracts on a number of projects, including a revised version of *Strike Up the Band,* which opened in mid-January 1930. This was followed almost immediately by another smash hit, *Girl Crazy,* which featured some of the Gershwin brothers' most enduring hits, including "I Got Rhythm" and "Embraceable

You." Their most successful show, *Of Thee I Sing,* ran for 441 performances in 1931. Gershwin's operatic masterpiece *Porgy and Bess* premiered in the autumn of 1935. Shortly thereafter, however, his health began to decline. He died of a brain tumor on July 10, 1937, two months shy of his thirty-ninth birthday.

Kathleen Ruppert

See also: Jazz; Music, Classical.

Further Reading

Greenberg, Rodney. *George Gershwin.* London: Phaidan, 1998.
Jablonski, Edward. *Gershwin.* New York: Doubleday, 1987.
Leon, Ruth. *Gershwin.* London: Haus, 2004.
Peyser, Joan. *The Memory of All That: The Life of George Gershwin.* New York: Simon & Schuster, 1993.

Gish, Lillian (1893–1993)

One of the most popular stars of the silent film era, and among the most influential actresses in the history of Hollywood, Lillian Gish is best known for her starring roles in the pathbreaking films of director D.W. Griffith, including *Birth of a Nation* (1915), *Intolerance* (1916), *Broken Blossoms* (1919), *Way Down East* (1920), and *Orphans of the Storm* (1922).

She was born Lillian Diana de Guiche on October 14, 1893, in Springfield, Ohio. Her father, a candy merchant, moved the family to New York when Gish was still a young girl. When her father abandoned the family, Gish's mother supported Lillian and her younger sister, Dorothy, by working in a candy stand, ice cream parlor, and theatrical boardinghouse before becoming an actress. Neither girl got much of an education, though Lillian briefly attended the Ursuline Academy in East St. Louis. When the two girls were old enough, they joined their mother on stage. Gish's first acting job was on an Ohio stage in the early 1900s. By 1905, she was a member of a touring stage show while her sister was part of another.

In 1912, Gish and her sister visited one of their mother's boarders, an actress working at Biograph Studios in New York. The actress's name was Gladys Smith, but that would soon be changed to Mary Pickford. Pickford introduced Gish to director D.W. Griffith, who signed Gish to appear in his short film *An Unseen Enemy* (1912). In the fast-paced studio production of the early silent era, Gish made dozens of films over the next couple of years, many under Griffith's direction and co-starring her sister Dorothy.

Under Griffith's guidance, Gish soon developed her film persona, projecting an image of purity, chastity, and quiet nobility. She became popular with audiences for her portrayals of idealized womanhood. By 1913, she was one of the public's favorite stars, along with Pickford.

In 1915, Griffith, now with the Mutual Film Corporation, hired Gish to star in *Birth of a Nation,* one of the most influential films in the history of American cinema. More than two hours long and using pioneering cinematography, it was Hollywood's first true feature-length film. By modern standards, the story is awash in racist stereotypes, depicting freed slaves running amok in the post–Civil War South. Contemporary audiences and critics, however, loved the film and hailed Gish's performance. Recognizing the publicity value, Griffith promoted Gish relentlessly, helping to establish the idea of the Hollywood movie star.

In 1916, partly in response to the charges of racism leveled against *Birth of a Nation,* Griffith directed *Intolerance,* another epic starring Gish, but this time one that emphasized brotherhood. When the United States entered World War I the following year, Gish starred in a number of propaganda films that Griffith made for the government.

Helping Gish develop as an actress, Griffith insisted she take dancing, fencing, and voice lessons. He also had her attend boxing matches and visit psychiatric hospitals in order to study the extremes of the human condition and lend emotional depth to her performances. Gish also learned about the technical side of moviemaking. She helped the director edit his films and select the appropriate scores. When he bought an estate on Long Island, Griffith asked Gish to oversee its conversion into a studio.

In 1920, Griffith provided Gish with $50,000 to make her own film; with *Remodeling Her Husband,* Gish became the first American woman to direct a feature-length film. Dorothy starred in the film, and Gish convinced popular writer Dorothy Parker to write the titles—the printed lines of dialogue and narrative that moved a silent film forward. *Remodeling* is a light-hearted comedy about a woman's attempts to convince her husband she has sex appeal by flirting with other men. While Dorothy's performance was hailed by critics, Gish's direction was not; she never directed another film. Over the next several years, Griffith and Gish would make three more features together: *Broken Blossoms, Way Down East,* and *Orphans of the Storm,* with Gish playing her typical innocent but wronged woman in each.

Gish's accumulated wealth allowed her to produce films of her own. As the financial backer of Inspiration Films, she produced *The White Sister* (1923) and *Romola* (1924). But when Gish began to suspect that Inspiration Film's president, Charles Duell, with whom she was romantically involved, was manipulating the books, the two broke up romantically and professionally.

For the rest of the 1920s, Gish remained one of America's favorite stars, avoiding roles that might undermine her image as the innocent young woman. This did not compromise her career; she was so popular, she could pick and choose her parts. In 1926, she moved to Metro-Goldwyn-Mayer (MGM), where she starred in *La Bohème* (1926), *The Scarlet Letter* (1926), and *The Wind* (1928).

When sound came to the movie business, Gish was reluctant to make the transition, preferring to return to the stage. She made only two films during the 1930s, but after World War II, she appeared in numerous television programs, and she made several films in her later years. Gish died in New York City on February 27, 1993, less than eight months short of her one-hundredth birthday.

Tim J. Watts and James Ciment

See also: Film.

Further Reading

Affron, Charles. *Lillian Gish: Her Legend, Her Life.* New York: Scribner's, 2001.

Gish, Lillian. *Dorothy and Lillian Gish.* New York: Scribner's, 1973.

Gish, Lillian, and Ann Pinchot. *Lillian Gish: The Movies, Mr. Griffith, and Me.* Englewood Cliffs, NJ: Prentice Hall, 1969.

Oderman, Stuart. *Lillian Gish: A Life on Stage and Screen.* Jefferson, NC: McFarland, 2000.

Gitlow v. New York (1925)

A landmark U.S. Supreme Court decision on free speech, *Gitlow v. New York* upheld a state law that banned speech deemed by authorities to be a threat to public security. The ruling confirmed and extended the Court's 1919 decision in *Schenck v. United States* that freedom of speech is not an absolute right. Criticized by civil libertarians at the time, *Gitlow* was ultimately reversed by the Court half a century later.

Plaintiff Benjamin Gitlow, a labor activist and New York state legislator, had become a member of the Socialist Party in New York in 1909, at the age of eighteen. Over the years, Gitlow gravitated toward the radical wing of American socialism, which was critical of the moderate democratic tactics of the party's mainstream. The radicals, many of whom, including Gitlow, organized the Communist Labor Party in the late 1910s, supported the idea of the class struggle and advocated strikes and social upheaval rather than the political process to bring about change. In 1919, Gitlow helped to prepare and circulate a document known as the "Left Wing Manifesto," which was published in the *Revolutionary Age,* the official publication of the radical Socialists.

The revolutionary views espoused in the manifesto and Gitlow's role led to his arrest; he was charged with violating New York's 1902 criminal anarchy statutes, which prohibited advocacy of the violent overthrow of the government. At the trial, his principal attorney, Clarence Darrow, pointed out that publication of the manifesto had had no discernible impact and that Gitlow had merely been exercising his rights of freedom of speech and of the press, which were protected under the First Amendment to the U.S. Constitution. Nevertheless, Gitlow was convicted and sentenced to five to ten years in prison. Gitlow's attorneys appealed his conviction, and the case made its way through the appellate process to the U.S. Supreme Court, which heard arguments in April and November 1923, handing down a decision on June 8, 1925.

As in other cases of the post–World War I era, such as *Schenck v. United States*—in which Justice Oliver Wendell Holmes set forth the "clear and present danger" doctrine (speech that creates a clear and present danger is not protected)—the justices held in *Gitlow v. New York* that freedom of speech is not an absolute right, but one that entails responsibilities and has certain limits. In *Gitlow,* they affirmed that a state has the right to prohibit speech and publications that tend to pose a threat to public security, even if that threat does not constitute a "clear and present danger." They concluded that although the "Left Wing Manifesto" did not specifically and immediately call for violent revolutionary action, it was no mere abstract or philosophical discussion of tactics to promote social change. Thus, the Court upheld New York's criminal anarchy legislation and Gitlow's conviction under its provisions.

The broader significance of the *Gitlow* decision was the Court's position regarding the relevance of the Bill of Rights to state actions. Traditionally, the

Court had held, as in *Barron v. Mayor and City Council of Baltimore* (1833), that the protections guaranteed in the Bill of Rights apply only to actions of the federal government and not to those of the states. In *Gitlow,* the Court held that the due process clause of the Constitution's Fourteenth Amendment, prohibiting states from depriving any person of life, liberty, or property without due process of law, applied to the First Amendment guarantees of freedom of speech and the press. The Court, in effect, accepted Gitlow's contention that his right of free expression was protected from state abridgement by the Constitution— but in the current case, public security superseded that right.

Many constitutional scholars regard the Court's position in *Gitlow* as the genesis of the "incorporation doctrine," under which most of the protections of the Bill of Rights have subsequently been "incorporated" into the due process clause and now apply to the states as well as the federal government.

Roughly a half century after the *Gitlow* decision, in *Brandenburg v. Ohio* (1969) and *Hess v. Indiana* (1973), the Court reversed its position, ruling that the constitutional guarantee of free speech prohibits states from banning the advocacy of unlawful or violent acts unless that advocacy is intended and likely to result in imminent unlawful action.

Robert F. Martin

See also: Anarchism; Law and the Courts; *Schenck v. United States* (1919); Socialism and the Socialist Party of America.

Further Reading

Gitlow, Benjamin. *I Confess: The Truth About American Communism.* Freeport, NY: Books for Libraries, 1972.
Renstrom, Peter G. "Benjamin Gitlow: Radical Leader to Fallen-Away Communist." In *100 Americans Making Constitutional History,* ed. Melvin I. Urofsky. Washington, DC: CQ, 2004.

Golf

Golf is a product of the British Isles where it was invented and developed over centuries. As English and Scottish champions historically dominated competition, the game remained largely unknown to most Americans until late in the nineteenth century. By the second decade of the twentieth century, however, Americans were the most important innovators in the game. In the Jazz Age, American golfers and golf organizations largely controlled the sport and were shaping its future.

The shift toward American dominance of the game began in 1913, when a relatively unknown twenty-year-old caddie named Francis Ouimet of Massachusetts, the working-class son of French Canadian and Irish immigrant parents, captured the U.S. Open, defeating legendary British golfers Ted Ray and Harry Vardon. Ouimet's stunning upset was credited with helping triple the number of American players within a decade. At the same time, World War I robbed Britain of many of its players and diminished fan interest in the game. As Britain was preoccupied with the war, Americans organized the Professional Golfers Association (PGA) in 1916, partly shifting fans' interest from amateur players to professionals.

Before the 1920s, golfers were rigidly defined by their status as either professional or amateur players. Amateur status was highly regarded by the golfing community. Thought of as gentlemen sportsmen, amateurs played purely for the love of the game. Professional golfers were not as respected; they were the people who instructed paying members at a golf course or country club.

Two golfers epitomized the distinctions between professional and amateur status in the Jazz Age, and both helped propel the game to levels of popularity greater than any previously known in the United States. Bobby Jones of Georgia represented the ideal of the amateur golfer, talented and competitive but unsullied by crass monetary considerations. Walter Hagen, born in upstate New York, was the quintessential professional; he made a living by his skills, and he lived well. Hagen's flamboyant lifestyle and style of play attracted fans' attention and, in the process, helped promote professional golf.

Jones's golf career largely coincided with the Jazz Age. He began playing on the national amateur circuit in the late 1910s, but he first made a name for himself by winning the U.S. Open in 1923. From then through 1930, Jones won a major tournament every year—thirteen of the twenty-one he entered. In 1930, he won all four major tournaments—then including the U.S. Open, British Open, U.S. Amateur, and British Amateur—a feat the Associated Press declared the greatest individual achievement in the history of all sports.

Hagen, too, had a sterling record. When Hagen began to play for money in the early 1910s, professional players were often snubbed at major country clubs, sometimes forced to use the service entrance at the clubhouse. At one tournament, Hagen made headlines by using a Rolls-Royce as his changing room when a country club refused him access to its facilities. Such antics helped win him a public following. But it was his skills and winning record that gradually broke down many of the institutional barriers to—as well as prejudices against—professional players. His victory in eleven majors ranks him third in the history of professional golf, behind Jack Nicklaus and Tiger Woods.

Women's golf also made significant strides during the 1920s, largely through the exploits of British golfers Charlotte Cecilia "Cecil" Leitch and Joyce Wethered, who between them won more than two dozen tournaments in the 1910s and 1920s. The preeminent American woman golfer of the Jazz Age was Glenna Collett of Providence, Rhode Island. Collett began competing at the age of sixteen, and she went on to win dozens of tournaments, earning six U.S. women's championships.

Women's golf was an entirely amateur affair in the 1920s. Professional women's golf did not emerge until the 1940s. African Americans and other minorities, because of segregation and prejudice, were largely kept off U.S. golf courses in the 1920s. The first black golfers did not emerge until well after World War II.

Patrick Mallory and James Ciment

See also: Jones, Bobby; Leisure and Recreation.

Further Reading

Burgess, Charles D. *Golf Links: Chay Burgess, Francis Ouimet, and the Bringing of Golf to America.* Cambridge, MA: Rounder, 2005.

Lowe, Stephen. *Sir Walter and Mr. Jones: Walter Hagen, Bobby Jones, and the Rise of American Golf.* Chelsea, MI: Sleeping Bear, 2000.

Wind, Herbert Warren. *The Story of American Golf.* New York: Callaway, 2000.

Grange, Red (1903–1991)

Football star Red Grange, an electrifying running back for the University of Illinois and a leading force in the establishment of the professional game while playing for the Chicago Bears in 1925, was one of America's first great celebrity athletes. He was born Harold Edward Grange on June 13, 1903, on a farm near the logging town of Forksville, Pennsylvania. After the death of his mother in 1908, his father moved the family to Wheaton, Illinois.

Grange first became involved in organized sports in the fourth grade, playing basketball for his school and the Boy Scouts. He went on to become an outstanding all-around athlete at Wheaton's Central High, lettering in four sports (football, baseball, basketball, and track) in each of his four years. He preferred basketball and track—in May 1922, he won the state title in the 220-yard dash and finished third in the 100—but it was football that would become the center of his life. His stellar high school career in Chicago's western suburbs and in Cook County helped to put high school football on the map.

Attending college at his father's insistence, Harold enrolled in the University of Illinois at Urbana-Champaign. He did not originally intend to play football in college, thinking he was not good enough. He tried out for the team only under the threat of paddling from his fraternity brothers. Initially placed on the freshman practice team, he was a full-fledged star by the time he was a sophomore.

Nicknamed the "Wheaton Iceman" because he worked summers hauling and delivering 75-pound (35-kilogram) blocks of ice, Grange was in much better shape than most other players. This was only one of his many nicknames; the most well-known nickname was "Red." He never really cared for the moniker, commenting once that his hair was not red, but more auburn. He much preferred Hal, the name he was called in high school. Grange put up with the name that the newspaper writers gave him, but he would always place it in quotes when he signed his name.

Grange would go on to become the premier running back in all of college football, astounding opponents with his speed and ability to elude tacklers. Perhaps his greatest performance came in October 1924, when he scored six touchdowns (four in the first twelve minutes) against the powerful University of Michigan defense. He scored more points in that one game than had been scored against Michigan in the two prior seasons combined. It was after this game that sportswriters such as Grantland Rice thrust Grange into national prominence. Rice is said to have bestowed on Grange another familiar nickname, "Galloping Ghost," because he wrote a poetic tribute that began, "A streak of fire, a breath of flame / Eluding all who reach and clutch / A gray ghost thrown into the game / That rival hands may never touch." However, credit for the nickname Galloping Ghost is truly owed to Warren Brown of the Chicago *Herald-Examiner*.

After the final game of the 1925 football season, amid great controversy, Grange dropped out of the University of Illinois a year early to pursue his professional career. Grange pointed to the financial difficulties of his childhood as part of the reason for his move. The controversy soon passed, however, as Grange continued to be a major attraction for national audiences and helped the young National Football League (NFL) gain a foothold in popular culture. Grange's first professional game was on Thanksgiving Day against the Bears' crosstown rivals, the league-leading Chicago Cardinals; 36,000 fans crammed into Cubs Park, with police driving away thousands of others.

Grange had so captured the attention of America that he was featured on the cover of *Time* magazine in 1925, the first athlete to be so recognized. Children looked up to him as a hero, reading about him in their books and comics. Grange's business agent, Charles C. Pyle, took every opportunity to cash in on endorsement offers. Grange's name appeared on candy bars, meat loaf, sweaters, and socks. He starred in *One Minute to Play* (1926), a hastily written silent film directed by Sam Wood and distributed by Joseph Kennedy's Film Booking Office, which quickly produced a second film, *Racing Romeo* (1927), that allowed Grange to indulge his one known vice—fast cars. Grange later appeared in the serial *Galloping Ghost* (1935), an early "talkie" (the only Grange film that survives today).

Red Grange retired from football in 1934 after a ten-year professional career with the Chicago Bears and the ill-fated American Football League's New York Yankees. He continued his involvement with football as a broadcaster, working for WJJD in Chicago, KCKN in Kansas City, and the CBS radio network. In 1951, he was elected a charter member of the College Football Hall of Fame, and in 1963, he became a charter member of the Professional Football Hall of Fame.

Moving from Illinois to Lake Wales, Florida, after a heart attack, the Galloping Ghost enjoyed a quiet retirement with his wife, Margaret, to whom he was married for fifty years. He died at the age of eighty-seven on January 28, 1991.

David B. Malone

See also: Celebrity Culture; Football.

Further Reading

Carroll, John M. *Red Grange and the Rise of Modern Football.* Urbana: University of Illinois Press, 1999.

Grange, Harold E. *The Red Grange Story: An Autobiography.* Urbana: University of Illinois Press, 1993.

Peterson, James A. *Grange of Illinois.* Chicago: Hinckley & Schmitt, 1956.

Schoor, Gene. *Red Grange: Football's Greatest Halfback.* New York: Julian Messner, 1952.

Haiti, Intervention in

For nearly two decades—from July 1915 to August 1934—the United States maintained a military occupation force in the Caribbean island republic of Haiti. Originally dispatched to deal with disorders following the assassination of President Jean Vilbrun Guillaume Sam, the U.S. Marines fought a counterinsurgency campaign against a rebel Haitian army known as the Cacos while helping to develop a national police force that could maintain order once the American troops left. The nature of counterinsurgency fighting—combined with the racism of the U.S. military in the early twentieth century—resulted in so many acts of brutality by Marines that a congressional commission was formed in 1922 to investigate the charges.

Since its founding as the Western Hemisphere's second republic in 1804, Haiti had been torn by coups, armed conflict, and political instability, largely resulting from the basic social divisions of the country. The new republic was ruled by a light-skinned mulatto elite who controlled most of the wealth and ruthlessly exploited the country's black masses; the latter were descended from the slaves who had successfully revolted against French colonial rule in the late eighteenth and early nineteenth centuries.

U.S. interest in the republic began in the 1890s with efforts to persuade the Haitian government to grant preferences for American businesses and allow for resupply of American naval vessels. To guarantee repayment of Haiti's substantial debt to American and European financial institutions, the United States took control of the country's customs operations—the main source of government revenue—in 1905.

Two events led to the Haitian intervention of 1915. One was World War I, which began in Europe a year earlier. Technically neutral in the conflict until its entry in 1917, the United States was concerned about growing German influence in Latin America and wanted to ensure that Germany did not take advantage of the turbulent conditions in Haiti to establish a military toehold in the Caribbean that might threaten the newly opened Panama Canal. In addition,

U.S. businesses active in Haiti wanted to prevent German competition in what they considered their territory.

A succession of coups racked the country, many instigated by the Cacos army, which helped Sam topple the government of Jean Davilmar Théodore in February 1915. For its part, the urban mulatto elite, who controlled the economy—in cooperation with U.S. business interests—feared the largely black and rural Cacos and their supposed leader, Sam. The Cacos had their concerns as well. Worried he might be toppled by a mulatto-led uprising, Sam moved against those he believed to be his opponents within the mulatto caste in a crackdown that culminated in a mass execution of 167 political prisoners in July. Among those killed was a former president being held in a Port-au-Prince jail. The executions triggered mass rioting in the capital and the capture and murder of Sam. Concerned that the anti-American politician Rosalvo Bobo might take power and make a deal with Germany, U.S. President Woodrow Wilson ordered 330 Marines, stationed on ships in Port-au-Prince, to occupy the capital.

The troops met little organized resistance at first. The new U.S.-backed Haitian government quickly signed a ten-year treaty—later extended—which gave the United States control of Haiti's politics and finances. In 1918, a new constitution was written, allowing for foreign ownership of land. The U.S. Marines helped create a new national police force, or gendarmerie, and allowed the traditional mulatto elite to resume power in Port-au-Prince.

While the Wilson administration claimed that it had acted in Haiti's interests, the vast majority of the population saw it as an attempt by the United States to establish hegemony through a mulatto client regime. Even public works efforts were objects of suspicion. As the projects used forced labor of black workers and peasants, many Haitians came to believe that the United States was trying to reintroduce slavery to the island.

All of this reinvigorated the Cacos. In 1919, under rebel leader Charlemagne Peralte, it launched a new rebellion against the Marines and the mulatto elite. It took the Marines, who now numbered about 1,300, and the Marine-officered gendarmerie more than a year to crush the rebellion. The conflict included atrocities by both sides. With the fighting largely over by the end of 1920, the Marines began to draw down their numbers, and by 1922, the force consisted of just 400 troops and remained at roughly that level for the next decade or so.

The Haitian intervention also had an impact on U.S. politics. The 1920 Republican candidate, Warren G. Harding, who argued for an isolationist foreign policy, made the situation a campaign issue in his successful run for the presidency. Still, neither Harding nor his successor, Calvin Coolidge, moved to end the occupation. It took the brutal suppression of the 1929 student and worker riots to open a congressional inquiry. Among the findings and recommendations of the committee were that Haitians did not have enough control over their own government and that the occupation should end.

Haitian elections in 1930 put moderate, pro-U.S. politician Sténio Joseph Vincent in power. That, and the election of Franklin D. Roosevelt to the U.S. presidency in 1932, led to the withdrawal of U.S. troops from Haiti. Under its "good neighbor" policy, the Roosevelt administration emphasized more cooperative relations between the United States and Latin America. The last Marine contingent left the country in 1934, although the United States maintained direct control of Haiti's finances until 1941.

James Ciment

See also: Dominican Republic, Intervention in; Latin America, Relations with; Military Affairs.

Further Reading

Renda, Mary A. *Taking Haiti: Military Occupation and the Culture of U.S. Imperialism, 1915–1940.* Chapel Hill: University of North Carolina Press, 2001.
Schmidt, Hans. *The United States Occupation of Haiti, 1915–1934.* New Brunswick, NJ: Rutgers University Press, 1971.

Harding, Warren G. (1865–1923)

Elected to the U.S. presidency in 1920 on a platform that promised to return America to "normalcy," Warren Gamaliel Harding was a popular figure during his lifetime and beloved during his tenure in the White House. However, the scandals that engulfed his administration and revelations of his marital infidelity forever tarnished his reputation.

Harding was born on November 2, 1865, in what is now Blooming Grove, Ohio. The oldest of eight children, he developed an interest in printing and newspapers at a young age. After graduating from Ohio Central College, he moved to Marion and purchased the *Daily Star* in the late 1880s. He made the paper a successful voice and supporter of the Republican Party, and it became one of the largest circulating papers in the state. In 1891, Harding married Florence Kling, an older divorcée and the daughter of a Marion business rival. She would become the perfect partner for her husband, helping him manage the paper and ensure its financial success.

Early Political Career

Harding served as an Ohio state senator from 1899 to 1903, winning election as lieutenant governor in the latter year. Returning to private life two years later, he lost a bid for governor in 1910 but was elected to the U.S. Senate in 1914. Present for less than a third of the roll-call votes, he missed the vote on the woman suffrage amendment and was largely silent on Prohibition, though he ultimately supported it. Overall, he was a centrist, favoring neither progressive nor conservative positions.

His most prominent effort in the Senate came when he threw his support behind Senator Henry Cabot Lodge (R-MA) in opposition to the League of Nations in 1919. While not a strict isolationist, Harding strongly criticized the proposed organization, calling it an affront to American democracy. With the issue of the League dominating American politics, and despite being relatively unknown outside his home state, Harding entertained the notion of running for president in 1920.

As the Republican Party met in Chicago that summer to nominate a candidate, Harding was seen as the unlikeliest of choices. But the convention was deadlocked among more prominent candidates, including World War I aid administrator Herbert Hoover and Massachusetts Governor Calvin Coolidge. Republican leaders met with Harding's campaign staff in a suite at Chicago's Blackstone Hotel (said to be the origin of the phrase "smoke-filled room") and agreed that Harding would be the logical choice to break the impasse, largely because he had no known scandals or enemies to tarnish his reputation. In addition, he supported both Prohibition and woman suffrage, which were seen as crucial to victory. He was chosen on the tenth ballot.

Harding's opponent in the general election was Ohio Governor James M. Cox. The voting was seen as a referendum on outgoing President Woodrow Wilson and Democratic leadership over the last eight years, particularly on the question of the League of Nations. Harding promised a "return to normalcy," which included a rolling back of progressive reforms, restrictions on immigration, and an isolationist foreign policy.

Harding was portrayed as above the political fray, largely running a "front porch" campaign, speaking to supporters and the press from his home in Marion, Ohio. With a media savvy ahead of its time, his staff released weekly photos of Harding with Hollywood and Broadway stars, and they used newsreels, films, and radio speeches to craft an image of the candidate as a respectable, dignified statesman. Florence Harding was especially important, actively coaching her husband and cultivating good relations with the press.

Harding won 16 million votes to Cox's 9 million. The electoral college tally was even more overwhelming, 404–127. Jailed Socialist candidate Eugene V. Debs received more than 900,000 votes. The largest Republican landslide to that time, the election of 1920 demonstrated the disillusionment most Americans felt regarding the state of the country and world affairs. It was also the first election in which women could vote; they overwhelmingly favored Harding and helped Republicans capture 301 House and 59 Senate seats.

Presidency

Harding's presidency closely reflected the platform adopted at the 1920 Republican convention. Probusiness, Harding shied away from government intervention in the economy but petitioned U.S. Steel to reduce its workday from twelve hours to eight. He also proposed a Department of Welfare and established the Bureau of Veterans Affairs, but he vetoed a Veterans Bonus Bill, fearing that it would break the federal budget. Along with passage of the Emergency Tariff Act of 1921 and the Fordney-McCumber Tariff of 1922, the administration's decisions helped lift the economy out of recession. By protecting certain industries and establishing the Bureau of the Budget, government spending was subject to oversight for the

first time. The economic boom of the 1920s went into full swing.

Another key component of the Harding administration was the growing isolationist sentiment that followed World War I. Although Harding was silent on the League of Nations during the campaign, he put the issue to rest in April 1921 by telling Congress, "the League can have no sanction by us." He proposed U.S. participation in the world court, but this measure was also defeated in the Senate.

It was left to Harding to formally conclude hostilities with Germany and the Central powers, as the Senate rejected the Treaty of Versailles. In 1921, he directed Secretary of State Charles Evans Hughes to call the Washington Naval Conference, which achieved the reduction of naval construction by the United States, Great Britain, France, Japan, and Italy but failed to prevent Japanese aggression against China in the 1930s.

Harding became the first president since Reconstruction to speak out for African American rights. On October 26, 1921, he accepted an honorary degree from the University of Alabama and addressed the audience on the virtue of racial equality. He also spoke out in favor of anti-lynching laws. These statements would repudiate later rumors that he had secretly been inducted into the Ku Klux Klan after his election.

Harding played golf and poker regularly, attended baseball games, and followed boxing. Although he voted for Prohibition, the White House had plenty of bootleg liquor on hand with which to entertain friends. The image of a president at play would lead to future criticism that he was disengaged from the day-to-day affairs of a scandal-ridden administration. There is no evidence that Harding personally benefited from any illegal activity, but it is also unclear how aware he was of the activities of his friends and allies.

Two Harding administration officials were convicted of bribery, two more killed themselves before their full involvement could be revealed, and Harding's secretary of the interior, Albert B. Fall, was directly involved in the infamous Teapot Dome affair. Fall had taken control of federal oil reserves at Teapot Dome, near Caspar, Wyoming, and had granted drilling rights to certain oil companies in exchange for money and other favors. Fall would later be convicted of bribery and became the first administration official ever to serve prison time.

In June 1923, Harding set out on what he called a "voyage of understanding," a cross-country trip to meet ordinary Americans and explain his policies. In doing so, he became the first sitting president to visit Alaska. On July 27, however, he developed what was first thought to be food poisoning. Upon his arrival in San Francisco, he developed pneumonia and a high fever. The fever broke on August 1 and he was feeling well enough to make plans for a fishing trip, but on the night of August 2, 1923, Harding died of what was believed to be a stroke; medical historians now believe that he suffered a heart attack brought on by end-stage heart disease. His body was brought back to Washington, D.C., where a state funeral was held on August 8. Harding was interred in Marion, Ohio.

David A. Serafini

See also: Coolidge, Calvin; Daugherty, Harry M.; Election of 1920; Hoover, Herbert; Mellon, Andrew; Normalcy; Republican Party; Teapot Dome Scandal.

Further Reading

Dean, John W., and Arthur M. Schlesinger, Jr. *Warren G. Harding.* New York: Times, 2004.

Mayer, George H. *The Republican Party, 1854–1966.* New York: Oxford University Press, 1967.

Russell, Francis. *The Shadow of Blooming Grove: Warren G. Harding in His Times.* New York: McGraw-Hill, 1968.

Sinclair, Andrew. *The Available Man: The Life Behind the Mask of Warren Gamaliel Harding.* New York: Macmillan, 1965.

Harlem Renaissance

The Harlem Renaissance, which lasted from the end of World War I to about the mid-1930s, was the twentieth century's first great outburst of African American cultural energy. Also referred to as the "New Negro movement," it produced a body of writing that brought black Americans to the world's attention and esteem.

Beginnings

The end of World War I and the demobilization of America's black soldiers may be identified as the origin of the Harlem Renaissance. The war and war production had brought hundreds of thousands of African Americans out of the countryside and into the cities, to factories, shipyards, and recruiting centers. In the Harlem section of New York City, the black population mushroomed. Other major metropolitan centers experienced similar growth. Black veterans, having served honorably in France, were aware that they had vanquished a mighty foe in the name of American ideals: freedom, democracy, and self-determination. They were also aware of the yawning divide that separated those ideals from the reality of the African American experience. Both the crusading spirit of the war years and righteous anger at a nation that continued to tolerate lynchings were evident in Harlem Renaissance intellectual W.E.B. Du Bois's 1919 article "Returning Soldiers." "Make way for Democracy!" Du Bois wrote. "We saved it in France, and by the Great Jehovah, we will save it in the United States of America, or know the reason why."

Far from being welcomed home as heroes, African American soldiers suffered alongside their civilian counterparts in a tension-filled climate. Demobilization, white fears about job security, and the worldwide specter of Socialist revolution proved a deadly combination. In the "Red Summer" of 1919, race riots flared in more than two dozen cities across the North and South, with Chicago experiencing the worst violence. By the end of the summer, seventy-six blacks were dead and hundreds more had been wounded. Lynchings of black soldiers, including several still in uniform, were widespread. This stark demonstration that African Americans were to resume their prewar role as second-class citizens was a major factor in the development of a new racial consciousness.

Unlike previous waves of antiblack violence, this one was met with concerted resistance. In the nation's capital, armed and organized self-defense groups fought back against white mobs. In Manhattan, which did not witness scenes of bloodshed, what emerged was an intellectual resistance. In 1919, Jamaican-born poet Claude McKay provided a refrain for the oppressed with his popular sonnet "If We Must Die." Three years later, he produced *Harlem Shadows,* a remarkable volume of poetry that placed both the poet and the nascent Harlem arts scene in the national spotlight. In his poem "America," McKay wrote: "Although she feeds me bread of bitterness, / And sinks into my throat her tiger's tooth, / Stealing my breath of life, I will confess / I love this cultured hell that tests my youth!" There was no clearer statement of the ambiguity that underlay African American cultural resistance.

High Renaissance

In the tumultuous years of 1919 and 1920, the African American struggle for justice inspired left-leaning whites. Eugene O'Neill's *The Emperor Jones,* a powerful play about a railroad porter who becomes the ruler of a Caribbean island, was staged in 1920 with black actor Charles Gilpin in the title role. The immediate and overwhelming acclaim accorded the play and its star marked a major step forward for black theater. More shows featuring "Negro" themes followed, and audiences flocked to see them. The musical comedy *Shuffle Along*—written, produced, and acted by blacks—was a smash success in 1921. *Runnin' Wild* captivated Broadway later that year and introduced the world to a dance called the Charleston.

Poet Langston Hughes derided the years that followed as the time "When the Negro Was in Vogue" (the title of a 1940 essay). While black performers such as Josephine Baker continued to enjoy immense popularity on the stage, the black cabarets of Harlem became a fashionable entertainment for white New Yorkers. Uptown, with its jazz, dancing, and aura of transgression, became the pulsating cultural center of Manhattan. By 1925, the African American novelist and musician Rudolph Fisher could write, "Time was when white people went to Negro cabarets to see how Negroes acted; now Negroes go to these same cabarets to see how white people act."

For many leading figures in the black intelligentsia, the opportunity represented by white interest and patronage was too important to be ignored. With the official support of the National Association for the Advancement of Colored People (NAACP) and the National Urban League (NUL), the arts movement that had taken root in Harlem began to flower. Poets such as Hughes and Countee Cullen, fiction writers such as Zora Neale Hurston, and scholars such as E. Franklin Frazier emerged from the prize competitions that these organizations sponsored. Howard University professor Alain Locke's 1925 anthology *The New Negro,* filled with the prose poetry of Jean Toomer, the artwork of Aaron Douglas, and dozens of other contributions, demonstrated just how wide-ranging the Harlem Renaissance had become. Painters such as Douglas, Palmer Hayden, Malvin Gray Johnson, and Laura Wheeler Waring, as well as sculptors such as Richmond Barthé, produced striking portraits of African Americans and representations of everyday African American life.

The Harlem Renaissance also witnessed a great outpouring of original African American music. Jazz

Many of the finest African American musicians and dancers performed at New York's Cotton Club in the 1920s, the entertainment epicenter of the Harlem Renaissance. *(Stringer/Hulton Archive/Getty Images)*

and blues, the two major black musical genres of the 1920s, had emerged out of another place and time—the South in the late nineteenth and early twentieth centuries. But they experienced a transformation during the Harlem Renaissance. At venues such as the Cotton Club in Harlem and Connie's Inn in Midtown Manhattan, jazz and blues innovators such as bandleader and pianist Duke Ellington, trumpeter Louis Armstrong, and singer Ethel Waters experimented with new motifs and styles, creating music for the Jazz Age.

Much of the literary, artistic, and musical vibrancy of the Harlem Renaissance was captured in *Black Manhattan,* James Weldon Johnson's 1930 retrospective. Like *The New Negro,* it highlighted the vitality of African American cultural life: the advent of a black-owned Harlem, the international success of stage figures such as Baker and Paul Robeson, and the ubiquity of black music and dance. Yet some, like Hughes, increasingly saw in the achievements of the Harlem Renaissance a travesty and a descent into self-parody.

Departures

Langston Hughes's reputation as the most innovative and original poet of the Harlem Renaissance was underwritten by a succession of works that were fiery in their intensity yet musical in cadence. His early poem "I, Too" evoked the lyrical Americanism of Whitman, while his 1923 "Jazzonia" echoed the "shining rivers of the soul" poured forth in cabaret jam sessions. Hughes's more overtly political poetry in the late 1920s marked not only a personal transition but also a new inflection for the movement as a whole. In the acid "Advertisement for the Waldorf-Astoria" (1931), Hughes invited the cold and ragged Harlem mob to "Drop in at the Waldorf this afternoon for tea" and "Give Park Avenue a lot of darkie color." Gone was the accommodating posture of the Harlem Renaissance's first optimistic years, replaced by the stern warning that "the new Christ child of the Revolution's about to be born."

With the onset of the Great Depression, money was tight, and white cabaret crowds disappeared, as did many of the prizes and fellowships for promising artists. While excellent work—such as Arna Bontemps's 1931 novel *God Sends Sunday*—continued to appear, there were signs of Harlem's slow decline. Hughes departed for the Soviet Union in 1932. Two years later, Du Bois abandoned Harlem to chair the Department of Sociology at Atlanta University. In March 1935, a deadly riot caused serious damage to New York's black enclave and signaled an end to the Harlem Renaissance.

The figures who brought Harlem notoriety in the 1920s exercised an enormous influence on the rising generation of African American writers: Richard Wright, James Baldwin, Ralph Ellison, and many others. They also brought black culture and entertainment into the mainstream, in a way that it emphatically was not during the first years of the century. Nevertheless, the collapse of the movement brought the reputation of its major practitioners into eclipse. In the 1960s, however, the Harlem Renaissance was rediscovered as a phenomenon worthy of attention in its own right.

Eric Paras

See also: African Americans; Art, Fine; Blues; Fiction; Hughes, Langston; Jazz; Locke, Alain; McKay, Claude; Migration, Great; Poetry.

Further Reading

Baker, Houston A., Jr. *Modernism and the Harlem Renaissance.* Chicago: University of Chicago Press, 1987.

Helbling, Mark. *The Harlem Renaissance: The One and the Many.* Westport, CT: Greenwood, 1999.

Huggins, Nathan. *Harlem Renaissance.* New York: Oxford University Press, 1971.

Johnson, James Weldon. *Black Manhattan.* New York: Alfred A. Knopf, 1930.

Lewis, David Levering, ed. *The Portable Harlem Renaissance Reader.* New York: Penguin, 1994.

Wall, Cheryl A. *Women of the Harlem Renaissance.* Bloomington: Indiana University Press, 1995.

Havana Conference of 1928

The Havana Conference in early 1928 was a landmark meeting of the Pan American Union (later known as the Organization of American States). For the first time in the organization's thirty-eight-year history, growing Latin American resistance to U.S. military intervention topped the agenda.

Formally known as the Sixth International Conference of American States, the meeting was held in the Cuban capital from January 16 to February 20, with delegates from twenty-one Western Hemisphere states in attendance. The U.S. delegation was headed by former Secretary of State Charles Evans Hughes. Other leading Americans at the conference included U.S Ambassador to Mexico Dwight Morrow and Ray Wilbur, president of Stanford University. The delegates were carefully chosen to present the United States in the best possible light, a response to growing anti-U.S. sentiment that had been evident at the previous conference in Santiago, Chile, five years earlier.

The military interventions of the previous three administrations built animosity in many Latin American states toward the United States. The invasion of Nicaragua in 1926 served as a recent reminder of heavy-handed American imperialism in the region. Many Latin American delegates were determined to pass a rule forbidding future interventions and remake the Pan American Union into more than a tool of the U.S. government. The U.S. representatives were aware of these attitudes and hoped to stall or stop any anti-U.S. provisions from being passed.

As at the Santiago conference, a resolution was proposed that no state had the right to intervene in another's internal affairs. Given U.S. interventions in Latin America in the previous quarter-century, it was obviously meant to condemn U.S. actions in the region. The statement went first to the Committee on Public International Law and was referred to a subcommittee. The subcommittee's chair, Peruvian delegate Victor Maurtua, was more sympathetic to the United States than many of the other delegates. He proposed a U.S.-inspired counterproposal that would allow for intervention when a state "interferes" with the rights of others. That loophole would allow Washington to continue interventions when it could make an argument for doing so.

When the new statement was brought back to the Committee on Public International Law, its chair,

Gustavo Guerrero of El Salvador, refused the changed language. Committee members bickered over the proper wording and eventually agreed to continue reviewing the proposal and try to reach a decision at the next conference. Refusing to let the issue die, an Argentine representative reintroduced the motion at the closing meeting. After a raucous debate, American delegate Hughes argued that the United States did not really want to intervene but was compelled to take action to protect American lives when order broke down in a neighboring state. With time running out, the delegates agreed to follow the original committee statement and decide the matter at a later conference.

In another challenge to U.S. hegemony, Mexico proposed substantial changes to the organization and powers of the union. A new structure called for each nation to have a representative on the governing board, with a chair chosen annually by rotating among the nations alphabetically. The board would serve as an independent international body with jurisdiction to settle disputes between member states. The proposal would make the organization more democratic and give Latin American states greater control over its agenda and decisions. It would also dilute the power the United States had held in the Pan American Union since the organization's creation. The proposal did not receive enough votes for ratification but again showed the growing tension between the United States and its Latin neighbors.

Beyond the challenges to U.S. hegemony in the region, the conference was notable for other reasons. It was not only the first conference attended by an American president but also the first time a sitting U.S. president visited another American republic. President Calvin Coolidge arrived in Havana aboard the SS *Texas* on January 15 and gave a speech on January 17 that focused on Columbus's arrival in the Americas and the consequences of that event. He left the following day.

Another notable attendee was Alice Paul, head of the National Woman's Party. None of the nations had sent a woman delegate to the conference, and Paul was initially told that she could not participate. But she and the women who accompanied her continued to demand a place at the conference and finally were granted an opportunity to address a plenary session. Paul proposed the creation of an international women's organization to push for equal rights for women. Although these women activists did not achieve their goal—passage of a Treaty of Equal Rights—they did achieve the establishment of the International Commission of Women and a charge from that commission to study and report on the rights of women in the Americas at the next conference.

Michael Faubion

See also: Canada; Dominican Republic, Intervention in; Haiti, Intervention in; Latin America, Relations with; Mexico, Relations with; Nicaragua, Intervention in.

Further Reading

Fagg, John Edwin. *Pan Americanism*. Malabar, FL: R.E. Krieger, 1982.

"Kellogg to the American Delegation," January 5, 1928. *Foreign Relations Papers of the United States, 1928*. Vol. 1. Washington, DC: Government Printing Office.

Louria, Margot. *Triumph and Downfall: America's Pursuit of Peace and Prosperity, 1921–1933*. Westport, CT: Greenwood, 2000.

Schoulz, Lars. *Beneath the United States: A History of U.S. Policy Toward Latin America*. Cambridge, MA: Harvard University Press, 1998.

Health and Medicine

Measured in terms of infant mortality and overall longevity rates, no period in American history saw greater improvements in public health than the first half of the twentieth century. While medical breakthroughs were important, many of the gains of the 1920s were achieved through basic public health measures and better diet. Americans of the Jazz Age reaped the benefits of two decades of progressive health legislation, from the turn of the century to World War I, as well as remedial measures instituted in the wake of the great flu pandemic of 1918.

The interventions and educational activities of local, state, and federal public health officials and agencies brought a wide number of diseases under control. The dissemination of information about the causes of typhoid fever decreased the incidence of this airborne disease from 100 per 100,000 people in 1900 to 33.8 in 1920, and 18 in 1930. In 1922–1927, a Michigan statewide prevention program aimed at nutritional deficiency diseases helped lower the goiter rate from 38.6 to 9.0 per 100,000 people. Vaccination programs were responsible for a dramatic reduction in the number of cases of virulent diseases. Diphtheria fell from 144.7 per 100,000 Americans in 1919 to 70.1 in 1929; tuberculosis declined from 125.6 in 1919 to 75.3 in 1929. In addition, influenza and pneumonia fell from just over 200 per 100,000 Americans in 1920 to less than 150 in 1929.

Women and Children

Nothing illustrates the impact of public health measures, improved diet, and an increased emphasis on personal hygiene and public cleanliness better than improvements in childbirth and early infant health. At the turn of the twentieth century, roughly 8.5 American women died for every 1,000 live births. Since the average mother gave birth to roughly 3.5 children, the average childbearing woman stood a one in thirty chance of dying in childbirth. And one in five babies born in 1900 would be dead before his or her fifth birthday. The leading killers were pneumonia, tuberculosis, and diseases of the intestines (resulting in death from dehydration caused by diarrhea). By 1930, however, the maternal mortality rate had fallen by nearly 30 percent, to about six women for every 1,000 live births. Given the roughly one-third drop in the number of children per woman, this meant that the average childbearing woman in 1930 stood about a one in seventy chance of dying in childbirth. Meanwhile, infant mortality rates dropped by roughly a fourth in the 1920s, from 86 per 1,000 live births in 1920 to 65 in 1930.

The decrease in death rates for women in childbirth was due to several factors. Improved obstetrics certainly helped, as did an increase in hospital births, particularly among middle- and upper-class women. Shrinking families contributed as well. Women who experienced childbirth less often were less likely to experience obstetric complications. However, most physicians in the 1920s looked down on obstetrics as a medical field, as the practice of assisting childbirth was seen as the purview of female practitioners, such as midwives, and most births continued to take place in the home. Even for those women who went into hospital, procedures like induced labor, episiotomies, and cesarean sections could be dangerous. Roughly 40 percent of women who died in childbirth did so because of sepsis (the spread of infectious bacteria).

Risks were also high for abortion, largely an illegal practice in the 1920s. Improved access to birth control information, a by-product of the educational work of Margaret Sanger, reduced the number of abortions in the 1920s, as well as the number of women who died from complications due to the procedure.

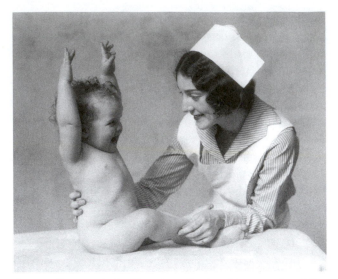

Among the most significant medical achievements of the 1920s was a dramatic decrease in the infant mortality rate, largely a result of improved prenatal and neonatal care. *(H. Armstrong Roberts/Stringer/Retrofile/Getty Images)*

Safer childbirth and improved infant health were the results of better diet and hygiene as well as improved public health measures. New local, state, and federal public health laws and increased spending on public works projects, particularly in urban areas, ensured improved waste disposal, sewage removal, cleaner drinking water, and safer foods. Laws concerning milk pasteurization, first adopted in Chicago in 1908, meant that toddlers who had been weaned from the breast were far less likely to drink contaminated cow's milk. The 1924 establishment of uniform sanitation standards for interstate shipping of milk was an offshoot of the Grade A Pasteurized Milk Ordinance created by the Public Health Service. By the end of the 1920s, the milk supply had become safe enough that the majority of pediatricians were recommending infant formulas based on cow's milk over mother's breast milk.

Government efforts to educate mothers and families, and to provide prenatal and postnatal health care services, also contributed to the drop in infant mortality rates and maternal deaths. Founded in 1912, the federal Children's Bureau provided guidance to local and state government entities in setting up comprehensive maternal and infant welfare services, including prenatal, birth, and postpartum home visits by public health professionals who would educate mothers in nutrition, hygiene, and basic health care, as well as monitor their health and the health of their babies.

The bureau's efforts were furthered by passage of the federal Sheppard-Towner Maternity and Infancy

Protection Act of 1921. The legislation provided small grants to states to provide maternity education and established regulations for federally funded health care. But the medical profession's resistance to external supervision of health care—combined with a growing ideological resistance in Congress to federal involvement in health care—led to the termination of the act in 1929.

Both the Children's Bureau and Sheppard-Towner had a significant impact on infant health. Between 1920 and 1929, mortality among infants in the first year of life fell 21 percent, with deaths among neonatal babies (0–27 days) falling by 11 percent and post-neonatal babies (28 to 364 days) dropping 31 percent.

Hygiene and Cleanliness

Several factors led to an increased awareness of hygiene, both personal and public, as a critical element of public health in the 1920s. One was World War I, with disease constituting a major problem in military mobilization. To increase America's fighting ability, the government undertook a massive effort to clean up military camps around the country. These efforts were successful in bringing down rates of illness and mortality away from the frontlines, convincing many in government that the same efforts, including improved access to clean water and proper sewage systems, could be applied in urban areas. It was not long before the lesson was to be applied.

In the wake of World War I, the United States—and the world—experienced the worst health crisis in human history, in terms of absolute numbers dead. The great flu pandemic killed an estimated 40 to 60 million people worldwide, including some 670,000 in the United States. Public health efforts broke down in the face of the epidemic, but the public, health care professionals, and government health officials quickly recognized the need for improved public health measures. Indoor plumbing became more widespread in the 1920s, for those who could afford it, and public health was improved by the spread of regular trash collection, which came to most larger municipalities in the first few decades of the twentieth century.

The pandemic also reinforced for many Americans the need to practice better personal hygiene and to maintain a cleaner home, as authorities continued to insist that the only way to fight the spread of the disease was to clean and sterilize anything contaminated by the sick and dying. Schools adopted health curricula and educated children and their parents about the need for regular bathing, washing of hands before eating, and brushing of teeth daily.

Advertisers capitalized on cleanliness to sell products. During the 1920s, advertisers made Americans more attentive to personal hygiene, and particularly the odors caused by poor hygiene. The makers of Listerine mouthwash and Lifebuoy soap, for example, saw sales soar as they turned "halitosis" and "body odor" into household phrases. While neither bad breath nor body odor was a true health issue, these conditions raised awareness of personal hygiene, which had benefits for overall health.

In 1921 the Johnson & Johnson Company introduced a new kind of bandage held in place by adhesive tape and marketed under the brand name "Band-Aid." The Band-Aid made it possible for people to keep small wounds cleaner and also raised people's understanding of the danger of infection. Another important breakthrough in personal hygiene was the Kotex brand feminine napkin, brought onto the market in the 1920s by Kimberly-Clark. Sterile and disposable, it decreased the chance of infection during a woman's menstrual period. Such infection had been a major source of illness for women throughout history. Like many other new products, it remained out of reach for many working and rural women, but its presence on the market and the advertising surrounding it raised overall awareness of feminine hygiene. Even those women who could not afford Kotex were conscious of the need for cleanliness in the rags, gauze, or cheesecloth they used to absorb menstrual flow.

Improved cleanliness in the home was a major theme of advertisers as they promoted electric-powered household appliances such as vacuum cleaners and washing machines. Cleaner homes meant fewer chances of infection. The new refrigerators reduced the chance of contaminated food. Most of these new appliances, however, would remain out of reach for working and farm families until after World War II.

Diet

The health of Jazz Age Americans benefited from improvements in diet and nutrition. With the exception of the very poorest rural sectors of the population, Americans were eating a more varied diet at the end of the 1920s than they had at the beginning. Some of

Invention of the Iron Lung

The prototype was big and clunky, jury-rigged from an iron cylinder and a couple of the newfangled vacuum cleaners that were becoming so popular in homes across America in the 1920s. The machine's dimensions and weight were like those of a modern sub-compact car. Built by Harvard University medical researchers Philip Drinker and Louis Agassiz in 1927, this ungainly contraption was the first iron lung. Drinker, the primary inventor of the machine, had initially envisioned the device as a way to clear lead and coal dust from the lungs of miners. Instead it would help save the lives of thousands of poliomyelitis victims.

"Iron lung" is the popular name for a negative-pressure ventilator, an external artificial lung that helps patients with severe paralysis breathe. While Drinker and Agassiz's prototype would be modified within a few years—made lighter, smaller, and cheaper—its basic design and operation have remained essentially the same to the present day. Patients are placed inside the chamber, with their heads exposed. A collar fits around the neck, securing an airtight fit. Sensors detect the chamber's internal air pressure. When the pressure falls, the sensors trigger external pumps that force air into the chamber; the increase in pressure pushes air into the victim's lungs. When the pressure in the chamber rises to a certain point, the pumps draw out air, lowering the pressure and pulling air out of the lungs.

The first version of the iron lung was installed at New York City's Bellevue Hospital in 1927, the same year it was invented. On October 12, 1928, at Children's Hospital in Boston, a girl who had suffered respiratory failure was placed in an iron lung and was able to breathe again in a matter of seconds. The success of the "Drinker respirator" was trumpeted in headlines across America.

It was not until the 1940s, when a polio epidemic paralyzed thousands across the country, that the term iron lung became familiar to most Americans. By the mid-1950s, hospitals had devoted entire wards to polio patients encased in rows of iron lungs. Drinker's name was not on these devices, however, as his version had been supplanted shortly after its invention by a cheaper and more effective model created by Boston inventor John Emerson. Drinker sued Emerson for copyright infringement, but the courts threw out the case, declaring his original patents invalid.

The iron lung ultimately became a museum piece, as the development of an effective polio vaccine in the early 1950s eliminated the disease in most of the industrialized world. Polio victims and others suffering from catastrophic paralysis would be put on mechanical ventilators that use positive pressure to pump air directly into the respiratory passageways. Nevertheless, a few survivors of polio remain in their home-based iron lungs more than half a century after first falling ill; they and their caretakers insist that the ungainly machines, introduced by Drinker in 1927, simply work better than modern devices.

James Ciment

this was the result of new scientific findings. Medical research had discovered the importance of vitamins and minerals to human health. Before, during, and after World War I, the federal government attempted to disseminate information about these findings, first to soldiers and then to the civilian population. Through wartime mess halls and health lectures, many poorer and particularly rural recruits were introduced to the importance of a varied diet. After the conflict, the government issued a number of reports emphasizing the importance of a mineral- and vitamin-rich diet that balanced proteins, carbohydrates, and fats.

Economic, demographic, and cultural factors also contributed to improved diets. Per capita income rose during the 1920s by an astonishing 37 percent, and food prices fell significantly from their wartime highs. Improvements in transportation, especially the proliferation of motorized and refrigerated trucks, carried fresh foods over greater distances. Preserved foods—largely canned and bottled, but also frozen food later in the decade—made varied diets more possible.

Also aiding the trend was the growth of the urban population. In most farming areas, diets were quite monotonous during most of the year and heavily influenced by falling food prices, which undermined farm incomes and farm health. The diet of Southern tenant farmers—many of them African Americans—was among the worst in the United States, consisting of fried salt pork, molasses, cornmeal, and a few fresh vegetables in season. Pellagra, a disease caused by a deficiency in vitamin B3, was among the most widespread illnesses in America in the 1920s.

The average American, however, was eating a far better and more varied diet in 1930 than in 1900, one richer in fresh vegetables and fruit as well as dairy. Better diet had an effect on height. Recruits in World War II—who were born or were children in the 1920s—were several inches taller than recruits in World War I.

The 1920s also saw a dramatic transformation in the perception of how much food one should eat. Prior to the 1920s, the emphasis had been on a healthy appetite, with physical rotundity viewed as a sign of health in adults and children. With the spread of fitness fads, diet books, film and advertising images of slim men and svelte women, and ironically, cigarette consumption, Americans began to slim down in the 1920s. Between the end of World War I and 1929, the average American was consuming roughly 5 percent fewer calories per day. Annual beef consumption fell from 72.4 pounds per person in 1900 to 55.3 in 1929.

Medicine

During the 1920s, medical breakthroughs, especially those concerning the treatment of several chronic diseases, contributed to improvements in American health. The decade's most significant finding due to medical research was the discovery of insulin. By the end of the decade, it was possible for people with adult-onset diabetes to control their illness. Other medical breakthroughs of the 1920s concerned new insights into hormones and body chemistry, though applications of this understanding for ordinary medicine would have to wait until later decades.

All of the improvements in health and medicine had one noticeable result—life expectancy rose in the 1920s. Between 1900 and 1930, life expectancy at birth climbed from roughly 47 years to nearly 60, with just over half of that achieved in the 1920s, the greatest gain of any period in American history. However, at the same time, the number of licensed physicians, while climbing in absolute terms by about 6 percent (from about 145,000 to 154,000) fell in per capita terms. At a time of rapidly rising population, the number of physicians per 100,000 Americans decreased from 136 in 1920 to 125 in 1930. In the end, formal medicine would not play a significant role in the improvement of American health until after World War II.

James Ciment and Leslie Rabkin

See also: Beauty Industry and Culture; Birth Control; Cigarettes and Tobacco; Drugs, Illicit and Illegal; Eugenics; Flu Pandemic (1918); Food and Diet; Population and Demographics; Psychology; Sanger, Margaret; Sex and Sexuality.

Further Reading

Duffy, John. *The Sanitarians: A History of American Public Health.* Champaign: University of Illinois Press, 1992.

Rosen, George. *History of Public Health.* Baltimore: Johns Hopkins University Press, 1993.

Star, Paul. *The Social Transformation of American Medicine.* New York: Basic Books, 1984.

Tomes, Nancy. *The Gospel of Germs: Men, Women, and the Microbe in American Life.* Cambridge, MA: Harvard University Press, 1999.

Hearst, William Randolph (1863–1951)

By the end of World War I, newspaper mogul William Randolph Hearst was already among the most famous and influential figures in the United

States, if not the world. He controlled a vast media empire, built on an ever-growing string of newspapers and such major magazines as *Cosmopolitan* and *Harper's Bazaar.* Lauded by some as a champion of labor and the ordinary person, Hearst was derided by others as an autocrat.

He was born on April 29, 1863, to Phoebe Apperson and George Hearst, a miner who had become wealthy. Educated at Harvard, Hearst left before graduating to take over as publisher of his father's *San Francisco Examiner* after his father entered the U.S. Senate in 1886. George Hearst had acquired the *Examiner* as payment for a gambling debt and used it to further his political ambitions.

The paper was a commercial disaster when young Hearst took it over. He proved a natural at the newspaper business, however, and the *Examiner* soon became the cornerstone of a new media empire. In 1891, following his father's death, Hearst expanded to New York, buying the struggling *Morning Journal.* That paper's ensuing circulation battles with media mogul Joseph Pulitzer, owner of the *New York World,* raised Hearst's profile but brought derision on both publishers for the lurid "yellow journalism" (sensationalism) practiced by their papers.

Although World War I led to a reduction in circulation, Hearst began to further expand his journalistic holdings soon after the war's end. In 1921, he bought the *Detroit Times, Boston Record,* and *Seattle Post-Intelligencer.* The following year, he started the *Oakland Post-Enquirer* in California and the *Syracuse Telegram* and *Rochester Journal* in New York State. In 1924, he would add a tabloid, the *Daily Mirror,* in New York City in an unsuccessful effort to undercut the surging *Daily News,* a pioneering tabloid founded in 1919 by another newspaper magnate, Joseph Medill Patterson.

All of these papers were financed with borrowed money. Hearst spent freely during the 1920s and took on a massive amount of debt. As early as 1923, Chase National Bank refused to lend money to Hearst's businesses after he substantially overdrew on his accounts.

Hearst was also an enthusiastic investor in the early film industry. In 1916 he founded the International Film Service, which produced newsreels, and in 1919 he created Cosmopolitan Productions. He was motivated in part to enter the movie business by his relationship with the actress Marion Davies, with whom he began having an affair in 1915, when she was an eighteen-year-old chorus girl on Broadway.

Hearst envisioned Cosmopolitan Productions as a home of "classy" films, such as *The Belle of New York* (1919) and *The Restless Sex* (1921), many drawn from stories in the pages of *Cosmopolitan* magazine. He fashioned a distribution deal with Paramount Pictures; MGM would later handle these duties.

Hearst harbored ambitions beyond journalism and Hollywood—and pursued them vigorously. A longtime member of the Democratic Party, he served as a U.S. congressman from New York from 1903 to 1907. He had been one of the state's only prominent Democrats to support the populist William Jennings Bryan in 1896 and, like Bryan, broke with Democratic President Woodrow Wilson over U.S. entry into World War I in 1917. Hearst regarded that conflict as a "war of kings" and believed the United States should stay clear. By 1922, however, Hearst returned to the Democratic fold and sought the party's nomination for governor of New York. His opponent was future presidential candidate Al Smith, who defeated the publisher in a grueling primary. Hearst's political career was effectively over. When the Democrats nominated the conservative John W. Davis for president in 1924, Hearst largely withdrew from the party for the rest of the decade.

Nevertheless, Hearst continued to impart his enormous political influence through the many major metropolitan dailies—nearly thirty by the end of the Jazz Age—that he owned. Hearst was not shy about using the news sections as well as the editorial pages of his newspapers to promote liberal causes and candidates, including support for the failed presidential candidacy of Al Smith in 1928 and the successful one of Franklin D. Roosevelt four years later. An early supporter of Roosevelt's New Deal, Hearst later turned against those policies and grew increasingly conservative as the 1930s progressed.

Meanwhile, his personal life became grist for the gossip mills. After his failed gubernatorial bid in New York, Hearst spent more time in California while his wife, Millicent, remained in New York. In 1920, he began construction of a massive summerhouse on his coastal San Simeon property, with famed California architect Julia Morgan overseeing the project. The magnate spent his days in San Simeon and in Los Angeles with Davies, overseeing his Hollywood investments.

This was not an easy time for Hearst. Cosmopolitan Productions struggled financially, and rumors began to spread about his relationship with Davies. It was said that Davies bore his illegitimate children—allegations that were never corroborated. More serious were rumors surrounding the death of Hollywood director and actor Thomas Ince aboard Hearst's yacht in 1924. While the coroner said the death had resulted from a heart attack, the non-Hearst press—always eager to tarnish the industry leader's reputation—printed rumors that Hearst had murdered Ince over a romantic affair with Davies.

By 1925, things began to look better for Hearst. That year, Cosmopolitan Productions was largely taken over by MGM, under very favorable financial terms for Hearst. The same year saw the release of *Zander the Great,* widely regarded as both Marion Davies's biggest artistic success as an actress and Hearst's finest hour as a producer. The year 1925 also witnessed the final rupture between Hearst and his wife. Although they remained married, they would now live largely separate lives. Hearst soon bought Davies a mansion for the two to share in Santa Monica. Davies also began spending time in San Simeon, where she had previously been forbidden out of respect for Millicent.

Hearst spent much of the rest of the boom years expanding San Simeon and collecting works of art. He had long been an aficionado of European art, and he began buying paintings, statues, tapestries, even whole sections of churches, at a furious clip. By the time of the 1929 crash, Hearst was deeply in debt but managed to survive the collapse of the stock market. Hearst died on August 14, 1951.

Guy Patrick Cunningham

See also: Democratic Party; Film Industry; Journalism.

Further Reading

Nasaw, David. *The Chief: The Life of William Randolph Hearst.* Boston: Houghton Mifflin, 2000.

Swanberg, W.A. *Citizen Hearst: A Biography of William Randolph Hearst.* New York: Scribner's, 1961.

Hemingway, Ernest (1899–1961)

One of the most prominent American authors of the twentieth century, Ernest Hemingway came of age in the 1920s and left a lasting imprint on literature and popular culture. His writing style captivated critics and readers alike, and his fiction—shocking at times in its subject matter—appealed to an American public that was struggling to find its way in the aftermath of the Great War. By the end of the Jazz Age,

Hemingway—just thirty years old—had published two of the greatest novels of his generation: *The Sun Also Rises* (1926) and *A Farewell to Arms* (1929). He was also a successful journalist, covering important world events in the interwar years, as well as a respected writer of short stories and nonfiction.

Born on July 21, 1899, the second of six children, Hemingway was raised in Oak Park, Illinois, an affluent Chicago suburb. His father, Clarence, was a doctor and an avid outdoorsman; his mother, Grace Hall Hemingway, was a professional musician who gave voice and music lessons. Hemingway attended River Forest High School, where he was a regular contributor to the school newspaper and literary magazine. When he graduated in the spring of 1917, the United States had just entered World War I. Too young to enlist, Hemingway accepted a job as a reporter for the *Kansas City Star.* His experience there, and later with the *Toronto Star,* contributed to the terse, forceful writing style for which he would become so well known.

Rejected from the U.S. Army because of poor eyesight, Hemingway enlisted with the American Red Cross in 1918 and drove ambulances on the Italian front. On July 8 of that year, he was severely wounded. The Italian government awarded him the Silver Medal for Military Valor, and he spent the next six months in the Milan Red Cross hospital recovering from his injuries. Hemingway's *A Farewell to Arms* would be loosely based on his experiences on the Italian front and in the Red Cross hospital, where he fell in love with his nurse, Agnes Von Kurowsky.

Hemingway returned to Oak Park in January 1919 and began writing short stories, none of which was accepted for publication at the time. After a frustrating year of professional and personal rejections (Von Kurowsky refused to marry him), Hemingway moved to Toronto, accepted a job as a tutor, and began writing freelance feature stories for the *Toronto Star.* He left for Chicago in May 1920 but continued to write for the newspaper.

In Chicago, Hemingway met Hadley Richardson, a St. Louis woman eight years his senior, who became the first of his four wives on September 3, 1921. The couple began making plans to move to Italy, but Sherwood Anderson (already an established author) convinced Hemingway that Paris was a more promising venue for an aspiring young writer. Hemingway and his wife sailed for France in December 1921, carrying with them Anderson's letters of introduction to Ezra Pound, Sylvia Beach, and Gertrude Stein, who would school Hemingway in the foundations of modernism. Once in Paris, Hemingway continued to write for the *Toronto Star* and was frequently sent on special assignment to cover important events in post-war Europe.

In August 1923, two months before the birth of his first son, Hemingway published *Three Stories & Ten Poems.* Shortly thereafter, he quit his job with the *Star* to concentrate on his creative writing. Three Mountains Press in Paris published a small collection of Hemingway's vignettes under the title *In Our Time* (1924). Hemingway was also working as an unpaid editor for Ford Madox Ford's *Transatlantic Review,* which published several of Hemingway's short stories. In April 1925, Hemingway met F. Scott Fitzgerald in Paris and the two began one of the most written-about literary friendships of the twentieth century. In October, New York publishers Boni and Liveright published *In Our Time,* a collection of Hemingway's short stories interspersed with the vignettes from the 1924 Paris publication of the same name.

Hemingway had finished a first draft of *The Sun Also Rises,* but, probably on the advice of Fitzgerald, he withheld the draft from Boni and Liveright and instead submitted *The Torrents of Spring,* a satire of Sherwood Anderson's work that he knew the publishers would reject. Free to negotiate a new publishing contract, Hemingway signed on with Charles Scribner's Sons in February 1926. Scribner's published Hemingway's first two novels, *The Sun Also Rises* (1926) and *A Farewell to Arms* (1929), which launched him to international fame. Both works, which centered on wounded war veterans, resonated with disillusioned survivors of the World War I era.

Unlike many of his contemporaries, Hemingway enjoyed fame and literary success beyond the 1920s. His 1940 novel about the Spanish Civil War, *For Whom the Bell Tolls,* was an enormous best seller, as was *The Old Man and the Sea* (1952). Hemingway was awarded a Pulitzer Prize in 1953 and the Nobel Prize in Literature in 1954. After suffering from considerable physical and psychological ailments, Hemingway took his own life in Ketchum, Idaho, on July 2, 1961.

Kathleen Ruppert

See also: Fiction; Lost Generation.

Further Reading

Baker, Carlos. *Ernest Hemingway: A Life Story.* New York: Collier, 1969.

Hemingway, Ernest. *A Moveable Feast.* New York: Collier, 1987.

Lynn, Kenneth S. *Hemingway.* Cambridge, MA: Harvard University Press, 1995.

Oliver, Charles M. *Ernest Hemingway A to Z: The Essential Reference to the Life and Work.* New York: Facts on File, 1999.

Reynolds, Michael. *Hemingway: The Paris Years.* Oxford, UK: Basil Blackwell, 1989.

Wagner-Martin, Linda, ed. *A Historical Guide to Ernest Hemingway.* New York: Oxford University Press, 2000.

Hoboes

A hobo was a migratory worker who took short-term, temporary jobs. Hoboes, mostly male and white, though there were a few African Americans and women among them, arose with the development of regional and national railroad systems in the mid-nineteenth century, as the train provided their primary form of transportation. Transcontinental railroads made it possible for people to traverse the country by surreptitiously hopping on freight trains and riding from one town to another.

Despite the relative prosperity of the 1920s, hoboes were prevalent during this time. Although the term "hobo" is sometimes used interchangeably with "tramp," "vagrant" and "vagabond," these other designations are more accurately applied to homeless men who wander aimlessly and steal or beg for money. What set hoboes apart from such homeless thieves or beggars was their willingness to work.

There were many opportunities for itinerant workers during the 1920s. The West was still being settled, new mines were opening, new railroads were being built, and farmers were in need of seasonal field hands. Hoboes would work in the mines, help build the railroads, pick crops, and take on other temporary jobs. When the work ran out, they would moved on to the next town and the next job.

Common methods of hitching a ride on freight trains included "riding the rods" (on the structural framework beneath a freight car), "riding the deck" (on top of a railroad car), and riding inside a boxcar. The last was the preferred and safest method of travel. Riding the rods or riding the deck could be dangerous, and often hoboes would be severely injured or even killed trying to negotiate this type of transportation. (Railroads eventually began using freight cars with no structural rods underneath, to end the practice of riding the rods.) When hopping trains, hoboes also had to find ways to outsmart the security staff employed by the railroads to prevent them from taking a free ride.

Hoboes often would establish places on the out-skirts of cities, where they would congregate. Called "jungles," these were stopover places that hoboes would use on their way to the next city or town. These gathering places became problematic for some cities, as they tended to attract unseemly types and often brought crime to the area.

When it was too cold to sleep outside, a hobo might pay fifty cents for a room in a cheap hotel. Or he might sleep in a "flophouse," where a dime would buy a spot on the floor or a bare wooden bunk. Such facilities were limited, however. The growing number of homeless men and hoboes became such a problem for the city of Chicago that on June 16, 1922, the municipal government established the Committee on Homeless Men to study the problem of casual migratory workers.

Hoboes had to carry all their possessions with them, so they lived simply. Pots, kettles, and reused cans were used to cook food or wash clothes. Generally, these and other cooking utensils would remain at a jungle or other campsite for use by the next hoboes who came along.

Hoboes had their own customs, traditions, and code of ethics. They developed a language riddled with slang terms for people and things related to life on the road. They also developed a set of written symbols to designate the personality of different places—places that were hospitable or hostile, places to get food or money, places with mean dogs, and the like.

In the early 1900s, with the rise of the labor movement, the working class began looking to unions for help with wages and working conditions. Hoboes were actively recruited by the Industrial Workers of the World (IWW), which had formed in Chicago in 1905. Although the IWW did little to improve working conditions for migrants, being a card-carrying member did help some of them. Hoboes riding freight trains in the West found that railroad workers were easier on card-carriers, often letting them ride unmolested. IWW membership cards also helped hoboes obtain emergency relief in some Midwestern cities.

People from all walks of life became hoboes, and for a variety of reasons. Some experienced difficulties with their families and were turned out. Others were not able to hold long-term jobs, because they did not have the skills or training, or they experienced racial or ethnic discrimination when seeking employment. Others suffered from a deformity or illness that prevented them from holding a long-term job. Some had problems with alcohol. And some who became hoboes simply had a case of wanderlust and enjoyed the freedom that life on the road gave them. Their numbers would peak during the Great Depression of the 1930s, at which time these homeless Americans would become, and remain, part of the public imagination.

Beth Kattelman

See also: Railroads and Railroad Industry; Wealth and Income.

Further Reading

Anderson, Nels. *The Hobo: The Sociology of the Homeless Man.* Chicago: University of Chicago Press, 1923.
Gypsy Moon. *Done and Been: Steel Rail Chronicles of American Hobos.* Bloomington: Indiana University Press, 1996.
Wallace, Samuel E. *Skid Row as a Way of Life.* Totowa, NJ: Bedminster, 1965.

Holmes, Oliver Wendell, Jr. (1841–1935)

One of the most influential jurists in American history, Oliver Wendell Holmes, Jr., served as an associate justice on the U.S. Supreme Court from 1902 to 1932. In his years on the nation's highest court and earlier, during his time on the Massachusetts Supreme Judicial Court, Holmes issued more than 2,000 decisions, many of which were based on his judicial philosophy that rulings should go beyond mere legal precedent and take into account economic and sociological factors.

Holmes was born into a socially prominent family in Boston on March 8, 1841. His father, a noted physician, poet, and writer, was one of the founders of *The Atlantic Monthly*. Holmes grew up in a freethinking household and rejected traditional religion at a young age, though he maintained a firm belief in God. Embracing both the natural and social sciences, he would take both into account in his judicial decisions. Moreover, he came to believe that society and social values change over time and that the law must reflect these changes.

Graduating from Harvard College in 1861, just as the Civil War was commencing, Holmes enlisted in the infantry and was wounded three times in combat before being discharged in 1864. He graduated from Harvard Law School two years later and was admitted to the Massachusetts bar in 1867. Even as he practiced commercial law, however, his family's wealth allowed him to focus much of his time writing on jurisprudence and legal theory. In 1881, he turned a series of lectures into an influential book, *The Common Law,* in which he argued that the law should emphasize real-life experience over abstract logic. This general philosophy, known as legal realism, argued that jurists should move beyond stale legal principles to consider social, economic, and even political forces in issuing their decisions.

In 1899, Holmes was appointed chief justice of Massachusetts's highest court but served there only three years before being tapped by President Theodore Roosevelt, a fellow progressive, for an associate justice position on the U.S. Supreme Court. Often in the minority, Holmes argued in his early decisions that justices should practice judicial restraint, putting aside their own legal preconceptions and attempting to understand what exactly legislatures were trying to do when they passed laws that were being tested before the Court. In one of his most famous dissents, in *Lochner v. New York* (1905), he argued that the Court should have accepted New York State's efforts to set maximum workday hours, in this case for bakery workers. He criticized his fellow justices for putting legal principle, in this case liberty of contract, ahead of the harsh realities of life for working-class Americans.

Some of Holmes's most important and frequently quoted decisions came during the Jazz Age and concerned civil liberties issues raised by federal legislation during World War I. In 1917, Congress passed the Espionage Act, making it a crime to interfere with the operation of the U.S. armed forces. In 1919, the Supreme Court heard *Schenck v. United States,* a case that involved the conviction of a local leader of the Socialist Party for distributing leaflets denouncing the military draft. These actions were said to be a violation of the Espionage Act and its 1918 amending legislation, the Sedition Act, which made it illegal to criticize the federal government during wartime. Writing for the Court, Holmes upheld the conviction, arguing that the government has the right to curb any free speech that constitutes a "clear and present danger" to the national well-being. In one of his most famous legal formulations, Holmes equated Charles Schenck's actions with crying "fire" in a crowded theater.

The "clear and present danger" test would be upheld by the Court throughout the Jazz Age and beyond, permitting the government to squelch free speech in certain instances. But just months after the *Schenck* decision, Holmes joined Justice Louis Brandeis in dissenting from the *Abrams v. United States* (1919) ruling, in which the Court upheld the conviction of Jacob Abrams for speaking out against U.S. intervention in the Russian Revolution. Holmes argued that the government had arrested Abrams for his political views and that no clear and present danger existed. In instances where there is no immediate danger to the republic, he argued, the free exchange of ideas should be protected, as it is essential to the proper functioning of democracy.

In 1928, Holmes backed Brandeis's dissenting opinion in *Olmstead v. United States,* in which the Court upheld the right of the government to wiretap people's phones. Both justices agreed that courts need to take into account technological advances when considering Fourth and Fifth Amendment protections against unreasonable searches and self-incrimination.

Holmes's defense of civil liberties was not absolute, as was seen in *Buck v. Bell* (1927), which upheld a Virginia law that allowed the forced sterilization of mentally challenged individuals. In writing for the majority, Holmes noted that the plaintiff Carrie Buck, her mother, and her illegitimate daughter all had low intelligence, and he infamously argued, "three generations of imbeciles are enough." Here, Holmes was weighing in on the side of the prevailing scientific thinking on eugenics—the attempt to improve humanity through selective breeding or the sterilization of individuals, particularly the mentally deficient and habitually criminal.

Holmes retired from the Court in January 1932, before having to decide on the constitutionality of liberal New Deal legislation. He died in Washington, D.C., on March 6, 1935.

Tim J. Watts and James Ciment

See also: *Gitlow v. New York* (1925); Law and the Courts; *Schenck v. United States* (1919).

Further Reading

Alschuler, Albert W. *Law Without Values: The Life, Work, and Legacy of Justice Holmes.* Chicago: University of Chicago Press, 2000.

Frankfurter, Felix. *Mr. Justice Holmes and the Supreme Court.* Cambridge, MA: Belknap Press, 1961.

Howe, Mark De Wolfe. *Justice Oliver Wendell Holmes.* Cambridge, MA: Belknap Press, 1957.

Novick, Sheldon M. *Honorable Justice: The Life of Oliver Wendell Holmes.* Boston: Little, Brown, 1989.

White, G. Edward. *Justice Oliver Wendell Holmes: Law and the Inner Self.* New York: Oxford University Press, 1993.

Homosexuals and Homosexuality

During the Jazz Age, homosexuals and homosexuality came to newfound prominence in the United States. In the late 1910s and 1920s, many gays and lesbians developed a sense of collective identity that in later decades would help facilitate movements for social and political equality. They did so, however, in the face of social and legal efforts to enforce heterosexual concepts of normality in response to the perceived threat of homosexuality. For many Americans, the increased visibility of homosexuality during the Jazz Age made it seem a significant problem, requiring aggressive tactics to criminalize and marginalize it.

Rethinking Sexuality

Reevaluations of social "normality," and increased concern with enforcing it, gained a new level of importance during the Jazz Age in part because of changes in perceptions of sexuality and gender. Through the first three decades of the twentieth century, single men and women began socializing with each other more and more, raising questions and affecting perceptions about how people should properly interact with one another. In the 1920s, many Americans became more interested in understanding and defining how people—especially women—should behave in the new, relatively permissive atmosphere of the Jazz Age.

Prior to the late 1910s and 1920s, most people thought relatively little about homosexuality. The concept of the homosexual as a type did not emerge until the late nineteenth century, when experts such as Austrian psychiatrist Richard Krafft-Ebing began studying homosexuals as a group biologically distinct from heterosexuals. Literature on the subject was often restricted to readers with a physician's certificate.

By the 1920s, however, attitudes toward homosexuality changed as psychoanalytical and pathological theories took precedence over biological ones, appealing to increasing public interest in psychiatry, psychology, and sexuality. By the end of the decade, scientific thought began to shift away from the idea that homosexuality is inherent. Instead, it was believed that homosexuals were made, not born, and that "normal" people could become homosexual under certain circumstances. Many people who once thought of homosexuality as an individual problem now thought of it as a social one, requiring broad reform efforts; heterosexuality was regarded as an attribute that needed to be aggressively protected.

City Life and Culture

World War I and the expansion of urban life made issues of sexuality seem even more urgent. The war introduced many young servicemen to urban America, where vices—especially prostitution—were cited by reformers as threatening to create a moral crisis. Among the perceived dangers was the spread of homosexuality; it was feared that soldiers could be corrupted by male sexual advances. In response, the police began to more aggressively pursue arrests for same-sex solicitation and activities. In 1919, a special enforcement squad in the navy arrested sixteen men in an investigation of homosexuality at a training station in Rhode Island.

Throughout the 1920s, open assertions of homosexuality by either men or women heightened fears of moral corruption and often led to legal measures against homosexuality—such as those against the Society for Human Rights. The society, founded in Chicago in 1924, was the first known chartered homosexual rights organization in the United States. Started by postal worker and German immigrant Henry Gerber, the society was short-lived. It published two issues of its journal before Gerber and three others were arrested and the organization disbanded. After that, the establishment of homosexual rights organizations in America during the Jazz Age was negligible, especially when compared to activity in European countries such as England and Germany.

Many homosexual men and women did not regard their sexuality as immoral or unnatural. But they could not express their sexual identities openly, and the obstacles to setting up formal organizations made informal or underground networks all the more important. Through their encounters with others in the armed forces or the urban environment, or due to comparatively liberal European attitudes toward sexuality, many young homosexuals realized that they were not alone and did not have to live in as intense a state of repression as they previously thought. Many relocated to cities because larger populations and relative anonymity made a homosexual life more feasible, and many created their own distinct communities.

In New York, for example, Harlem and Greenwich Village became nexuses for the homosexual community. Drag balls, in which participants could dress as members of the opposite sex and openly dance with same-sex partners, emerged in Greenwich Village in the 1910s and spread during the Prohibition era. Attendance at these balls sometimes numbered in the thousands. The Harlem Renaissance became famous for, among other things, lavish interracial parties featuring same-sex activities and shows. Other elements of the homosexual community, however, were far more subtle. Many gays and lesbians worked in ostensibly straight occupations, such as the theater or fashion, that were actually homosexual enclaves. Many found homosexual friends within supposedly straight atmospheres or kept their daily lives separate from their discreet social networks.

The Arts

Literary works about gays and lesbians entered the American mainstream during the Jazz Age, contributing to and deriving from increasing popular interest in the subject. Earl Lind, writing as Ralph Werther and Jennie June, published books in 1919 and 1922 based on his experiences as a gay man. Sherwood Anderson's "Hands," a short story in his 1919 collection *Winesburg, Ohio,* is the sympathetic portrayal of a gay protagonist who is ostracized because of his sexuality. Edouard Bourdet's 1926 play *The Captive* portrayed lesbians who appeared to be outrightly feminine and therefore "normal"—which makes them even more threatening to many people.

In 1928, British writer Radclyffe Hall published *The Well of Loneliness,* perhaps the most successful and best-known twentieth-century novel to deal with lesbianism. The book reflected many of the period's stereotypes of lesbians in telling the story of its main character, Stephen Gordon, who is recognizably homosexual even in childhood. She is athletic, mannish in appearance, dress, and mannerisms, and doomed to unhappiness by her sexuality. The book portrays Gordon as an essentially sympathetic character, however, and became a critical text in the discourse on lesbianism because of how explicitly it dealt with its subject matter.

Navigating Censorship

Most artists in the Jazz Age who produced works with candidly homosexual characters enjoyed relatively small circulation and risked possible criminal charges. In 1926, for example, stage star Mae West announced her intention to stage *The Drag*, a play she had written that defended the right of gays to live as they chose and that concluded with a drag ball. The play had already run in Connecticut and New Jersey, but *The Drag* would not be produced on Broadway during the 1920s. The police also raided West's show *Sex* in early 1927, along with *The Captive* and the play *Virgin Man,* arresting members of all three casts.

While none of these three plays was primarily about homosexuality, they did contain allusions to homosexuality. West fought to keep *Sex* going for another six weeks but was eventually convicted and sentenced to ten days in jail. Soon thereafter, the New York state legislature passed a law banning all plays featuring overtly homosexual actors or content. The measure did not succeed in eliminating implicit homosexual themes from Broadway.

In response to censorship, many writers masked the sexuality of their characters. It was a technique employed by Virginia Woolf, Gertrude Stein, and other Jazz Age writers. Henry Blake Fuller, in his novel *Bertram Cope's Year* (1919), left the sexuality of the main character unstated while ironically portraying the strains caused by a life of repression. Implicit subversions of rules and customs about sexuality became more critical to homosexual expression as explicit portrayals of homosexuality became increasingly more difficult to produce.

Beginning in the late 1920s and continuing through the 1930s, arrests related to homosexuality increased, along with censorship and other forms of suppression. The Jazz Age, however, saw important advancements in the development of homosexual identity, most importantly in the simple recognition that it was a part of human sexuality. But for many people, the greater public recognition of homosexuality only made it seem more dangerous. Later decades would witness great strides toward the legal and social recognition of homosexual rights, but important elements of the struggle began to take form during the Jazz Age.

John Fiorini

See also: Bohemianism; Sex and Sexuality; Stein, Gertrude.

Further Reading

Adam, Barry D. *The Rise of a Gay and Lesbian Movement.* New York: Twayne, 1995.
Chauncey, George. *Gay New York: Gender, Urban Culture, and the Making of the Gay Male World, 1890–1940.* New York: Basic Books, 1994.
Fone, Byrne R.S. *A Road to Stonewall: Male Homosexuality and Homophobia in English and American Literature, 1750–1969.* New York: Twayne, 1995.

Lauritsen, John. *The Early Homosexual Rights Movement, 1864–1935*. Ojdi, CA: Times Change, 1995.

Terry, Jennifer. *An American Obsession: Science, Medicine, and Homosexuality in Modern Society*. Chicago: University of Chicago Press, 1999.

Hood, Raymond (1881–1934)

One of America's most highly regarded architects of the early twentieth century, Raymond Hood came to prominence amid an unprecedented commercial building boom. A pioneer of the art deco style, Hood resisted traditional ideas concerning design and aesthetics, believing that the intended purpose of a building should heavily influence its design. He also considered the positive impact that publicity and advertising would have on his designs. In his view, a building that "stimulates public interest and admiration" is more "profitable to the owner" and therefore enhances the value of the property.

Raymond Mathewson Hood, born on March 29, 1881, in Pawtucket, Rhode Island, attended Brown University but later transferred to the Massachusetts Institute of Technology (MIT), where he studied architecture. During the course of his education, Hood developed a preference for the unconventional and a disregard of tradition for the sake of grandeur that would manifest itself repeatedly in his later designs. His senior thesis project, *A Design for the Parish Church* (1903), challenged the traditional, conservative, English-influenced American church design as too reserved. Instead, he proposed a heavily Gothic design because it "typified the majesty and power of God" and was therefore better suited to the church's purpose. After graduation, Hood worked briefly at Cram, Goodhue, and Ferguson, a leading Boston design firm, before continuing his art education at the École des Beaux Arts in France, where he earned a degree in 1911.

Upon completing his education, Hood struggled with small design jobs for a number of years. His big break finally came in 1922 with the design competition for a new *Chicago Tribune* office building. The owners of the newspaper wanted a design that used workspace efficiently, was architecturally innovative, and portrayed a sense of power and authority; *Tribune* owners wanted to convey the impression that they were kings of the industry. The winning design was worth $50,000, and the building would be con-

structed in a prime downtown Chicago location. The international competition drew more than 260 applicants. Hood collaborated with fellow architect John Mead Howells, submitting a design that showcased Hood's neo-Gothic design preference. Their work narrowly beat out the submission of Finnish architect Eliel Saarinen. Winning the Tribune Tower competition established Hood as a leading figure in American architecture.

Hood's use of lines, zigzags, and angular shapes as decorative elements in his designs had a formative influence on the art deco movement in America. Art deco, introduced in 1925 at the Exposition Internationale des Arts Décoratifs et Industriels Modernes in Paris, is an eclectic mixture of international styles characterized by geometric elements, streamlined curves, intricate ornamentation, and innovative use of colors and textures. A key component of art deco is the use of nonstructural decorative elements, purely for aesthetic purposes.

As the style developed in America, architects were faced with the challenge of complying with city ordinances that required building setbacks, step-like recesses in the façade intended to promote the flow of light and air through the street below. The result was terraced designs that gave many American skyscrapers a pyramid appearance. Hood's cutting-edge step-back designs, with their angular ornamentation, manifested an art deco flair even before the technique swept the international world of architecture.

The American Radiator and Standard Sanitary Company, impressed with Hood's work on the Tribune Tower, commissioned him to design its Manhattan office tower in 1923. Although short by skyscraper standards at a mere twenty-two stories, the building's innovative art deco color and ornamentation created a sense of grandeur commonly found in taller structures. The black brick façade emphasized the building's mass and hid what Hood called "the depressing effect of monotonous regularity" of windows contrasting with the building face in many other skyscrapers. Ornamentation was highlighted by gold neo-Gothic trimmings at key intersections between the building, its roof, and its base, with gold foil plating toward the top. The base was encased in black granite, with the main entry adorned in bronze. Light fixtures positioned on the roof to radiate upward created a striking contrast between the dark building and the night sky.

Members of the architectural community praised the American Radiator (now American Standard) building as "a bold and worldly piece of experimentation." Others, noting its striking unorthodox black and gold colors, criticized it as a monstrosity. Nevertheless, the finished design was in keeping with Hood's philosophy of purpose, as the building constituted a creative piece of advertising for the company. Unique in design and set across the street from Bryant Park, the building called attention to itself and therefore the company whose headquarters it housed.

In addition to skyscrapers, Hood designed public monuments, churches, residential buildings, asylums, and commercial structures, including a Masonic Temple in Scranton, Pennsylvania, at the end of the 1920s. In 1929, he published *Nation's Business,* a proposal for a futuristic city designed to manage traffic congestion while promoting urban growth. In the book, he proposed the construction of enormous buildings spanning many city blocks that would house all the components of a prosperous city: industry, entertainment, housing, and retail space. Hood intended to alleviate traffic congestion by constructing streets below the open, elevated building (a design influenced by the Swiss French modernist Le Corbusier).

Hood again teamed with John Mead Howells in 1929 for the design of the New York Daily News building, which was far more streamlined and less ornamented than most of Hood's other work. He continued to design and publish into the 1930s, with Rockefeller Center and the McGraw-Hill buildings in New York City being his two best-known works of the decade. Hailed as a genius of design, Hood was ever the pragmatist, asserting that style is as much a result of problem solving as of intentionally striving for aesthetics. He died on August 14, 1934, in Stamford, Connecticut.

Jennifer Aerts Terry

See also: Architecture; Design, Industrial; Technology.

Further Reading

Bayer, Patricia. *Art Deco Architecture: Design, Decoration, and Detail from the Twenties and Thirties.* London: Thames & Hudson, 1992.

Goldberger, Paul. *The Skyscraper.* New York: Alfred A. Knopf, 1981.

North, Arthur Tappan. *Raymond M. Hood.* New York: Whittlesey House, 1931.

Stern, Robert A.M., and Thomas P. Catalono. *Raymond Hood: Pragmatism and Poetics in the Waning of the Metropolitan Era.* New York: Rizzoli, 1982.

Hoover, Herbert (1874–1964)

The last American president of the Jazz Age, Herbert Hoover was inaugurated on March 4, 1929, at a time of unparalleled prosperity in the nation's history. Less than eight months later, the stock market crash sent the country plummeting into the Great Depression, which lasted well beyond the remaining years of Hoover's term. His unwillingness to commit the federal government to direct relief for the poor and unemployed in the early 1930s earned Hoover a reputation as an arch-conservative. However, Hoover came out of the progressive wing of the Republican Party and was best known through much of the 1920s as the innovating head of the Department of Commerce, a position that gained him widespread acclaim as the architect of the decade's economic prosperity.

Herbert Clark Hoover was born to working-class parents in the small, Republican-dominated town of West Branch, Iowa, on August 10, 1874. His father, Jesse, was a blacksmith. His mother, Huldah Randall Minthorn, died when he was a young boy, and Hoover was sent to Oregon to be raised by his Quaker uncles. A bright student, he was admitted to Stanford University, earning a degree in mining in 1895. For the next twenty years, he worked around the world, setting up his own mining consulting firm in 1902. He retired from the business a wealthy man in 1914.

Relief Work

At the outbreak of World War I, American officials in London—where Hoover was then living—asked him to head the American Relief Committee, an organization set up by the government to rescue the 120,000 Americans stranded in Europe by the war. Once that task was achieved, he was made head of the Commission for the Relief of Belgium, which provided food and other aid to some 9 million people in that war-torn country. Hoover's extraordinary organizational success earned him a national reputation and an appointment by President Woodrow Wilson to run the nation's food administration for the duration of America's participation in the war.

Through his work providing relief to civilian victims of World War I, Hoover developed his belief in voluntarism, the idea that the best role for government was providing guidance and encouragement to busi-

Herbert Hoover, formerly a mining engineer and successful entrepreneur, established a national reputation for humanitarianism and efficiency as head of U.S. efforts to supply food and other aid to Europeans impoverished by World War I. *(Topical Press Agency/Stringer/Hulton Archive/Getty Images)*

nesses and ordinary citizens rather than establishing rigid regulations or new laws to promote social goals. By war's end, Hoover was hailed in the press as the "Great Engineer." In 1919 Wilson appointed Hoover to serve on the U.S. delegation to the Paris Peace Conference.

Hoover's work during and after the war won him a high-profile position as head of the U.S. Food Administration, which sent millions of dollars in food and other aid to war-torn Europe and even to Communist Russia, which was torn by civil war in the early 1920s. His decision to provide aid to Communists garnered him much criticism but also evinced his pragmatic, humanitarian side. "Twenty million people are starving," he said. "Whatever their politics, they shall be fed."

A nationally renowned figure, Hoover was considered presidential timber by both Democrats and Republicans in 1920. Rejecting overtures from both parties, the Republican-leaning Hoover supported Warren G. Harding's bid for the White House. His help on the campaign, along with his demonstrated organizational skills, won him an appointment as secretary of commerce in the Harding administration, a position he retained after Harding's death and through both terms of Calvin Coolidge's presidency.

Commerce Secretary

Created in 1903 to promote economic growth, the Department of Commerce had never been as important as the older and more powerful Department of the Treasury as far as setting economic policy was concerned, and most secretaries of commerce preferred to keep a low profile. Hoover, by contrast, reorganized the department and set up conferences on a number of economic problems, including labor relations, trade, housing, child labor and welfare, and industrial policy. He also served as chair of the President's Conference on Unemployment during the recession year of 1921. Hoover's voluntaristic principles were on full display as he tried to persuade industry to adopt policies that would ease unemployment and spur growth during times of economic hardship. To get industry to avoid the cutthroat competition that lowered prices, reduced profits, and triggered unemployment, he advocated establishing informal, government-sanctioned cartels.

Hoover was also active in setting government policy for emerging industries in the 1920s, particularly radio and aviation. In 1926, he advocated passage of the Air Commerce Act, which established a Bureau of Air Commerce (predecessor to the Federal Aviation Administration), promoted airport construction, and established guidelines for the industry. A year later, he helped push through legislation establishing the Federal Radio Commission (FRC), given responsibility to regulate the nation's airwaves, and worked with the industry in establishing guidelines for the nationwide growth of radio. (The FRC was supplanted by the Federal Communications Commission in 1934.)

Hoover also put his war relief experience to good use in helping the government cope with the aftermath of the Great Mississippi River Flood of 1927, one of the worst natural disasters in twentieth-century America. Responding to a request from the governors of the six states most affected, President Coolidge assigned Hoover to lead the Special Mississippi Flood Relief Committee. In addition to providing relief, the committee set up programs to deal with health problems such as malaria and typhoid in the lower Mississippi Valley.

Hoover's last task as commerce secretary was to serve as chair of the Committee on Economic Changes, endorsing the group's recommendation that government spending on public works be used for relief in case of economic hard times. This, ironically, was a policy that Hoover failed to promote as president at the onset of the Great Depression. Indeed, it was Hoover's reluctance to get the federal government involved in relief that contributed to his landslide defeat by Franklin D. Roosevelt in the 1932 presidential election.

Presidency

When Hoover ran for the presidency in 1928, the economy was roaring—perhaps even overheating, according to economic historians. As the high-profile, activist secretary of commerce, Hoover had won acclaim for his stewardship of American business, and he had no serious rivals for the Republican nomination. His Democratic opponent in the general election was New York Governor Al Smith, a moderate Democrat with roots in the immigrant-based machine politics of New York City. Smith was the first Catholic to run for president on a major party ticket, and anti-Catholic prejudice permeated much of America, particularly in rural areas.

Hoover refrained from making Smith's religion a campaign issue, but his underlings stoked fears of a president beholden to the pope. Hoover also supported continuation of Prohibition, a plus in much of rural America, while his opponent wanted to end it. With the economy booming and Smith's Catholicism an issue, there was little contest in the election. Hoover won the popular vote by 21 million to 15 million, and the electoral college by 444 to 87.

Promising a continuation of the good economic times, Hoover appointed a number of businesspeople to his cabinet, including six millionaires. To the lower ranks of the government bureaucracy, he appointed a host of technocrats, mostly young, college-educated professionals. What Hoover wanted was an efficient and cost-effective government that would not interfere in the natural workings of the marketplace. In foreign affairs, Hoover mended fences with Latin America, going on a tour to promote better relations in the wake of a series of military interventions taken in the Caribbean and Central America by his predecessor.

Hoover's probusiness approach was much appreciated on Wall Street, as stocks soared to new highs, but many shares were traded at prices far in excess of their underlying value. Other economic trouble was brewing as well. Throughout the 1920s, farm areas—still home to nearly half of the American population—suffered from low crop prices and depressed incomes. Debt was rife throughout the economy, as businesses borrowed to expand and consumers took out loans to buy the many new durable goods coming onto the market.

When the stock market crashed in October 1929, Hoover told Americans not to worry. The underlying economy, he insisted, remained sound. As the crash reverberated throughout the economy, setting off mass bankruptcies and unemployment, Hoover remained reluctant to get the federal government involved in relief, either to industry or to the unemployed. He did authorize some public works projects, such as dam building, and his Reconstruction Finance Corporation eventually provided $2 billion in loans to failing banks, insurance companies, railroads, and state and local governments.

As the economic depression worsened and criticism of Hoover grew louder, the president became more dour and angry. When veterans came to Washington to demand early payment of their bonuses, Hoover had the army evict them from their makeshift camps, a public relations disaster. In the 1932 election, presiding over the worst economic crisis in the nation's history and facing buoyant New York Governor Franklin D. Roosevelt, Hoover did not stand a chance. He lost in a landslide; Roosevelt won 22.8 million votes to Hoover's 15.8 million, and 472 electoral votes to Hoover's 59.

Humiliated, Hoover withdrew from public life, though he campaigned for Republican candidates in subsequent elections and criticized many aspects of Roosevelt's activist New Deal policies. Hoover's reputation was somewhat resurrected when he headed committees to reorganize the executive branch during the administrations of Harry Truman and Dwight Eisenhower. He also established the Hoover Institution, a conservative think tank, at his alma mater, Stanford University. Hoover died in New York City on October 20, 1964, at the age of ninety.

James Ciment and Andrew J. Waskey

See also: Commerce Department, U.S.; Coolidge, Calvin; Economic Policy; Election of 1928; Food Administration, U.S.; Mellon, Andrew; Smith, Al; Stock Market.

Further Reading

Burner, David. *Herbert Hoover: A Public Life.* New York: Alfred A. Knopf, 1978.

Fausold, Martin L. *The Presidency of Herbert C. Hoover.* Lawrence: University Press of Kansas, 1985.

Smith, Richard Norton. *An Uncommon Man: The Triumph of Herbert Hoover.* New York: Simon & Schuster, 1984.

Wilson, Joan Hoff. *Herbert Hoover, Forgotten Progressive.* Boston: Little, Brown, 1975.

Hoover, J. Edgar (1895–1972)

J. Edgar Hoover was the director of the Federal Bureau of Investigation (FBI) from 1924 (when it was still called the Bureau of Investigation) to his death in 1972—so long that his name became almost synonymous with that organization and federal law enforcement. Although he freed the FBI from political patronage and transformed it into a professional police force, he also introduced institutional rigidities that would later prove a major liability as society changed.

The second son and third child of a government employee, John Edgar Hoover was born on January 1, 1895, in Washington, D.C. He was devoted to his mother and would continue to live in his childhood home until her death forty-three years later. Hoover's upbringing was strict, and he is remembered as a studious young man who never participated in common adolescent mischief. After graduating as valedictorian from Central High School in 1913, he worked as a file clerk with the Library of Congress while studying law at George Washington University. Obtaining his degree four years later, he took a position in the U.S. Department of Justice.

During America's involvement in World War I, Hoover worked in the alien registration section and was profoundly angered to find that some foreign nationals living in America despised the United States and sought to undermine its culture. In 1919, Attorney General A. Mitchell Palmer appointed him head of the General Intelligence Division of the Justice Department, which investigated radical political groups. Hoover then created an index of alleged political extremists that eventually numbered 60,000 individuals he considered dangerous.

During this period, he became convinced that communism was the great adversary of the American way of life. As a result, Palmer put him in charge of the campaign to round up and deport large numbers of aliens involved in radical political groups. The Palmer Raids entailed widespread abuses of police power and swept up a large number of innocent people along with the few radicals who were actually found. Many of the prisoners were beaten or otherwise abused, and the National Civil Liberties Bureau (predecessor of the American Civil Liberties Union) called for an investigation of the government's actions. Palmer refused to apologize, and Hoover's career did not suffer.

In 1924, Attorney General Harlan Fiske Stone appointed Hoover as acting director of the Bureau of Investigation, with the stipulation that Hoover stop the investigations of political activities and concentrate on actual lawbreaking. Many critics thought Hoover too young for the position, but Stone considered Hoover's youth an asset, since he would not have so many preconceived notions to overcome. Hoover spent seven months rebuilding the Bureau of Investigation to restore the public's confidence. He was then named its permanent director.

His first change was to put an end to the patronage system, the practice of giving jobs in return for political favors (making a clean sweep of agents who could not pass demanding background checks). He instated a rigorous training program to ensure that all agents would meet his standards of professionalism. In addition to improving the quality of his personnel, Hoover instituted modern scientific methods of handling evidence. He introduced the use of fingerprints for identifying criminals and oversaw the creation of a file of millions of fingerprints, organized to facilitate rapid identification. He also forged links with state and local law enforcement agencies, enabling police at all levels of government to share information efficiently. In addition, he launched a public relations program intended to build an image of the FBI as America's number one crime fighter and the protector of ordinary, law-abiding citizens.

The last years of the 1920s saw the rise of a new brand of criminal activity—organized crime—and new levels of violence. Many Americans questioned the government's ability to fight these new criminals, some of whom became folk heroes. Many of the criminals were the product of Prohibition's ban on alcohol. But illegal liquor and organized crime were not the entire problem. The period also brought a spate of bank robberies, kidnappings, and other criminal felonies whose perpetrators included the likes of Charles Arthur "Pretty Boy" Floyd, Lester Gillis "Baby Face" Nelson, Kate "Ma" Barker and her family of thugs, and John Dillinger. New technology such as the automobile made it possible for such criminals to strike over wide areas and escape across state lines.

Hoover's new, professional FBI systematically tracked down and arrested or killed these notorious gangsters, helping create the image of the "G-man"—the government agent who always got his man. There was a dark side to Hoover's success, however, which would lead to major problems in later decades. Hoover grew vain about his reputation, unwilling to share the glory, and hounded some of his best agents out of the agency. In his high-profile pursuit of bank robbers and kidnappers, he largely ignored organized crime.

Worst of all, Hoover and his organization became increasingly rigid, unable to change with the times. His successes during World War II in hunting spies, influenced his obsession with communism and the FBI's renewed investigation of political dissent. After the demise of Senator Joseph McCarthy (R-WI) brought an end to the anticommunist witch hunts of the 1950s, Hoover used the FBI to investigate and attack civil rights activists and Vietnam War protesters. When J. Edgar Hoover died on May 2, 1972, the FBI was under a cloud of suspicion for illegal and unconstitutional investigations of political dissent. Even so, Hoover was given a military funeral with full honors, and the new FBI headquarters in Washington, D.C., was named the J. Edgar Hoover Building.

Leigh Kimmel

See also: Bureau of Investigation; Crime, Organized; Criminal Punishment; Palmer, A. Mitchell; Prohibition (1920–1933); Red Scare of 1917–1920.

Further Reading

De Loach, Cartha. *Hoover's FBI: The Inside Story by Hoover's Trusted Lieutenant.* Washington, DC: Regnery, 1995.

de Toledano, Ralph. *J. Edgar Hoover: The Man in His Time.* New Rochelle, NY: Arlington House, 1973.

Denenberg, Barry. *The True Story of J. Edgar Hoover and the FBI.* New York: Scholastic, 1993.

Potter, Claire Bond. *War on Crime: Bandits, G-Men, and the Politics of Mass Culture.* Piscataway, NJ: Rutgers University Press, 1998.

Housing

Housing played an important role in the economic prosperity of the Jazz Age, as the construction of single-family homes proceeded in unprecedented numbers, along with that of apartment buildings and duplexes in the nation's burgeoning cities. Housing also played a role in the period's cultural divide between suburban homeowners living in single-family bungalow houses and urban renters living in multifamily apartment complexes near public transportation. As the demand for housing increased, so did prices, encouraging investors to purchase houses—like other commodities—for the purpose of speculating, hoping to sell at a substantial profit in a short period of time. By 1926, the housing supply in

America exceeded demand, causing a drop in prices and leaving speculators with a loss. The weakness in the housing market foreshadowed the structural weaknesses of the economy at large.

Supply and Demand

In 1920, Secretary of Commerce Herbert Hoover identified a housing shortage in America. The shortfall was due to a sharp decline in the number of new houses built during World War I and the recession that followed. Housing starts fell from 437,000 units in 1916 to 240,000 in 1917 and 118,000 in 1918, primarily due to rising costs and the diversion of capital and materials to war production. Following the war, production recovered to 315,000 units in 1919 but then fell again to 247,000 units in 1920. The latter decline resulted from the postwar recession, a shortage of mortgage money, rising costs, and a railway strike that curtailed the movement of building materials.

After the recession of 1921, the construction industry built new houses in unprecedented numbers, rising from 449,000 in 1921 to 937,000 in 1925. A total of nearly 6.3 million new homes appeared during 1921–1928, an annual average of 785,000. About 3.8 million (60 percent) were single-family houses. Toward the end of that period, however, there was a pronounced trend toward multifamily structures comprising three or more units, due to the ready availability of mortgage money for that purpose. From 1921 through 1925, large rental structures accounted for 20 percent of the units started; from 1926 to 1928, they accounted for 30 percent.

Much of the new housing took the form of detached, single-family houses built on undeveloped, less expensive land on the periphery of large metropolitan cities. Unlike urban dwellings, these suburban houses were not located near places of employment. Nor were they generally accessible by bus, trolley, or other forms of public transportation. The growth of suburban housing was made possible by the advent of reasonably priced automobiles.

Urban and Suburban Landscapes

Most suburban homes adopted the new architectural style of the bungalow: a single-story house with a low-pitched roof and a porch. Entering the front door of a typical bungalow, a visitor would step into a large room with the dining area on the right and the living area on the left. The living room had a fireplace with built-in bookcases on either side. Behind the dining room was a small kitchen with counters, a sink, and a refrigerator; a small closet in the kitchen contained a built-in, fold-down ironing board. Behind the living room and separated by curtained French doors was the master bedroom. Two other bedrooms were designed for children. A bathroom and hallway made up the rear of the house.

Whereas single-family houses dominated the suburbs, multifamily apartment buildings and duplexes dominated the inner city. Suburban communities were based on extensive planning, with rows of houses that were nearly identical in size, shape, and color. But land in urban areas was subdivided and sold for whatever purpose the owner desired. By the 1920s, apartment buildings, duplexes, and houses found themselves next to factories and other commercial enterprises. Suburban lot sizes averaged 5,000 square feet (465 square meters). The average lot size of a single-family urban home was 3,000 square feet (280 square meters).

The interiors of urban and suburban homes changed significantly with the advent of household electricity. By 1927, 63 percent of the U.S. population lived in dwellings with electric lights. Households now were equipped with vacuum cleaners, irons, refrigerators, stoves, fans, and floor waxers. Sockets were installed at convenient places so that an electric toaster no longer had to be plugged into the ceiling light fixture. Although labor-saving electrical appliances benefited urban and suburban residents, electrical power was not available to many rural households until the 1930s.

Planned Communities

Among the notable developments in American housing during the 1920s was the planned community. Real estate developers purchased large tracts of land on the outskirts of major metropolitan areas, then divided the land into smaller units. Before selling any of these subdivisions or building a single house, the developer planned nearly every aspect of the community, from the size of the lots and the width of the streets to the style of houses and the types of trees and other plantings. Then the developer would either build the houses according to the specifications or sell the subdivided lots to individual owners, who would carry out construction. The contract usually contained a restriction clause, providing that the devel-

oper's stipulations would continue indefinitely unless a majority of owners in the subdivision voted to change them at some point in the future.

Planned communities benefited from effective use of zoning ordinances. Such regulations banned industry and even commercial enterprises, reinforcing the residential nature of the development. In 1926, the U.S. Supreme Court ensured in *Village of Euclid, Ohio v. Ambler Realty Co.* that residential zoning would be a permanent fixture of land planning when it upheld an ordinance that banned industry from residential sections. Zoning boards relegated luncheonettes, clothing stores, garages, and movie houses to commercial strips on the outskirts of the subdivisions, though grocery stores and a few shops were generally permitted within the residential areas. By 1930, zoning ordinances affecting more than 46 million people were in operation in 981 cities, towns, and villages throughout the United States.

Restrictive covenants and zoning ordinances contributed to various kinds of economic and social segregation. Restrictive covenants, for example, might prevent the sale of property to such minority groups as Asians, Hispanics, African Americans, and Jews. In 1917, in *Buchanan v. Warley,* the Supreme Court struck down segregationist municipal residential ordinances. As a result, real estate boards and property owners' associations turned to covenants restricting who could purchase a specific property or house in the subdivision. In suburban areas, regulations setting minimum lot sizes and house prices reinforced economic segregation. In urban areas, municipal zoning restrictions reinforced class segregation. These laws prevented nuisances, such as noise and pollution, but might be used to bar certain groups, such as Chinese families operating laundries.

Market Decline

By 1928, the U.S. housing market clearly was overbuilt. The increase of 6.3 million units from 1921 to 1928 was nearly 50 percent greater than the corresponding increase in the number of households (4.7 million). The national vacancy rate in 1928 rose to 8 percent, and the number of foreclosures of nonfarm properties had risen from 68,000 to 116,000 in just two years. The residential construction industry, which had the capacity to produce at least 1 million units annually, produced nearly 750,000 in 1928. New household formation was only a little over

400,000 annually. Thus, a drastic reduction in residential construction was necessary.

In 1929, production dropped by one-third, contributing heavily to the onset of the Great Depression, as housing investments plummeted. The resulting housing crisis set the stage for the revolution in housing finance brought to fruition by the federal government's willingness—through the National Housing Act of 1934 and the GI Bill of 1944—to provide mortgage guarantees so that lenders could offer mortgages on more favorable terms, thereby leading to the boom in private housing development after World War II.

Michael McGregor

See also: Appliances, Household; Real Estate; Suburbs.

Further Reading

Clark, Clifford Edward, Jr. *The American Family Home, 1800–1960.* Chapel Hill: University of North Carolina Press, 1986.

Doan, Mason C. *American Housing Production 1880–2000: A Concise History.* Lanham, MD: University Press of America, 1997.

Jackson, Kenneth T. *Crabgrass Frontier: The Suburbanization of the United States.* New York: Oxford University Press, 1985.

Weiss, Marc A. *The Rise of Community Builders: The American Real Estate Industry and Urban Land Planning.* New York: Columbia University Press, 1987.

Wright, Gwendolyn. *Building the Dream: A Social History of Housing in America.* New York: Pantheon, 1981.

Hughes, Langston (1902–1967)

Langston Hughes was a key figure in the Harlem Renaissance, an African American arts movement that included Claude McKay, Zora Neale Hurston, Countee Cullen, and other noted writers, artists, and musicians of the 1920s. Best known for his poetry about the African American experience, Hughes was strongly influenced by Walt Whitman and Carl Sandburg as well as by the folk art and music of African Americans in the rural South and industrial North.

Hughes was born James Mercer Langston Hughes in Joplin, Missouri, on February 1, 1902. His parents divorced when he was a boy, and his father moved to Cuba and later Mexico. For a time, Hughes was raised by his maternal grandmother, Mary Langston, in Lawrence, Kansas. Her celebration of African American culture influenced Hughes's later interest in ethnic and social issues.

Hughes began writing poetry at age thirteen, by which time he was living with his mother in Lincoln, Illinois. After graduating from high school, Hughes lived for a short time with his father in Mexico. In 1921, he began undergraduate studies at Columbia University in New York. His father agreed to pay for his university studies on the condition that he work toward a "practical" degree, in this case engineering. Hughes complied for one year and then dropped out of college.

Between 1923 and 1924, Hughes worked as a crew member on the merchant steamer SS *Malone* and traveled to West Africa and Europe. Living in Paris, the budding scholar and student of American literature and poetry spent most of his time in the African American expatriate community rather than with Americans of the Lost Generation, such as Ernest Hemingway and F. Scott Fitzgerald.

Upon his return to the United States in 1924, Hughes wrote poetry that emulated Carl Sandburg's democratic idealism and modernist free verse. He later described Sandburg as his "guiding star." His first two books were a melding of modernist poetry with traditional African American verse patterns. *The Weary Blues* (1926) and *Fine Clothes to the Jew* (1927) concentrated on the plight of poor African Americans in urban and rural America; a number of the poems also decried divisions based on skin color within the black community itself. These subjects led to attacks from the mainstream African American press, which was focused on political activism and influenced by the Niagara movement of W.E.B. Du Bois, who published many of the early works of Harlem Renaissance authors, including Hughes, in his journal *The Crisis.* But Du Bois's faith in the "talented tenth" as the means to racial uplift had exacerbated tensions within the African American community and encouraged divisions based on skin color and class.

In 1926, Hughes published "The Negro Artist and the Racial Mountain," which many critics consider a manifesto for the Harlem Renaissance. In the essay, first published in *The Nation,* Hughes argued for a racial pride that would unite African Americans across economic lines and called for artists to celebrate these shared cultural traditions and contemporary social concerns. Hughes subtly placed himself and the artists of the Harlem Renaissance between the activism of the National Association for the Advancement of Colored People (NAACP) and the exclusionary politics of Marcus Garvey's black nationalism. Specifically, Hughes defined new artists as proud of their "dark-skinned selves" and wanting to express themselves from this racially conscious context. According to the poet, it did not matter whether white people were supportive or not, or even whether black people were supportive or not. Instead, African American artists were to build "temples for tomorrow" and "stand on top of the mountain free within ourselves."

Whereas earlier black intellectuals had focused on liberating African Americans through political action or economic improvement, Hughes celebrated individual black identity. Thus, he advocated a liberation program that spoke to one individual at a time. Hughes wrote not only for African Americans but also for the right of an African American to be free of the opinions of both white and black America and, in this way, to be truly free.

Hughes earned a B.A. degree from Lincoln University in Pennsylvania in 1929 and would earn a doctorate there in 1943. During the interwar years, Hughes, like many writers, was interested in communism as an alternative to American capitalism and entrenched racism, and he began writing poems with a more overtly political tone. In "A New Song" (1932), he imagined that "The Black / And White World / Shall be one! / The Worker's World!" In 1932, Hughes traveled with the American Negro Film Group to the Soviet Union to make a film that was to depict blacks living in the United States. Although the film was never made, Hughes traveled throughout the Soviet Union. He returned to the United States after traveling through China and Japan.

Hughes published often in the *Daily Worker* and supported Communist-sponsored campaigns to free the Scottsboro Boys, a group of black Alabama men and boys accused of raping two white women in 1931. However, Hughes never officially joined the Communist Party. He initially opposed U.S. entry into World War II, pointing out the paradox of African Americans, victims of U.S. racism, fighting a racist Nazi regime in Germany. But by 1942, Hughes moved closer to the American political center and came to view the war as an opportunity for African Americans, who, by fighting for their country, would earn the moral leverage to overcome prejudice and discrimination.

During the war, Hughes began a popular weekly column for the *Chicago Defender* that featured the fictional character Jesse B. Semple, or Simple. By using this character as a foil for his own voice as the narrator, Hughes waged a weekly war against racism and reached a wide audience that may not previously have been familiar with his poetry.

Hughes lived in Harlem for much of the remainder of his life. He died from surgical complications during an operation for prostate cancer on May 22, 1967.

Jason Stacy

See also: Harlem Renaissance; Locke, Alain; Poetry.

Further Reading

Gates, Henry Louis, Jr. *Langston Hughes: Critical Perspectives Past and Present.* New York: Amistad, 1993.

Hughes, Langston. *The Collected Works of Langston Hughes.* Columbia: University of Missouri Press, 2001.

———. *Good Morning Revolution: Uncollected Social Protest Writings by Langston Hughes.* New York: Lawrence Hill, 1973.

Rampersad, Arnold. *The Life of Langston Hughes.* New York: Oxford University Press, 1988.